Daniel J. Evans

An Autobiography

Washington State Archives

Front cover photo: Washington State Archives
Back cover photos:
Mary Levin/UW *Columns* alumni magazine;
Evans Family Collection
Title page photo: Washington State Archives
Dedication page photo: Washington State Archives

Cover and Book Design by Amber Raney
Edited by John C. Hughes

Printed in the United States of America by Gorham Printing, Centralia, Washington.

Other Legacy Washington books:

An Election for the Ages: Rossi vs. Gregoire, 2004
Booth Who? A biography of Booth Gardner
Nancy Evans, First-Rate First Lady
Where the Salmon Run, A biography of Billy Frank Jr.
Lillian Walker, Washington Civil Rights Pioneer
The Inimitable Adele Ferguson
Pressing On: Two Family-Owned Newspapers in the 21st Century
Slade Gorton, a Half Century in Politics
Across the Aisles: Sid Snyder's Remarkable Life
A Woman First: The Impact of Jennifer Dunn
John Spellman: Politics Never Broke His Heart
Korea 65, the Forgotten War Remembered
Washington Remembers World War II
1968: The Year that Rocked Washington
Ahead of the Curve: Washington Women Lead the Way, 1910-2020
Julia Butler Hansen, a Trailblazing Washington Politician

For Nancy

April 1959: Our wedding day was two months away. *Washington State Archives*

CONTENTS

DANIEL JACKSON EVANS

"I would rather cross the political aisle than cross the people."

Born in Seattle, Oct. 16, 1925

Achieves Eagle Scout rank, 1941

Roosevelt High School graduate, 1943

U.S. Navy, 1943-1946; 1951-1953
(commissioned officer, 1945)

Engineering degrees,
University of Washington:
bachelor's 1948, master's 1949

Washington State Rep., 43rd District,
1957-1965

Running for governor in 1964. *Washington State Archives*

Married Nancy Bell, June 6, 1959

Daniel Jackson Evans Jr.,
born November 25, 1960

House Minority Leader, 1961-1965

Mark Lawrence Evans,
born September 20, 1963

Washington's 16th governor, 1965-1977

Bruce McKay Evans, born August 21, 1966

President, The Evergreen State College,
1977-1983

Named one of the 10 outstanding U.S. governors of the 20th century in a 1982 study conducted by a Harvard researcher.

U.S. Senator, 1983-1989

Co-founder with Mike Lowry, Washington Wildlife & Recreation Coalition, 1989

Regent, University of Washington, 1993-2005

Daniel J. Evans School of Public Policy & Governance, founded at UW, 2000 (present name adopted, 2015)

Named UW *Alumnus Summa Laude Dignitatus*, 2007

Olympic Wilderness renamed Daniel J. Evans Wilderness, 2017

Receives 2018 Margaret Chase Smith American Democracy Award, together with Ralph Munro, for assisting refugees displaced by Vietnam War

Introductions

A remarkable life

"When one man, for whatever reason, has the opportunity to lead an extraordinary life, he has no right to keep it to himself." So said Jacques Cousteau, the famed oceanographer and filmmaker. The extraordinary life of Daniel J. Evans unfolds on these pages—from the Great Depression to the Smartphone, and everything along the way, with all of life's ups and downs. For Dan, mostly ups. Not many downs.

Paul Newman, the gifted actor, was once asked how he would like to be remembered. "As being a part of my time," he replied. What does that mean? I believe Newman was trying to say that during his time on planet earth he wanted to be a part of what's happening. He wanted to be remembered as being involved—as someone whose time here meant something.

Who can deny that Dan Evans has not been a part of his time? He still is. Not only a part of his time, he significantly shaped his time. The Eagle Scout became

Evans with Bill Jacobs, twice his chief of staff. *Bill Jacobs Collection*

a lifelong outdoorsman; the civil engineer turned legislator drafted a "Blueprint for Progress" and became a three-term governor; the college president became a U.S. senator; the university regent mentored young people pursuing public service.

Mike Royko, the Pulitzer Prize-winning Chicago columnist, wrote this wonderful remembrance of things past:

> When I was a kid, the worst of all days was the last day of summer vacation, and we were in the schoolyard playing softball, and the sun was down and it was getting dark. But I didn't want it to get dark. I didn't want the game to end. It was too good, too much fun. I wanted it to stay light forever, so we could go on playing forever, so the game could go on and on. C'mon, c'mon. Let's play one more inning. One more time at bat. One more pitch. Just one? Stick around, guys. We can't break up this team. It's too much fun.

That's the way it has been with Dan. His fans—Republicans, Democrats, and our state's highly independent independents—have always championed him to run again. Go for it all. One more time on center stage. One more time to show us the way.

He has always answered the call in his own way. And shown us the way. So here it is, a vivid history of his time and ours. Dan Evans is on the ballfield again—hiking, campaigning, governing and teaching. It's his story. The story of a remarkable lifetime.

—**Bill Jacobs**

William C. Jacobs was Evans' chief of staff twice, from 1976 to 1977 in the Governor's Office, and from 1983 to 1989 in the U.S. Senate. Jacobs is also a former director of the State Department of Labor & Industries and a former executive director of the Washington Forest Protection Association.

62 years and counting

Our wedding day, June 6, 1959. *Evans Family Collection*

On a Sunday evening in October of 1958, Dan suggested we walk to the park near my apartment to enjoy the pleasant weather. As we sat on the baseball field bleachers, I soon realized he was proposing marriage. Totally surprised, I was thrown into an inward panic. I didn't know what my answer would be! He was very handsome and obviously smart. He had done so many interesting and important things in his young life. A true gentleman, he was kind and solicitous to me, but he was also shy. At times he could be so quiet.

I had to return to my apartment and think about it—for three days!

It's hard now to believe it took me that long to realize how much I loved Dan. When I said "Yes," I soon realized my life would change forever. And change it did! We have had an amazing life together—62 years and counting. Three superb sons and their wonderful wives have given us nine grandchildren who keep us entertained and young as we watch them grow into interesting, wise and adventurous young adults.

So, why has it worked for so many years?

In many ways, Dan is the same man I married on June 6, 1959: steadfast, adventurous, thoughtful and wise, with a deep love of family, friends and his country. Washington state and the mountains and trails he has hiked and climbed most of his life have been a huge influence. He led major efforts to protect our natural environment. A huge bonus has been the many opportunities to meet and work with so many amazing and dedicated citizens. We cherish the many friends we have made during this journey. But when you add all those years of rich experience to his very productive young life, it's not surprising that Dan is such a successful leader. He works hard for his fellow citizens without seeking praise, just the satisfaction of a job well done.

And so, much of it is now on paper. This is his story. I think you will learn some things that will surprise you! Enjoy!

—**Nancy Evans**

1
ROOTS & BRANCHES

They came to America in trickles, then a flood, from Scotland, England and Wales, excited to leave behind poverty and persecution; frightened of the unknown and the realization they would never again see their parents or "home," hard life though it was.

When my forebears finally arrived in "the Oregon Country," the wagon ruts across the prairies were still fresh. The Columbia River rolled, wild and free, past the ancient Grand Coulee, over Celilo Falls and down to the sea. Their letters and diaries testify to how hard it was to get here, and that it was worth the grueling journey.

My evergreen roots run four generations deep. I was born here in 1925. And when I die, I hope all the mountains are out—Rainier looming majestically; the Olympics arrayed like craggy sentinels, snowcaps sparkling in the sunshine. I'd like to expire with a smile on my face after skinny dipping in an alpine lake.

I've traveled the world, met presidents, premiers, and kings. For me, there's no place like home. I inherited this sense of place and purpose from my grandparents. They were descendants of a long line of New Englanders, most of whom arrived in this country in the 1600s. They tilled rocky fields for almost 200 years and raised large families. They were active in their communities. In their day, people and goods moved no faster than during Greek and Roman times. My 18th-century ancestors probably never traveled more than 50 miles from where they were born.

Two events in the early 1800s revolutionized American history: Thomas Jefferson negotiated the Louisiana Purchase, which doubled the size of the nation. Then he sent Lewis and Clark on their historic journey to map a viable land and water route to the Pacific Coast. The Corps of Discovery was tasked with exploring the vast, unknown expanses of the newly acquired territory while establishing "peaceable" trade with Native American tribes. Lewis and Clark helped stake America's claim to hegemony on the Northwest coast.

Next came the agents of John Jacob Astor, the shrewd New York merchant, intent on extending his fur-trading empire. The British, through the powerful Hudson's Bay Company, countered forcefully. The tide began to turn as ever-increasing numbers of American settlers began arriving in the Northwest. By 1843, the wagon trains were making their way west along the Oregon Trail. Within seven years, practically everyone in America had heard the stories: fertile western farmland just waiting for homesteaders; mountains of gold in California. And never mind the natives. The notion of peaceable trade was supplanted by relentless migration that many whites saw as "manifest destiny." We gave the Indians our diseases, took their land and livelihoods, and attempted to eradicate their rich culture.

The power of steam was being linked to machinery. Railroads—the iron horses of Western expansionism—began connecting a new continental nation. In one generation, each of my grandparents trekked across America to Washington Territory.

My great-grandfather, Daniel B. Jackson, whose names I bear, was an adventurer. He went to sea at 14 and roamed Mexico for a time before returning to East Machias, Maine, where he married Mary Rowell and fathered three children. The lure of the West was still powerful. In 1858, Jackson booked passage on a sailing ship and journeyed around Cape Horn to San Francisco, leaving his family behind with a promise they would be reunited in an exciting new place. A year later, he made his way north to Puget Sound and settled at Port Gamble along the Kitsap Peninsula. He found steady work as a timber buyer for Pope & Talbot's screeching lumber mill.

Capt. Daniel B. Jackson, my great-grandfather, in the 1890s. *Evans Family Collection*

After a six-year separation, Jackson sent for his wife and children. We can only imagine the excitement of their reunion 3,200 miles from rocky Maine in an evergreen land. My grandmother, May Jackson, was born in 1866 at Port Townsend, the booming little town where Puget Sound flows into the Strait of Juan de Fuca. Port Townsend seemed to have it all, including a deep-water port, a U.S. Customs House, and 500 citizens. Many believed it was sure to become the great city of the Northwest.

Daniel B. Jackson prospered in the timber business and branched out to shipping. Starting with three small vessels, he built the Puget Sound & Alaska Steamship Company. Now he was "Captain Jackson." In 1890 he commissioned an elegant steamer, the *City of Seattle*, which became his flagship. It was the envy of his competitors. Some 5,000 spectators hailed its first arrival on Puget Sound.

The *City of Seattle*, Capt. Jackson's flagship steamer. *UW Special Collections*

THE EVANS BRANCH of my family tree was transplanted from Wales to Connecticut. For many generations, the Evanses scrabbled their sustenance from the thin New England soil. My great-grandmother died early. The children were parceled out. Sixteen-year-old George Evans was sent to live with a farm family that had settled on Puget Sound. He made the arduous journey by steamer to the Isthmus of Panama, crossed it on a teetering train, and hopped another steamer to Seattle. He landed at Stanwood, a raw-boned settlement in Snohomish County.

Tired, hungry and apprehensive, he set out on a wooded trail to meet his new family. That night, he huddled cold and lonely beside the trail. At dawn, he discovered he was only a few hundred feet from the clearing surrounding the farmhouse that was his goal.

George Evans, sturdy and industrious, worked at many jobs with increasing success, eventually signing on at the Pope & Talbot mill in Port Gamble where Daniel B. Jackson was now a leading citizen. Evans met the captain's daughter, May, and must have impressed her parents. George Evans and May Jackson were married in the Jackson home at Port Gamble. It was a gala event, by all accounts, and a fortuitous match. The bride was bright, attractive and attentive, the groom an upwardly mobile young man with an influential father-in-law. Evans was sent with Cyrus Walker to open a new mill at Utsaladdy on Camano Island.

While the great fire of 1889 wiped out much of downtown Seattle, the can-do "Seattle Spirit" emerged from the ashes. Captain Jackson built an imposing new family home—it had 14 fireplaces—at 8th and Pine. My father, Daniel Lester Evans, was born in his grandparents' house in 1894, the fourth of five children.

"Les" Evans grew up in a rapidly changing community. One wag wrote that Seattle grew so fast its socks didn't fit. With the discovery of gold in Alaska, Seattle became a lusty, teeming port city. Its population nearly doubled to 80,000 between 1890 and the turn of the century. By 1917, it had grown to nearly 300,000. That was the year Dad received his civil engineering degree, with honors, from the University of Washington. The U.S. declared war against Germany a month before his graduation. Dad volunteered for the U.S. Army Air Service, the forerunner of the Air Corps. He had almost earned his pilot's wings when the war ended in 1918. Given the choice between mustering out or completing flight training, Dad always told us he said, "Show me the gate." He returned home to begin a long, eventful career as an engineer for King County.

MY MOTHER'S PARENTS were Clarence Ide (pronounced "I'd") and Dora McKay. Clarence's father had moved from Vermont to Wisconsin where Clarence was born. Apparently, that was not far enough west. In 1878, the Ides, including 18-year-old Clarence, joined a wagon train. My great-grandmother, Lucy Loomis Ide, kept a diary. It is a marvelous exposition of birth, death and survival as the bedraggled settlers inched toward Washington Territory. One entry is a testimony to their stubbornness and ingenuity:

> July 8. Over the mountains this morning we started; came to another toll bridge; they asked 50 cents a team to cross it, and we concluded not to give it; it was not a wide stream, but the water ran like a torrent at that particular place. We informed them that we preferred fording it rather than give them their price. In a short time the stream was running full of railroad ties; they had gone above us a short distance and were shoving them off as thick as they could. This looked rather bad for fording the stream; but … several members of our party went above the bridge a little ways, and with heavy poles held the ties back while the teams crossed.

It took them nearly six months to reach Dayton, the county seat of Columbia County. Wedged between Walla Walla and Garfield in the jigsaw puzzle of Washington's counties, Columbia boasted fertile soil and, early on, a railroad depot.

Perhaps Dayton was becoming too citified because the Ides and other members of the wagon train soon resolved to homestead in Lincoln County, to the north. They were part of a settlement they named Mondovi after their hometown in Wisconsin. The Ides opened a general store. Lucy taught school. With the coming of the railroad, a land boom erupted in Spokan Falls, a town of around 400. Before long, Spokan gained an "e" and lost its "Falls." Sent there to buy supplies, Clarence instead bought several lots. When he returned to Mondovi, his father exploded.

The pair set out for Spokane to retrieve their money. On arrival, they discovered the investment had already doubled. My great-grandfather's anger evaporated. That investment changed their lives.

The family moved to Spokane. Clarence and his father began developing building lots. When statehood was achieved, in 1889, Clarence became active in Spokane politics. In 1892 he was elected to the State Senate, where he "distinguished himself as a man of unusual legislative ability." In that era, legislatures chose U.S. Senators. Ide managed the Senate campaign of John L. Wilson, a mustachioed Republican lawyer who earlier had been a legislator in Indiana. The Legislature was staunchly Republican. The *State Senate Journal*, in dry prose, tallied 26 ballots for seven candidates over five days. Wilson was rarely ahead but never far behind, with a loyal cohort of supporters spurred on by Senator Ide. The weary Legislature took an overnight breather. The next

Grandpa Clarence Ide, a state senator in 1893.
Washington State Archives

morning Wilson was elected with 75 percent of the vote. How I wish I could have asked my grandfather "What went on the night before?" Eighty-eight years later, I was elected to the U.S. Senate seat Wilson once held. (Happily, it took only one ballot.) My grandfather's reward was appointment as U.S. Marshal for Washington at Tacoma. Later, he served as U.S. Collector of Customs at Port Townsend. He remained a leader in Republican state politics and a strong supporter and ally of President Theodore Roosevelt. When I entered politics, Teddy Roosevelt, the progressive reformer who loved the outdoors and "the strenuous life," was one of my heroes.

Donald Douglas McKay, my maternal great-grandfather, was from Glengarry, Canada. In his youth, he made his way to Memphis, Michigan. My grandmother Dora was born there. Her mother died when Dora was but a year old. She went to live temporarily with family friends while her father regrouped from the loss. Reunited, they moved to Spokane. It was there that 19-year-old Dora met Senator Ide. They were married in 1896. Dora presided over a household deeply involved in Republican politics and entertained widely while tending a growing family.

My mother, Irma Alice Ide, was born in Spokane in 1897, the eldest of seven children, six daughters and a solitary son. She spent her early school years in Port Townsend, acquiring a fascination with politics that would last a lifetime. The Ides moved to Seattle after Clarence's U.S. Customs appointment ended. Irma attended Lincoln High School. When her father died unexpectedly in 1917, everything changed for the Ides. Irma dropped out of school to help support the large family.

MY PARENTS MET ON A BLIND DATE and were married a year later, on October 21, 1921. It was the beginning of a 57-year partnership for Les Evans and Irma Ide. They spent their first summer in a tent in a cow pasture near the Tolt River east of Seattle. Dad was supervising construction of a new bridge. Their first child, a daughter, died at birth. Two years later, that heartache was displaced by

joy. I was born on October 16, 1925, and christened Daniel
Jackson Evans. My brother Bob arrived in 1927. We lived in
a small rented bungalow near Roosevelt High School. My
folks stretched their resources to buy a home in Hawthorne
Hills, closing on the deal almost on the day the stock market
crashed.

Life is punctuated with might-have-beens. My father
had passed up a chance to play a role, likely lucrative, in
the birth of modern commercial aviation. One of his UW
classmates was a Norwegian kid—from Ballard, of course—
named Claire Egtvedt. He urged Dad to join him at a small
airplane company along the Duwamish River. Egtvedt was
a superb draftsman. Bill Boeing had snapped him up to help
engineer his new "aeroplanes." By 1920, Egtvedt was his
chief engineer. Given the post-war glut of surplus airplanes,
my dad wasn't convinced the fledgling Boeing Airplane
Company had a secure future—he laughed about that one
for years—and opted for the security of the King County
Engineering Department. Egtvedt would become chairman
of the Boeing Company.

At 3, I loved to ride my springy hobby horse.
Evans Family Collection

By 1930, the year my brother Roger was born, Dad was Deputy King County Engineer. America was in the throes of the Depression. Along the grubby industrial flats just south of downtown,
where Seattle's state-of-the-art sports stadiums now stand, homeless people erected a "Hooverville"
of tarpaper and tin shacks.

AT OUR HOUSE, we learned early on that voting was a special privilege. Dad often recalled that he
cast his first vote in 1916 for Woodrow Wilson because the professorial Democrat pledged to keep
us out of the carnage sweeping Europe. A year later we were at war. My father never again voted for
a Democratic candidate for president.

Mother, the real politician in the family, was as gregarious as Dad was quiet. An exuberant organizer, mother would become a Republican precinct committee person. When I decided to run for
office, she was an enthusiastic supporter, always certain I would win.

I remember my excitement as a seven-year-old in 1932. The neighbors were coming over to help
celebrate Hoover's re-election, confident his policies would end the Depression. I helped put out
hors d'oeuvres. That party ended early when KOMO Radio relayed news of the Roosevelt landslide
gaining steam in the East.

As the Democrats swept into office across the country, Dad and all other senior county engineers were replaced. There were no Civil Service regulations in King County back then. Thirty-eight-
year-old Les Evans was jobless, with a wife, three young children, and a mortgage on a new house.
He was grateful to find employment with the Public Works Administration, one of FDR's "alphabet"
agencies to spur recovery through construction projects. Keynesian projects like the WPA and the
Civilian Conservation Corps were brilliant quick stokes to lower unemployment. While money was

occasionally scarce, we never felt the despair of the Depression.

In second grade I was advanced half a grade, which forever created an academic no-man's-land for me. I entered Roosevelt High School in February of 1939, not as a member of the Class of 1942 or 1943 but somewhere in between. Awkward at the time, it turned out to be an advantage a few years later.

My teachers at Laurelhurst School were a succession of formidable spinsters. They were hard-nosed yet kind, dipping into their meager salaries to give us little extras. Miss McCullough distributed postcard-size Renaissance paintings. Miss Pearl passed out harmonicas and taught us all how to play. Miss Audett taught from a temporary portable building and created a prize from a chore. The child she chose as the day's best pupil—whether in academics or deportment—won the right to stoke the small furnace with coal. Miss Thulon demanded good penmanship. I had a hard time following her graceful Spencerian example. I tried to blame our scratchy wooden-pen nibs.

NEIGHBOR KIDS were lured to our back door when cookies came out of the oven. Danny, Bob and Roger were lucky to have a stay-at-home mom, and a dad with a job. We always sat together for dinner and talked about the day's events. As we grew older my brothers and I would challenge our parents, especially on politics. Mostly we were playing devil's advocate, yet the exchanges were lively. Today, when I'm in a restaurant, I often see kids hunched over their iPhones, twittering away, or playing games in between bites. Call me a fossil, but it bothers me.

My mother was a splendid cook. And at our house, no one left the table until Dad was finished. Evans family holidays and traditions

With my brothers, Bob, center, and Roger, in 1933. *Evans Family Collection*

continue in our home today. Christmas trees have to touch the 12-foot ceiling. At Thanksgiving, youngsters clamoring for another drumstick are reminded, "No seconds until father has firsts." It's funny how things like that—snippets of dialogue, sights and smells—stick in your mind forever.

Family was exceptionally important to my mother. Holidays were gathering times for a growing clan. Irma Evans also believed strongly in community service, actively supporting the Red Cross and PTA. In the early 1950s, a site near Laurelhurst east of the University of Washington was chosen for a new Children's Orthopedic Hospital. The neighbors opposed its construction, citing the residential character of the area and the noise and traffic a new hospital would create. Mother was part of a small group that supported the location. "We all have to do our part," she said. "If every neighborhood said no, then nothing would ever be built." I often thought about her wisdom many years later when our eldest granddaughter, Eloise, spent much of a year at Children's Hospital, successfully fighting cancer.

WHEN PEARL HARBOR finally brought the U.S. into World War II, my Dad served as Seattle District Engineer for the U.S. Army Corps of Engineers. In 1946 he was appointed King County Engineer. During my years as a civil engineering student at the University of Washington, it was instructive to tour county projects with my father. I was proud to be the County Engineer's son, especially because the road-crew guys doing the grunt work of public works respected his courtesy and expertise. He taught me the important difference between just spending budgeted money ("use it or lose it") and investing the public's money as a public trust.

My Dad was impeccably honest. Long before the introduction of public-service ethics laws, he had his own unwritten code. One Christmas, a courier delivered a splendidly wrapped present to our house. My brothers and I gathered around eagerly as Dad opened the box. He lifted out a handsome snap-brim wool fedora and placed it jauntily on his head. We shouted how good he looked. Then we learned an important lesson: He put the hat back in the box, shrugged and said, "I'll have to send it back." I exclaimed, "Why?" If I close my eyes, I can still see his face and hear his voice. "Because the hat came from a man who contracts for road work with the county." I was still confused. "But he's a good friend of yours." Dad smiled. "Yes he is, and the best way to keep him as a friend is to show no favoritism or even an appearance of favoritism. The next gift might be larger and harder to reject. That is a road you must never even start down." I have never forgotten that homily. And if you're imagining that he didn't say it just like that, you never knew my Dad.

Les Evans was a skilled craftsman, measuring every board. Early on I learned the joy and satisfaction of sawing and hammering as we constructed a summer home on Hood Canal. The whole family participated. Dad, ever the engineer, was the superintendent. He and I agonized over each measurement while my less fastidious brothers, Bob and Roger, groaned, "Let's build!"

My Dad retired in 1959 as the longest-serving chief engineer in King County history. He had presided over the construction of a permanent road system to serve the rapidly growing suburbs. In that era, the three County Commissioners supervised their road districts, often jealously. Dad fought hard to invest in high-quality concrete arterials while most commissioners wanted maximum miles. On rural roads, a pre-election application of fresh gravel was known as a "vote coat." Many of the main roads of King County today, crowded though they are, are a legacy of my dad's insistence on quality.

2
"Be Prepared"

In the fourth grade at Laurelhurst School, I learned it isn't easy to wear a crown—a cautionary tale for all who aspire to higher office. The occasion was my coronation as king during the annual school pageant, a major event of the school year. The 1934 production was a medieval coronation. There I was, resplendent in a purple cambric robe, its faux ermine edges trimmed with cotton dotted in black ink. The archbishop wielded a golden cardboard miter decorated with gumdrop jewels. I had rehearsed to perfection my first address to my subjects. When I declared, "I promise not to raise taxes," a parent at the back of the crowded room yelled, "Atta boy!" The audience roared. I promptly forgot my lines and have never uttered the phrase again.

Our new house, just two blocks from the two-story brick school, abutted the neighborhood playfield. With four boys my age as neighbors, it was paradise. We were perched on a hill above Lake Washington, with the university to the west and lots of undeveloped land in between. We were in awe of Husky Stadium, which seated 30,000. Along the Montlake Cut stood the Husky Shell House where Coach Al Ulbrickson was methodically assembling the ingredients for greatness. The 1936 varsity crew, in one of George Pocock's exquisite racing shells, put Seattle on the map at the Olympic Games in Berlin. Coming as it did in the middle of the Depression, that Gold Medal was a huge tonic for Seattle and a thrill for a 10½-year-old who always knew where he wanted to go to college. I have hundreds of books in my library, none better than Daniel James Brown's *The Boys in the Boat*.

There were no Little League teams when I was a boy. After school, we all hurriedly changed clothes and headed to the playfield. Baseball derivatives like "500" and "Workup" put everyone in the field, challenging the batter. A pop fly was dangerous since all nearby fielders were converging on the ball, attempting to get their turn at bat. During World War II, when Army troops occupied the neighborhood park, the ball field was adjacent. It was an automatic double if you hit a ball into the machine gun nest.

The city's only organized competitive sporting events for kids under 13 were sponsored by *The Seattle Times*. Pitching to "Old Woodenface" was a highlight of summer; "Old Ossie" meant it was fall. Old Woodenface was a scarred lumber frame, its interior dimensions equal to a strike zone. "Woody" was set up at home plate and each boy (only rarely did girls ever try out) attempted to throw three strikes before missing four times. The winner was the kid with the most strikeouts. The event always drew more than a hundred boys to Laurelhurst Playfield. We eagerly scanned the next day's edition of *The Times*, which featured the names of all the participants, not just the winner from each playfield. The city championship of Old Ossie—the equivalent of today's Punt, Pass & Kick competition—was also hotly contested. Winners received tickets to Husky football games.

I was never a good pitcher or passer. Checkers was my game, thanks to my dad. He taught us all the strategic moves. I won the playfield championship and entered the city finals, advancing to the checkers equivalent of Wimbledon's center court—in 1930s Seattle at least. The checkerboard was painted on a concrete pad; the checkers were the size of dinner plates. Spectators surrounded the board, my father prominent among them. Finally, it came down to three or four checkers. After pondering my next move for what seemed like minutes, I slid my giant checker onto a square. Out of the corner of my eye, I saw my father turn away in dismay. The end came swiftly. I shook hands with the new city champion and walked away with my dad. He consoled me on the long ride back home but also made sure I understood how to avoid making the same mistake ever again.

SUMMERTIME MEANT BASEBALL. I was a huge fan of the Seattle Indians of the Pacific Coast League. The legendary Leo Lassen was the radio voice of the team. He was famous for reading tele-type bulletins from away games and making it sound as if he was actually in Portland, Sacramento or Oakland. He took us all on the road. Lassen would have been a great baseball announcer in any era. We all tried to imitate his distinctive nasal twang, especially his home run call: "Back, back, back and it's over!"

My dad and Grandfather Evans took me to my first Indians game. We sat on the splintered boards that served as bleachers at Civic Field where Memorial Stadium now stands in the shadow of the Space Needle. The dirt field—there was not a shred of grass—extended from home plate to the center-field wall. Unfortunately, for all our hopes and cheers, the Indians weren't very good. Real hope came to Seattle when Emil Sick, owner of Rainier Brewery, bought the team, renamed it the Rainiers and produced championship baseball. Freddie Hutchinson was the Rainiers' young pitching star, the King Felix of his day. In 1938, my dad, brother Bob and I joined an overflow crowd of 16,000 at Sick's Stadium in the Rainier Valley to watch Hutch win his 19th game of the season on his 19th birthday. I can still hear the roar of the crowd every time he fired a strikeout.

Summers also meant camping. My uncle, Cameron Will, owned an abandoned logging camp on Camano Island. He built a lovely cottage. My cousin, Bob Will, my brothers and I spent hours fishing, swimming and exploring the seemingly endless forests that blanketed the hills. We had a few important chores: a hike up a winding dirt road to the neighbor's farm to get bottles of fresh milk; a trip to the well for water. My uncle carved a wooden yoke that we carried on our shoulders, with hooks for two buckets. The old pump sat in a glorious glade of maidenhair ferns. We vied to work its handle, stopping only to taste the cold, sweet water.

MY NEIGHBORHOOD PAL, Art "Pokey" Polson, always had good ideas. Shortly after I turned 12, Pokey said, "Let's go up to the fieldhouse and check out the Boy Scout troop." Troop 180 was a long-established institution in Laurelhurst. Sponsored by the local Community Club, it was led by Ross Williams, a banking executive, and later by William Douglas, an engineer with the telephone company. Douglas became one of my most important mentors. I led his son Bill on Scout trips. We still hike together 70 years after we first met.

The troop leaders—older boys from the neighborhood—played a key role in Scouting. Shortly after Pokey and I joined the troop we took our first hike, a November climb to Silver Peak, near Snoqualmie Pass. That was the day I learned the meaning of the Scout motto: "Be prepared." You could say it's a motto for everything, including politics.

I was apprehensive about the trip since the older boys laid it on about the perils ahead: Our legs and lungs would ache; cougars and bears lurked in the brush. "Stick together and stay alert," they warned. The first few miles along a forested trail were a delight. When we arrived at timberline, however, it began to drizzle. I shivered and began to wonder why I was there. As we climbed higher, the rain turned to sleet, then snow. I swore under my cold breath that my first hike would be my last—if I lived to make it home.

Eventually, the slope lessened. I caught my breath and cleared my head. Soon we stood atop Silver Peak. At 5,600 feet, we huddled in a blanket of freezing fog, Tenderfoots and Eagles alike, buffeted by snow and wind. "I did it!" I told myself. "I climbed the mountain." Pokey was smiling, too. As we descended, the rain stopped, the air grew warmer and the sun played peek-a-boo with the clouds.

When I burst through the front door, I couldn't wait to tell my folks and kid brothers what it was like up there. I can still conjure up practically every mile of that first Boy Scout hike. It was the beginning of a lifelong love affair with the magnificent mountains and wilderness of the Northwest.

I SET OUT, eagerly yet methodically, to master the requirements to move up through the ranks of Scouting. A mapping test designed to measure a Scout's compass and "pacing" skills was required to achieve First Class rank. Pacing was the way to pinpoint distances without a measuring tape. Carefully calculating the length of our strides, we counted our steps as we walked each leg of our map route. My father, ever the engineer, suggested a traverse that circled the area now occupied by University Village, the upscale shopping mall below the main campus of the University of Washington. The route was over a mile in length. My father patiently taught me how to locate buildings and landmarks along each leg of the map. Soon I tired of the tedious work and trudged along, complaining, "Dad, the other kids didn't do anything like this and they passed." Dad wasn't buying that. He urged me on, saying precision was important.

The fieldwork—a reconnaissance, if you will—was just the beginning. When we got home, Dad said, "Now you will find out how accurate your pacing and compass work was." We set up a card table and taped a large sheet of tracing paper to the top. With growing excitement, I began to translate directions and distances to the map. When we finally arrived at the last leg, Dad said, "Now we will discover your error of closure." I had no idea what that meant. "Even with good instruments," he explained, "a competent engineer won't come up with exact measurements. The difference when you return to your point of beginning is called the 'error of closure.' Now draw your last leg." I measured it carefully and found, to my delight, only a very small error. That test produced one of the most detailed maps in Scouting history. I kept it for many years. Somewhere between the area now occupied by dozens of University Village tenants, including the QFC supermarket, Din Tai Fung and Molly Moon's Ice Cream, I earned my stripes in mapping and pacing. That exercise also boosted my desire for a career in engineering. My dad was a very wise man.

A HIGHLIGHT OF EACH YEAR of Scouting was a two-week stay at Camp Parsons on Hood Canal. My first year there, 1940, featured a full-scale hike into the Olympic wilderness. Olympic Nation-

At Camp Parsons on Hood Canal in 1940. *Evans Family Collection*

al Park had been created two years earlier.* Our goal was the summit of Mt. Deception, the second-highest peak in the Olympics. A dozen scouts, led by Chief Ranger Grant Wilcox, started up the Dosewallips River trail. We soon veered into the woods and began a grueling climb through an old-growth forest of towering Douglas fir. As the trees thinned, we emerged on an emerald meadow tattooed with wildflowers. The cliffs of Mt. Deception loomed dauntingly before us. I couldn't imagine any feasible route to the top, 7,789 feet.

We circled the base of the cliff and discovered a steep gully that we climbed with great care. Higher and higher we climbed. Finally standing on top, I was awestruck by what I saw as I swiveled my head: Rank upon rank of craggy, majestic peaks in every direction, broken only by a commanding view of Puget Sound and faintly, so far in the distance, Seattle. Below us beckoned Royal Lake, our destination that evening. As our leader identified each mountain and river valley, I made a mental note of destinations for scores of future expeditions. I never imagined, however, that I'd be hiking there for the next 80 years. I was hooked on the Olympics. That was one of the greatest days of my life.

BY NOW I WAS EAGERLY QUALIFYING for merit badges leading to Eagle Scout, the highest achievement in Scouting. Only about four percent of Scouts make it that far. You're required to demonstrate proficiency in an array of life skills, including hiking, camping, swimming and lifesaving. Earning the merit badge for citizenship, especially community service, is important. I was asked to join the staff at Camp Parsons, where I spent two years as a junior staff member.

After the war, I was an assistant camp director while finishing college. I loved it. Every two weeks during those summers I led young scouts into the river valleys and peaks of the Olympics. Our equipment was pretty primitive. Sleeping bags were heavy, bulky kapok; tents nonexistent. Trapper Nelson packboards, which resemble a ladder with only three rungs, hung from our shoulders. The pull of gravity from your gear was unrelenting. Hikers develop strong backs, and Scout leaders learn how to herd cats—and cook. Preparing a campfire dinner for a dozen ravenous youngsters is no small feat. Our ad hoc cookware made the chore even more challenging. It consisted primarily of No. 10 tin cans—big enough to serve a large group and cheap enough to discard after the hike ends. We

---

* We have both Roosevelts to thank for preserving this international treasure. Though Theodore delighted in wantonly blasting big game on three continents, he was also a visionary conservationist. T.R. created Mount Olympus National Monument in 1909, and Franklin designated the monument as a national park in 1938. FDR liked to list his occupation at Hyde Park as "tree farmer."

strapped the cans on the outside of our backpacks. Their clanging sounded like cowbells on a Swiss mountainside.

The Recreational Equipment Cooperative, Seattle's legendary R.E.I., was nirvana for hikers, climbers and campers. In 1941, when R.E.I. was only three years old, and I only 15, I proudly became Member No. 1819. The mountaineering equipment neatly arrayed on shelves was generally beyond our means and ability. Now and then, however, we'd find affordable stuff to add to our gear—padded socks or a nifty pocket knife. When World War II ended, R.E.I. was a veritable treasure chest of war surplus equipment. Down sleeping bags, lightweight tents, air mattresses, contoured packs and gas stoves transformed our mountain expeditions. Comfort soared and pack weights plummeted.

I'M CERTAIN THAT SCOUTING also made me a better student. It was scary at first to leave the comfortable familiarity of Laurelhurst. Marked as achievers, 11 of us departed grade school at midyear in 1939. We boarded a belching orange school bus and joined 2,500 other Roosevelt High School students. They all seemed a lot older. But I quickly learned the classroom routine and settled in, excelling in science and math. I liked English, too. Registration each semester was a chaotic race through the hallways to sign up for classes taught by the popular teachers. Sam Glass was a gregarious, entertaining English teacher who set high standards. When a mob of students gathered outside his door to register, I climbed into his classroom through a first-floor window. Scouts are resourceful!

Miss Wilcox, who taught algebra, had my mother in her class at Lincoln High School 25 years earlier. "I wasn't very good at algebra," mother told me, "but I learned to follow directions. Make sure you pay attention." From Day One, Miss Wilcox set exacting standards. "Draw a vertical line 1½ inches from the left margin of the page (we were using unlined paper) and put a box around all your answers," she ordered. Other, seemingly silly, requirements followed. I was stunned and furious to receive only an average grade on my first test when I had all the answers right. When I complained to Miss Wilcox, she pointed out that I had not followed her rules on presentation. My answers were not boxed. I grumbled under my breath. In time I would realize that accuracy and order are vital in mathematics—and many other endeavors, most assuredly engineering. Politics, too, if you want to be effective.

Physics, algebra and chemistry were my favorite subjects. Some things definitely did not come easy. To fulfill part of the graduation requirement for English, I chose a course called Oral Expressions. The teacher, Minnie Moore McDowell, was popular. I discovered to my dismay, however, that it was a speech course with a heavy emphasis on individual participation. Deep down, I'm shy. The prospect of giving a speech to the rest of the class was terrifying. Each day found myself slumped down in my chair at the back of the room. I prayed for a fire drill, even an earthquake—anything to keep me from that dreaded moment when Miss McDowell would say, "Dan, it is your turn."

I joined the Roosevelt High School Minute Service, a boy's community service club, and proudly wore its green sweater. We went tree planting in the Snoqualmie National Forest. After the forest ranger showed us how it was done, we started the tedious climb up a barren slope. We stopped every few feet to drive a pickaxe into the soil and insert a young seedling. After a long, hard Saturday, we gathered along the road and looked up at a still barren hillside, wondering if our effort would ever pay off. Fortunately, I have lived long enough to know the answer. When I'm driving along Interstate-90 with my grandchildren I enjoy pointing out the lovely mature forest that now covers the once-barren slope. When we planted the trees, we were told it would be a 60-year forest. In other words, it would be ready for harvest and another cycle. Sustained yield forestry is an important practice. I also learned early on that some trees are more valuable to the ecosystem and our quality of life when they're left standing. The Mountains to Sound Greenway created by my friend Jim Ellis and nurtured by hundreds of volunteers will preserve this vital forest. I hope my grandchildren will show their grandchildren an old-growth forest that once was planned as merely a crop to be cut.

MY FOLKS WERE STRONGLY OPPOSED to Roosevelt's decision to violate tradition by seeking a third term in 1940. We were all excited by the dark-horse candidacy of Wendell Willkie, a charismatic former Democrat, who opposed the isolationism espoused by Robert Taft. Willkie was also a steadfast foe of racism, defying the powerful Ku Klux Klan in his early days as a Midwest lawyer and calling for legislation to deter lynching and ban poll taxes. I can still see myself sprawled on the floor in front of the radio with my two brothers, charting the delegate count at the GOP Convention in Philadelphia as Willkie gained momentum. "We want Willkie!" the galleries chanted. When Willkie won the nomination on the sixth ballot at 1 a.m. East Coast time, we leaped to our feet and cheered.

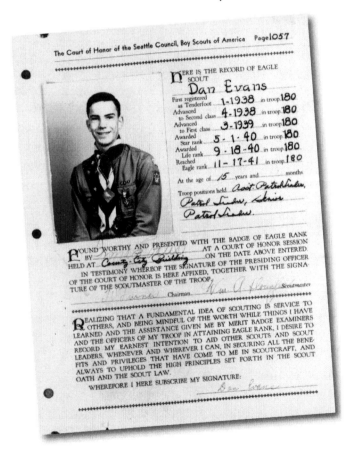

I became an Eagle Scout in 1941 after achieving my 21st merit badge. *Evans Family Collection*

In the spring of 1941, I decided to run for Sophomore Class Vice President. It was a huge class; nearly 700 students. We gathered in the auditorium to hear the candidates make their two-minute speeches. I listened nervously to my opponents—six bright girls. When it was my turn, I made my case, concluding with "May the best man win." The crowd chuckled and I won in a close runoff. The next year, my appetite for politics whetted, I ran for Junior Class President. That would be the only election I ever lost.

My enthusiasm for the outdoors gave me more and more opportunities to prove my Scouting skills. A good thing, too, as the Eagle Scout tests were challenging. Finally, I achieved my 21st merit badge and was summoned to a Court of Honor in the chambers of King County Superior Court Judge John Frater. He presided over the ceremony in his judicial robes, intoning our oaths in a deep baritone. A half dozen Eagle Scout candidates from troops across the city stood before him, ramrod straight. Jim Corlett joined me from

Troop 180. His father, Don, was my dad's longtime physician. My family looked on, radiating pride, as my mother pinned the Eagle badge on my 16-year-old chest. I was proud, too. I had realized a goal I had set as a Tenderfoot Scout four years earlier. I learned a lot about responsibility and goal-setting.

That ceremony took place on December 3, 1941. Four days later, on a quiet Sunday morning, our family set out to gather Christmas greens and a tree. While the others were looking for a perfectly proportioned 11-foot tree to grace our living room, I returned to the car to get some equipment and idly flipped on the car radio. I listened incredulously to a news bulletin and sprinted back through the woods shouting, "The Japs bombed Pearl Harbor!" We hurried home without a tree—that no longer seemed important—listening to the accounts of devastation in Hawaii, and ominous speculation that the Japanese would soon attack the Pacific Coast, likely landing along the beaches at Grays Harbor.

Municipal and military officials ordered a blackout of Seattle that evening. Our Boy Scout troop was deputized to serve as wardens to ensure no lights showed to guide enemy planes. I was standing on the corner of 43rd Avenue Northeast and East 41st Street at about 6:30 p.m. when Seattle suddenly went dark. The street lights were extinguished; the bright lights of the university blinked out. The glow of downtown vanished and an eerie silence settled over the city. I went home and listened to the radio with my folks and brothers. Like thousands of other Seattleites, we were hunkered down behind our shades and curtains. We wondered what would happen next.

The world changed forever that day. The innocence of my Eagle Scout youth evaporated overnight. The war was practically at our doorstep as Laurelhurst Playfield was occupied by an anti-aircraft battery. The soldiers lived in tents pitched on the old baseball diamond. Roger, my 12-year-old brother, walked a morning paper route that led him across the playfield. "Who goes there?" came a shout the first day he traversed battle lines before dawn. The unit became Laurelhurst's own. The soldiers were inundated with cookies and dinner invitations. The battery never fired a shot. The real war drew us all in, one way or another.

3
ENSIGN EVANS

As young men by the thousands left Seattle for the military in 1942, I found a Saturday job in a sailmaker's loft on the waterfront, earning 35 cents an hour to paint canvas lifeboat covers. They had to be blue on one side, yellow on the other. Blue was for camouflage against enemy aircraft swooping down to mop up survivors; yellow was a beacon to rescuers. I was eager to do my part to help win the war, but it was a messy job. I watched other workers splicing cargo netting and told the supervisor "I can do that." My Boy Scout training in knot-tying paid off in more ways than one: Splicers got 50 cents per hour.

A few months after Pearl Harbor, the war hit home at Roosevelt High School when we learned a member of the Class of 1940 had been killed in combat. Then a Scouting hero of mine was gone, too, his submarine missing in action in the Pacific. The newspapers began featuring casualty columns that grew longer by the day. Grieving Gold Star Mothers placed memorial banners in front-room windows. Boeing's big factory along the Duwamish River began cranking out B-17 bombers bristling with machine guns. The shipyards clanked around the clock.

That fall, with the war raging on multiple fronts, Washington's apple crop was imperiled by a picker shortage. I joined several hundred other high school kids on a train trip to Yakima to help with the harvest. The grateful growers met us at the station. Several of us jumped aboard an old pickup and bounced out to an orchard ringed with primitive shacks. Our bunks were little more than boards, and we washed up with cold water. Mornings were freezing, afternoons hot and dusty. Our pay, 10 cents a basket, translated to 7 or 8 dollars a day if you worked hard. We were all glad to return home.

When I was governor, I visited several migrant-worker camps and was shocked and disgusted that most were much the same as I had experienced 25 years earlier. And many of those families had young children; they weren't just a bunch of high school kids. When I returned to Olympia I asked my staff and agency directors to push for more humane conditions in the camps. We developed a bill setting responsible standards for farm housing. Some growers were irate, arguing they couldn't afford to make a major investment in temporary housing. "We cannot afford to do nothing," I shot back. "Adequately housed workers will be more productive and we should take pride in doing what is right." Developing new housing standards was an arduous task and it took several legislative sessions to produce the first appropriate bill protecting farmworkers.

AS HIGH SCHOOL WOUND DOWN, I was eager to get in uniform, never imagining I could become a teenage officer. Art Polson, my enterprising classmate, showed me some brochures describing a new naval officers' training program called V-12. The Navy, short on officers with degrees in engineering, math, sciences, and foreign languages, was offering qualified applicants full-ride college scholarships. Those accepted would carry a heavy course load and attend classes year-round. If you fulfilled all of the attendant military training requirements, you could earn a place in Officers' Can-

Seaman Evans, 1943. *Evans Family Collection*

didate School and a commission. We talked with our parents, visited the teeming Navy headquarters downtown and passed muster. Evans and Polson, both 17, were sworn into the U.S. Navy and ordered to report for duty on July 1, 1943. My awkward mid-year graduation status finally paid off. I finished high school on a Friday in February and enrolled at the University of Washington the following Monday to get a head start. Come July, when I officially became a V-12 officer candidate student, I already had one quarter of engineering classes under my belt.

Housing for V-12 trainees at the University of Washington was supplied by fraternity houses, now emptied of their military-bound brothers. We didn't look like frat boys. All V-12 recruits received standard apprentice seaman uniforms. Learning how to manipulate the infamous 13-button fly on Navy bell-bottom trousers took some doing.

We alternated nine credit hours of engineering with nine hours of naval studies. As we progressed, most cadets were transferred to officer training schools. Some of us were sent to Naval ROTC programs at other universities. In February of 1944, I was transferred to the University of California at Berkeley, then as now one of America's great universities.

The war was always out there. It dominated our lives. Every three months, new officers were commissioned. Most received orders to join amphibious forces preparing for the day when our island-hopping advances would move us to the threshold of Japan.

On D-Day in Europe, June 6, 1944, I followed every newscast on the fate of our forces storming the beaches at Normandy. I listened to my radio under the blankets long after lights out. Over the next 10 months, the allies ground out victories in Europe and advanced steadily in the Pacific. Then on a spring day came the stunning news of President Roosevelt's death. In office for an unprecedented 12 years, FDR was the only president millions of Americans had ever known. The nation grieved. And we wondered about our new and untested president, Harry Truman. It was reassuring to learn the plain-spoken former haberdasher had served with distinction as an artillery captain on the front lines of World War I.

IN THE LAST MONTH of my studies, we watched a training film that was anything but boring. "Fighter Direction" focused on the officers who had front-row seats in the ship's Combat Information Center. They used radar to direct our carrier-based fighter planes to intercept enemy aircraft. Well before the movie was over, I knew that's what I wanted to do. Qualifying for extra training was tough. One part of the exams was especially daunting. It tested speed and accuracy in spatial analysis. Two of us passed. We eagerly awaited our new assignment.

On graduation day in June of 1945, we gathered in the Greek Theater, a replica of an ancient stadium, in the heart of the Berkeley campus. Resplendent in our brand-new dress blue uniforms glistening with gold ensign's stripes, 55 of us stood and repeated the oath that made us officers in the United States Navy. When I Googled how much we were paid, I had to smile: $150 per month. But the money was secondary. We were now *officers*. And there was a war on.

The farewells were emotional. We had studied, marched and lived together for 16 months. Our fates were uncertain. Would we ever see one another again? The war in the Pacific was reaching a climax. If we entertained the thought that some of us wouldn't live to see victory, that possibility was quickly displaced by our excitement; 19 and 20-year-olds think they're immortal.

ENSIGN DANIEL J. EVANS, serial number 457409, was sent the other direction: Hollywood Beach, Florida, for radar training. I was there on August 6, when a Boeing B-29 dropped an atomic bomb on Hiroshima. We were incredulous that the Japanese still balked at surrender. Three days later, Nagasaki was flattened with a bomb triggered by plutonium from Hanford in Eastern Washington. The emperor told his imperial cabinet it was over.

At the Potsdam Conference following Germany's defeat, General Eisenhower learned of the plan to drop atomic bombs on Japanese cities. He voiced his "grave misgivings" to Secretary of War Stimson, saying that Japan "was already defeated." My admiration for Eisenhower has only grown over the years. When he became president, he often challenged the saber-rattlers. "If we have a nuclear exchange," he warned, "we're not going to be talking about reestablishing the dollar. We're going to be talking about grubbing for worms." However, I believed then, as I do now, that the atomic bombs, horrific weapons though they were, saved thousands of American lives. American losses at Okinawa from Japanese suicide pilots were devastating. The warlords were even mobilizing civilians, including women and children, to defend the home islands to the last gasp, with sharpened bamboo sticks if need be. FDR and Churchill had insisted on "unconditional surrender," and Truman wasn't about to budge from that posture when he became president.

Happily, the Marshall Plan to resuscitate Europe after World War II was American diplomacy at its finest. Likewise, Douglas MacArthur's performance as our temporary czar in postwar Japan. While hubris sometimes clouded his judgment, in this role he was a consummate statesman. MacArthur's even-handed wisdom was instrumental in Japan's adoption of a democratic constitution.*

On V-J Day I joined one of the wild celebrations that erupted all over America, from Miami to Mukilteo. No one would ever forget Pearl Harbor, least of all a Navy man.

My naval service was not over. I advanced to a Fighter Director school at Saint Simons Island, Georgia, then made the long trek to Pearl Harbor to be assigned to sea duty. I served on two aircraft carriers but never got the chance to direct a fighter plane. The planes were snug below decks. Our job was to bring home planes and troops from the Far East.

On Christmas day 1945, our ship, the *U.S.S. Puget Sound* (CVE-113) entered Manila Bay. As we moved gingerly toward the pier, we saw the masts of scores of sunken ships. They were pointing skyward like the ghostly gray remnants of a demented forest. The city lay in ruins, though cleanup

---

* The first postwar friendship mission to Japan was under the leadership of Seattle Mayor William Devin. By the time I became governor some 15 years later, Washington had established a much closer relationship with Japan than almost any other state. Trade was thriving and sister-city bonds were forged. People asked how I felt about the devastation we inflicted on Hiroshima and Nagasaki. I said I regretted it had come to that, but wouldn't second-guess President Truman.

was well underway. Food and fuel were still scarce, but for the first time in five years Christmas was a holiday of hope and celebration for the people of the Philippines. They had endured some of the worst of the war.

I RETURNED TO SEATTLE in July 1946, and like thousands of other discharged servicemen, signed up for the G.I. Bill to help finance my return to the University of Washington to complete my studies for a Bachelor of Science in Civil Engineering. The campus was jammed with vets, all eager to make up for lost time. I hadn't expected the competition to be so tough. Virtually all of my courses were upper-level engineering. However, there was a new course designed to give engineering students a taste of the humanities. Our instructor was Amy Violet Hall, a talented, demanding professor. Cramming literature, history, writing and verbal communication into the heads of engineers accustomed to thinking of a world filled with numbers, was no small feat. For me, the class became a delight and a revelation rolled into one. She opened the door to a world of learning beyond the geometry of engineering and naval tactics.

As graduation approached in 1948, I pondered grad school. My goal was either a Master of Science in Civil Engineering or Law School. The challenge of mastering law intrigued me. I decided instead on graduate work in engineering, mostly because it would require only one year of additional college, while law school meant three. The three years I'd spent in the Navy, though invaluable in the larger scheme of things, felt like time lost. That made law school seem impossibly long. I was, after all, 22.

A year later, I landed my first professional job in the City of Seattle's Engineering Department. I was soon asked to join a design team working on a major new project. For the next two years, I carefully calculated stresses and design elements for the Alaskan Way Viaduct. It was touted as a major new transportation artery for Seattle. Auto sales were skyrocketing. The central waterfront at the time was a marine industrial center dominated by deteriorating wharves serving a declining steamship industry. Long gone were the days when my great-grandfather's steamer, the *City of Seattle*, docked daily after a 70-minute trip from Tacoma. Grass grew through unused railroad spurs, and gaunt facades of industrial buildings faced Elliott Bay. Seattle had turned its back on its glorious heritage. The new Alaskan Way Viaduct offered fast transportation and, high above a grimy waterfront, an extraordinary view of the bay and the Olympic Mountains.

With my dad (UW Class of '17) on my graduation day at the UW in 1948. I received my master's in civil engineering a year later. *Evans Family Collection*

In any case, that project was much more interesting than being assigned to tedious design work on street intersections. The viaduct was by far the biggest project attempted in the Seattle area up to that time.

To be part of the design team, even as a junior member, was pretty exciting. I delighted in watching the construction of columns and beams I helped design and the transformation of paper plans into reality.

In 2017, with its demolition on the horizon, the executive director of the Museum of History & Industry acknowledged that the viaduct was a "triumph" of civil engineering. "It was actually an elegant solution," a downtown bypass that reduced traffic along the formerly choked surface streets below, Leonard Garfield said.

As I watched one of the last sections crumble under the wrecking ball two years later, I told a TV reporter I had mixed emotions: I was sorry to see it go because it was a piece of what I helped accomplish as a young engineer. But the prospect of creating a spectacular front door for the city I love outweighed nostalgia. In 1995, I had advocated replacing the Viaduct with tunnels.

The Alaskan Way Viaduct under construction at the north end of the waterfront in the spring of 1950. *Seattle Municipal Archives*

4
COUNTING NOSES

ouse Speaker Tip O'Neill, who famously observed that "All politics is local," could have been talking about my political coming-out party. Our next-door neighbor, Bob Robinson, dropped by one spring evening to ask my parents to accompany him and his wife to the Republican precinct caucus. The Robinsons were avid supporters of U.S. Senator Robert Taft, the flinty conservative from Ohio. Bob Robinson wanted to be chosen as a delegate to the 1948 King County Republican Convention. My mom and dad agreed to go. When Bob asked if I wanted to tag along, I said, "Sure."

Precinct caucuses are, or at least ought to be, the foundation of citizen involvement in our democratic society. Maybe it's just nostalgia, but caucuses seemed more civil back then, though fierce discussions occasionally erupted. I've seen some nasty infighting in my day. Still, I don't remember anything like the vitriolic shouting matches that erupted when supporters of Trump and Cruz and Sanders and Clinton squared off in 2016. What I know for certain is that we all knew our neighbors' names.

Besides being local, politics is counting noses. As our committeewoman greeted us at the door and took our coats, I glanced around her front room. There were only two others in attendance. *We had the votes.* Bob Robinson was quickly elected a county convention delegate, with five votes to our hostess's three. Then she noted that we were entitled to two delegates. Bob leaned over and asked me if I'd like to join him at the county convention. I said that would be great. By an identical 5-3 vote I crossed the line from observer to participant. Robinson, however, had made a major political error. He assumed I was for Taft.

Senator Taft's leading opponent for the GOP presidential nomination was New York's governor, Thomas Dewey, a former racket-busting prosecutor. For me, Taft was too conservative and too old—nearly 60—and Dewey too stiff, with his Fuller Brush mustache and thin-lipped smile. Alice Roosevelt Longworth, Teddy Roosevelt's acid-tongued daughter, said Dewey looked like "the little man on a wedding cake," and it fit.

I supported Harold Stassen, who had been elected governor of Minnesota a decade earlier at 31. Stassen was a Navy man, serving in the South Pacific during the war. He and Eleanor Roosevelt were leading members of the U.S. delegation to the organization meetings of the United Nations. Stassen's perennial candidacy would become a running joke in the decades to come. In 1948, however, he was the Republican equivalent of his fellow Minnesotan, Hubert Humphrey, the Young Democrats' civil-rights champion. I was eager to join the small band of Stassen supporters who held the balance of power between the dueling delegations supporting Taft and Dewey. I thought we could leverage our position to gain extra delegates to the state convention. When I arrived, I was dismayed to learn that our brain trust had already reached a deal with the Taft and Dewey forces. For rolling over, we received a miserably small number of delegate spots that were immediately appropriated by our self-serving leaders. I felt betrayed. Ray Moore, the instigator of the sell-out, later served as King County Republican Chairman. Then he switched parties and served as a Democratic state senator for many years. Jumping ship at an opportune moment was just Ray's style. He was a wily character who loved to pontificate.

Dewey, who had all but ordered new drapes for the Oval Office, lost to Truman that November in one of the greatest upsets in American political history. "Give 'em hell, Harry" won Washington's electoral votes after whistle-stopping the state with Governor Monrad "Mon" Wallgren, one of his favorite poker pals. When I was governor, visitors to the Mansion always wanted to see Truman's signature in the guestbook.

The great political parlor game is "What-ifs." Suppose Stassen, with a boost from the Washington state delegation, had won the nomination? He was a forceful stump speaker. Could a moderate who appealed to military veterans have beaten Truman?

The 1948 election whetted my appetite for politics and taught me some important lessons. One was that smoke-filled rooms are hazardous to your health. Fresh air is an elixir.

I LEARNED TO SKI the hard way when I was a Boy Scout. We packed our rented or borrowed skis to a mountain cabin and set out the next day for a large clearing atop a forested hillside. With little concept of technique, I pointed my skis downhill. Like a kid handed the keys to a Porsche, I soon reached speeds way beyond my capacity. Trees ahead, I opted for a spin-out that created a windmill of skis, legs and arms. Glad to be in one piece, I grinned sheepishly as the other scouts hooted. By the end of the day I had learned how to execute a crude turn, and of greater importance, how to stop.

A truckload of war surplus ski equipment arrived in Seattle after the war. The skis from the European theater—painted white for camouflage—were almost new. We meticulously removed the paint and varnished the natural wood to perfection. It was a thrill to speed down the slopes, a rooster-tail of powdery snow in my wake.

As the spring and summer sunshine opened routes for hiking and mountain climbing, I volunteered to lead an Explorer Post of teenage scouts. We studied the history of early-day climbing in the Northwest, particularly the expedition that attempted to cross the Olympic Mountains in 1890, with Army Lieutenant Joseph O'Neil as its leader. After a winter of research and preparation, we set out from the Skokomish River trailhead in August of 1950. Bill Douglas, Tom Winter, Bob Thwing and I began a six-day trek, mostly off-trail. Following the route of the O'Neil expedition, we crossed the Olympics. The weather was spectacular. We saw hundreds of elk, viewed the world from the top of Mt. Olympus and emerged at the Hoh River trailhead within an hour of our predicted time. It was the trip of a lifetime. We later calculated that we had climbed and descended a total of 21,000 feet. That is the height of Mt. McKinley (Denali) from sea level.

WHEN THE KOREAN WAR ERUPTED in the summer of 1950, I was apprehensive about being recalled to active duty. Soon, however, the tide turned with MacArthur's brilliant amphibious landing at Inchon. U.N. forces chased the North Koreans to China's doorstep. At the rate things were going,

MacArthur said, the troops might even be home by Christmas. Then suddenly, in overwhelming numbers, the Chinese swarmed down from the hills along the Yalu River. With the onset of a brutal winter that saw temperatures plummet to 35 degrees below zero, U.N. forces at the frozen Chosin Reservoir barely escaped annihilation. The war was far from over.

I came home from work on a sunny August afternoon and leafed through the mail. A letter in a crisp U.S. Navy envelope jumped out. I was instructed to report for two weeks of Combat Information Center training in San Diego. This was a puzzling development. I had not applied for that program. Then my eyes darted to the final paragraph: "On completion of refresher training, report to the Commander, Pacific Fleet for further assignment." I was perplexed, dismayed, even angry that my carefree world was being interrupted. Then I sublimated my selfishness and took stock of the Navy's view: I had received two years of training during my previous three years of service. It wanted a return on its investment. There was a war on. And I had taken a naval officer's oath. The next two years rate as perhaps the most valuable of my life. I learned leadership skills, sailed the Pacific, fought in a war, and discovered a desire for public service.

I reported for duty in San Diego in the fall of 1951. After two weeks of refresher training, I was assigned as a Combat Information Center officer aboard the *U.S.S. Leonard F. Mason*, a destroyer. The Combat Information Center on our ship was a small darkened room filled with radar scopes and beeping sonar equipment. The CIC was the hub of information-gathering and electronic navigation. During the next year, we completed two tours of duty in the Far East.

Task Force 77 operated in the Sea of Japan. Our ship's assignment was to help protect the aircraft carriers and battleships. Nighttime operations required extraordinary seamanship, especially during air operations. The fleet commander had a biblical bass voice that matched his radio call sign. We knew air operations were about to begin when we heard "This is Jehovah. Turn to course 320 degrees." The armada of blacked-out ships began to turn into the wind, an intricate maneuver. The big aircraft carriers turned ponderously while the speedy destroyers raced ahead to take new positions. I loved the mathematical challenges involved in maneuvering our ship to its new position. I knew that those in command on the darkened bridge above could see little of the ships around them in the endless void of a starless night. They depended on the radar and technical agility of those of us below in the humming CIC.

During one daytime flight operation, the aircraft carrier *U.S.S. Boxer* caught fire. Cornered by flames, terrified sailors began jumping overboard. A black plume of smoke rose hundreds of feet as the fire spread. The radio began crackling with orders to search for 63 men identified as missing. I was responsible for navigating our search track. As I squinted at the coordinates, I felt sure it was a mission with no happy ending.

Miraculously, after almost an hour of searching, we saw splashing. We scrambled to lower the whaleboat and soon brought aboard an almost naked survivor who gasped that he had been treading water with a buddy. Then we spotted the half-dead second sailor. Unable to shuck his clothes, he was barely able to move. Despairing, they had watched the task force sail over the horizon. We learned that we had rescued the last pair of the missing men. The other 61 were safe as well.

THE *LEONARD F. MASON* later was temporarily assigned to patrol the Chinese coast along the Straits of Formosa. We were ordered to remain 12 miles offshore in international waters. Twice we accidentally maneuvered to within 10 miles of islands in the Chinese sphere. The captain was furious. After the second incident, I was in the wardroom having a cup of coffee when the squawk box erupted: "Lieutenant Evans, report to the captain's cabin immediately!" I took the ladder two steps at a time. Our red-faced skipper declared that messy navigation was intolerable, given the strict limits of our mission. With that, he summarily relieved the navigator and appointed me as his replacement. "Aye, aye, captain!" I declared, suppressing a gulp. I was already Operations Officer, supervising all of the ship's electronic communications—radio, radar, sonar and decoding machines.

I went in search of our Chief Quartermaster. "Chief," I beseeched, "I haven't done any navigation since my midshipman days. Give me a crash course." Every naval officer worth his salt knows Chief Petty Officers are the backbone of the Navy. Chief Hunt that evening handed me a sextant and patiently guided me back through the basics of celestial navigation. Today, practically every vehicle has a talking GPS "nav system" linked to satellites. You can get coordinates on your iPhone. But in 1952, electronic navigation was in its infancy. Sextants and chronometers were a sailor's essential instruments. Little had changed in hundreds of years.

I carefully recorded the angles of several stars at twilight. Accurate sextant readings required not only seeing the star but also having a clear horizon. We retired to the navigator's

The *Leonard F. Mason*'s newly appointed navigator gets a crash course in sextant reading from the destroyer's Chief Quartermaster along the Straits of Formosa in 1952. *Evans Family Collection*

post just behind the bridge and began the mathematical tasks to translate the angle of each star to a line on our chart. The first two lines crossed close to our estimated position. To my horror, the third line created a triangle 20 miles across. Half of it bisected the Chinese mainland. I had flunked my first try. Practice makes perfect. Finally, the lines crossed in a point. Soon, even when the ship pitched and rolled in heavy seas, I was confident I had the hang of it. Celestial navigation required that I take sights each dawn and dusk. I thrived on the challenge of making accurate readings and the responsibility of guiding the ship to its destination. Engineers and navigators learn early on that painstaking attention to detail is crucial.

My navigational skills were severely tested when our destroyer division transited Shimonoseki Straits, the narrow, twisting waterway between Honshu and Kyushu, the main islands of Japan. I was on the bridge, navigating by taking bearings on prominent points of land and buoys. Our ship was third in line that day. I watched in consternation as our lead ship, with the division commander on board, steamed straight ahead just past a marker buoy. The second destroyer turned to port around the buoy. The skipper turned to me and exclaimed, "OK, Evans, what do I do?" I gulped and replied,

"Turn to port. The second ship is on course." At that moment the radio crackled and the division leader reported "I am aground." That was the end of naval careers for the skipper and the navigator of that destroyer.

IN MIDWINTER 1952 we were detached from the fleet to provide gun support off the coast of North Korea. Our destroyer eased in close to the coastal cliffs while the battleship *U.S.S. Iowa* sailed slowly up the coast 10 miles offshore, firing her main batteries at a railroad line clinging to a steep hillside. We listened to the eerie whistle of 16-inch shells flying overhead, gauged the results and sent gunnery corrections back to the battleship. Our teamwork regularly destroyed the rails. The North Koreans regrouped, hiding their trains in a maze of tunnels. Every night they would mobilize an army of workers to repair the track and move their trains to another tunnel. It was an intricate chess game of guns and locomotives, of spotters and repairmen, neither side claiming checkmate.

The *Leonard F. Mason* was sent next to join the siege of Wonsan Harbor, a vital North Korean transportation hub at the narrow neck of the peninsula. It was a dangerous and difficult assignment. The hills surrounding the harbor were speckled with gun emplacements connected by tunnels. It was the railroad cat-and-mouse game all over again. The Koreans timed their fire to our mealtimes, assuming it would take us more time to react. After a few shots, they would retreat into the tunnels, only to pop up some distance away to give it another go. One afternoon, I thought we were in real trouble. Sailors were lined up for the evening meal when we heard the clamor of the bell sounding General Quarters. I raced for the bridge, the navigator's battle station, and clapped on my helmet just in time to see a geyser of water erupt a hundred yards away. All along the destroyer's deck, binoculars scanned the hillside searching for the menacing gun. A second shot hit about 50 yards short of our ship. "My, God," I thought, "he has us bracketed!" By that time we were hammering the enemy gun emplacement. To our immense relief, the shooting stopped. We were lucky.

We were part of the longest siege of a port in U.S. naval history. American ships pounded that critical center of transport for the North Korean Army for 861 days.

OUR ASSIGNMENT OFF WONSAN finished, we joined the three other destroyers in our division for the long voyage back to Long Beach, California. On arrival, we immediately began reprovisioning and making repairs. The crew also received more training. As we awaited redeployment to Korean waters, I regularly decoded messages. One morning, my name suddenly appeared on an incoming message. Typing furiously, I was dismayed to read orders transferring me to a job I hadn't sought and certainly didn't want: "Aide and Flag Lieutenant to the Commander Destroyer Forces Far East." My only contact with aides was watching them fetch their admirals' hats as they left the Officers Club. Destroyer sailors, on the other hand, were special—daring, smart, and most importantly, informal. I had no desire to trade that for the formality of an admiral's staff.

The next day I reported to the flagship. It was moored right across the pier from the *Mason*. Rear Admiral William K. Mendenhall was ramrod straight and balding, with a bristly white mustache and piercing eyes. I would come to admire his wit and penchant for cutting to the chase. Our conversation went like this:

"Lieutenant, have you ever been an aide?"

"No, sir!"

"Well, I have never had an aide, so let's learn together."

With that, he grinned disarmingly. I smiled too.

Admiral Mendenhall was a wise mentor. He gave me major responsibilities on shore and at sea. A few months after my arrival, a message arrived for the admiral, one that had huge consequences for me. Mendenhall was ordered to report to General Mark Clark's headquarters in Tokyo as one of five members of a newly formed Military Armistice Commission. Korean War armistice talks were underway. The orders authorized one staff member to accompany the admiral. I delivered the message to his office and stood at attention with fingers crossed as he read the orders. Leaning back, he smiled and asked if I would like to accompany him. "Yes sir!"

Lieutenant Evans as an admiral's aide in 1952. *Evans Family Collection*

Events unfolded quickly. Admiral Mendenhall promptly left for Tokyo. I followed a few days later with some tools we'd need. Soon we were engaged in preparing maps of the demilitarized zone, preparing for our move to the truce camp, and getting acquainted with other members of the commission. President Eisenhower, who as a candidate in 1952 had vowed, "I shall go to Korea," was determined to end the war. We all expected an early armistice.

We moved to the United Nations truce camp at Munsan-ni, a few miles from Panmunjom where the truce was to be signed. My quarters were a walled tent shared with the aide to General Blackshear Bryan, the head of our five-member commission. We worked closely with the aide to a Thai general who also served on the commission. Except for interpreters, we were the only staff allowed to accompany commission members to Panmunjom.

It was a short but harrowing helicopter ride, following a narrow, predefined route. Below us we spotted North Korean soldiers, guns at the ready, apparently hoping we would stray from the authorized flight path.

Final preparations for the signing ceremony were virtually complete when Syngman Rhee, the mercurial president of South Korea, unilaterally released thousands of anti-communist prisoners of war. Tensions rose dramatically, peace talks ceased, and we waited. For two months, negotiations continued, now between UN commanders and Rhee, who wanted to continue the war.

I spent much of the time helping prepare for the visits of dignitaries to the truce camp, and writing letters home detailing my adventures. They were increasingly filled with my youthful anger over the military and political stalemates in Korea and the conflicts back home over Eisenhower's new initiatives. In one letter to my dad on Father's Day, I expressed my love and respect for him before launching into a diatribe over politics. He kept the letter and showed it to me years later after I became governor. I was fascinated to read what I had written:

"I feel completely frustrated sometimes when I think of how far down the path we have gone toward collectivism and how little my one vote seems. I think the place to begin reversing this trend lies right in our state governments. I wish that I was home for this election for I would be greatly tempted to run for the state Legislature from the 43rd District."

It was my first expressed desire to run for political office. I suspect I was voicing a long-hidden thought.

PRESIDENT EISENHOWER'S PATIENCE had its limits. Syngman Rhee agreed to armistice conditions after we threatened to remove him from office. In the space of 48 hours, North Korean and UN teams constructed a new building for the signing ceremony. Dignitaries from the United Nations, China and North Korea filled the cavernous hall on July 27, 1953. Medals gleamed and jingled as military officers marched to their seats. Leaders of the two sides moved swiftly to a small table and scratched their signatures to an armistice agreement. As I observed the arrogance of the North Koreans and the obvious distaste of UN commanders, I realized this was neither peace nor truce, simply an armistice or cessation of battle.*

The simple ceremonies concluded quickly and we prepared for the first meeting of the Military Armistice Commission to be held the next day. We three aides were to join the interpreters and the five members of the commission as the only UN representatives to the discussions at Panmunjom. The site of the talks was a small wooden building astride the armistice line. The boundary split the negotiating table right down the middle. I peeked through a window at the green felt-covered table adorned with nameplates of the 10 delegates, five from each side. Two small table flags identified the United Nations and North Korea. A young North Korean aide entered the building and surreptitiously slid a small wooden block under the North Korean flag to raise it above the UN flag. When he left, we crept in, removed the block and snuck out just in time to escort the delegates in. We were elated for days, reveling in our small triumph for the good guys.

A month after the truce was signed, my tour of duty ended. I began the long journey home after a final farewell to Admiral Mendenhall. I admired and respected him greatly as a mentor and a commanding officer. His final advice was to encourage me to remain in the Navy. He predicted a bright future for me as a senior officer, but when it was apparent I was determined to return to the Northwest, he offered his best wishes. "Young man," he said, "you can do anything you want to do."

---

* As a U.S. senator, I visited Panmunjom 33 years later. Not much had changed physically, and the Armistice Commission was still meeting. Instead of five top-ranked officers, the UN representative was an American lieutenant colonel. The belligerency and polemics of 1953 were undiminished. We still had found no peace and the armistice continued.

5
THE REFORMERS

As I plunged into civic life in 1953, the Municipal League, Jaycees and Young Republicans were infused with the energy of college-educated veterans eager to build better communities. City Hall and the Courthouse were patronage mills; the police department winked at corruption, and Seattle's burgeoning bedroom communities were dumping raw and partially treated sewage into Lake Washington at the rate of 20 million gallons per day.

A young engineer with a growing interest in politics. *Washington State Archives*

The Municipal League was a lively mix of lawyers, accountants, engineers, contractors, real-estate developers and businessmen—upwardly mobile men getting married and having kids, though I was a late bloomer on that score. The Jaycees—short for Junior Chamber of Commerce—combined activism with irreverent fun. No old guys need apply. At age 35 you were declared an "exhausted rooster" and relegated to the sidelines.

With the Alaskan Way Viaduct under construction, our design team at the Seattle Engineering Department was developing specifications for a new bridge across the Duwamish River at First Avenue South. I loved being an engineer. It's a profession where precision, problem solving and teamwork matter. Being single, I also had energy to spare.

While many of us harbored political ambitions, the Municipal League and Jaycees were nonpartisan. I acquired a slew of smart new friends, Democrats as well as Republicans. Jim Ellis, the League's 32-year-old attorney, wasn't very big, yet he was one of the most persuasive human beings I've ever known. His vision for a model community—clean air and water, world-class transportation, parks and recreation accessible to all, a flowering of the arts—was coupled with painstaking preparation. Ellis put in so much work ahead of time that he knew the answers before you came up with the questions. Wiry, with intense eyes and a warm smile, he became the greatest civic activist in Seattle history.

THE MUNICIPAL LEAGUE had been a fixture of the "good government" movement in Seattle since 1910. In a city known for its "tolerance policy" toward gambling and prostitution, the league set out to combat patronage and graft by championing Civil Service for the police and other munici-pal employees. It was also an early advocate of land-use regulation. The league's most influential, and perennially controversial, role was its election-year rating of candidates. It sent out questionnaires and conducted forums to weigh their qualifications.

Undaunted by a losing campaign to modernize the King County charter—mossbacks in both political parties had staged a full-court press to defeat the measure in 1952—Jim Ellis was embark-ing on a crusade to clean up Lake Washington. The project was a huge engineering scheme and a dramatic political challenge. I was entranced with both aspects and signed up on the spot when Ellis issued his call for volunteers.

Heartache propelled Jim's sense of mission. Jim and his brother Bob—just two years apart—were as close as twins. When Bob Ellis died in combat in Germany just 11 weeks before VE Day, Jim was an Army Air Forces meteorologist, far from harm's way at a base in Idaho. Losing his brother brought Jim to his knees, literally. "I could not understand how God could permit something like that to happen," he told me and hundreds of other friends over the years. Each time he told the story, his grief—and lingering guilt—were heartbreaking. Though the war was almost over, Jim wanted to be sent into combat, hell-bent on revenge, or at least catharsis. Finally, his wise wife, Mary Lou, sat him down. She wrapped an arm around his shoulders and put her face inches from his. "You have to get hold of yourself," she said. "You're trying to throw your life after his. Why not make your life count for his?" Jim told us it was the defining moment of his life. He resolved to "do something ex-tra" to improve his community. Bob was Jim's silent partner.

Another new friend was motivated by a similar loss. John Spellman was an affable, pipe-smok-ing labor lawyer, an Eisenhower Republican, and one of the leading young Catholic laymen in the Northwest. He had studied for the priesthood before attending Georgetown Law School, where he was a member of a national champion moot court team. While my destroyer was shelling the coast of North Korea, John's brother David, a West Pointer, was leading a company of paratroopers toward an important enemy rail terminal when a sniper picked him off. John Spellman, like Jim Ellis, was imbued with a sense of mission. I was, too. Thousands of other men our age had never made it back home.

We were all energized by the Pritchard brothers—Joel and Frank—as witty as they were bright. Army veterans both—Frank in Europe, Joel in the South Pacific—they were moving up in the print-ing business and retail politics. Frank, five years Joel's senior, was in his element in a backroom or basement with a mound of voter-registration lists. Joel, an engaging public speaker, could have earned a decent living doing standup comedy. His Bob Newhart imitation was deadpan hilarious. The Pritchards made their mark as part of Governor Arthur B. Langlie's King County campaign brain trust in 1952 when the former Seattle mayor won a third term in Olympia. They were also foot soldiers in the Eisenhower campaign that year, raising money, recruiting doorbellers, distributing fliers.

Gordon S. Clinton, a World War II naval officer, was another popular Municipal Leaguer. Clin-ton, 33 in 1953, had graduated from the University of Washington and Harvard before attending UW Law School after the war. He was a fellow Eagle Scout and Navy man, as well as a former FBI agent. A foe of "tolerance," he instigated a Municipal League probe of Seattle City Hall.

In 1956, the year Municipal Leaguers elected Clinton mayor, we recruited another foot soldier—a slender, witheringly bright Ivy Leaguer named Slade Gorton. He had no desire to enter the family's legendary fish business. He was intent on a career in public service in a state that welcomed newcomers.* Gorton joined our Municipal League speakers' bureau, the Town Criers.

When "no swimming" signs were posted on Seattle's beaches, citizens demanded action. Ellis led a Municipal League study that proposed a new regional entity, the Municipality of Metropolitan Seattle. "Metro" would have the power and taxing capacity to create sewage treatment plants for the entire region. It was my first involvement in civic activity. Inspired by Ellis, I learned the joy and commitment of volunteer action. I also learned that big ideas are hard to sell to suspicious voters, especially in the suburbs.

I JOINED THE CAMPAIGN to elect a new state Jaycee president. Jaycee political conventions were boisterous affairs, replete with vote-wooing and shifting alliances as delegates advanced their candidates. I made new friends from Jaycee chapters around the state, many of whom later helped in my campaign for governor. I also learned some practical politics. Seattle was the largest chapter in the state and carried the most votes into the state convention. We were confident our candidate for state president would win, only to discover, much too late, that voting strength was not based solely on membership. Each club was assigned an equal base vote. The winning candidate assembled a coalition of smaller clubs and prevailed in a close vote. We big-city guys learned an important political lesson that day: Always know the rules before you start the contest, and never ignore even the smallest community in either political or legislative affairs. Elma can matter as much as Everett.

Seattle Jaycees spearheaded a campaign for Daylight Savings Time. We soon discovered that influential legislators from farming districts opposed the plan. Their constituents maintained it was tinkering with the Earth's natural rhythms. My teammate in the push to enlist the support of other Jaycee chapters was Brock Adams, who went on to serve as a Democratic congressman, Secretary of Transportation, and my seatmate in the U.S. Senate.

We found that most rural clubs wanted no part of our plan. So we began the signature-gathering with an all-volunteer crew. Suddenly, in what amounted to a rescue scene from a Hollywood Western, an ardent supporter arrived: the Motion Picture Operators. They promised to fund the campaign once enough signatures were gathered to get the measure on the ballot. Pleased with their support, we were also puzzled. Why would they care about daylight savings? It didn't take long to discover why. Movie theatres were in hot competition with drive-ins, which sprouted after World War II as millions of Americans acquired autos. Daylight savings time would extend daylight hours and force the outdoor theatres to begin their programs later in the evening.

Initiative 193 qualified for the ballot through our efforts, but the promised financial support for the campaign never materialized. In November 1954, the Grange and other farm groups crushed our proposal. Daylight Savings Time finally was adopted by Initiative 210 six years later. The cows survived; drive-ins not as well.

THE WASHINGTON ATHLETIC CLUB offered superb athletic and workout facilities. It was also

---

* The post-war Municipal League would produce two governors (Evans and Spellman), three U.S. senators (Gorton, Evans and Brock Adams), a congressman and lieutenant governor (Joel Pritchard), and numerous legislators.

A climbing expedition in the 1950s. *Evans Family Collection*

a free, get-acquainted pass to the Toastmasters Club at the WAC. When I walked into my first meeting, I spotted two of my grade-school classmates, Pat Goodfellow and Art Bishop. Friendly faces helped me shake my apprehension over public speaking. Every session was a verbal workout as we critiqued one another. I was a Toastmaster for the next 10 years.

I was asked to join the WAC's Membership Committee as a representative of the younger members. Before we began sifting applications, a pompous longtime member cleared his throat and proceeded to reveal the unwritten rules: "Ah, for the benefit of new members of the committee you should know that, ah, we must be careful about admitting certain kinds of members." There was an uncomfortable silence before the proceedings continued. It was only after we adjourned that I fully realized what he meant: No Jews or other minorities would be welcomed to our august club. Women were only allowed as associate members. Stunned and appalled, I was ready to resign from the committee. I talked it over with my father. "Stick with it," he counseled. "You can help change things more from the inside than the outside." He also told me that the WAC had teetered on the edge of bankruptcy during the Depression until several of Seattle's prominent Jewish families provided financial help. They were the club's only Jewish members for many years.

My father was right. Working from within, I became a more effective voice for inclusion than if I had resigned on the spot.

THE KING COUNTY REPUBLICAN headquarters was a dingy office in the Arcade Building on Second Avenue. I visited one day, eager to volunteer, yet not knowing quite what to expect. Joseph Lawrence, the county GOP chairman, sat alone at an old oak desk under framed photos of President Eisenhower and Governor Langlie.

The party organization was debilitated by the 1952 feud between Taft and Eisenhower supporters. Langlie and Don Eastvold, a silver-tongued young Eisenhower delegate, had played key roles in a fight over delegates at the National Convention. The Eisenhower forces prevailed but Senator Taft's embittered conservatives were busy building grass-roots strength to take control of the party organization.

Lawrence was startled that an eager volunteer had presented himself at headquarters. He wasn't quite sure what to do with me. Finally, he suggested I call John Barnard, the leader of the 43rd Legislative District. Barnard, a Boeing engineer, was a dedicated yet inexperienced political district leader. That made two of us. It was the beginning of a long and successful political friendship. Neither of us knew what was expected so we read books on political organization. Building precinct strength was the prevailing advice. We set out to fill precinct committeeman vacancies. Along the way, we recruited some extraordinary workers, including Edith Williams, a granddaughter of President Theodore Roosevelt. Janet Tourtellote and Emily Kirk were also amazing. Tourtellote and Williams later served as national Republican committeewomen. And many years later, I was delighted to appoint Edith to the Board of Regents at the University of Washington and Janet to the board of The Evergreen State College.

Before long, virtually all precincts were organized. John Barnard would become King County Republican Chairman. And I was off and running for the Legislature.

6
THE CANDIDATE

I borrowed a reverse Polk Directory from the public library and traced the boundaries of the 43rd Legislative District on a service station map—the GPS of America in the 1950s.* I wrote down the names of everyone I knew on every street. It was a political treasure hunt. When the last street was checked off, I had more than 600 names. They were parents of Boy Scouts, fellow Jaycees and Municipal League members, Young Republicans, friends and neighbors. Each name was coded as a potential donor, doorbeller or organizer.

State Senator Will Shannon, State Representative Newman "Zeke" Clark and a dozen senior advisers met at Chairman Barnard's house. I was 20 years younger than any of them. Each suggested a potential replacement. When it was Barnard's turn, he said, "Why not young Dan Evans? He's smart and has worked hard in the district." The silence was deafening. Then began the winnowing. One by one, candidates rose and fell: "He's too conservative." "He wouldn't run." "He doesn't fit the district." Barnard kept suggesting I had real potential. But in that crowd my bandwagon had no wheels, let alone horses. After several hours, the meeting broke up with no favorite, precisely as Barnard expected. "You ought to run," he urged, "and announce soon to get a head start."

Two years earlier, I had been a volunteer in Congressman Thomas Pelly's re-election campaign. That's when I got to know Frank and Joel Pritchard, the masterminds of Pelly's massive doorbelling effort. My assignment was to distribute Pelly potholders. "Potholders?" you say. Go ahead and laugh. But each time one of those potholders pulled a pie out of the oven people saw Tom Pelly's political message. Joel Pritchard organized the teams that ventured forth with his evening benediction, a map, a bag of Pelly potholders and the promise of beer and pretzels on return to headquarters. I learned a lot from that campaign and gained a friend and mentor in Joel.

The primary election was the key race in my bid for the Legislature since a Republican victory in the final was virtually assured. In those days, the top two finishers in each party advanced to the general election. Newman Clark, a shoo-in, was running for re-election. My opponents for the second seat were Jack Lycette, a young attorney, and Joe Holmes, a community leader in the Capitol Hill neighborhood.

The fledgling Evans campaign raised $300 for the primary. We printed a two-color brochure and organized doorbelling parties, targeting every corner of the district. Sometimes only six or seven supporters would show up. On good nights there'd be more than thirty. When our troops returned after an evening in the field they regaled us with stories—slammed doors, inebriated constituents

---

* A reverse directory was a list of phone numbers, followed by the corresponding street addresses.

and, sometimes, much more than they'd bargained for. Brochures and potholders in hand, one volunteer rang a doorbell and waited patiently for what seemed like minutes. Finally, a young woman in a negligee opened the door. He stuttered out our campaign message. "Come on in," she said, "and let's discuss this." He fled. That story may have bolstered our recruits.

We marked off the canvassed precincts on a large map. Soon, most of the district had been covered. Now the challenge was to reach every precinct by primary day. My youngest brother, Roger, played a big role in this first effort, as he would in all of my campaigns. He was particularly skilled in drawing the maps. He also devised an impressive chart to tally the precinct votes on election night. Our brother, Bob, was an excellent artist. He designed the silk-screen for our yard signs, which volunteers churned out by the dozens.

The Municipal League's ratings were enormously influential. When I appeared before the evaluation committee, I emphasized my engineering background. If elected, I said I would apply for the Highways Committee because urban areas had been shortchanged for years by rural legislators who teamed up to thwart the big-city lawmakers. That impressed the committee. I received its highest rating, "Superior Candidate."

As we approached the primary, I wondered whether we had done enough. When I walked to Laurelhurst School to cast my first vote for myself, I was suffering from a typical case of rookie-candidate jitters. The big green mechanical voting machines stood in a row, one for each precinct. I pulled the hefty lever that drew a privacy curtain, took a deep breath and contemplated the first ballot to ever feature my name. The candidates' names were arrayed by party, each with a small lever above the name. A large bar at the back of the machine impressed a tally sheet with the final vote for each candidate.

My mother and Irene Robinson, our next-door neighbor, presided over the polling place in my home precinct. Few people voted absentee back then and polling places were crowded with neighbors greeting one another. Today every county in Washington state votes by mail. I know that's better in most respects, but the community celebration of democracy has disappeared from voting.

By 8 p.m. on the day I first sought public office, half a dozen voters were still patiently waiting to cast ballots. When the last one left, the machine was locked and I peered anxiously over my mother's shoulder as she slowly drew the bar down the back of the machine. The precinct election officials tore off the tally sheet and spread it on a table. I could barely conceal my excitement. Not only had I defeated my competitors, I was also ahead of Newman Clark, the incumbent. I hurried home to join a growing group of my jubilant campaign volunteers, each one carrying new precinct returns. When the results were certified, I was ahead of Clark by 393 votes, 5,899 to 5,506. Lycette and Holmes were both some 3,000 votes behind. I was now an odds-on favorite to prevail in the general election.

Six weeks passed quickly. Most of the headlines focused on the Eisenhower-Stevenson rematch. Come November, Ike won re-election in a landslide, carrying Washington and 40 other states. Democrats swept the rest of the ballot. State Senator Albert D. Rosellini, the charismatic son of Italian immigrants, was elected governor. Warren Magnuson crushed the outgoing governor, Art Langlie, to win re-election to the U.S. Senate.

Eight of Washington's nine statewide elected officials were Democrats, and the D's were in solid control of the Legislature. I had received 13,049 votes to Newman Clark's 11,739. We handily outpolled a pair of Democrats to claim the 43rd District's two seats in the House where we would be outnumbered 57-42. The Democrats had a 31 to 15 margin in the State Senate.

Being a Washington state legislator carried few trappings of office in 1957. The pay was $100 per month, plus $20 per diem for each day of legislative action. I traveled to Olympia—population then about 17,000—and searched for a place to stay that fit a young engineer's tight budget. Rooms close to the Capitol were expensive and generally snapped up by lobbyists. I finally found a room at the Holly Motel on the outskirts of town. Rod Moreland, the owner, helped me get acquainted with Olympia. I enjoyed his friendship for many years.

In late November, the Republican caucus gathered for its traditional organizational meeting. I met my new colleagues and immediately began to forge friendships with lawmakers from every corner of the state. Farmers taught me the seasonal cycles of agriculture and why adjourning early in the spring was vital to their livelihoods. Fishermen, loggers, businessmen, teachers, and attorneys all shared their experiences. I began to better understand our state's extraordinary diversity and vitality. Lincoln Shropshire, an attorney from Yakima, was chosen as our leader, and my seatmate, Newman Clark, as his assistant.

A 1958 clipping featuring me with my 43rd District legislative colleagues, William Shannon and Zeke Clark. *Washington State Archives*

I was pleased to join the Highways Committee, my number one goal. I was also appointed to Forestry, State Lands and Parks, where I could work on my environmental interests. As a lowly freshman, I was also assigned to committees I neither chose nor wanted. Liquor Control was saddled with some prickly bills, and the dreaded Legislative Process Committee was the home of all freshman members of the minority party. Our task was to proofread every bill that passed to ensure that the final engrossed measure was identical to the bill adopted on the floor. This mind-numbing, eye-glazing task was a rite of passage for beginners.

On January 14, 1957, I was sworn in as a member of the Washington State House of Representatives. Our Capitol is formally inscribed in stone as the Legislative Building. It's one of the nation's most impressive capitals. Inside, the House Chamber's marble walls glowed in the Klieg lights of television cameras, bulky contraptions on dollies back then. Each small legislative desk was arrayed with empty folders marked "House Bills" and "Senate Bills." Only leadership had offices back then. Our desks were piled high when things got rolling as hundreds of bills were introduced. On the floor beside each desk was a shiny brass spittoon. Though seldom used, they were visible reminders of an all-male political past when tobacco chewing was a common habit.

My parents and brothers sat in the packed balcony galleries on opening day. At precisely noon the gavel banged and the Chief Clerk called the House to order. We all stood. Supreme Court Justice Hugh Rosellini administered the oath of office. Tears of joy, awe and anticipation filled my eyes. I knew at that moment what my future would be. Engineering was a fine profession, but the challenge of politics, the ability to help make laws, and the opportunity to guide the future, created my lifetime goals.

7
GERRYMANDERS & JULIA

T he first thing I learned is that if you want to see a politician's head explode, start tampering with his district boundaries. Redistricting was the most pressing issue facing the Washington State Legislature in 1957. New boundaries hadn't been drawn since 1933. The U.S. Supreme Court's landmark "One person, one vote" ruling was still six years off. That decision and others to follow would eliminate the most outrageous electoral-map mischief, as howls of anguish rang from every capitol dome.

Redistricting in many states remains steeped in horse-trading, though the districts that result from computer modeling are nowhere near as bizarre as the ones hatched by cronies of Massachusetts Governor Elbridge Gerry in 1812. *The Boston Gazette*, observing that one new district resembled a salamander, called it a "Gerry-mander." A new word entered the American political lexicon.

Like every other Washington state legislator, I knew precisely where my supporters and opponents lived. Now, however, things were in flux. The end of World War II initiated great migrations of families, especially to the suburbs where legislators happily expanded their influence. They usually had the votes to control vital spending issues such as highway construction and school appropriations, all at the expense of big-city representatives.

In Washington state, to the horror of politicians, citizen groups entered the fray. The League of Women Voters, which featured some of the smartest, most determined activists I'd ever met, painstakingly researched census tracts. The League created new boundaries that equalized district populations. Next, it gathered the signatures that propelled Initiative 199 to the 1956 General Election ballot. Fifty-two percent of the voters endorsed the plan, which created three new legislative districts and mandated census data as the benchmark for apportionment. Faced with extinction, some legislators attempted to override the initiative.

The Senate majority leader was R.R. "Bob" Greive, a shrewd Democrat from West Seattle's lunch-bucket 34th District. A legislator since 1947, Greive boasted that he got ahead by "working twice as hard as anyone else." When it came to hardball politics, Greive was masterful—and a fanatic about redistricting, devoted to protecting senators who supported him as leader, and much less concerned about his House colleagues.

R.R. "Bob" Greive, the shrewd Senate Majority Leader. *Washington State Archives*

The minute the 1957 legislative session was gaveled to order, Greive introduced Senate Bill 374, which purported to correct mistakes in Initiative 199. What it did was gut the hard work of the League of Women Voters. The bill quickly passed the Senate but faced furious opposition in the House. I joined two fellow freshmen Republicans, Chuck Moriarty and Rocky Lindell, and numerous young Democrats in strenuously opposing Greive's land grab. We were soon to learn a lesson in power politics.

When SB 374 came to the floor of the House, Speaker John O'Brien did some tactical scheduling. He placed it just ahead of HB 264, which authorized the City of Tacoma to build a dam on the Cowlitz River. It was never proven the two issues were linked. However, nine of the 10 representatives from Pierce County voted to support Greive's gerrymandering. With their support, the politically charged redistricting measure reached its required two-thirds vote. Ironically, the dam was later defeated 50 to 49. Pierce County got nothing, a citizen mandate was overturned and the redistricting battle had only just begun. Round One went to Greive and O'Brien. King County's Republicans did emerge with a new North Seattle district with no incumbents. Greive would rue the day we received that crumb.

FIREWORKS OVER, I settled into the routine of committee action. I found the Highways Committee fascinating and quickly developed enormous respect for Julia Butler Hansen, the Democrat who headed the committee. This savvy, plain-spoken woman from tiny Wahkiakum County had served in the House since 1939. To her constituents and fellow legislators on both sides of the aisle in both chambers, she was just "Julia." In 1955, her bid to become the first-ever female Speaker of the House fell short when O'Brien's men pulled out all the stops. "No hard feelings," she told the guys who had engineered her defeat, "but I'll get even with you SOBs!" While Julia had a long memory, she was more principled than partisan. She would have been a great Speaker.

Rep. Julia Butler Hansen, a force of nature, presides at a meeting of the Legislature's Joint Fact-Finding Committee on Highways, Streets & Bridges in 1959. Sen. Louis Hofmeister is in front of me, Rep. Lincoln Shropshire to my left. *Washington State Archives*

As a nationally recognized proponent for interstate highways, Julia was a power in the Legislature at a time when the highest priority for most members was the roads in their districts. I was surprised and thrilled to be asked to serve on her Joint Fact-Finding Committee on Highways, Streets and Bridges, a plum assignment. I was a civil engineer, and Julia wanted someone with expertise. But it was a Republican slot. The Republican leader protested that a prestigious seat like that should not go to a freshman. "Appoint him!" Julia ordered. He did. There was no arguing with Julia. She mentored me and other newcomers on the intricacies of the legislative process. We quickly learned to ask her for help on bills that had nothing to do with highways. One day I complained about the fate of a rather modest bill I was sponsoring. It had passed the House but was going nowhere in a hurry in the Senate. Julia casually opened her desk drawer. As I looked on in amazement, she began thumbing through scores of original drafts of bills pending before her committee. Finally, she extracted a Senate bill that just happened to be of great interest to the chairman of the Senate committee to which my bill was assigned. "I think your bill will move shortly," Julia said with a sly little smile. Within a week, my bill passed the Senate. From a master, I had learned an indelible lesson in power politics: Committee chairmen decided which bills were to be heard in committee. They were virtually never challenged on their decisions. Julia Butler Hansen used that power with great skill to advance her agenda. In 1960, she became the second woman ever elected to Congress from Washington state, serving with distinction for the next 14 years. Her admirers included Lyndon B. Johnson and Republican Congressman Gerald Ford. When Julia retired from Congress, I jumped at the opportunity to appoint her to a commission she had created, the Washington State Toll Bridge Authority and the State Highway Commission. It was one of my best decisions as governor.

Another thing I learned early on was that when it came to staff, I was pretty much a one-man-band. Freshmen legislators had no offices other than their desks in the House Chamber. A secretarial pool of about 20 highly skilled women handled correspondence for all House members. When each day's session adjourned, the doors were locked for an hour. Legislators hurriedly dictated letters and studied pending legislation. Time up, the doors were opened and we were inundated by lobbyists, tourists and constituents. Sometimes the only sane thing to do was flee to the protection of the House lunchroom, a small dining area reserved for legislators one floor below. It was often an oasis of calm during long floor sessions and a place to gather at night to share stories, eat ice cream and study bills.

Lobbyists flooded Olympia for every session. You soon learned who had clout and who didn't. The Good Roads Association and the State Grange had clout that was magnified on road issues because they worked together. Lars Nelson, the state Grange Master, had a bone-crushing handshake. It was hard not to wince. Ed Weston, Labor's beefy lobbyist, and Ed "Deke" Davis, a crafty, pipe-smoking leader of the Association of Washington Industries, were quite a pair. They would testify vociferously on opposite sides of an issue and then retire together to hash out a compromise. Their success rate in forging labor-management agreements both sides could live with was phenomenal. There weren't many female lobbyists in those days. Everyone respected Margaret McClellan, whose clients were local sewer and water districts. She spent many years in Olympia and became a lifelong friend.

I was one of the few Republicans endorsed by the Teamsters. Granted, most of us were from districts that never elected Democrats. It was a coveted endorsement nevertheless. When it came to clout, the Teamsters had it. They also staged terrific steak dinners at a large house they rented in Olympia for the session. The editor and columnist for the union's widely read house organ was acerbic Ed Donohoe. He had a knack for nicknames. When I emerged as a comer in the Legislature, he seized on my Eagle Scout resume and dubbed me "Straight Arrow." Sometimes this was delivered with praise for probity; more often mockingly. It all depended on Ed's mood. He could be a hard-nosed investigative reporter or a curmudgeon; sometimes both in the same column. Ed's annual Catholic Seaman's Luncheon became the Washington state equivalent of the White House Correspondents' Dinner. It was a roast and fundraiser rolled into one. Governors, mayors, Supreme Court justices, legislative leaders and county officials all turned out to be lampooned by Ed to the hooting of a huge crowd. Ed is long gone, but the luncheon still draws a full house.

AS FRESHMEN, we heard all the war stories and were taught the traditions that enriched the history of the Legislature. In time, we added a few of our own. Committee Room X was a secretive place sporting a reputation far beyond reality. It was a small, unmarked room on the fourth floor of the Legislative Building, presided over by longtime Representative Ralph "Brigham" Young, a barber from Cle Elum with Brylcreemed hair. "Brig" offered free haircuts and libations as the days droned by. Definitely not a Mormon, he maintained a small inventory of liquor that some members and reporters occasionally sampled. Some more than occasionally. One day a member slipped into Committee Room X and poured himself a healthy shot from an unmarked bottle. He gagged and sprayed the liquid all over the floor. Storming up to Brig, he sputtered, "What kind of gin do you have up there?" Brig asked him to identify the offending bottle. "Good God," he declared, "you got the formaldehyde I use to sterilize my combs."

Committee Room X died a headline-making death several sessions later when Don Miles, a first-term representative from Olympia, blew the whistle on the evils of extracurricular activities in the hallowed halls of the Capitol. While his bill to close it down went nowhere, the bad publicity spelled the end of Committee Room X. Members lost their free haircuts, and the place turned as dry as a church social hall. When Miles lost in his bid for re-election many old legislators raised a toast to the electorate.

Most of the early action was in committees where issues were debated, sometimes vociferously. As I settled in, I began to hear more often from constituents seeking my support for their causes or projects. One of my earliest supporters was Emily Haig, a longtime leader of the Audubon Society. She came to Olympia to ask me to sponsor a bill protecting Mourning Doves. I was familiar with the lovely small birds whose call sounded like a lamentation. All hell broke loose when I introduced the bill. I learned that Mourning Doves, small and fast, were prized by hunters. Letters of protest flooded in. Undeterred, I introduced the bill again in the next session, only this time I identified the dove only by its Latin name, *Zenaida macroura*. Protest letters arrived by the score from San Juan County. They thought the Latin name described jackrabbits, a troublesome pest on the islands.

John Biggs, the assistant director of the Game Department, told me there was no way a bill protecting Mourning Doves would become law. He suggested an alternative. The Game Department would support a bill protecting hawks, owls and eagles, none of which were protected at the time. I agreed and introduced the bill. It passed quickly. Emily was ecstatic, the Audubon Society was grateful and I was proud of the result. I also learned an important lesson: Don't be stubborn; listen to the experts and find alternative ways to progress.

8
THE BATTLE OF THE BRIDGES

The ancient Chinese built pontoon bridges. Caligula, the mercurial Roman emperor, erected one that stretched two miles in 37 A.D. History's earliest, inventive civil engineers still would have been awed by the first Lake Washington floating bridge. Called "a marvel of modernity" when it opened in 1940, it was the world's largest, longest floating structure and the first to feature a draw span. The bridge transformed the east side of Lake Washington, especially sleepy little Bellevue. "But by the early Fifties," Seattle historian Roger Sale observed, the bridge "was clogged morning and night."

With my dad, the King County Engineer. *Evans Family Collection*

The biggest highway issue of the 1957 legislative session was a proposed second Lake Washington floating bridge. If the need was abundantly clear, the location generated huge controversy. My father, as King County Engineer, suggested a route from Kirkland to Sand Point. It was the shortest crossing and halfway between the existing floating bridge and the north end of the lake. Real estate developers and business leaders demanded a bridge from Evergreen Point to the Madison Park neighborhood in Seattle, coupled with a new North-South freeway that would tear the heart out of the Washington Arboretum. The Seattle approach to their proposed bridge bisected my legislative district.

Seattle officials, led by Mayor Gordon Clinton, supported a bridge parallel to the existing structure, citing its ability to use reversible lanes in concert with the existing span to maximize traffic flow. That plan called for Bellevue to be served by a special bridge running northeast from the north end of Mercer Island.

The battle of the bridges occupied center stage for much of the session. Advocates of each bridge proposal sought my support. Though I was a freshman in the minority party, I was also the only engineer in the House.

While the Sand Point route had its advantages, I concluded it was unlikely to win approval to traverse the Naval Air Station at Sand Point. I discussed the various proposals at length with my father and constructed many of my arguments on his advice. He quietly challenged each of my points until he was convinced I could defend my position. I decided that the parallel floating bridge made the most sense. It would enhance the main highway to Snoqualmie Pass and, in tandem with a Mercer Island-Bellevue bridge, create a shorter route to downtown Seattle. My constituents were vehemently opposed to a bridge approach that would rip the heart out of the legislative district. I offered my support to the group advocating the parallel bridge. We began preparing for a long, hard fight.

Our proposal became House Bill 145. My co-sponsors were my seatmate, Newman Clark, and Max Wedekind from West Seattle. Representative Al Leland from Kirkland, joined by Vernon Smith of Medina and Eric Braun of Cashmere, countered with HB205, a bill backing the Evergreen Point location.

The opening salvo was a report by a nationally recognized engineering firm, DeLeuw, Cather & Company. This report, commissioned by the state Toll Bridge Authority, favored a bridge parallel to the existing floating bridge. The State Highway Commission issued a rebuttal and recommended the Evergreen Point route. So even the experts disagreed. The debate soon turned nasty. Al Leland wrote, "I would like to get some of these birds on the witness stand under oath. Then perhaps we could find out who is financing whom." He branded the DeLeuw report "either biased in their studies or at least most inept."

The Argus, Seattle's venerable weekly, identified major backers of the Evergreen Point route as large property owners in the vicinity. Seattle City Hall, the Municipal League and a variety of civic organizations supported the parallel route. Governor Rosellini backed his highway engineers and pushed hard for an Evergreen Point span. Later, however, in a speech to the Good Roads Association, the governor declared, "We need a bridge so badly, I don't care where it is built." Al knew how to hedge his bets.

The opposing forces clashed before a joint House-Senate hearing. When 600 advocates descended on Olympia, the hearing had to be moved to the House Chambers. I made the case for the parallel bridge, an unusual opportunity for a freshman legislator. The air was electric with tension. Julia Butler Hansen calmly maintained control. She knew well the power of seniority, the chairmanship and how influential her vote would be.

I was pleased with our arguments and the audience support. However, we were fighting a powerful coalition: the members of the State Highway Commission, none of whom were from King County; the State Highway director, William Bugge, and the governor. Ultimately they prevailed. The Evergreen Point bill moved out of committee and was adopted by the House 74-21. The wishes of Seattle-area legislators were shot down by lawmakers from the rest of the state, many eager to "show Seattle who's boss," at the urging of the Highway Department and governor. That attitude is even more intense today, especially between rural and urban counties and east of the Cascades. The bipartisan Seattle legislative delegation of 1957 has morphed into a solid Democrat monopoly.

The bridge was delayed by a State Supreme Court ruling that struck down its financing plan. It opened in 1963, and 15 years later was fittingly named in honor of Al Rosellini, who had championed its construction. By then I was a U.S. senator, and the differences between two old adversaries had been distilled into cordiality by the passage of time.

WHILE THE BRIDGE FIGHT raged, I also learned the ropes of the tedious legislative process. Each bill was read the first time and sent to a committee for analysis and modification. The second reading opened bills for floor amendments. Next, they were delivered to the Rules Committee, which had absolute power over which could appear on the daily calendar. And its meetings were private. The third reading consisted of debate on the final version of a bill and final passage. Fifty votes were required to send a bill to the State Senate where the process was repeated. After passage by both houses, a bill was transmitted to the governor for signature or veto. Overriding a veto required a two-thirds vote of each house. About 20 percent of bills introduced became law.

This famous photo was part of the campaign to clean up Lake Washington by creating a new municipal agency—Metro—to oversee sewage treatment. *Seattle Municipal Archives*

I was intensely interested in the proposal to establish "Metro," Jim Ellis's proposed metropolitan King County agency to clean up Lake Washington. The postwar growth of the East Side, propelled by the first floating bridge, had also accelerated pollution of the lake to the point that its ecosystem was endangered. Ten sewer districts poured excrement, motor oil and the other byproducts of unregulated growth into Lake Washington. Beaches were befouled by human waste and black bacterial slime. No less than 29 governmental units bore some responsibility for the mess.

Campaigning for Metro as a member of the Municipal League had been my introduction to political activism, with Ellis as a mentor. Now my goal as a freshman legislator was to help secure its passage.

I was astonished at the vehemence of the opposition. Metro was condemned by arch-conservatives as "Communism in disguise" and the slippery slope to One-World Government. It was too expensive, they said. Too intrusive. Besides, it wouldn't work. Some local officials believed their power would be usurped by a Seattle-centric cabal. Finally, the bill reached the floor for final passage. I rose to offer an overview and attempted to defuse the opposition's arguments by citing the consequences of inaction. "Any further remarks?" Speaker O'Brien inquired. None offered, he started the electric roll call machine that had been installed for the 1957 session. When the Speaker locked the machine, no votes could be changed. I was crestfallen to see only 49 "yes" votes. Passage required a constitutional majority, or 50 votes, of the 99-member House. Zeke Clark rose to change his vote from "aye" to "nay" to prompt reconsideration. (Rules required that the person making a motion to reconsider had to vote on the prevailing side.) In a split second, I saw the tally move to 50 positive votes. I raced down the aisle shouting, "Sit down, Zeke!" He looked astonished but sat down. O'Brien, a Metro supporter, quickly locked the machine. He had seen the same magic number.

The final vote on Metro was 51 to 36, a thin margin for a proposal of such magnitude. As a freshman legislator, I had helped guide Metro's enabling legislation to victory. It remains one of my proudest moments in public life. Within a decade, Lake Washington was teeming with fish and splashing youngsters.

AS THE SESSION neared adjournment, everything speeded up; bills passed or failed as lobbyists cursed, legislators fumed and the press corps attempted to make sense of the melee. In those days, a swarm of reporters covered the Legislature. The Associated Press and United Press International had dueling Olympia bureaus. Even the smaller dailies had correspondents.

The budget and taxes were always the last issues resolved, except for sought-after appointments to important interim committees. When Julia Butler Hansen demanded my appointment to the Highway Interim Committee, I was elated and thrilled. My first session as an elected official was heady stuff. I was named the "outstanding freshman legislator of 1957."

I returned to my job as assistant manager of the Mountain Pacific Chapter of the Associated General Contractors and began a fascinating term as a member of the Highway Interim Committee. Serving on Julia's committee was an education in itself. We met in communities around the state. For the first time, I experienced the endless rolling vistas of the wheat fields in the Palouse, the productivity of orchards and forests, and the vitality and friendliness of small-town citizens.

The committee thoroughly examined the route and feasibility of a cross-Sound bridge and in November of 1958 issued a report favoring construction. It was to be the major highway issue of the 1959 session.

9
NANCY BELL

There were only eight or nine stools in the diner when our ski party stopped for burgers. I made sure I sat next to the teacher with the luminous smile. I knew immediately she was the one. It took her longer. Little wonder, given the number of eligible guys asking her out.

She was 25. I was almost 33. My friends were ribbing me that I was destined to be a confirmed bachelor.

Nancy Bell was born in Spokane on the first day of spring 1933. Her witty father, 54 when she was born, joked they should name her Vernal Equinoxia—"Vernie" for short. Her mother suggested "Elizabeth Ann." But the obstetrician said, "She looks like a Nancy." The doctor was right. Frank Sinatra's wonderful song about "Nancy with the laughing face" fit Miss Bell to a T. Her eyes are blue, her laugh a contagious chuckle.

AFTER THE 1957 LEGISLATIVE SESSION, I had spent every spare hour on *Challenger*, my 32-foot sloop, which required a four-man crew for racing. There was no shortage of volunteers. Snapping sails, the creak of the windlasses tightening and frequent cries of "Starboard tack" punctuated each event, followed by beer and bragging as all the crews got together.

We sailed into spring and reveled in summer. When fall turned to winter, snow blanketed the Cascades. Out came our skis. On that memorable day in early 1958, Nancy was among several carloads of friends and acquaintances who trekked to Stevens Pass. All the experienced skiers, including Nancy's date, headed for the top of the mountain. I started to follow. When I spotted Nancy lagging, I asked her if she wanted someone to ski with. She did. When she veered under a clump of trees, I pulled her out. We

Our friend David Faires joins us for a sail on *Challenger*, my 32-foot sloop. *Evans Family Collection*

laughed. She had a wry sense of humor.

By day's end, I learned she was a grade-school music teacher in Shoreline and a graduate of Whitman College, one of America's top liberal-arts schools. The woman who became the youngest and, in my view and that of many others, the greatest First Lady in Washington state history, has been aptly described as "simultaneously down-to-earth and sophisticated. But she always reminds herself that no matter where she is or who she's with, she's still just Nancy Bell from Spokane."

Nancy's first impression of me was that I "was very quiet and shy.… Each time I went out with him I learned something new," she told a historian years later. "I saw a man of depth. He grew on me. He was not one of these people who just came on the first time and you learned it all. I found that very intriguing. … I loved everything I learned. He already had done a lot of interesting things: He was an engineer, interested in politics, athletic, very competitive, served in the Navy. There were all these things that he'd done. I also learned to love sailing."

I WAS MAKING MORE HEADWAY than I imagined. However, that wasn't apparent from the glimpse I got at her calendar. One night when I arrived at her apartment to pick her up for a date, I had to make a phone call. Her datebook was right by the phone. She had a little rubber stamp embossed with "Bob"—the name of one of her many boyfriends. I opened the datebook and saw "Bob" everywhere. There were other guys too. So I carefully marked down all of the free nights I could find and made sure that I asked her out on those days.

One Sunday night that October, after a wonderful outing to Victoria, I asked Nancy if she would like to take a walk. We strolled several blocks to the Laurelhurst playfield and sat on the bleachers behind the baseball diamond. There, in possibly the most incoherent speech I ever gave, I asked her to marry me. Little did I know that she had politely rejected a proposal a week earlier in the same place.

I didn't get an outright "No." She asked for time to think it over. Those were agonizing days. But on Wednesday she said "Yes." As I left her that night I jumped for joy, swung around a lamppost like Gene Kelly in *Singin' in the Rain*, and dashed to my car. I had to tell someone so I drove to my parents' house, even though it was close to midnight, quietly let myself in and knocked on their bedroom door. My mother dissolved into tears of joy. My reserved old dad even shed a tear. They probably wondered whether I would ever get married. Better yet, they adored Nancy, and she had grown fond of them.

A few weeks later, Nancy's parents arrived from Spokane. I was invited to her apartment for dinner and introductions to Lilith and Lawrence Bell. Nancy and her mother headed for the kitchen and I was left to chat with Mr. Bell, a very impressive-looking, 80-year-old. He squinted at me for a moment before noting that his other sons-in-law had sought his consent before proposing marriage. Taken aback, I mumbled some inane reply. I discovered later that he was enjoying a devilish put-on at my expense.

The Bells were a marvelous couple. Lawrence Bell graduated from Stanford University in 1900 and became a mining engineer in Peru and Bolivia. Later, he gravitated to Montana to oversee the Butte Highlands mine. His spouse efficiently oversaw a household of four children, served on Spokane's motion picture censor board and managed a small greeting card business.

My mother-in-law was a very wise woman. Nancy had called her the night I proposed. "What should I do?" Nancy pleaded, deeply conflicted. Her mother laughed heartily. "Dearie," she de-

My parents, Les and Irma Evans, at left, and Nancy's folks, Lilith and Lawrence Bell, look on as we toast our new life together. *Evans Family Collection*

clared to Nancy's chagrin, "that's your decision, not mine!"

After 62 years, three fine sons, amazing daughters-in-law and nine grandchildren, I submit that Nancy Bell made the right decision. I know I did.

We were married on June 6, 1959, at the Congregational Church in Spokane. Our honeymoon trip took us to San Francisco and Carmel in the first new car I'd ever owned, a gold 1957 Plymouth with huge fins.

Few couples anticipating marriage think much about the in-laws they're acquiring. I could not have chosen better. "Bampa" Bell was a wise man and wonderful raconteur; "Gam" a strong, loving force during her 94 years. After her husband died in 1962, she agreed to stay with us for a short time to help take care of our firstborn, Dan Jr., while Nancy joined me in the early days of my campaign for governor. Lilith Bell remained an integral part of our family for 20 years as the resident grandmother for three boisterous young boys. She also played an important part in the Olympia community. As governor, in one act of gentle nepotism, I appointed her to the Hearing Aid Advisory Council. She was hard of hearing and vigorously led the fight for better treatment of consumers. When Gam's health began to fail, our sons stayed with her when we traveled. That completed a cycle of care and love that none of us will forget.

Nancy Evans claims she knew what she was getting into when she married a politician. But neither of us imagined so much would happen so fast. Or that the glee of our engagement would be followed by a Republican disaster in the 1958 elections.

10
REMARKABLE ROOMMATES

For the second election in a row, tone-deaf conservatives intent on undermining organized labor placed a "right to work" measure on the ballot. Washington was the most heavily unionized state in the nation. Voters once again crushed the initiative, and Republican candidates went down to defeat all across the state in 1958. We now held only 33 of the 99 seats in the state House of Representatives, our lowest number since the depths of the Depression.

Given a crystal ball, we would have felt a whole lot better. The good news was a quintet of freshmen Republican legislators destined for bigger things. Slade Gorton would become a three-term attorney general and serve in the U.S. Senate for 18 years; Joel Pritchard was a member of Congress for 12 years and lieutenant governor for eight; James "Jimmy" Andersen from Bellevue became chief justice of the Washington State Supreme Court; Don Moos from Lincoln County went on to head the State Department of Agriculture and later served as director of Fisheries and Ecology, while Jack Hood from Whatcom County became director of Banking and chairman of the State Liquor Control Board. Our sixth teammate was Charles Moriarty from Seattle's 36th District. Re-elected to the House despite the Democratic tide, Chuck later moved to the State Senate where he served as Republican Leader in 1965. He gave up a promising political career to return to the practice of law. Otherwise, I'm confident his political ceiling was as high as the others.

With, from left, State Reps. Joel Pritchard, Chuck Moriarty, Jim Andersen and Slade Gorton in 1959. *Washington State Archives*

During the 1959 legislative session, Gorton, Pritchard, Moriarty and I roomed together in a rented house near the Capitol. Our den mother was Slade's wife Sally, a former *Seattle Times* reporter. "We went out to dinner practically every night and they talked politics," Sally remembered. "They were so young; so full of energy to change things."

Every night over dinner, we studied and debated bills, chafing under the weight of a massive Democratic majority. Pritchard counseled that we needed to forge alliances across the aisle. His wisdom was infused with strategy: Good ideas with Republican sponsors were routinely defeated; the same proposal advanced by a Democrat would often pass.

When I joined Julia Butler Hansen as a co-sponsor of legislation authorizing a $200 million cross-Sound bridge project, some old-guard members of the Seattle Chamber of Commerce groused that I had been co-opted by the "cow county" Democrats. Ross Cunningham, the powerful *Seattle Times* columnist, begged to differ. He wrote that Julia and Senator Nat Washington, the Highways Committee vice-chairman from Grant County, had "fought our battles for such projects as the Seattle freeway while many legislators from this area were overly busy with problems more closely associated with their political careers." That the redoubtable Highways Committee chairwoman liked me was another sign I was going places, Cunningham wrote.

My view, as both civil engineer and politician, was that the cross-Sound bridge project made bipartisan sense and cents. Consultants had told the Joint Fact-Finding Committee on Highways, Streets and Bridges that a network of Puget Sound bridges could substantially reduce the need for expensive ferries. Governor Rosellini strongly endorsed the plan.

A newly-formed group, the Gasoline Tax Protective League, opposed any legislative effort to guarantee toll-revenue bonds for the project by pledging motor-fuel tax collections as collateral. When the Good Roads Association also announced its opposition to the bridge funding plan, its opponents had the momentum. Dueling bridge bills emerged. The Hansen-Evans bill never made it out of committee. It fell one vote short of making it to the floor of the Senate. Eyes flashing daggers, Julia was livid.

In hindsight, the longest of the proposed floating bridges—across open saltwater for two miles from West Seattle to the north tip of Vashon Island—likely would have faced far more difficult weather problems than the Lake Washington and Hood Canal bridges subsequently damaged in storms. Undeniable is that the state is committed to ferries for a long, long time.

SINCE THE REPUBLICAN PARTY apparatus was focused on defeating Governor Rosellini in 1960, we resolved to aggressively recruit first-rate Republican candidates for the Legislature. In one of his memorable "Joelisms," Pritchard declared, "No one looks past the next election." We had to set aside any personal political ambitions for the common good. The outcome of the 1960 election would give us more insight into what to do next. And if we could make substantial gains in the Legislature, the way forward would be clearer yet.

The session ended with no perceptible Republican influence. We returned home determined to add to our numbers. We made lists of emerging community leaders, young professionals and accomplished businessmen from all over the state. Eastern Washington was a key stop on our road trips. We applied only one political litmus test: Could they win? Pritchard conducted campaign workshops to give promising neophytes a head start.

I returned to my job at Associated General Contractors and soon realized there was tension among the members over my service in the Legislature. In the summer of 1959, the manager summoned me to his office and started to explain the problem. I stopped him practically in mid-sentence and said, "I think it's time I resigned." I'd had an epiphany. Nancy, however, was not exactly thrilled that evening when I told her what I had done. Two months earlier, she had married a well-employed young engineer. Now he was out of a job. While I knew I wanted to enter the practice of structural engineering, here was an opportunity for a carefree interlude I knew we'd never regret.

"Why don't we plan a trip?"

"Well, jeepers," she said, "don't you have to get a job first?"

I said I wasn't worried. Besides, both of us had worked hard and saved some money since college. Nancy had been especially frugal.

We began sending itinerary requests to tourist bureaus all over Europe. Before long, we had filled a big cardboard box with enticing brochures and road maps. Our bible was Arthur Frommer's best-selling guidebook, *Europe on $5 a Day*, now still in print, revised to $50 a day.

On New Year's Day 1960 we were at the Rose Bowl to watch my Huskies trounce Wisconsin. It was the perfect start for what would be a stunningly successful year. We boarded a plane for Copenhagen the next day with all our gear for six months. I was wearing my ski boots and Nancy carried a purse as big as a shopping bag.

We skied for a glorious month in Austria and Switzerland, then hit the autobahn. Our wanderings took us to Marrakech in Morocco and virtually every country in Western Europe. We stayed in castles and private homes, a small hotel on the beach in Nice, and many small villas, all chosen carefully to stay within our budget. We pulled it off, too. Today, $5 a day wouldn't pay for parking.

After six spectacular months of delayed honeymoon, we sailed from London to New York on the brand new *S.S. Rotterdam*. Nancy was pregnant with our first son, I was looking for a new engineering career and the elections of 1960 were fast approaching.

IT SHAPED UP TO BE a close election, here in Washington state and across the country. Nixon and Kennedy were neck and neck in every poll. We watched the first televised presidential debate with a group of friends. When the camera first focused on Nixon, we gasped at his pallor. Though still recovering from knee surgery, he had refused makeup. His 5 o'clock shadow was amplified by black-and-white TV. Kennedy, tanned and relaxed, appeared young and vigorous. Television's extraordinary power was revealed. Those who watched the debate on TV told pollsters Kennedy won; those who listened on radio chose Nixon. It was hard to say whether either would have coat-tails. We campaigned energetically in all but a few legislative districts, the ones where Democrats were shoo-ins.

Nixon carried Washington but lost the presidency in a photo-finish. Governor Rosellini was narrowly elected to a second term. We gained seven seats in the State House of Representatives. Pritchard, Gorton and I decided it was time to challenge our caucus leadership. Since I had served one more session, I became our upstart candidate for Republican leader. We fanned out to contact legislators, concentrating on those we had helped elect. Then, at a Republican State Central Committee meeting, we hit a speed bump: Tom Copeland, an ambitious legislator from Walla Walla County, was also running for the leader's position. We had entered the Legislature together. Tom was a fellow rebel, and no one to take lightly. He had been a tank destroyer commander during World War II.

Pritchard said I had to persuade Copeland to step aside and back me. "If he splits the votes, the old-timers will win." Joel was right. I protested that I still couldn't do it. "He's a friend. Besides, I don't think I'm very good at this."

They virtually shoved me into a hotel room with Copeland. I sat on the bed, gulped and looked him in the eye: "Tom, I have the majority of the votes of the rebels. Join me and be part of the leadership. Otherwise, we all lose." He asked for the names of my supporters. "Go check them out," I said. "See for yourself." He returned several hours later and agreed to join my team. Now we were closer to victory, but I still could count on only 18 votes from our 40-member caucus.

The Republican organizational caucus was traditionally held in Spokane the weekend of the Apple Cup football game between the Huskies and Cougars. The entire caucus, plus spouses, gathered for dinner after the game as a prelude to the business meeting on Sunday morning. During the cocktail hour, Spokane's Ed Harris and Elmer Johnston drew me aside and grilled me on issues vital to Eastern Washington's largest city. Then they waylaid my leading competitor, Damon Canfield from Yakima County, the assistant leader in the previous session. The next morning, Johnston corralled the three representatives from Spokane County and advised, "We're voting for Evans." It was Evans 21, Canfield 18.

Pritchard was our candidate for assistant floor leader. However, just before the next vote he turned to me and whispered, "Let's elect Damon Canfield. It will unite the caucus." Damon was duly nominated and unanimously elected. That move helped shape the caucus into a powerhouse influential beyond its numbers. It would become a key element in the 1964 governor's race. Joel Pritchard's selfless act reflected not only his political genius but a personal strength unusual in political leadership. One of his often-quoted axioms became our mantra: "It's amazing what you can get done if you don't care who gets the credit."

We immediately elected Don Eldridge from Mount Vernon as caucus chairman and Tom Copeland as whip. I chose Damon Canfield as head of a new Republican Policy Committee charged with developing a comprehensive GOP agenda. We would go on to introduce bills and argue amendments with little hope of success, but we built morale and created the foundation for the next campaign.

When I returned to my in-laws' house in Spokane after the caucus I was greeted on the front steps by Nancy's brother, Bill Bell. "What happened?" he demanded. I held up two fingers in the V for victory sign. Bill thought I meant I had been elected to the number two position. "Heck no," I grinned. "I won!"

Days after my election as House Republican leader, Nancy gave birth to Daniel Jackson Evans Jr. When I first held this tiny pink human in my cupped hands, he squinted up at me for a second. Then his lower lip quivered and he began to cry. Who could blame him? The lights were bright, and strangers were inspecting him. The nurse assured me he was just hungry. I felt an enormous sense of joy and optimism.

11
AN ELECTRIFYING SESSION

The Democrats were a house divided as the 1961 legislative session convened. We watched the machinations with fascination, sensing opportunity. The open warfare that broke out, then festered, ultimately would topple Speaker O'Brien and launch my campaign for governor.

Leonard Sawyer, a crafty young lawyer from Puyallup, wanted to be Speaker. His ambition was fueled by a turf-protection war chest from the state's private power companies. Most Democrats backed public power. They hoped to create more public utility districts. Most free-enterprise Republicans (including me) supported private power. Party affiliation mattered little to Washington Water Power of Spokane, the largest private utility east of the Cascades. It was out to corral all the votes it could. In the summer of 1960, Sawyer toured the state in a white Thunderbird convertible, doling out private power money to sympathetic legislative candidates.

When Sawyer challenged John L. O'Brien for the speakership, their caucus deadlocked 29-29. O'Brien was a powerful and controversial Speaker, first elected to the Legislature in 1940. Frantic efforts to unseat him continued until minutes before the session was called to order. O'Brien made just enough concessions to keep the gavel. Fifty years old, he was tall, immaculately dressed, and Irish to the core—a plucky, self-made man.

One concession extracted by the Sawyer forces was the appointment of Dick Kink of Bellingham, a private power supporter, to head the House Committee on Public Utilities on which I served. This was an opening salvo in the renewed fight between public and private power.

OUR FIRST OPPORTUNITY to tweak the fracturing majority came quickly. Governor Rosellini had used his line-item veto to delete a gubernatorial pay raise from a bill setting salaries for elected officials. My friend Don Moos

At my desk in the House. *Washington State Archives*

jabbed, "If he thinks he is only doing a $15,000 job, I'm not going to argue with him." But enough Republicans joined me and the Democratic majority to override the governor's politically correct veto. The press ate it up. Then, when Rosellini proposed a budget that would require nearly $58 million in new taxes, he failed to specify what kind of new taxes, saying that was the Legislature's responsibility. I countered with a resolution asking the governor to suggest specific new taxes and/or cuts to balance his budget. To our astonishment, the resolution passed on a standing vote, 56 to 35. Rosellini was fist-shaking furious; O'Brien was embarrassed and the fissure in the Democratic caucus widened.

The split became a sinkhole when House Bill 197 was reported to the floor for second reading and amendment. Backed by private power, the bill said, "No public utility property used for the generation, transmission, or distribution of electric energy shall be condemned without submission of the question to the voters of the utility district." The impetus was a move by the Thurston County Public Utility District to grab part of Puget Power's territory. We began floor debate on HB 197—the "Right to Vote" bill—with Slade Gorton as our legal strategist and a clear bipartisan majority. The fight was on.

The Grange and the State Labor Council joined the Public Utility District Association in a passionate defense of public power. The State Democratic Party damned private power as rapacious and greedy.

The private power bill was reported out of Kink's committee 13-11. The five Democrats who joined our eight Republicans in approving the bill were all part of a game-changing coalition that would emerge in the 1963 session. Spokane Democrats William "Big Daddy" Day and Margaret Hurley were key players.

We didn't expect the bitter conflict that would erupt on the floor of the House. Legislative historian Don Brazier called it "the most contentious standoff in the history of the Washington Legislature." Amendments by the dozen, mostly frivolous or irrelevant, piled high on the chief clerk's desk. Oral roll calls were repeatedly demanded as a delaying tactic. A blizzard of motions sought to refer the Right to Vote bill back to other committees, where its death was certain. Almost lost in the turmoil were serious efforts to improve the measure. When I noted that the bill was nothing more sinister than requiring a public vote before any county could shift from private power to a PUD, public power lobbyists said we were out to take power from the people, literally and figuratively.

Speaker O'Brien, who adamantly opposed the bill, lost control of the House after 21 tedious roll calls. Private power supporters refused to surrender. Late one evening, the Democratic majority was rebuffed in an attempt to defer the issue until the next day. Mark Litchman, the Democrats' floor leader, moved to adjourn. As outraged "no's" reverberated through the chamber, O'Brien shouted, "The House is adjourned!" and slammed down his gavel. We both watched in astonishment as the head broke loose and spun into the aisle in front of my desk. I was incredulous. As he stalked off the speaker's platform, we exchanged thin smiles. Clusters of furious legislators milled about the House Chamber thumbing through the rule books and clamoring for O'Brien's removal. I believed he had abdicated his responsibility to follow long-established rules. "I don't believe the members of the House will tolerate such actions again," I told a gaggle of reporters.

I had learned the power of the gavel, though I abhorred the use of that power to perpetuate a minority position.

THE CONTEST RESUMED the next morning with more of the same, including five roll calls. On and on we went, departing the Capitol tired, hungry and frustrated each night. The pressure on individual legislators was enormous, especially from labor and the Grange, with its deep roots in rural counties. A motion to refer the bill to the Rules Committee carried 51 to 47. The fight was over. Forty-eight roll calls consumed four days. Though the Democrats claimed to have won, they knew their unity was in tatters. O'Brien was in trouble. We rejoiced in our newly discovered leverage: a minority could forge a majority.

The Democrats who had sided with the evil Republicans were pawns in a plot to "deal a fatal blow to the economic future of the State of Washington," Litchman fumed. I scoffed, saying the dispute was not a public/private power issue, "but a principle of people having a right to vote on issues that affect them deeply. Like Hamlet's ghost, this issue won't go away. It will reappear as a bill, or as an initiative, surely as a campaign issue two years from now." I did not realize how prophetic I was.

Tension oozed away over the next few days. Gorton, Pritchard and I teamed up to pass a billboard control act. Garden Clubs and environmental groups had joined the cause as unsightly billboards began popping up statewide with the advent of new highways. We built a surprisingly large bipartisan majority to outflank strong opposition from business groups and Chambers of Commerce.

THE 1961 LEGISLATURE wrestled with two more major issues when it went into overtime. Governor Rosellini proposed a graduated net income tax to balance his budget. Republicans bristled that the governor had refused to propose specific new taxes until late in the regular session. Then he dropped the income tax bomb on us during the special session as a way out. There were no reductions in other taxes or protections against future tax increases. I branded the plan "a thing of beauty and a nightmare forever." No attempt was made to gain the Republican votes needed to produce the two-thirds majority necessary for a constitutional amendment. Eight years later, I was to learn just how difficult an income tax could be.

As the special session neared the end, we scored an unexpected triumph. I urged the Highway Committee to dedicate a half-cent of a proposed gas tax directly to the cities. Counties, especially the ones in rural areas, divvied up a huge share of gas tax revenues. Realizing a Republican initiative would probably lose, I enlisted the support of Representative Avery Garrett, a well-respected veteran Democrat who also served on the Renton City Council.

We were rebuffed when we proposed the amendment in the Highway Committee. One last opportunity remained. We collected signatures on a minority report. Virtually all the Republicans and several Democrats signed. When the gas tax bill reached the floor, Garrett proposed the minority report containing our amendment. The committee chairman, W.J. Beierlein, frantically tried to regain control. (He had succeeded Julia Butler Hansen, who was elected to Congress in 1960.) Beierlein was no match for Garrett, who methodically proposed our amendments. Miraculously the King County delegation coalesced around our proposal and propelled us to a surprising bipartisan victory.

Heading back to our regular lives, we savored our few victories, relived our frustrations and realized that governing required majorities. We set our sights on winning control of the Washington State House in 1962.

The extended legislative session had derailed my engineering business. I needed to re-establish

With Al Bluechel, surveying a project at Crystal Mountain. *Washington State Archives*

a consulting practice. I talked with Vic Gray, a former design teammate when I worked for the City of Seattle. We decided to form a partnership, Gray & Evans. Within six months we reached our first milestone, hiring an engineer to help handle our workload.

12
THE COALITION

The Olympia press corps was working overtime on January 13, 1963, a drizzly Sunday on Budd Inlet. Rumors were rife that something big was brewing as legislators gathered at a downtown hotel for the traditional pre-session dinner. The freshmen and their spouses mingled with veterans. When the crowd began to thin, I summoned my team.

"Meet me in the Elks Club parking lot after dinner," I whispered, moving from Slade Gorton to Don Eldridge and Tom Copeland. We piled into my car and headed toward Cooper Point, the gooseneck peninsula that pokes into Puget Sound west of the Capitol. We looked over our shoulders several times to make sure no one was following us. The detailed directions we'd been given heightened the intrigue of a moonless night.

We were headed for a rendezvous that set in motion "arguably the single most dramatic series of events in the political history of the State and the Territory," wrote Don Brazier, who spent countless hours researching his two-volume history of the Washington Legislature.

But I'm getting ahead of myself: This story actually begins a few months earlier.

AS CHAIRMAN of the 1962 Republican State Convention, I presided over a united party eagerly anticipating the next election. Joel Pritchard, Gorton and I spent much of the summer on the road, from Port Angeles to Pullman, recruiting candidates for the Legislature.

The Democrats were in disarray. At their convention, left-wingers pushed through an ultra-liberal platform with a strong public power plank and a call for weakening the anti-communist federal McCarran Act. Several conservative delegates ignored John O'Brien's pleas for unity and stomped out of the convention hall. "This platform is the Communist Manifesto," snorted Spokane delegate Joe Hurley, spouse of Representative Margaret Hurley. Most of the renegades were from Spokane County—the same legislators who had joined us in the fight over

With Joel Pritchard, a political genius, on the floor of the House in 1963. *Washington State Archives*

the private power bill. As the elections approached, we distributed thousands of copies of the Democrats' platform, highlighting in red the most liberal planks. Many of their candidates tried to distance themselves from the document. At Lincoln Day banquets and campaign events, my message was that we needed to gain control of the House. The media styled me as a clean-cut young engineer with a cohort of button-down insurgents. For the first time, I was beginning to think about the governor's race in 1964. If Al Rosellini sought a third consecutive term, he would be fighting precedent; if he bowed out, the race would be wide open.

ON ELECTION DAY, 1962, we came tantalizingly close to gaining control of the House. An agonizing week of counts and recounts gave us eight new seats. We were only 228 votes short of two more. I was disappointed and excited all at once. Republican House candidates had polled 53 percent of the popular vote statewide. The Democrats now had a fragile 51-48 majority.

My team helped elect two talented women, Mary Ellen McCaffree of Seattle and Marjorie Lynch from Yakima. Mary Ellen had served as president of the King County chapter of the League of Women Voters. She could size up a redistricting map in a glance. Few freshmen have ever made their mark as quickly. Marjorie was a natural-born politician with a fascinating life story. Born in England, she had served in the Royal Air Force during World War II. In 1967, during our stunningly successful expansion of higher education, Marjorie headed the House Higher Education Committee. She later served as undersecretary of the Department of Health, Education & Welfare during the Nixon administration.

Our impressive freshman class also included Bob Brachtenbach of Yakima, a future member of the Washington State Supreme Court; Duane Berentson of Burlington, a future longtime secretary of the Department of Transportation and candidate for governor; Bob Earley, a longtime Port of Tacoma commissioner, and my 43rd District seatmate, Bill Young, who would later serve as supervisor of Savings and Loans.

A surprise winner was Herb Hadley, a Cowlitz County insurance man. Sid Snyder, the genial deputy chief clerk of the House, aptly described Herb as "a classic go-getter in the Jaycees mold." Herb was a great addition to our caucus. We also welcomed the first of a new breed of young conservative legislators, Charles Lind of Bellingham, Robert Eberle of Seattle, Mike Odell of Spokane, and Walt Reese of Kennewick. They often voted more conservatively than "Evans Republicans," but on crucial issues they were loyal members of a caucus united in a desire to govern, not just oppose.

Republicans also made gains in the Senate, though the Democratic majority there was still solid. Gaining a say in redistricting was imperative for us. A federal court had branded the lines drawn by Democrats six years earlier "invidiously discriminatory." It ordered the 1963 Legislature to achieve "rational" redistricting based on data from the 1960 Census. Joel Pritchard, Slade Gorton and I well knew that it was now or maybe never. If we couldn't gain control of the process, or at least more leverage, Bob Greive, the Senate majority leader, would make sure we remained a minority party for at least another decade.

I WAS TRYING TO FIGURE OUT our next move when Gorton called with intriguing news. He had been contacted by Representative Bob Perry, one of the private power supporters who had bolted the Democrats' state convention. Gorton and Perry had struck up a seemingly curious friendship when they sat across the aisle from one another in the House. Perry was a big, enigmatic guy who loved intrigue. He was also a voracious reader, which impressed Slade. A former Seattle business agent for the Electrical Workers union, Perry had been a union man on the rough and tumble docks of San Francisco. He told me his favorite persuasive device was a baseball bat. I was surprised when he revealed we shared a love of classical music. Perry knew his Bach as well as backstreet politics. Joel Pritchard—right, as usual—suspected he was a paid agent of Washington Water Power.

Perry told Slade he should ask me whether we were interested in forming a coalition to seize control of the House. Perry and Margaret Hurley, together with "Big Daddy" Day, the chiropractor from Spokane, had sworn they would never again vote for John O'Brien as Speaker. "He didn't play fair," Margaret fumed. "He's gotten to be a dictator."

This was heady stuff. Joel, Slade and several other members of our team gathered at my house to decide how to respond. We were joined by Jim Dolliver, the brilliant young lawyer who served as attorney for the House GOP caucus. We all agreed that Slade should tell Perry we were interested, just not quite ready to commit.

We held our traditional reorganization caucus in Spokane on the eve of the 1962 Apple Cup game. As Slade related his meeting with Perry, there were a lot of raised eyebrows. Some said it was too risky, arguing that we shouldn't stake the integrity of our caucus on a few dissidents. Slade outlined what was at stake. The federal court demanded a redistricting bill that would pass constitutional muster. The Supreme Court's "One person, one vote" rulings meant we could no longer create small rural districts to save incumbent legislators. "Democrats control the House of Representatives, the Senate and the Governor's Office," Gorton said. "A coalition may be the only way to avoid a Democratic gerrymander that could relegate us to minority status for years." I reminded the caucus that although we had won a clear majority of the popular vote, we were still in the minority. "We need a fair redistricting plan."

After several hours of intense debate, the caucus gave us the authority to continue talking with the dissident Democrats. Meanwhile, the Democrats' organizational caucus descended into rancor. John O'Brien's hold on power was tenuous.

THE TIRES ON MY BIG-FINNED PLYMOUTH crunched on the gravel as we left the main road at Cooper Point. We slowly made our way down a winding lane through a stand of towering Evergreens. When we emerged into a tiny clearing, I cut the engine and turned off the headlights. Suddenly enveloped by darkness, we half-expected to hear twigs snapping. I chuckled to myself that it was all too much. It felt like we were caught up in some grade-B film noir movie. Fedoras and trench coats were the only missing elements.

A light flickered through the front window of a cabin. I knocked. The door creaked open, and there, illuminated by the fireplace, stood William Day. At 6-3 and 300 pounds, he looked every inch of his nickname.

"Big Daddy" grinned and beckoned us in. Though we had served together for two sessions, I did not know him well, just that his bulk and affability masked his political agility. Day was the de facto leader of several restless Democratic legislators. He had rented the cabin for the 1963 session.

Arrayed around the fireplace were Margaret Hurley, Bill McCormick, Dick Kink, Chet King and Bob Perry, Day's go-between with Gorton. McCormick, a business agent for the Ironworkers Union, and "Maggie" Hurley were both from Spokane. Kink was a commercial fisherman from Bellingham; King a logger from Raymond on Willapa Harbor. Looking back on a lifetime in politics, including three terms as governor and a stint in the U.S. Senate, they were six of the hardest bargainers I've ever met.

We were joined by Silas "Si" Holcomb, the longtime chief clerk of the House, and his popular assistant, Sid Snyder. They were crucial to our plans since under House rules the chief clerk presided until a Speaker was elected. Holcomb chafed under John O'Brien's often abrupt and abrasive leadership and was eager to see him deposed. Having learned the ropes at Holcomb's elbow, Snyder was an expert on the Legislature's rules and traditions.*

Slade wasted no time in getting down to business: "We have 48 solid seats. Evans should be the coalition's Speaker."

"That's a non-starter," Day growled. He wanted the job.

"None of us on the Democratic side will vote for a Republican Speaker," Hurley said. They were solidly behind Big Daddy.

"Don't mistake Bill's likability for wimpishness," Hurley said, emphasizing that we could count on him to keep his promises.

None of this came as a surprise. We knew going in that my candidacy was a long shot. Besides, if I had been elected Speaker with the votes of a small group of dissident Democrats the political fallout would have been far greater.

We quickly conceded Big Daddy should be Speaker. Then it was our turn. We went for a potentially bigger prize—control and chairmanship of the Constitution and Elections Committee where any redistricting bill would be written. As an extra safeguard, we also demanded full control of the Rules Committee. In the 1960s it met in closed session and occasionally voted by secret ballot to determine the fate of bills it controlled. Members of the committee were called upon in rotation. Each could request a bill to be placed on the next day's calendar. A member's wishes were generally respected. The most controversial bills, however, required a committee vote. Many bills died in the Rules Committee.

Day and his team agreed to everything we wanted. Hurley was especially loaded for bear, bristling that O'Brien had "a very quizzical way of looking at you, as though he was superior in knowledge, ability, power and authority—and you were nothing but a worm."

We jointly decided that committee chairmanships should be divided equally between Republicans and Democrats, including O'Brien's supporters. As reformers, we proposed drastically reducing the number of standing committees and scheduling committees, with a minimum of overlap.

The plan was this: I would be nominated for Speaker, with all 48 Republican votes in my corner. Day's candidacy would prevent O'Brien from reaching a majority. We would wait and see if Day gained votes on succeeding ballots before we made a final decision to switch.

As we shook hands all around the room, I was still skeptical of the dissidents' strength. Yet Big Daddy was confident. Hurley more so.

---

* A grocer from Long Beach, Snyder's first job at the Capitol was running the elevator on the swing shift for $10 a week in 1949. From there he was always on his way up, ultimately becoming majority leader of the Senate Democrats. Sid was revered on both sides of the aisle for his fair-mindedness and institutional memory. I trusted him.

THE NEXT MORNING, our caucus convened promptly at 10 to make plans for the noon opening of the 38th session of the Washington State Legislature. I shut the door, turned the key and slipped it in my pocket.

As I revealed the clandestine events of the previous evening, Don Eldridge and the others who had been at the cabin chimed in. There were a lot of flabbergasted faces around that old oak table when we announced that we had agreed to help elect Bill Day Speaker of the House. Some old-guard Republicans would have sooner voted for a yellow dog before Big Daddy.

I let them hash it out for nearly an hour before asking, "What the hell do we have to lose? If O'Brien manages to get re-elected, we'll still have our 48 votes and the promise of help from across the aisle from dissident Democrats who will be madder than ever. If we win, we'll gain key committee chairmanships and above all the power to oversee redistricting." Gorton and Pritchard emphasized that redistricting was our only path to an outright majority and a Speaker of our choosing. The dissident Democrats were our ideological soul mates on education funding and private power. We said we trusted that Day and the others, especially Maggie Hurley, would keep their part of the bargain.

They came around—even Alfred O. Adams, a retired orthopedic surgeon from Spokane. Doc had to swallow hard to digest the thought of voting for a chiropractor who was also a card-carrying Democrat. "Dr. Adams is the first Republican name on the roll call," I said. "Follow his lead."

Rumors were echoing beneath the rotunda. Adele Ferguson, the freewheeling reporter for the *Bremerton Sun*, had scored a scoop that some sort of plot was brewing to deny O'Brien a fifth term as Speaker. She quoted Bob Perry as boasting that O'Brien was toast. O'Brien, seemingly confident, was busy shoring up the faithful in his office.

There was still an hour left before the session began. I wanted no leaks, so I kept our caucus talking. Old-timers told stories of past sessions; Pritchard was his usual entertaining self; we even sang a few songs. The reporters and O'Brien spies lurking outside were amazed to hear strange noises emanating from behind the closed doors as the caucus dragged on.

At five minutes to noon, I declared that "no comment" was our mantra and unlocked the door. We emerged to a jabbering gaggle of inquisitive press and filed into the House chambers. The galleries were packed with spectators, the wings crowded with senators drawn to potential fireworks.

O'BRIEN, DAY AND I were duly nominated. A tiny clue of what was about to happen came from Chet King, who seconded Bill Day's nomination saying, "I don't think the Speaker of the House has stumpage or homestead rights to that particular position for all time."

On the rostrum, Sid Snyder's right eyebrow twitched.

The first ballot was Evans 48, O'Brien 45, Day 6. An immediate second ballot saw Day gain one vote. Dr. Adams was one row behind me. I swiveled around and said, "Doc, it's time to switch to Day."

The chief clerk launched the third ballot:

"Adams?"

"Day!" said Doc.

Savvy onlookers in the galleries gasped. O'Brien furrowed his brow and stood up. He had been sitting on an upside-down wastebasket next to the Democrats' floor leader, Mark Litchman, who was poised to tally the votes.

House Speaker John L. O'Brien, about to be deposed, pleads for a recess. "School's out, John," I said. *The Argus*

As the roll call continued, Adele Ferguson watched O'Brien's face collapse "like a jiggled soufflé." He stormed down the center aisle, placed a hand on Adams' shoulder and beseeched him to reconsider. Doc was unmoved by the stricken patient.

O'Brien glanced around the rows of our stony-faced Republicans and said we should talk things over. "There's nothing to talk about," Pritchard said. When O'Brien locked eyes with Gorton, I think he truly realized he'd been outflanked.

One of the most dramatic photos in the history of the Washington Legislature shows O'Brien looming over my front-row desk. "We'd like a recess," he begged. "Give us some time, Dan. Do us this courtesy. Can't we work something out?"

I just shook my head: "School's out, John."

Holcomb announced that Day had been elected Speaker, with 57 votes to O'Brien's 41.*

Outrage erupted across the aisle, with O'Brien loyalists moving for reconsideration. Our whip, Tom Copeland, challenged the validity of the motion, as per our carefully scripted plan. Si Holcomb, a master of parliamentary procedure, peered down through his thick eyeglasses. Suppressing his satisfaction at O'Brien's imminent ouster, he declared, "The authority of the Chief Clerk in presiding over the House of Representatives is limited to one thing. That is the election of a Speaker. A Speaker has been elected by your vote on the last ballot. While the Chief Clerk is presiding, the motion is declared out of order."

Bill Day was sworn in immediately by Supreme Court Justice Robert Hunter. He appealed for the members to "put aside personal ambitions and partisan causes" and promote a "responsible, and productive legislative session."

I spoke next, hoping to dispel the rancor. Congratulating Day on his election, I outlined the dissatisfaction that gave rise to the coalition. "We on this side of the aisle will advocate the principles we hold dear—that individual liberty is the cornerstone of our democracy; that the local government which is closest to the people can best serve the people; that fiscal responsibility is not an end in itself but a means to an end, a means to give to our children a government that is free from debt caused by the spending sprees of their fathers."

Now that political talk has become so coarse, I guess that sounds flowery. It's also true that we

---

* I received one vote. It was from Dwight Hawley, a longtime lawmaker from King County, who had made it clear in caucus that come hell or high water he couldn't stomach voting for Bill Day.

had engaged in backstage intrigue to advance our agenda. O'Brien called it "dishonest and immoral." I liked John O'Brien, but he knew better. And all these years later, I still cherish the principles I shared on the House floor that fateful day in 1963. I am dismayed that Republican administrations and Congresses in the 21st century have strayed so far from these tenets. Huge and growing deficits threaten our financial futures. They threaten the integrity of state and local governments. Worse, we are all plagued by blatant attempts to restrict individual liberty in arenas as diverse as national security, free speech and moral conscience. Bombast and "tweets" now pass for political discourse. And God save us from "alternative facts."

O'Brien, voice quavering with emotion, rose to denounce what had happened as "a low type of political maneuvering" by double-dealing Republicans and traitorous Democrats. Only through such perfidy had we thwarted his re-election as Speaker, the post he loved. "There should be a code of ethics," he said, "even among legislators." That last line struck me as both ironic and revealing: *Even* among legislators?

Speaker Day interrupted him: "Let's not impugn the motives of anyone."

O'Brien didn't blink. He thanked his loyal supporters and warned, "The blame and whole responsibility is going to be placed on the Republican Party. ... I can tell you this right now, you are in for the most interesting 60 days you have ever had."

OBrien, right, contests the Coalition's committee assignments with harsh words for me and the new Speaker, William "Big Daddy" Day, left, of Spokane. Rep. Elmer Johnston looks on between us. *The Seattle Times*

Adele Ferguson wrote that as O'Brien continued to rail, "voices rose, and the man who once was king was obviously just another House member talking too long."

Once the smoke cleared, the 1963 session was dominated by redistricting. Our coalition pushed through a plan that was summarily rejected by the Democrats who controlled the Senate. In retaliation, we stonewalled their plan. We were determined to create districts where both parties could be competitive.

The main House bill was debated day after day, often late into the evening. Occasional moments of levity punctured the tension. Don Moos, our wise and witty wheat farmer from Edwall, population 500, frequently claimed to represent the AFL—as in Adams, Ferry and Lincoln counties. One weary night, our bill was being dissected, section by section. When Moos' proposed new Eastern Washington district popped up, John L. O'Brien, the deposed Speaker of the House, inquired, "Mr. Moos, what is the population of the new district?"

"It will have roughly 25,000," Moos said. Then, furrowing his brow theatrically, "Hummm, let's see—the last time I counted it was 25,983. Now that my wife and I are over here it is 25,981."

"How many Democrats?" O'Brien asked.

"The last time I counted them? Let's see. My wife is over here..."

Everyone laughed. But the stalemate endured. Our failure to reach a compromise tossed the issue back to the federal court, which ruled that no more elections could be held based on the existing district lines. The decision was later modified to give the Legislature one more chance to craft a constitutional bill when it next met, two years hence. The judge also stipulated that no bills beyond routine housekeeping could pass the Legislature until a satisfactory redistricting bill became law. (As luck would have it, that ruling would be an enormously powerful tool for me during my first few months as governor.)

AS THE SESSION neared adjournment, Governor Rosellini asked the Legislature to pass a bill eliminating a law that barred the sale of intoxicating beverages in a one-mile zone around the University of Washington. Enacted years earlier, the law was a major roadblock to the construction of quality restaurants and hotels close to the university. After the bill passed with a bipartisan majority, the governor piously vetoed the measure. I thought it was pure political duplicity by a man seeking an unprecedented third consecutive term.

After a contentious 60-day regular session and a 23-day special session featuring more of the same, the Legislature adjourned, exhausted. Against long odds, the Coalition had survived, confounding the skeptics. We had pushed through a balanced, no-new-taxes budget.

For the first time in a decade, Republicans had steered the House of Representatives. The Coalition controlled the Rules Committee and thwarted repeated attempts by the Democrat-controlled Senate to redraw legislative boundaries. Though the courts were demanding a solution, we were unwilling to sign our political death warrants.

When appointments were made to major interim committees, Governor Rosellini erupted over the number of Republicans on the prestigious Legislative Council. In a fit of pique, he vetoed appropriations for all interim committees, fearing that Republicans were intent on conducting investigations of his administration. We responded by agreeing to meet voluntarily, without compensation, but soon found we were crippled by a lack of staff and travel money. The governor had prevailed. Temporarily. His veto would become a campaign issue in 1964. We could not investigate but we constantly did ask, "What is the governor trying to hide?"

I was having the time of my life. As Republican leader, I had a small office in the Capitol. I could look out on the Governor's Mansion. Sometimes, I'd bring 2-year-old Danny to the office. One day he peered out the window, spied the Mansion and shouted, "Daddy's house!" I explained that the governor lived there, but he kept insisting it was mine. Little did either of us know that two years later it would be our house.

NANCY WAS NOW PREGNANT with our second son. With the session over, there was more time to delight in Dan Jr.'s growth. We bought a gangly black puppy, promptly named Tigger, who became Danny's constant companion. Each night after we tucked Danny into bed, we would shut Tigger into a basement room close by. Early each morning we awoke to rustling sounds, followed by doors opening and a clatter of young feet and paws racing up the stairs. When the bedroom door

Ski trips recharged our batteries. *Washington State Archives*

slowly opened, a small face appeared. Then we were engulfed in a tangle of legs, arms, boy and dog. It was a wonderful way to greet each day.

Vic Gray had ably carried on our growing engineering practice while I was gone in Olympia or campaigning. He was a remarkably patient and skillful engineer. I was a little rusty but soon re-engaged in engineering design. Politics was on the back burner, for the time being at least. Or so I thought.

13
DRAFTED

I was at my drawing board on a breezy early-May afternoon, wishing I was on my sailboat, when the phone rang. It was Sally Ryan, an enterprising young reporter for the Associated Press: "What's this about a Draft Dan Evans Committee?" Taken by surprise, I guffawed, *Draft Dan Evans for what?* Sally laughed too. "Why, governor, of course."

Sally had in hand a press release from a "Draft Dan Evans Committee" in Cowlitz County. I told her this was all news to me. I was not running for governor, I said, but it was nice to know someone thought I should. I promised to check out the story.

I had given the idea some thought after the success of the Coalition session but hadn't taken any steps. Now, it seemed, someone was intent on giving me a kick in the slats. I called Joel Pritchard and Slade Gorton. We soon discovered that the Draft Dan Evans Committee was the brainchild of Herb Hadley, a freshman member of our House caucus. Affable and whip-smart, he had won his seat in a heavily Democratic district. Herb had coffee practically every morning with R.L. Corbin, Pat Gygi, other young Republican activists, and a group of Cowlitz County business leaders. Without asking me, they just decided I should run for governor.

Nancy's brother, Bill Bell, joined Pritchard, Gorton, Jim Dolliver and several other supporters at my house to consider what to do next. Though I'd made some headlines, I was still a relative unknown statewide. The hard-core conservatives and old bulls in the party resented the "Evans Cohort" of whippersnappers. "Look," Pritchard said, "invite 200 friends to a 7 a.m. breakfast. Tell them upfront that you're going to ask for money and see how many show up." I said a 7:30 start would generate a bigger turnout. Joel shook his head: "Nope. You want to make it tough. That way you'll see who your friends really are."

JOEL AND I ARRIVED extra early for the mid-June breakfast at the Washington Athletic Club in downtown Seattle. We hadn't a clue as to the turnout. Joel sized up the room as the waiters unfurled white tablecloths. "Take two tables away," he declared. I protested, saying I thought we'd fill them. "Probably," he replied, "but always set tables for fewer people than you know will attend. Then when extra tables have to be set up, everyone will say it was an overflow crowd, regardless of how many come." Pritchard was a political genius. I have even seen this strategy work with an audience of 10 arriving in a room where there were only six chairs.

As the crowd grew, I felt the first frisson of campaign fever. I shook hands and worked the room as extra chairs and tables were set up. We had attracted 140 supporters. Most were young, their enthusiasm far exceeding their pocketbooks. I spoke about the failures of the Rosellini administration,

Alan Pratt of *The Seattle Times* portrayed me as David vs. two Goliaths. *The Seattle Times*

outlining my goals for education, equitable taxation, and orderly growth. It was an earnest plea but I was still a clunky orator. Thousands of speeches later, I was much more at ease and knew better how to connect to an audience. But I would never be in the same league with Joel Pritchard. His enthusiasm wowed the crowd as he exhorted each attendee to pledge at least $50 or go forth to raise that much. We needed shoe leather, too, he said, pointing to signup sheets for volunteers. We collected scores of pledge envelopes from the tables. Pretty soon, I started receiving calls from friends complaining, "How come I wasn't invited?" A second breakfast was quickly scheduled. One volunteer made the rounds at a Young Republican cocktail party asking each guest for a dollar. She brought in 60 one-dollar bills. My good friend Jimmy Andersen had run for Attorney General in 1960. He transferred the remainder of his campaign fund. That $250 was the largest single donation to my

fledgling campaign. The two breakfasts raised more than $12,000—a lot of money in 1963. That funded the campaign for the next six months. "We felt like we were on a mission," Gorton remembered. Pritchard said, "We all were pretty young, and we were taking on giants. We were working full-tilt, all out."

Dolliver, the attorney for the House GOP Caucus, was my immediate choice for campaign manager. Jim was politically astute and well respected by our fellow House members. They were the early strength of our campaign.

We realized that someone needed to coordinate our volunteers. Pritchard recruited Esther Seering, the widow of a King County Superior Court judge. She had served as a key staff member for Seattle Mayor Gordon Clinton. Promising that the campaign would be "a great adventure," Joel talked her out of accepting a $600-per-month job at Children's Hospital.*

Esther was soon joined by Meredith Morris, a talented young woman just out of college. Dolliver, Seering and Morris were the only paid members of the campaign during the next six months as we built a cadre of several thousand volunteers.

The State Republican organization was led by W.Y. "Billy" Walters of Tacoma. He carefully managed the widening gulf between supporters of Nelson Rockefeller, New York's liberal governor, and Arizona Senator Barry Goldwater, who had written a best-selling manifesto, *The Conscience of a Conservative*. They were the leading contenders for the 1964 Republican nomination to oppose Kennedy's bid for re-election. Embraced by the John Birch Society, Goldwater was a Cold Warrior

---

* Esther was a genius at scheduling. When the campaign was over, I asked her to come to work with me in the Governor's Office. She spent the next 10 years, until her retirement, as an extraordinarily valuable team member. Unflappable, wise and witty, she oversaw my schedule with precision and finality.

whose bellicosity worried General Eisenhower, one of my political heroes. I was determined to stay clear of that fight and try to appeal to all Republicans. Walters supported my candidacy but kept a neutral public stance.

IN PREPARATION FOR the 1964 elections, the party commissioned a series of polls. The first, taken in June 1963, listed six prospective Republican candidates for governor:

Richard G. Christensen was a 33-year-old Lutheran minister with flashing eyes. To him, every lectern was a pulpit. Pritchard dubbed him *"Christ*-ensen." The fiery preacher had given Warren Magnuson the fight of his life in the 1962 U.S. Senate race, accusing Maggie of being soft on communism. Energized by his showing, Christensen quickly turned his ambition to the governor's race. His righteous army of supporters included a contingent of "Women on the Warpath" who dressed in Indian costumes.

The Rev. Christensen in a classic pose. *Washington State Archives*

Gordon Clinton had just concluded eight successful years as Seattle mayor. A reformer, he had been a strong proponent of Metro

Joe Gandy was a popular Seattle businessman who had presided with skill and vigor as president of Seattle's Century 21 Exposition world's fair. Our grandfathers had served together in the Washington Legislature in 1895.

Tom Pelly, an early environmentalist, was the incumbent congressman from Seattle's 1st District. Before running for Congress, he was a civic and business leader honored as Seattle's "First Citizen" in 1950.

Catherine May, from Yakima, in 1958 became the first Washington woman elected to Congress. Smart, articulate and charming, she had morphed into a moderate during her years in the Legislature after rooming with Julia Butler Hansen.

So, all I needed to do was wrest the Republican nomination for governor from two members of Congress, a mayor, a headline-making business leader, and a charismatic minister who had almost knocked off one of the nation's most influential senators.

The envelope, please: 37 percent of those polled favored Christensen; 17 percent picked Pelly and 12 percent were for Clinton. Gandy and May each had 6 percent. I was dead last, so to speak, with 5 percent, while 17 percent were in the "don't know" category. A second question assessed name familiarity: Christensen registered 38 percent. Pelly and Clinton were tied at 15 percent. May was a blip back at 14 percent, while Gandy was at 8 percent. Only 2 percent of those polled had heard of Evans, whoever he was. Another 13 percent had never heard of any of us.

At our next campaign committee meeting, we mulled the sobering results. Finally, one optimist piped up, "Look, you have more people for you than know you!" We all laughed, resolving to redouble our efforts to build name recognition and establish a statewide network of volunteers. I had two critical assets: My colleagues in the Legislature knew their districts well and helped recruit campaign leaders in their counties. Whitman College proved to be a stronghold. Nancy, her two sisters and her brother were alumni. Hundreds of Whitman graduates were active in community affairs around the state. They became enthusiastic Evans Campaign volunteers.

Nancy's mother—"Gam" to her beloved grandkids—was now living with us, still determined to stay in Seattle only temporarily while the campaign progressed. Mrs. Bell became an integral part of the campaign, sharing tips on protocol and offering advice on issues. Most importantly, she was a loving grandmother, making it possible for my amazing young wife—just turned 30—to play a key role in the campaign. With her disarming smile and easy manner, Nancy created much of the spark in the opening months. She charmed everyone she met, from elderly, white-gloved ladies to college kids. Her moxie helped us recruit many new volunteers. My inner circle early on grasped something I had known from the beginning of our marriage: Nancy Bell Evans was a quick study when it came to politics and a natural-born campaigner.

My first campaign appearances were mostly coffee hours, opportunities the Kennedys seized instinctively when they set out to elect young JFK to Congress. Our first few were highly successful. Soon the campaign team was scheduling several a day. Addressing groups from five to 50, I spoke about the issues but enjoyed answering questions even more, although my answers were often too detailed. Nancy counseled that I was telling people more than they wanted to know. "When you're rambling on too long I'll cough discreetly," she said after one event. "You'll know it's time to wrap it up." In audiences large or small, I was attuned to Nancy's signals, buoyed by her smiles or chastened by the tell-tale cough. Our system worked almost perfectly, except for the day years later when I was moving confidently into the heart of what I perceived to be one of my most persuasive talks. Just then, Nancy coughed. I ignored it and pressed on. A few minutes later, she coughed again. Secretly confused, I shortened my remarks, stumbled to a conclusion and sat down. Event over, I asked her what the heck was wrong with my talk. "Nothing," she said, staring back blankly. "I thought it was great. Why did you quit so early?" "Well, you were coughing!" She frowned. "I had a tickle in my throat! Our signal needs fine-tuning."

AS THE SUMMER WANED, we decided it was time to visit other parts of the state. We'd been concentrating on King, Pierce and Snohomish counties. When we were organizing the campaign, I had visited Pat Goodfellow, a grade school friend who was now in the automobile business. "I could help with money, but I have a better idea," Pat said. "Why don't you look over my used car lot and pick a car to use during the campaign." I chose a nondescript white Plymouth sedan—the automotive equivalent of the "respectable Republican cloth coat" Nixon had touted as fiscally appropriate in his famous "Checkers" speech. The car was an inspired contribution. However, I suspect Pat had little idea how large a contribution he was making. We returned the car after the election with 60,000 additional miles on the odometer. During the last half of 1963, Jim Dolliver and I drove that Plymouth to every corner of the state. We started with the home towns of my legislative colleagues, visiting the swivel-stool corner cafés where townsfolk gathered for morning coffee. It was a crash course in the diversity of our state. In Eastern Washington, where Republicans are strongest, then as now, I learned the unique problems facing apple growers, wheat producers, cattle ranchers, and the score of other specialty farmers wet-siders too often take for granted. I rode combines, picked apples, sniffed hops and developed a new appreciation for the taxpayers of our complex, productive, beautiful state.

Travels with Jim were never dull. Dolliver was a renaissance man. During our long hours on the road that year, our friendship deepened into a virtual brotherhood. We talked of favorite hikes in the Olympic Mountains, explored political issues that divided the state, and mapped campaign strategy. I discovered his enormous intellect and passion for books. His secret Mario Andretti complex took some getting used to. It's a good thing we were never intercepted by the State Patrol because Jim may have set some speed records as we were invariably running late for the next engagement. We made it from Spokane to Colfax one day in what seemed like a cloud of dust.

Frequently we would arrive in a town knowing no one and having no appointments. We'd circle the streets looking for the antenna tower of the local radio station and pull our trusty second-hand Plymouth into the lonely parking lot. The station was usually manned by one guy who was the disc jockey, newsman, transmitter repairman and janitor rolled into one. When I'd introduce myself, explain I was running for governor, and volunteer to sit for an exclusive live interview right there and then, the response was often puzzlement. Looking up from his turntable, one fellow noted, "But there is no election this year." True, we said, but we were there early in his town because his listeners mattered. "I don't even know what questions to ask," he protested. Dolliver was always equal to that task.

Our second small-town must-visit was the weekly newspaper. Often the owner was the editor, reporter, typesetter, and circulation manager. The Linotype machine, a wheezing dinosaur, squatted in the corner, clanking and whirring as it disgorged lines of hot type into a tray. Unlike the lonely disc jockey, weekly newspaper owners were acutely aware of approaching elections and the potential

Parades at community celebrations were a staple of campaigning. *Washington State Archives*

for revenue from campaign advertising. They were flattered, too, to be visited by a bona fide candidate for governor. They almost always gave me a good story, frequently accompanied by good advice. They knew their towns, including idiosyncrasies, hot-button issues, and who to see down the street.

Nancy, now eight months pregnant, was still campaigning daily.

IN MID-SEPTEMBER, Dolliver and I headed out for a two-day swing around the Olympic Peninsula. After a luncheon speech in Aberdeen, we headed for a banquet at Forks, a hundred miles north in the shadow of the Olympic Mountains I knew and loved. Organizers of the event promised 200 people, which would be by far the largest meeting of the campaign and a stunning turnout for a small logging town. An hour out of Grays Harbor, we stopped at Humptulips, a wide spot in the road, to check in with Nancy. I brushed cobwebs from the receiver in a lonely phone booth and called home, dropping coins in the slot until I heard the voice of Mary Sidwell, Nancy's upbeat sister. "Hi, Dan," she said without an ounce of drama, "we're just leaving for the hospital. Nancy is about to go into labor." I sputtered that we would start for home immediately, then ran to the car to tell Jim the news. We studied the roadmap to see how long it would take to get back to Seattle. There were no shortcuts. It looked like five hours minimum, whether we continued around the "loop" to Port Townsend and caught a ferry or headed back the way we'd come. We called the organizers of the Forks event and told them of my dilemma. It turned out that one member of their committee was a pilot who owned a plane. Hightail it to Forks, they said. I could speak before dinner, then they'd fly me to Seattle.

The hall was packed when we arrived, the drama adding to the expectation. The minute my abbreviated stump speech was over, the sponsors approached with bad news. The weather over the Olympic Mountains had turned bad. Many phone calls later, I jumped into a State Patrol car and took a terrifyingly high-speed ride along narrow, winding Highway 101 from Forks to Port Angeles where a private plane was waiting. At Boeing Field, I was met by Nancy's brother Bill and Joel Pritchard. They told me I was a new father of a baby boy. As we raced to the hospital, Joel quipped, "Couldn't you have had a minor crash landing? We need the publicity!"

I burst into the hospital room to embrace a radiant Nancy, busy holding court, family all around. "You're late!" she declared, laughing. It wasn't the last time during that 18-month campaign or my 12 years as governor.

Accompanied by Pritchard and my brother-in-law, I walked down the hall to gaze on a healthy squirming boy. We named him Mark Lawrence Evans, his middle name honoring Nancy's late father, William Lawrence Bell. The next day's papers featured a story detailing my travails getting home. Joel wasn't missing a beat.

14
THE BLUEPRINT

At 5 percent in that first poll on the 1964 race for governor, we were so far back we had nothing to lose and everything to gain from what Joel Pritchard called "creative thinking." Joel's broad definition of "creative" embraced ideas ranging from goofy to brilliant. It's a shame we never tape-recorded meetings of the Evans Campaign Committee.

One of Pritchard's good friends was John Murray, the publisher of the weekly *Queen Anne News*. It took little persuading to enlist Murray in the campaign. He practically donated the cost of printing 95,000 tabloid-size newspapers outlining my platform. Every page featured heartwarming family photos: Me as an Eagle Scout and 19-year-old naval officer; Nancy and I with our two active boys, hiking, camping, sailing, romping with puppies.

A hundred volunteers manned each intersection in downtown Seattle during the evening rush hour when our paper hit the streets on November 5, 1963. Election Day was a year away. "EVANS ELECTED GOVERNOR," the banner headline declared. In smaller type came this question: "Will this be the headline a year from now?"

Bill Bell, Nancy's brother, recruited another important volunteer. John Haydon was the publisher of the *Marine Digest*, a magazine devoted to the maritime industry. Later a member of the Seattle Port Commission, Haydon had a Rolodex filled with influential contacts and a head full of ideas to boost our campaign. He was also an active Democrat. John and his wife Jean hosted a reception for us in their West Seattle home. The event drew a sizable crowd, mostly Democrats who had no particular love for Al Rosellini. They felt he was over-reaching to seek a third term. Rich White, a veteran Seattle attorney, and Gerald Hoeck, a former aide to Scoop Jackson, cornered me in a hallway.

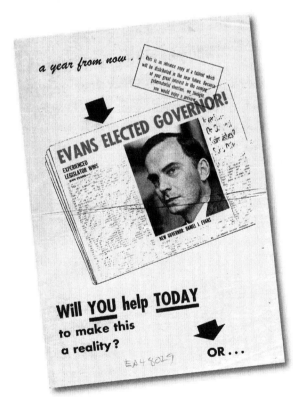

On Nov. 5, 1963, with Election Day a year away, our campaign distributed 95,000 tabloid-size newspapers outlining my platform. *Washington State Archives*

Blueprint for Progress

FOR GOVERNOR DAN EVANS

From the day of the Governor's inauguration just 57 crucial days remain in the legislative session . . . 57 days in which a new program must be shaped, introduced and acted upon if we are to curb the downtrend brought about by the Rosellini administration.

The time is critically short. It demands leadership experienced in state government and the legislative process. Dan Evans will give our state this leadership. He has a "Blueprint for Progress" for Washington State that can make these 57 days an historic turning point for all of us. Let's give our state the forward thrust we need—now. Vote for Dan Evans for Governor.

REPUBLICAN

James Dolliver, Director, Dan Evans for Governor, 820 3rd Ave., Seattle, Wn.

One of our Blueprint for Progress fliers. *Washington State Archives*

Several other Democrats huddled around as they grilled me on issue after issue: Where did I stand on labor? Taxation? Higher education? Fighting back tears, Nancy fled to the kitchen. Her brother consoled her, warning, "This is the way it is." In other words, "Toughen up, Sis." She was soon back on the stump, speaking at coffee hours. I'm certain we won over some Democrats that night, most importantly John Haydon, who became an enthusiastic supporter.

Tony Frederick, a longtime friend who was an investment broker, signed on as campaign treasurer. My brother Roger, a school counselor whose enthusiasm for politics equaled mine, became a key player, together with Dan Ward, the banker for our engineering firm. Dan's wife Marilyn was serving as the State Republican Committeewoman for King County, so she could not directly serve on our committee, but she was a stalwart. Another energetic volunteer was Walter Williams, my grade school compatriot, legislative seatmate, and later state senator from the 43rd District. Frank Pritchard, Joel Pritchard's equally enterprising brother, and Helen Rasmussen, one of the most nimble volunteer coordinators in the history of Washington politics, were tasked with coordinating our growing corps of volunteers. Ritajean and Fred Butterworth and Mary Ellen and Ken McCaffree also contributed mightily to our grassroots organizing. Mary Ellen had made her mark as a legislator in the tumultuous 1963 session, while Ritajean personified the "housewife" political activist of the era. Those two women were tireless and tough. Their spouses proved invaluable, too. Fred Butterworth was a sharp young Seattle attorney. Ken McCaffree taught economics at the University of Washington.

Isla Morris and her daughter Meredith, assisted by Dorothy Engel and Elizabeth Wright Evans (no relation, but a jewel), assembled a huge team of headquarters volunteers who mimeographed, addressed, stamped, sealed and mailed more than a million pieces of mail during the campaign. Back then, virtually everything was done by hand. Those old, hand-cranked mimeograph machines were the workhorses of every campaign.

ON NOVEMBER 22, I was at campaign headquarters, getting ready to catch a ferry for a speech in Bremerton when a volunteer rushed in, sobbing that President Kennedy had been shot. Stunned, we turned on the radio and listened to the voices of horrified motorcade spectators and the cluster of Secret Service agents outside a Dallas hospital emergency room. When a somber Walter Cronkite announced that the president had died, I told Dolliver to cancel the luncheon appearance and assemble the campaign committee. We decided to suspend campaigning until after the State Funeral for President Kennedy on November 25.

I was moved by Lyndon Johnson's pitch-perfect speech to Congress in the wake of the assassination. "All I have I would have given gladly not to be standing here today," the new president said. "The greatest leader of our time has been struck down by the foulest deed of our time." I did not regard John Fitzgerald Kennedy as the greatest leader of our time, but that thought never entered my mind in those sobering days before the tarnished Thanksgiving of 1963. My president had been murdered. Like Pearl Harbor and 9/11, that day in Dallas lives in infamy. In 2017 as America commemorated the 100th anniversary of his birth, I found it hard to imagine JFK as a codger. But then there are days when I can't believe I'm this old—born just eight years after Kennedy.

I voted for Nixon in 1960 and did my bit to promote the ticket that year, though I sensed something disquieting about the man. If Ike could have run for a third term, I would have been an enthusiastic supporter. Kennedy styled Eisenhower as a relic of America's yesterdays, yet Ike was only 70 when he left office. Eisenhower's steady hand and vision are now coming into sharper focus, particularly his farewell address warning of the pervasive influence of the military-industrial complex. Ike also worked masterfully across the aisle with House Speaker Sam Rayburn and LBJ, the Senate majority leader, to advance important legislation. The Interstate Highway Act of 1956 was one of the greatest public works projects in American history.

IN DECEMBER, we resumed campaigning. It would be several months before it felt normal.

As Election Year dawned, we eagerly awaited the results of a poll commissioned by the State Republican Party, confident that our battalion of volunteers and six months of hard campaigning had closed the gap. We were thunderstruck to learn that Christensen, who had done practically no campaigning, still led by a huge margin and we had made only modest progress. While my support level had doubled to 11 percent, I still had abysmal name familiarity. I was now ostensibly in third place in the GOP race, a point ahead of Congressman Pelly and a point behind Mayor Clinton. Christensen was sailing along at 34 percent.

Luckily for us, C. Montgomery Johnson had joined the cause as chairman of the Campaign Strategy Committee. "Gummie" was an old friend from our days as staff members at Boy Scout camp. He didn't smoke Churchill-size cigars back then or cuss like a sailor, at least in front of the kids, but he was already a force of nature. His fertile mind was always working overtime. A skilled lobbyist, Gummie was now on the executive payroll of the Weyerhaeuser Company. He decreed that the campaign now needed an ad agency. We heard a lot of pitches before settling on Soderberg & Cleveland of Spokane. Stan Soderberg and Bob Cleveland were energetic young guys with lots of good ideas. They were excited about the prospect of propelling a dark horse to the Governor's Mansion. They would prove to be as loyal as they were creative.

Two new volunteers, Bruce Baker and Jim Lane, took on key roles. They were both in the advertising business. Lane became a speechwriter, contributing heavily to my major speeches over the next six years, including the keynote address to the 1968 Republican National Convention. What we needed now was professional press assistance. *Seattle Times* reporter Wayne Jacobi, a Roosevelt High School classmate of mine, signed up and helped us land another important ally—Walt Woodward, publisher of the *Bainbridge Review*.* After interviewing me and Christensen at length,

---

* Woodward and his wife Milly were bravely supportive of Bainbridge Island's Japanese Americans at the outbreak of World War II, opposing mass incarceration.

Woodward had written thoughtful columns about each campaign. He finally concluded I was the better candidate, writing an endorsement editorial that included a line I'll never forget. "Glib goodness will not solve state problems."

We had assembled a superb team and seemed to be building momentum, only to screech to a halt at a roadblock that has stalled many promising campaigns. We were out of money. The exuberance generated by the easy money raised in June and the donated labor of an army of volunteers had collided with the reality that the growing ranks of professionals crucial to our success expected to be paid. Our campaign committee gathered glumly in a basement room of the Roosevelt Hotel in downtown Seattle. After Dolliver and Johnson explained our dilemma, I chimed in to say I was unable to contribute personal money to the campaign, for two reasons: "I do

Alan Pratt's cartoon in *The Seattle Times* summed up Gov. Rosellini's big frundraising lead. *The Seattle Times*

not believe in doing so. Besides, I don't have any." That lightened the mood for a moment before I added that I was dead set against taking out loans. "We must pay our bills. If we can't, we'd better close down."

Cleveland and Soderberg exchanged whispers. "We've come this far," one said as the other nodded. "We're willing to forgo our fee for a few months to see whether we can make real progress." The mood brightened. We filed out, determined to see if we could scare up some money.

IT WAS SLOW GOING. Business leaders, bankers, and all the other old-reliable Republican campaign contributors were waiting to see if Joe Gandy, their favorite, would enter the race in earnest—and hedging their bets to see if we could gain steam on our own. "Show us some progress," they'd say. And we'd say, "We can't do it without money." It was our Catch-22.

I went to see Ross Cunningham, the associate editor at *The Seattle Times*. Cunningham had been Republican Governor Art Langlie's executive secretary during the 1940s. When he rejoined the city's influential afternoon daily, everyone knew he was the publisher's favorite. Cunningham's columns could sway a lot of votes. He was feared and respected, holding court in his cluttered office to parades of supplicants. He beckoned me to sit down and sized me up through wire-rimmed glasses. I told him all about our campaign, its wonderful volunteers and the progress we were making until we ran out of money. He listened politely, nodding his bald head now and then. With a practiced hand, he slowly re-packed his pipe and lit it with care. "If I were appointing a governor I would appoint you," he said. "You have the experience and smarts to succeed, but you can't win the election." Inwardly furious, I played it cool. "I'll bet you a dollar I'll be the next governor," I said, reaching across his desk. Cunningham smiled indulgently as if to say, "Right you are, my boy." We shook hands, and I departed the newspaper's block-long fortress determined to prove him wrong.

Resuscitation arrived in the nick of time a few days later when we received a $500 check, our largest donation to date by far. The identity of the donor was much more important. It was from John Hauberg, a member of the Weyerhaeuser family. He was a successful lumberman in his own right and state finance chairman for the Republican Party. Tall, slim, patrician and soft-spoken, Hauberg was widely respected in both business and political circles. I immediately called him to express our gratitude, asking if we could meet. "Come right over," he said. When I explained our financial dilemma, he volunteered to help. Soon larger donations began arriving from leaders across the state. Washington state history had turned on one donation.

Fred Baker, a hugely successful advertising executive, volunteered to temporarily serve as our finance chairman. His firm represented leading Northwest companies. Baker opened doors and cajoled his friends and associates to donate to this promising young Republican.

I chose the annual meeting of two journalism groups, Sigma Delta Chi and Theta Sigma Phi, to formally announce my candidacy on January 22, 1964. The audience was loaded with the people I wanted to reach. Dolliver, Johnson, Jim Lane and I worked hard on what I'd tell a room full of reporters, editors, and publishers. It turned into a massive press conference. Reporters like fresh faces and a good story. I declared that Rosellini's administration had created a "fumbling, bumbling political apartheid," especially "between the legitimate governmental concerns of organized labor and those of industrial management." The Legislature had appropriated millions of dollars to help the administration diversify the economy and create new jobs, I said, "but there are fewer jobs today … than in 1957 when the governor first took office or any year since." In answer to a pointed question, I also made it clear I would not accept support from the John Birch Society.

WHAT BEGAN AS a winter of discontent gave way to an upbeat spring. We still needed a slogan. We were working our way through a thicket of clunkers one night when the group's not-so-shining Eureka moment was the realization that its candidate was a civil engineer. "How about 'Blueprint for Progress'?" someone said. I wish I could remember who. We knew instantly it was right. From Day One of its roll-out, the slogan began appearing in papers. When the opposition referred to it derisively, we knew it was a winner.

By now it was apparent that only three candidates would actively seek the Republican nomination for governor: Joe Gandy, Richard Christensen, and me. Gandy threatened to divide the anti-Christensen vote and deprive us of victory.

A delegation of our campaigners, led by Jim Dolliver, met with the Gandy braintrust and found that both sides had the same concern. Each wanted the other out of the race. An agreement was reached that the State Republican Party would take another poll in June. Whoever was ahead—Gandy or Evans—would stay in the race; the other would step aside. Though it was a big risk, we were confident.

I DIDN'T NEED A SOOTHSAYER to understand the implications of the King County Republican precinct caucuses during the Ides of March 1964. The average attendance was the highest since 1952 when Republicans were energized at the prospect of winning their first presidential election since the Hoover debacle. But with Barry Goldwater at the top of the ticket, I feared it was going to be 1932 all over again, and we'd be collateral damage. Goldwater's coattails "would be more like lead weights," Joel Pritchard sighed.

A narrow majority of the caucus-goers in my home county, the most populous in the state, now backed me for governor. But they were head-over-heels in love with Barry, who outpolled Nixon and Rockefeller more than 2 to 1. The good news for me was that I was ahead with motivated voters—50.4 percent to Christensen's 32.9 and Gandy's 16.7. Given our statewide organization, I was gaining confidence we would win the nomination. The tricky part would be keeping our distance from Goldwater, without alienating his conservative faithful. Al Rosellini, a seasoned campaigner, didn't need a weatherman to know which way the wind was blowing. He began referring to his trio of Republican challengers as "carbon copies" of Goldwater.

Mark, our second son, brightened the campaign. *Washington State Archives*

15
MOMENTUM

Joel Pritchard surveyed the platoon of sign-makers in his garage and issued a directive: "We want vertical signs. When they're too wide they get in the way of the demonstrators."

The 1964 State Republican Convention at the University of Puget Sound Fieldhouse in Tacoma would be our coming-out party. The three-horse race for the GOP nomination for governor ensured extensive media coverage. Christensen and Gandy were determined to halt our momentum. With Don Moos as permanent chairman of the convention, we had a leg up on the competition.

The electric atmosphere inside that cavernous old gymnasium, the site of so many exciting high school basketball tournaments, equaled that of any national political convention I've ever attended. Rival delegations jockeyed for position as the speeches began. Moos had arranged for me to go last, just where I wanted to be. Though Nancy Evans hates hoopla, she's a trouper. After watching Laurene Gandy march down the main aisle hand in hand with Joe to the strains of a brass band, Nancy resolved to follow her example.

The Gandy demonstration was surprisingly brief. Joe touted his experience as an attorney, auto dealer, and civic leader, emphasizing the success of the Seattle World's Fair on his watch as president of Century 21. He vowed to run the state in "a business-like manner."

Next came Christensen. The doors to the auditorium swung open and a throng of the pastor's supporters surged into the hall. The "Women on the Warpath" led the way to the beat of tom-toms. I noticed, however, that few delegates left their seats to join the demonstration. Christensen's speech was typically bombastic, filled with applause lines and slim on specifics about what he would do if elected governor.

Up next, Nancy and I strode to the podium as voting delegates poured into the aisles to join our volunteers in a sea of bobbing signs. Ours were unmistakable. (Pritchard was a genius!) It was the largest, most enthusiastic demonstration of the day. Christensen's make-believe In-

Nancy close behind, I make my way through a throng of supporters at the 1964 state GOP Convention. Joel Pritchard specified that our signs be vertical for better visibility. *Washington State Archives*

Nancy joins me on the convention rostrum. She was a trouper. *Washington State Archives*

dian maidens scrambled to get out of the way. I spotted my staid old engineer father, an Evans sign in each hand, pumping his arms up and down as he marched with the crowd. Nancy did a double-take, too. She saw the tears well up in my eyes. My love and admiration for my father was never greater.

My speech outlined our Blueprint for Progress, emphasizing the need for tax reform, educational excellence from kindergarten to grad school, and a diversified economy that would generate new jobs. Nearly one of every 10 employable Washingtonians was out of work.

IN EARLY JUNE, right on schedule, Central Surveys conducted a comprehensive statewide poll for the State Republican Central Committee. Forty percent favored Christensen. My support had nearly tripled to 28 percent, and Gandy, at 11 percent, was now a distant third. It was time for Joe to go. With him out, it shaped up as a dead heat, and we were gaining on Christensen by the day.

Dolliver led our delegation to a powwow with the Gandy braintrust while I cooled my heels at our campaign headquarters. When Jim returned, much later than expected, he slammed his briefcase on the table and muttered, "They won't get out!" Since I was only 38, they insisted I should be content to bide my time and run for lieutenant governor. Gandy, 59, would agree to serve only one term, if elected, then enthusiastically back me as his successor. "It doesn't work that way," Dolliver shot back. "Besides, you made a promise that the person in third place in the June poll would drop out." Joe had changed his mind—or more likely his backers had changed it for him. We were all mad as hell. The unanimous verdict from Team Evans was "Don't quit. We can beat them both."

Three weeks later I was in a small plane, heading home from a campaign appearance in Spokane. As we crossed the Cascades I looked down longingly on the snow-capped crags and icy lakes. My reverie about future hikes was broken by the pilot: "I just received a radio message telling you to call campaign headquarters as soon as you land and before you talk to anyone else." Puzzled, I raced to a phone when we arrived at Boeing Field. I could hear bedlam in the background as Dolliver picked up the receiver. Gandy had withdrawn. He was now endorsing me, telling the press he was unwilling "to decimate the finances available to the Republican Party by forcing a three-way primary race" to the finish. I immediately arranged to meet Joe. He graciously offered to write an enthusiastic fundraising letter and followed up with radio and television appearances to support my candidacy. Some of his key campaign aides in Eastern Washington joined our team. Business leaders now had a single candidate to support. Money began to roll in.

Goldwater won the Republican nomination for president on the first ballot, his supporters roaring as he declared, "I would remind you that extremism in the defense of liberty is no vice! And let me remind you also that moderation in the pursuit of justice is no virtue!"* Rosellini declared that Evans and Christensen were right-wing peas in a pod, and the Republican Party was turning into "a blueprint of the John Birch Society, led by the enemies of labor."

THE FILING FEE FOR GOVERNOR was $225. Always striving for free publicity, we tacked that many one-dollar bills on a sandwich board. Campaign volunteers signed on to walk a mile apiece, Olympic torch relay-style, to cover the 60 miles from Seattle to Olympia. Former Seattle mayor Gordon Clinton, now chairman of the Citizens for Evans Committee, walked the first mile with a scrum of reporters in tow. I hefted the board to walk the last lap to the Secretary of State's office in the Legislative Building. Our volunteers were churning out thousands of mailers every day. Mary Ellen McCaffree reported to the committee that we now had 10,000 volunteers around the state. The press sensed an upset in the making. We began emphasizing the "most important 57 days for Washington." That was the length of time between Inauguration Day and the scheduled end of the legislative session. The next governor would have a little over eight weeks to select his cabinet and

Former Seattle mayor Gordon Clinton prepares to walk the first mile from Seattle to Olympia as part of a relay to register my candidacy for the 1964 governor's race. We tacked the $225 filing fee in dollar bills on the sign volunteers wore. I walked the last lap to the Secretary of State's office. *Washington State Archives*

department heads, sell his budget and gain political capital for bigger things. Redistricting loomed as unfinished business.

Christensen's campaigners put him through a crash course on state government. He was still inclined to go off the rails. His speeches sounded like sermons. His magnetism registered as sanctimonious. By mid-August, most editorial writers were backing me. The *Marysville Globe* dismissed Christensen as "woefully lacking" in managerial experience. The *Bremerton Sun* concluded that "the job of being governor cannot be filled by just a personality." And *The Seattle Times*, the state's largest paper, wrote: "Of the three Republicans, Evans, of course, is the best qualified by experience in government."

The temperatures were well over 100 as Nancy and I wooed voters throughout Eastern Washington, attending fairs, rodeos, picnics and coffee hours. "You've got a fine milking hand," said a dairy farmer as we shook hands. Nancy's smiling face kept my brain from bouncing as I tried to give my stock campaign speech a new spin at each stop.

In mid-August, a writer for the weekly *Kitsap County Herald* came to a prescient conclusion: "If Christensen continues to tumble and Evans continues to gain at the rates indicated by the three

---

* That line sent shivers down the spine of the GOP's moderate wing. General Eisenhower played the good soldier during the campaign but privately worried that Goldwater might start World War III. "I have the feeling that that man is dangerous," he confided to a reporter he trusted.

polls, I think you'll find the date Evans passes Christensen is around August 21st." Ever the engineer, I had already plotted the polls on a chart of my own and come to the same conclusion. I would catch Christensen in mid-August and keep climbing, my rise culminating in a big victory on September 15, Primary Election Day.

Most pundits were still saying it was too close to call.

SHORTLY BEFORE THE POLLS CLOSED, I joined Nancy, her brother Bill and his wife Tina at Rosellini's 610. Owned by Victor Rosellini, the governor's cousin, the 610 was downtown Seattle's finest restaurant, with a bipartisan clientele. While everyone else chatted, I surreptitiously plugged an earpiece into a transistor radio to listen to the news. The first returns were from a precinct in Grant County, wedged in the middle of the state. Christensen had a hundred-vote lead. I was dismayed but kept quiet. A few minutes later, several thousand absentee votes from King County were announced. I was ahead by almost 2 to 1—a very good omen. I gleefully reported the returns to the table and the party really began. My lead in Spokane County was greeted with special jubilation. I toasted the anchors of my Inland Empire support group—Nancy Bell Evans, her brother and her mother.

When the counting was done, I was resoundingly the 1964 Republican nominee for governor. We outpolled Christensen by nearly 110,000 votes, 39 percent to 25.8 percent, and ran well ahead of the governor, who received 29.44 percent of the total vote in the blanket primary.

Giddy with success, we all traipsed a few blocks to our campaign headquarters to be greeted by an ecstatic crowd of volunteers. Phones rang constantly. I talked to county chairmen from around the state and gave interviews to a swarm of reporters. Finally, I stood on a chair to say that in the space of 15 months we had come from nowhere—barely 5 percent in that sobering first poll—to score what amounted to a landslide. We had waged one of the greatest political campaigns in Washington state history. But we were only halfway there.

All the polls were predicting a Democratic landslide in the General Election. LBJ's lead over Goldwater was holding steady at 15 percentage points. I said we'd have to work even harder in the weeks ahead. "I know we can do it!" They cheered. And I went home to get some sleep.

WE MOVED IMMEDIATELY to capitalize on the euphoria of Election Night. Christensen, for all our derision of his pious persona, issued a gracious statement of support, which helped unify the party and generate more money for ads, signs, campaign buttons and all the myriad other expenses I'd never thought much about before I found myself in a hot statewide campaign.

Our campaign team focused on three priorities: Effectively deploying an army of volunteers whose ranks would swell to 14,000 by November; expanding our Blueprint for Progress, and walking the political tightrope strung across the canyon that divided the hard-core Goldwaterites from Teddy Roosevelt progressives like us. In the years to come, I would be aptly described as "passionately moderate."

A snapshot telephone poll gave us a 10-point lead. For a reality check, my brother Roger sent his team out to canvass voters in King County shopping areas. The results were the same.

Joel Pritchard and John Haydon masterminded the volunteer effort. Evans signs popped up everywhere. Endorsement ads signed by thousands of supporters appeared in weekly and daily newspapers. Radio and newspapers were the prime political advertising targets in the mid-1960s. We did produce some half-hour TV specials—laughably clunky by today's standards—where I detailed the "five E's" of the Blueprint for Progress: Economic Growth, Educational Opportunity, Equitable Taxation, Efficiency in Government, and Energetic Leadership. In speeches around the state, I expanded on those themes, proposing 35 bills and executive actions I would embrace if elected. I advocated streamlining the bureaucracy by consolidating departments; equalizing property taxes statewide to enhance support for public schools; ending politically appointed estate appraisers; professionalizing the Board of Prison Terms & Paroles and expanding opportunities for higher education, including more community colleges.

I was eager to debate the governor, unsurprised at his reluctance. Incumbents seldom want to debate challengers. (A suggestion that we'd still be squaring off eight years later when our roles were reversed would have boggled my mind in 1964.) Rosellini did some hemming and hawing about his busy schedule and the demands of being governor that a neophyte like me could not grasp. Finally, the Washington State Newspaper Publishers' Association brokered the rules for a joint appearance at their convention in Spokane on October 3, one month from Election Day.

With Rosellini after our first debate in 1964. *The Seattle Times*

As I took the stage, I was astonished to see Al at the podium, almost hidden behind a stack of documents. The rules hadn't addressed crib sheets. I ad-libbed my opening statement: "Governor, take a good look at those notes you have in front of you— the product of your 27 public-relations men …because it's the last time you'll use them in a debate with me." We sparred over taxes, liberalized gambling, and government priorities. I lit into him over state employees soliciting campaign contributions from firms they regulated. Looking nervous early on, the governor now bristled. The practice was "wrong," he said, but not illegal. He asserted that the contributions solicited for his 1960 campaign were made without his knowledge and accused me of shaking down lobbyists, truckers, and "big" Seattle establishments. My record in office was "more negative" than Goldwater's, the governor said. In his final statement, Rosellini quoted statistics from his pile of documents to assert that Washington's economy was doing fine. "Certainly I have papers and notes. It's the only way you can keep some people honest—to cite the facts and specifics against the generalities that this man has been dealing with in his so-called regressive invisible dew point or blueprint …." I resisted a smile. When your opponent refers to your platform, you know it's getting under his skin.

The publishers called it a draw but admired my calm demeanor. They said I had held my own against an "old trial-lawyer" who had been in politics since 1939. Ross Cunningham wrote that I represented "a combination of pragmatism and idealism." And the *Post-Intelligencer's* popular columnist, Emmett Watson, identified with my "sincere abhorrence of political lunacy." Joel Pritchard read that one aloud and pronounced it bipartisan manna from Heaven.

Most of my colleagues on the statewide ticket were running hopeless races, especially Lloyd J. Andrews, who lost a close race to Governor Rosellini in 1960. Now, Andrews was running against Senator Jackson, a virtually invincible centrist Democrat popular with business, labor, the military, and environmentalists.

Our only other real hope was 32-year-old A. Ludlow Kramer, running for Secretary of State against Victor Aloysius Meyers, a former bandleader more than twice his age. "Lud" was a liberal Seattle City Councilman. Meyers was a character. In the 1930s, he showed up for a candidates' forum dressed as Mahatma Gandhi and leading a goat. Elected Secretary of State in 1956, the former long-time lieutenant governor had continued his practice of adding relatives to his payroll. At campaign events, Lud would pull out a pair of scissors and begin cutting a folded sheet of paper. With each snip, he would describe another of Vic's relatives supping at the public trough. Finally, with a flourish, he'd unfold an accordion string of paper-doll cutouts.

Our volunteers had the rural vote covered. We concentrated on the larger counties. Our pollsters reported that people were tired of negative campaigning, so we had a late-night summit at the Olympic Hotel in downtown Seattle where Joel Pritchard's brother Frank and Gummie Johnson—two of the savviest campaign operatives I've ever known—were holed up doing opposition research in a haze of cigar smoke. We decided to close out the campaign with a slew of positive newspaper ads.

At a campaign stop in Yakima, I was having lunch with Dolliver when Don Brazier, our county chairman, arrived to ask if we would like to meet Will Bachofner, the newly appointed chief of the Washington State Patrol, who was in town to address the Rotary Club. We said that would be great. Don brought him over to our table. Though it was a short conversation, I was immensely impressed with Bachofner. He was a tall, dignified, career state patrolman, much respected by his troopers. I would discover that Bachofner was one of several fine cabinet appointments Governor Rosellini had made.

WHEN WE LEARNED that Goldwater would be making a campaign stop in Spokane on October 10, Pritchard, Dolliver and the rest of the campaign leadership urged me to stay as far away as possible. With Rosellini claiming I was a Goldwater clone masquerading as a moderate, it would be stupid, they said, to give him any ammunition. Besides, it was abundantly clear that Goldwater hadn't a prayer beyond Arizona and the Deep South. It was all true, I conceded. "But if I am leading our party's ticket in this state I can't duck out."

I dutifully arrived at the Spokane airport with a busload of Evans campaigners and mingled with the crowd. I was asked to join other state and local candidates on a truck trailer that would double as the podium. Don Moos had won the Bronze Star and two Purple Hearts in some of the deadliest combat of World War II. In Spokane that day he was a resourceful political soldier.

Goldwater's people and Rosellini operatives were equally eager to get a photo of me shaking hands or, better yet, embracing Barry. When Goldwater's jet taxied to a stop, Moos and I were sitting together on a riser across from Bob Timm, a GOP national committeeman, and a row of other Republican officials and civic leaders. Goldwater was methodically working his way down the line with a photographer in tow, motorized Nikon whirring. Moos craftily stood up at exactly the moment Goldwater shook my outstretched hand, blocking the photographer's view. "I did a pivot and his lens hit me right smack in the middle of my backbone," Moos remembered with a chuckle. "The guy exclaimed, 'You dirty S.O.B.!'" For the life of me, I can't remember what Goldwater told me as we shook hands. I was about to crack up over the photographer cussing out Moos.

After the most intense 18 months of my life, only one event remained. In what would become an Evans campaign tradition, I shook hands with voters in front of the Frederick & Nelson department store at the corner of 5th Avenue and Pine Street in downtown Seattle. Shortly before the polls closed at 8 o'clock, I learned Governor Rosellini was shaking hands nearby in front of the Bon Marche, another retail landmark. I walked over to greet him. We exchanged good wishes and a warm handshake.

IT WAS LBJ ALL THE WAY as polls closed in the East and Midwest. No candidate for president since has equaled or surpassed Johnson's percentage of the popular vote, 61.1 percent. He was running even stronger in Washington. Democrats had steamrolled their way to two-thirds majorities in both houses of Congress.

We had not just survived a Democratic tsunami, we had won handily, with nearly 56 percent of the vote while carrying 36 of the state's 39 counties. Albert D. Rosellini and John W. Reynolds Jr. of Wisconsin were the only two Democratic governors defeated in their bids for re-election. Eight partisan state offices were on the ballot. Evans and Kramer were the only victorious Republicans.

As our lead surged past 100,000, Nancy and I worked our way through a boisterous crowd of supporters, pausing every few feet to thank volunteers. Their hard work had sealed a victory that featured gallons of coffee, thousands of handshakes, countless speeches, and 60,000 miles in Pat Goodfellow's Plymouth loaner. Watching Nancy exchange hugs with old and new friends, I realized for the umpteenth time that I had an extraordinary partner. She had taught me a lot about campaigning. The headline writers played up the fact that at 39 I would be Washington's youngest-ever governor. Nancy was only 31. And we'd been married for only five years.

The next morning we slept late. When I finally got around to retrieving the *Seattle Post-Intelligencer* from the doorstep I stared in awe at the headline: "Evans Elected Governor." The cheeky headline on the campaign tabloid we had distributed a year earlier had come true. When I surveyed our front yard I saw scores of campaign signs and hand-painted greetings from our neighbors. They had been up late creating a display of their affection and congratulations. As I pored over the election news, I was particularly saddened that Herb Hadley was losing in the 18th District.* His Cowlitz County "Draft Evans" committee had started it all. Losing Herb italicized the reality of the task ahead. With redistricting looming, Democrats had tightened their control of both houses of the State Legislature.

---

* Hadley ended up losing by 15 votes to Alan Thompson, a young weekly newspaper publisher from Castle Rock. Alan earlier had been Congresswoman Hansen's administrative assistant. It was Julia, the master politician, who wanted Hadley's ascendancy halted in its tracks, lest he become a future opponent. I hated to see Herb go, but Thompson was a Democrat I came to admire. He became a fine legislator who put his principles above party.

16
SETTING THE AGENDA

This governor-elect's easiest decision was choosing a chief of staff. Jim Dolliver was one of the brightest, wisest, most principled human beings I've ever known. The son of a former Iowa congressman, Dolliver was a naval aviator during World War II. He had excelled at Swarthmore, one of America's elite colleges, and worked summers as a ranger in Olympic National Park before law school at the University of Washington. In 1953, Washington Congressman Jack Westland picked Dolliver as his administrative assistant. When Jim signed on as attorney for our GOP Caucus in the House, we instantly clicked. He would become my most trusted legal and political adviser and a friend for life.

Born in 1924, Dolliver was almost exactly a year older than me. Later, when his neatly-trimmed beard turned gray, he looked like a mountain man in a three-piece suit. Around Olympia in the eventful years we shared, Dolliver

With Jim Dolliver, my newly appointed chief of staff, at a post-election press conference in 1964. *Washington State Archives*

came to be seen as the "assistant governor." His "energy and efficiency was the stuff of legends," Justice Gerry Alexander would write years later after he and Jim became colleagues on the Washington Supreme Court.

When a gregarious young man named Ralph Munro joined my staff, he asked Dolliver, "What is the real role of a governor?" Without a moment's hesitation, Jim said, "To set the agenda. Governors who don't set the agenda really don't govern."

We set out to set the agenda.

STATE PATROL CHIEF WILL BACHOFNER called to say I was being assigned executive security. I chuckled at the notion of bodyguards and said that would be unnecessary. Bachofner reminded me that the Legislature had enacted a law requiring the State Patrol to ensure the security of the governor and his family. Nancy rolled her eyes. Our lives were changing.

Sergeant Bill Lathrop reported for duty the next day. He was in his early 40s; imposing in his immaculate blue uniform, deferential yet also easy to talk with. I was reminded of my terse interview with Admiral Mendenhall in 1951. This time the roles were reversed. I asked Sergeant Lathrop if he'd ever been a governor's security aide. "No, sir." "Well," I said, smiling, "I've never had a security aide before so let's learn together." Bill and I would spend countless hours together in the governor's official auto, a black Lincoln Continental. In the beginning, it bore Washington license plate Number 1. Drivers in the next lane would slow down and peer into the windows attempting to see who was inside. Nancy hated it, and Lathrop decided that for security's sake we needed new plates. A detail man, he became an indispensable member of the Governor's Office, always in close touch with Dolliver and Esther Seering, my personal assistant. Lathrop supervised the development of a 24-hour security force at the Governor's Mansion as the 1960s grew more turbulent. We traveled together throughout the United States and on many international missions. Bill Lathrop became like the older brother I never had. He was my confidant, adviser, security officer, and friend for almost 12 years, retiring as a State Patrol colonel.

If you ever get elected to high public office you're going to discover how much you need a Bill Lathrop of your own. There are a lot of little surprises—details that never before entered your mind. From the day he first ran for Congress, John F. Kennedy famously never carried any money. Though he was rich, his aides were always paying out of pocket—and seldom reimbursed—for newspapers, cigars, and chewing gum; lunch was always on someone else. I wasn't rich, to put it mildly, but Lathrop observed early on that there were awkward moments when the check arrived. Someone was always eager to pick up the tab for coffee or a sandwich with the governor. Bill suggested I give him $100 for a private, small-expenses kitty, from which he would discreetly pay the waitress or cashier. He kept meticulous accounts of every expenditure and let me know when our "bank" needed a deposit.

THE STATE DID NOT PROVIDE any resources for gubernatorial transition. Governor Rosellini graciously offered us office space in a state office building at the Seattle Center. We used surplus campaign funds to cover expenses and salaries for the next two months. Esther and Jim set up shop and started handling the hordes of requests for appointments. On November 11, 1964, Esther's first day as my personal assistant, her desk calendar was speckled with appointments. I heard entreaties about highway safety, insurance, workman's compensation, banking, stevedoring, libraries, and advertising. And that was before lunch. I was reminded of Thomas Jefferson's observation that "Every appointment made gives me one ingrate and 100 enemies." It was a constant battle to create order out of chaos, grant access to those who deserved it, console those we couldn't accommodate, and use every hour wisely, saving time for family and the physical exercise I'd need to stay healthy, mentally and physically.

After 18 months of nonstop campaigning, Nancy and I needed to get away. We flew to Hawaii to spend a few days basking in the sun. When we de-planed in Honolulu, reporters were waiting. There would be no place to hide for the next four years.

We returned home to find a packed schedule and a long list of decisions to be made concerning appointments. Dolliver and I met with Governor Rosellini, who was cordial and genuinely helpful in discussing personnel and the budget. We spent two days meeting with his department heads, assessing them for potential retention as they aired the challenges facing their agencies. Besides Chief Bachofner, two other Rosellini appointees stood out. Dr. Garrett Heyns, director of the Department of Institutions, had attained a national reputation for his work in Washington state, while Warren Bishop had created a modern State Budget Office. Bishop decided not to remain, which created an urgent decision. I wanted to strategically revise the budget the outgoing governor was obliged to present to the Legislature, and I needed someone who could help me decipher Rosellini's priorities. Fortunately, Jim Ryan, Bishop's deputy, agreed to serve temporarily while we conducted a national search for a new director for the Central Budget Agency. Ryan was an experienced manager and a vital link for me during the tempestuous 1965 legislative session.

Wayne Jacobi officially became my press secretary. George Kinnear, a good friend and key player in the campaign, became chairman of the Tax Commission. Tall and gregarious, Kinnear was a seasoned lawyer who understood Washington politics. He and his father had both served in the Legislature. George and his wife Carolyn moved to Olympia and became active in the community. That set an example for other department heads. Their involvement, together with Nancy's activism in the arts, would help elevate Olympia to a more engaging city. When the Legislature wasn't in session, the capital was a pretty sleepy place, its population barely 20,000. It pains me that many current state leaders are commuters who fail to give either the Olympia community or their administrations the full benefit of living where the action is.

IN EARLY DECEMBER the Republican Governors Association met in Denver. Dolliver, Jacobi, and the Pritchards joined me as I jetted off to meet my new colleagues. We arrived in a blinding snowstorm and were waylaid by a group of national political reporters who wanted to size up Washington's young governor-elect. Only 17 Republican Governors had survived the Democratic landslide. Fortunately, several were giants.

Governor John Love was our host for a governors-only dinner and strategy session. It was a collegial yet ambitious group. George Romney of Michigan, a former automobile company executive, had built a reputation as a reform governor. Bill Scranton of Pennsylvania, smart, able and genial, quickly asserted his influence. John Chafee of Rhode Island and Mark Hatfield of Oregon—later also colleagues of mine in the U.S. Senate—became important role models. Chafee, a combat-hardened former Marine Corps officer, became an ardent environmentalist. Hatfield was handsome and articulate, with a stentorian voice and gracious manners. The quintessential Lincoln Republican, Hatfield was a champion of civil rights and a deeply committed Christian who nevertheless opposed government-sponsored school prayer. In his keynote address at the 1964 GOP convention in San Francisco, Hatfield was roundly booed by right-wingers when he denounced the John Birch Society.

Midway through dinner, New York Governor Nelson Rockefeller burst into the room. He greeted everyone with his famous backslapping "Hiya, fella!" and regaled the room with his white-knuckle landing. We repaired to the living room to mull what we could do to help rebuild the party. Goldwater's landslide loss disqualified him as a unifying leader. Nixon, having lost the California governor's race in 1962, had only just begun to resuscitate his reputation by collecting IOUs on the service-club circuit. Our congressional ranks stood decimated. Assigned to a small group tasked with drafting a path-forward resolution, I found myself kneeling on the floor alongside veteran governors. Our statement was adopted by the group. We urged Dean Burch, who had presided over the

Goldwater debacle, to step down as chairman of the Republican National Committee. We wanted a new, inclusive national leader.

A National Republican Coordinating Committee was formed. It included congressional leaders, former presidents, presidential nominees, and five governors, one of whom was me. I was awestruck at our first meeting to be seated around a table that featured General Eisenhower, Thomas Dewey, Nixon, Goldwater and an array of GOP congressional leaders I had only read about. Ray Bliss, our newly chosen party chairman, was a blunt political professional from Ohio. He cared little about factions and philosophical purity. His mantra was "Can he win?"

The road back to the statehouses—and White House—was shorter than any of us imagined. Vietnam spelled the difference. The jungle war was a cancer that would metastasize through the nodes and organs of Lyndon Johnson's otherwise uplifting presidency. I especially admired his historic civil rights legislation.

AS MY ADMINISTRATION took shape, I discovered that Washington's Constitution and laws splintered the executive function. Successful governors need to understand the issues and punctuate persuasion with cajolery and, most of all, patience.

Rosellini-appointed commissions governed Highways, Parks, Game, Liquor, Taxes, Utilities, Universities, and Paroles. Of the seven other partisan state elected offices, Secretary of State Lud Kramer and I would be the only Republicans. I began to wonder what department I did control. I soon found the answer: Budget. If I could come up with progressive budget priorities and use my legislative experience and bully pulpit to champion my choices, I could influence even the most obtuse and independent department head.

I also needed to assert my influence over the Republican Party apparatus statewide, especially King County. Gaining control of the Legislature, or at least more leverage, was crucial. Come January, Democrats would control the State Senate 32-17 and the House 60-39.

In mid-December, King County Republicans met to select a new chairman. I was supporting John Besteman, a 29-year-old Boeing manager who had been one of our stalwarts during the campaign. The Goldwaterites, undaunted by their hero's shellacking, backed 34-year-old Ken Rogstad, a staunch conservative who was no fan of Evans, Dolliver, and the Pritchard brothers. We were confident we had the votes to elect Besteman even though the conservatives controlled the convention mechanism. I was invited to address the convention but not until after a new chairman was selected. The Rogstad forces were fearful I might affect the outcome. The phone rang while Dolliver and I were cooling our heels. Jim answered, listened for a few moments, shook his head and hung up. Besteman had lost to Rogstad, 505 to 497. Furious, I barked, "I'm not going to let them rub it in! I refuse to speak to them." Jim tried to change my mind but I was adamant. With our largest county controlled by a bullheaded faction that would be of little help in our efforts to rebuild party strength, I knew the road ahead was riddled with potholes.

I came to realize that my refusal to appear was a dumb decision. I could not change the results but a gracious speech would have heartened our supporters and maybe even won over some of the less doctrinaire. Rogstad crowed to reporters that the party organization should be controlled from "the grassroots up, not from the top down." (Later, several delegates told us they had made other plans for that day because they thought we had the votes to elect Besteman.) That missed opportuni-

To prepare for the 1965 legislative session, we set up a command post in the Secretary of State's offices across the hall from the Governor's Office. The outgoing Secretary of State, Vic Meyers, had graciously invited Lud Kramer, his successor, to move in as soon as he wated. Lud looks on as Jim Dolliver and I read a letter that must have been amusing *Washington State Archives*

ty dogged my first term as governor.

In 1966 and again in 1968, we ran massive campaigns to unseat the crafty ringleaders of the King County conservative faction. Mary Ellen McCaffree's basement served as headquarters for a task force to field precinct committeeman candidates in every corner of the county. The reactionaries reacted. Soon pitched battles erupted for the most obscure but collectively powerful of all elected offices. We twice lost close votes for control of the party apparatus. The smaller counties, plus Spokane and Yakima, remained loyal to the Evans bloc, with King County leading the opposition. For years to come, philosophical divisions would vex the Republican Party in Washington state.

The Evans family tradition of finding a tree that touched the ceiling gave way to endless interviews, right up to Christmas Eve. Nancy was immersed in plans for moving to Olympia and her transition to First Lady. Dan Jr. had just turned 4; Mark was a toddler. We decorated a three-foot fir perched on our piano and vowed the Christmas of 1965 would be back to normal.

17
HIGH NOON

The newly strengthened Democratic majorities in the Legislature were plotting to push through a highly partisan redistricting bill during Governor Rosellini's final 48 hours in office. The lame duck's last quack might be a game-changer unless we were fast on our feet.

My inauguration was scheduled for noon on day three of the 1965 session. We set up a command post in the Secretary of State's suite of offices across the hall from the Governor's Office. Vic Meyers, having tasted defeat more than once in his 30 colorful years in politics, bowed out with class. He had invited Lud Kramer to move in as soon as he wanted. That gave us a strategic spot to contact legislators and design our defense. We knew the Senate Democrats, led by Bob Greive, would pass their version of redistricting the first day. Our only hope lay in delaying House action. Slade Gorton—Greive's nemesis—was our point guard.

Greive was a fascinating adversary. He epitomized the politics of building power by doing favors. A slender man who wore horn-rimmed glasses and jaunty bow ties, he was a devout Catholic, attending Mass every morning. He was also a polished dancer (or so Nancy told me). As governor, I dealt with Greive frequently on budget issues. The first time I watched him lean back in his chair with his eyes closed, I thought he was sleeping. Then as arguments raged around him, he'd sit bolt upright, eyes flashing as he entered the fray. When we reached an agreement, Bob always produced what he had promised. He met his match in Gorton. Always poised and prepared, Slade dazzled us with his knowledge of the geography and politics of each legislative district, virtually block by block.

HOWARD McCURDY, a 23-year-old University of Washington grad school student, was holed up in Mary Ellen McCaffree's basement, crunching numbers and drawing new legislative district boundaries on service station roadmaps. In our wildest dreams we never could have imagined Google Maps and laptops.

Our task seemed impossible. We needed to convince 11 Democrats to vote against a bill that favored

Howard McCurdy, the redistricting aide for the House GOP Caucus, draws boundary lines in 1965. Looking on from left are Joel Pritchard, Damon Canfield, Mary Ellen McCaffree, me, Tom Copeland and Slade Gorton. *Howard McCurdy Collection*

their party. A cartoon in the *Seattle Post-Intelligencer* portrayed me as a knight astride a white horse, poised to joust with hostile lawmakers. My lance was captioned "veto." If the Democrats had their way, I'd never get to use it. We took some comfort in the knowledge that federal judges wielded a real sword. The 1965 Legislature was under orders to enact a redistricting plan that met the U.S. Supreme Court's equal representation mandate before it could take up any new legislation, "other than housekeeping."

We scored a sorely needed victory when the Republican State Central Committee met to select a new chairman. I strongly supported C. Montgomery Johnson. "Gummie," a self-described "fanatical moderate," trounced Charles Hinshaw, the conservatives' choice. Johnson ran the State Republican Party aggressively for the next decade, despite obstinate opposition from Ken Rogstad's King County conservatives. They viewed us as ideologically suspect, to put it mildly. To the John Birchers, we were "communistic."

AS GAVELS FELL in both legislative chambers on Monday, January 11, 1965, Gorton and Dolliver reported they had discovered something very interesting while scrutinizing the State Constitution: It does not specify a time for the swearing in of a new governor—just that the oath will be administered on the second Wednesday of January. We could hold a swearing-in ceremony in the Visitors'

Spokane's *Spokesman-Review* forecast daunting ski-slopes for the governor-elect, given the hefty Democratic majorities in the Legislature. *Shaw McCutcheon/ The Spokesman-Review*

Gallery of the House Chambers at 12:01 a.m. Wednesday. That might foil the Democrats if they remained intent on rushing a redistricting bill to Rosellini's desk. I called Richard Ott, the Chief Justice of the Washington Supreme Court. Ott was a short, stocky lifelong Republican who had served in the Legislature during the 1930s. I explained the situation and asked if he could swear me in. "Absolutely," he said.

The House was up late on Monday and spent all day Tuesday in heated debate over redistricting, interrupted only by frequent party caucuses. Slade told me his heart sank as he pored over Greive's bill. "It's constitutional," McCurdy glumly confirmed after running the numbers several times.

Greive proceeded to make what proved to be a fatal tactical blunder: He was so devoted to protecting the Senate Democrats who supported him as majority leader that he forgot to weigh the needs of his fellow party members in the House.[*]

To gain time, we offered countless amendments, much as the Democrats had done in 1963 after our

---

[*] Senate Democrats being punished for not supporting Greive were also growing more militant. Bob Charette of Aberdeen, a centrist Democrat who counted Scoop Jackson as a close friend, stood to be redistricted right out of his seat under Greive's plan. Accusing Greive and his allies of placing self-interest above party loyalty, Charette introduced my plan as a substitute. "As long as the Democratic Party has been sold a bill of goods, we might as well go all the way with Dan," Charette said.

Coalition seized control of the House. Brandishing maps, we waylaid nervous House Democrats and outlined what they stood to lose—in most cases important turf. "If a wavering Democrat was disgruntled with his district, Gorton or Pritchard would hint that better things might come from negotiations later," McCurdy remembered. Don Moos contacted fence-sitters and conservative Democrats from rural districts.

As night fell over the Capitol on Tuesday, we learned that House Speaker Bob Schaefer and John O'Brien, now the majority floor leader, had informed Senator Greive that victory was at hand. I called Nancy in Seattle. "You'd better get down here," I said, "if you want to see my inauguration!" It took her several frantic calls to round up a neighbor to babysit our two boys. A State Patrol trooper scooped up Nancy, her mother and my parents and headed south. At the Temple of Justice across from the Capitol, Chief Justice Ott was standing by with a Bible and the State Seal.

Tom Copeland, the scrappy Walla Walla lawmaker who succeeded me as floor leader of the House Republicans, prepared to deliver what became known as "the best speech never given." It would have concluded like this: "Before you make a final determination on my suggestion that we adjourn, I wish to advise you that here inside this Capitol at this very minute, a Judge of the Supreme Court is prepared to administer the oath of office to Governor-elect Daniel J. Evans, and he will thereupon assume the office as provided by law. The new governor would prefer to be sworn in at the joint session as is usually done. The decision is yours to make. Let's show the people that we know how to be statesmen."

When Copeland informed Schaefer of our contingency plan, the Speaker gulped, "You're not kidding, are you?"

"I'm absolutely dead serious."

"How would it be if we adjourned right now?" Schaefer offered.

"You've got a deal," said Copeland.

The halls were buzzing with rumors that something big was brewing.

At 11 p.m. the House adjourned. The gerrymander so confidently hatched in the Senate had been thwarted, for now at least. The news was radioed to the State Patrol cruiser carrying Nancy and our parents. They returned to Seattle to try and get some sleep. It would be a short turnaround.

ON JANUARY 13, 1965, the future First Lady's morning was a lot more complicated than mine. Nancy got the kids dressed and fed, dismantled Mark's crib and muscled it into our station wagon, which was filled with clothes and household goods. Up and down the block neighbors had gathered to say goodbye. She smiled and waved as she carefully placed her Inaugural Ball gown on top of the crib. "Then," she told me that night,

Former colleagues from both sides of the aisle greet me as I enter the House chamber to deliver my inaugural address. The tall man wearing glasses is Chuck Moriarty. *Washington State Archives*

Daniel J. Evans Jr., his mother and grandmother listen intently to my inaugural address in 1965. *Evans Family Collection*

"as I accelerated up the hill in front of our house, I glanced in the rearview mirror. People were waving their arms, yelling, jumping up and down, so I screeched to a stop. The tailgate had flown open and everything was spilling out onto the street, including my dress. Fortunately, it was in a plastic bag. Tire tracks on a ball gown would have been quite a fashion statement."

At noon, the joint session convened. A ceremony still virtually unchanged since statehood in 1889 began. I fiddled with the pages of my address. Finally, I heard the good-humored voices of my escort committee—eight friends and colleagues from the Legislature. We waited outside while the House Sergeant-at-Arms boomed, "The governor-elect of the State of Washington!" The double doors swung open, and we made our way down the aisle to thunderous applause. I glanced up at a gallery filled with beaming family and friends. I felt triumphant and humbled all at once, a bit incredulous that it was really happening.

As I listened to the invocation by Dale Turner, our minister from the University Congregational Church, I began to realize the enormity of my new responsibilities. I framed Dale's handwritten prayer. It has been on my office wall ever since:

> Deliver him from love of power and motives of personal gain; from considerations of man and money in place of the demands for justice and truth, and losing patriotism in partisanship. Guide him to an ever-larger version of the truth and an ever deeper sense of the demands of righteousness. That through his faithfulness the life of our people may be lifted to higher ideals and nobler achievements. Deliver us all from every influence that would break down our reverence for law and corrupt our sense of corporate responsibility.

I placed my left hand on my great-grandparents' Bible, raised my right hand and repeated an oath taken by 15 governors before me and seven since, solemnly swearing to "faithfully discharge the duties of the Office of Governor of the State of Washington to the best of my ability." Then, speaking directly to my former colleagues, I began my term by saying, "This administration brings to office no commitment except to the people, no interest except the people's. It does bring and shall retain the highest regard for the Legislature. I shall never mistake deliberation for disinterest nor compromise for weakness." Writing those words more than half a century later, I'm struck by the fact that "shall" is now out of date. That's a shame, for it conveys gravitas. I was striving for cadences that conveyed my covenant with the taxpayers and my respect for bipartisan civility in the legislative process. In today's poisonous political climate, civility has given way to intemperate tweets and polarizing invective.

Reprising my "Blueprint," I advocated more financial aid to schools to reduce special levies, urged construction of new community colleges, and said it was time to begin planning for another four-year college. I proposed a new Foreign Trade division for our Department of Commerce and endorsed a reformed Unemployment Compensation program. I said we needed Community Health Centers and expanded services for the developmentally disabled. Open Housing and Equal Employment legislation were high on my list of priorities. I asked the Legislature to enact comprehensive ethics and public-disclosure legislation and proposed extensive legislation protecting the environment and our cultural heritage. I called for construction of a third Lake Washington floating bridge. My proposals for governmental reorganization included three new departments: Motor Vehicles, Water Resources, and Transportation. I urged the Legislature to authorize a Constitutional Convention to modernize our State Constitution. It was an ambitious package.

I ended my inaugural address by saying, "I will not ask this Legislature to lay aside the convictions of party; only that it support the needs of progress. ... This administration is not frightened by the word 'liberal' nor is it ashamed of the word 'conservative.' It does not believe that the words 'fiscal responsibility' are old-fashioned, nor will it ever fear to spend money if money needs to be spent."

I detoured on my way out of the chambers to hug Nancy, her mother and my parents. My mother was overcome with emotion and pride. From the very beginning, she was the one most certain I would win. Former colleagues on both sides of the aisle reached out to shake my hand, but the relationship was now different. As a legislator, I had mused that the Prime Ministers' Questions tradition, where the British PM fields questions weekly in the freewheeling House of Commons, would be interesting to try here. However, as I left the chamber I realized it couldn't work. The Prime Minister of Great Britain is a member of the House of Commons. He or she enters into debate as a colleague and equal. A governor retains a different, more distant relationship with the Legislature, as I was soon to fully discover.

"GOOD AFTERNOON, GOVERNOR!" Ruth Yoneyama declared, phone in one hand, notepad in the other, as I entered the foyer of my new office. Every phone seemed to be ringing at once. Within a few months, Ruth could recognize scores of callers by their voices and greet them by name. She was a superb first contact for people visiting the office and her cordiality eased the pain of those who ended up cooling their heels. My hectic schedule routinely ran late.

As Joel Pritchard and Slade Gorton looked on in bemusement, I spun around in my new desk chair like a kid on a soda fountain stool and declared, "What do I do now?" We all laughed. Then Esther Seering reminded me I needed to get with the program. Several people were waiting to see me. Then I needed to sprint over to the Mansion for a live TV interview, followed by two receptions and the Governor's Ball.

Our new house was a 19-room Georgian Revival mansion built for $35,000 in 1909. On our first day as its new tenants, it reverberated with the happy chatter of extended family and children's laughter. Our guests soon discovered there was no restroom on the main floor. That was just one of our disconcerting surprises. It was a grand old place that desperately needed modernization. Looking back, I am reminded of Governor Mike Lowry's quip that "one of the perks of being governor is public housing." As Nancy sized up the Mansion I could see the wheels turning.

As I struggled with white tie and tails, I turned from the mirror to see a dazzling Nancy, trans-

At the Governor's Mansion with Danny and Mark. *Washington State Archives*

formed into a princess in white satin. We grandly descended the staircase and were met by Charles Herring, KING–TV's veteran broadcaster. In the drawing-room, 4-year-old Danny sat between us, squirming with excitement as Herring began the interview. When he commented that Nancy, at 32, must be the youngest First Lady in state history, Nancy set him straight with mock indignation: "I'm 31!" We all laughed and set off on a tour. Danny slid past us on the ballroom's freshly waxed floor, stealing the show.

The Governor's Ball was held in Olympia's old National Guard Armory. We wearily shook the last hand at 12:45 a.m. Years later when I saw a photo of Nixon wincing in a reception line when someone gave him the old iron grip, I could feel his pain.

We had invited good friends to come back to the Mansion for a late get-together. At 3 a.m., we finally slumped into bed. Barely four hours later, it began bouncing. Danny and Mark were eager to explore their new house and the tree-filled yard outside. It was their dad's first day at the office. Their mom had a daunting new job of her own.

18
"DANNY VETO"

State Senator August P. Mardesich, an influential Democrat from Everett, was a darkly handsome 45-year-old with sharp eyes. The son of Yugoslavian immigrants, "Augie" had been a legislator since 1950, appointed to replace his brother Tony, who was lost at sea in a fishing boat accident together with their father. No fan of Bob Greive, Mardesich was a lawyer with street smarts. Now that I was governor, he took to calling me "Boss."

In its dying days, the Rosellini administration had sent to the State Senate scores of nominations to boards and commissions. Two nominations to the State Highway Commission were particularly onerous. If I couldn't derail them, there would be no way to gain traction on highway policy until close to the end of my term. Mardesich saw an opportunity of his own. "Boss," he said, "there are two Highway commissioners we haven't confirmed. One has to come from my congressional district, the other from Eastern Washington."

Senator August P. Mardesich, who called me "Boss." *Washington State Archives*

Augie had done his homework. The law stipulated that the five commissioners had to come from different districts, with at least two from Eastern Washington. There could be no more than three from one political party.

"If we reject the current nominees, you get to make the Eastern Washington appointment and we will give you a name for the 2nd Congressional District."

"Give me a name," I said, "and I'll let you know."

The next day he brought me a name. It was a fellow my top supporter in Everett described as too political. I called Augie. He laughed and said, "OK, Boss, I'll try again." The next day he had a new name—Harold Walsh, a well-respected automobile dealer from Everett. We had a deal.*

Rosellini's two nominees were promptly rejected by the Senate. I appointed Walsh and Elmer

---

* Years later, when Mardesich was being interviewed for an oral history, he remarked that he always liked to "kick stuff around" with me. "One thing about Dan, if he told you he was going to do something, he did it. ...he was a man of his word—no question." The feeling was mutual.

Huntley from Whitman County, a longtime member of the Senate Highway Committee.

I KNEW IT WAS IMPORTANT to be accessible to the media to advance my agenda, but I was clueless about how often we should have press conferences. "How about one a week?" I suggested to Wayne Jacobi, my press secretary. Won't work, he said. "You've got morning dailies and afternoon dailies. You'll always end up with unhappy reporters if you slight one news cycle." We settled on three a week during legislative sessions, two a week the rest of the year, and press availability on every out-of-town trip, no matter how small the town. We conducted more than 1,200 press conferences during my 12 years as governor. Being accessible, candid and quotable worked to my advantage.

The written press was dominant in the 1960s. Practically every daily paper around the state—some weeklies, too—had a legislative correspondent. Old notebook-wielding newsies like Stub Nelson of the *Seattle P-I* viewed the TV people, with their big cameras, cables and microphones, as disruptive and pushy. Robert Cummings, an Olympia old-timer who published a political journal, hated TV. He smoked a big briar pipe. I could gauge his level of frustration by his puffs. One day when a TV reporter asked a question Cummings viewed as particularly inane, he blew a huge cloud of smoke across the TV camera's line of sight just as I began to answer.

SEVERAL WEEKS AFTER THE INAUGURATION, I called a meeting of my cabinet. I gaped in astonishment as I entered a room packed with more than 50 people. I had expected department heads and chairmen. Every member of the Liquor Board, Parole Board, and Public Utilities Commission showed up, together with a slew of subordinates. No one wanted to be left out. "How do I govern with this mob?" I asked Jim Dolliver. We decided to form sub-cabinets: Education, Natural Resources, Public Safety, Social Services, and General Government. From then on, I usually met once a week with a sub-cabinet group. I could work with department heads, seven or eight at a time, who had similar program responsibilities. Significant new proposals for interdepartmental cooperation emerged.

Lacking time to prepare a new budget, we made course corrections to Rosellini's. Every state was struggling with Johnson's "Great Society" program. Intent on placing his own stamp on history, LBJ created Medicaid and Medicare, as well as broad new programs for education, social services, and welfare. These innovative federal initiatives brought new dollars to state governments. The catch was that most required matching money and state-funded administration. America was absorbing the full impact of the post-World War II Baby Boom. It seemed as if every member of my generation except me had started having kids—lots of kids—by 1952. These children were overwhelming the capacity of our schools, creating new demands for aid for the developmentally disabled, welfare assistance and all of the social services aimed at the young. Government was engulfed by the demographic tidal wave.

Even though Washington state was recovering from a recession, I believed new taxes were necessary to react to this double-barreled challenge. In my first budget message to the Legislature, I unwittingly fomented a bipartisan uprising by advocating the extension of the sales tax to services, including barbers, attorneys, and engineers. "Good God, governor," one legislator moaned, "can't you just hear all the barbers yapping at their customers? They'll see every voter once a month. This dinosaur egg will never hatch." That was one of the polite messages.

The Democrats had a field day pointing out that my budget proposal was $167 million higher than Rosellini's. Counter-attacking, they jammed through a redistricting bill that hit my desk with a D.O.A. thud on January 20, 1965. By now hundreds of bills were clogged in the legislative pipeline. Lobbyists clamored for action, legislators wailed and editorial writers chastised the Legislature for inaction. This pitched battle gave me early credibility as governor. Republicans were gratified I was intent on preserving their chances for re-election, and the Democrats openly acknowledged we knew how to play hardball.

SLADE GORTON AND HOWARD MCCURDY were squinting at maps in the redistricting war room.* After a lot of thrashing, we reached agreement on all districts except those in Seattle and Spokane. Late one night, Greive and Gorton filed into my office with two worried-looking Democrats from Spokane. John Cooney and Karl Herrmann were two of the majority leader's staunchest supporters. Greive was intent on protecting them, while we were out to create as many competitive Spokane-area districts as possible. I watched with fascination as the combatants pored over easel-mounted maps of the senators' districts. It was street-by-street warfare. Gorton and Greive knew the political makeup of each neighborhood just as well as the incumbent legislators. After hours of mind-numbing map-making, we shook hands on a deal. Seattle became the final battleground.

Gorton and McCurdy drew two sets of maps. One maximized the number of swing districts in Seattle, including Greive's 34th District. The other created a safe Democratic district for Greive but gave Republicans fighting chances in the rest of greater Seattle. I looked on as Slade pushed the first marked-up map in front of Greive. "This won't work!" the senator sputtered. "We might as well quit negotiating." We let him vent for a few minutes. "OK," we said, "how about this one?" Greive squinted at the map, eyes darting over McCurdy's Magic Marker borders. "This one needs a lot of changes," he finally said, "but maybe we can work it out." At that moment we knew we had won. Greive was now working from our map. Every time he demanded a change that helped his senators, we pushed for changes that aided our Republicans. The debate continued for several days, each change smaller than the one before, until block-by-block minuscule modifications ended the fight.

With Greive on board, the compromise plan cleared the Senate with ease. But John O'Brien urged his fellow Democrats in the House to reject it, railing that Greive had made a devil's pact with Gorton and Evans to protect his pals by hanging House Democrats out to dry. The former Speaker—still smarting over being deposed in 1963—branded me "a power-hungry" dictator "grossly abusing" my veto power. I had manipulated my Republican colleagues "like a master puppeteer," O'Brien charged. Tom Copeland, my successor as minority leader, shot back that there were winners and losers on both sides of the aisle. This was no gerrymander, he said, but it was still "a lousy bill. We have to go through the painful process of redistricting our friends out of a job."

When the final vote finally came, all 39 Republicans joined 14 Democrats to pass House Bill 196. Within an hour, I signed it, handing Gorton and Greive souvenir pens. For the first time in U.S. history, a governor and legislative majorities from an opposing party had adopted a comprehensive re-

* Bob Greive had his own sorcerer's apprentice in 23-year-old Dean Foster, who went on to serve as chief clerk of the House and chief of staff for Governor Gardner. In the 21st century, Foster and Gorton were members of the bipartisan Redistricting Commission. As the staff churned out computer-generated alternatives, Dean and Slade reminisced over what it was like to labor over service-station maps and adding machines.

The smile on my face speaks volumes as I prepare to sign the redistricting bill in 1965. From left, Tom Copeland, John Ryder, R.R. "Bob" Greive, Howard McCurdy, Bob Bailey, Lud Kramer, Hayes Elder, Slade Gorton, Dean Foster, Mary Ellen McCaffree and Don Moos. *Washington State Archives*

districting bill. Two years later, Republicans won 16 additional seats to take control of the state House of Representatives. We maintained our majority for the next six years.

AFTER 47 tension-filled days, the legislative logjam broke. Both houses worked overtime to pass hundreds of bills. My desk was piled high with bills waiting to be analyzed. Dolliver couldn't handle all that work in addition to his duties as chief of staff. Ray Haman, an astute Seattle attorney, agreed to serve as my legal counsel, assisted by Walt Howe, one of his young colleagues. Dolliver, Haman and Howe became a superb team. I read each bill in its tedious entirety before we sat down to hash things out. To the frustration of the majority Democrats, I used my veto pen frequently to counter what I viewed as partisan or inept legislation. One senator quipped bitterly, "We have another Italian Governor—Danny Veto."

The last major proposal of my first legislative session as governor was a complex five-part program to build a solid financial base for public education, the state's "paramount duty," in the words of our constitution. I wanted to equalize property tax payments to schools throughout the state, modernize the distribution formula for state school support, and adjust the constitutional lid on property taxes. The goal was to eliminate or drastically reduce the need for "special" levies to support schools. The levies had long since stopped being special. They were a budgetary life preserver.

The package proved to be too complex. Another two years were required to ease the pain of special levies. By that time, it was apparent to me that public education would be permanently shortchanged without major reform of our regressive state tax system, too dependent on the sales tax and property taxes. I would risk a lot of political capital in the years to come trying to make my case for tax reform.

WHEN THE 1965 SESSION dragged on, I faced a dilemma. Washington was a major participant in an International Trade Fair in Kobe, Japan. We had financed a pavilion, the only state to do so. Our exhibit was as impressive as those sponsored by major nations hoping to cash in on blossoming Pacific Rim trade. The governor of Hyogo Prefecture, Washington's sister state, had invited a delegation of Washington business and political leaders to join him on a day honoring Washington state.

Our delegation, including Secretary of State Lud Kramer, former Seattle mayor Gordon Clinton, and 30 prominent Washingtonians, was scheduled to leave on April 13. When the legislative session showed no sign of adjourning, I said goodbye to Nancy and the others, promising I would join then them in a few days. I never got out of town.

The legislators were tired and cranky after the protracted battle over redistricting. Adjournment proved elusive.

I wouldn't call it a wake-up call, but just after breakfast on April 29, the Capitol received a timely jolt. I was sitting in the Governor's Mansion, talking strategy with Chuck Moriarty, the GOP leader in the Senate, when the room began to shake. That old house groaned and rattled as a magnitude 6.7 earthquake rumbled across Puget Sound. Realizing that my 18-month-old son was asleep in his crib, I lurched toward the stairs and raced to the second floor as a hailstorm of crystals fell from the ballroom chandeliers. When I reached Mark's room, he wasn't there. Petrified, I scrambled down the back stairs. Lorna Leidy, the Mansion's longtime housekeeper, was standing outside the back door with Mark in her arms. Lorna was slight and elderly. But when the shaking started, she was a woman on a mission.

As I inspected the Legislative Building with state engineers, we saw that major cracks laced the concrete structural panels of the Capitol's dome. The legislative chambers were littered with shards of glass from the decorative skylights. Property damage was remarkably light around the region, but three people were killed by falling debris in King County.

I was at my desk the morning after the quake when the White House called. "Hello Dan, this is Lyndon!" came the unmistakable earthy Texas drawl. I instantly recalled Rosellini's full-page ads during the 1964 campaign. The bottom half depicted the governor shaking hands with LBJ. The top half showed the president on the phone with someone. The caption said, "Dan who?" I was sorely tempted to say, "Lyndon who?" but instead breezily replied, "Hello, Mr. President!" Johnson asked about the earthquake and solicitously offered whatever federal help we needed. It was my first of many conversations with LBJ over the next four tumultuous years.

THE 1965 SESSION, with Democrats in control of both houses, enacted much of my "Blueprint for Progress." The legislature endorsed my call for a reorganization of the community college system and created a commission to study a new four-year college. The Legislature also commissioned studies for a third Lake Washington bridge and allocated funds to hire 150 more State Patrol troopers and build four new ferries. The AP's Leroy Hittle was a baseball fan. He concluded that my batting average was .600. I had won 18, lost 11, and tied on 6. The redistricting victory was huge. We had done well on education and economic development but failed to achieve meaningful governmental reorganization or real progress in meeting human needs. (Almost all the remaining Blueprint bills would pass in the 1967 session.)

A few days after the Legislature adjourned, Louis Bruno, the Superintendent of Public Instruction, told me there had been an error in calculating appropriations for K-12 education. He believed another special session would be necessary to rectify the shortfall. His aides handed me their calculations. Everyone looked on intently as I examined the reports. I retrieved my trusty slide rule from the top drawer of my desk. With the practiced dexterity of a civil engineer, I quickly checked their math. The room grew quiet. Finally, I announced, "Gentlemen, I think you have a mistake in your calculations." The accountants protested that it could not be so, but they acceded to their governor's request to review their figures.

The next morning, I received a call from a sheepish Bruno. They had made a mistake, he admitted. No special session would be necessary. The story of Evans' slide rule quickly spread around the capital campus. During budget debates in the years to come, I sometimes extracted it with a little flourish, like a conductor with his baton. That worked every time. Well, most of the time.

NORTON CLAPP'S POWER as president of the Weyerhaeuser Company was buttressed by his bulk. He stood 6-4 and weighed 230 pounds. The scion of pioneer lumbermen, Clapp gave his time and money generously but strategically. He loathed government inefficiency. And he was a Navy man. So he liked me.

Most of our 1964 candidates were still licking their wounds from a disastrous year. Our total GOP deficit was the equivalent of nearly $1.4 million today. Fortunately, many of the top business leaders in the state served on the party's state finance committee, including Clapp.*

Norton offered to help resolve our financial problems by assembling business and professional leaders for "a little lunch" at the Governor's Mansion. I was treated to a lesson in leadership and influence.

When Norton arrived, he asked for a large glass bowl. I retrieved one from the kitchen and, at his direction, placed it on a card table near the door to the ballroom, where lunch was being served. After I welcomed the group, Norton made a short, powerful speech. Against long odds, we had elected a Republican governor, he said. It was important to give me and the Republican Party a fresh start. "Dan tells me the combined deficit of our party is $160,000. By my nose count, there are 40 of us here today. That means each of us should be responsible for $4,000. I ask you to deposit your share in the glass bowl as you leave." Within a week, the deficit was eliminated. We could move forward politically without the handicap of a heavy debt load.

DURING MY FIRST SCONE-FILLED SUMMER as governor, Nancy and I attended a dozen fairs and festivals. Our boys loved parades but hated waving incessantly from an open car. Sometimes we passed glum-faced onlookers who didn't like their dad. "Pick out someone in the crowd ahead, look straight at them, and wave," we'd say. "I'll bet you can get them to wave back." It became a family game.

At the Militia Ball, the Washington National Guard's grand formal event, we were dazzled by the glint of gold braid, ribbons and medals. When the Grand March began, a loudspeaker boomed the name and rank of each officer and dignitary. "Major General Howard McGee, Adjutant General of the Washington National Guard!" the announcer declared. Then came, "The Commander in Chief, Washington National Guard!" Nancy leaned toward me and whispered, *Who's that?* I chuckled. "You're holding his arm!" We still laugh about that one.

Losing privacy comes with the territory. It still takes getting used to. The people we met spontaneously over the next 12 years were great 99 percent of the time. One of my most awkward public moments occurred after a UW Husky football game. I was standing at a urinal when a young man

---

* Clapp's 29-year-old stepson, Booth Gardner, had just received an MBA from Harvard Business School.

sidled up to the one beside me and gazed over at me with a grin. He must have maintained his aim with his left hand, for he reached across with his right hand and jauntily declared, "Hello, Governor!" I was mortified but could not ignore the proffered hand. I shook it weakly with a thin smile and washed my hands vigorously afterward. As I returned to the reception, I heard a loud voice proclaim, "I won! It *was* him."

THE WESTERN GOVERNORS CONFERENCE was held in Portland in the summer of 1965. I was chatting with some of my new colleagues when a happy-faced man zipped across the room. "I'm Pat Brown from California," he declared, pumping my hand, "and I want to talk to you about water." Oregon's Mark Hatfield was close by. Practically in unison, we said, "Take all you want from the mouth of the Columbia, but don't touch a drop upstream!" We all laughed, though it was a serious matter. Water, specifically the lack of it, was becoming a huge issue throughout the West. Southern California was "one thirsty camel whose nose we should let into our tent with the utmost caution," Hatfield observed. As things developed, I was even more adamant.

On the Fourth of July weekend, I escaped for a long-awaited personal adventure. From my earliest years as a Boy Scout, I had climbed many Washington peaks. Mount Rainier, the highest in the Cascades at 14,410 feet, was an unmet challenge. Bill Bell, my brother-in-law, and Frank Pritchard signed up for the climb. Our leader was Joel Pritchard's business colleague, George Senner, an experienced Rainier climbing guide.

Early on a sunny morning, we set out for our overnight destination, a hut at Camp Muir at 10,000 feet. Far below as we steadily ascended was the evergreen expanse of Western Washington, punctuated by Puget Sound's inlets and islands. Soon the rocky trail disappeared under the permanent snowfield. As we approached the camp, the enormity of the mountain captured us. Huge glaciers gripped the rocks underneath, gnawing at Rainier's volcanic dome. Crevasses beckoned on the glaciers we would traverse.

We cooked an early dinner and bedded down, fidgeting for the call to start our climb to the summit. At midnight, we roped up in groups of three. Headlamps glowing, we moved out under a

With Nancy's brother, Bill Bell, left, climbing guide George Senner, and Frank Pritchard, right, atop Mount Rainier in 1965. *Evans Family Collection*

star-studded sky. Then, plodding higher, we saw the first streaks of dawn. When the sun emerged over the horizon like a mammoth orange ball, we looked west and saw the shadow of Rainier covering a huge expanse of the land below. We needed to hurry now to avoid the heat of the day.

At mid-morning we reached the crest and crossed the huge summit crater to Columbia Crest.

We all signed the register, and looked out in awe at the stunning panorama. All of Western Washington was beneath us. We could see all the way to the sea. After a few souvenir photos, we began the long descent to Paradise. We were giddy, but it was no time to be careless. Crevasses laced the glaciers. The snow softened in the sun's heat. We carefully picked our way back down to Camp Muir, reloaded our packs and joyously marched down the snowfield to Paradise, 4,500 feet below.

That climb remains a highlight of my life. It was also one of the rare private moments of my first six months as Washington's 16th governor.

THAT FALL, NANCY AND I plopped down in the living room of the Mansion after a large reception. I wondered how many people we had entertained since January. Nancy retrieved a journal in which she had carefully recorded the details of each event. We were staggered to discover nearly 10,000 people had visited the Mansion for special events. We weren't counting the routine tours. The largest by far was Nancy's first open house as First Lady. Once a longstanding tradition, the event had been abandoned for years. People were excited not just to visit the Mansion but to see a new First Family with young children. The tricycles on the porch drew smiles.

My engaging young wife was an attraction all by herself. I walked from my office to the Mansion late one afternoon and was astonished by the crush of people waiting to enter. As excited people shook my hand, I glanced inside. Nancy was graciously talking to visitors in between quick trips to the kitchen to see what could be done about the rapidly disappearing supply of coffee, tea and cookies. Some 1,500 visitors passed through the Mansion that afternoon. The events were mostly a treat— and the ultimate home improvement challenge. Nancy's goal was to make the creaky old house more livable and presentable. She ended up saving it—certainly one of the most historic achievements of her 12 years as First Lady.

19
VICTORY WAS NOT AT HAND

Fifty velvet-covered chairs were arrayed in a semi-circle around the podium as the nation's governors entered the chandeliered East Room of the White House. Lyndon B. Johnson looked pensive. The president was joined by Secretary of State Dean Rusk, Secretary of Defense Robert McNamara, National Security Adviser McGeorge Bundy, and General Earle Wheeler, chairman of the Joint Chiefs of Staff. As each aide spoke, Johnson fidgeted like a caged lion. Finally, he burst from his chair, strode to the front of the room and took over the briefing. Stalking back and forth, slamming a huge fist into the palm of his left hand, he exuded passion and power as he declared that

Secretary of State Dean Rusk briefs the nation's governors on the progress of the war in Vietnam in 1967 as a pensive President Johnson surveys our faces. *LBJ Library/Yoichi Okamoto*

boosting our troop strength from the present 75,000 to 125,000 would finish the job in Vietnam. He told us he needed our counsel and support.

My mind flashed back to the Governor's Day Review of the ROTC, an important tradition at the University of Washington. The 1965 review took place on a sunny spring day on the grassy expanse in front of the Suzzallo Library. Hundreds of proud parents were there to watch the cadets march in review. Suddenly, student protesters dressed in black and wearing death masks streamed through the procession, disrupting the march. I grasped for the first time that escalation of the war could divide America, not just its youth. I never imagined then, however, that I'd soon have a front-row seat for that tense presidential briefing.

The 1965 National Governor's Conference in Minneapolis began with several days of entertainment and sightseeing but little substance. I told Jim Dolliver events like this were a colossal waste of time. My mood changed overnight after our new chairman, Bill Guy of North Dakota, outlined his agenda. The plainspoken farmer was elected governor in 1960 on a Democratic Nonpartisan League ticket and immediately set about modernizing state government. Guy proposed that henceforth we should also meet in Washington, D.C., every February and concentrate on federal-state relations. We needed streamlined working committees, he said. I immediately volunteered to help.

We interrupted our proceedings to watch a televised presidential news conference. Peppered with questions about Vietnam, Johnson said our involvement was crucial to deter "communist aggression" in Southeast Asia. Seconds after the TV was switched off, Governor Carl Sanders of Georgia, an LBJ ally, offered a resolution to put the conference "on record in support of the president and the policies he has just announced." After a lively debate, it was adopted by voice vote. Mark Hatfield of Oregon and Michigan's George Romney were the only dissenters. Romney, a contender for the 1968 GOP presidential nomination, said the endorsement amounted to a "blank check." Hatfield asserted that LBJ had abandoned President Kennedy's view that "in the final analysis," it was the war of the Vietnamese people to win or lose. The president should place the issue before the U.N. or ask Congress for a declaration of war, Hatfield said. He understood war. As a Naval officer during World War II, Hatfield commanded landing craft at Iwo Jima and Okinawa. He was also one of the first Americans to survey the devastation at Hiroshima at war's end.

The last event of the conference was a barbeque at Vice President Humphrey's rural home. Hubert was a wonderful host and a great storyteller. His stand for civil rights in 1948, when Dixiecrats bolted the party, was the stuff of political legends. We were all astonished, however, when Humphrey announced that President Johnson was sending *Air Force One* to Minneapolis to take us to Washington, D.C. The president wanted to brief us on the war in Vietnam.

That briefing was one of those watershed moments where you sense you're caught up in something extraordinary. Johnson went on to ask Congress for an additional $1.7 billion for the war. I wondered if that would be enough.

IN 1966, THE GOVERNORS were again invited to the White House for a briefing on the progress of the war. "I know Vietnam is in our minds," the president said gravely. "This is the greatest challenge which faces us in the world today. Today our wise and able Secretary of State, Dean Rusk, our brilliant Secretary of Defense, Robert McNamara, and General Ellis Williamson, a combat commander who just returned from Vietnam, are all here to talk to you about that challenge. We will answer any questions any of you may have."

This time, we were told 150,000 more troops would ensure victory. To the surprise of all, Ohio's Republican governor, James Rhodes, had drafted a resolution of "wholehearted" support for Johnson's conduct of the war. Also surprising was that Nelson Rockefeller seconded the motion. Many of us by now

LBJ in a classic pose—leaning forward with all his bulk to make a point. Secretary of Defense Robert McNamara is seated at left. *Washington State Archives* had serious reservations about Vietnam, but the unexpected resolution and the looming presence of LBJ produced stunned silence. The resolution carried unanimously among the 38 governors on hand. (Hatfield was home in Oregon with the flu.) It was reported that we stood "four-square behind the President of the United States."

I had a growing, gnawing feeling that Vietnam, like Korea, was a war we'd be hard-pressed to win. However, when the full membership of the National Governor's Conference met in Los Angeles that summer, I didn't speak out. We Republicans watered down the resolution of "absolute support" authored by Texas Governor John Connally to "resolute support." It was an exercise in hair-splitting. In the face of a full-court press by Johnson and Humphrey, the final vote was 49-1. Mark Hatfield stood alone once again.

That same day, the Defense Department announced that the draft quotas for July and August would be boosted by a total of 6,000 due to "insufficient voluntary enlistments." And in August, the Pentagon said it would need to draft 46,200 men in October, the largest call-up since the Korean War. The generals also wanted the draft modified so that 19 to 20-year-olds were taken first because "combat commanders prefer the younger age group."

IN 1967, THE PRESIDENT summoned us once more. Victory clearly was not at hand. Knowing what was coming at the White House, Republican governors had drafted a statement balking at total support for the president's conduct of the war. Two nights before the briefing, Mark Hatfield, a newly-elected U.S. senator, addressed a capacity crowd at a forum sponsored by Harvard University's Young Republicans. He assailed both the conduct of the war and the president himself, calling for "an alternative to the tyranny of no alternatives."

Our frustration over the war and its impact on the nation was evident at the briefing. The president, aware that the Republican governors had caucused, said he was not seeking renewed support from the governors. But he was resolute. This time we were told it would take 500,000 American troops to win the war.

America was roiling. Protest marches took place in 30 cities across the country. On October 21, 1967, 100,000 people marched on the Pentagon. Nuns and priests, professors, combat veterans, and clean-cut college students joined the hippies and Black Nationalists. Dr. Benjamin Spock—America's pediatrician—branded President Johnson "the enemy."

In February 1968, when we trooped back for another session on Vietnam, LBJ's haggard face was like a death mask. "All of us are trying our dead-level best to find answers to the war," the president said wearily. The formal briefing took place at the State Department. Dean Rusk pointed to charts and posters detailing 36 ways we were trying to end the war. When the secretary of state said the administration was debating calling up reserves, several governors said that with the growing unrest in the country that would be a big mistake. The president took little part in the briefing. Iowa Governor Bob Ray was next to me as we left the building. "I don't think they know what to do next," I said. "I don't either," Ray said, shaking his head.

Thirty days later, a somber president ended a televised address to the nation by saying, "I shall not seek nor will I accept the nomination of my party for another term as your president." Vietnam had destroyed his presidency and ended the expansion of his domestic "Great Society." It was an American tragedy. And it was going to get worse.

IT BECAME NIXON'S WAR. Fear and loathing gripped America in the spring of 1970 when Governor Rhodes sent National Guard troops to the campus of Kent State University to quell student unrest. Four students were killed and nine others wounded when the jittery young Guardsmen opened fire. The events still seem so vivid that I can hardly believe they occurred a half-century ago. I can hear Walter Cronkite's voice and see the images—the war raging on the nightly news; students burning draft cards. In Lynn Novick and Ken Burns' riveting documentary on the Vietnam War, a soft-spoken veteran from small-town Missouri relates that virtually all the adult men he knew, from his father to his teachers, were World War II vets, "revered for their service." When it was time to fight the communists in Southeast Asia, "he simply figured it was his turn." He joined the Marine Corps. "We were probably the last kids of any generation," he says, "who actually believed our government would never lie to us."

Vietnam, the Pentagon Papers and Watergate left us "reflexively cynical about our leaders, quick to take sides," one reviewer said. The abiding lessons we can learn from the documentary are these: "Alternative facts" and the politics of polarization threaten democracy.

KENT STATE essentially ended James Rhodes's ambition for higher office. He was a big, blustering veteran politician, but not without good ideas. During the 1964 Republican Governors' Conference, he had touted his efforts to streamline Ohio government by appointing a team of business leaders to examine state agencies and recommend cost-saving strategies. I liked that.

In the spring of 1965, I met with business leaders and proposed assembling a group of talented managers to review state agencies. They were enthusiastic. Don Johnson, an aluminum company executive, agreed to lead the effort. Soon, we had a terrific collection of managerial talent from the private sector, 100 volunteers in all.

The Commission for Reorganization of Washington State Government returned with 640 recommendations covering every aspect of state government. Some were dramatic, long-term proposals that would have required changing the state constitution. The commission advocated creating a unified executive branch, with the governor as its only statewide elected official. The lieutenant governor, secretary of state, treasurer, auditor, attorney general, commissioner of public lands, and superintendent of public instruction would be de facto members of the governor's cabinet. That idea, not without merit, and some other proposed innovations would have been politically difficult. The group also over-reached in estimating how much money could be saved by streamlining.

During the next year, many of its recommendations were successfully adopted. We saved millions by reducing paperwork and eliminating redundancy. However, the press constantly measured progress against the ballyhooed target number instead of the substantial actual savings. The "Blueprint for Progress" governor found himself on the defensive at several press conferences. The commission was a genuine success, but we could never gain full credit. I learned an important political lesson: When appointing volunteer commissions, explicitly outline your marching orders. Otherwise, they may stray far afield from the mission and create unexpected difficulties when the final report arrives. If you let volunteers romp around, barking up the wrong trees, the story likely will go astray.

At a Republican Governors' Conference in 1967, I had lunch with Ronald Reagan, the newly-elected governor of California. I told him about the commission and mentioned the difficulties I had handling the final report. He was enthusiastic about the idea and promptly created a government efficiency commission in California. Its conclusions were similar to ours. Reagan, however, was much more successful in managing the results by touting each successful initiative to save the taxpayers' money, all the while downplaying the overall goal. "The Great Communicator" was a quick study.

20
"LET THEM LEAVE"

Shelby Scates, a veteran political reporter with a novelist's eye, wrote that Aggie's Motel alongside Highway 101 at Port Angeles seemed like "an unlikely place in which to make history." It was "an informal assemblage of bedrooms, parking lots, dining halls, lunch counters and kitchens, put together to handle the river of tourist traffic that pours past its dining room windows." There, however, "amid visiting Shriners in green sateen bloomers and overnight tourists with carsore kids," Washington Republicans sensed a showdown was at hand.

My political goal was to gain control of the Legislature to advance my Blueprint for Progress. King County, the state's most populous, and Snohomish, Kitsap, Yakima, Okanogan, and Asotin counties were hotbeds of radical conservatism. While top volunteers from my 1964 campaign were at the reins in most counties, we had determined, doctrinaire enemies everywhere. Fran Cooper of Seattle, our new national committeewoman, had been elected at the Goldwater lovefest state convention of 1964. At a Republican Club meeting, she was asked to explain how the likes of Dan Evans and

Lud Kramer could get elected on the Republican ticket. "We'll give them a chance to prove themselves before we get rid of them," Cooper declared. "Don't forget Evans is supported by the Ripon Society, and everyone knows they are dominated by communists."*

"Everyone knows" was a line Joe McCarthy and Albert Canwell, Washington state's own unreconstructed red-baiter, would have loved.

C. Montgomery Johnson, though a gunslinger, seldom shot from the hip. As state GOP chairman, he had counseled patience in our efforts to build a broad-based Republican organization. But by the fall of 1965, after we turned back efforts by John Birch Society members and other right-wingers to gain control of key county organizations, Johnson publicly announced it was time to challenge the "irresponsible, irrational right." The Republican Party "must repudiate the Birchers to make it honorable again to be a conservative," Gummie declared.

C. Montgomery "Gummie" Johnson, our astute State GOP chairman. *Washington State Archives*

---

* Founded in 1962 by grad-school students and young academics, The Ripon Society supported civil rights legislation and set out to rally "the new generation of Republicans."

We chose the mid-September meeting of the 78-member Republican State Central Committee in Port Angeles atop the Olympic Peninsula.

Expecting fireworks, reporters from the state's major papers and wire services hovered on the sidelines of the motel's packed banquet room as I was introduced. The first two-thirds of my speech emphasized the importance of building an inclusive party and meeting "the Crisis of Federalism." By 1975, I said, more than half of the nation's population would be under 30. "If we are to win in 1966 or 1976, we will have to be a party whose ideas and ideals appeal to youth." The Crisis of Federalism was also easy to grasp. It was the growth of centralized control by the federal government and the concurrent decline in the importance of state government. In other words, a dagger to the heart of Republican Party dogma. I said our goal should be to "combine progressive action and conservative thought; to take the best of America's past and present and apply it with resolute courage to America's future. ...We must convince the people that a Republican Party—diverse in its viewpoints, united in its principles—can come up with sensible, workable solutions."

I offered a litmus test for the kind of groups worthy of being called Republican:

> Is the group motivated by faith and hope or by fear?
> Does it use the tools of truth or promote lies?
> Does it teach trust in our established political institutions?
> Or preach distrust?
> Within its own organization, does it follow democratic procedures?
> Or practice militant authoritarianism?
> Does it understand the art of political compromise?
> Or deal only in unrelenting absolutism?

Looking out at the crowd, I saw some fidgeting and frowns. Never more determined, I plowed ahead:

> The John Birch Society and its frightened satellites, as shown by their methods, their leadership and rash policies, meet none of the tests and follow none of the traditions of the Republican Party. Let me be specific: The Republican Party did not achieve greatness nor will it regain greatness by being the party of radicalism or a lunatic fringe. Extremists of neither the right nor the left contribute to the strength of America or her political institutions. Both feed on fear, frustration, hate and hopelessness. Both have lost faith in themselves and the American dream, and both quite openly predict an American disaster. Our party embraces this "philosophy" only at its peril. I do not intend to watch silently the destruction of our great party and with it the destruction of the American political system. The false prophets, the phony philosophers, the professional bigots, the destroyers, have no place in our party. Let them leave!

A handful of state committee members rose and stomped out of the room. Those remaining cheered loudly as I ended by describing what being a Republican means to me:

We must be the party that is responsive and responsible to the needs of people; the party that believes in local self-government and is willing to take the risks and endure the sacrifices to make it work.

We must be a party that is colorblind, which has no exclusions of race, geography, status, or creed; a party that welcomes a diversity of opinions within the broad American political tradition, but refuses to become the captive of the narrow demands of the fanatic few; a party of and for the people, not pronouncements, propaganda, and promises.

If this is our stand, if this is our party, we need not worry about the departure of the extremists. They will leave of their own accord, overcome by the vitality of a strong, united party.

Response to the speech was immediate and overwhelmingly positive. After 90 minutes of often heated debate, the GOP State Central Committee voted 43-15 in favor of a resolution saying groups like the Birchers hurt the party. Fran Cooper declined to say how she voted but denounced the action as tantamount to a "kangaroo trial" of the John Birch Society.

All this drama escaped the "six be-fezed Shriners" Shelby Scates encountered crooning *In the Evening by the Moonlight* in an adjacent bar.

The national publicity director for the John Birch Society branded my remarks "hysterical and misinformed." But editorial-page comment, both local and national, was gratifying. Hearst's *Seattle Post-Intelligencer* and the Blethen family's *Seattle Times*, whose publisher had once soft-pedaled coverage of the Birchers, hailed the speech. *The P-I* wondered, "Will this step split the party asunder, or will it start the Republican Party back toward a cohesiveness it so long has lacked?" Writing in *The Times*, political reporter Lyle Burt observed that "severe surgery is sometimes the only cure for cancer." And Herb Robinson, the newspaper's political columnist, concluded that "even nonpartisan observers" were saying the speech was "a singular demonstration of political courage" that might prove to be a "make-or-break" factor for my political future. The *Argus* said I had gained "national stature."

I received hundreds of letters, including some that criticized my stand. Interestingly, the critics invariably began by stating, "I am not a member of the John Birch Society." They then proceeded to praise its objectives. Not one letter I received came from a writer who admitted belonging to the John Birch Society.

Within days, Montana Governor Tim Babcock, a conservative Republican, read the John Birch Society out of the Montana Republican Party. U.S. Senators Thomas Kuchel of California, Thruston Morton of Kentucky, Everett Dirksen of Illinois, and Congressman Gerald Ford of Michigan agreed that there was no place for the John Birch Society in the Republican Party.

Though Gonzaga's Chad Mitchell Trio had a hit with their recording of "Barry's Boys"—a ditty that declared, "Barry, Barry, make your bid; I love John Birch, but oh you kid!"—by 1966 even Barry Goldwater was disenchanted with the Birchers. In the middle of an Arizona Republican Party power struggle, our 1964 standard-bearer declared, "I tell you, the worst job of politics is done in districts run by the Birch people. If you gave them control of the state organization, you wouldn't have a

Republican candidate elected in the state." Both locally and nationally, we had set the stage for a Republican comeback in the midterm elections of 1966.

SHORTLY AFTER the Port Angeles speech, I traveled to Washington, D.C., to attend a meeting of the Republican Coordinating Committee. Much of the discussion focused on the John Birch Society and other extremists within the party organization. Chairman Ray Bliss constantly preached the "big tent" concept and set out to bridge the chasm between the Rockefeller and Goldwater wings. He was an architect of Nixon's 1968 comeback victory.

With my newfound celebrity, I was chosen as chairman of the National GOP Gubernatorial Campaign Committee. I found quickly that most of the money available was aimed at congressional races. However, we were able to independently raise some money and convince the national party that we deserved a significant infusion of funds to be competitive. There would be 35 statehouse races in 1966. We had a great opportunity to expand our numbers. The debacle of 1964 had left us with only 17 governors. I enlisted the support of fellow GOP governors. We met with potential candidates and encouraged those we judged particularly promising. We couldn't offer a lot of money, but we promised to join them on the campaign trail.

THE BRAIN TRUST Joel Pritchard had dubbed the Dan Evans Group of Heavy Thinkers—DEG-OHT for short—thought it high time to stage a fundraiser to boost Republican Party finances and sock away some money for my re-election campaign in 1968. The group hatched a plan to celebrate my 40th birthday with a fundraising dinner. Attendees would receive a commemorative photo of me conferring with President Eisenhower—a national icon as both soldier and statesman, and our only Republican president since Herbert Hoover.

With General Eisenhower at Gettysburg in 1965. *Evans Family Collection*

After the meeting of the Republican Coordinating Committee, Jim Dolliver and I drove to Gettysburg. Ike's large white farmhouse was as quintessentially American as the president himself. Mamie offered us coffee. And the picture-taking was soon accomplished. For the next hour, I had an extraordinary opportunity to talk with the five-star general about his role in the D-Day landings, his decision to cut our losses in Korea, and the challenges he faced during his presidency. He was a gregarious, fascinating storyteller, often flashing his inimitable grin. As we prepared to leave, he asked if we had time to visit the Gettysburg battlefield. Absolutely, we said. Eisenhower asked his aide to lead us on a tour. Ike's aide, a major general, was a Civil War buff, and we were treated to a splendid commentary of the details of the historic battle. I left Gettysburg with even greater admiration for President Eisenhower. The picture of the two of us together was a popular memento—one I've always treasured—of what became a highly successful fundraising event.

Eventful as it was, my first year as governor was primarily one of defense. We staved off gerrymandering, managed to moderately amend the state budget, and advanced parts of my "Blueprint." I realized it would be several years before my appointees constituted majorities on major policy commissions.

The state Constitution mandated 60-day legislative sessions in odd-numbered years. The Legislature wouldn't be back in town until 1967, but the midterm elections would be crucial. My resolution for 1966 was to go on the offensive.

21
FLYING HIGH

In 1966, Washington was beginning to emerge from a nagging recession. Boeing was flying higher than ever, developing a new wide-body jetliner, the 747, and playing a major role in the Apollo program aiming for the moon. A revolutionary Supersonic Transport was on the drawing board. Most of us had no inkling that Seattle was just three years away from its worst downturn since the Great Depression of the 1930s.

A model of Boeing's ill-fated Supersonic Transport. *Washington State Archives*

The state's traditional resource industries, timber and farming, were expanding. The state continued its rise to prominence in foreign trade, especially along the Pacific Rim. Happily, the deficit I inherited shrank rapidly as tax receipts grew. But the demands were many. Washington had added 556,000 citizens since 1960. Boeing alone had recruited 50,000 workers for the 747 project. This population bulge created new needs for our state's already hard-pressed K-12 public school system, as well as higher education. The needs of the developmentally disabled and mentally ill were also underfunded. Our prisons were old and overcrowded. I was puzzled by the rise in crime until corrections officials reminded me that crime is mostly the province of young men. Our youth population was exploding. I became an avid student of demography and urged both my cabinet and legislative leaders to recognize the unusual population pressures that would challenge state government for the next several decades.

The growing civil rights movement targeted red-lining, demanded equal opportunity for decent-paying jobs—union membership in particular—and called for an end to de facto school segregation. The Berkeley free speech movement was spreading to campuses throughout the country. Students protested, with increasing intensity, a war they saw as unnecessary, unwinnable and racist. With every escalation of troop strength and every revelation of Pentagon dissembling, my own doubts grew.

I had no doubts about America's growing environmental consciousness. Our success in rescuing Lake Washington demonstrated the power of activism. Metro's sewage treatment plants were just a start. Citizens saw harbors, bays and rivers befouled by industrial effluents and open sewers. Beaches were walled off by developers, freeways clogged. The Seattle skyline was gray with smog.

Scores of environmental organizations vied for legislative attention, but the complex nature of the problem and a multitude of issues diminished their effectiveness. That was about to change with the founding of the Washington Environmental Council, an umbrella-group that eventually proved hugely successful in lobbying for environmental legislation.

THE MOST IMPORTANT ITEM on my 1966 agenda was the need to be able to govern. That required Republican legislative majorities as well as a willingness to work across the aisle to forge support for the big issues. My kitchen cabinet—Gummie Johnson, Jim Dolliver, Joel Pritchard and Slade Gorton—had met six months earlier to discuss how to make the most of our hard-won redistricting victory. Our new team member was Mary Ellen McCaffree. She was a rookie state representative but an old hand at redistricting, thanks to her days as a member of the Seattle League of Women Voters.

Ritajean Butterworth, who played a key role as a volunteer coordinator in the 1964 campaign, assured us that the army of Evans-for-governor volunteers was just as eager to work for candidates who backed my Blueprint. Slade and Mary Ellen said the new swing districts held the key. Having identified potential candidates, we were now ready to conduct campaign schools and mobilize volunteers around the state.

Education was a pressing issue when we reassembled at the Governor's Mansion early in the new year. Elementary classrooms in fast-growing suburban areas were overcrowded. The expected surge in high school enrollment meant we'd need new secondary schools, too. Colleges and universities would soon feel the surge of Baby Boomers. My four-part program for the 1967 legislative session called for reorganization of the "junior" colleges into a state community college system; creation of a new four-year college; developing a bond issue for school construction, and establishing a commission on tax reform. It was now abundantly clear that our public schools could not be funded primarily through a rickety property tax system. We needed to modernize and equalize property taxes, but also identify new state tax revenues to reduce the rapidly increasing dependence on special levies in local school districts.

The Washington Education Association over-played its hand, styling the funding issue as an impending catastrophe. I had already decided to meet with the WEA and other concerned educators. Ten days after what I viewed as a productive meeting, I was astonished to receive a nasty letter from the WEA. Cecil Hannan, the WEA's executive secretary, and Jack Hill, the association's president, were "deeply disappointed" by my failure to call a special session of the Legislature. They were "seriously concerned that Washington might be held up before the nation as a state in a condition of educational chaos, which could result in the collapse of industrial expansion for which we had all hoped. Our fingers are crossed hoping to avoid nationwide disgrace." The accompanying news release was equally belligerent: "It appears to us as if the governor is playing a numbers game with the educational future of every child in the state. He has dumped an insoluble problem in the lap of every school board in the state. It is strange, indeed, that the governor leading the cheers for industrial expansion and economic boom expects the price of progress to be paid by schoolchildren."

Though furious, I did not respond until a month later, when an analysis of school funding was complete. I told them I was amazed they hadn't bothered to double-check their funding figures before making incendiary public statements. The Washington Education Association was morphing from a professional organization to a craft union. I feared its tub-thumping could destroy the coalition I was attempting to build to make the case for tax reform. Absent reform, there was no way to build a solid funding base for education

Fortunately, Hannan shortly left the state to take another job. Gladys Perry, a second-grade teacher in Seattle, was installed as the new president. She had supported my candidacy for governor in 1964. Gladys was a healer. Soon the WEA was working in close cooperation with the administration on tax reform as the long-term answer to dependable school support.

THE ANXIETY IN K-12 EDUCATION was matched by enormous growth in higher education. The Temporary Advisory Council on Public Higher Education, which I had proposed in my inaugural address, was now deeply involved in developing proposals to improve funding and promote excellence. I named Mary Ellen McCaffree to the council. On the basis of a report by Nelson Associates, the council recommended establishing a new four-year college that would admit its first freshman class by the 1969-70 academic year "or as soon thereafter as is feasible." What became The Evergreen State College was now on the drawing board.

The future of community colleges was not as clear. The Advisory Council was deeply involved in developing proposals. Two other groups were also hard at work. Louis Bruno, the Superintendent of Public Instruction, oversaw one committee, and a legislative Interim Committee on Education was reincarnated under the chairmanship of State Representative Frank "Buster" Brouillet, a cheerful champion of public education. It quickly entered the melee on community college management.

Community colleges were attached to individual school districts and received their funding from them. Rapid student growth now forced the districts to seek additional funding from the state. School superintendents were adamant, however, in their demand that management of community colleges remain with the districts. Labor leaders opposed the transfer of technical institutes to any new state community college system. I strongly believed in a new statewide community college system, funded and managed at the state level. During 1966, legislators and the press received dozens of competing reports, all touting reform. The coming legislative session would be the battleground for decisions, but the coming election would decide the generals.

IN EARLY APRIL, undeterred by the legislative logjams that kept me home in 1965, I embarked on an economic tour of the Far East. Nancy, pregnant with our third son, was the one who stayed home this time. I led a group of 46 business and governmental leaders on visits to Tokyo, Osaka, Kobe, Seoul, Taipei and Hong Kong. In Tokyo, I had an audience with Emperor Hirohito, who reminded me of a kindly grandfather. My mind wandered back to the first postwar photo of the Emperor, looking so tiny and formal beside a towering General MacArthur in khakis. Through the royal interpreter I told him about our state pavilion at the Osaka international trade fair. An avid student of marine biology, he was aware of marine research being conducted at the University of Washington.

I looked forward to our visit to Kobe, Seattle's sister city, and Hyogo Prefecture, Washington's sister state. Nancy told me of her delight, a year earlier, meeting Governor and Mrs. Motohiko Kanai of Hyogo Prefecture. Governor Kanai had been in office for many years. His chiseled face radiated wisdom, patience, and authority. Mrs. Kanai, standing shyly beside her husband, was dressed in a formal kimono. On our way into the hotel she asked about Nancy and Nancy's mother whom she had met a year earlier. Nancy was right. The Kanais were a charming couple.

On our short flight from Japan to Korea I looked down at the tranquil Sea of Japan and day-dreamed about 1952. I could almost see the armada of Task Force 77, its huge aircraft carriers surrounded by cruisers and a protective arc of destroyers as it spit planes into the wind.

The Seoul I remembered was mostly rubble. Now, a modern city gleamed in the sun with scores of construction cranes dominating the skyline.

Our mission divided into teams to make business calls. I paid a visit to President Park Chung-hee. The former general had first gained control of the government in a 1961 military coup d'état. He was an autocratic yet effective leader, extremely proud of South Korea's progress. Korea was intent on becoming a leader in world trade and technology, he emphasized.

The next day we met with government ministers, extolling Washington's products, with particular emphasis on wheat, apples, and other agricultural products. Red Delicious apples were particularly desirable as red is the color of good luck in China. Taiwan ultimately became a very large importer of Washington apples.

Hong Kong, still a British Crown colony, was the last stop on our whirlwind tour. At the hotel before yet another banquet, Bill Bell, my brother-in-law, remembered me saying that my destroyer had visited Hong Kong during the Korean War.

"What was the number of your ship?"

"852."

"It's out in the harbor," he exclaimed.

"Come on, Bill," I said. "Quit kidding me."

I looked out the window. There, riding at anchor, was the *Leonard F. Mason*, my old ship! I was soon on the phone with its captain. The next day, as I climbed the ship's ladder to the deck, I was greeted by the chirping of the bos'ns' pipe. This was the Navy's traditional greeting of dignitaries, usually senior naval officers, but seldom accorded on smaller ships like destroyers. Two to eight "side boy" sailors lined the entry to the deck, depending on the rank of the visitor. A governor rated eight side boys. I smiled as I imagined the officers madly thumbing through the protocol book to decide how many side boys were appropriate. As the captain greeted me, I looked with amazement at the changes in the ship. The traditional 5-inch gun turrets were gone, replaced by missile launchers. The mast bristled with scores of new electronic antennas.

The living quarters had not changed much in 14 years. As we passed through the galley we met a sailor cooking chicken wings. When I was introduced, he cheerily declared, "Here Governor, have a wing. It'll make your dick as hard as a 19-cent chisel!" The captain's face reddened. I quickly ducked down the passageway to the uproarious laughter of the sailors in the galley.

I KNEW I WOULD RETURN to some difficult decisions. Shortly before departing on the trade mission, I was contacted by State Senator Martin J. Durkan, one of the state's most influential Democrats. "Jim" to his friends, Durkan smoked cigars and loved deal-making. The 43-year-old Seattle lawyer was also extremely bright and a man of his word.* We had arrived in Olympia in 1957 as freshmen in the House of Representatives. Now, nine years later, he was a powerhouse as chairman of the Senate Ways and Means Committee, with his sights set on running for governor. "Governor," Durkan said, his tone grave, "you have some real problems in your Budget Office." He did not elaborate, but it was obvious he was giving me a heads-up about a brewing political storm. As a former chairman of the Budget Interim Committee, Durkan could have caused me real political trouble, but he cared more about having the Budget Office run properly.

I appreciated his warning and asked Dolliver to investigate the Budget Office. He concluded we needed a new director. The right man turned out to be close at hand. It was Walt Howe, my legal counsel. I trusted his judgment. He understood the tricky politics of a crucial position—one that can make or break an administration. When Howe took over as budget director he quickly settled in for a superbly successful run as head of what was now known as the Office of Program Planning and Fiscal Management.

Members of the Senate Democrats' Committee on Committees meet with Lt. Gov. John Cherberg before opening day of the 1967 legislative session. Seated from left, Cherberg, August P. Mardesich of Everett and John Cooney of Spokane. Standing from left, Martin J. Durkan of Issaquah, Robert C. Bailey of South Bend and Al Henry of White Salmon. *Washington State Archives*

During my early years as governor, Nancy and I took short vacations, trying to avoid returning to piles of work. As I built a dependable team, however, I discovered that longer absences actually meant a cleaner desk on my return. Decisions that could wait a few days could not wait for two weeks or longer. I had absolute confidence in Dolliver, Esther Seering and the rest of my team, and was never disappointed by their decisions made in my absence. It's a valuable lesson taught in all the best MBA programs: Hire talented subordinates and learn to delegate.

---

* Durkan's daughter Jenny, a bright former U.S. Attorney, was elected mayor of Seattle in 2017, a job she soon found daunting. During the Black Lives Matter movement, demonstrations over police practices often erupted into violence. A "head tax" on Amazon and other major employers was hotly debated as the homeless crisis escalated. She chose to not seek re-election.

22
NEW SON, NEW MAJORITY

Bill Lathrop, my State Patrol aide, was at the wheel as we drove through the Capitol campus on a muggy July day. I spotted Peggy, our enormous Irish wolfhound, with my barefoot wife close behind, maternity smock billowing as she tried to keep up with the dog. It seemed a bit odd that they were so far from the Governor's Mansion, but we waved gaily as we drove by. A half hour later, I was relaxing in the Mansion when Nancy—Peggy reluctantly in tow—burst in, furious at the dog and me:

"You saw me chasing that damn dog! Why didn't you stop?"

"I thought you were just walking the dog."

"I wasn't *walking* the dog! Peggy's in heat and she got loose. I chased her for almost an hour! It's hot! I'm nine months pregnant, and the governor and his trusted aide just waved and kept on go-

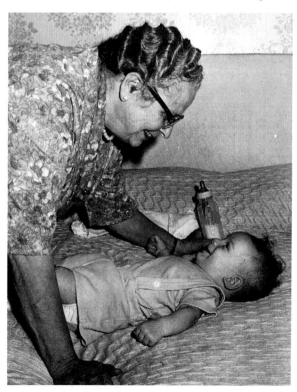

Grandma Bell with baby Bruce. *Evans Family Collection*

ing!" I couldn't keep from laughing. "Well, there aren't many male dogs in this neighborhood that are going to give an Irish wolfhound problems!" The First Lady was unamused. It was several days before Peggy and Dan got out of the doghouse.

Nancy's due date came and went. She shook me awake at 1 a.m. on August 21, 1966, and said it was time. "Hurry." We made a mad dash to St. Peter's Hospital—luckily nearby, because Bruce McKay Evans, 10 pounds, four ounces, arrived within 45 minutes. The head nurse wasn't about to let the governor in the delivery room. But I got to hold Bruce minutes after his birth.

The next few weeks were a cacophony of late-night feedings coupled with an extraordinarily full calendar. Dan Jr. and Mark delighted in their new brother. Nancy's mother, whom the boys called "Gam," made it possible for Nancy to resume a busy official schedule. Mrs. Bell deftly handled her three grandsons when we were away. Gam was a godsend.

I RESUMED CAMPAIGNING for legislative candidates and helped boost Republican gubernatorial candidates around the country. I also began the practice of conducting budget hearings for every department of state government. That added up to more than a hundred hours of meetings. It was worth it. By the last hearing, I knew more about the budget than anyone else, inside or outside state government. I was able to set priorities and base decisions on first-hand knowledge. Department heads were quizzical at first, but the word spread that I was serious: "You'd better be prepared to defend your request or face cuts to meet priorities elsewhere." Even departments overseen by commissions or independently elected officials participated. They realized it was difficult to convince a legislature to spend more than a governor had proposed.

Quite by accident, I found another budgetary weapon. We hired close to a hundred college and university students each summer. I was enthusiastic about the program, and set out to tap all that youthful energy and inquisitiveness. Once a week we assembled the interns for a brown-bag lunch on the Mansion lawn. These impressive young men and women asked lots of questions, occasionally challenging me about goings-on in the departments where they worked. "I don't see why this regulation is necessary," one might say. Or, "It seems like a waste of money to do this." Insightful inside stuff emerged. At meetings of my sub-cabinet I often asked about issues raised by the interns. I know many department heads left the meeting wondering, "How the hell did he know about that?" The curiosity of whip-smart interns gave me valuable insight into the mechanics of my administration.

Lud Kramer had been a civil rights champion as a Seattle City Council member. Now, as secretary of state, he had assembled an Urban Affairs Council. Lud told me I needed to visit the Tri-Cities in Eastern Washington and see for myself the impressive things being accomplished by the East Pasco Self Help Association. It was there that I first met Art Fletcher, who in 1950 had been the Baltimore Colts' first Black player. Art's charisma matched his intelligence. Audiences were mesmerized by his anecdotes. Some generated gales of laughter; others brought us to tears. Fletcher told me of his work with the desperately poor of East Pasco. He was an apostle of the power of education to build self-esteem and change lives. He inculcated young people with the importance of a strong work ethic. I was thoroughly impressed with Art, his work and everything he stood for. Our first meeting was just the beginning of a lifelong friendship.

AS A FRESHMAN LEGISLATOR in 1957, I had fought hard to defend equitable redistricting, only to see Bob Greive dismantle the initiative approved by the voters. In 1963, we formed our Coalition to thwart gerrymandering. And in 1965, our Republican minority, aided by my veto pen, fought for 47 days to create a fair redistricting plan. Now, on Election Day 1966, that 10-year effort would be tested at the polls. Could Republicans, after 14 years in the minority, win a majority of seats in the Legislature? It was my mid-term reality check.

We were encouraged by the early returns from across the country. Republicans were making a huge comeback after the debacle of 1964. GOP candidates for governor were winning in state after state. It was apparent we would add substantially to our hardy caucus of 17.*

Sorting out legislative returns usually took several days back then, but we had scores of vol-

---

* Twenty-three Republicans won statehouses in 1966, including Ronald Reagan in California and Winthrop Rockefeller in Arkansas, the state's first Republican governor since Reconstruction. America's statehouses were now evenly split—25-25.

unteers all over the state tracking down precinct returns or watching the counting of paper ballots in rural courthouses. Our 39 incumbent GOP legislators were running strong races. After all of the close House races were settled, we celebrated a smashing victory, gaining 16 seats for a comfortable 55-to-44 majority. For the first time in 14 years our House caucus would select a Republican Speaker. We gained three seats in the state Senate but were still in the minority, 20-29.

Republicans gathered in Spokane for the traditional Apple Cup caucus. Tom Copeland of Walla Walla savored the election results,

With Speaker Don Eldridge, right, and Speaker Pro Tem Tom Copeland. *Washington State Archives*

and with good reason. He had helped recruit solid candidates and tutored them at freewheeling campaign schools. As Republican leader during the 1965 session, Copeland helped unify the Republican caucus and pushed hard for our Blueprint for Progress legislation. Now, however, he had competition for Speaker. And I was conflicted.

Don Eldridge had served ably as GOP caucus chairman the previous session. A former seatmate of mine, Eldridge owned a stationery store in Mount Vernon. Amiable, with a quick wit, he had served as state Jaycees president.

Slade Gorton suggested to Don that he run for Speaker. Soon after the election, they hit the road rounding up commitments. Spokane's *Spokesman-Review*, the East Side's major daily, accused me of manipulating the election, charging that I wanted to see Gorton as Speaker but lacked the votes and settled for Eldridge at Copeland's expense. That was totally untrue. I hotly denied the accusation.

Everyone in the caucus admired Eldridge. They felt comfortable with him as Speaker. Copeland was selected as Speaker Pro Tem and given substantial responsibility for the internal operation of the House. Gorton became our floor leader. We had a terrific team. Copeland loved the management side of the House. He streamlined the committee structure and established schedules that minimized conflicting hearings and meetings. New Republican committee chairmen were selected. My office immediately began to contact them to outline our proposed Executive Request legislation. We finally had the power to initiate ideas and fully implement the Blueprint for Progress I had proposed two years earlier.

I WAS INVITED TO APPEAR on *Meet the Press*. Now the longest-running program in TV history, it was then the most prestigious and most-watched political interview show. Although columns and articles about my improbable 1964 victory had already appeared in *Time* magazine, *The New York Times* and *The Washington Post*, it was my first opportunity to speak to a national audience. I was excited but also apprehensive as I contemplated facing a panel of the nation's most influential newsmen: Herb Kaplow, Tom Wicker, David Broder and James Kilpatrick. Their probing questions ranged from the war in Vietnam and national domestic policy to my views on the basic philosophy of the Republican Party.

Kaplow wanted to know what civil rights advice I would give the next Republican nominee for president. I said he should reiterate that in the Party of Lincoln "we clearly and completely believe in equal opportunity for every citizen of this nation."

Wicker asked the last question: "Governor, you made it clear that you want to attack the problems of your own state. What are the main points of the program you will present to try to achieve these things within the State of Washington?" I said we needed to combat air and water pollution, expand mass transit and promote conservation, including open space and recreational areas. "You move right from here through the whole sweep of government. We are consciously trying to do the job at the state level rather than just waiting for the federal government to suggest action."

I was about to have the first state budget of my own creation. Unemployment had dropped from 7 percent to 4 percent in the space of two years. The state's population was on track to reach 3.4 million by 1970, up 43 percent from the 1950s. The downside was that farm land was disappearing as subdivisions sprouted all over King and Snohomish counties. And road building couldn't keep pace with two-car families.

SNOW SKIING was our family's favorite outing—and a chance to forget all the number-crunching and political posturing. On the slopes, in a parka, goggles and hat, I thought I'd be relatively anonymous, but my distinctive baritone voice usually betrayed me.

It was a thrill to survive Crystal Mountain's Giant Slalom course. *Evans Family Collection*

Over cocktails one night on Crystal Mountain, friends convinced me I should make the forerun on the Giant Slalom course for the Women's National Ski Championships.* Heading up the mountain the next day, I realized it was a very dumb idea. I had skied for 30 years and thought I was pretty good, just not good enough for a course that demanded precise, high-speed skiing through many gates down steep terrain. Bill Lathrop, my State Patrol security aide, adamantly opposed the idea. It was his first time on skis. For me, down was the only way out. I donned the bib marked "F" for Forerunner, now con-

---

* "Forerun" is the skiing term for a pre-race check of the course—often by a former ski racer, but in this case a nut who thought he was one!

vinced it would be my grade—if not for skiing at least for wisdom. At "Go!" I pushed out of the starting gate and made the first few sweeping turns with aplomb. It was glorious. The bright blue sky framed the brilliant white of the slopes. Flags marking the gates whipped in the breeze. The snow sang under my skis.

I felt like Superman for at least 30 more seconds. Then my legs turned to lead. I was out of gas less than halfway down the course. Suddenly, one ski caught in a rut, the binding popped and I careened into a snow bank. I dusted myself off and sprang—to use the word loosely—back into action. Fortunately the next part of the course was relatively easy. As I crested the last hill, I gulped when I saw a forest of flags marking the last steep pitch, and a crowd along the finish line. Somehow I staggered through the gates. Danny, who had been watching my run on television, jumped into my arms and whispered, "Daddy, you fell." As if I needed confirmation.

23
TURNING POINTS

With Washington growing faster than any other state, we needed to confront the most compelling questions of our time. In my 1967 State of the State message I spoke of our growing prosperity and the challenges it created:

Can we have our growth and live with it, too?

Can we become urbanized and remain civilized at the same time?

Can we achieve continuing economic growth without relentlessly exploiting our resources and destroying our natural beauty?

Can we devise an educational system that provides both equal opportunity and unlimited individual attainment?

Can we preserve an effective structure of local government and at the same time recognize the urgency of regional and metropolitan needs?

Can we both reorganize and refinance the foundations of state government in a manner that preserves the best of past principle and prepares us for the changing tasks of the future?

I proposed a series of measures in five broad arenas—urban affairs, the environment, government reorganization, transportation and human needs. "Blueprint for Progress Chapter 2" featured 40 specific bills. To help coordinate local planning, I asked for an Office of Community Affairs in the Governor's Office. Recognizing our cities' serious financial difficulties, I proposed, for the first time, an appropriation of $25 million from the state's general fund to assist municipalities. I advocated a Court of Appeals to relieve congestion in our legal system and called for an environmental quality commission "empowered to coordinate all efforts to maintain high standards of air and water quality." For starters, I proposed a $50 million bond issue to acquire and preserve scenic and recreation areas and called for establishment of a Seashore Conservation Area embracing all state lands along the coast, from the Columbia River to Cape Flattery and along the Strait of Juan de Fuca to the Elwha River. I also advocated a system of Scenic Recreation highways, protection of sites of historic significance, and preservation of open spaces. For the first time, I asked for an investigation into regulation of strip mining and endorsed in principle the concept of preserving "wild rivers."

Two years had not dimmed my conviction that a governor elected by the people should have the prerogative to pick the manager of a Department of Transportation. Having a highway commission set road priorities was just another brand of politics heavily influenced by the Good Roads Association and its myopic allies. "The impact of transportation is now too great to allow its management to be scattered among separate agencies," I told the Legislature.

The House quickly passed the bill, but the Senate refused to give the governor the ability to pick a transportation secretary. That would take another 38 years.* Meanwhile, freeways became virtual parking lots and mass transportation took a back seat to the automobile.

EDUCATION WAS A CENTERPIECE of my address and the tax-reform message that followed. The leaders of the Legislature's Higher Education committees—two experienced legislators—were key allies. In the Senate, Gordon Sandison, a gregarious Democrat from Port Angeles, led a united bipartisan committee. Sandison's passions were education and fishing. The round-faced Marine Corps veteran strived to lead by consensus rather than political power. Gordon would soon serve as chairman of the Western Interstate Commission for Higher Education. (My star-crossed successor, Dixy Lee Ray, named him fisheries director in 1977. It was one of her best decisions.) In the House, Republican Marjorie Lynch from Yakima County assumed the chairmanship and quickly built respect within her committee and with Senator Sandison. She later moved to Washington, D.C., where she became undersecretary of the department of Health Education & Welfare, a new but increasingly powerful cabinet office.

Between sessions, Sandison's Temporary Advisory Council on Public Higher Education conducted hearings around the state on the location of a new four-year college. Communities from Arlington to Vancouver vied for the new institution. The advisory council featured 14 citizens and 10 legislators. After meeting with representatives from each community, it reached consensus on the site criteria and recommended the new college be built "within 10 miles of Olympia." I was delighted, saying that a state college near the capital would help state government, and state government would help the college. I endorsed a bill establishing the college and providing a budget for a president and 18 founding faculty, plus an ample initial capital budget. While there was little opposition in the Legislature to the creation of the new college, there was considerable grousing over the location, with Snohomish and Clark counties especially aggrieved they had lost out. In the end, large majorities favored Thurston County.

Sandison told the college's new board of directors, headed by T.L. Schmidt of Olympia, they should decide what kind of school they wanted, then select a site. "If the college is to emphasize oceanography, a site on Puget Sound probably would be the best," he said, while a downtown site would be tailor made for an emphasis on government and political science. Among the evergreens at Cooper Point, just a few miles from the Capitol dome, we ended up with the best of both worlds.

The Temporary Council proposed a new type of public liberal arts college, one the two higher-education chairpersons and I heartily endorsed. We proposed that the founding faculty be given a year before startup to design and then institute a new curriculum that would unshackle "educational thinking from traditional patterns." The Evergreen State College, which welcomed its first freshman class in 1971, was the result. Instituting "narrative evaluations" in place of grades and encouraging political activism, it proved to be too liberal for some—at times even for me. But the legislators and

* In 2005, at the beginning of Chris Gregoire's first term, the Legislature granted governors the power to appoint the Secretary of Transportation, subject to Senate confirmation.

other critics who decried a campus of "long-haired hippie kids and their wet dogs" discounted a bold experiment in public higher education. I never imagined that in 10 years I would become Evergreen's second president.

CONCURRENTLY, a decisive battle over the future of the "junior" colleges raged in both chambers and in Ulcer Gulch, the hallway where lobbyists plied their trade. Earlier laws prohibited establishment of any two-year college within a county with a four-year institution. The two-year schools, which sprang up in rural areas like Grays Harbor and Lewis County during the Depression, were funded by community donations until 1940 when Governor Arthur B. Langlie signed a bill granting the seven pioneer junior colleges a total of $200,000 from the General Fund, around $6 million in today's dollars. By the 1960s, the combination of tuition and per-capita funding made these newly designated "community" colleges cash cows for the local school districts.

Adele Ferguson, the *Bremerton Sun's* inimitable reporter, and Frank "Buster" Brouillet, a future Superintendent of Public Instruction. *Adele Ferguson Scrapbook*

Restrictions on location having been lifted in previous sessions, the debate turned to oversight and management. In 1965, the Legislature authorized a comprehensive study of community colleges. The consultant recommended a new independent community college system. That report now entered the political whirlpool. Four competing forces descended on the Legislature. Louis Bruno, the superintendent of Public Instruction, produced a bill to greatly expand the number of community colleges while leaving them under the umbrella of their school districts. Representative Frank "Buster" Brouillet, chairman of the Joint Interim Committee on Education, pushed his committee to endorse the report with one notable exception: Control would remain under the State Board of Education. That was a concession to the state school superintendents' strong lobby. Labor union leaders, meantime, were protective of the vocational technical institutes, and demanded they be separated from any proposed new community college system.

The dominant force on this issue was the Temporary Advisory Council. I believed it was important to examine all of the pieces of higher education before embarking on a statewide community college system. The council, with Senator Sandison as its chairman, did its homework. After creating The Evergreen State College, it recommended a new State Community College system, separate from the "common" (K-12) schools. Charles Odegaard, the sagacious president of the University of Washington, played a crucial role on the Advisory Council. He understood both the need for community colleges and the dramatic change the new system would bring to higher education.

The factions squared off at a series of pivotal legislative hearings. Labor succeeded in keeping local control of its beloved vocational technical institutes, but the State Board of Education was crushed in its efforts to retain control of the community colleges. Ultimately, a new, comprehensive state community college system was adopted by the Legislature. I had the opportunity to appoint more than a hundred trustees to the community college districts and seven members of the state community college board. My staff worked hard to identify outstanding citizen leaders recommended by legislators. The success of this new and controversial system would depend on early decisions by these policymakers.

Helping create a modern community college system, an affordable gateway to higher education, is one of my proudest achievements.

THE REMAINDER OF MY STATE OF THE STATE message dealt primarily with human needs. I advocated major new facilities for the developmentally disabled, the establishment of community mental health centers and consolidation of social service agencies. The unemployed and persons on public assistance deserved more support, and I called for initiatives to ensure equal opportunity for Washingtonians of all races. I asked once again for a Constitutional Convention and proposed annual sessions of the Legislature. The state's needs were too pressing to let two years pass between sessions.

"The governor was feeding us an agenda that would normally choke a horse," Tom Copeland recalled. "We were ready for the challenge." Some conservatives questioned whether such activism was in keeping with our party's philosophy. Always a strong supporter of our federal system, I also believe government close to home is more responsive and more understanding of the needs of its citizens than a central government several thousand miles away. That belief requires a vibrant state government. I summarized the dilemma and challenge:

> State governments are unquestionably on trial today. We have been derelict in the past in meeting our basic obligations. This has both required and encouraged intervention by the federal government. If we are not willing to pay the price; if we cannot change where change is required; if we cannot prepare and carry out the programs so necessary to the conduct of expanding state affairs—if these things are not possible, then we have only one remaining recourse, and that is to prepare for an orderly transfer of our remaining responsibilities to the Federal government.

Paying the price was the sticking point. The state's General Fund had rebounded from a $24.3 million deficit on June 30, 1965, to a projected surplus of $81.9 million by June 30, 1967. It wasn't enough, however, to do what I strongly felt needed to be done over the next two years. For one thing, as I had foreseen two years earlier, many local school districts were experiencing voter backlash over now routine "special" property tax levies.

My budget proposal for the 1967-69 biennium exceeded projected revenues by $49 million. I opposed tapping into the surplus to eliminate the shortfall, believing that one-time revenues should not be used to support the ongoing operation costs of state government.

I did endorse using the surplus for grants to the financially strapped cities and for capital projects such as new school buildings and parks.

Our tax system was skewed, putting excessive burdens on small business and people with modest incomes. A year earlier I had appointed a Tax Advisory Council headed by Seattle lawyer Keith Grim. I enthusiastically adopted its proposal for comprehensive tax reform in an address to a joint session of the Legislature: "In approaching any major reform of Washington's tax structure, our three major considerations must be responsibility, responsiveness and equity," I said. "Our present taxes are not responsible in terms of practice; they are not responsive in terms of the economy, and they are not equitable in terms of people." I offered five tax-reform proposals, including:

A constitutional amendment creating a single-rate income tax, together with a statute setting the rate at 3.5 percent.

A second constitutional amendment establishing the property tax limit at 40 mills on an assessment level of 25 percent of true and fair value. If the income tax proposal failed, the property tax millage would increase to 50 mills.

If voters approved the income tax proposal, sales taxes would be reduced from 4.2 percent to 3.5 percent and removed from food and pharmaceutical drugs.

Upon passage of an income tax, the base rate of the business and occupation tax would be reduced to two-tenths of 1 percent. The Department of Revenue then would be directed to enforce uniform application of rates to all property in the state, both real and personal.

I could see legislators whispering to one another and scribbling notes. Some looked stunned as they grasped the magnitude of my proposal. I acknowledged it was a tall order. "In the history of every state and its people, the truly significant acts of government are few in number and rare in nature," I said. "Because they are significant, they are seldom easy, and their accomplishment requires not only wisdom but courage. I believe that this is one of those significant times. If the legislature sees fit to place the amendments on the ballot—and if the people approve—we will be changing a tradition of taxation that dates back to the early days of statehood."

Reaction was swift and polarizing. Some Democrats opposed the entire proposal, holding out for a graduated net income tax. A few Republicans opposed the whole plan, yet almost all were willing to send a proposal to the voters.

Hearings were packed. Lobbyists cornered every legislator they could track down. Finally, the bill and constitutional amendment came to the House floor for a showdown vote. Seattle Democrat Sam Smith, the son of a Baptist preacher, loved metaphors. "This is like mixing orange juice with castor oil to make the medicine easier to take," Smith said. "Let's add a little more orange juice by making it a graduated net income tax." Slade Gorton's comeback prompted chuckles: "The single rate tax is the middle ground between two ancient positions—Democrats favoring a graduated net income tax; Republicans opposed to any kind of an income tax. But Republicans are probably taking a bigger dose of castor oil than Democrats."

During a 52-day special session, our plan fell one vote short of the two-thirds majority required to pass a joint resolution to send a constitutional amendment to the voters.

Politics played a big role in the defeat of my tax reform plan. Democrats generally opposed it because they favored a graduated tax or simply did not want to see a Republican administration get the credit for reforming our highly regressive tax system. A graduated income tax on individuals, businesses and corporations was approved by 70 percent of the electorate in 1932, with the Depression paralyzing America, only to be ruled unconstitutional by the Washington Supreme Court. In ensuing years, Democrats had sent income tax proposals to the ballot several times and were rebuffed repeatedly by the voters. My old friend and mentor, Julia Butler Hansen, who was now a member of Congress, said it was a lost cause. She had been there and done that as a member of the Legislature. Republican colleagues told me I was lucky my plan had failed because if I ran for re-election in 1968 an income tax would be an albatross. I was undeterred. "Look," I said, "this is already my baby and I would rather have a real goal to fight for than try to explain a failed proposition."

I reappointed the Tax Advisory Council and asked it to review its work and to propose new legislation for the 1969 session.

My proposals for a Constitutional Convention and annual sessions of the Legislature also fell short of two-thirds majorities. However, the new Court of Appeals was sent to the ballot, where it was endorsed by the voters, and the Department of Community Affairs was created. Clean water laws were enacted, together with stricter regulation of air pollution. We boosted the gas tax from 7.5 to 9 cents per gallon to fund highway construction. I was delighted to sign the open housing law Sam Smith had championed since 1958 when he became only the third African American ever elected to the Washington Legislature. It was a modest first step on the road to equality.

ONE OF OUR MOST FAR-REACHING legislative achievements in 1967 was shepherding a dozen "Forward Thrust" bills to final passage. Forward Thrust was an offspring of Jim Ellis's push to clean up Lake Washington, culminating in the creation of Metro in 1958. Seattle was at a crossroads, Ellis declared in a memorable 1965 speech at the Downtown Rotary Club. It could usher in a "golden age" of livability and become one of the world's great international cities, Ellis said, or, in the immortal words of Joni Mitchell, pave paradise and put up a parking lot. With the freeways and byways growing more crowded by the month, King County's suburbs had a major stake in the outcome, Ellis emphasized. His "Committee of 200" drafted a manifesto for a massive investment in public works,

including a multipurpose civic stadium, community centers, swimming pools, sewer and storm-water control projects, enhanced fire protection, arterial highway improvements and, crucially, a rapid-transit program. But first, the Legislature had to authorize a special bond-issue election in King County.

I saw Forward Thrust as one of the most visionary quality-of-life projects in U.S. history. Joel Pritchard and Slade Gorton, two foot soldiers from the Metro campaign, felt the same way. Jim had a trio of determined supporters at the Capitol. Pritchard ran interference in the Senate, outmaneuvering Bob Greive, who was no fan of Ellis. Gorton took over in the House

Jim Ellis in downtown Seattle in the 1960s. *The Seattle Times*

and masterfully staged what amounted to a full court press.

At the polls in February of 1968, voters around King County backed Forward Thrust's marquee attraction, a $40 million bond issue for a domed stadium. They approved another $118 million for parks and recreation projects, including 25 swimming pools, and supported sewer bonds, fire stations and $81.6 million for arterial highway projects. But, gallingly, the rapid transit proposals we viewed as the centerpiece of Forward Thrust fell far short of the necessary 60 percent supermajorities. Ellis was crestfallen. Gorton called it "the stupidest 'no' vote the people of Seattle ever cast." Mayor Dorm Braman, an avid supporter of rapid transit, predicted there would be "tragic results." Sharing all those sentiments, I commiserated with King County's new county commissioner, future governor John Spellman. "We left a lot of federal money on the table," John said, shaking his head. That was spot on. With matching funds, we could have parlayed $385 million in local bonds into a total of $1.15 billion and built a rapid-transit system in 1970 that would have saved us a lot of 21st century frustration and grief.

WITH DON ELDRIDGE as speaker and Slade Gorton as majority leader, our Republican House caucus produced great leadership, but the intensity of the tax reform fight created a backlash among some members. Helmut Jueling, a stalwart Republican from Pierce County, spoke to the GOP luncheon club in Tacoma and predicted that House Republicans rather than Senate Democrats would give me trouble in the next session. "Because we have a governor from our own party, many of them have laid themselves across the rack and compromised their principles to give the governor his programs. What grieves us is that all he has done is appease a bunch of Democrat liberals. I will not go along anymore, and I told the governor this to his face."

In reality, when the session ended with generally high marks from newspaper editorialists all over the state, tensions eased and the caucus united to expand its strength in the next election. In my own backyard, however, I would never be Republican enough for King County's diehard band of right wingers.

After the historic 114-day session in 1965, the 112-day marathon in 1967 underscored that "the biennial 60-day session the founding fathers had envisioned was clearly an outdated concept," Don Brazier, a freshman House Republican from Yakima in 1967, wrote 30 years later in the second volume of his comprehensive history of the Washington Legislature.

24
THE RIOT DIDN'T HAPPEN

"Governor, if I had a gun right now, I'd shoot you!" The angry Black teenager aimed an index finger at my head and pretended to pull a trigger. The meeting room turned deathly quiet. I waited a second to steady my voice. "What good would that do?" "One less honky to deal with," he said.

Our eyes were locked across a table at the East Madison YMCA in Seattle's largely Black Central Area. It was August 2, 1967, the beginning of one of the hottest months in Seattle history. The tension was as palpable as the humidity. It was like that all across America.

On June 23 in Los Angeles, 10,000 war protesters had gathered to hear a speech by Muhammad Ali, stripped of his heavyweight championship for defying the draft. On average, 500 U.S. soldiers were dying in Vietnam every month. As the crowd advanced toward a hotel where President Johnson was addressing a $500-a-plate fundraiser, a phalanx of nightstick-wielding police intervened. All hell broke loose. America's inner cities "began exploding one after another like a string of firecrackers," Walt Crowley wrote in *Rites of Passage*, his memoir of the 1960s in Seattle. In Detroit, seething discontent over the war and racial inequality left 40 dead, 2,000 wounded and 5,000 homeless after a week-long riot quelled by 13,000 federal troops and National Guardsmen.

Seattle and Tacoma were the focal points for potential unrest in Washington state. Young Black activists began to challenge their communities' traditional leadership, rejecting all things "Negro" as remnants of slavery. James Brown gave them an anthem: "Say it loud! I'm Black and I'm proud."

In the spring of 1967, Black Power activist Stokely Carmichael spoke at the University of Washington and addressed a crowd of 4,000 at Garfield High School in the Central Area. Carmichael flailed the mainstream press for distorting the Black Power movement and denounced "institutionalized racism."

The Black Panthers, founded in Oakland in 1966 by Huey P. Newton and Bobby Seale, had branched out to Seattle. Counseling non-violence, the Rev. Dr. Samuel B. McKinney, pastor of the Mount Zion Baptist Church, was seen as too conservative for some of the firebrands—never mind that he was a brave, forceful champion of civil rights. The Rev. John Adams, a more recent arrival at First AME Church, was more combative than some of his colleagues. He rejoiced that the civil rights movement "had finally leaped the Cascade Mountains."

I MET FREQUENTLY with leaders of various civil rights groups, intent on doing what I could to forestall violence as the national turmoil intensified. We announced that I would be at the East Madison YMCA on the afternoon of August 2 to meet with anyone from the community. I was accompanied that day by Alfred E. Cowles, the newly appointed head of the State Board Against Discrimination. We recruited Al to Olympia after a nationwide search. He was a splendid young man, thoughtful and articulate.

Over lunch, we met with 22 leaders from the Black community. They aired a long list of concerns and proposed a program to boost jobs for at-risk teenagers and young adults and create more recreational facilities. Adopting the urgency of younger activists, they demanded a response within two days. "Government and business must act now as a demonstration of good faith," the Rev. Adams declared. They were no longer content to play by the white power structure's rules, he said. "If we can't make the rules, we won't play the game!" They warned me to be careful who I listened to and question who some self-appointed spokesmen really represented.

We left the luncheon and headed for my open-door session at the YMCA. It was now in the mid-80s. A large crowd was waiting to meet their governor. I was led to a small, un-air-conditioned room furnished only with a table and a half-dozen chairs. I greeted the first person in line, an older Black gentleman. He had a problem with Social Security. I listened intently, then led him out to meet with a staff member who could help him cut through the agency's red tape. Most of the people I met that day had individual problems with one level of government or another. However, one group of charming ladies in white gloves and dignified hats wanted only to welcome their governor to the neighborhood. I ordered coffee and tea, and we had a delightful conversation about the importance of family and community. As they departed, Bill Lathrop, my State Patrol aide, said there was one last group waiting to see me.

Six combative youths marched in. I had barely managed to say hello before the tirade began. Several talked at once, but the message was clear. They hated conditions in their community and demanded a change. Finally, one of the most outspoken pulled his chair around to the other end of the table to grow closer. When he squeezed the imaginary trigger it was one of the most electrifying moments of my life.

His "One less honky" statement was too confrontational for his friends. Concluding that their audience with the governor was now over, they stood almost in unison. As they filed out, one of them extended an invitation: "Governor, why don't you come home with me tonight for dinner to see how we have to live." I said I had another speaking engagement, but if we could find another mutually convenient time I would be honored to have dinner with his family. "I'll have to ask my mother first," he replied with a shy smile. That broke the tension. The fledgling Black Power zealots, even the angry kid who "shot" me, suddenly reverted to who they really were: teenagers—frustrated teenagers, and with good reason, but teenagers just the same. I gave them a challenge and an invitation of my own: "You've spent your time with me talking about all that's wrong with your community. I need to know what to do about it. I would like you to come to my office a week from now with some ideas that would help."

I doubted they would come, but they made an appointment. A week later they showed up as part of a delegation of 12 young people representing the Central Area "Grass Roots Committee." In suits and ties, they came armed with a long list of "Concrete Proposals." Their demands included 18 astonishingly pertinent items, and they were clearly prepared to argue them in depth. They asked that African-American history be included in the school curriculum and that Central Area teachers be given training to deal with racial problems. Further, the school district needed more Black classroom aides. As we debated the allocation of school funds, they claimed, with considerable evidence, that schools outside the Central Area were better equipped. Emphasizing that minority students, other than standout athletes, were handicapped in gaining entrance to the University of Washington and other colleges, they demanded more minority scholarships and financial aid. Further, they said the university needed to recruit Black professors and tap into its faculty talent to research interracial problems.

Infanta Spence, spokesperson for the group "WE" of the Grass Roots Committee, and four members of the Central Area Committee of Peace and improvement (CAPI) talk with reporters after meeting with me in August of 1967. Behind Spence are, from left, Jim Franklin, Bob Redwine, and Robert Isabel, and seated at right, Les McIntosh, chairman of CAPI. *MOHAI, Seattle Post-Intelligencer Collection, Image 2000.107.131.22.07*

When we turned to job opportunities, they pointed to bias in civil-service testing and complained that Black job-seekers in particular were foreclosed from labor union apprenticeship programs—the gateway to family-wage jobs. With little chance to land lucrative government contracts, there were few minority contractors. Training programs for women with young children were in short supply. More day-care centers were needed.

When they mentioned that welfare assistance was reduced with even modest increases in income, including money earned by kids with paper routes and other odd jobs, I was astonished at their savviness. They had focused directly on a technical problem we had with the federal government. Their complaint was well founded.

Likewise, when Seattleites groused that the Central Area looked run-down, the Grass Roots Committee said few white people understood how hard it was for a Black homeowner to secure a low-interest home improvement loan.

Their number one issue was a request for a centralized state office in the Central Area. They asked, with considerable passion and logic, why they had to take two buses to get to the public assistance office near Queen Anne, and then two more to reach the state Health Department office in the Rainier Valley. "Why can't all of the offices that serve our community be located in one place in our community?" I said that was a great idea, and promised to open a new office in the Central Area within 30 days. Further, we would weigh all their requests and make sure the community stayed in the loop.

THIRTY DAYS LATER, the Multi-Service Center opened its doors. It soon had a director who understood the community. Vince Hayes, a young man recommended by Al Cowles, had grown up in the Central Area. Hayes came home from Utah to manage the center, joined shortly by Robert Flowers, another native of the district who was finishing up his graduate work at the University of

Washington's School of Public Affairs. Both in their mid-20s, they had virtually no administrative models for such a center, and no direct appropriation. What they had in abundance was intelligence, energy and street credibility: They knew their community. Hayes later had a long career with the Social Security Administration and Flowers eventually retired as a senior vice president from Washington Mutual Bank.

I insisted that the new center be attached to the Governor's Office since there was no department in which it would fit. That gave Vince and Bob the clout they needed. When the center opened, there was a central intake counter and desks for the representatives of many state agencies. Before long, the City of Seattle asked to be included. A little while later, the federal government brought in a Social Security representative as well as workers from several other agencies.

A few weeks after the center opened, we held a formal reception and invited an array of public officials. There was also an open invitation to people of the community. The place was packed when I arrived, and as I circulated through the room I was greeted by an elderly lady. "Governor," she said proudly, "how do you like *our* center?" I had a lump in my throat as big as a tennis ball. "I think it's terrific," I said. With one word she had captured government's obligation to public service.

I was already thinking about a major reorganization of state government, including a unified social service agency and would soon appoint a Commission on Reorganization. The concept of one-stop citizen service agencies in communities of need throughout the state was now my goal. The six angry teenagers had good ideas, but they had to shout to capture my attention. I reflected wryly on the old adage, "You have two ears to listen and one mouth to talk, so it's a good idea to listen twice as much as to talk." The age of citizen activism was in full throat. I was determined to let the voices of all citizens be heard.

In the months to come I met with the Central Area Committee for Peace and Improvement, a hundred-member group formed to help further the goals of the Grass Roots Committee. Its members were mostly 20 to 30, with a smattering of 40-somethings who stood ready to help the "young turks" like the Student Nonviolent Coordinating Committee.

A little over a year later, a ribbon-cutting ceremony took place at Liberty Bank, the state's first Black-owned bank. During the middle of the reception an uneasy silence suddenly fell over the crowd. I saw a half dozen young people approaching me. One was carrying a machete encased in a leather sheath. Bill Lathrop eyed them warily. "Governor," their spokesman said, "we really liked what you did in opening the Multi-Service Center so we made this machete for you as a thank-you gift." The audience let out an audible sigh of relief. I marveled at the sharpness of its blade and

I help cut the ribbon for the opening of Liberty Bank in Seattle, the Northwest's first Black-owned bank. From left, Dr. James E. Jackson, chairman of the board; Mayor Dorm Braman; Mardine Purnell, secretary of the board; City Councilman Sam Smith; Patrinell Wright, a bank employee and singer. *Ron De Rosa/The Seattle Times*

the leather work on the sheath. I used that machete for many years to cut brush, remembering each time the extraordinary events of that long, hot summer of 1967.

"THE BIG STORY IN SEATTLE," Walt Crowley wrote nearly 30 years later, "was the riot that didn't happen." In 1967, Walt was a leading contributor to *Helix*, the freewheeling "underground" Seattle newspaper founded that year. Before my meeting with the angry youths, the *Helix* had interviewed two Black activists who said "establishment attempts to defuse tensions had actually inflamed the situation. ...We had people who wanted to see a riot, who were dead set on seeing a riot that Saturday night. There were 'volunteers' in our own group who would have gone down and gotten their brains blown out just to see the whole thing off." What defused the situation, they said, was my immediate response to the militants' demands for more services and facilities. "A new multiservice center came together within days of the meeting, an earned income credit of $50 a month was approved for the Central Area's 2,600 AFDC mothers, and Black History was added to the Seattle Public School curriculum for the coming year," Crowley wrote.

My Central Area listening session was followed shortly by similar meetings in Tacoma and Spokane. The Tacoma meeting was particularly important because there was a large, activist minority community. After spirited meetings with a wide variety of residents I spoke to a dinner meeting packed with 400 concerned citizens. My message on racial tolerance was punctuated by the need for cooperation. "Labor and industry ought to be marching hand in hand because they are not combatants, not contestants. ... All of our other efforts really mean very little unless we can achieve this goal of brotherhood." Black folks were not seeking handouts, I said, just opportunity—"better training, better education, a better chance for better lives." To me it was what Washington state, enriched by immigrants from so many lands, should stand up for.

Those dramatic meetings with justifiably frustrated Black people in the Central Area also underscored my commitment to ban racial discrimination in housing. In one of the most shameful events in Seattle history, city voters in 1964 overwhelmingly rejected an open housing referendum. The City Council had balked at enacting an ordinance to overturn red-lining, despite the prodding of Councilmen Wing Luke and Lud Kramer. I said it was time to rectify that wrong, telling *The Seattle Times*: "I think all citizens of this state must search their own conscience, their own background, to recognize that people ought to be able to live where economics and their desires would put them. There is no question in my mind that it is very difficult, if not impossible, for some citizens of our Central Area to live where they might wish to. This is an area where every citizen must join in because legislation alone cannot solve this problem."

The success of the Central Area Multi-Service Center left me optimistic. Still, given the unrest festering across the country, I sensed that riots were going to happen. Looking back, 1967 was a relative cakewalk compared to what 1968 had in store. And I found myself on the national stage.

25
THE MANSION

It would have been the height of arrogance for the Evanses to complain too loudly about the condition of their public housing. The kid who invited me to dinner at his house in the Central Area surely would have been impressed by our red brick, 14,000-square-foot abode next door to the Capitol. Like one of those elegantly decrepit English country homes that look wonderful from the circular driveway, the Governor's Mansion was a dangerous money pit periodically infested with bats.

The Mansion was constructed in a hurry in 1908 to give the governor suitable quarters to entertain dignitaries attending the Alaska-Yukon-Pacific Exposition, Seattle's first world's fair. When work on Wilder and White's stately new Capitol Campus got underway in 1912, it was expected that the governor's "temporary" mansion would be torn down. The master plan envisioned the site being occupied by a twin to the neoclassical Insurance Building. In the wake of our never-ending debates over budget balancing and the priorities of government, the Mansion stayed put in a state of perceived benign neglect.

Governor Ernest Lister, a cranky Democrat elected in 1912 in a photo-finish reminiscent of the Gregoire-Rossi battle 92 years later, was so fed up with the mansion and

Inspecting the antiquated plumbing in the basement of the Governor's Mansion in 1966. *Washington State Archives*

the lack of privacy that he threatened to move out in 1913. He actually did in 1915, living intermittently in a downtown hotel in 1917. Lister said the plumbing was bad, the wiring worse and the heating system a joke. The paltry budget the Legislature provided for maintenance and operations only ensured further decay, the governor warned. Adding insult to injury, the state auditor wanted to dock the governor $1,500 for overspending the Mansion Fund. In what became one of Nancy's favorite quotes, Governor Lister pronounced the Mansion "a monument to the high cost of low bids."

When First Lady Ethel Rosellini graciously gave Nancy the cook's tour of the place after I was elected in 1964, she warned that the Mansion had major problems. Ethel related that one night during a big formal dinner, every fuse in the place blew when the caterers plugged in their 50-cup coffee pots in the tiny kitchen. The portable heaters needed to heat the place in the winter strained the ancient wiring. There was one bathroom on the first floor where public events occurred. The roof leaked every winter, the radiators clanked and the furnishings were a mishmash of mostly pedestrian faux antiques.

One day when I opened the "Urgent" file on my desk, I found a formal memo to the governor from the First Lady. "Subject: Wallpaper: The decor of one particular bedroom probably was appropriate when the room was occupied by a daughter of Governor Rosellini. But now an Evans son has that room. And the wallpaper of pink ballerinas has got to go!"

I made a decisive gubernatorial decision to promptly remove the wallpaper.

With the pittance the Legislature appropriated for its operation, I was dazzled by Nancy's resourcefulness in making the place feel like home, yet presentable for thousands of visitors. She welcomed everyone, including Cub Scouts, J.P. Patches, D.A.R. ladies, Dairy Princesses, and Vice President Spiro Agnew.

The Nixon administration's lightning rod came to Olympia in 1971 to address the Legislature on behalf of the revenue sharing program. After the joint session, I invited Agnew to the Mansion. Nancy had arranged a small reception. Dan Jr., who was 11, and 8-year-old Mark dutifully complied with their mother's orders to dress up to meet the Vice President of the United States. Four-year-old Bruce balked. He put on his gray flannel shorts, knee socks and blue blazer but refused to come downstairs. Nancy was insistent that he meet Agnew, certain it would be a memorable moment in years to come. How right she was.

Press photographers captured Agnew crouching to shake hands with a sobbing little boy whose mother was gently prodding from behind. Lower lip quivering, Bruce wouldn't even look up. The picture went nationwide. At the time I was chagrinned, but as things turned out we concluded that Bruce—with intuition way beyond his years—smelled a rat. Our distinguished guest turned out to be a nattering nabob of hypocrisy. Agnew resigned in disgrace three years later, pleading no contest to a charge of income tax evasion. Bruce Evans went on to become head of the staff for the U.S. Senate Appropriations Committee in Washington, D.C. He still gets teased about the photo.

Bruce balks at shaking hands with Vice President Agnew in 1971. He was only 4, but he already could smell a rat. *Evans Family Collection*

DURING THE SUMMER OF 1967, the Washington Newspaper Publishers' Association met in Olympia. Publishers' wives and members of Washington Press Women toured the Mansion and heard Nancy explain the problems she dealt with daily. "The safest thing in the whole house is the tree fort my husband built for the children," she said. The tour led to a flurry of articles in papers across the state, including a front-page story in the Sunday edition of the *Seattle Post-Intelligencer*. "This house should be brought up to code," a deputy state fire marshal told the paper. "I wouldn't want my kids to live in it. I would not sleep easy in it." Nancy said the key questions were: "Is it worth refurbishing? Is it historically important? Is it attractive?" Her answer to all three was "An emphatic Yes! Let the executive Mansion be restored. Let the rooms be decorated with the quality furniture original with the house whenever possible and new pieces of value added to complete it."

Unfortunately, The State Capitol Committee, composed of the governor, lieutenant governor and commissioner of Public Lands, could not agree on a plan to proceed with renovations. Seattle architect Ibsen Nelsen reported it would cost $375,000 to renovate and expand the Mansion and $1 million to build a new one. Lands Commissioner Bert Cole pushed hard for a new Mansion, while Lt. Governor John Cherberg would only support minimum repairs. I strongly supported Nancy's proposal for preservation and renovation and tried to persuade Cherberg to change his mind. He wouldn't budge. So the committee was deadlocked and the project was set aside. Seven years later, with the problems mounting daily, the Capitol Committee voted for preservation and renovation. Costs had risen to more than $1 million, but further delays would have driven the cost higher yet.

The Evanses outside the mansion with Peggy, our Irish wolfhound. *Washington State Archives*

Nancy's common sense ultimately carried the day. The Governor's Mansion was likely saved by her persistence. "If you tear it down," she warned, "it will never have historic value." Nancy wasn't shy about lobbying lawmakers visiting the Mansion. Watching her in action sometimes gave me pause. When the guests were gone, I'd scold, "Did you have to buttonhole that one?" She would just smile and say that "some of our 17th century legislators" needed a reality check.

The people of Washington and a succession of First Families have my extraordinary wife to thank for giving the Governor's Mansion a new lease on life. Nancy created a Foundation for the Preservation of the Governor's Mansion. She asked Laurene Gandy, the widow of Joseph Gandy, president of Seattle's 1962 World's Fair, to head what emerged as a remarkably talented and devoted committee. Its task was to acquire appropriate period furniture, rehabilitate the public rooms and find private funding for the entire enterprise. They were strikingly successful. That old house is now a home and a public trust rolled into one, lovingly maintained by hundreds of volunteers. The Palladium window in the renovated downstairs of the Mansion has a replica in the home we built in Seattle after I retired from the U.S. Senate, a reminder of the happy years we spent in the Mansion with three rambunctious boys and their grandmother, plus Peggy, the Irish Wolfhound, two cats, plus bunnies, gerbils, Gam's guppies and, at one time, a couple of turkeys.

Another of Nancy's key projects was the Governor's Festival of the Arts. Our friend Lud Kramer, the Secretary of State, hatched the idea in 1966 and found an enthusiastic supporter in Nancy. Teaming up with the Olympia Fine Arts Guild, the festival brought in diverse entertainment—from Fred Waring and his Pennsylvanians to "La Bohème," Puccini's immortal opera. That was heady stuff for the capital city back then.

Nancy was also founding trustee of Planned Parenthood of Thurston County. She supported the 1970 statewide referendum to make abortion "legal and safe" in the early months of pregnancy. She also backed the Equal Rights Amendment and has been a lifelong activist for the mentally ill and developmentally disabled. During the 1964 campaign, Slade Gorton and Joel Pritchard were amused that the press was preoccupied with Nancy's youth. They knew the truth about Nancy Bell Evans: She could have been a formidable elected official in her own right. She may have misspoke, however, when she hailed the tree fort as a triumph of my civil engineering skills.

The boys wanted to climb into the branches of the huge maple tree in the front lawn of the Mansion. I nailed a few cleats onto the trunk so they could reach the lower branches. About 10 feet up, the trunk divided, providing a great base for a tree fort. I drew a sketch for a design of a two-story structure with a trap door and firemen's pole for a quick return to the ground. It was a chance for me to return to my engineering roots. I eagerly undertook construction. The boys watched with great anticipation and occasionally picked up a hammer to pound nails.

I was putting the finishing touches on the fort on a sunny Sunday in 1967 when 4-year-old Mark pleaded to join me up the trunk. I helped him climb to the lower floor of the structure. He looked on attentively as I went back to work. Suddenly there was a thump and a scream. Mark had accidentally stepped backward through the trap door. He was sprawled on the ground, face covered with blood. I yelled for help. The state trooper on duty came running. Mark had a deep gash in his forehead that required 23 stitches. Luckily, he had not sustained a concussion. I was finding out that raising three boys included assorted bumps, bruises and broken bones. The tree fort became a favorite spot for our three boys and their friends for the next nine years.

OUR DOMESTIC CHALLENGES were but breadcrumbs in comparison to the lives other Americans were living. I created an Urban Affairs Council in 1967. "Our time is up," I told reporters. "We can no longer ignore the fact that our towns have become cities, and that our cities have become regional urban sprawls. We cannot ignore the freeways tearing through the hearts of our cities, the pollution clouding both our horizon and our lakes, the rotting slums creeping into our cities."

I appointed Kramer to oversee the council. A former member of the Seattle City Council, the Secretary of State was intimately familiar with urban problems. For executive director, we recruited future Secretary of State Sam Reed, who had just completed a master's degree in political science at Washington State University. Sam earlier had worked as an academic intern for us. He was bright, young and steeped in state history, his grandfather, Wenatchee attorney Sam Sumner, having been a respected legislator. One of Sam's assignments as an intern was to work with Kramer, Slade Gorton and Jim Ellis, the legendary Seattle civic activist, to draft an urban affairs report and conceptualize legislation for the 1967 legislative session. Reed was the obvious choice to play a key role with the Urban Affairs Council. He put together a blue ribbon council that featured community leaders from around the state, including Pasco City Councilman Art Fletcher, Pacific Northwest Bell president Tom Bolger, labor leader Austin St. Laurent, Seattle Mayor Dorm Braman, King County Judge Charles Z. Smith, Seattle City Councilwoman Phyllis Lamphere, Spokane Mayor David Rodgers, Spokane civic leader King Cole and Yakima County Commissioner Lenore Lambert.

The council's report made recommendations regarding job training, housing, health care, education, the environment and the non-urban sector. With the assistance of an extraordinary summer intern, Harvard student Rollie Cole, Reed wrote a 62-page report explaining the recommendations. Then, working with my talented legal assistant, Dick Hemstad, he put together an extensive legislative package for the 1969 legislative session. Remarkably, most of the package was adopted.

The Urban Affairs Council found racial problems

Sam Reed, a future secretary of state, was an academic intern from the WSU Graduate School of Political Science. *Washington State Archives*

underlying most of these issues, so it created a Commission on the Causes and Prevention of Civil Disorder to focus on racism in Washington state. Reed recruited another future secretary of state, Bruce Chapman, to be its executive director. The work of the council and commission paved the way for many of my legislative proposals in the 1970s.

THE GOP GUBERNATORIAL CAUCUS formally recommended to the Republican National Committee that I be named keynoter for the 1968 convention—an honor that was also a daunting responsibility. We also pushed for stronger representation for governors on the platform committee in response to the huge gains we had made in the 1966 election.

As the year ended, I still had not announced my candidacy for re-election, but I was certain I would seek a second term. The economy of the state was booming, and a Republican majority in the House of Representatives made legislating a whole lot easier. We had made good progress in many areas but were still struggling to finance the huge growth in school enrollment. A rising citizen interest in the environment coincided with new initiatives I was eager to propose. We were also deeply involved in the massive construction of the interstate highway system.

26
HISTORY CRACKED OPEN

My 90 years of Seattle memories can be stirred by the simple act of driving past a building on a street corner. If you live in the town where you were born and raised, you know the feeling. There are ghosts everywhere. Sometimes on Denny Way, I flash back to a sea of marchers filling two street lanes for 10 blocks. We were headed for Seattle Center, our numbers growing by the block, in a show of solidarity after one of the darkest days of a cataclysmic year. It was the seventh day of April in 1968, "the year America shuddered, history cracked open and bats came flapping out," as *Time* magazine put it so well.

In January, the North Vietnamese launched their surprise Tet Offensive. In February, the Pentagon reported a one-week casualty total that topped 3,000 for the first time. CBS News anchor Walter Cronkite returned from Vietnam to pronounce it a deceit-filled mess. And the "New Nixon" announced his candidacy for president. In March, Eugene McCarthy nearly won the New Hampshire Primary. Bobby Kennedy, smelling blood, jumped in. And a haggard-looking Lyndon B. Johnson bowed out.

In the middle of all that I announced my decision to seek a second term. Governor John Love, my splendid colleague from Colorado, introduced me at an "appreciation" banquet attended by 2,500 cheering supporters who in one night donated $200,000, almost half of the funds needed for the 1968 campaign. I told them our Blueprint for Progress had become a reality. We had created 100,000 new jobs in each of the past three years, with record personal incomes, strong industrial development and capital expansion.

> This is an administration that cares—cares enough to recommend a record budget for schools, colleges and universities; cares enough to lead the way for strong air and water pollution control legislation; cares enough to obtain the preservation of our ocean beaches for recreational uses; cares enough to bring direct aid to our cities and urban areas; cares enough to talk with people face-to-face and to bring new hope, dignity and jobs to hundreds of people in urban areas; cares enough to develop new and dramatic programs for the mentally ill and the mentally retarded.

Preaching to the faithful is one thing; hitting the streets quite another. I was finding out that citizen activist voices grow more strident in an election year. One day you're a hero, the next just another politician running for re-election.

The Rev. Dr. John Adams, chairman of the Central Area Civil Rights Committee, lambasted me over my efforts on civil rights, saying, "What Governor Evans did last summer is the biggest fraud in the history of the Central Area. He put up a big office but he didn't create the jobs." The truth was that 5,000 Central Area residents had visited the Multi-Service Center in its first six months, and we had connected more than 700 people with new jobs. I told the crowd at the grand opening of the expanded center that "until discrimination is driven from the heart and mind of every American we will continue to have turmoil in our communities." We needed to work together to create an America "where every citizen can make his way based on his ability, his background and his willingness to work."

In the struggle for civil rights I discovered a continuing conflict between the older more established leaders and the young rebels. Both struggled to be heard but often would not listen to each other. The firebrands frequently seemed to have better ideas but were less capable of translating them into reality. It was a precarious balancing act to listen to all and then choose an appropriate direction.

APRIL 4, 1968, had been an uneventful Thursday at the Governor's Office until staff members burst in to say that the Rev. Martin Luther King Jr. had been shot dead on a Memphis motel-room balcony. That morning's edition of the *Seattle P-I* had carried a story about Dr. King's address the night before to a throng gathered in a Memphis church. He had come to Memphis to support striking sanitation workers. Cautioning them to avoid violence, he said peaceful demonstrations would underscore the justice of their cause. The strike was just another skirmish in the battle for equality promised by the Declaration of Independence and the Constitution's Bill of Rights. Be resolute, Dr. King counseled. Though there had been countless threats against his life and violence against people peaceably assembled to seek justice, "We aren't going to let dogs or water hoses turn us around. We aren't going to let any injunction turn us around. We are going on," he vowed, adding:

> We've got some difficult days ahead. But it really doesn't matter with me now, because I've been to the mountaintop. … Like anybody, I would like to live a long life. But I'm not concerned about that now. I just want to do God's will. And He's allowed me to go up to the mountain. And I've looked over. And I've seen the Promised Land. I may not get there with you. But I want you to know tonight, that we, as a people, will get to the Promised Land. So I'm happy, tonight. I'm not worried about anything. I'm not fearing any man. Mine eyes have seen the glory of the coming of the Lord.

It struck me then—as it does now, all these years later—as one of the bravest, most eloquent speeches I'd ever heard. And tragically prophetic.

Dr. King's murder prompted a paroxysm of fury—the antithesis of his ministry. Riots erupted in more than 100 cities in 29 states. Over the next 10 days, 46 people were killed nationwide, 2,600 injured and more than 21,000 arrested. In Chicago, Mayor Daley ordered police to shoot to kill if they encountered arsonists. I was deeply concerned about our state, particularly the urban centers of Seattle and Tacoma. Sporadic violence was reported, with warnings that worse was yet to come. I met with two decisive yet cool-headed men—Major General Howard S. McGee of the Washington State National Guard and Will Bachofner, Chief of the Washington State Patrol. Both agreed with my view that it was vital that local civic, political and religious leaders speak out against violence.

Fortunately, clerical and community leaders from the African American community joined city and state leaders in reminding citizens that Dr. King's enormous strength came from his preaching of nonviolent protest.

That Sunday, I joined the Rev. Adams and the Rev. Samuel McKinney—both good friends of Dr. King—and other African-American clergy in leading a peaceful procession that grew by the block. "Little streams of humanity that began moving toward the Seattle Center Arena grew into rivers," Don Duncan, *The Seattle Times*' award-winning feature writer, wrote. The Seattle Center Coliseum was picked for a city-wide memorial service honoring Dr. King. It turned out to be too small. The program was delayed by nearly an hour as the throng moved to the High School Memorial Stadium.

My friend Sam Smith, Seattle's first Black city councilman, surveyed a sea of faces—people of every color and creed from every walk of life, including protestant, Catholic and Jewish clergy. He rested a hand on the shoulders of his 11-year-old son and said, "This is the essence of a country." With a lump in my throat, I told the crowd that violence was the way of the coward; nonviolence was the way of the hero. "Does it always take martyrdom to cause concern?"

The Rev. Adams drew a standing ovation when he called for passage of an enforceable open-housing ordinance in Seattle as a memorial to Dr. King. Five-thousand petitions were distributed that day to support the ordinance sponsored by Sam Smith. Eight days later, it was unanimously adopted by the City Council and signed by Mayor Braman. "The arc of the moral universe is long, but it bends toward justice," Dr. King famously observed.

Thanks to wise community leaders who spoke out, and distraught citizens who listened, we were spared the violence that wracked America.

GIVEN HIS STRONG SUPPORT by Black voters and anti-war liberals of all stripes, Robert F. Kennedy seemed to be on a roll. Then Gene McCarthy showed the breadth of his appeal, winning the Oregon primary on May 28 with help from mischievous maverick Republicans. (Senator Hatfield, mentioned as a possible Nixon running mate, had urged friends to temporarily change their registration and back McCarthy, whom he viewed as "a true anti-war lawmaker.") It was the first time a Kennedy had ever been beaten in direct competition in any primary or general election. Nixon, meantime, trounced Reagan and Nelson Rockefeller, who had dithered to the point he was reduced to a write-in.*

In California a week later, buoyed by surging crowds of Black voters, Kennedy decisively defeated McCarthy. As he was leaving a Los Angeles hotel ballroom following a victory celebration, Kennedy was shot in the head by a Palestinian zealot. My campaign paused again, as it had five years earlier when his brother was murdered in Dallas. The TV footage of Robert F. Kennedy mortally wounded on the floor of a hotel kitchen, a rosary in his hand, his distraught wife kneeling alongside, was soul searing. Thinking about Nancy and our three sons, I seriously considered whether it was worth continuing to face the turmoil and danger of political office. The State Patrol regularly reported death threats aimed at me. Most we shrugged off as bluster. A few required serious investigation. As I weighed Dr. King's bravery and my commitment to public service, I realized that danger was

---

* Oregon Governor Tom McCall, a Rockefeller supporter, rebuffed Nixon's repeated requests for an endorsement, even after Nixon dangled a cabinet seat, Secretary of the Interior.

part of the job and that I was probably at greater risk traveling the freeway than facing an attacker.

THE POLITICAL CALCULUS of my re-election bid was tricky. My administration was embroiled in a controversy involving the Department of Institutions and the Rainier School for the Developmentally Disabled at Buckley in rural Pierce County. For years, each state institution was budgeted separately and some superintendents developed delusions of power. There was little effort at coordination from Olympia and each institution became its own fiefdom.

Dr. Garrett Heyns, head of the Department of Institutions under Governor Rosellini, was the first to try to rationalize programs between institutions with some success. When Heyns retired at 73 in 1966, he recommended his assistant, Dr. William Conte, a Tacoma psychiatrist, as his successor. Soon, I was faced with an open revolt from Charles Martin, the superintendent of the Rainier School. The Buckley Citizens Committee, a group created to help support its local institution, joined in the fray, charging Dr. Conte with harassment. Fortunately, Dr. Martin took a job in Texas and the furor dissipated. When the Legislature, through the Legislative Council, held a hearing on the issue before a large crowd in a politically charged atmosphere, Dr. Conte defended himself well and noted that Heyns had also criticized Superintendent Martin, saying he had been "less cooperative than any other superintendent in the system." A blue-ribbon group of witnesses also testified in favor of Dr. Conte's leadership.

IT WAS APPARENT EARLY in the year that my Democratic opponent would be either State Senator Martin J. Durkan or our three-term attorney general, John J. O'Connell. A good looking, affable Irishman from Tacoma, O'Connell had tested the waters against Rosellini in 1964, but made little headway. He backed off and waited for his next chance. An agile debater, he was also a good attorney general, assembling a strong team of deputies. Durkan, however, knew the ins and outs of state government far better. After several terms in the House he moved to the Senate and quickly became a force, rising to head the Ways & Means Committee.

Either man would be a formidable opponent. From the beginning of the campaign, however, I felt confident I would win. Unemployment was near an all-time low. We had delivered on most of our Blueprint for Progress.

I chose John Barnard, a Boeing engineer, as my campaign manager. He was my first political mentor as Republican chairman of the 43rd Legislative District and later served as King

John J. O'Connell, a three-term attorney general, was a tough opponent. *Washington State Archives*

County Republican chairman. Barnard excelled at organizing tasks and managing volunteers. Predictably, King County would prove challenging. The county chairman, Ken Rogstad, and his band of right-wing stalwarts were now infatuated with Ronald Reagan and more disenchanted than ever with me. They had hosted a Reagan love-fest at the Olympic Hotel in downtown Seattle the previous winter. Bill Boeing Jr. and 1,100 other cheering conservatives hailed Reagan as the second coming of

Barry Goldwater. They maintained that GOP State Chairman Gummie Johnson and other operatives from the liberal "Evans crowd" were out to purge my opponents and gain control of the party so I could "do some horse-trading in national politics in 1968" and perhaps gain the vice-presidential nomination. Nothing of the sort was on my agenda, especially with my friend Mark Hatfield as a legitimate vice-presidential contender representing the West and our wing of the party.

Nixon campaigns in Olympia in 1968, telling reporters I was "definitely among those who'll be considered for the number two spot." My press secretary, Neil McReynolds, arms folded, looks on at right, together with Bill Lathrop, (bald man at center left), my State Patrol security aide. *Washington State Archives*

A NUMBER OF PROMINENT moderate Republican governors had been touted as potential presidential candidates in 1968, including Rockefeller and Romney. A tall, square-jawed Mormon, Romney had shot himself in the foot by declaring he had been "brainwashed" by the generals when he visited Vietnam. Nixon, meantime, had rebounded from his humiliating 1962 loss in the California governor's race by becoming a tireless fundraiser for GOP candidates. No event was too small. Nixon "logged 127,000 miles visiting 40 states to speak before more than 400 groups," Tom Wicker noted in *The New York Times*. That's a lot of IOUs.

Unconvinced Nixon was the right man to bring us victory in 1968, I urged Bill Scranton, the centrist governor of Pennsylvania, to seek the nomination. He was an appealing leader with good ideas. Despite my prodding and the support of many other Republican governors, Scranton balked. "My children are entering their teen years and we only have a little time before they begin to leave home," he told me. I remembered his dedication to his family when I was faced with a decision on whether to seek a fourth term as governor in 1976.

Republican governors had sized up the contenders earlier in the year during the National Governors' Conference in Washington, D.C. Most of us were dissatisfied with Nixon and the incipient campaign of Reagan, who had been governor of California for only a year. We urged Nelson Rockefeller to begin an active candidacy. It was a hard sell. Eighteen months earlier, Rocky had declared he was "out of national contention, completely and forever, without reservation." Sort of like Nixon's famous "last press conference" in 1962. My enthusiasm for Rockefeller was undiminished. He coupled long experience in a variety of leadership roles in the federal government with his outstanding reputation as governor. I admired his moderate, yet activist politics. Interestingly, one of the strongest advocates for Rockefeller's candidacy at the Governors' Conference was Spiro T. "Ted" Agnew, Maryland's new governor. Agnew asked me what he could do to push the Rockefeller candidacy. "Work the phones," I said. Agnew and I contacted as many of our colleagues as possible, trying to create enough broad support to prompt Rocky to run.

Shortly after returning to Olympia, I received a call from Rocky, who had just met with a group of backers. He wanted my advice. "You should run," I said without hesitation. "Romney's campaign is stalled, and I think it's important to have an alternative to Nixon and Reagan." Rocky chuckled. "That's the same advice the whole group gave me yesterday. I really have to think this one through." The next day I received a telegram from Rockefeller. He had decided not to run and was going to announce his decision at a press conference that afternoon. I was deeply disappointed but forewarned. Agnew had been left out of the loop. Anticipating a Rockefeller declaration of candidacy, the governor had assembled the press corps in his office to watch the announcement on TV and add his fulsome endorsement. Hugely embarrassed by the deflating surprise, Agnew immediately shifted his support to Nixon.

I had already decided not to make any public announcement of my choice for the nomination until after I presented my keynote address at the National Convention, which was five months away. It seemed appropriate to speak on behalf of the party as a keynoter and not as an advocate of one candidate.

In April, Rockefeller changed his mind, alerting me with yet another telegram: "My purpose is to give our party a choice of candidates and of programs. I have become convinced that I can present it within a framework of party unity. This I pledge to do."

It was too late. Some of his supporters had already shifted to Nixon.

DELIVERING A KEYNOTE ADDRESS to a national convention was an opportunity to spotlight everything I believed in. However, if I blew it by droning on too long, millions of TV viewers likely would switch to reruns of *The Flying Nun*.

Early in 1968 I contacted Jim Lane, who had worked with me on speeches for several years. I read a number of keynote speeches by both Democrats and Republicans, including William Jennings Bryan's mesmerizing "Cross of Gold" speech, which propelled the 36-year-old Nebraskan to the 1896 Democratic presidential nomination. I wasn't going to come anywhere close to matching that, but I was determined to make it the best speech of my career. Jim Dolliver and Neil McReynolds, my press secretary, joined us as we developed my themes. I received a letter from Emmet John Hughes, an eloquent Rockefeller speechwriter, who offered to help. He added some excellent ideas. Interestingly, I never received any direction from the Republican National Committee or any other party official on the content of my speech. I liked being on my own.

Just before we left for Miami Beach, someone sent me a copy of Ed Donohoe's column in *The Washington Teamster*. Donohoe tweaked me relentlessly, but I usually enjoyed it because he was such a clever writer. This time, he really let me have it:

> I firmly doubt that Evans is any great shucks as an orator who will send the Grand Old Party on its drunken way. Frankly, if there is a worse public speaker than Dan Evans it must be former Gov. Albert D. Rosellini when he chose not to follow his script. ... If there is a lesson here for Evans it might be this: Come up with throat trouble while you're still ahead. Evans isn't going to be re-elected governor even if he addressed the Republican Convention every night in Sodom-by-the-Sea."

My speech team had a good laugh over Ed's benediction.

27
KEYNOTER

Nancy frowned slightly as she squinted at the August 9, 1968, edition of *Time* magazine. The cover featured her husband, the keynote speaker for the Republican National Convention. "The mouth and chin are all wrong," Nancy observed. Given a tight deadline, the artist probably did the best he could with my visage. He nailed my nose, eyes and thinning dark hair beginning to gray at the temples, but gave me a curiously fat lower lip.

Twelve years earlier I was a relative unknown running for the state Legislature. Now we were jetting toward Miami Beach, and I was on the cover of America's most influential weekly news magazine, with 10 million readers.

The convention preview cover story described me as "an idealist of uncommon rectitude" and the prototype of the GOP's dynamic, yet pragmatic "New Breed." *Time* also recalled historian Mark Sullivan's observation that the interminable keynote speeches of yesteryear amounted to "a combination of oratory, grand opera and hog

Washington State Archives

calling." TV had changed everything. I was determined to limit my address to 25 minutes and avoid the partisan diatribes and boasting I'd heard so often from keynoters.

As if I didn't need more pressure, *Time* set the stage like this, contrasting the "eve-of-execution" atmosphere at the 1964 GOP convention with 1968: "This time the Democrats are in decline, taxes and living costs are up, the cities are seething, and Viet Nam has turned into the nation's longest, least popular war. The heady awareness of opportunity that infects the entire GOP assemblage is a measure of the distance the party has come since the dismal post-Goldwater days. ... Not since 1952 has the party in power been so vulnerable."

Our convention entourage included my parents, Jim Dolliver, speechwriter Jim Lane, press secretary Neil McReynolds, Gummie Johnson and Bill Jacobs, one of my most agile and politically smart aides. Our high spirits at deplaning to the cheers of a mob of Young Republicans—some backing Nixon, others Rockefeller—dimmed a bit as we sped by the massive Fontainebleau Hotel, convention headquarters. Seven miles down the road, we were deposited at a rather shabby hotel that served as headquarters for the Washington state delegation.

On the Sunday evening before opening day of the convention, the Fontainebleau hosted a Republican gala for 1,500 guests in formal dress. I received a lot of back-patting compliments about *Time's* cover story—and some razzing, too. Gummie had told *Time* my nickname during the 1964 governor's race was "Old Gluefoot" because I was still a shy campaigner. Instead of mingling with crowds, Gummie said, I'd "go off in a corner to talk to some old guy about how to redesign a bridge."

Newsweek's "Nixon and the Veepstakes" article was creating the biggest buzz. I was included in the roster of 12 potential running mates. That was heady stuff, though I harbored no illusions I was an actual contender. The bulk of the article detailed Reagan's whirlwind trip through the South. It claimed he had yanked about 30 votes away from Nixon, who had a "Southern Strategy" of his own. Rockefeller maintained that his own efforts, coupled with Reagan's, left Nixon about a hundred votes short of a first-ballot majority. Uncommitted delegates were wined and dined all evening by each camp.

Monday afternoon, I roamed through the hall and found, to my dismay, that from many areas it was difficult to hear the speaker. That confirmed my decision to speak primarily to the television audience. I wanted to reach the maximum audience back home, so we worked with the convention committee to have the keynote address set for 9 to 10 p.m. Eastern Time, 6 to 7 on the West Coast.

When the evening session convened, it was apparent that the committee had overloaded the schedule. We heard first from President Eisenhower, speaking from Walter Reed Hospital where he was recuperating from yet another heart attack. Ike received a heartfelt ovation. A raft of pro-forma welcoming speeches by the GOP chairman, assistant chairman and the convention's temporary chairman droned on for 40 minutes.

As Barry Goldwater strode to the podium, the bored auditorium erupted. And when he lit into the Johnson Administration, chopping the air with his right hand, they cheered their lungs out. Up next was New York Mayor John Lindsay, tall, good-looking, unapologetically liberal. Viewed as a vice-presidential contender, Lindsay had been deputized to introduce me. By now it was nearly 11 p.m. I listened with growing frustration as Lindsay spoke for 20 minutes in words that virtually paralleled my keynote address, particularly on the divisiveness of Vietnam. He finally concluded with a nice

I take the rostrum at Miami Beach in 1968. *Evans Family Collection*

introduction. As I stepped forward into the spotlight and waited for the applause to subside, I had the disconcerting experience of seeing some delegates and spectators leaving the hall. But it was still prime time back home. And I had a lot to say about the sad state of America and our chances in November:

> In a very real sense, this is the Republican hour. Today, as never before, the nation demands new leadership; the fresh breeze of new energy; a full and honest assessment of national goals; a new direction for its government, and a new hope for its citizens.
>
> We are frustrated by the fourth most costly war in our history—a war in which we spend $1 million every 20 minutes; a war which under the present administration we have not won in Saigon, cannot negotiate in Paris and will not explain to the American people. But we are even more burdened by the crisis in the main streets of America—a crisis of violence and stolen hope; a crisis of lawlessness and injustice; an impulsive reckless dissatisfaction with what we are and a desperate outcry for what we could be once again.
>
> Above all, we are now witness to the disintegration of the old order. Our system of welfare, so long promoted as a cure for social ills, has eliminated nothing, with the possible exception of pride and incentive and human dignity. The increasing dominance of the federal government has accomplished little except the destruction of local initiative. The steady erosion of our cities has left us a legacy of physical decay and human misery.
>
> In this process we have robbed the nation of its great resource of individual initiative and public responsibility. We have become creatures of the system instead of the engineers of progress. We are a nation muscle-bound by its power, frustrated by the indecision of its leadership and fragmented by its great differences.
>
> It is from this point that the Republican Party must now proceed. For it is leadership, not the fundamental strength of this country, that is at issue. We must be where the action is.

It was obvious to me that many delegates were straining to hear my words. So I kept reminding myself that I needed to reach the millions watching on TV. Lindsay may have stolen some of my thunder, but I wasn't about to miss my opportunity to italicize the fact that Vietnam was stealing from us the opportunity to create a more just society in America:

> We have stood for 20 years in defense of the free world. We have given as no other nation to the securing of world order and the pursuit of human progress. And for that we have paid a heavy price on the ledger of neglect. Not neglect in terms of ignorance but neglect in terms of priorities. This does not mean that the United States should abandon its international commitments. ... To have entered the war by the path of error does not mean we can leave through the door of default. But it does mean that the first priority of the United States is the resolution of our own internal

conflict—the recognition that if we can't unite our own nation we can't preserve the hope of others. It is time now to reach inward—to reach down and touch the troubled spirit of America.

That line generated rousing applause. Heartened, I turned to the party's challenge and "a new agenda" focused on minorities, the poor and our youth:

The problems of environment, of congestion, of urban decay and rural stagnation did not suddenly occur. They are the residue of years—even of decades—in which we devoted too much of ourselves to size and quantity and too little to shape and quality.

They are the residue of years in which we believed that welfare was a substitute for pride and that public charity could replace individual opportunity. But Black America and poor America are teaching us a new language—the language of participation. They say, "Let us share in your prosperity. Let us have not another generation of servitude but a new generation of opportunity." And in this process we are being reminded of something we very nearly forgot: the nobility of the American dream. There is no place in that dream for a closed society, for a system that denies opportunity because of race, or the accident of birth or geography or the misfortune of a family.

For each of our youth who has dropped out, there are a hundred more who have stayed in; some radical, some demanding, some searching, some hoping—but all concerned. To break that spirit would be to bankrupt our future. These are not the pleadings of a weak and useless generation; they are the strong voices of a generation, which—given a chance—can lead America to a new unity, a new purpose and a new prosperity.

For our direction and our leadership we must turn, not alone to government, but to a new partnership; a partnership of government, private enterprise, and the individual citizen. …The problems of urban growth and rural stagnation; the need for low-cost housing, for restoring our central cities, for creating new communities, for retraining the unemployed—these needs are not apart from private enterprise. They are its newest and perhaps most significant challenge. Government can establish a direction, but it can't construct the solutions of the next three decades. Private enterprise and free labor can build, but they can't write and administer the laws that create profit opportunities and business incentives.

The challenge to the Republican Party lies within the problems of America, not outside of them. It lies in the prevention of wars and not their prosecution; in the advancement of man and not the destruction of mankind. It lies in the ghetto just as surely as the suburbs. In the factories just as clearly as on the farms. In the hearts of all our people and their great and growing aspirations. The protest, the defiance of authority, the violence in the streets are more than isolated attacks upon the established order; they are the symptoms of the need for change and for a redefinition of what this country stands for and where it is going. This opportunity now rests with the Republican Party. ...Let us unite to rally a great party in the cause of a great nation—to seek progress with victories; to find not a way out, but a way forward.

I'm proud of that speech. I think it is the best of my career. Re-reading it today, I am struck by the sad fact that it is still so relevant. I believe that in 1968 I offered a genuine prescription to actually make America great again—in contrast to the polarizing "hog calling" and dog-whistle rhetoric we Republicans heard a half century later.

The applause at the end of my remarks was generous but muted. It was almost midnight. The delegates had been listening to speech-making for more than six hours.

THE PRESS REACTION the next day was decidedly mixed. Many newspapers commented on the inattention of the audience and said I was too soft on the Democrats. Others declared it one of the most important keynotes of recent history. It seemed to me that response to the speech depended on whether the observer was paying attention to the audience or to the speaker.

The Chicago Tribune, house organ for the unreconstructed Taft wing of the party, dismissed my speech as "flat and without passion" and declared that "everyone" knew I was a "liberal placed in his slot to give balance to the program." Gummie Johnson reminded us that *The Tribune's* place in the dubious achievements hall of fame had been cemented 20 years earlier by its "Dewey defeats Truman" headline.

The Miami Herald, covering the convention with a platoon of reporters and photographers, observed, "When Gov. Evans finished at 11:24 p.m. any hopes he might have had for a vice presidential nomination were also finished. Evans had issued a call for the party to look to the future … and the party faithful ignored him."

The Washington Post's editorial writers were more circumspect, saying my speech "afforded a sort of key to the convention—in three distinct respects. For one thing, it was singularly free from the flatulence and the stem-winding rhetoric that has seemed so inescapably a characteristic of this peculiar art form. Second, he wasted little time lambasting the opposition or exalting his fellow Republicans; on the contrary, he dealt with the real and immediate social problems, exhorting his party to 'rise to the challenge created by the winds of a new direction.' That kind of talk hasn't been heard in Republican conventions since Teddy Roosevelt. Third, the delegates seemed almost completely to ignore him."

Being compared to Teddy Roosevelt, one of my political heroes, was a thrill. And what's not to like about a review that includes the line "singularly free from flatulence"?

Ralph McGill, the legendary anti-segregationist publisher of the *Atlanta Constitution*, called my speech "a magnificent address, but a majority of the convention's delegates had ears only for the Nixon mind and strategy. One of the small straws that indicated the direction in which the convention wind would blow came on the day before the first gavel fell. A Nixon emissary showed up at a Southern delegation caucus with the assurance that Mr. Nixon would not select a vice presidential candidate who would, in any sense, offend Southern sensibilities."

McGill's political antennae rarely failed him. Yet few of us, perhaps even McGill, suspected that Nixon's choice—calculated to not offend those sensibilities—would be such a shocker.

James J. Kilpatrick, the nationally known conservative commentator, gave me an even-handed review: "Gov. Evans, from whom much had been feared, proved that much could be delivered. Like the platform, his keynote address, dwelt upon free enterprise and individual opportunity. He bore down, in the old tradition, upon the 'help yourself society' and denounced the 'increasing dominance of the federal government.' It wasn't what you would call pure Goldwater, but it wasn't far from vintage Ike."

"Vintage Ike" suited me just fine.

IT WAS ALMOST 1 A.M. when we finally returned to our hotel, but I met with my team to discuss reaction to the speech—but more importantly my upcoming press conference. After only a few hours of sleep, I would announce which presidential candidate I was backing. They urged me to endorse Nixon, the candidate supported by most of our fractious state delegation. The first ballot was going to be close, but Nixon was sure to prevail, they all said. Besides, I was in what shaped up as a tight race for re-election. Backing Nixon could help solidify the party. Tired though I was, I listened intently before summing up my feelings: "I didn't ask you who would receive the nomination. *I asked who you thought would be the best president?* I want to support the person I think would be the best president." That was Nelson Rockefeller. For all of his "Tricky Dick" dark side, I also admired Nixon's intellect and foreign policy expertise.

The next morning, to Rocky's delight and the dismay of my advisers, I announced my support for Rockefeller at a press conference that drew more than 800 onlookers. Though I knew Rocky had little chance of being nominated, I wanted to demonstrate my respect for his qualities as a leader. With the clarity of hindsight and history, I think I was right, but the choice created temporary consternation within our state Republican Party organization. Reagan, the darling of our conservative bloc, had announced his last-minute decision to actively seek the nomination, while Governor Agnew—finger to the wind—was renouncing his favorite son role to endorse Nixon.

The GOP philosophical schism in Washington state was bound up in my ongoing struggle with doctrinaire conservatives headed by King County GOP Chairman Ken Rogstad. King, Pierce, Spokane and Snohomish, the state's four most populous counties, were in conservative hands when the delegate-choosing process for the 1968 national convention began. Bill Boeing Jr., a Rogstad ally, was Reagan's ex-officio state chairman, hoping that the California governor would make an all-out bid for the nomination. That spring, the King County GOP Convention had made its antipathy for me crystal clear by calling for an amendment to the Washington State Constitution prohibiting a state income tax. Gummie Johnson countered shrewdly, rallying our supporters to rewrite the delegate allocation formula to reduce the strength of the big four counties. Rogstad, realizing he had been out-maneuvered, cried foul. When the state GOP convention convened in Seattle in June, the conservatives claimed we had "stolen control" and threatened to walk out.

With Reagan on the fence and the conservatives thwarted, Nixon was the clear choice of the 24-member Washington State Delegation selected for Miami Beach. The real battle was now for the delegation's second choice. If Nixon fell short of a first-ballot majority, all bets might be off. Rogstad and Frances Cooper, the hard-nosed state GOP national committeewoman, wanted a delegation ready to switch to Reagan. They also suspected that if Nixon faltered, I would prod the delegation to back Rockefeller.

Mad as hell at losing the delegate-seating battle in the credentials committee, Rogstad and his allies had considered holding a "rump" convention to elect their own slate of delegates and carry their challenge all the way to Miami. They decided instead not to bolt. "That way they could at least send six Reagan delegates to Miami Beach from the two congressional districts located primarily within King County."*

WHEN THE NATIONAL CONVENTION balloting began at 1:17 a.m. on August 8, 1968, the three contenders "personified the evolving Republican Party," James Cannon, a veteran reporter and White House aide, wrote: There was Richard Milhous Nixon, "the heir to the old order." Nelson Rockefeller, "the symbol of the once dominant, almost extinct East Coast Republican establishment," and Ronald Reagan, the once washed up matinee idol who had become "the rising star of the new order—a small but soon-to-proliferate cadre of conservative Republicans."

I was a man in the middle with deeply mixed emotions. The "stop Nixon" movement, waged from both the right and the left, faltered because Nixon had "assiduously collected and banked the most delegates" during his comeback from the depths of defeat. The Reaganites unsuccessfully lobbied the convention chairman, Michigan Congressman Jerry Ford, to delay the first ballot until the next day due to the lateness of the hour.

As the roll-call of the states advanced, it was apparent that Nixon's Southern strategy was a winner. Even though most Southerners loved Reagan, they had committed to Nixon. When Washington was called, I reported 15 votes for Nixon, six for Reagan and three for Rockefeller, including me. Wisconsin's 30 votes put Nixon over the top, giving him three votes more than the 667 he needed. Rocky finished with 277, Reagan 182.

Nixon's campaign slogan was "Bring Us Together." Instead, he would tear us farther apart, though that hardly seemed possible in the tragic summer of '68. I have often pondered what Richard Milhous Nixon might have accomplished if his festering childhood resentments and paranoid demons could have been subdued by advisers with the integrity to help him conjure up his better angels. And what if he had picked as his vice president Mark Hatfield, who understood that Vietnam was a quagmire? Or Jerry Ford, another man of probity blessed with the common touch? The trajectory of national, indeed world history, might have been dramatically different—and surely for the better.

THE MORNING AFTER Nixon clinched the nomination, our delegation met in caucus. I was asked if I thought I had been left standing at the station when the train pulled out because of my endorsement of Rockefeller. Laughing, I said, "I ran down to the next city and got on board. We're all going to be in the same place—Washington, D.C.—in January." The delegation applauded, Rogstad smiling thinly.

From a glassed-in booth high above the convention floor, I appeared on CBS' highly rated *Capital Cloak Room* the next morning. During the middle of the interview with Daniel Schorr, Neil McReynolds, my press secretary, held a sign against the window: "It's Agnew." I was astonished—so

---

* In the Summer 2016 issue of *Columbia* magazine, historian Gene Kopelson analyzed that "Decade of Turmoil" between liberal and conservative Repbulicans in Washington state.

was Schorr—since Agnew had not been mentioned prominently as a possible running mate for Nixon. Agnew seemed like an affable, yet opportunistic fellow. He had been governor of Maryland for just over 18 months. It was later that we discovered Ralph McGill's sources were spot on. Wily old Senator Strom Thurmond, the Dixiecrat candidate for president in 1948, had informed Nixon the litmus test was this: "If we support your candidacy, will you promise us a vice president acceptable to the South?" Agnew was an acceptable mediocrity who would in time prove to be a bombastic, hypocritical "common extortionist," as Slade Gorton later put it so well. One thing was for sure: Even if I had strongly supported Nixon there was no chance he would have picked me as a running mate, despite his declarations early on that I was a contender. Hatfield, likewise, as another strong supporter of civil rights, would have been anathema to the South. I confess, however, that in the next few years as the Nixon administration crashed and burned, my mind sometimes played its own what-if game. Hatfield did too.

As we left Miami Beach, and flew home I reflected on Cinderella, whose fairy-tale evening ended at the stroke of midnight when her magical horse-drawn coach turned back into a pumpkin. The intensity, excitement and celebrity of my prominent role at the 1968 Republican National Convention were abruptly over. I faced a fierce campaign for re-election.

When the Democrats convened their convention in Chicago three weeks later, fear and loathing erupted on prime-time TV. Mayor Daley allowed his baton-wielding police to savagely attack antiwar protesters. Poor Hubert Humphrey, an honorable man dogged by his loyalty to LBJ and the ghost of Robert F. Kennedy, had bigger problems than I.

28
THE ACTION TEAM

Sam Reed and Chris Bayley, two of the brightest young guys I'd ever met, launched a political action movement in 1968 that harnessed the restless energy of a new generation of moderate Republicans. They were frustrated by Vietnam and passionate about civil rights. "Action for Washington" staked out a big tent approach. "We didn't care if you were a Republican, Democrat or Independent," Reed remembers, "but most of us considered ourselves 'Dan Evans Republicans.'"

Sam Sumner Reed, the grandson of Wenatchee's leading lawyer, became executive director of my Urban Affairs Council in 1967. He was 27 years old. Christopher T. Bayley, 29, was a descendant of one of Seattle's most respected old-line families. He arrived back home from Harvard in 1966 and landed at Perkins Coie, a top Seattle law firm. Bayley had extensive contacts among King County's young reformers, not to mention large donors. Reed had a network of energetic young Republicans on campuses around the state.

One of Reed's first assignments when he joined my staff as an intern was to work with Secretary of State Lud Kramer, House GOP leader Slade Gorton and Seattle civic activist Jim Ellis to draft an urban affairs report. When Reed met Pasco City Councilman Art Fletcher, he saw a rising star. After moving to the Tri-Cities to work at the Hanford nuclear site, the former NFL player organized a community self-help program in predominantly Black East Pasco.

Action for Washington quickly attracted more than 2,500 idealistic young people from around the state. The group's leadership included Dale Foreman, Jim Waldo, Steve Excell, John Giese, Gary Smith and two Young Republican stalwarts from Hoquiam, H. Stuart Elway and Jack Durney.

One of the volunteers was a UW dropout named Ted Bundy, who attended the 1968 GOP National Convention as a Rockefeller supporter. Bundy served as Art Fletcher's driver during the 1968 campaign and went on to volunteer with my third-term campaign in 1972. I can't recall ever meeting the man who in 1975 was revealed to be one of the most horrific serial killers in American history. People have written that Bundy and I were "so close" that I wrote a letter endorsing his application for law school and that he babysat one of our sons. It's total malarkey.

THOUGH POLLS INDICATED Nixon was leading Humphrey nationally, they also forecast a Democratic trend in our state. Regardless of which Democrat emerged from the primary—O'Connell or Durkan—I was facing a tough race.

Kramer's road to a second term as secretary of state looked easier, but Gorton was in a tight race for attorney general. Fletcher, whom we recruited to run for lieutenant governor, was in uncharted waters as a credible African-American candidate for statewide office.

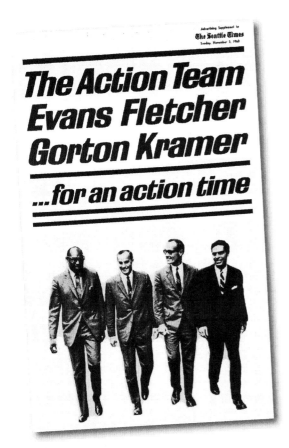

A full-page "Action Team" ad from the 1968 campaign. Our GOP ticket also featured Art Fletcher for Lt. Governor, Slade Gorton for Attorney General, and Lud Kramer for re-election as Secretary of State. *Washington State Archives*

The Reed-Bayley masterstroke was to create the first, and to date only, effective party ticket in Washington state history. They dubbed us "The Action Team for an action time." Each flier, full-page ad and TV spot featured our foursome, "striding forward side by side with clean-cut confidence." While some of the verbiage struck me as over the top, the ads were a compelling departure from the old grip-and-grin stuff that still dominated political advertising, especially in newspapers. They billed me as "Arrow-straight, disciplined, combining the vigor of youth with the wisdom of experience." Gorton was "The Lawyer with a Cause—young, tough, with a mind like a steel trap" and a deep concern for making Washington "safe and sane." Kramer was "The Get Things-Done Guy" who had been "where the action is," from the Seattle City Council to the state Capitol. Art Fletcher, 43, was "The Man With a Plan—tall, fluent, with a grasp of problems as broad as his hands"—an ex-pro football player with two college degrees who could "transform the office of lieutenant governor just as he transformed the ghetto of Pasco."

IN LATE JULY, on an intense campaign swing through Western Washington, I received an urgent phone call from Harold "Hi" Tollefson, a former mayor of Tacoma and brother of former longtime congressman Thor Tollefson. He said we needed to talk—privately—when I arrived in Tacoma. I interrupted my schedule to find out what was up. Tollefson informed me there was something very strange about John O'Connell's personal finances, especially for an attorney general. Tollefson said he had no proof and could not be specific but warned me to be alert. It was all very mysterious. I reported the conversation to Jim Dolliver and promptly forgot about it.

During the next 35 days, I participated in 133 events in 46 communities. One typical overnight venture in late August began with an Action for Washington breakfast in Spokane. I raced to a rented helicopter and flew to Newport on the Idaho border, where I toured Main Street with my local campaign manager, ending up at a popular café to greet a coffee group. I had long since learned that these were vital stops in small towns. Every community had a group that gathered daily to share gossip and friendship. News that the governor had dropped by quickly spread around town.

This campaign was a lot tougher than 1964 when I was running full time with no other official responsibilities. Now it was just as important to visit the entire state, yet I also was responsible for governing. While I was confident we were well ahead, that was no excuse for relaxing. Nancy was an enormously important asset and I wanted her to join me on most campaign activities. But now we had three young sons who were old enough to know what was happening and young enough to be dismayed by our absence. I finally had a tough talk with our campaign committee. I wrenched most Sundays out of the campaign schedule and insisted on time to build the next biennial budget.

MY BREAKFAST ON AUGUST 21, 1968, was rudely interrupted by a huge headline on the front page of the *Seattle Post-Intelligencer*: "PINBALL KING IS TAILED TO HOME OF PROSECUTOR." Hearst's morning daily and KING Broadcasting's sophisticated new *Seattle* magazine had teamed up to investigate Seattle's longstanding "tolerance" policy toward gambling. The probe focused on the relationship between King County Prosecutor Charles O. Carroll and Ben Cichy, an official with the King County pinball operators' coalition. The group had held the master license for pinball operations in the county since 1942, with annual revenues estimated at $5 million. The *P-I's* story, complete with surveillance photos, asserted that Cichy visited Carroll's home monthly. "What could possibly be the nature of such liaison between men of such diverse callings, a prosecutor and a pillar of the pinball fellowship?" the *P-I* wondered. Carroll said he was "too busy" to discuss the issue.

Seattle magazine called for the removal of the county prosecutor. *Washington State Archives*

As for his friendship with Cichy, Carroll kept stonewalling, even when KING-TV offered air time for a rebuttal. The exposé ballooned into a distraction that affected me both as campaigner and governor.

"Chuck" Carroll, a legendary halfback for the University of Washington in the late 1920s, was in his 20th year as prosecutor. He was King County's "Mr. Republican," with Bill Boeing Jr. as an ally. Now, however, he was facing a withering media attack, and his hold on courthouse patronage was being challenged by reformers like John Spellman, the new Republican county commissioner. Carroll and the King County GOP chairman, my nemesis Ken Rogstad, were especially intent on derailing Gorton's campaign for attorney general. There was no telling what sort of mischief someone so bright and independent could unleash, they feared. I was well aware of Carroll's back-stage antipathy for me and the whole "Evans crowd," yet whenever we met he was cordial.

When the *P-I's* story hit the news-stands, O'Connell and Durkan jumped into the act, portraying all Republicans as birds of a feather. Senator Durkan, who headed a legislative interim committee, vowed to hold hearings. Attorney General O'Connell resolved to launch "a full-scale investigation into strong suggestions of organized vice in King County." However, under state law, he needed my approval. I was determined to keep a King County brouhaha out of the race for governor. The *Post-Intelligencer* prodded me to conduct my own investigation. I proposed that any pertinent material in the hands of the newspaper, O'Connell or Durkan be given to King County's senior Superior Court judge, who could determine if a Grand Jury should be called.

Absent hard evidence of cronyism, I saw the case against Carroll as largely innuendo. Clearly, he was haughty and indiscreet—an old-school power broker. But was he really taking payoffs? I wanted facts. I met with him twice—the second time at his home at his invitation. He offered to show me his financial records. It was an uncomfortable session for me. Although Carroll was extremely candid and displayed his extensive banking and investment reports, I felt like a financial voyeur. Carroll said Cichy was merely a longtime friend, and indignantly denied the media's inference that he was in the pinball operators' pocket. I found no clear evidence he was on the take. All the numbers seemed to match up with his income from his county salary and inheritances. I strongly suggested he issue a public statement that in my view could have muted the controversy. Carroll wouldn't do it, figuring he could ride it out. But his reputation was badly tarnished. (When he ran for re-election in 1970, he was defeated in the Republican primary by Chris Bayley.) O'Connell, meantime, balked at sharing his information with a judge, saying a Grand Jury would be premature. Durkan's hearings never got off the ground.

WITH ALBERT F. CANWELL, the old red-baiter from Spokane, as my token opposition in the Republican primary—he maintained I was "actually a socialist"—I was eager to see who my real opponent would be.

In a surprisingly close contest, O'Connell outpolled Durkan. I was somewhat relieved. Durkan understood the intricacies of state government and budgeting far better than O'Connell. In John J. O'Connell, however, I was now facing an experienced campaigner. The three-term attorney general was an accomplished public speaker who worked crowds with Irish wit. Gorton reminded us that O'Connell could point with legitimate pride to the creation of an aggressive Consumer Protection Division in the AG's office. Nevertheless, polls taken before the primary had me with a strong lead over O'Connell. I was pleased with the size of my

Art Fletcher and I celebrate our primary election victories in 1968. *Washington State Archives*

vote in the primary (43.4 percent), which ratified the poll results. The Democrats had outpolled me, but that was no surprise. All the action was on their side in an open primary.

The entire "Action Team" advanced to the general election. Art Fletcher handily outpolled Bill Muncey, the famous Gold Cup hydroplane racer, to win the GOP nomination for lieutenant governor against the two-term incumbent, Johnny Cherberg. For attorney general, Gorton would face

John G. McCutcheon, an old-guard Democrat from Tacoma, who squeaked past longtime state legislator Fred Dore and three other credible challengers. We had regarded Dore as a far more dangerous opponent. Lud Kramer, meantime, was renominated for secretary of state in a landslide.

THE CONVENTIONAL WISDOM is that an incumbent—particularly one with a substantial lead—should avoid debates. "They're unpredictable and dangerous," Dolliver and others warned. "Don't do it." I plowed ahead, confident in my knowledge of state government. I also believe debates offer voters a real opportunity to size up candidates head to head. By 1968, TV's ability to bring the news into everyone's front room was a game changer, witness the coverage of Vietnam and the horror-show Democratic National Convention.

In a press conference a week after the primary, I said O'Connell's recent statements about my "half-baked" tax reform plan, "failed environmental agenda" and alleged coziness with Carroll lacked any semblance of substance. "The easiest and best and most direct way to bring this to the attention of the people is to meet with him face-to-face," I told reporters, noting that I had already contacted the state's network affiliates.

O'Connell happily agreed. The first of three debates was sponsored by KOMO-TV, with the station's news staff as moderators. For openers, I said the paramount issue in the campaign was whether I was living up to the promises I'd made in 1964. I said I was proud of what we had achieved—a dynamic economy, new initiatives to promote educational excellence, improve transportation, reduce pollution, expand recreation and reform mental health and mental retardation services. "It's a new concept of government—a concept that says the problems of Washington are not in Olympia. The problems of this state and the challenges of this state are in its local communities, its cities, its counties and its farms."

O'Connell responded forcefully, dismissing my "so-called Blueprint" as smoke and mirrors. "The trick of this administration is to sloganize; to coin words; to study us to death. We have government by press agent. And the truth is we have made no substantial progress in the financing of our state government, in the control of our environment [or in combatting] crime, civil disorders and air and water pollution. None! I say we can't stand another four years of doing business at the same counter."

O'Connell was asked how he would pay for his own wide-ranging program. "We could make a tremendous effort to clean up the dirty water of Puget Sound right now without any massive expenditure of funds on the part of state government," he insisted as a for-instance. "I'm not sure that we need any more money from new taxes in the next biennium."

"Not sure" struck me as especially lame. "I just wonder how many of the programs and new ideas carried out in the past four years you would turn away from. Which teachers' salaries you would cut back? Which new programs for our mentally retarded you would eliminate? Which parts of our old-age assistance you would cut back? …The important thing is that in four years we have done precisely what I said we could do and would do in office, and that was to change an 18-year-old general fund deficit that prevented us from really accomplishing things to a good fiscal situation—a program where today we are in the black."

O'Connell stumbled badly in response to a question regarding welfare-law reforms designed to encourage recipients to seek work. "Of course, most of the money we get in our state to defray the public assistance costs, or welfare costs, comes from Uncle Sam. ... I don't think welfare, if I can use that term, is a serious problem in the state."

I pounced. "The federal government doesn't handle most of our public assistance problem. Every dollar that comes from the federal government to this state is matched by a state dollar. But the important thing is that all the money comes from the taxpayers, and it would be foolish in the extreme for anyone to believe welfare abuse isn't really a serious problem. ..."

O'Connell shrugged it off.

The Seattle Times headlined its story "Evans demolishes O'Connell on first TV debate." Ross Cunningham, the newspaper's agile political editor—he liked me *and* his old friend Chuck Carroll—wrote: "When the timekeeper rang finish to the first of the gubernatorial election television debates Friday night, the challenger looked like a mauled boxer who had been saved by the bell."

The next round took a sensational turn. In a front page story headlined "O'Connell queried on Vegas check," *The Times'* ace investigative reporters, John Wilson and Marshall Wilson, reported that the attorney general had a $10,000 line of credit at a Las Vegas hotel in 1965. Gambling is legal in Las Vegas, of course, as a livid O'Connell immediately took pains to point out. But $10,000 was far from penny-ante stuff. To many, the revelation suggested that the vice-fighting attorney general had suspect proclivities. Also, there was "the innuendo that Vegas gamblers could do O'Connell favors by forgiving debts and persuading hotel staff to cover up embarrassing stories."

O'Connell issued a 6,000-word "white paper" declaring that my campaign had ferreted out his visits to Vegas, leaked the news to *The Times*, which was already "transparently" in my corner, and drummed up a bogus scandal in an attempt to derail his probe of vice in Seattle and defeat his bid for governor.

We had known for years that O'Connell liked to gamble, just not for such high stakes. Several weeks before the primary, we received an anonymous package containing a smudged photocopy of a $10,000 line of credit check. Dolliver and I examined the virtually unreadable document. It was O'Connell's signature, all right. But since we had no additional information, we locked it in the office safe. The photocopy *The Times* received was much clearer. They didn't get it from us. When the Wilsons asked to see ours, we showed them what we had received. We had no advance knowledge of the article. O'Connell scoffed, saying "Straight Arrow" Evans loved low blows. "I have heard this was in the offing. It is a political gambit on the part of the GOP's state chairman and the governor."

I told Gummie Johnson to release a statewide poll we had just received from Central Surveys. It showed me leading O'Connell 52-37 with 11 percent undecided. We didn't need a scandal to seal the deal. In fact, a tactic like that would have been risky. Why would we give O'Connell an opportunity to tar us as playing dirty-tricks and generate a backlash?

Next, *The Times* revealed that another check, this one for $12,625, had been cashed by O'Connell at the Hotel Tropicana. The credit manager there told reporters O'Connell "won the money down the street." The next day he reversed himself, saying he didn't know O'Connell. But perhaps he misremembered, he added, because he had taken medication prior to entering the hospital to have some teeth removed. It was obvious that the casino operators in Las Vegas were determined to put a lid on this story.

I WON A SECOND TERM with nearly 55 percent of the vote, carrying 29 of the state's 39 counties, including King by nearly 93,000 votes. (How times have changed.) Spokane, Nancy's home town, gave me a 13,000-vote victory. We all had a laugh at my puny 600-vote margin in Lewis County, a conservative stronghold. To them I was a Republican in name only.

On election night, Kramer was on his way to a 64 percent landslide, while Fletcher and Gorton were running very close races. We had cultivated the absentees, and I began to think Action for Washington might score a clean sweep. When all the ballots were tallied nine days later, Slade had won the race for attorney general by just over 5,000 votes out of 1.2 million cast. Sadly, Fletcher came up short. After leading through the early returns, he lost to Cherberg by 48,000 votes. Tellingly, the Democratic incumbent carried King by 2,100 votes, while Kramer, Gorton and I won handily in the state's most populous county. Cherberg also won conservative Lewis County. Race clearly mattered in the race for lieutenant governor. I was enormously disappointed. I thought Fletcher was clearly the best candidate and expected he would be a close partner in the coming administration. We were appalled when we discovered that a right-wing Yakima weekly backing George Wallace for president had produced a racist smear against Fletcher. The flier was circulated in working-class white neighborhoods during the closing days of the campaign.

In the days immediately after the election, I was inundated with congratulations, but deeply dismayed by comments I heard from a number of enthusiastic, mostly older supporters. They would pull me aside and say, "Governor, I just couldn't vote for Art Fletcher because I was afraid of what might happen to you." I didn't fully grasp the message until a gentle, elderly woman said, "If Mr. Fletcher was lieutenant governor, radicals might assassinate you to get a Negro governor." I was stunned, saddened and furious that the tentacles of discrimination, some overt, some unknowing, still gripped Washington state. Nearly 97,000 Washingtonians were among the 10 million Americans who cast their votes for George Wallace in 1968. I'm confident that if Art Fletcher had been elected lieutenant governor he would have succeeded me as governor, perhaps in 1977. In any case, sooner rather than later.

Happily, Fletcher's political career was far from over. President-elect Nixon named him Assistant Secretary of Labor. He went on to serve in the Ford and George H.W. Bush administrations and became known as the "father of affirmative action." Fletcher headed the U.S. Commission on Civil Rights, and as president of the United Negro College Fund helped craft the wonderful phrase "A mind is a terrible thing to waste." Those were historic achievements. Yet I wish Washington could have been the first state in the union since Reconstruction to elect an African-American governor. That would have been a proud boast. I'm confident Fletcher would have been a first-rate governor.

I WAS PLEASED that the GOP had scored a net gain of five statehouses. Thirty of the 50 states, including most of the 10 most populous, would have Republican administrations. Our Republican Governors' Campaign Committee was now an effective force. I was proud of what we had accomplished and looked forward to working with my new colleagues.

Nationally, for only the second time in 40 years we had elected a new Republican president. But Nixon had won only 43.4 percent of the vote. He knew he needed to create an aura of bipartisanship, starting with his cabinet. He wanted Henry M. Jackson as his Secretary of Defense. Scoop's defense and foreign policy credentials were impeccable. He had admirers on both sides of the aisle. Naming him to the cabinet might also shrewdly pre-empt having Scoop as an opponent in 1972. So I wasn't surprised when I received a post-election call from John Ehrlichman, the newly appointed White House counsel. John was a friend. After graduating from Stanford Law School in 1951, he had developed a reputation as one of Seattle's leading land-use lawyers. He was active in the Municipal League and joined our campaigns to clean up Lake Washington and modernize King County government. After we exchanged congratulations, Ehrlichman got right down to business:

"If it were a condition of Scoop accepting the appointment that you appoint a Democrat to succeed him in the Senate, would you do it?"

"Well, I would consider anything to help the president, but I hope you never have to agree to that as a condition."

At a press conference a few days later I was on the hot seat, with Adele Ferguson trying to pin me down:

"Did you agree to appoint a Democrat if Senator Jackson became Secretary of Defense?"

"It didn't get that far. …My response was that I would do anything I could to help the new president get the kind of cabinet he wanted."

"The Associated Press said you 'reluctantly agreed to name a Democrat to Senator Jackson's position.' Are they just making that up, governor?"

"I would do anything I could to help him achieve the kind of cabinet he wanted. … It did not come right down to an actual question to do that."

"Would you be in trouble with the Republicans if you appoint a Democrat?" Mike Flynn of United Press International asked.

"I would say right now, if that were a requirement, certainly it would be difficult. I would be in trouble with the Republicans, but I might say it wouldn't be the first time."

The next day, to my immense relief, Nixon appointed Congressman Mel Laird as Secretary of Defense.*

FOR THEIR YEAR-END EDITIONS, the Hearst Corporation's newspapers asked me to join Senator Ted Kennedy, San Francisco Mayor Joseph Alioto and Cleveland Mayor Carl Stokes to comment on the most serious problems facing the new Nixon administration and the nation. I was asked to write about "The Outlook for States." It was another opportunity to speak nationally, and I was eager to advocate a new partnership between the states and the federal government. Chafing under the rigidity of federal mandates, activist governors like me were proposing new concepts. "None of this means we should hoist the tired and tattered banner of states' rights," I wrote. "Usually those who promote this phrase are more interested in inactivity on the part of state government than in asserting any rights of the states. It does mean, however, that if the federal system is to survive and if government is to serve the people, all governmental resources must be applied to the solution of the problems of our country." I proposed replacing many of the federal single-purpose categorical grants with block grants for broad general purposes or general revenue sharing without any mandates. "By using block grants and by giving states the direct use of some federal tax sources we not

---

* In his biography of Henry M. Jackson, Robert G. Kaufman asserts that I "finally relented" to naming a Democrat to Scoop's Senate seat if he joined the Nixon cabinet, "but not before extracting a quid pro quo from Nixon: he would name Representative Tom Foley, a protégé of Jackson's, to replace him and a Republican to replace Foley." I agreed to no such thing, as I outlined above. Further, it's ridiculous to suggest that a governor can appoint someone to the U.S. House of Representatives.

only allow a better use of resources by the states but also avoid the danger of federal rules that search for the lowest common denominator in their application, rules that often tend to stifle state initiative and do not allow state solutions that may be an improvement on the federal standards."

The column was carried in Hearst newspapers across the country and became an important agenda item at the Republican Governors Conference, which met in Palm Springs that December. There were now 31 Republican governors. They enthusiastically backed "revenue sharing." It was the beginning of a long, difficult campaign to convince Congress and President Nixon to share relatively unrestricted federal revenue with the 50 states.

AT THE END OF THE YEAR I received the report of my Advisory Council on Urban Affairs, headed by Lud Kramer. Its talented staff was led by young Sam Reed. The council brought me nearly 200 recommendations in six areas: Housing, Education, Physical Environment, Health, Employment and the Non-Urban Sector. It recommended a statewide Open Housing law; tax reform to eliminate special school levies; creation of a Department of Transportation, and more relevant high school vocational-technical courses. There were more than 40 recommendations on health that underlined one of my observations in that tumultuous year: "It is still possible in our affluent society to be too young to qualify for Medicare, too poor to afford insurance, too ignorant to ask for help and too sick to care one way or the other." This was the core of a new Blueprint for Progress. More than 40 bills were prepared for the 1969 legislative session.

I met with all our Republican legislators in Yakima in mid-December. We had a solid House majority, 56-43, with experienced leadership. The Democrats still controlled the state Senate, 27-22, but we had gained two seats. It was time to push hard on tax reform. School levies were failing all across the state. Property taxes were soaring and there was no good alternative source of revenue for our overcrowded schools. In the House at least, I sensed a possible breakthrough. Representative Robert Charette, the Aberdeen Democrat I admired, was the House Democrats' organization leader. "As a responsible minority, we can't merely be against things," Bob said. "We must have our own proposals. If we adopt it, we'll have something to counter the Republican proposals." Stu Bledsoe, our Republican floor leader, replied, "When the Democrats come up with their package we'll have the cattle in the ring. Then we can start bidding." Bledsoe, a cattle rancher from Ellensburg, was noted for his pungent remarks. I trusted and admired him, and so did his caucus. I knew we had a rare opportunity to bring a bipartisan tax reform proposal to the voters.

29
TAXING TIMES

I had a mandate and planned to make the most of it. As legislators gathered in Olympia for the 1969 session, Washington was in the third year of an extraordinary economic boom, led by the aviation industry. Boeing's Lunar Orbiter team was helping NASA select landing sites for American astronauts. The new jumbo jet plant at Everett was the largest building in the world. Unemployment statewide was at an all-time low. My old seatmate, Don Eldridge, had been re-elected Speaker of the House. Slade Gorton was now attorney general. Little did I know from this heady vantage point that the year ahead would feature a rising tide of citizen protests on multiple fronts and usher in the worst economic downturn on Puget Sound since the 1930s.

My team prepared an ambitious package of executive-request legislation, highlighted by a new tax reform proposal. Relying heavily on sales taxes, our tax system was—and today remains—

Speaker Eldridge offers congratulations after I take the oath of office for a second term. *Washington State Archives*

one of the most regressive in the nation. The average workaday Washingtonian pays a higher percentage of his or her income on taxes than the well-off. This time I intended to reach out early to Democratic leaders and build bipartisan momentum for another ballot measure. I laid out the challenges we faced in an unprecedented trio of joint-session speeches in the space of eight days, beginning with my second inaugural address.

It had been 12 years since I arrived in the Legislature as the determined grandson of a pioneer legislator. Washington was poised to celebrate the 80th anniversary of statehood. What I knew for certain, I said on January 15, 1969, was that the challenge at hand transcended party politics. Our duty was to protect and enhance the "quality of life" that made Washington so attractive to newcomers and longtime citizens alike—and ensure efficient delivery of taxpayer services, starting with our "paramount duty" under the State Constitution: quality public education. One thought came to mind when I read the speech again for the first time in nearly half a century: I could give whole portions of it today. Judge for yourself:

> Our metropolitan areas are expanding at record rate, and parts of them are deteriorating with equal speed. The land which once seemed inexhaustible is disappearing—some of it consigned forever to the tragedy of perpetual blight.
>
> Our transportation system is threatening to tie itself in a suicidal knot—a system in which our ability to build new freeways is exceeded only by our ability to fill them beyond capacity.
>
> In our cities we are confronting the sometimes visionary, sometimes violent problems of social upheaval. Many are searching for human dignity and equal opportunity under physical conditions which are barely more than adequate and barely less than impossible.
>
> And while our problems have multiplied, we have steadfastly refused to modernize our state government; failed to come to grips with the necessary task of constitutional reform and failed to meet the responsibilities of revising our taxing system.
>
> I pledge to you today that this administration enters the arena with an open mind. There are no closed corridors, no rigid formulas, no backroom agreements—only my commitment and the commitment of this administration that we shall do what is reasonable and what is right.

My Urban Affairs Council had recommended a comprehensive package of legislation to cope with urban challenges. I urged its passage, saying that Forward Thrust, the visionary capital-expenditures program adopted by the citizens of King County, needed to be attempted at the state level. Within the next 60 days, I said I would promote the formation of a broadly-based statewide organization charged with analyzing "the total needs of the state." Its mandate would be to present an action plan by 1970.

It was a huge agenda all around. I ended my inaugural address by announcing I would convene an extraordinary session of the Legislature in January of 1970, regardless of how much we accomplished in the months ahead. It was time for annual sessions. Given the challenges facing the state, I was going to initiate them on a de facto basis. We simply couldn't wait until the issue was placed before the voters. We had reached the point where a Legislature could not deal with 24 months of change in two months of activity every two years. Having been in their shoes, I said I knew what I was asking meant vastly increased legislative responsibilities. I said their salaries should be at least doubled to $600 per month. That line prompted the loudest and most sustained applause of the entire address.

My budget message two days later noted that while I was submitting the largest budget in the state's history, it required no new taxes. The booming state economy created ample new revenue, and when combined with our population growth, meant a small decrease in the per-capita tax burden. But this relatively austere budget offered no promise that we could go on as we were, I said. And the day of reckoning likely would be here by the second year of the biennium. For one thing, inflation was on track to reach 5 percent by 1970. While revenues were up substantially, the appropriations authorized by the Legislature in 1967 had not kept up with the actual increasing costs of government programs, said Don Burrows, former executive director of my Tax Advisory Council. Further, over the past eight years the federal government had systematically shifted the burden of public service programs, notably welfare, back to the states. Many of LBJ's "Great Society" programs were monumental, but the states were paying large portions of the tab. The states needed "block grants" and revenue sharing, I said, as well as a role in national decisions. "But it is both idle and inaccurate to cast all the blame on the federal government. We must get our own house in order. The Legislature—and ultimately the people of Washington—must decide what kind of state they want and how much and by what method they will pay for it."

The follow up was my tax reform message. We had swept tax reform under the rug for decades, adding new burdens to old taxes and taxing what was convenient. "We have worried so long about pleasing the people," I said, "that we have ended up failing to serve them instead." One thing was abundantly clear: The people weren't pleased by their escalating property taxes as school districts with rapidly growing enrollments struggled to meet modern educational demands with an anti-quated tax system. "Special" levies were now essential levies. And taxpayers around the state were in revolt. When levies failed—sometimes repeatedly—everything "extracurricular," including band, sports, field trips and the yearbook class, was in jeopardy, together with counselors, courses not deemed "basic" and educational materials. Drop-out rates were rising. Some schools were threat-ened with loss of accreditation. Higher education, likewise, was struggling. Community college en-rollment had increased by an unprecedented 49.5 percent during the previous two years.

Since the voters had resoundingly rejected income tax proposals five times since 1934, I said it was clear, to me at least, that whatever tax reform plan we put on the ballot had to include iron-clad constitutional limitations—"a specific set of safeguards" to prevent lawmakers from jacking up the rates willy-nilly. I backed the single-rate income tax endorsed by my Tax Advisory Council headed by G. Keith Grim, a former assistant attorney general in the Tax Division. "It can be applied to a broad base," I said. "It is by definition limited. And, above all, it is fair. Not more fair; not less fair—but fair in every sense of the word." I believed a single-rate income tax had at least two other compelling advantages. It would be the least expensive income tax to collect and it wouldn't penalize incentive.

> I am not referring to the very wealthy, who already have high federal income taxes, or the poor, who have little income tax liability. I am referring to the wage earner, the average worker, who by his ability and through the great productivity of our economic system, and, yes, with the help of his labor union, is finally enjoying some small measure of affluence. I fail to see the wisdom of giving him greater affluence on the one hand, only to take it away on the other by imposing higher and higher graduated tax rates.

I called for full funding of basic education by state government, with limits on the amount of voter-approved maintenance and operation levies; elimination of the business and operations tax and lowering the constitutional limit on regular property taxes.

That evening, in a half-hour statewide television broadcast, I urged people to contact their leg-islators without delay. Our ability to function as a quality state government was at stake. "The alternatives of increased sales taxes or increased property taxes bearing no relationship to ultimate tax reform are simply not acceptable."

The most vociferous response came from State Senator Mike McCormack, the Democrat from Richland who headed the Revenue Subcommittee of the Senate Ways and Means Committee. "Neither the Legislature nor the people will accept a flat rate income tax," he declared. "The tax system Evans proposes, with graduation through exemptions, will only encourage people to have more children." Coming from the chairman of the committee where my plan was headed, it was a disquietingly bizarre commentary. I quickly determined that McCormack's view was not shared by many members of his committee or the Senate as a whole.*

We began the biennial legislative dance to find majorities for these complex proposals. It would require a two-thirds majority of the House and Senate to send the constitutional tax reform proposal to the ballot.

IN BETWEEN those addresses to the Legislature, Nancy and I escaped Olympia for three days. Hand-calligraphied invitations to attend Nixon's inaugural were too enticing to ignore. I thought Nixon's most eloquent words were these:

> Greatness comes in simple trappings. The simple things are the ones most needed today if we are to surmount what divides us, and cement what unites us. To lower our voices would be a simple thing.
>
> In these difficult years, America has suffered from a fever of words; from inflated rhetoric that promises more than it can deliver; from angry rhetoric that fans discontents into hatreds; from bombastic rhetoric that postures instead of persuading. We cannot learn from one another until we stop shouting at one another—until we speak quietly enough so that our words can be heard as well as our voices.

I know what you're thinking: Those words would have been equally appropriate coming from Joe Biden on January 20, 2021. If only we could lower our voices and open our minds.

Unfortunately, Nixon's darker impulses won out after some genuinely visionary initiatives. At the time, however, we had high expectations for the first Republican president elected since 1956. And Spiro T. Agnew, if not presidential, seemed benign.

WITH THREE YOUNG SONS, Nancy scheduled a limited number of public engagements. But given her strong support for women's rights, she accepted an invitation to participate in a Women's Day celebration at the University of Washington, never suspecting it would devolve into a raucous event. First, she appeared on a panel with faculty and students. I was proud of Nancy's remarks. Expressing her solidarity with the push for equal rights and equal pay, she stressed that women must be able to argue with facts, figures, and ideas–not just emotions. "There are those students who see wrong in society and work to destroy that society," she said. "They don't offer any alternative. And then there

---

* I was unhappy a year later when McCormack was elected to Congress, defeating our excellent five-term GOP congresswoman, Catherine May of Yakima.

are those who see wrong in society but probe deep into the causes of those wrongs and then propose alternatives. It doesn't take any skill to destroy. It does take skill to build something new."

When a student-led fashion show started, members of the UW chapter of Students for a Democratic Society, a New Left activist group, jumped onto the stage, heckled the audience and put on a skit deriding the garment industry. "You can be pretty as a model if you're as wealthy as the governor's wife," one protester shouted. Robbie Stern, an SDS leader, harangued Nancy in a 15-minute exchange. Finally, Nancy set down her coffee cup and walked away saying, "You don't want to hear the facts. I'm sorry."

Asked about the incident the next day at a news conference, I related that when she arrived home from Seattle, Nancy said, "You're a sissy down here working with the Legislature!" Neither she nor I were prepared for the volume and intensity of the citizen response to the incident. Nancy received scores of letters, applauding her cool and blasting the protesters. Editorial writers and commentators praised her. The shouting in America over the war, racial and gender inequality and the power of "The Establishment" was going to get a lot louder.

ALMOST LOST IN THE DEBATE over budget and taxes was a proposal for a new Court of Appeals. The counties' Superior Courts, our trial courts, had almost doubled in size in the previous decade to handle the problems of our rapidly increasing population. Appeals were now overwhelming the Washington Supreme Court. Justice suffered through increasing delays. A bill to create a new Court of Appeals languished quietly in the State Senate until I received a request for a meeting with two Senate Democrats. William Gissberg, a hard-charging Swede from Snohomish County, was a senior member of the Judiciary Committee. First elected in 1952, Gissberg was respected on both sides of the political aisle. He was joined by Wes Uhlman, the young Seattle lawyer who was now chairman of the Judiciary Committee. Gissberg got right down to business: "We have a choice to make concerning the Court of Appeals bill. Twelve new appellate judges are to be chosen. We can allow them all to be selected at the next election, or allow you to make the initial appointments. We would rather not delay until the next election but we're interested in what kind of appointments you would make if given the opportunity to name all 12." In other words, would a Republican governor jump at the chance to appoint 12 judges of the Republican persuasion?

I didn't hesitate, saying I would depend on the recommendations of the State Bar Association. "But I can assure you I will be fair in the political makeup of these first appointees."

"How many Democrats will you appoint out of these first 12?" Uhlman prodded. Before I could even answer, Gissberg stood up. "Come on, Wes," he said, heading for the door. "I've heard all I need to know." Uhlman was grumbling a bit as they exited my office, but the bill began to rapidly advance.

A month later, I signed the legislation and began the process of selecting 12 new members of the court. We received excellent recommendations from the State Bar Association, suggestions from a variety of professional organizations, and a host of applications from self-starters. I was especially careful in this selection process and interviewed a number of prominent candidates. Eventually, I made my choices from both sides of the political aisle, tilted understandably to Republicans. The new court was established in four panels of three judges. To keep their seats, all were required to run at the next election. I was pleased with the positive editorial commentary about the new court and especially gratified when not one of the 12 judges had an opponent at their first election.

THE STATELY ROW of Japanese Cherry Trees on the Capitol Campus bloomed in mid-April and faded while the legislative session droned on. I spent an increasing amount of time meeting with the leaders of both Houses trying to find the magical two-thirds majority required to pass the constitutional amendment authorizing tax reform. Finally, the main operating budget was passed by an overwhelming vote in both houses, followed by the capital construction budget and the Omnibus Highway bill. Now the focus was on tax reform and everyone seemed to get into the act. Joe Davis, the wily head of the State Labor Council, demanded that the constitutional amendment require a graduated net income tax. He also pushed to have unemployment compensation included in any final agreement.

In a long and intense meeting with legislative leaders, I suggested a compromise. The constitutional amendment would authorize a single-rate income tax but would also contain a provision for an automatic referendum in November 1975, when the people could change it to a graduated net income tax. I also demanded passage of a bill mandating annual general elections so the proposal could be voted on that November.

In a truly bipartisan vote, the Senate by 34 to 15 reached the necessary two-thirds margin. The amendment was quickly sent to the house where there was little debate. When the 84 to 12 vote was announced there was a resounding cheer by the exhausted members. Now the House and Senate negotiated furiously on details of the bill that would implement the constitutional amendment.

The 60th and last day of the special session dawned with a huge unfinished calendar. The House had completed its agenda and waited impatiently for the Senate to act on important legislation. Lobbyists gathered in the Senate gallery, bleary eyed and frustrated. Finally, the Senate passed the annual general elections bill but authorized only two elections, in 1969 and 1975. That clearly would not pass constitutional muster and the House modified it to allow elections every year until 1975. The Senate would not accept the House version and the bill died, delaying a vote on tax reform until November 1970. One senator admitted, "We didn't want this vote in 1969. We wanted it in 1970 when legislators are running for re-election." It was obvious that partisan politics had crawled into what otherwise was a bipartisan accomplishment.

Nancy, strongly pro-choice, closely monitored Joel Pritchard's efforts to pass legislation protecting a woman's right to choose an abortion. A throng of women who supported Joel's Senate bill marched to the Capitol, only to be denied admission to the building by the Senate's sergeant at arms. Outraged, Pritchard contacted Slade Gorton, who ruled that the women could not be barred from the Capitol, only to the Senate Chambers. The abortion bill squeaked through the Senate Rules Committee on an 8-7 vote, but advanced no farther.

Several of my major proposals received serious attention, only to bog down in the down-the-stretch wrangling of a tiring 120-day session, namely creation of a Department of Transportation and a Department of Ecology. I felt sure, however, that we had laid the groundwork for success sometime soon. And they'd be back in less than a year.

The longest legislative session since statehood in 1889 was monumental in that a Republican House and a Democratic Senate had joined in proposing, by a two-thirds vote, an income tax as part of a broad tax reform.

SAVVY LOBBYISTS and many citizen activists well understood that the bills they had shepherded through the legislative process were now on the desk of a governor who had liberally used his line-item veto power during his first term. Practically my entire staff was involved in analyzing the form, content and constitutionality of the several hundred bills passed by the Legislature. Ray Haman, a versatile Seattle lawyer, once again came to Olympia to help my valued legal counsel, Dick Hemstad, plow through the mound of legislation. Even so, I was determined to read every bill in its entirety after I received the staff analysis. Though there were times when my eyes glazed over, I occasionally spotted errors.

One of the bills I signed into law without much fanfare in 1969 had economic consequences beyond my wildest expectations.

When Prohibition was repealed in 1933, the Washington State Legislature enacted a series of laws that amounted to tariffs on California wines. The industry here revolved around a handful of wineries that produced sweet and high-alcohol "fortified" wines. Fast forward to the 1950s. "The booming California wine industry was pushing to enter Washington," wine industry historian Andy Perdue notes, "even threatening to block Washington apples if California wines weren't let into the state." The restrictions left Washington's wines mired in mediocrity. Slade Gorton and I had lobbied for their repeal practically every session. The California wine growers finally made headway in 1966 when they hired Tom Owens, a popular lawyer who lobbied forcefully for repeal of the exclusionary legislation. Tommy's wife Angela was the daughter of Angelo Pellegrini, a legendary UW English professor, food writer and winemaker who helped found one of the state's first premium wineries. Owens said competition wouldn't destroy the Washington wine industry, it would transform it. How right he was. The analogy that comes to my engineer's mind is what happened to the American automobile industry when Japan's cars began setting new standards for quality at unbeatable price points. The Big Three domestic automakers—GM, Ford and Chrysler—were forced to produce better cars. Protectionism was not the answer. Today, Washington is second only to California in the production of premium American wines. We now have an $8.5 billion wine-grape industry, with more than a thousand wineries producing some of the world's finest wines and providing 30,000 jobs. We're also leading the way educationally, with internationally respected viticulture and enology programs at WSU and Walla Walla Community College.

I'll drink to all that.

30
"F**K EVANS!"

I was intensely interested in the 1969 race for King County Executive. It marked a comeback attempt by Al Rosellini, who figured the new "second most important job in the state" was his for the taking, especially since his opponent was a first-term county commissioner, John Spellman.

Early on, County Prosecutor Chuck Carroll and his friend Ken Rogstad, the county GOP chairman, had pegged Spellman as too mild-mannered for King County's hardball politics. But when he arrived at the Courthouse in 1967, Spellman denounced Rogstad's divisiveness and faced down Carroll's attempts at intimidation. When Rosellini entered the race for county executive, he was assured he could count on Carroll and Rogstad for behind-the-scenes support. The Spellman camp countered with some of the top people from my campaigns, including Joel Pritchard's brother, Frank, Helen Rasmussen, Ritajean Butterworth and Joe McGavick.

In their decisive last debate, Rosellini pledged there would be no new taxes in King County on his watch and made it clear he still had a score to settle with me. "We're being taxed to death right now under

Joel and Frank Pritchard, two amazing peas in a pod. *Washington State Archives*

the present governor," Rosellini declared. If Al was looking past Spellman for a rematch with me, he miscalculated the opponent at hand. John Dennis Spellman, 42, had quiet gumption and a deep social-justice conscience. And on March 11, 1969, he became the state's first elected county executive. Republicans also won a 5-4 majority on the new King County Council.

The ashes of the legislative session and the King County elections had hardly cooled when citizen unrest stoked new fires. By fall, Spellman and I had weathered protest marches left and right.

THE BLACK STUDENT UNION at Seattle Community College, prodded by the Students for a Democratic Society, staged a rally to demand appointment of a Black trustee. The college had a large African-American enrollment. In 1968 I had appointed Edwin Pratt, a distinguished African-American who headed the Seattle Urban League. Unfortunately, his residence turned out to be outside the boundaries of the college district. And on January 26, 1969, he was assassinated in the doorway of his home.

I was mulling my next appointment when the Black Student Union turned up the heat.

When the rally turned unruly, Seattle Police dispersed the crowd with volleys of tear gas. The group reassembled at predominantly Black Garfield High School, where several hundred students joined the throng. Efforts by police and demonstration leaders to calm the crowd failed when someone lobbed a chunk of concrete, followed by a couple of Molotov cocktails. That prompted more tear gas and several hours of skirmishes that left nine policemen and a number of protesters injured.

Intent on choosing the best candidate, regardless of color, I came to Seattle, listened to what the trustees had to say and told them I had full confidence in their judgment concerning the upheaval. In a 13-hour marathon session that followed, the board met with protest leaders. The newest member of the board, Carl Dakan, a vice president at Pacific National Bank, offered his resignation, saying, "I differed with the board over its policy of appeasement. The only way for the board to be right and prove me wrong is for the Black students to abide by their statement that a Black appointee is the one thing they want and refrain from future violence."

A. Frank Williams, the leader of the Black Student Union, demanded that I immediately appoint a Black trustee. The next day, Adele Ferguson was characteristically blunt during a press conference:

"You're not going to be blackmailed into naming a Black man to that board ... just out of fear of what people might think?"

Asserting that Marvin E. Glass, my appointee to the Seattle Community College Board of Trustees was "a white Negro," students protest outside the Seattle hotel where the Western Governors' Conference was in session in the summer of 1969. They wanted me to instead appoint David Mills, president of the United Black Front. *MOHAI, Seattle Post-Intelligencer Collection, Image 1986.5.50972.1*

"No, but I might very well name a Black man because I did originally and because I thought it was a good idea. There are more Black students attending Seattle Community College than all of the other colleges, universities and community colleges in the state put together, public and private. ... And I'm not going to eliminate consideration of a Black man because of a backlash or citizen pressure either."

I was flooded with recommendations for a new trustee and letters from all over the state. Most were from angry citizens who, in the words of one, said, "Under no circumstances appoint a Black trustee." I let things cool down for a month while I weighed the credentials of potential appointees. Then I announced the appointment of the Rev. Willie Jackson. Formerly a college professor in the South, he was a relative newcomer to Seattle yet already a leader in the community. The reaction from the Black Student Union was swift and negative. He wasn't their preferred candidate. Jackson called to say that with great regret he was going to withdraw. Now I was determined to find a Black person both qualified and tough enough to withstand this kind of dogmatic pressure. That was Marvin Glass, a young executive at Pacific Northwest Bell. He was smart, even-handed and not easily intimidated. The firebrands didn't like him either. When the Western Governors Conference convened in Seattle a few days later, David Mills, the new president of the Black Student Union, led a group of some 25 protesters parading in front of the Washington Plaza Hotel, blasting Glass as "an Uncle Tom—black on the outside but white on the inside." I did not budge, and Glass served his term as a trustee with distinction.

That was just one in a series of campus protests across the state. I was concerned, not just about the protests, but by the intense blowback. It was a pitched battle between often obstreperous students—with legitimate concerns about the war and civil rights—and their parents' generation, which the Nixon-Agnew "law-and-order" ticket had targeted. I was simultaneously young enough and old enough to understand both sides of the equation. That turbulent summer I spoke at Dr. Gordon Bjork's investiture as president of Linfield College in Oregon. Focusing on campus turmoil, I said:

> In more than one measure, the campus is a mirror of our deeply troubled society. It is the place where the larger issues are being debated …and where society itself is being subjected to an intense, uncomfortable examination.
>
> Right or wrong, for ultimate good or permanent evil, this is the point of abscess; this is where young minds are rebelling, where a new and uncommitted generation… sees no honor in war, no justice in poverty and no hope for their solution. This is where the battle for reason is being fought. And this is where presidents, governors and others charged with responsibility belong. No more than the ghettos can the campuses be walled off—left to spend their reckless energies against barricades erected by a fearful and misunderstanding outside world. We cannot surrender to anarchy, but neither can we insulate ourselves from the voices that call for change.

NIXON, in his first few months in office, proposed a broad restructuring of domestic programs. He called it "The New Federalism." He also successfully began to desegregate Southern schools by involving local biracial committees, added many women to high positions in government and ordered that sex discrimination be addressed in the Federal Contract Compliance program. In response to growing environmental pressure, Nixon instituted a massive Clean Air Act, and with advice from our people in Washington state proposed a new Environmental Protection Agency. These were huge steps. What really grabbed my attention, however, was a proposal for General Revenue Sharing. The president said he believed that strong state and local governments were a vital part of a true federal system and that government closer to the people would be more efficient and responsive. He proposed replacing many categorical federal programs with Revenue Sharing, and appointed Agnew chairman of the committee to oversee the effort. I was impressed. Revenue Sharing fit exactly with my views on federalism.

During the Western Governors Conference, I was asked to head a special committee to urge passage of Revenue Sharing. I quickly realized that cities and counties were deeply concerned about money coming from the federal government directly to the states. Unless there was some specific proviso that would ensure a pass-through to city and county governments we stood little chance of success. The Democrat-controlled Congress was not enamored with the idea to start with, and any division between state and local governments would doom the project. I began conversations with the presidents of the National Association of Counties and the U.S. Conference of Mayors, seeking to build a coalition that could agree on the specifics of Revenue Sharing.

Shortly after the conference, I attended a meeting featuring Nixon, Agnew and Arthur Burns, the noted economist. Soon to be named chairman of the Federal Reserve, Burns was then serving as counselor to the president. It was clear that Nixon was serious about Revenue Sharing. I was concerned that the mayors and county officials on the committee would demand direct payments, bypassing the states. But the meeting turned into an excellent work session with all of us agreeing that there should be some pass-through of funds from states to local communities. Afterward, reporters quizzed us on the potential for a state/local standoff. Taxpayers were all in the same boat, I said. They wanted police and fire protection, potholes fixed and efficient government, from city hall to the courthouse to the statehouse. "And they are paying the taxes," I said, "whether to the local units of government or the federal government through the income tax. Revenue Sharing should incorporate incentives for the states and cities to work together more closely and efficiently."

I left Washington, D.C., feeling that the odds for Revenue Sharing had gone up considerably.

The euphoria from landing men on the moon that July, was soon replaced by a series of crises unlike anything I had faced in my five years as governor—and a very personal close call.

THE CAR RADIO BLARED "Washington State Patrol One!" I had just finished giving a speech in Everett and was headed toward Paine Field to fly back to Olympia. The regular call sign was "WSP1." When the words were spelled out it indicated an emergency. Our 3-year-old son Bruce had run through a glass door and suffered a deep laceration.

The patrol car made a high-speed run from Everett to Swedish Hospital in Seattle, with my heart in my throat every second of the way. "He's OK! He's OK!" Nancy said as we embraced in the corridor. Our three boys and their cousins had been to the circus that day and were playing "circus" at a home rented by Nancy's brother, Bill Bell. As the children raced in and out of the house, one closed a glass door. Bruce hit it face first at full speed. A large shard of glass descended like a guillotine and sliced open his abdomen. He began to bleed profusely. Fortunately, a State Patrol trooper was there. He administered first aid and rushed Nancy and Bruce to the hospital. Luckily, the laceration was more like the stroke of a scalpel. It had gone through skin and muscle but left his stomach untouched. A couple of inches deeper and Bruce's life might have ended before his fourth birthday. Ironically, I had already signed a law requiring that patio doors be equipped with safety glass. But doors in thousands of older homes around the state still had the old glass. That scary incident was yet another reminder that when a tragedy occurs some plaintive pleas to "get government out of our lives" are often superseded by "Why didn't government do something?"

With Bruce safely on the mend, I reflected on that wild ride, with the trooper skillfully maneuvering through heavy traffic on Interstate 5. "How would you like to go to work at 3 a.m. every day?" I asked a teachers' conference. Staggering work shifts to avoid traffic jams might be one of the alternatives by the year 2000, I predicted, if the state's population and the number of vehicles grew at the pace projected and nothing was done to alleviate the gridlock. It might even get to the point where Seattle restricted auto access to its downtown core and banned cars carrying only one person, I said. "It is impossible for this state to accommodate so many vehicles."

ON OCTOBER 15, 1969, an estimated 2 million people paraded, protested and prayed in cities across America, calling for an end to the war in Vietnam. I was in Pullman, expecting to address a small gathering of Young Republicans. I had scheduled the trip months before, little knowing that the date would turn out to be national Vietnam Moratorium Day.

Addressing 2,000 WSU students in Pullman on National Vietnam Moratorium Day, Oct. 15, 1969. *WSU Evergreen/Office of Publications*

When I arrived at the airport I was met by WSU President Glenn Terrell, a marvelous leader, and a visibly shaken Young Republican chairman, who stammered, "Governor, there are more than 2,000 students packed into the Student Union building waiting for you." One of the most profound and rewarding experiences of my career in public office was about to unfold.

Nixon, increasingly defiant, had been quoted two weeks earlier as saying that "under no circumstances" would he be affected by the growing opposition to the war, especially on college campuses. Dismayed by his attitude, I believed the students were sincerely motivated and deeply concerned. When I entered the main auditorium of the Compton Union Building I was greeted by thunderous applause. The students, many wearing black armbands, filled every seat, sat on every inch of floor space and stood in packed rows around the room. Expressing my support for the president's domestic initiatives, including welfare reform and Revenue Sharing, I said I backed his stated goal of de-escalating the war in Vietnam. "The question is, 'Have we moved far enough and fast enough?' I say no. The question is not what has been done but what must be done. We must end the war that has bled this nation not only in dollars and lives but in terms of national purpose."

I spoke for only about 10 minutes, emphasizing I was there to listen. Hundreds of hands shot up. The questions were passionate and intelligent. As we left the building two hours later, I told Terrell, "That is some student body you have. I am really impressed." Turning to the student who had promised to round up at least a hundred Young Republicans if I visited the campus, I quipped, "Well, you sure got me the crowd. I hope they are all Young Republicans." Highly unlikely. But I left Pullman energized and hopeful on the eve of my 44th birthday.

THE NEXT DAY, I was back at the Capitol to greet a jeering crowd of 4,000 hard-hats who had descended on Olympia to protest quotas for minority on-the-job trainees. Hoping to break the tension with some levity, I announced, "It's my birthday, and I'm glad you came to help me celebrate!" Ralph Munro, my state volunteer services coordinator, was standing nearby on the Capitol steps. He swears that a lot of them laughed, but all I heard was even louder booing and taunts. "Fuck Evans!" one guy shouted, red in the face with anger as he cupped his hands into a megaphone.

The tension between Black contractors and white construction workers had been building for months in Seattle. It began to boil in August when the newly organized Central Contractors Association demanded more work and apprenticeship opportunities for minorities. The Black contractors shut down work on the new King County Administration Building and a research facility at Harborview Medical Center. John Spellman asked the new King County Council to pass an ordinance requiring minority hiring on all county projects. And I warned that discrimination would not be tolerated by any company, union or contractor doing business with the state. The state's 15 building trades unions had only seven non-white apprentices among their 29,000 members. We had an influential ally in demanding compliance with the Equal Employment Opportunity provision of the 1964 Civil Rights Act. Art Fletcher, our only "Action Team" casualty from the 1968 campaign, was now assistant secretary of labor and Nixon's designated point man in his push for Affirmative Action. Washington state's loss in not electing Art lieutenant governor turned out to be America's gain.

By September, the Central Contractors Association had shut down practically every publicly-funded construction project in the county, idling some 700 white workers. Some 3,000 white construction workers marched 20 blocks through the heart of Seattle to the King County Courthouse, chanting "Impeach Spellman!" and "Whites have rights, too!" Standing on a truck, Spellman tried to address them through a bullhorn. When they kept shouting and booing, he decided it was fruitless. As he pushed through the crowd to return to his office, someone threw a punch that was barely deflected.

I knew what to expect when the protest reached Olympia a week later.

Thousands of angry construction workers rally outside the capitol. Bill Lathrop, my State Patrol Security aide, literally has my back. *Washington State Archives*

A temporary podium was placed halfway down the Capitol steps. As I descended toward the podium, the booing, hissing protesters surged forward. I hoped the few state patrolmen in attendance could maintain some semblance of order. Fortunately, the protesters had their own security force, which proved critical in keeping control.

Leroy Mozingo, chairman of V.O.I.C.E. (the Voice of Irate Construction Employees) read a letter demanding that I "stop interfering with bona fide, federally recognized and supported apprenticeship programs" and reconsider the construction cutbacks I had ordered to deal with a slowing economy.

They jeered when I declared we had not attempted to destroy apprenticeship programs and were evaluating the Outreach Program. They booed when I said I had no intention of backing down on my call for increased minority representation in construction unions. And when I said the cutbacks—hopefully short-lived—were necessary to balance the state budget and fight inflation, shouts of "Impeach Evans!" rang out.

Munro had spotted two of his cousins in the angry crowd. "We talked later in the cafeteria," he told me, shaking his head. "They were adamant that no minorities should be hired. The ironic thing was that the older cousin was an immigrant from Scotland and in many ways a minority himself."

The combination of a federal court order, continued pressure by minority contractors and the work of some wise labor leaders eventually pried open the door of opportunity. Unfortunately, the economic downturn was closing thousands of doors.

SINCE THE STATE had no official economic analyst, I had appointed a Council of Economic Advisers, carrying forward a concept created by Governor Rosellini. The council provided predictions on economic growth for the coming biennium, from which we prepared our revenue estimates. The Legislature also used the estimates as a baseline for its budget proposals. I felt we needed more details on leading indicators since monthly budget receipts varied widely. Sales tax revenue was highly seasonal and state property taxes were almost all paid in April and October. I asked Walt Howe, the director of the Office of Program Planning & Fiscal Management, to prepare monthly estimates for the biennium and began to carefully examine each month's receipts.

A delegation from Boeing visited my office in September to warn they were facing a substantial reduction in employment. Environmental and cost-benefit opposition to the company's prototype of a Supersonic Transport, the SST, was growing and jetliner sales were slowing as the global economy began to stall.

I called a meeting of my entire cabinet, plus statewide elected officials, representatives of higher education and the courts to give them the sobering news and our proposed reaction. The Legislature had overspent our revenue estimates. We were also obliged by federal court decisions to spend more on welfare, which we had not budgeted. The slowing economy would continue to slice into our revenues, since the sales tax quickly responds to an economic downturn. In addition, the national economy was plagued by a tight money supply, which increased inflation. Nixon asked the governors to cut capital spending to reduce pressures on borrowing. The combination of these elements created a $53 million budget gap.

A week before, the Superintendent of Public Instruction, Louis Bruno, had unilaterally raised the per-student allocation of state funds to each school district in the state. Although it was legally within his authority, I was furious. I had discussed school financing issues with Bruno's top aides and asked for their feedback, only to be blindsided.

I suspect I cursed our lawmaker forefathers, who wrote our state constitution during a period of extreme suspicion of government. They created a multi-headed executive branch destined to create stalemates. I was attempting to create a cohesive response to our budget crisis with a separately elected Superintendent of Public Instruction in full revolt. I was also trying to slow down highway construction and respond to the president's request but could only cajole a Highway Commission I did not yet, and never did, fully control. My edicts limiting hiring and out-of-state travel only applied directly to a fraction of state employment. Education, higher education, natural resources, highways and state parks were all controlled by either separately elected officials or appointed commissions. Countless times in the course of my career, I was asked, "Why don't you run government more like a business?" No business would last long with the kind of splintered executive Washington's Constitutional Convention created for its governor.

A report recommending a dramatic overhaul of our state's then 80-year-old constitution was plopped into this vortex of uncertainty. I had appointed the Constitutional Revision Committee 18 months earlier. Headed by retired WSU president C. Clement French, the committee concluded that the present state constitution "was designed more to restrain government action than to permit it." In fact, "it provided for its own obsolescence, inasmuch as the constitution's inflexibility in the face of newly felt needs has resulted in the adoption of 54 constitutional amendments."

The committee's report called for abolishing most statewide elected officials and strengthening the power of both the governor and a full-time Legislature. The governor would have "wide ranging power to tailor the executive branch to meet his needs, subject to the veto of the Legislature." The committee also backed a "gateway amendment" to allow the constitution to be amended more easily. I was an enthusiastic supporter of the report and proposed a constitutional revision to the next session of the Legislature.

The story detailing the committee's report got relatively little exposure, given the looming economic crisis. By year's end, Boeing had laid off 25,000 workers. The slowdown chilling the state's economy turned to an epidemic of pneumonia.

31
"WHAT PRICE TO PAY?"

Only a few bills survived from the flurry of environmental legislation proposed in the marathon 1969 legislative session. Regrouping from that disappointment, the fledgling Washington Environmental Council shared my view that 1970 could be a pivotal year for the environmental movement in Washington state.

Before the Environmental Council's birth in 1967, the movement was splintered into scores of groups. All well intended, they nevertheless lacked the knowhow to transform their passion into legislative success. The movement now spoke with one voice—for the time being at least. If you put a hundred environmentalists in one room you never knew if they would sing *Kumbaya* or start fighting over priorities. I was eager to call a special session in 1970, hoping to pass major environmental legislation. I also hoped to build momentum for a constitutional amendment on annual sessions. Legislative leaders groused that since they had passed a biennial budget in 1969, a special session was unnecessary. Some old-timers declared it would be their last roundup, since the increased legislative workload was impeding their ability to practice law, sell insurance and adjust vertebrae.

In the fall of 1969, when the Environmental Council invited me to speak at one of its first conferences, I eagerly accepted. It was an opportunity to set the stage for one of the most productive legislative sessions in Washington history. I sensed we were at a crossroads:

> The problem, of course, with a deteriorating environment is that we never see it as a day-to-day priority. It never comes before us with the demand for solution that some other crises do. One more minor increment of pollution in our air or one more lake lost among hundreds, one more acre of scenic view property removed from public access—these are small losses in a time marked by some major problems. And yet they do add up, like the toll of a crippling disease, until one day the enormity of neglect becomes all too visible, and the resources of government all too inadequate. No issue or no combination of proposals that we could present to a Legislature could be more bipartisan in nature or even perhaps more non-partisan in nature. Clean air is certainly no province of just one political party—although hot air seems to be a province of both. This is an opportunity to join everyone together, citizen and legislator alike, to prove that here in Washington state at least, we can do a real job.

The speech was well received, I talked strategy with my trusted aide, Jim Dolliver, who shared my love of the outdoors. We decided to hold a weekend retreat at Crystal Mountain, assembling leaders of the Legislature and the environmental movement. Tom Wimmer, who headed the Washington Environmental Council, said it was a great idea.

We assembled six Republican legislative leaders and state agency department heads with environmental responsibilities. I wish we had been smart enough to ask some Democratic legislators to join us. That would have made the legislative session a lot easier. There's a message there for today's lawmakers, whether in Olympia or the other Washington.

Sixty proposals were identified in two days of lively discussion in that beautiful setting, far from the noise and exhaust fumes of traffic jams and the clamor of a legislative session. I asked each participant to identify his top three issues. As we worked our way around the room, there was an air of contagious enthusiasm.

Six issues emerged with overwhelming support: The need for a new "Department of Environmental Quality"; oil spill regulation; a thermal power plant siting council; scenic river protection and shoreline management; property taxation based on actual land use, and strip mining regulation. We needed to be certain we didn't bite off more than the legislators could chew, especially in a short session. I asked Wimmer and his colleagues from the Environmental Council, "If I call a special session for 1970 will you agree to focus on these six and leave the remainder until the regular session of 1971?" They protested mightily that all those issues were important. True enough, I said, but if you push more than six you might end up with none. They agreed to concentrate on the big six. Turning to the legislators on hand, I asked if they would give those core issues top priority for hearings and make sure they made it to the floor. Yes, they said, reminding us they could not promise passage. That was up to the members. I asked the department heads to help draft legislation, and to be prepared to testify convincingly. We left Crystal Mountain on a Cascade high.

I issued a special session proclamation in December, pointing to the unfinished business regarding the environment, unemployment compensation, welfare funding, executive branch reorganization and lowering the voting age. By now, however, with the dark clouds of recession more menacing by the month, it was also clear that we faced a major revenue shortfall—perhaps as much as $25 million for the biennium. The New Year's Day edition of *The Seattle Times* featured its annual appraisal of the year in the rearview mirror and predictions for the road ahead. Miner Baker, the president of Seattle-First National Bank, wrote about "the Soaring '60s" when Puget Sound's economy "lived up to every promise and then some." He warned that 1970 would be "a painful year of readjustment."

GRUMBLING, THE LEGISLATURE gathered on January 12. Most members questioned the need for a session. I asked to speak to a joint session on the morning of their first day. After posing the challenges of a new decade, I summed things up with a series of questions:

> What price must the people pay for 12 more months of chaotic abuse of our saltwater beaches?
> What price must they pay for 12 more months of stripping the mountains and polluting our lakes and streams and open spaces?
> What price must they pay for 12 more months of inadequacy in meeting the responsibilities of unemployment compensation, or in meeting the housing needs of

low-income families?

What price must they pay for 12 more months of leaving our cities and counties the choice between beggaring and bankruptcy?

I outlined a six-point program to meet the challenges, including bills to protect the environment, modernize unemployment compensation, reorganize state agencies, enact an optional local sales tax for cities and counties, promote affordable housing, and lower the age of majority and voting to 18. Outside the Capitol, supporters of a woman's right to choose an abortion were staging a large demonstration. Bob Dylan was right. The times *were* changing—and in so many ways. By spring, 20 million Americans would participate in rallies across America on the first "Earth Day," demanding a healthy, sustainable environment.

AS LEGISLATIVE COMMITTEES began sifting legislation, I flew to Oakland with a worried team of Seattleites, hoping to save the Seattle Pilots, our bankrupt, year-old Major League Baseball franchise. I was joined by Slade Gorton, a passionate baseball fan since his childhood, rooting for the Cubs at Wrigley Field; John Spellman, who, like me, had grown up watching the minor-league Seattle Rainiers at Sick's Stadium; Wes Uhlman, Seattle's young mayor, and Eddie Carlson, the chairman of Western International Hotels, aptly described as "a pint of dynamite" in his high school yearbook.

We met with American League owners and proposed a community-owned team, much like the Green Bay Packers. We noted that our new domed stadium, approved by the voters in 1968, was expected to be ready for the Pilots' 1973 home opener. Negotiations continued

With King County Executive John Spellman, hotelier Eddie Carlson, Seattle Mayor Wes Uhlman, and Attorney General Slade Gorton in Oakland on January 27, 1970. We urged the American League owners to accept a local ownership plan to keep the Pilots in Seattle. *Washington State Archives*

throughout the day, with separate sessions followed by joint meetings where the duplicitous owners alternatively tossed us curve balls and walks. "There are only about three of these guys I would even invite to dinner at my house," Carlson observed after one tedious session.

"We didn't come down here to strike out," I told John Owen, the *Seattle Post-Intelligencer's* ace sportswriter. But we did. The franchise was moved to Milwaukee—on April Fools' Day no less. What the American League owners hadn't counted on was our attorney general's indignation and persistence. Gorton viewed their arrogance as an affront to the Northwest, as if Seattle was some backwater led by a bunch of rubes. He assembled a brilliant legal team headed by Bill Dwyer, one of the greatest trial lawyers in Northwest history, and sued the American League in federal court for breach of contract. It took nearly seven years, but this time Major League Baseball capitulated. Seattle was granted a new franchise that became the Mariners.

MANY OF MY executive request bills were sent to the House Natural Resources Committee headed by Representative Sid Flanagan. Sid was a gravelly-voiced rancher accustomed to handling bills on agriculture, forestry and irrigation. Now he was responsible for bills on water pollution, open-space protection and environmental regulation. Like the Marlboro Man, Sid's tanned, lined face testified to a life spent outdoors. And he was rarely seen without a cigarette drooping from a corner of his mouth. He seldom looked up from the bills spread before him on a conference table. Environmental zealots looking on at committee hearings shook their heads, viewing Sid as an inept rustic. They were monumentally wrong. Sid Flanagan was an honest, extremely intelligent leader imbued with common sense. I think he sometimes pretended to be hard of hearing, especially when fielding a question he didn't particularly want to answer.

Charlie Roe, a savvy yet always congenial senior lawyer in the Attorney General's office, had developed much of the water-related environmental legislation I proposed.

Two weeks into the session, our priority bills were all stalled in committees. I was in Seattle for an interview with KING-TV and bumped into Eric Bremner, the station's general manager. He asked how things were going. Not good, I said, explaining that the environmental bills were my main reason for calling a special session. "Well," he said, "why don't you make a direct appeal to the people? We might be able to give you a spot on the 5 p.m. newscast." I said that would great. A couple of days later, I was given six minutes—an eternity in broadcasting terms—to make my case. I appealed to viewers to contact their legislators so their voices could be heard over the din of special-interest lobbyists intent on derailing new environmental regulations. It was a dangerous gambit since I was going beyond the normal practice of a governor lobbying a Legislature through its leadership. But we were already half way through a scheduled 30-day session.

Maybe it was a slow news day. Maybe my zeal was contagious. The next morning's *Seattle Post-Intelligencer*—increasingly progressive on environmental issues—featured a front-page story about the TV interview and the stalled legislation. The story listed the members of the appropriate committees, even putting X's and O's after the lawmakers' names to indicate whether they supported or opposed the environmental bills. I now had activist media allies in KING Broadcasting and the *P-I*, but I knew the story spelled trouble. That morning all hell broke loose. Legislators stormed into my office demanding to know why I said they were opposed to legislation when, by gosh, they were supporters. I said it was the *P-I's* decision to assign individual blame for stonewalling the bills, but it was nice to know I had more support than I assumed, given the logjam. The electorate definitely got the message. All morning long, teenage pages in their crisp blouses and blazers hauled in sacks of mail and distributed telegrams to members. Over the next two days more than 5,000 telegrams were received. It was the most robust citizen reaction on any issue anyone could remember. Telephone lines were jammed and legislative hearings were packed with irate citizens.

Legislation began to move although there was still strong opposition to many of the bills. Flanagan, a crafty committee chairman if there ever was one, remained confident he could convince a majority to support him. It was still a tightrope. After a hearing on one of our executive request bills, a conservative Republican legislator declared, "They might as well hang a hammer and sickle from the Capitol dome."

MY REQUEST FOR a Department of Environmental Quality was our top priority. Gathering all the environmental regulatory responsibilities of state government into a single department was the only way to achieve uniform oversight. When the bill was debated in the Senate, it ran into serious headwinds. Martin Durkan, defeated by John J. O'Connell in the 1968 Democratic primary, was intent on making another run for governor in 1972. As chairman of the Ways and Means Committee, Durkan had a bully pulpit. Luckily, he was also cultivating a greener image. It was Durkan who christened the proposed new agency the Department of Ecology to dilute its identification with me. "You dope," one of Durkan's senate colleagues observed wryly, "the new initials are 'DE.' Now Dan Evans will be enshrined forever." When the bill came to the Senate floor, one

Senator Martin J. Durkin, a formidable opponent and man of his word, played a key role in establishing the State Department of Ecology. *Washington State Archives*

senior lawmaker puzzled by "ecology" exclaimed, "Is this a department of social diseases?" I told my staff I didn't give a damn what they called the department. "Let's just get the bill passed!"

Our priority bills gradually began to move, boosted by skillful lobbying by environmental groups and thousands of citizen telegrams. Senator Durkan's support helped us create the nation's first state agency dedicated to protecting the environment. The Department of Ecology developed comprehensive oil-spill regulations, measures designed to preserve open spaces, a nuclear plant siting protocol, and strong controls on strip mining. Many other states asked for our advice. And we consulted with the Nixon Administration on development of the U.S. Environmental Protection Agency, which was born On December 2, 1970. The EPA's first administrator was a man I would come to admire and value as a friend, Bill Ruckelshaus. He moved to Seattle in 1975 to oversee legal affairs for the Weyerhaeuser Company.

THE LAST ISSUE DEBATED on the floor of both chambers was the Shorelines Management Bill, opposed ferociously by developers, real-estate interests, port districts and some local governments. Getting the bill to the floor was no small achievement. I had asked Representative Flanagan if I could speak directly to his House Natural Resources Committee. It was the first time since taking office as governor that I engaged directly in the legislative process—and one of the last times, too. Though many members were still angry over my TV appearance pushing environmental legislation, the committee received me graciously. They asked probing questions before unanimously approving the bill for floor action. However, the concept of managing development and protecting all of the state's shorelines, including those along navigable lakes and rivers, was too big a step for the Legislature in a frenetic session. We ran out of time.

In 32 pressure-packed days, weary legislators produced landmark legislation. Five out of six of my environmental proposals became law. In addition to the new Department of Ecology, the Legislature created a Department of Social & Health Services and authorized referenda on an income tax, legalizing abortion and granting 19-year-olds the right to vote. Cities and counties received authority to levy a local sales tax, and a comprehensive unemployment compensation bill was passed after more than a decade of setbacks.

On the last day of the session, I asked for the unprecedented opportunity to address the House and Senate. I had the same message in each chamber: In my five years as governor and 13 years in state government I had never seen a legislative session where so much of real consequence to the people of the state was accomplished; where there was a spirit of bipartisanship despite some severe partisan differences:

"I came to say 'Thank you' for leaving your homes and making real history for our state."

32
HISTORY ON THE MARCH

The euphoria from the success of the 1970 special session was short-lived. Boeing was laying off 1,500 workers per month and college campuses were roiling with dissent. The anti-war and social-justice demonstrations angered conservative voters and legislators. Tacoma Republican Helmut Jueling, a longtime member of the House Appropriations Committee, charged that the administration of the University of Washington was knuckling under "to demands made by a small group of communist-oriented hoodlums."

The militant Black Student Union and Seattle Liberation Front staged demonstrations that drew 2,000 UW students outraged over the university's willingness to play teams from Brigham Young University. BYU's beleaguered athletes were being harassed by student protesters on campuses throughout the West because the Church of Jesus Christ of Latter-day Saints barred Black men from its priesthood.* UW administrators worried that any action to sever the agreements would amount to infringing on the church's religious freedom. When administrators said they were seeking legal counsel on cutting ties with BYU after the current agreements expired, the dissatisfied protesters invaded several buildings on campus. The Black Student Union demanded that the administration "not only sever all relationships with BYU, but also make a statement denouncing BYU as a racist institution."

In March of 1970, university administration asked the Seattle Police Department to enter the campus for the first time to engage in a police action. I received a torrent of letters and calls from people who admired Governor Reagan's move a year earlier to send in armed police and National Guardsmen with fixed bayonets to disperse demonstrators at Berkeley. But that action left one person dead and scores injured. I was determined to open doors, not close them—convinced that was the way to head off violence.

I appointed Dr. Robert Flennaugh to the UW Board of Regents. A 1964 graduate of the university's School of Dentistry, many remembered Bob as the drum major of the UW Marching Band during the 1959 football season that culminated in the Huskies' resounding Rose Bowl victory over Wisconsin. At 32, Flennaugh became the youngest member of the board and its first ever African-American regent. He was to play a crucial role during some of the most intense student protests.

Seattle's assertive new mayor, 34-year-old Wes Uhlman—touted as a possible opponent should I seek a third term in 1972—proposed that the State Patrol and National Guard be called on to handle major difficulties on the UW campus "because it's a state facility." I attended a summit featuring

---

* The ban was rescinded in 1978.

top law enforcement officials, Mayor Uhlman, King County Executive John Spellman and UW President Charles Odegaard. The mayor emphasized his opposition to "deploying all our police in one area." I reminded him that the city had prime responsibility for police protection inside the municipality, including the sprawling UW campus. "However, when the problem grows beyond the city's capacity we've always responded and will continue to respond." That had been my agreement with his predecessor, Dorm Braman. As an exponent of free speech, I was unwilling to mobilize the State Patrol or National Guard to rein in student protests except in dire circumstances. My stance was fortified by a meeting with Howard McGee, Adjutant General of the Washington National Guard, and Will Bachofner, Chief of the Washington State Patrol. Both emphasized that their personnel were not trained in urban policing. Bachofner said communications support to fully engaged city police was one thing, direct action quite another. General McGee was adamant that he did not want armed 19-year-old Guardsmen facing down emotional 19-year-old college students. His statement proved tragically prescient. Less than two weeks later, on May 4, 1970, Ohio National Guardsmen, called to the campus of Kent State University to quell a mass protest against escalation of the war in Vietnam, killed four unarmed students and wounded several others. Four million students staged protest strikes across the nation.

The meeting established an important set of priorities that proved valuable for the bigger protests yet to come. But I was out of the country when the biggest trouble began.

A WORLD'S FAIR, EXPO 70, opened a six-month run in Osaka on March 15. Washington state had its own Pavilion, underscoring our relationship with Japan, especially at a time when Boeing needed all the help it could get—and Canadian lumber exports were on the rise. I was scheduled to lead a trade mission to Japan and other Asian nations in May and take part in a special presentation at EXPO 70. The early spring unrest made me reluctant to leave the state, but the campuses seemed to be quieting. The opportunity to advance our leadership in Pacific Rim trade was too important to miss. So in early May I embarked with a 26-member trade mission to visit Japan, Singapore and Australia.

Kobe, Japan, population 1.3 million, was the main city of Hyogo Prefecture, our sister state. There, the trade mission broke into small teams. Over the next several days we made some significant trade and business contacts. When the weekend came, we were invited by Gov. and Mrs. Kanai to join them on a visit to Awaji, a resort on a remote island. After a traditional Japanese dinner and striking entertainment, we retired that night looking forward to the events planned for the next day. It was not to be.

A few days earlier, President Nixon had authorized an incursion into Cambodia to eliminate a sanctuary for North Vietnamese troops. The surprise escalation of the war triggered a series of massive protests throughout the U.S. Early Sunday morning, Japan-time, I received a call from Dolliver back in Olympia. Nixon had called a meeting of the nation's governors for Monday. Jim urged me to attend. It was then that I learned more details about the Kent State shootings and a huge protest at the University of Washington that spilled over onto the Interstate-5 freeway. A sea of students flowed around stalled trucks and cars. As they approached the crest of the bridge crossing Lake Union, a thin line of state troopers stretched across the lanes blocking their path. I spoke later with one of the troopers. "Governor," he said, shaking his head in wonderment, "when we saw the number of students and their determination, we stepped aside and let them pass." I told him that was a wise decision. Police were able to lead the students off the freeway at the next off-ramp, but they continued to block surface streets as they continued their march to the Federal Courthouse in downtown Seattle. Some 5,000 students jammed the lawn and surrounding streets, cheering fiery speeches. Although a few radical stragglers threw rocks through store windows, the protests were remarkably peaceful considering their size and intensity.

I said a quick goodbye to Nancy and our hosts, grabbed an overnight bag and embarked on a terrifying ride over a sinuous two-lane highway to reach a ferry. A prefectural official hurried me to the airport in time to board a plane for Anchorage and then on to Washington, D.C.

The meeting with Nixon was strained throughout and occasionally testy. Many governors were dealing with disruptive demonstrations that threatened to erupt into violence. Others, like me, were increasingly skeptical of the war itself. The meeting reminded me of the annual Governors' Association visits to the embattled Johnson White House, with a haggard LBJ declaring victory was in sight if we just stayed the course. Now, the Nixon-Kissinger plans for victory sounded hollow, while the financial and human costs of the war—dead and maimed soldiers—and national upheaval escalated. The meeting was unimpressive and inconclusive. I departed for yet another airport, disappointed in the lack of cohesive war plans and dismayed at the president's determination to ignore the rising tide of angst engulfing the nation.

HOME AGAIN AT LAST, I met with Dr. Odegaard, a former history professor with a Ph.D. from Harvard. He had elevated my alma mater to the first rank of American universities. Odegaard said a great university was about more than lectures, theses and degrees. He praised the students for their intense interest in peace and social justice and hailed the way in which they conducted the largest student protest ever held at the University of Washington. While Odegaard refused to close the campus in spite of repeated demands by students to join a nationwide strike of university students, he did close school for one day as a memorial to the students killed at Kent State. He also told me he had written a letter to Nixon urging a quick end to the conflict in Vietnam.

It was important for me to hear directly from students, faculty and other college presidents. I scheduled meetings and invited legislative leaders to join me. The meeting with students lasted more than six hours. I was impressed by their intensity and intelligence. They hated the war, especially the inequality of the draft, and had strong feelings about the relevance of their education.

I received several thousand letters from citizens in response to the freeway protest. The messages were intense and troubling, for they were advocating violence against student protesters. The chilling irony was that student protests against the violence of the war in Vietnam created a response from ostensible "grownups" suggesting violence to end protests. I called KING-TV and asked if I could see the evening news report on the day of the freeway-blocking protest. Management sat with me as the film rolled. The first scene, on campus, showed thousands of students listening to the fiery remarks of protest leaders. Next, an aerial shot from a helicopter showed students surging around stopped traffic on the freeway, followed by a scene at the Federal Courthouse with additional provocative speeches. The final shot was of several downtown store windows shattered by a handful of protesters.

Now I understood. Forty-five intense seconds of speeches, a panorama of thousands of marching students and close-ups of shattered windows caused viewers to believe the protesters had just ransacked downtown Seattle in a massive, violent protest movement. Those who watched the broadcast received a misleading, incomplete version of what actually occurred. I thought the impression needed to be corrected. KING-TV management offered me a 30-minute time slot to address viewers. I accepted on the spot. Yet when I returned to Olympia with news of this development, several advisers counseled, "Don't do it! You'll just stir up more antagonism. Let things die down." I said I had to give it a try. If people didn't get a better sense of the true picture, we could have open warfare. In the months to come, Crosby, Stills, Nash & Young's anthem "Ohio," with its refrain "Four dead in O-hi-o," became part of the enduring soundtrack of 1970. I told Dolliver I didn't want to speak from a script or Teleprompter. I just wanted to talk to the people, informally, and try to sort out their misconceptions.

On the evening of June 4, 1970, I sat behind a simple desk. A red light on the TV camera flashed on as the floor director pointed at me. I looked into the unblinking lens and began:

Events of the last few months have left citizens of this nation and citizens of this state emotionally drained and probably as confused as they've been in a long, long time. A war continues in Southeast Asia, seemingly without let-up. Unemployment is rising. Inflation continues. Campus unrest has intensified, particularly over the past month since the first announcement of our involvement in Cambodia, followed closely by the killings at Kent State. Many, I think, feel that the combination of all of these events occurring in such a limited period of time is leading to a disintegration of the order they have known. Let me read for you excerpts from some of the many letters I have received—letters from angry, confused and frustrated citizens:

"Now that the Ohio State National Guard has taken a positive approach at Kent State University it is time for the authorities at campuses all over the United States to follow suit."

"As a salesman, I talked to many people from all walks of life and know that if the government will not protect our rights, we will do it ourselves."

"I'm fed up with paying taxes to support an educational institution headed by someone who bows to the minority. I say that if it takes killing of these radicals, let's kill them all. Gov, I have not talked to anyone yet who is not fed up with this bunk."

And finally: "My family is 100 percent behind you in stopping the student riots regardless of how harsh it is."

These letters frightened me. I think they should frighten you, too. They frighten me just as student violence frightens me. And the growing gulf that exists between the generations in the state frightens me. They are symptoms of a void we must somehow bridge if we are to have any hope for a productive and progressive future in our state or in our nation.

We like to categorize. But all students are not radical. All police are not brutal. All adults have not lost their idealism. I think, by and large, all students, law enforcement officers and older citizens in our society look for essentially the same thing: An ability to live a life of their personal choice; to live it in a free society that is strong and vital, and a nation that has a real future. ...

The real question is where do we go now? The answer is nonviolence. I abhor violence by those students who have chosen to be revolutionaries, who have chosen to tear down and destroy a system that it has taken more than 200 years for this generation and the many generations preceding it to build up. By the same token, I cannot condone violence by vigilantes. Any action to repress, restrict or in some fashion strike out blindly at the actions they dislike is as reprehensible—perhaps even more reprehensible—than the actions of some of this fringe of today's college students.

Here's a letter from a student, one dramatically different than the ones I quoted earlier:

"The very essence of this new education is nonviolent action. Those who press for violence as a means to bring about peace have lost the struggle. Attempting to end the war in Vietnam by violence, even if successful, will not eradicate the inhuman attitude that causes war but will actually help to sustain that cruel attitude. The end is conditioned by the means. Violence to gain peace will require violence to retain peace, and there still will be no peace."

It's important for all of us to take the time to communicate with the youth of today. Invite them into your homes; listen to them and speak to them. The wisdom of age and the enthusiasm of youth ought to work together toward the progress of our state and not at cross purposes.

Let me finally speak to every citizen of the State of Washington: Government simply can't do the total job it's being called upon to do today. It's important for citizens to contribute something far more important than their taxes: *Time*. We need you to contribute your time as volunteers in the scores of fields across the state where volunteer support, coupled with governmental action, could bring success where today we see continued failure.

The voice of moderation in the state has been too quiet over the past months. If it is heard, I think we all have far more hope than hopelessness.

When I finished, I was emotionally drained. The reaction to the speech was immediate and intense. Lieutenant Governor John Cherberg, a former UW football coach, disputed virtually everything I said. His attitude was to deploy riot-trained police or the National Guard to control protests. State Representative Carlton Gladder, a Republican from Spokane, huffed in a long ranting letter that I was a wimp. Over the next few days I received hundreds of letters and telegrams. More than 80 percent were supportive. I was particularly pleased by a letter that declared, "Your speech tonight was your shining hour as governor," and a postcard that concluded, "What a contrast to VP Agnew," who had denounced war protesters as drug-addled malcontents.

Hundreds of citizens responded to my speech. We matched them with programs throughout the state. A year earlier, in 1969, I had initiated a volunteer program and asked Ralph Munro to become its coordinator. A large, ruddy-faced young man fizzing with energy, Munro was only 26, but he exuded confidence and put his heart and soul into the effort. For starters, Munro put out a pamphlet aimed at UW students. Its headline was an eye-catcher: "Where the hell were you last spring?" That was a reference to campus demonstrations. But when you opened the pamphlet, this was the message: "It's not so much where you were last spring that counts, but where you're going to be this fall." A plea followed for volunteers who wanted to help to improve society. Several thousand students responded. Soon, many were tutoring underprivileged pupils in elementary schools and helping the developmentally disabled, one of Munro's passions. Designated 4-F by his draft board, Munro had resolved to serve his country by volunteering to work with disabled kids. The statewide volunteer program that sprang from our efforts ultimately became the model for a national effort.

Many of you know the rest of the story: Munro went on to become my assistant on education and social service issues, authored a referendum that funded construction of more than 100 facilities for the disabled and saw to it that terms "idiot" and "imbecile" were removed from the state Constitution. He also campaigned to open public-school classrooms to the developmentally disabled and promoted legislation to require sidewalk curb cuts and wheelchair ramps. Ralph served five terms as Washington's Secretary of State, becoming a bipartisan icon. Introducing him on one occasion, I remarked that he was the man who taught me how to care.

After graduating from College at Bellingham in 1966, Ralph became interested in two developmentally disabled boys who were largely mute and on occasion had to be restrained by the staff at Fircrest School to calm them down. Ralph contributed hundreds of hours to nurturing their socialization. One eventful day in 1971, he brought them into my office to introduce them to me. They were both shy, but one easily shook my hand. We conversed for several minutes. Looking on intently, his friend finally followed his lead. It was a wonderful meeting. Ralph suggested that I visit the Fircrest School without the publicity and trappings of an official tour by the governor. I loved the idea. I dressed in slacks and a turtleneck sweater and we piled into a State Patrol car one morning. "Don't be surprised if many of them know who you are because they do watch a lot of television," Ralph said during the ride to Shoreline, just north of Seattle. "Also, some may greet you with a hug even though they are in their twenties and probably bigger than you are. Many are mentally still children."

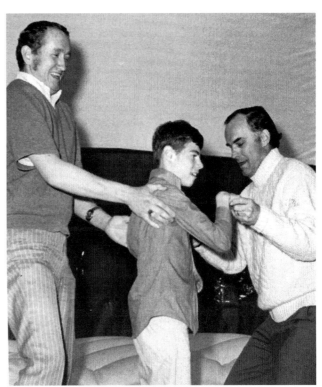

With Ralph Munro and Darwin Neely, a developmentally disabled boy, at Seattle's Fircrest School in 1971. *Washington State Archives*

When we arrived at the school, many of the students converged on Ralph like the old friend he was. But a number of the youngsters recognized me, and a tall young man immediately wrapped his arms around me. It was an electric moment. The residents were proud to show us around. When we came to a large room with a soft, bouncy floor they urged me to join them. I shucked my shoes, climbed into the chamber and thoroughly enjoyed a bouncing spree with Ralph and the students. Munro is a big kid at heart in any case, but his joy that day was infectious. Spending several hours in close contact with those developmentally disabled students gave me a lesson in their potential capabilities. I regularly remembered that experience as we pushed for "Education for All" legislation that would revolutionize educational opportunity for all developmentally disabled children.

WITH THE 1970 GENERAL ELECTION fast approaching, my tax reform plan was the major topic of every speech and press conference. The ballot issue, HJR 42, called for amending the state Constitution to reduce the maximum allowable rate of property taxation to 1 percent of true and fair value and constrain special levies. Concurrently, the Legislature would be authorized to enact a single-rate income tax. The plan was hammered by opponents who warned it was a blank check for tax increases. In truth, the plan was designed to be revenue-neutral, with low-and middle-income citizens and small businesses benefiting most. Opponents also asserted there was no constitutional protection on rates of the proposed income tax. I argued that the only constitutionally protected tax was the property tax. "Which tax has risen faster, has become more of a new burden and continues to rise faster than any other in our state?" I asked. It was the property tax, of course.

The League of Women Voters, Washington Education Association, School Directors' Association, Association of Counties and most daily newspapers endorsed tax reform. Nevertheless, polls showed the fight was all uphill. There were times during my three terms when I felt like Sisyphus rolling that boulder up a hill time after time.

AFTER A PARTICULARLY EXHAUSTING WEEK, I returned to the Governor's Mansion and crawled into bed, all but pulling the covers over my head. In the middle of the night I awoke from a deep sleep, laughing out loud. Nancy was startled. I had just experienced a dream that could have set psychiatrists' tongues wagging for weeks. In my dream, I was groping for a way to convince voters to support tax reform. Finally, in desperation, I announced that if tax reform passed I would walk stark naked down 3rd Avenue in downtown Seattle. They responded wonderfully, and the next day a huge, expectant crowd gathered as I arrived from Olympia, a small dog trotting behind me on a leash. I announced that this was my new pooch, "Stark," and I was going to walk Stark naked down the street. That's when I woke up. Nancy and I resolved that it ought to be our own little secret moment.

On Election Day, tax reform stood naked and alone, rejected by 68.45 percent of the electorate. I was not surprised it lost but disheartened by the margin and enormously disappointed that funding common-school education would grow substantially more difficult—especially given the deteriorating economy. I pored through the returns in Seattle and discovered a number of precincts that supported the measure. I was fascinated that these precincts were generally in higher-income neighborhoods. It was apparent that they were enthusiastic advocates of their schools and were convinced that the measure would give them sustained and dependable school support. Some of the most intense opposition came from low-income precincts where residents would unquestionably benefit from lower taxes. It seemed that their skepticism of government overcame the promise of lower taxes. With the defeat of HJR 42, Washington voters had rejected tax reform plans incorporating income taxes six times since 1932 by an average margin of nearly 68 percent. Still, I wasn't ready to abandon tax reform.

There is little question that the delay of a year in voting on the tax reform measure played a significant role in its defeat. The state Senate's refusal to pass an annual elections bill meant it was impossible to submit HJR 42 to the voters in November of 1969. The booming economy of 1969 turned into an economic freefall by November of 1970.

The 19-year-old vote was rejected by nearly 55 percent of the electorate; 56 percent backed legalizing abortion within four months after conception.

My party also lost several seats in the Washington State House, barely retaining the majority at 51 to 48. I knew the coming session would be brutal, since unemployment kept climbing, thousands of new students crowded our schools, revenue fell below expectations and voters were in a surly mood.

At the Western Governors Conference, I was riding in a bus with Oregon Governor Tom McCall, bemoaning the thumping I had absorbed on tax reform. Tom leaned back and roared with laughter: "Hell, Dan, I just tried to get a sales tax in Oregon, and got beat 8 to 1!" It is ironic that Oregon depends more heavily on a state income tax than any state in the nation and has no sales tax, while Washington depends on a sales tax more than any other state and has no income tax. We are neighbors and rather similar politically but hugely different on tax policy. It seems apparent that voters are more satisfied with the poison they know than the new one they haven't yet tried.

AT YEAR'S END, I sat down with Richard Larsen, the even-handed political writer for *The Seattle Times*, for a wide-ranging interview. He asked if I was deliberately moving my party away from traditional Republican positions on an income tax and unemployment compensation. "I think, if anything, maybe it's a return to the Republican Party of 100 years ago ... under Lincoln," I said. "They were initially successful as—in the words of so many in those days—a 'radical' party. They weren't so much radical as they were really progressive. The trouble with some forces in politics is that they're matching one group against another and trying to put together a coalition that makes a majority... That constantly carries with it the necessity of confrontation and polarization... My view is to see where the trouble points are today and try to get at those. But you don't back away from doing something because it happens to help a group that isn't part of your original coalition or constituency."

Larsen asked if I would run for a third term in 1972. It was a question I was thinking about frequently. I told him the whole truth: I didn't really know. At times it occurred to me that I would be happy to totally turn my back on politics. But then there were other times when the challenge of accomplishing something important—unfinished business—seemed irresistible.

I debated with myself for much of 1971 before finally deciding that the challenges and opportunities, especially with a recovering economy, were too great to walk away from. I would seek a third consecutive term, something no governor had yet achieved. But that announcement was a year away.

Unfortunately, almost more bad breaks than we could stand were still ahead.

33
SIGNS OF THE TIMES

The legendary dangling lightbulb billboard went up in April of 1971 across from a cemetery near Seattle-Tacoma International Airport, which in retrospect seems fitting. The sign said:

Will the <u>last person</u> leaving SEATTLE – <u>Turn out the lights.</u>

Bob McDonald and Jim Youngren, who sold real estate, intended it as "a spoof on all the gloom-and-doom talk" over Boeing's brutal layoffs. They wanted to emphasize Seattle wasn't dead yet. But the national media had a field day with Seattle's plight. The pain remained long after the sign came down. Having tried to do too much too fast, Boeing "came within an eyelash of bankruptcy," its CEO admitted years later. Seattle-area unemployment soared to 17 percent—worst in America—at the peak of what we ruefully remember as The Boeing Bust. Boeing employment on Puget Sound—100,000 in 1967—fell to 38,000 around the time the billboard message appeared.

When *Time* magazine and *The Wall Street Journal* ran stories about the billboard, it was the first topic at my next press conference:

"Would you say we are now a one-industry town?"

"No," I said, suppressing a sigh, "we are a no-industry town."

That was the low point, though we didn't know it at the time. Boeing employment began to slowly recover. I was intent on doing what we could to spur economic diversification and boost overseas markets. For the time being, however, weathering the storm was foremost on my mind. The defeat of my tax reform proposal and the Boeing layoffs created a dismal start to a new year and a new Legislature.

WE LOST FIVE HOUSE SEATS in the 1970 elections and now clung to a 51 to 48 majority. The Democrats boosted their Senate majority by two seats to 29-20. Bob Greive was chosen majority leader once again. More worrisome would be his role as the Rasputin behind the Democrats' efforts to control redistricting. The population numbers were in from the 1970 Census. No bill was exempt from becoming trading stock if Greive believed it could become a weapon to help pass a plan favorable to the Democrats. That Greive's old adversary, Slade Gorton, was now attorney general pained him deeply. Greive charged that Gorton was using "in-house facilities, including computer data," to give Republicans an unfair advantage. It wasn't true, but we certainly tapped Slade's expertise on political district line-drawing. The showdown was a year away.

A fascinating new influence on the House of Representatives was the sizable batch of freshmen elected from the Seattle area. As the 1971 session dragged on and partisan fights erupted almost daily, they forged a bipartisan coalition of sorts. The group featured four Republicans: Scott Blair, John Rabel, Paul Kraabel and Michael Ross. And six Democrats: Don Charnley, Jeff Douthwaite, King Lysen, Al Williams, Peggy Maxie and Jim McDermott. As they became better acquainted, they objected to the volatile partisanship they experienced and decided to erase the political boundary on a number of issues. Since the House was closely divided, the "Seattle 10" gained influence far beyond their scanty seniority. One of the most interesting members of the group was Mike Ross, a young African-American activist. Ross was elected as a Republican from the Democratic 37th District in Seattle's largely Black Central Area. He had participated in the protests at Seattle Community College and later at construction sites when members of the Black community demanded a chance at union apprenticeships. Ross became an eager member of the Seattle 10 and an important addition to the Republican House Caucus. Many in the caucus had little if any experience with a person of color and were oblivious to the root-causes of the urban issues that brought thousands of citizens to the streets. Ross helped immensely to educate and advise his colleagues about the conflicts facing the nation.*

I was impressed with these bright young freshmen. In mid-session I invited them to the Governor's Mansion for cocktails. We had a lively, constructive discussion on some of the major issues of the session. On some issues, they returned to their partisan roots, but on issues I cared most about they were united and powerful. They were concerned about the environment and farsighted on highway issues. Rabel summed it up as "the whole concept of balancing priorities between concrete and people." The Seattle 10 supported my Department of Transportation bills and demanded open-government reforms. Ross shocked his colleagues by sponsoring a bill legalizing recreational use of marijuana. He was 40 years ahead of his time.

FIGHTS BROKE OUT over my proposed budget even before the 1971 session got under way.

We had experienced a rapid decline in the number of patients at our three mental-health hospitals. This corresponded to similar drops across the nation as new drugs and community treatment centers were developed. I proposed the closure of Northern State Hospital in Skagit County and moving its patients to Western State Hospital in Pierce County. I also advocated adding dollars for traveling mental health teams and for community-based health centers, which struck me as a better investment than funding two large, half-full hospitals. The Skagit County community erupted in opposition and held a standing-room-only protest meeting. Dr. William Conte, deputy secretary of the newly formed Department of Social & Health Services, was the object of their wrath. Conte was a brilliant physician, though a somewhat scratchy administrator. Nevertheless, I believe he proposed a practical, modern and money-saving move—one I strongly endorsed. The fact that Skagit County— and the rest of the state—voted more than 2 to 1 against tax reform never seemed to dawn on those vociferously protesting cuts of any kind in the middle of a recession.

I knew it was going to be a long, tedious session, especially when the executive director of the Washington Education Association proposed a 19 percent salary increase for teachers in the new biennium. I was proposing no salary increases for anyone during an economic emergency. The WEA

---

* Ross's tenure in the House was unfortunately short-lived. The 37th District Democrats were not going to allow this electoral aberration to persist. Ross was defeated in his bid for re-election in 1972. It was a real loss, for he had the ability to become a legislative leader.

was so bizarrely out of line that it became almost irrelevant in legislative budget discussions. The Office of the State Superintendent of Public Instruction wasn't much better.

I caused more consternation with an appointment to the Washington State Game Commission. Traditionally, governors chose appointees from a list of candidates submitted by the State Sportsmen's Council. I made my own choice: Glen Galbraith, a member of the Spokane Tribal Council. Galbraith was a lifelong hunter and fisherman with an impressive background in civic and tribal affairs. Since the resolution of Indian fishing rights was one of the most significant issues facing the commission, I believed it was highly desirable for a respected Native American leader to serve on the commission. Ultimately, Galbraith helped create better understanding between two conflicting forces—tribes and sportsmen.

THE BOEING LAYOFFS amounted to a two-pronged crisis: lower tax revenues and higher demands for public assistance, unemployment compensation, and education as jobless workers sought re-training. A thousand welfare recipients marched on Olympia to demand additional benefits. The political dilemma was summed up by a freshman legislator who told me, "I believe in cutting fat out of the budget but I didn't know part of the fat was in my district." I reminded the legislators that since 1967 Washington was one of only five states without a major state tax increase. Our top priority was to avoid a deficit at the end of the biennium, which was only six months away.

My next move would prove controversial for years to come. I proposed revising the state's accounting procedure to treat both expenditures and revenues alike at the end of each biennium. We were measuring expenditures when they occurred, even if the bills were paid after the end of the biennium. Tax revenues, meantime, were counted when received, even though taxable sales occurred earlier. If we rationalized budgeting and counted 24 months of expenditures and 24 months of tax receipts for a biennium's activity it would give us a one-time gain. Twenty-five months of revenue would be counted against 24 months of expenditure. After that, every biennium would match 24 months of revenues and expenditures occurring during a biennium. Opponents dismissed it as "Evans jujitsu." It was something of a gimmick, but those were perilous financial times. I also requested that payments to the state employee and teacher retirement systems be suspended during the last six months of the biennium. Those moves would balance our budget and give us a chance to start a new biennium with no deficit. Other states were facing bankruptcy. But I warned the legislators that in the next biennium current expenditures would create a $565 million gap measured against anticipated revenues. In today's dollars, that was the equivalent of a $3.7 billion budget gap.

I felt strongly that we could not just cut budgets to lift ourselves out of recession. It was imperative to put people back to work. I proposed a two-stage economic recovery program— "Jobs Now" and "Washington Future." Jobs Now was designed to attract new businesses to the state during the next two years. The effort would be funded by extending the 4.5 percent sales tax to gasoline. After the next biennium, these revenues would be used to fund a series of bond issues for important capital investments. The focus would be on water pollution control, water supply, mass transit, storm-water drainage, recreational land acquisition and community college construction. The bond issues would total $500 million and would qualify for at least that much in federal and local matching funds. Washington Future advocated placing a series of major capital-improvement bond issues on the 1972 General Election ballot.

I caught hell from all sides. Predictably, Louis Bruno, the mercurial Superintendent of Public Instruction, claimed disaster for the public schools, and our pension actuaries warned against delaying payments into the state retirement systems. Fortunately, lower birth rates were now reflected in a declining school enrollment. Consolidation of institutions would bring more focused service and save substantial money.

A NEW CRISIS threatened to derail our budget when the Nixon Administration announced it would close the N-Reactor at Hanford. The weapons-grade plutonium the reactor produced was no longer needed, yet steam from the reactor fueled a generator that produced 500,000 mw of electricity, a substantial contribution to the region's power grid. When I contacted officials with the Atomic Energy Commission, I learned they were only concerned about the nuclear material produced. They had not considered the loss of electric power. The administration agreed to delay a shutdown until we had an opportunity to make our case. I assembled a bipartisan task force composed of legislators, public and private power leaders, Hanford business and labor representatives, and a nuclear scientist. We met with Nixon's science adviser, representatives of the Atomic Energy Commission and the Office of Management & Budget. In a White House meeting with the president, we pointed out that the proposed closures would put 6,000 people out of work at Hanford while another 3,000 to 5,000 manufacturing jobs could be at risk with the loss of the electrical power. The corresponding loss of revenue would unravel the precariously balanced state budget. We also offered to pay the Atomic Energy Commission $15 million a year to keep the N-reactor running to produce heat for electrical generation. We headed home with some hope our arguments would prevail.

The federal government offered to keep the reactor running for $31 million a year. After weeks of negotiation, we reached agreement to pay $20 million per year for three years. I was immensely pleased with the performance of our quickly mustered task force, especially with the joint effort of management and labor.

The bad news was the major blow we suffered a week earlier, when the U.S. Senate voted 51 to 46 to end development of Boeing's Supersonic Transport. The environmental coalition of SST opponents was led by Senator William Proxmire, the gadfly Wisconsin Democrat. Proxmire famously bestowed "Golden Fleece" awards on projects he felt wasted taxpayer money, including practically anything to do with space exploration. A decade of research and investment of millions of dollars ended, together with 15,000 jobs.

EACH WEEK, the recession deepened and state revenues ebbed. Soon the voices of the wishful thinkers on revenue were silenced and the Legislature focused on creating a balanced budget with no significant tax increases. In hundreds of hours of budget hearings over 120 days, we made the decisions that gradually closed the gap. However, having spent most of its stamina on the budget and measures to combat the economic crisis, the Legislature rejected two-thirds of my executive-request legislation. It did pass a landmark mandatory unemployment compensation bill covering state employees, as well as an alternative to the shoreline management initiative proposed by environmental enthusiasts. The citizens' initiative vested state government with most of the control for shoreline management. The legislative alternative gave more control to local government, with some state supervision. I strongly supported the legislative alternative, believing that local initiative was vital if this dramatic change was going to succeed. It would be left to the voters to decide between the competing proposals.

The Legislature sent me a gambling bill that would have opened opportunities for cardrooms, pinball machines and punchboards. I vetoed that section but allowed bingo games and raffles by nonprofit organizations. It was time to end the sleaze-promoting "tolerance policy" that plagued local police departments. In all, I vetoed 34 items, trimming more than $20 million from the legislatively passed appropriations.

TWO WEEKS LATER, Nancy and I took a memorable trip to the Soviet Union. It was the inaugural flight in Alaska Airlines' concentrated attempt to open air routes to Siberia.

In 1971, I signed into law a landmark Mandatory unemployment compensation bill covering state employees. Five House members played key roles in the bipartisan effort: Standing, from left, future Speaker Leonard Sawyer, D-Pierce; Hal Wolf, R-Thurston; Vaughn Hubbard, R-Walla Walla, and Gary Grant, D-King. Seated is future congressman Sid Morrison, R-Yakima. *Washington State Archives*

The lush architecture of the palaces of the Czars and the onion-domed ancient churches clashed with the gray monotony of Soviet workers' tenements and sterile government buildings. The scarcity of automobiles was notable, but the Moscow subway system, which carried seven million passengers per day, featured exquisite stations and modern railcars. Speedy hydrofoils traveled the urban rivers. In each city we were housed in modern hotels but invariably found the finished workmanship, especially in the bathrooms, particularly shoddy. I pondered how they could put satellites in space when they couldn't even lay tile properly. The inefficiency of the communist system was striking.

At Sochi, the stunning resort area on the Black Sea, we were treated to gypsy dancing and a fine meal at a traditional restaurant. A table of young Russians close by started singing Russian songs. We responded spontaneously with American songs. They moved our chairs over to their table and we all sang late into the night. The blustering of political leaders and threats of nuclear annihilation faded as people from homes 10,000 miles apart joined in a magical evening. The external view of a Soviet monolith disappeared when we heard the disparate voices of villagers who had no connection, love or respect for the central government. I saw a fragile assemblage of divergent states that could not last, yet it took almost 20 more years for the Soviet Union to splinter.

On my first day back in the office, I discovered a letter from a boy at Mount Vernon. He had written it just before I departed. I always liked to read the letters to the governor from everyday people. This one was priceless:

> Dear Govner Evens, My Dad says you are the only friend we have in Olympia and the legeslatur is Lousy and without you they would ruine our state and my dad attends meetings where he learns these things and he says now you are going to fly to China on a jet Plane and I worry for you because you know how these jets are always

crashing and falling in the water and so me and my friend Jimmy found these plastic blocks and we thought maybe you could put them in your pockets so you would float until the USA Navy could save you, and please be careful we need you. –Zelator Joven, Jr.

I kept those plastic blocks in my office display case for years. Whenever I concluded the "legeslatur" was lousy they made me smile.

THE OLYMPIA PRESS CORPS wanted to know whether I'd made up my mind about a third term. I had no intention of announcing a decision before the 1972 legislative session. If I said I wasn't running, I would instantly become a lame duck.

Martin Durkan was the Democrats' early frontrunner. Jim McDermott, brimming with self-confidence, was also making candidate noises. And Al Rosellini, despite losing to John Spellman in the race for King County executive, missed few opportunities to attack my administration.

Democrats scoffed that I was dissembling. I was still genuinely undecided. The continuing refusal of the Nixon Administration to respond to our economic crisis was my overwhelming concern. Focused on curbing inflation, Nixon's brain trust simply did not understand the depths of the recession in the far corner of America. With national inflation rates at 6 percent, Nixon decided to slow the economy by drastically limiting highway construction. At the Western Governors Conference in Wyoming in July of 1971, I pointed out that Washington's 12 percent unemployment rate was twice the national average. Yet our state was prevented from spending $150 million in available highway construction funds. "That would put a heck of a lot of people to work," I said. Labor Department officials were defensive and noncommittal.

Two days later, the U.S. Department of Agriculture refused to allow distribution of surplus commodities to needy Washington families. It was a total reversal of what I had been told 24 hours earlier. Tons of surplus food commodities were warehoused at Sand Point Naval Air Station in Seattle. We were mired in an unprece-

In the pool with Danny, 10, top, and Mark, 7, at the 1971 Western Governors' Conference in Grand Teton, Wyoming. *Evans Family Collection*

dented aerospace recession and they were worried about "setting precedents." I was as angry as I've ever been. Senator Magnuson called it "a callous disregard of the basic human needs." When Congressman Brock Adams, an influential Democrat, and Thomas Pelly, the veteran Republican from the 1st Congressional District, chimed in, our bipartisan indignation finally began to reach ears at the White House.

I asked Walt Howe, director of the Office of Program Planning & Fiscal Management, to assemble a list of programs that could help us jump-start a recovery. The list was long, ingenious and costly—almost $1 billion. I knew we had no chance of any response approaching that amount, but a fraction of that and some changes in federal policy, coupled with our own efforts, would add up to substantial relief.

Walt and I met with John Ehrlichman, Nixon's chief domestic adviser. The former Seattle lawyer was an old friend. He made sure we had a working session with George Schultz, director of the Office of Management & Budget. Schultz listened carefully and asked probing questions. Schultz seemed genuinely troubled by the statistics we cited. The jobless rate in Seattle was 15.7 percent; 180,000 people were out of work, and about 85,000 of them had no unemployment insurance. The number of people not on welfare but receiving food stamps had zoomed from 5,000 before the Boeing Bust to 36,000 in King County alone. Aid to Families with Dependent Children quintupled; home repossessions were up eight-fold. The state's unemployment compensation fund had dropped from $302 million to $122 million in the past year and was expected to be totally depleted in 1972. It was apparent that the Nixon Administration's major national concern was 5 percent inflation and 6 percent unemployment. I implored Schultz, to imagine national unemployment at 12 percent and inflation at 15 percent. We were in a unique mess.

The up-side, we emphasized, was our state's assets. Washington probably boasted the largest pool of skilled labor of any state in the nation, with a productivity rate 20 percent above the national average. We cited an abundance of clean water and agricultural land, foreign trade opportunities across the Pacific Rim, a good transportation system and low-cost hydro power. I told Schultz we were developing a major infrastructure investment program. Federal dollars would be well spent, and the state would happily shoulder its share.

Within a week the U.S. Senate overwhelmingly passed the Economic Disaster Relief Act of 1971, sponsored by Magnuson and Jackson. I was grateful that we had two of the most powerful senators in American history. The bill authorized temporary housing, mortgage or rent payments for up to a year, expanded food stamps, surplus commodities, extended unemployment compensation, job relocation assistance and medical services. The proposal treated "economic disasters" much the same way as hurricanes, floods or massive wildfires.

34
CAPTIVITY

The warden, looking nervous, gave me a briefing, told the guards to be vigilant and led me to a back gate at the Washington State Penitentiary. The maximum-security fortress at Walla Walla had been "troubled by idleness, violence, and overcrowding" practically since its first prisoners arrived in 1887. Some of its 1,300 inmates—ones who'd been incarcerated there more than once—called it "concrete mama." The humanizing reforms I supported were denounced by hardline conservatives.

It was the summer of 1971. Bloody prisoner revolts erupted at San Quentin in California and Attica in New York. Many warned Walla Walla could be next. Six months earlier, the prisoners at Walla Walla had refused to leave their cramped cells for 10 days. I wanted an unscripted tour of the 20-acre compound. And I was determined to go in alone.

Leaders of the inmates' Resident Council greeted me in the prison yard. I was a little apprehensive until I met my lead guide. His nickname was "The Crusher." Dressed in a T-shirt and shorts and carrying a clipboard, he looked more

B.J. Rhay, the warden at the State Penitentiary, talks with Johnny Harris, center, president of the inmates' Resident Government Council, and Gordon Allen, a council member, in 1972. *The Seattle Times*

like a camp counselor than an inmate, except his biceps bulged like a bodybuilder's. He'd spent a lot of time in the weight room.

I spent four hours with the prisoners, visiting their cell-blocks, listening to their hopes and grievances. They said the prison infirmary was so pathetic that getting sick in prison might be a death sentence. I was surprised by their intelligent questions and the lively debate over prisoner-shared governance of the institution, including how it could work better and what the limits should be. Unsurprisingly, they all viewed our new furlough program as a major incentive for good behavior. If things kept improving, one said, Washington could avoid an Attica.

The Crusher delivered me safely back to the exit gate. We shook hands. The warden looked relieved.

EARLIER IN THE YEAR, I had several meetings to see if the reforms were effective—or making things worse by letting "the tail wag the dog," as some wary guards put it. First, I met with the superintendents of our correctional institutions. We discussed the implementation of partial self-governance among inmates, and the lack of educational and vocational programs, especially at Walla Walla and the State Reformatory at Monroe on the west side of the state. At Walla Walla, the license-plate factory was the only meaningful work. Even that was haphazard.

The superintendents also admitted health care at their institutions was mediocre at best.

Since virtually all prisoners eventually will be released, it seems logical to better prepare them for a return to society. I felt strongly that except for the most vicious, recidivistic criminals, the future of corrections in Washington—and across the nation—ought to be smaller, community-based facilities with no more than 200 inmates. Dr. Karl Menninger's 1966 book, *The Crime of Punishment*, summed up all of my misgivings about patently punitive incarceration.

William Conte, the psychiatrist who headed the state Department of Institutions before his tenure with the Department of Social & Health Services, fervently believed humane treatment was crucial to rehabilitation and lower recidivism. I shared his view, especially given the baby boom explosion of young men being incarcerated at record numbers—minorities in particular. Conte remembered a late-night meeting in 1969 with Bobby J. Rhay, the longtime warden at Walla Walla, as a pivotal event. "One thing stands out in my mind very clearly," Conte recalled. "It was my prediction that something horrible could occur in Walla Walla…and that I thought it was within our power to prevent it. That prevention, of course, rested on our developing humane treatment." Conte sensed that the warden—hard-nosed yet open-minded—could be a game-changing ally.

The reforms Dr. Conte prescribed allowed inmates to dress as they pleased, grow beards and let their hair grow as long as they wanted. "Fair hearings were required before guards could punish inmates for rule infractions." And on visiting days, the inmates "could interact freely with their families and friends, rather than having to talk though glass partitions and screens," John A. McCoy wrote in *Concrete Mama*, an award-winning book that featured Ethan Hoffman's evocative photographs of life inside the penitentiary.

A month after Attica, Warden Rhay told CBS news, "I think we're writing history here."

Less convinced were the correctional officers. When I met with them to discuss their working conditions, the recession had caused staffing cutbacks that amplified their worries about the reforms. I excluded prison managers from that meeting so I could get a more candid response. Some of the guards feared for their lives, believing crafty inmates could gain control of the institution and run amok.

Having promised the corrections officers I would visit the penitentiary, I resolved that it would be just me and the inmates. Warden Rhay and the State Patrol chief said that was a bad idea. So there I was, in the custody of "The Crusher." Afterward, I knew I had made the right decision, though I fully realized reform would be anything but smooth sailing.

Prison management attempted to roll back some reforms when it felt inmates were abusing privileges. That led to a tense incident where inmates took over a wing of the prison and held officers hostage for several hours. Dr. Conte and I were denounced as dangerous Pollyannas.

A KEY PART of our prison reform program was to help ease the transition back to society by granting up to 30 days of outside leave to inmates who exhibited good conduct. With my support, the 1971 Legislature created a furlough program that drew national media attention. By the winter of 1972, some 2,000 inmates "had spent at least a day or two away from prison while out on furlough. Forty-two had failed to return, but nothing [had] happened to bring adverse attention to the program," Christopher Murray wrote in *Unusual Punishment*, a history of the prison reform movement at the state penitentiary.

Something terribly adverse happened on the night of February 5, 1972, when State Patrol Trooper Frank Noble, the father of six, pulled over a speeder near Zillah in Yakima County. It was a routine traffic stop. What Noble didn't know was that the man behind the wheel was a furloughed Walla Walla inmate who had just committed an armed robbery. Trooper Noble was shot three times, the last a .357 bullet to the head execution style. The inmate, serving time for a 1970 car theft, was soon apprehended and ended up being sentenced to life in prison.

"One incident, however tragic, cannot by itself end a program which has been considered promising," I told a news conference. Within days, we announced an eight-point plan to tighten the furlough program. That was cold comfort to a grieving widow and six children. I attended Trooper Noble's funeral in Sunnyside, together with State Patrol Chief Bachofner and more than 400 law enforcement officers from around the state. I met with Trooper Noble's wife, young son and mother. Though I'd given thousands of speeches, I found it impossible to express in a few words my anguish over their loss, and my distress over the errors that allowed it to happen.

More errors compounded the controversy.

Several weeks later, a Walla Walla inmate serving a life sentence was allowed out for the evening as part of Warden Rhay's "Take a Lifer to Dinner" program. The inmate escaped through a bathroom window and managed to make his way across the state to Tacoma, where he attempted to rob a pawnshop. In a gun battle with the owners, he was badly wounded but killed the owner and shot the man's wife before being apprehended. The inmate, Arthur St. Peter, was a notorious escape artist who should have been watched like a hawk. A judge who had presided over one of St. Peter's trials declared that letting him out for the evening was "the most flagrant example of bad judgment in prison management I have ever seen."

I totally agreed. It was yet another tragedy for law-abiding citizens and an election-year nightmare. I felt strongly, however, that a return to a highly punitive program of incarceration would do nothing to foster public safety because inmates would be returning to their communities unchanged after their release and commit further crimes. "Unfortunately, even in the best of well-regulated programs there will be failures, since there are significant risks involved," I told reporters. "If the prospects of a successful return are improved, then public safety is enhanced."

Though we never had a serious prison-wide outbreak in any of our correctional institutions during my 12 years in office, security at the antiquated penitentiary remained chaotic. Inmate gangs increasingly were preying on vulnerable first offenders. In 1979, a new warden gutted the furlough program. Violence ensued. A prisoner and a corrections sergeant were killed. A lockdown that lasted 146 days "was the pretext to institute a far more punitive prison," wrote Dan Berger, associate professor of Comparative Ethnic Studies at the University of Washington-Bothell.*

Today, I am even more convinced that soul-sapping warehousing hardens criminals. And the incidence of rape and other non-consensual sexual acts, especially against young inmates, remains appalling. Prisons, in other words, turn a lot of people into criminals or otherwise broken human beings.

IN THE FALL OF 1971, I felt like a judge trying to preside over two disputes—redistricting and fishing rights—where the litigants insisted on their own rules.

The U.S. Court of Appeals for the Ninth Circuit ruled that if the Legislature failed to enact a "constitutionally valid" redistricting plan by February 25, 1972, it would appoint a special master to do the job. The ruling complicated my plan for a January special session, though I took comfort in the realization that Bob Greive would have a tough time ramming a partisan redistricting bill past a Republican House. And if necessary, I could use my veto pen.

A states' rights issue added a new wrinkle to the fishing rights dispute. The Committee to Save Our Fish, a sportsmen's group, wanted the state to officially declare a policy on Indian net fishing. The Washington Supreme Court earlier had ruled that the state's Fish and Game departments could regulate off-reservation fishing by the Puyallup Tribe when necessary for conservation. It also ruled that the Puyallups no longer had a reservation. Now, however, the U.S. Department of Interior asserted that the Puyallup Reservation had never been terminated. It also ruled that the bed of the Puyallup River within the reservation was owned by the tribe. The conflicting decisions created a complex dilemma.

I told the Save Our Fish contingent that opinions of the Department of Interior did not over-rule decisions by our State Supreme Court. But we couldn't just ignore the fact that the Puyallups were relying in good faith on the legal advice of the federal government. The tribe believed it had an exclusive right to fish portions of the Puyallup River. The U.S. District Court was reviewing the case. Until we had a decision, arresting Indian fishermen and confiscating their property would be a harsh and inhumane way to contest the federal government's denial of state police power. I was hopeful the state, the Puyallups and other citizens could work together to honor treaty rights and preserve fishing resources for all. We needed joint management based on science rather than passion.

THE NEXT CHALLENGE—one with huge consequences for the Northwest—evolved from the commission formed by President Johnson in 1965 to attack poverty in Appalachia. It wasn't long before other states demanded the same kind of regional planning mechanism and federal assistance. The Nixon Administration created regional planning commissions for the entire country. Oregon Governor Tom McCall and Idaho's Cecil Andrus, two insightful partners, joined me for the first meeting of the Northwest commission. Someone dubbed us "The Three Musketeers."

---

* Governor Dixy Lee Ray scolded the ACLU for calling the penitentiary "the shame of the nation." However, she did ask the Legislature to authorize $29 million in bonds to renovate the penitentiary, build a new medium security prison, add a wing at the Shelton Corrections Center, and complete a mental health unit at the Monroe Reformatory. Increasingly at odds with the Legislature, she opposed proposals to ease overcrowding by having the state take over the federal prison at McNeil Island. The otherwise contentious 1979 Legislature appropriated a record $80 million for new correctional facilities. Two years later, when John Spellman became governor, the state signed a lease with the federal government to take over McNeil Island. Two new prisons were authorized in 1982.

We debated how best to use the planning funds. It was clear that an enormous battle was brewing between electric power producers and fish and environmental advocates over plans for huge new dams on the Snake River. In a letter to the Federal Power Commission, we voiced our concern over the potential for virtual elimination of salmon runs—a priceless Northwest treasure. Construction of additional dams in Hells Canyon would not be in the best interest of the people of the Northwest or the nation, we said. If all the dams proposed on the Snake were built, they would not make a significant dent in the impending power shortage. Hells Canyon was an archaeological treasure with unique combinations of plants and wildlife. It was time to seek protection for Hells Canyon and the Middle Snake River.

Our announcement brought jeers from electric power producers and cheers from fishermen and environmental advocates. It probably wasn't what Nixon and Congress had in mind when they created regional commissions. We bent the rules, but the result was dramatic. The dams were never built, extreme power shortages did not develop and Hells Canyon was preserved. I wish I could write that fish runs were also saved, but too many dams were already in place.

THE CRUSHING DEFEAT of my tax reform proposal in 1970 left unsolved the problems of a patchwork tax system. It was unable to keep pace with rapidly rising school enrollments—not to mention overcrowded prisons—and continuing high inflation. Some legislators urged another attempt at tax reform. While I agreed that another attempt under somewhat better economic circumstances might be worthwhile, I did not want it to be another "Dan Evans tax plan."

Mary Ellen McCaffree had just finished eight years in the state House of Representatives, recently as chairman of the Committee on Revenue and Taxation. I hired her to complete a study on how best to plan for a new tax reform campaign. I knew the odds of success were slim, but I could not accept the current tax system. It was unfair, unresponsive and unproductive.

Mary Ellen reported back with a comprehensive agenda for a Committee for a New Tax Policy for Washington state. The group was charged with studying ways to finance high-quality basic education without special levies; remove business and occupation and inventory taxes; explore alternatives for an equitable tax system, and recommend a new tax policy to the 1972 Legislature. An outstanding group of citizens from business, labor, agriculture and education agreed to serve on the steering committee, including T.A. Wilson, president of the Boeing Company; Arnie Weinmeister, head of the Joint Council of Teamsters, and Jocelyn Marchisio, president of the state League of Women Voters. The group also included eight legislators. They were all enthusiastic, though well aware it would be an uphill battle to win over voters suspicious that the Legislature would boost taxes regardless.

THE YEAR ENDED with a preview of the 1972 campaign for governor. Senator Durkan proposed extending unemployment benefits and granting a cost-of-living raise for state employees. His theory was that extra dollars in people's pockets would create "an immediate infusion into the state's economic bloodstream." He claimed the cost could be met with a tax-free loan from the federal government, coupled with a tax increase on liquor sales. I countered with my Jobs Now and Washington Future programs, which could be financed with a sales tax on gasoline.

The irony was that Senator Greive, the Democrats' majority leader, headed an interim committee that for several weeks conducted hearings on Jobs Now and Washington Future. Greive recognized the depth of the recession and was trying to build a responsible legislative program. Richard Larsen summed things up with this perceptive paragraph in his *Seattle Times* column: "Greive, an arch Democrat who savors his ability to muscle lawmakers on redistricting and on other issues, suddenly loomed, by contrast, as a statesman on economic recovery. But Greive finds himself in a weird dilemma: He's been laboring all these weeks for a program wanted by his arch foe, the governor. Now the gubernatorial candidate of his own party, Durkan, starts chopping at it. 'I just can't figure it out politically,' Greive moaned today. He isn't alone."

It was going to be a fascinating year.

35
"DOING SOMETHING!"

Some pundits were still nursing New Year's Eve hangovers when the first political shot of the 1972 election year was fired: Victor Gould, an anti-tax activist, announced his candidacy for governor. The Bellevue businessman denounced both Republicans and Democrats as peas in the same tax-and-spend pod. Gould declared he would run on the "Taxpayer$ Party" ticket and hoped to attract other no-new-taxes candidates. While it was obvious he had no chance of winning, he would prove to be a substantial help to me in the General Election. Voters adamantly opposed to tax reform could vote for Gould instead of a Democrat.

I knew the massive defeat of my tax reform plan in 1970 would become a major political issue in 1972. Many advisers urged me to lay low on tax reform if I was going to seek a third term. But I was so identified with the issue and so committed to modernizing the state's dependence on sales taxes and B&O taxes that I decided to ask the Legislature to try again.

As part of my push to usher in annual sessions of the Legislature, I called an even-year extraordinary session for the second time in state history. Our public schools were in deeper trouble, "special" property tax levies having increased almost tenfold in the previous decade. Many more were failing. In addition to tax reform, I wanted to counter the Boeing Bust recession with job-producing investments in our state's infrastructure. Statewide unemployment was hovering at 12 percent.

In the 1971 session I had pushed unsuccessfully for a series of six "Washington Future" bond issues—capital projects for waste disposal, water supply, recreation, health and social services, public transportation and community colleges. I believed it was a way to jumpstart our construction industry and ultimately modernize our state's infrastructure. Legislative leaders balked at referring the package to the voters, saying it would be DOA in the middle of the worst economic downturn since the 1930s. They were probably right. The issues were so vital, however, that every speech I gave emphasized the importance of building ourselves out of our recession.

Al Rosellini, given up for dead by many after he was defeated by John Spellman in the 1969 race for King County executive, was busy giving speeches around the state, to the obvious irritation of Martin Durkan, who saw himself as a shoo-in for the Democratic nomination for governor. Rosellini boasted that if he secured the nomination he would be all "set up to go back to Olympia."

TO EMPHASIZE THE URGENCY of our economic challenges, I asked the Legislature for permission to speak to a joint session on its first night. The prime time TV broadcast was an opportunity to speak directly to taxpayers about the need to revive the Washington Future program. I proposed extending the sales tax to gasoline to fund the state share of the bond issues. While watching the counters spin on the gas pump, citizens could say, "It's a quarter for me, for my state, for my children and my neighbor's children and for our future health and economic welfare." Economic recovery required a public investment in productive jobs. "It isn't the easy thing to do, but it's the right thing to do," I said, "and now is the time to do it."

Durkan called my plan "fiscal legerdemain," and Len Sawyer, the House minority leader, claimed I had just offered "the most fiscally irresponsible and factually misleading report from a governor in the modern history of the Legislature."

Nevertheless, the Legislature scheduled a major hearing on the economic development program. The House chambers were jammed with spectators, lobbyists and scores of legislators. For the second time in seven years I asked to testify before a legislative committee. I urged passage of the Jobs Now and Washington Future programs. Making the investment might be difficult, I said, but it would bring enormous rewards and ultimately cost less than doing nothing. Baker Ferguson, chairman of the Highway Commission, stunned the lawmakers by saying a majority of the commission had "considerably greater enthusiasm for the programs than for the method of funding." Absent "a fairer, better form of tax," the majority favored extension of the sales tax on gasoline over loss of programs. My rejoinder was that if someone could come up with a more equitable source of income I'd listen. Even the Good Roads Association, adamantly opposed to my plan earlier, now supported the proposals if a different financing source could be found. If we failed to act, our current troubles would only compound. The post-war kids flooding our schools would soon enter the workforce. We'd need 200,000 new jobs during the 1970s just to stay even.

Durkan was worried. He invited Larry Kenney, director of research for the State Labor Council, to testify on economic recovery. Kenney dutifully praised Durkan's proposal to raise unemployment compensation and state workers' wages and blasted my proposals, saying, "I don't think Washington Future is an economic program. It's a political program." If any taxes were needed to fund economic recovery, the B & O tax should be increased by 25 percent, he asserted. Kenney ended his bizarre testimony by proposing the elimination of the Department of Commerce and Economic Development. Many senators on the committee seethed with indignation. Senator Jim Andersen, an old friend, growled, "It's political jobbing, pure and simple." That same day, the House State Government Committee approved all six of the proposed Washington Future bond issues. I seized the moment, telling legislative leaders I was not adamant about the details of the taxes to finance the program, or even all of its elements. Given the state of the economy, what mattered was doing something meaningful. I also reminded them that they were under court order to pass a redistricting bill. Absent an adequate recovery program, there was no way I'd sign it. To Democrats in the Senate that was a chilling possibility. The alternative would be redistricting by a court-appointed master unconcerned about the political fate of incumbents.

I WAS IMMENSELY PLEASED when the entire package I proposed was adopted by the Legislature. The Jobs Now initiative gave me great flexibility to invest the state appropriation wherever it could help produce new jobs speedily. We focused on extending sewer and water lines to plant sites where pending construction was halted by lack of infrastructure. Within months new manufacturing facilities were rising in communities across the state. The six Washington Future bond issues were sent to the voters for the fall election of 1972. Collectively the issues totaled $450 million. Most were matched by significant federal and local funds. The total investment would be almost $2 billion. It was the most important—and most contentious—program I had presented to the Legislature in my seven years as governor. Happily, bipartisan legislative leadership took charge and produced a first-class result.

The disappointment was that tax reform failed after intense political warfare in the last hours of the session. It was a two-pronged plan, and both elements were vital. The first was a constitutional amendment authorizing an income tax while setting significant limits on all taxes. The second was an implementing bill setting the statutory levels on all taxes. I argued vehemently that without a constitutional amendment and an accompanying bill, tax reform would almost certainly fail at the polls. The Republican-led House passed a constitutional amendment authorizing an income tax with strong constitutional limitations on other taxes. A companion measure established rates on all taxes. An ad hoc committee representing the four caucuses met for hours and approved a compromise very much like the original House-passed proposal. The Senate then adopted the proposal and sent it to the house—but without an implementing bill. House leadership argued against adopting only one part of the package. After a contentious meeting, the constitutional amendment was rejected. Tax reform was dead for the session.

Now the finger-pointing began. Senators claimed they only agreed to pass the constitutional amendment and the implementing bill could come later. Republican leadership compared it to the Legislature signing a blank check for the future. Durkan was happy that the proposal would not be on the ballot when he ran for governor. And Joe Davis, head of the State Labor Council, trashed the entire package. Ironically, in a complete reversal of tradition, the Republican leadership joined me in pushing for tax reform, including an income tax, while Democrats and labor opposed it.

Redistricting was also a standoff. Bob Greive, intent on retaining his post as Senate majority leader, was locked in combat with Sid Morrison of Zillah, the House Republicans' point man. With Slade Gorton, Greive's old adversary, as attorney general there was no way we were going to let the Democrats gain the upper hand. The impasse cast a long shadow over the session. What was needed was a bipartisan, independent redistricting panel. The federal district court took us to the first step by appointing a professional geographer to oversee the process.

STILL BIDING MY TIME on a third term announcement, I resolved that tax reform would be my major campaign issue. It would be an uphill battle, especially after the ballot box debacle in 1970 when tax reform was rejected by 68 percent of the voters. In any case, the Democrats were going to paint me as the man out to inflict an income tax on the beleaguered citizenry. I strongly believed tax reform was necessary to adequately fund K-12 education. Now was the time to find out what people were thinking.

In the next 40 days, I visited all 39 counties. Hundreds of times people would tell me, "We need to find a better way than special levies to fund our schools, but I can't afford to pay any more in taxes." Sometimes the message was more direct. One spring morning I stationed myself outside the gates of the Weyerhaeuser pulp mill at Cosmopolis on Grays Harbor. One sturdy-looking young fellow, lunch pail in hand, was startled to encounter his governor. He did a double take before shaking my outstretched hand. "My wife always votes for you," he said. "I might too, but I'm not going to vote for any fucking income tax!"

Here's some advice from an old campaigner: Don't run for political office if you're thin-skinned. And never underestimate your opponent, especially if he's Irish.

When I strolled into the Sears store in Renton on St. Patrick's Day, Senator Durkan was already working the crowd. He was sporting a bright green sport coat and matching slacks. My pale green carnation seemed so inadequate. "Welcome to the 47th District, governor!" Durkan declared. Clearly his people—a young guy named Mike Lowry was his campaign manager—had studied my schedule. Durkan proceeded to shadow me as I pitched tax reform to shoppers, interjecting his own views. When the TV crews packed up, he headed for his next stop.

"Thanks for helping me out," I quipped.

"Any time!" Durkan grinned.

"Maybe I'll come back next year," I offered.

"That's what I was afraid of!"

MOST OF THE PEOPLE who attended our tax reform meetings asked intelligent, often probing questions. Most expressed their support for tax reform at the end of the sessions. It was apparent that slogans and TV ads weren't going to change people's minds. Somehow we needed to develop a comprehensive educational campaign to give voters a clear idea of what tax reform would mean to them. Looking back—and ahead—there's one big constant: Washington voters believe politicians will find clever new ways to raise their taxes after promising to make things better.

I met thousands of people on that tour and rediscovered some

Campaigning for tax reform outside the Weyerhaeuser pulp mill on Grays Harbor in 1972. *John C. Hughes/The Daily World*

fundamental facts about citizens and voters. Their attitudes depended on whether they viewed themselves as "taxpayers" or "tax users." Virtually everyone is both. Teachers, school administrators, and parents of schoolchildren supported tax reform knowing that the focus of new money would be on education. They seldom told me about high taxes. Older citizens, and those without schoolchildren in their families, declared they were being taxed out of their homes. They were skeptics that property taxes would be lowered under tax reform and seldom understood that property taxes funded most of local government, including basic fire and police protection. People continuously told me that taxes were soaring, looking skeptical when I responded that overall it wasn't true since the ratio between average income and the average tax bill was the same as it was six years earlier. "Realities aren't necessarily what people think they are," I told a reporter in Spokane, "but that's the way they will vote."

As I neared the end of my month-long tour, the drumbeat of skepticism about tax reform was brightened by an unexpected development. The five student body presidents of our four-year colleges and universities issued a statement urging me to seek a third term because I had "demonstrated moral and intellectual strength, political courage and honesty." They touted Representative Jim McDermott as a second choice. Surprisingly, they said they had "little respect" for Durkan. And none of them mentioned Rosellini. Every year since taking office, I had invited the student body presidents to the Governor's Mansion for a luncheon. It was energizing to know they appreciated what I was trying to achieve. I would need the youth vote.

IN A TELEVISED STATEWIDE BROADCAST at the end of the tax reform tour, I reported what I'd learned. I also met with 40 legislative leaders to determine whether two-thirds of both houses could ratify a specific tax reform package in a one-day special session. I reported that people were more distressed about property taxes than I expected. They were also adamant about constitutional limits on taxation. "We're in the middle," people told me. "The poor are getting the benefits; the rich are getting tax exemptions. We're getting stuck." The interest in tax reform was more intense in the areas where property tax levies were the highest and strangely least popular in low-income communities that would benefit from tax relief. Washington's tax system is inherently regressive. The unhappiness and confusion over taxes was best expressed by a citizen who wrote, "Do something—even if it's wrong."

Legislative leaders could not reach agreement on a specific package, so plans for a special session were abandoned. I think most legislators were uneasy about tax reform being on the ballot when they were running for re-election.

THE GOOD NEWS WAS that the economy was beginning to rebound. State tax revenues and employment were exceeding previous estimates. The timber and agricultural industries were expanding. Boeing even rehired a few hundred workers, though its sales were still way down.

I waited until June to make a formal announcement that I would seek re-election. I wanted it to be a family moment because the next five months would test us all. Nancy, 11-year-old Danny, 8-year-old Mark and Bruce, who was 5, joined me on a whirlwind tour of the state. We were surrounded by enthusiastic supporters during each press conference, but the three boys were bored stiff by mid-afternoon. When Mark was asked if it was fun to campaign with his dad, he replied, "You have to get up too early!" At our final event in Spokane, Nancy's home town, Bruce stuck his tongue out at a photographer—an editorial comment on the joys of campaigning if there ever was one. It was the day's best photo-op.

Accompanied by Nancy, Danny, Mark and Bruce, I announce my candidacy for a third term in a campaign stop at Vancouver in 1972. *Evans Family Collection*

Initiative 276, the sweeping public disclosure measure championed by citizen activist Jolene Unsoeld, would be on the fall ballot. I released copies of my federal income tax returns for the seven years I had served as governor and reported my net worth was $85,000. I also released the names of all of my campaign contributors, together with the amount of their donations, and waited with interest to see how my challengers would respond.

I received an unexpected call from W.A.C. Bennett, the Premier of British Columbia. He was interested in creating an agreement to cooperate on cleanup of oil spills. It was the first official contact from the province during my time as governor. I learned that Bennett was about to call an election and wanted to burnish his environmental credentials. The idea was a good one, however, and our staffs worked together to create a joint action plan when oil spills threatened both sides of the border. The official signing ceremony, appropriately, occurred at the Peace Arch monument on the border between British Columbia and Washington. The meetings opened an opportunity for much closer relationships with British Columbia, which proved valuable—although not for Premier Bennett, who lost his bid for re-election. I was worried about my own chances.

There were days when I felt like sticking out my tongue the moment I looked at my daily schedule. I pleaded for family time, finally demanding that Sundays be reserved for Nancy and the boys. I grabbed one choice breather when I discovered that the City of Yakima sponsored a mass climb of Mt. Adams each year. Slade Gordon signed up, too, together with a sizable contingent from Olympia. It was a joyous, two-day adventure that drew nearly 500 climbers in all—hundreds of potential voters who shared my love of the outdoors. I stood atop the mountain, basking in glorious sunshine, followed by 15 minutes of sheer exhilaration in a 2,000-foot sitting glissade down a snow slope that had taken three hours to climb earlier in the day. I returned to Olympia refreshed and ready for the last two months of the campaign.

A RELATIVELY PEACEFUL—for a change—Republican state convention elected a unified slate of delegates to the 1972 GOP national convention. I was selected to head the delegation. We returned to Miami Beach, this time devoid of drama. Nixon was re-nominated by acclamation. Outside the convention hall some 6,000 mostly mellow protesters occupied a park. Jack Pyle, a political writer for the *Tacoma News Tribune*, invited me to accompany him on a visit to the Yippies, hippies and assorted other discontented youth bivouacked outside. We wandered through hundreds of small encampments featuring makeshift sun shelters. No one realized I was a governor. I was offered a "joint" several times, declining each with a polite smile. What a photo-op that would have been! I sat down with several groups to hear what was on their mind. It was Vietnam, of course. I said I had shared their concern for years, but felt the war was winding down. It was no longer viable, politically or militarily. How about life after the war? Their response was inspiring. They seemed less concerned about their individual lives than ending

California Gov. Ronald Reagan buttonholes me during the 1972 GOP National Convention at Miami Beach. *AP*

poverty and ensuring equal opportunity for minorities and women. It was an eye-opening experience, in vivid contrast to the drone of speeches across the street.

As we left Miami Beach, I noticed a relatively small headline in *The New York Times*: "Stans Swears He Can't Explain $114,000 Switch." Maurice Stans, the former Secretary of Commerce, was President Nixon's chief fundraiser. He swore under oath that he did not know how $114,000 in contributions to the Committee to Re-elect the President ("CREEP" for short—an unfortunate acronym if there ever was one) ended up in the hands of a man arrested in a burglary attempt at the Democratic Party headquarters in the Watergate complex.

There was a cancer growing on the presidency, as John Dean would put it later. I had deeply mixed emotions about Richard Milhous Nixon, but no inkling of his practically pathological paranoia and crude anti-Semitism—no suspicions that he and his White House confidants, including men like John Ehrlichman, whom I knew and liked, would go to any lengths to obliterate political opposition. If the public and the convention delegates had known in August of 1972 what they learned in August of 1974 the course of history would have changed radically.

36
DANNY BOY

With bounce in his step and a rosebud in his lapel, Albert D. Rosellini was the happy warrior of the summer of '72. He kissed babies, ate cotton candy, posed with rodeo queens and waved gleefully from street corners when motorists honked and cabbies yelled "Hi, Al!" He denounced Durkan and Evans as a pair of reckless "spenders," styled Jim McDermott as a wet-behind-the-ears McGovernite and himself as a conservative populist who would cut $100 million from the state budget and push through property tax relief.

By Labor Day, Durkan's shamrock had wilted. He was so convinced it was going to be his year that he couldn't grasp the reality of Rosellini's momentum. Durkan's springtime poll showed him way out in front in the race for the Democratic nomination. And his mid-August sampling maintained he was the only Democrat who could beat me. Our polls had Rosellini pulling ahead of Durkan but losing to me if he won the nomination. I was taking nothing for granted. Rosellini's relentless attacks on "The Two faces of Martin Durkan" demonstrated that at 62—spoiling for a rematch with me—the former governor was still one of the savviest old pros in the history of Washington politics. Though outspent by more than $50,000, he had Durkan on the defensive.

Shortly after the first primary election returns were reported, the crowd was stunned by Rosellini's lead. I knew I was now in the toughest fight of my political career. While I was rolling up a two-to-one margin over conservative state Senator Perry Woodall, who attacked me as a spendthrift, Al was crushing Durkan and running well ahead of me in total votes. Democrats, in the final count, had captured nearly 64 percent of the votes cast in the open primary.

Rosellini was exultant, Durkan furious and McDermott also angry over Al's bare-knuckle campaign. Both reserved judgment on whether they would now support him. I took solace that at least the third term issue was dead. The Evans-Rosellini rematch pitted a pair of two-term governors.

AT OUR FIRST POST-PRIMARY campaign committee meeting it was unanimous that we would challenge Rosellini to debate—and the more the better. Rosellini, now supremely confident, claimed to have conflicts on every date we suggested. He attacked me on tax reform, saying an income tax was unnecessary—just another way to fund "bloated" liberal government. He said the state budget on my watch was 137 percent higher than when he left office. I was soft on crime, "coddled" convicts and opposed the death penalty, Rosellini asserted. Prison reform might be well-intentioned, he said, but it was jeopardizing law-abiding citizens. He painted the Department of Social & Health Services as a monolithic disaster and charged that I had installed freewheeling cronies on the Liquor Control Board.

A month from Election Day, our polls agreed with his: He had a double-digit lead. In a move to distance their candidate from George McGovern, a sure-loser at the top of the ticket, the Rosellini brain trust even issued a campaign button featuring Rosellini's trademark rose below Nixon's name.

We finally found an event where it would be difficult for Al to dodge a face-to-face debate. North Seattle Community College was sponsoring a candidates' fair on Saturday, October 14, with speeches scheduled every half-hour. Rosellini had agreed to speak late in the morning. Our team negotiated with his team and asked KOMO-TV if it would host a debate. KOMO was delighted. The negotiations ended when Rosellini's team insisted the time period proposed for a debate was assigned to their guy. If I wanted a debate I would have to issue a challenge, presumably for some other date. Rosellini's camp maintains he was blindsided by the events that unfolded, but the record is clear.

At a well-attended press conference that Friday I charged that the former governor was insulting the voters. Tomorrow, I said, there was a golden opportunity to let the public judge which candidate was being transparently candid about the issues facing our state. "Instead of hiding in the shadows, it's time Albert Rosellini stepped out into full daylight—not only to debate the issues but also to be totally candid in his campaign finance reporting. In contrast, we have reported every dollar, every donation." I had released my tax returns for every year in office as governor. Al had refused.

THE COLLEGE GYMNASIUM was lined with candidate booths and festooned with bunting, balloons and posters. A platform had been erected for the speechmaking. Hundreds of voters mingled with candidates. Tipped to possible fireworks, a sizable contingent of my supporters was on hand. At 11 o'clock, when Rosellini was introduced, I pushed through the crowd and approached the steps to the platform. A short, barrel-chested man blocked my path. I don't know whether that was part of a plan to keep me at bay or if he was just a Rosellini stalwart who leapt into action. Little matter. "Get out of my way, you S.O.B.!" I barked. He grudgingly stepped aside. I sprinted up to the platform just as Rosellini was declaring, "Well, good morning ladies and gentlemen!" I interrupted him. "Governor Rosellini, as was printed in the *P-I* this morning and as you very well know from remarks I made yesterday, we have been searching for the time for us to appear on the same platform and answer the same questions, to discuss the issues before the people of the state. ... I am ready. You are here. I think it's time to conduct a debate." Two podiums were in place, I noted, and KOMO's Art McDonald, a fair-minded reporter, was on hand to serve as moderator.

When our eyes met, Rosellini's flashed annoyance for a few seconds. Then he put on a bemused face and smiled at the crowd as if to say he was going to indulge a pathetic act of scene-stealing by a desperate junior opponent. The crowd pushed toward the stage as the red lights on two hulking television cameras blinked on. The former governor's condescending first words were the opening salvo of one of the most amazing gaffes in Washington political history:

"Well, thank you very much, Danny Boy. I am delighted to have you here. I really am because maybe you can learn something about state government. ... Certainly I will engage in a debate or whatever Danny Boy wants to call it."

That first "Danny Boy" was astonishing to me. Irritated at being cornered, Rosellini had made an inexplicable blunder for such a seasoned campaigner. He was mocking not just me but the office of governor. I was determined to not respond in kind.

"Mr. Rosellini," I said, "the only way to do..."

"Danny," he interrupted, "I wish you would quit these childish [acts] like you have been all this campaign so far."

Some onlookers booed and one student shouted "Chicken!" Rosellini frowned. I could tell he was nervous.

"I think it's pretty clear," I said, "that you are not willing to stand up …with Mr. McDonald sitting right here, and make a presentation of three or four minutes, then allow me to make a presentation."

Smiling again, Rosellini said we should have at it. He protested, however, that the three-minute statement-and-rebuttal format outlined by McDonald was "basically unfair" because he had prepared for a speech, not a debate.

I jumped right in, asserting that spending more than doubled during his two terms as governor. "But more importantly he presented four budgets to a Legislature and so did I. His four budgets included deficits at the end of every single biennium. Mine had surpluses at every single biennium. And the state Senate, in its wisdom, cut each of his four budgets and raised each of my four budgets. So much for who is a fiscal conservative in office."

Rosellini regretted his "Danny Boy" quip.
Washington State Archives

Rosellini shot back: "I am delighted to have the chance to try to get Danny Boy to be specific at some issues. Up till now he has resorted to nothing but distortions and name calling and trickery—trickery to try to confuse the public …"

As we sparred on taxes, social services, education and openness in government, the former governor persisted in calling me "Danny Boy" or "Danny"—10 times in all, including in his closing statement. The crowd responded derisively each time—and not just the Evans partisans. The press didn't need an applause meter to declare a winner. At the end, my ovation was twice as long and loud. A telephone poll of 500 registered voters a few days earlier indicated I was gaining yet still a half-dozen percentage points behind. On Sunday night we polled the same voters. Some 300 of them had watched TV coverage of the debate. The shift overall was dramatic. I was now leading by 10 percentage points.

Rosellini didn't need a poll to grasp that he had made a grave error. A torrent of calls and letters to his campaign headquarters sufficed. During a speech at a Tacoma high school a few days later, Rosellini said he regretted his "facetious tone" in the heat of a debate. I had called him "Taxellini" in the past, he said, but "Danny Boy" was inappropriate. "I feel I should not have done it. I don't like name-calling. I have high respect for the office of governor, and for people who hold that office. I have respect for Dan Evans as a man. I meant no offense."

For several years afterward, at political and community events, I was frequently greeted by the audience singing "Danny Boy." I learned to hate that song.

I had some profound regrets of my own when one of my supporters—an insurance salesman in Wenatchee—all on his own, printed up a batch of "Does Washington Really Need a Godfather?"

bumper stickers. It was an appalling stunt. The son of hard-working Italian immigrants, Rosellini was a self-made man, justifiably proud of his ancestry. He had overcome not just racial but religious prejudice to become Washington's first Roman Catholic governor. Events that would play out in the last days of the election added to the spurious charge that Gorton and I "grossly played on the public's worst fears of Italians." The fact was, I had respect for Albert D. Rosellini, not just as a man but as a progressive governor.

WE SEEMED TO BE ON A ROLL. The economy was recovering, with unemployment projected to drop from 8.7 percent to 7 percent during 1973. Washington's foreign trade was booming. I announced that I foresaw no need for new taxes during the next biennium, which would mark the fifth year for no general tax increase. Few governors could make that boast.

Considering all the gibes I had endured over the years from Ed Donohoe, the acerbic editor of the Teamsters' house organ, I was tickled when the powerful union strongly endorsed my re-election, saying I had always kept my promises and been "truly a friend of labor." As we racked up editorial endorsements, I now really felt confident I would win.

It was becoming clear that the candidacy of Vick Gould of the Taxpayers Party was actually doing me a favor by giving opponents of tax reform an alternative to Rosellini.

What we definitely didn't need was another loose cannon in our midst.

When Gorton announced he had suspended Keith Dysart, his bright but headstrong chief deputy in the Attorney General's Office, for political intrigue, the Rosellini campaign charged there was now fresh evidence the "Godfather" smear was part of an "obvious conspiracy."

Dysart was conducting an unauthorized off-duty investigation of rumors that Rosellini was seeking help for Hawaii associates of Seattle's notorious Colacurcio family. When Dysart shared his tips with our campaign committee, it hired a private detective to track down the rumors. I knew about the detective but nothing about Dysart's extracurricular activities. Nor did Slade. Dysart, meantime, had shared his sleuthing with the *Seattle Post-Intelligencer* and KING Broadcasting's ace reporter, Don McGaffin, who concluded the evidence was "too flimsy to warrant a story." The *Post-Intelligencer* kept digging. Its executive editor, Lou Guzzo, saw credibility in the Rosellini-Colacurcio rumors. He viewed the Colacurcios as "our own little mafia" and believed "something needed to be done … to demonstrate to the Italian community and others that at least some Italian Americans…were on the right side of the law."

What a tangled web. I was furious that we were being painted as racist junior G-men in the last week of a campaign we appeared to be winning. Rosellini declared he was the victim of a "Joe McCarthy guilt-by-association" "Watergate West" "Gestapo" operation and a "terrifying type of terrorism" rooted in bigotry and innuendo. Scoop Jackson joined him at a press conference, angrily declaring, "I would have no time for those who spread bigotry… it's political genocide by national origin." However, when asked about the testimony of witnesses in a Colacurcio trial linking Rosellini to Colacurcio, Jackson said he would not go into the facts of the trial. And Rosellini acknowledged he "might have" phoned an old friend, a Honolulu police sergeant, concerning the Colacurcios, but the friend was also celebrating his 25th wedding anniversary and he'd made "several calls to offer his best wishes."

On October 30, when I walked into a scheduled press conference, the podium bristled with microphones from no less than 14 radio and television stations. The horde of reporters, poised with pads, pencils and tape recorders, included a visitor from *The Washington Post*. I announced that the Atomic Energy Commission was planning to build a new uranium fuel processing plant and that we would undertake a major effort to have it located at Hanford. "Now that you are out of film," I said with a thin smile, "let me turn to a comment on what seems to be on everybody's mind." Addressing Senator Jackson's accusations, I said that never in my entire life had I engaged in racial slurs. My record of two decades in politics spoke pretty clearly for itself, I said. "I have fought for and will continue to fight for not only racial equality and brotherhood but would not stoop to any such innuendo. To suggest anything differently is totally uncalled for in this campaign." I was unapologetic, however, about the campaign hiring a private investigator to investigate rumors affecting both our administration and the opposition, emphasizing that there was no wire-tapping or any other illegal activity.

The second I finished, 25 hands shot up. The questions were intense, probing and skeptical. Many revolved around a private investigator's report: What did it say? Had I read it? Who hired the investigator? Could they see it? I had not seen a report, I said, and was not even sure there was one. If a report existed, I said I would examine it and decide whether it was worth publicizing. I did not want to further spread unconfirmed rumors that might be contained in such a report. Dick Larsen of *The Seattle Times* pressured me on whether powers of the state were used in any investigation. I said I had found nothing that would indicate that was so.

When the grilling ended, I couldn't resist a quip: "No questions on uranium?"

On November 7, 1972, I became the first Washington governor elected to three consecutive terms. I outpolled Rosellini by 117,000 votes—50.78 percent to his 42.82 percent. Even Vick Gould's 86,800 votes wouldn't have given him the victory. But it would have been close.

I was immensely pleased that five of the six Washington Future bond issues were passing with substantial majorities in a record voter turnout. Unfortunately, the $50 million transit issue failed narrowly. There was an ironic twist: Western Washington voters backed the water supply bond issue, a portion of which would be used for irrigation projects in Eastern Washington, while Eastern Washington voters opposed the transit measure. Once again the farmers outmaneuvered the city slickers. However, the five bond issues approved by the voters gave us a major economic boost for the next five years, including construction of more than $1.5 billion in infrastructure improvements.

In all, voters faced 24 separate issues, an all-time record. A resounding 72 percent of the electorate endorsed Initiative 276, the open government reforms.

Dan Jr. dances with his mom at the 1973 Inaugural Ball. *Evans Family Collection*

Also approved were new campaign finance rules and controls on lobbyists, together with measures limiting property taxes, allowing combined county-city governments, mandating gender equality, easing requirements on excess levies, changing constitutional debt limits, promoting litter control and regulating shoreline use. Nearly 62 percent backed legalization of lotteries, but privatization of liquor sales was rejected.

IT WAS NOT A GOOD NIGHT for Republicans in legislative races, even though the playing field was now more even.

The federal court had ordered the 1972 Legislature to pass a redistricting measure based on the 1970 Census. When the lawmakers failed to act, the court turned to a special master. Richard Morrill, a distinguished geographer from the University of Washington, was under orders to pay no attention to legislative incumbents. His job was to divide the state into districts of equal population (within 1 percent) and to avoid dividing districts by rivers, lakes or other natural geographic barriers. He accomplished the task in 30 days. Democrats and their organized labor allies howled that the plan was tilted toward Republicans. Slade Gorton, our redistricting expert, was satisfied with the results. The plan passed constitutional muster.

The Democrats proceeded to steal a page from our playbook. In three previous elections, GOP state chairman Gummie Johnson and Republican legislative leaders had teamed up to find good candidates, run campaign schools and raise money for advertising and campaign support staff. Republicans won majorities in each of those elections. But in 1972, Republican legislative leaders were involved in difficult races themselves; Gummie had retired as state chairman and I was grappling with a tough re-election campaign. This time, the Democrats found the right candidates, schooled them well and out-paced us in fundraising. The result was Democratic control of the House, 57 to 41, and the Senate, 31 to 18. I would face formidable challenges in the 1973 legislative session.

I HAD A NEW NATIONAL ASSIGNMENT. I was appointed by President Nixon to the Advisory Commission on Intergovernmental Relations. I served as its chairman for several years. The 26-member commission was composed of four governors, six members of Congress, three members of the executive branch, plus state and county officials and leading citizens from around the nation. We met quarterly, debated issues of national importance and made recommendations to the president.

Nixon, a year earlier, had asked the commission to give him advice on the need for property tax relief, namely what role could or should the federal government play? We met a week before Christmas and almost unanimously stated that the issue should remain the primary responsibility of the states. It was a major surprise to the administration as well as the political press corps. I strongly supported the decision since I consistently believed that strong and independent state governments were the best weapon against the concentration of power in Washington, D.C.

Power in Olympia was far from concentrated.

37
CROSSING THE AISLE

I worked hard on my third inaugural address. It was an opportunity to set the direction of state government far beyond my four-year term. The House galleries were packed and an overflow crowd watched via television in the Capitol rotunda as I began by reviewing the events of the previous eight years—a roller coaster ride featuring exhilarating prosperity and a scary recession. Though the Boeing Bust was over, I reminded the Legislature of our unmet needs:

My address to the 1973 legislative session emphasized six compelling challenges. Speaker Leonard Sawyer appears skeptical. *Washington State Archives*

"So long as hunger and poverty still exist; so long as a medical catastrophe can destroy life savings; so long as we provide inadequate care for those with special needs; so long as the forgotten aged are cast aside; so long as true brotherhood is an elusive myth—so long as all these exist, we have work to do." We had an opportunity to make Washington the most progressive state in the nation. I outlined our six most compelling challenges:

The management of growth: Passage of the Washington Future bond issues gave us the chance of a lifetime—a mandate to improve social services, invest in community college and vocational programs, control pollution, modernize waste disposal and boost water supplies, including irrigation.

The management of government: Since statehood in 1889, more than 1,500 local governmental units had been created. We needed to streamline local government while loosening the regulatory bonds of 600 federal grant programs by endorsing federal revenue sharing. I again proposed annual sessions of the Legislature and annual elections to relieve ballot congestion. I repeated my request for the creation of a Department of Transportation and an Office of Community Development.

Government's relationships with its citizens: I spoke of the institutionalization of the handicapped, the developmentally disabled and the mentally ill. In the next four years, we needed to replace "the isolated and impersonal institutions of yester-day" with community-based facilities. "At the local level, the potent combination of dedicated volunteers, local professional expertise and state financial assistance can combine to provide fuller, richer, lives for all of these less fortunate citizens."

Tax reform: This time, I proposed no specific bill, emphasizing instead the ne-cessity of "a prohibition against special property tax levies for the maintenance and operation of basic education." We needed to substantially reduce property tax bur-dens, enact a constitutional limitation on all major taxes, and institute an income tax "with an initial revenue sufficient to replace, but not exceed, reductions made in other taxes."

Innovation: Notably, we had neglected early childhood development. No child should be cheated at the beginning of an opportunity for a full and successful life. I also proposed examining the possibility of instituting state-level insurance against catastrophic illness.

Quality of life: It's more than compassion, I said, "more than economic oppor-tunity; more than social justice. It is all of these. Let us hope that the compassion we found in a time of economic misfortune does not disappear in a time of progress, but remains as a continuing principle of our mutual regard and concern."

I closed with a bipartisan declaration that has become part of my legacy: "I would rather cross the political aisle than cross the people," I said. "That must be our common pledge."

Conservatives tut-tutted that I was advocating "swollen state employment."

Leading Democrats gave the speech positive reviews, saying I had offered them an "olive branch."

FOR THE FIRST TIME in eight years, Democrats controlled both chambers of the Legislature. Rep-resentative Leonard Sawyer from Puyallup, having worked hard to elect new members, was reward-ed with the speakership. August Mardesich finally deposed Bob Greive as Senate majority leader after a bitter fight.

Len Sawyer, like Mardesich, was an adroit politician and UW Law School graduate. Sawyer had arrived in the House in 1955, two years ahead of me. We were the same age—47—and Navy veter-ans. Ambitious and resourceful, Sawyer resented the activism I had brought to the Executive Branch during my two terms. He proposed a continuing legislative session concept that would remove the power of the governor to call special sessions. Mardesich, meantime, immediately streamlined the Senate's committees and installed supporters as chairmen.

Two enterprising Democrats now ran the branches of the railroad one floor above me in the Capitol. I knew this was likely my last term as governor but I did not intend to be a caretaker.

The Democratic majorities in the House and Senate were sharply divided. Meantime, nearly half of the minority Republican House caucus created a new group called the "Renaissance Club." Future Speaker William Polk and future Attorney General Ken Eikenberry joined with a group of mostly rural and Eastern Washington Republicans in espousing a conservative agenda. "Perhaps we should think about the maxim that government which governs best is that which governs least," Eikenberry declared. I always thought that was a simplistic cliché, and that the real goal should be neither big government nor small government. The goal should be smart government. I knew I would need to woo varying coalitions to enact my program. I also kept my red veto pen handy.

Shortly after the inaugural we received a delegation from British Columbia. I invited the new Premier, David Barrett, to visit Olympia with a team of his senior ministers to develop closer working relationships between our state and his province. Barrett had just defeated the long-term premier, W.A.C. Bennett, and brought a socialist-leaning majority to power. He was a young, freewheeling activist with new ideas.

For the first time in history, a B.C. premier addressed a joint session of the Washington Legislature. Barrett was candid, advocating joint efforts on pollution control, salmon fishing and coordination of tourist promotion, while warning of the dangers of additional oil tanker traffic in the Strait of Juan de Fuca. It was the beginning of a much closer working relationship between British Columbia and Washington state.

WHEN THE NATIONAL GOVERNOR'S CONFERENCE held its semiannual meeting in Washington, D.C., Nixon's revenue sharing plan was hotly debated. Many domestic grant programs would be replaced by a broad, issue-oriented revenue sharing concept. This idea would strengthen state and local governments and allow each to focus on their priorities, rather than marching in lockstep with federal programs. It would radically change some of President Johnson's Great Society programs and make them more responsive to local needs.

Many Democratic governors opposed revenue sharing, including Jimmy Carter of Georgia, already weighing a run for president in 1976. Carter told a Senate subcommittee headed by Ed Muskie that unless the president's budget cuts were reversed "we're going to have retarded children out in the streets." I testified that Washington state also felt the pinch of budget cuts "but I can guarantee you there'll be no retarded children on the street." Republicans were preaching the validity of government close to the people; Democrats were advocating centralized management. "The President is on absolutely the right track," I told the subcommittee. "He recognizes local and state government is more aware of problems of the people than Washington, D.C., can be." I was leading the fight for a fundamental Republican principle, laughing wryly to myself that my testimony was surely going to confuse conservative Republican legislators back home. The right-wing editorial page of Lewis County's Centralia *Chronicle* called me "Dr. Jekyll and Mr. Hyde."

THE LEGISLATURE FINALLY ran out of steam in mid-April and adjourned sine die rather than recessing. Speaker Sawyer's grandiose plan for a continuing session was rejected by his colleagues, an omen of future problems for an ambitious politician. My call for creation of a Department of Transportation failed for the sixth time. Legislative leaders asked me to call them back into session in September to prepare a tax reform bill to carry out the constitutional amendment they had just proposed.

One of the most controversial bills to emerge from the 1973 session tripled legislative salaries and granted much more modest raises for state elected officials. (My budget plan had called for a doubling of legislative salaries to $7,200, while a State Salary Committee had recommended boosting the governor's salary from $32,500 to $47,300.) The bill passed late at night in the closing hours of the session and carried an emergency clause to prevent a referendum. Many citizens were outraged by the secrecy of the vote. Bruce Helm, a young furniture salesman from Snohomish County, challenged the emergency clause before the Supreme Court. He lost, but immediately started a signature campaign for an initiative that substituted tiny salary increases for those the Legislature adopted.

Mr. Helm proved to be a very enterprising fellow.

After 10 days of travel and long meetings, I walked into a gaggle of reporters and TV cameras at Seattle-Tacoma International Airport. What was this all about?

A reporter thrust a microphone toward my weary face: "Do you have any comment on Bruce Helm turning in 665,000 signatures on Initiative 282?"

I was astonished by the record number of signatures opponents of the salary increases had gathered in just three weeks. I expressed my concern that initiatives do not go through the legislative process, are not subject to amendment and only represent the ideas of the sponsor. "We are literally in the position of having the salaries of elected officials, as well as legislators, set by the whim of a furniture salesman from South Snohomish County."

I should have just said "No comment" and got some sleep.

The next day's headlines screamed "Evans says initiative 282 is 'whim of a furniture salesman.'" All my explanatory answers were on the cutting room floor, replaced by a catchy phrase blurted by a tired governor. I received plenty of letters hotly defending the initiative and several from furniture salesman defending their craft. At my next press conference, Adele Ferguson, the *Bremerton Sun's* feisty columnist, asked, "Do you have any further words for the furniture salesman of the state today?" I repeated my careful explanation about the rigidity of initiatives. Another reporter said people were saying my comment belittled furniture salesmen.

"No," I frowned. "If it had been a fisherman who had started the initiative, I would've said 'fisherman.' If it would've been a banker, I would've said 'banker.' If it would have been a millionaire, I would've said 'millionaire.' It was just a description."

"How about a civil engineer?" Adele jumped in, eyes twinkling.

"I would've said 'civil engineer,' " I nodded with a smile.

My inept comment reached legendary status. I finally wrote a letter to Bruce Helm commending him for being an activist citizen and closed by saying that if I was ever in the market for furniture I would probably look him up.

That November, Initiative 282 passed in a landslide. More than 80 percent of the voters rallied to Helm's cause, stipulating that raises for state elected officials be limited to 5.5 percent over 1965 levels. As one newsman wrote, "Some whim, some furniture salesman." Legislators have been careful ever since to avoid passing self-serving, controversial legislation in the closing hours of a session.

I never suspected that someone like Tim Eyman would come along to elevate government-by-initiative to an art form in the 21st century. Bruce Helm's motives were pure populism.

I WAS GENERALLY PLEASED with the Legislature's actions on budgetary bills and my executive request measures. The constitutional amendment for tax reform included a graduated net income tax, as opposed to the flat income tax of 1970. There were many new constitutional limits on other taxes. However, I knew we would still have a hard time passing tax reform. The state's economic recovery was accelerating, but there were growing troubles nationally. The inflation rate reached 7 percent, interest rates soared and drastic energy shortages developed from a Mideast oil boycott.

Congress weighed proposals for gas rationing, speed limit reductions and even a meat boycott.

I had 10 days to scrutinize the 200 bills passed by the Legislature.

Speaker Sawyer ranted against my veto power, claiming that line-item vetoes without public hearings subverted open government. That was ironic, I suggested, since the Legislature had fast-tracked many bills with few public hearings. Moreover, the line veto was enshrined in the State Constitution.

One of the bills I vetoed was a landlord-tenant act. Committee hearings produced emotional testimony from tenants who complained about dictatorial landlords. Property owners retorted that tenants damaged property, engaged in illegal activities and walked away from their responsibilities. The Legislature concocted a bill heavily tilted toward landlords. The bill was punctuated with provisos intended to make it difficult for me to engage in any kind of line-item veto. I examined it with great care and was tempted to veto it entirely. Instead, I attempted to remove the most egregious elements. When I was done deleting, the bill looked like a GI's imprudent battlefield letter edited by a military censor. The eruption was wonderful to behold when I sent my veto message to the Legislature.

The lawmakers counter-attacked on two fronts: The validity of the governor's line-item veto was challenged in an appeal to the Washington Supreme Court. And a referendum was sent to the voters. In November of 1974, 54 percent of the voters backed limiting the item veto to sections of a bill or items in appropriations acts. They believed—or were persuaded—that I had been too aggressive in dissecting the landlord-tenant act. In so doing, they tilted the relative powers of governors and Legislatures back toward the Legislature. On many occasions I had used the item veto to correct errors in bills. It would now require a total veto and resubmission of a new bill. I still believe the item veto is a useful and appropriate tool for the governor. And it's always subject to override by two-thirds of the Legislature.

THE END OF THE LEGISLATIVE SESSION coincided with the loss of the first member of our closely knit Governor's Office team. Esther Seering, my executive assistant, was ready to retire. It was like losing a close family member. In the hectic, high-tension atmosphere of a governor's office, Esther was a calming influence, always able to disarm the most irate legislator or persistent citizen. Any career success I've enjoyed depended immeasurably on a succession of extraordinarily talented and devoted executive assistants.

38
ROPED IN

Exhilaration replaces apprehension as I rappel the clock tower at The Evergreen State College in the spring of 1973 to dedicate the college's new recreation building. *The Evergreen State College Archives*

Willi Unsoeld, the intrepid Mount Everest mountaineer, was now a member of the faculty at The Evergreen State College. Exuding energy, he bounced into my office one day after the Legislature adjourned and invited me to take part in the dedication of the new activities building on campus. I expected a ribbon-cutting. Willi had a better idea.

"This is an athletic activities building," he declared. "Why don't you rappel down the college clock tower?"

"You've got to be kidding!" I said, laughing.

"Hey, you're a climber," he said, couching it as a challenge.

Gulp. I had done some rappelling during my years of mountain climbing, so I agreed. But when the day came I wondered about my sanity.

Willi and I climbed to the top of the tower. A team of his students was there to handle the rappelling rope and the safety harness. I buckled in and peered over the edge. Thirteen stories below, the campus plaza was filled with spectators.

Now there was no escape. I spread my feet on the cornice of the tower with the rappel rope between my legs, over my chest and shoulder, and leaned back into space. With one hand on the rope in front and the other on the trailing rope behind, I made the first bounce outward, letting the rope slide so I could descend several feet.

Exhilaration replaced apprehension and I joyfully bounced my way down to the rising applause of the crowd. Willi was right behind me. For him, this was a piece of cake. Halfway down, he turned upside down and slid the rest of the way face first.

Willi was right: that's the way an activities building should be dedicated. But once was enough for me.

LEST YOU THINK politicians and celebrities had it easier in the days before social media and the 24-hour news cycle, I have an anecdote from life in the fishbowl 1970s style:

When letter writers wrote the Governor's Office to complain that Nancy's skirts were too short, she laughed it off. As mini-skirts went, hers were still conservative. Now a group from Grandview in Yakima County maintained my hair was too long, though by my young sons' standards I was still pretty square. My sideburns were lower but my ears were in plain sight. (When I look at photos from 1973, I marvel at how much hair I had!) The letter writers took up a collection and sent me $8 to "go downtown to a *good* barbershop and have a haircut." They recalled that a little girl made a suggestion "that resulted in an improvement in the looks of the greatest Republican of all time, Abraham Lincoln."

A few days later, students at Central Washington College wrote to say they liked my hair just the way it was and enclosed eight cents for postage to mail the $8 back to my critics. I sent a letter to the *Yakima Herald-Republic*, noting, "If I remember correctly the little girl's suggestion to President Lincoln was to grow a beard. I wonder if the Grandview group is suggesting this as an alternative for me." This also controversial alternative would soon occur.

APPOINTMENTS TO BOARDS and commissions were a constant concern. Legislatures over the years constantly created new boards and almost never eliminated one. I now faced decisions on over 500 slots each year, many with quite specific requirements. Fortunately, we assigned a talented young woman, Jo Garceau, to manage the appointments and she quickly created a system that produced excellent candidates for organizations as diverse as the Mattress and Bedding Advisory Commission and the Supreme Court. I was particularly careful with appointments to judicial posts since I knew that these nominees could serve long after I left office. During my three terms I appointed more than 100 lower court judges and six members of the Washington Supreme Court.

During the summer of '73, a judicial vacancy occurred in Thurston County. I decided on a young Olympia attorney named Gerry Alexander. He proved to be a wise choice. After serving on the Superior Court, he was elected to the Court of Appeals and ultimately the Washington Supreme Court, where he served as chief justice for nine years, retiring in 2011. Alexander served on the bench for 35 years after I left office. He is a splendid example of the long-term legacy a governor can leave.

THE ANNUAL MEETING of the National Governors' Conference was held on the Nevada side of Lake Tahoe. The slot machines, roulette wheels and marquee lounge acts offered a bizarre respite to the escalating problems governors faced: Inflation, rising interest rates and energy shortages. Watergate was always lurking, like the ghost of Hamlet's father.

I had strong misgivings about Nixon's candor: What did he know about Watergate—and when did he know it? "I wince every time there's a new statement from the White House," I told the reporters covering the conference. "I want to believe the president, but I find myself becoming more and more distressed as new information comes out." The possibility of his resignation slithered into hallway conversations.

During 1972, I had contacted nearly all of my Republican colleagues, asking for their support for my candidacy as chairman of the conference. The chairmanship alternated between Republican and Democratic governors. It was a Republican's turn. I was elected by acclamation at the end of the conference. I had strong ideas about the future of the conference as an independent force and intended to urge support for the Nixon Administration's General Revenue Sharing program.

President Johnson's "Great Society" programs were now fully operational. Most, like Medicaid and welfare, required state dollar matching and management by state government. I told my colleagues that if we couldn't convince the leaders of the Council of State Governments to more fully support the needs of governors we should form our own organization. I strongly recommended that we resign from the council and form a separate organization. I also suggested that we needed a permanent presence in Washington, D.C., since Congress was generally ignorant of the operation and needs of state governments. The nine-member National Governors' Conference Executive Committee enthusiastically agreed and a new and independent organization of governors was born.

FINALLY IT WAS TIME for an extended family vacation, including a backpacking trip. There were no official events planned for three weeks so I decided to quit shaving until I returned to Olympia. During the first week it was itchy. Nancy refused any caresses, claiming it was like kissing a porcu-

pine. Time flew, the beard grew, a special legislative session loomed and it was time to return to civilization. Our son Danny was attending a Boy Scout National Jamboree in Idaho. I was invited to attend, together with dignitaries. I thought, "Well, there won't be any press so I'll just wait and shave off the beard when I get home." Was that a mistake! Reporters and cameramen greeted us as we arrived at the Jamboree site, and my photo with a scraggly, three-week-old beard was spread countrywide by Associated Press. I began to receive hundreds of letters from people with extremely definitive views on beards.

Ultimately some 600 citizens expressed their opinions, with college students enthusiastically in favor. Most older citizens vociferously opposed. It was a record expression of opinion—one that ironically far surpassed the number of letters com-

Sporting a controversial beard, I join Dan Jr. at the National Boy Scout Jamboree-West at Farragut State Park, Idaho, in 1973. *Evans Family Collection*

menting on the tax reform resolution set for the November ballot. The prize letter came from a skeptic who saw the two white patches on either side of my chin in an otherwise black beard and wrote with great glee, "I always knew the Governor had skunk blood in him."

A MILD WINTER and warm summer had combined to drain our hydroelectric reservoirs. Energy experts reported that our hydroelectric system capacity was 15 billion kWh short of normal. I declared an electric power emergency and ordered state agencies to cut consumption by 10 percent. I also urged voluntary cutbacks by citizens and proposed that in the coming session of the Legislature I be given power to mandate broader cuts if necessary. Legislative leaders generally agreed that mandatory powers were necessary but they were divided on whether the governor should wield that power. "I'm not looking forward to it," I said. "There's no way anyone can win on that one."

The Legislature convened that September for a mini-session, an experiment aimed at easing the intense lawmaking at the end of regular legislative sessions. Sawyer and Mardesich believed that effective interim study, followed by short legislative sessions, could minimize the chaotic endings of extended sessions. Eight days later the Legislature adjourned, completing work on the tax reform proposal, giving me authority to act on energy shortages, passing a supplemental appropriations bill and acting on numerous proposals developed during the interim. The session was a pleasant surprise—a credit to both Houses and parties, I said. The Legislature also received high marks from editorial writers around the state. But the praise didn't dissuade the voters from trashing those legislative salary increases, come November.

ON OCTOBER 10, 1973, the nation was jarred by the resignation of Vice President Agnew, who pleaded no contest to charges of tax evasion and corruption during his years as a county executive and Governor of Maryland. "It was like getting hit between the eyes," I told reporters. Governors generally had been supportive of his selection as vice president, hoping that a former governor close to the president would be helpful to the states. Our enthusiasm eroded as Agnew became Nixon's bulldog, a shrill provocateur not only during the campaign but more intensely after taking office.

Fortunately, Agnew was forced to resign before Nixon's own downfall. Otherwise the chaos of rapid presidential succession could have both national and international consequences. For the first time, the 25th amendment to the U.S. Constitution took effect. Section 2 states: Whenever there is a vacancy in the office of the Vice-President, the President shall nominate a Vice-President who shall take office upon confirmation by a majority vote of both Houses of Congress.

Democrats piously suggested a caretaker vice president who would agree not to run in 1976. They did not want a Republican to get a head start on the next election. Oregon Governor Tom McCall suggested Nixon choose a senior governor like me or Rockefeller. The nominee should be "someone of value to the country... not just some doddering caretaker," McCall said.

I knew that I was not close enough to Nixon or his advisers to receive much consideration. Admirers sometimes ask if I still wonder about the roads not taken in American history. Had I been selected as vice president, I would have become president less than a year later. My answer is that it wasn't going to happen. And life is too short to waste time on what-might-have-beens.

Oregon Governor Tom McCall looks on as I address the opening session of the 1973 Western Governors' Conference in Gleneden Beach, Oregon. *Washington State Archives*

A few days after Agnew's resignation, I was in Washington, D.C., on a trip scheduled weeks earlier. My schedule included a White House meeting with Roy Ash, Nixon's budget director, to discuss funding for the Columbia Basin Project. A pack of TV cameramen was encamped outside the West Wing, ready to pounce on anyone who might have a clue on the identity of the new vice president. With my full beard as a disguise, I strolled by without recognition.

A day later, Nixon nominated Congressman Gerald Ford for vice president. It was a wise choice. Ford was an honest man with the common touch, and popular on both sides of the aisle. With his briar pipe and self-effacing sense of humor, he reminded me of my friend John Spellman, the King County executive.

39
SATURDAY NIGHT FEVER

The Watergate investigation accelerated after the infamous "Saturday Night Massacre" on October 20, 1973. Nixon had ordered his attorney general, Elliot Richardson, to fire Special Prosecutor Archibald Cox. Richardson resigned on the spot. Nixon then instructed Deputy Attorney General William Ruckelshaus to carry out the order. Ruckelshaus refused and resigned.* Next in line was Solicitor-General Robert Bork, who followed orders. It was a Category 4 political hurricane.

At a press conference three days later, I revealed that I had received a head's-up call from Ken Cole of the president's Domestic Council before the news broke. I supported the president in his decision to seek a judicial review of the constitutional question of separation of powers, I told reporters. But I hadn't changed my mind on a key issue of credibility and transparency: If the courts ruled Nixon did not have to release the Oval Office tape recordings, he ought to surrender them voluntarily.

The questions came like bullets:

"Do you feel at this point that there are grounds for impeachment?"

"Are you saying he should consider resigning?"

My response was that the federal courts would resolve the issue over the tape recordings. As for resigna-

Deputy Attorney General Bill Ruckelshaus leaves his office on Oct. 20, 1973, the day of the "Saturday Night Massacre." *Bill Ruckelshaus Collection*

tion, "If the president honestly comes to the point where he feels that the vast bulk of the people have lost confidence in him and are unlikely to regain it, then I think he ought to give serious consider-

---

* In a memoir, *Saving Justice*, published in 2013 a few months following his death, Bork wrote that after he complied with Nixon's order to fire Cox, the embattled president promised him the next Supreme Court vacancy. Whether Nixon actually believed he still had the political clout to get someone confirmed to the court was hard to discern. Perhaps, one historian speculated, he "was just trying to secure Bork's continued loyalty as his administration crumbled in the Watergate scandal." In 2018, Ruckelshaus told state historian John C. Hughes that he and Richardson encouraged Bork to carry out the president's order to fire Cox "if his conscience would let him. ...We were frankly worried about the stability of the government."

ation to that as a political step."

NIXON HUNKERED DOWN. The Republican Governors' Association was scheduled to meet in Memphis. I urged our leadership to invite the president to meet with us in private session. We gathered anxiously in a small room on the mezzanine level of the hotel. Finally, we heard the wail of the sirens of the presidential motorcade.

Nixon greeted us heartily and sat down at the end of the table. No staff, no press—no tape recorders—just the embattled, brave-faced 37th President of the United States and 17 worried, influential Republicans. As Nixon surveyed the room, he saw not one but two would-be presidents, Nelson Rockefeller and Ronald Reagan. This was an opportunity for candor, a chance to seek the advice of fellow Republicans in high places. Nixon began with remarks on his international and domestic programs and his hopes for the future, but he finally addressed the elephant in the room. As he proceeded through the litany of charges and denials, evidence, innuendo and rumors, I realized he was telling us nothing more than we had already learned through the media, including the press conference two days earlier where he declared, "I am not a crook." At last, he invited our questions. When my turn came, I focused on his domestic programs, particularly Special Revenue Sharing. I wanted to know where they stood on his priority list. Nixon said domestic policy was now number one on his priority list since the war in Vietnam was winding down. He put special emphasis on Revenue Sharing.

The last governor to speak was plain-spoken Tom McCall. "Mr. President, have you told us everything you know about Watergate, and is there anything else that we should know?" Nixon paused for several seconds that seemed like minutes. Then, jaw set, he glanced around the table and said, "No. I have told you all I know."

As Nixon departed, the rest of us filed out to a balcony overlooking the hotel lobby. It was a surging mass of reporters and photographers, TV cameramen and curious onlookers. We descended a circular staircase and stepped into a mass of eddy currents in a sea of curious press. Most of us said we believed the worst of Watergate was over and that we could refocus on important domestic programs.

Twenty-four hours later came another bombshell. Watergate investigators reviewing subpoenaed Oval Office tapes found an 18½ minute gap. Rose Mary Woods, the president's loyal, longtime secretary, said she must have caused it when she tried to answer the phone while transcribing the tape. The contortions necessary to do this made the explanation dubious.

I felt betrayed. Nixon had squandered an opportunity to be candid with the nation's Republican governors—ostensibly some of his staunchest defenders—and ask for their opinions on how best to proceed. He embarrassed us all by his lack of candor.

NEVERTHELESS, Nixon's Advisory Commission on Intergovernmental Relations met for two days that fall. It was difficult not to be distracted by the drama of the high-stakes battle over the White house tapes. But I was impressed with the caliber of those serving on the Advisory Commission and the thoughtfulness of the studies and reports they issued. We began to develop a policy brief regarding Revenue Sharing to present to the embattled president. It was hard to proceed cautiously since I was so enthusiastic about the program. However, I recognized the apprehensions of cities and counties about state government control.

Earlier I had received a call from David Rockefeller, who had an idea for a new commission. He recognized that there was significant political, economic and social interchange between Europe and the United States but very little with Japan, which was emerging as an economic powerhouse. David told me that he was engaged in creating a Trilateral Commission composed of business and political leadership in Europe, the United States and Japan. I thought it was a great idea and that we on the West Coast were particularly aware of the rising importance of Japan. He told me that the founding members wanted to add two governors and two senators to the commission's North American contingent. Their proposed choices were Jimmy Carter and me, and Senators Walter Mondale of Minnesota and Robert Taft Jr. of Ohio. My answer was an enthusiastic yes.

The organizing session in New York took place in an elegant hotel ballroom. A huge U-shaped table was set for 70. As each commissioner was introduced, I recognized that this was potentially an enormously powerful and influential group. I served on The Trilateral Commission for about 10 years and thoroughly enjoyed the interchange between bright and able leaders of three continents. I also noticed that Carter was enthusiastically building relationships. Clearly he was preparing to run for president and was intent on building a team of advisers. Ultimately he chose fellow Trilateral Commission member Fritz Mondale as his running mate, and, when elected, chose several cabinet members from the commission membership.

Commission meetings were private and off the record, which attracted interest from a fascinating collection of skeptics. Conspiracy theorists were joined by wackos from the extreme right and loonies from the equally extreme left in demonizing the commission and its members. The research reports and policy statements of The Trilateral Commission were all publicized and presented to the national governments of the three regions as proposals for action. A half century after its creation, The Trilateral Commission's membership includes representatives from more than 30 European countries, all of North America and some 15 Asian nations. I believe it has been a positive force.

I WAS PLEASED to return the visit of B.C. Premier David Barrett, and brought a retinue of cabinet officers and legislative leaders to Victoria for a continuation of talks on our common problems. It was a remarkably positive and candid visit. Barrett and I stated our shared opposition to a proposal to raise Ross Dam on the Skagit River because an important British Columbia valley would have been flooded as a consequence. But we disagreed on oil tanker traffic and sharing of natural gas resources. We commiserated that our relationships with our federal governments was problematic. Meantime, our department heads and ministers met for serious discussions on forestry, fishing, tourism, energy and conservation.

A rare event occurred the next morning. Strong tradition dictates that no one but a member of the British Columbia Assembly is authorized to speak from the floor, but for the first time in memory the Governor of Washington was given "leave to speak" to the Assembly. I emphasized that we had an opportunity for cooperative action on a host of mutual challenges. We should meet regularly and more informally, I said, especially since our fishery and natural resource challenges ignored geographical boundaries. This first exchange was followed by successful meetings every year for the remainder of my term.

WATERGATE HAD CONTRIBUTED to a growing distrust of government in general as Washingtonians went to the polls that November. After deep-sixing the salary increases for legislators and state officials, 77 percent rejected HJR 37, the tax reform package. That was the end of tax reform for a generation since the people had spoken twice, decisively, to put it mildly. At this writing, we continue to struggle with an unfair, inadequate, anti-business tax system that fails to help produce jobs and places the heaviest burden on those least able to pay.

A family ski trip to Crystal Mountain was a breath of fresh air after a fitful year. I arose early on the morning of January 1, gazed in the mirror and decided to greet 1974 clean shaven. My 10-year-old son, Mark, was also up, eager for a day on the slopes. I handed him our Polaroid camera to record the shearing. First, I shaved my chin and neck, creating a marvelous mutton-chop beard. Mark faithfully recorded each style, including a goofy Fu Manchu. The last strokes of the razor did away with a Hitler-style Fuller Brush mustache. I told Mark not to say anything to the rest of the family. Gradually they all joined us for breakfast. It took almost an hour for Nancy to notice.

40
"GOVERNOR EVIDENCE"

*A*ir Force One touched down at Fairchild Air Force Base on May 4, 1974, a sparkling day. Spokane was festooned with flags and bunting to celebrate the opening of Expo 74, the world's fair that rescued the city's urban core from the dowdy cluster of train tracks, trestles and bridges that hid Spokane Falls. We were there to welcome the Nixons to Nancy's home town.

Embattled though he was, Nixon greets me with a quip as he arrives in Spokane to help open Expo 74 on May 4. He resigned three months later. *Washington State Archives*

A small platform had been erected at the sprawling B-52 base on the outskirts of the city. I opted for simplicity in my introduction, booming, "Ladies and gentlemen, the President of the United States!" Nixon turned to me, smiled broadly and declared, "Thank you, Governor Evidence"—a Freudian slip that became the stuff of legends. The audience let out a collective little gulp, but Nixon instantly corrected himself as the presidential press corps scribbled furiously.

Downtown, 85,000 awaited us. I noted that on the way to Fairchild I had spotted a reader board with a simple message that summed up the theme of Expo 74: "Let's stop treating the earth like it's rented." The president's speech, fittingly, focused on the environment. He mentioned the frequent conflict between creating jobs and preserving a clean environment. "We can have both," he said, "and we shall have both."

Several hundred protesters clamoring for impeachment gathered outside the fairgrounds. Nixon appeared to ignore them as he and the First Lady headed back to the airport. That cloudless day in Spokane, with a sea of friendly faces, must have been one of the last purely enjoyable events of his presidency. He had only three more months.

I invited all of my fellow governors to attend the fair, with a special "state day" planned for each. I thought only a few would make the trip, but 32 accepted the invitation. Much of my summer was spent in Spokane. The permanent value of the fair is the reclamation of Spokane Falls and creation of a wonderful park and civic center in the heart of the city.

SPOKANE'S ACTIVISM set a good example. To deal with the challenges facing a rapidly growing state, I proposed a massive effort to involve citizens directly in planning. We called it "Alternatives for Washington." The Brookings Institution in Washington, D.C., was chosen to oversee the Growth Policy and Development process, in partnership with the University of Washington, Washington State University and state government agencies. We appointed a diverse group of 150 citizens to spearhead the process, and Brookings used a questionnaire to involve several thousand more citizens. Our chairman was Ed Lindaman, the president of Whitworth College in Spokane and an acclaimed futurist. He created extraordinary enthusiasm in our citizen team, often quoting Wayne Gretzky, the famed hockey player who said, "I skate to where the puck is going to be, not where it is."

The Alternatives for Washington committee gathered for several intense retreats. Late one evening I strolled through the halls of our retreat building and discovered two team members—a high-ranking banker and a welfare mother—kneeling on the floor, scribbling ideas on butcher-paper for the next day's presentations. I knew something special was happening and that we had an opportunity to rebuild people's confidence in their government and the future.

I CALLED THE LEGISLATURE back into session in 1974 to reassert my belief that we needed annual sessions to handle the complex problems of a rapidly growing state. Speaker Len Sawyer again proposed a "continuing" session where a Legislature could recess and then return on its own volition. At one point, I agreed with the concept. Watching it in practice gave me heartburn.

The Legislature finally adjourned after a second mini-session. It was another disaster. I had never seen a collection of bills with more errors and inconsistencies. In terms of veto overrides, the special interests had run rampant. Many legislative leaders, Republican and Democrat, expressed the hope that this would be the last of this experiment.

Fed up with the pettiness, I was happy to focus on a real crisis. The OPEC oil embargo, enacted in retaliation for the U.S. support of Israel during the 1973 Yom Kippur War, created a gasoline shortage throughout the U.S. As chairman of the National Governors' Conference I led a team of governors in a meeting with William Simon, the federal energy director. Concerned about the rigidity of the federal allocation system, we urged Simon to give us more flexibility to cope with gasoline shortages in our states. We were facing long lines at every gas station as nervous drivers kept topping off their tanks. We eventually initiated an "odd/even" system where motorists could refuel only when the last number on their license plate matched the day of the month in being odd or even. Gradually panic subsided, gas lines diminished and oil supplies gradually recovered.

THAT SPRING, Nancy and I joined five other governors and their wives for a trip to China. It was only the third official U.S. trip after Nixon's historic reopening of diplomatic relations. I brought the voluminous transcript of the Watergate Oval Office tapes with me. I was appalled by the foul language, deceit and duplicity.

None of us were fully aware of the turmoil and the struggle for leadership as Chairman Mao's health declined, but we were informed by Liaison Office experts that Deng Xiaoping appeared to be gaining strength. Some of our most rewarding visits were to farm communities where commune leaders bragged about consistent increases in productivity. Well-built sties were filled with piglets. Philip Noel, the governor of Rhode Island, politely asked why they didn't raise some to maturity and expand production, rather than sending them all to a regional slaughterhouse. It was obvious this was a foreign concept. Our hosts protested that they were following orders. A lively discussion about pig raising ensued. It wouldn't be long before China embraced economic expansion and capitalist efficiencies.

SEATTLE HOSTED the annual meeting of the National Governors' Conference. Five governors joined me in a one-hour episode of *Meet the Press*. The group included Tom McCall, my freewheeling Republican colleague from Oregon, and Democrats Jimmy Carter of Georgia, Daniel Walker of Illinois, Wendell Anderson of Minnesota and Wendell Ford of Kentucky. We were all eager to talk about the role of states in our federal system. To our dismay, half the questions focused on Watergate. It made us all aware of the need to excise that cancer as quickly as possible and turn the nation's attention to the challenges of a weak economy, inflation and troubling international tensions. I was determined to show the public and the 400 reporters covering the conference that state governments were stable, innovative, good managers and an essential link in our federal system.

Our nine-member executive committee endorsed a transformation of the National Governors' Conference. We separated from the Council of State Governments, which was dominated by state legislators, and created an independent National Governors' Association. We doubled our dues from each state, created an independent staff and expanded our presence in Washington, D.C.

WHEN I ADDRESSED the State Republican Convention in Richland that July, some conservative activists were happily handing out buttons declaring, "Cheer up, it's Dan Evans' last term." I grabbed one, put it on and at the beginning of my speech advised, "Save it—you might need it in 1978." That created plenty of press commentary about whether I was considering running for a fourth term.

Delegates were split, as ever, between the loyalists and the arch-conservatives, but I gave them a unifying speech by tearing into the Democratic leadership in the state and the Democratic Congress. The reaction was probably the best I had received at a GOP state convention in years. It was a reasonably harmonious convention but the shadow of Watergate was dark and growing.

As the House Judiciary Committee was refusing to settle for edited transcripts of the Oval Office tape recordings, Nixon traveled to Egypt and Israel, where he was hailed as a peacemaker. It was tonic for an embattled president. I was deeply troubled by the dichotomy of Richard M. Nixon, vilified at home and revered abroad; intellectually brilliant—a seasoned statesman—yet given to crude "screw our enemies" paranoia and situational ethics. Months earlier, Slade Gorton had publicly declared Nixon should resign.

I was scheduled to address a banquet of the National Conference of Christians and Jews in Seattle. At the last minute I set aside my prepared text and wrote a new speech. Gazing out at the expectant audience, I said my message would be brief but from the heart:

> We seem to be hurtling down a road with three equally difficult and perilous
> forks. First, that of resignation, which unquestionably would dismay those who sim-

ply do not believe the president is guilty of high crimes. The second, perhaps even more difficult, is impeachment—a road which unquestionably will lead to increasing turmoil and dismay at a time when America's leadership is so desperately needed in the cause of international peace. The third perilous course is acquittal—unacceptable to many who believe passionately in the guilt of the president. The long and torturous trial would fascinate but gradually paralyze the nation.

Perhaps there is a fourth fork. Maybe it is too late. Perhaps emotions are too aroused. But tonight I suggest to you, and all my fellow citizens, that the fourth road is amnesty. Look in the dictionary and you'll find the basic definition of what amnesty really is: *A general pardon for offenses against the government; an act of forgiveness for past offenses against the people as a whole; to grant a pardon.*

I noted that political amnesty had been granted by almost every wartime president—from George Washington to Harry Truman—to those who refused to serve in the military. "It is for all three groups—those who believe him guilty; those who believe him innocent, and the larger majority, those who are uncertain and confused—that we need to end the turmoil and the paralysis that grips us now," I said. "So my plea tonight is really not for a man or even for an office. It is a plea for a country and its people. It would take a perceptive and understanding people to say, 'We forgive you, Mr. President.' It would take a great and humble president to say, 'I am sorry.'"

The speech generated headlines across the state. The editorials were thoughtful but just as divided as the country. Clearly, there was little mood for amnesty. My wishful thinking was heartfelt, but it was too late for forgiveness.

The U.S. Supreme Court unanimously rejected the president's claims of executive privilege. The damning evidence of Nixon's complicity in the attempted cover-up was on the table. He had lied to the American people. "Even the president of the United States sometimes must have to stand naked," as Bob Dylan put it. In a visit to the Oval Office, it fell to Senate Republican leader Hugh Scott, House Minority Leader John Rhodes, and Barry Goldwater to give Nixon the unvarnished truth: He had no chance of surviving an impeachment trial.

August 9, 1974, was an important day in American history for it proved once again that our Constitution is inviolate. As Nixon's plane flew over the Middle West, Gerald Ford took the oath of office. The 38th President of the United States was the first to take office without having been elected by the people, either as vice president or president. "I am a Ford, not a Lincoln," the former Michigan congressman humbly said when he became vice president. Now he offered one of the most eloquent inaugural addresses in American history: "My fellow Americans, our long national nightmare is over. Our Constitution works. ... As we bind up the internal wounds of Watergate, more painful and more poisonous than those of foreign wars, let us restore the Golden Rule to our political process and let brotherly love purge our hearts of suspicion and of hate."

Attention focused almost immediately on the vice presidency. That decision would be Ford's first major action. We were on a boating trip in the San Juans when the radiotelephone started ringing off the hook. It was Jim Dolliver, my chief of staff. He was fielding reporters' calls from all over the country. "They're hot on the trail of vice presidential candidates and think you're in the mix." My response was that I had to be the darkest dark horse in the race. Be that as it may, Dolliver said I needed to get back to Olympia pronto. A State Patrol plane was waiting at Friday Harbor. I was mad at Nixon all over again for interrupting our vacation.

I decided to call Congressman Joel Pritchard, one of my oldest and wisest friends. Judging from Capitol Hill scuttlebutt, Joel said my chances for selection as Ford's veep were slim since I was a continent away. Other viable candidates were closer to the new president, literally and figuratively. Nevertheless, Joel suggested I call fellow governors and local political and business leaders to see what kind of support I might gather.

I called Nelson Rockefeller. George Hinman, the National Republican Committeeman from New York and a close confidant of the former governor, said Rocky could not come to the phone just then, but he would relay any message I might have. I said I was interested in being considered for the vice presidency and hoped I would have Rockefeller's support. "Nelson thinks you are the best governor in the country and would be qualified to hold any office," Hinman replied. I was pleased by the accolade, yet instantly realized it was no endorsement for the job at hand. I had no idea Rockefeller was seeking the office himself since I had heard him say many times that he was not "standby equipment." In fact, he once famously declared, "I've never wanted to be vice president of anything."

I talked things over with a number of my fellow governors and was gratified by their enthusiastic support. Eddie Carlson, a longtime friend who was chairman of United Airlines, called to offer his help, especially with several members of the Republican National Committee. A number of Midwestern Republican leaders weighed in, urging me to actively seek Ford's nomination.

When White House staffers asked me about my recommendation for vice president, I said I thought Rockefeller would be a splendid choice.

Several days later, I left for Washington, D.C., and a meeting with Ford. The new president had asked me to arrange a meeting with the executive committee of the National Governors' Conference. We were delighted for this early opportunity to share our concerns and ideas. The Washington state press corps engaged in tantalizing speculation, not quite believing the meeting was only for consultation on policy with the governors.

When the president announced Rockefeller was his choice, I had mixed emotions. I wanted the job, but I was a realist from the get-go. I had long admired and supported Rockefeller. Mostly, I was relieved we could get the country back on track.

FORD'S FIRST MAJOR PROBLEM was the sorry state of the economy. America was gripped by "stagflation"—inflation escalating to 12 percent, unemployment nearing 9 percent and sluggish economic growth. I was invited to join 200 business and professional leaders for a presidential forum dubbed "Whip Inflation Now." We wore our WIN buttons as we worked through a two-day brainstorming session on ways to reduce inflation. I was disappointed at the general nature of the recommendations and the apparent unwillingness of Congress to respond to presidential leadership. Predictably, things got worse. "The economy fell into the steepest recession since World War II, coupled with an upward price spiral that was faster than at any time in modern memory," *The Washington Post* wrote.

Shortly after returning to Olympia, I decided to speak out on the nation's economic problems at a luncheon sponsored by the State Restaurant Association. "It's time to turn to what's important," I said. "We must recognize that we can't continue to indulge as we have in recent years. Let's cut the production of frills. Let's quit driving ourselves to an early death by overeating and over-drinking and instead take care of pressing health care needs. The people of this country have the potential for saving more petroleum than will be produced by the North Slope of Alaska if they lower thermostats and watch their auto travel."

I spent hundreds of hours with cabinet and department heads to develop a responsible budget for the 1975 legislative session. It would probably be my last biennial budget and I was determined to set some long-range direction that would last beyond my time as governor.

A thorny dispute over Indian fishing rights would outlast my three terms, as well as my years in the U.S. Senate.

SOME 800 ANGRY COMMERCIAL FISHERMEN descended on Olympia just before the 1974 General Election. They were desperately worried about their future in the wake of a ruling earlier in the year by Federal Judge George Boldt, who reaffirmed that treaty tribes had a right to harvest up to 50 percent of salmon and steelhead runs in their "usual and accustomed places." Further, Boldt ordered the state to take action to limit fishing by non-Indians to ensure the tribal fishermen got their share.

The Boldt Decision was a bombshell. The judge's ruling was his interpretation of the Medicine Creek Treaty signed in 1854 by Territorial Governor Isaac Stevens and Puget Sound tribal leaders. There was little commercial fishing in the early territorial days and most citizens bought salmon from the Indians. As commercial and sports fishing grew on Puget Sound, so did conflict as the catches endangered the runs. The exquisitely obtuse wording of the 120-year-old treaty gave each side a main argument from the same phrase. Indian fishermen focused on "in their usual and accustomed places" to mean fishing when and where they had fished historically. Commercial and sports fishermen retorted that "in common with other citizens of the Territory" meant that Indian fishermen must follow the seasons and limits created for the commercial fishery. Judge Boldt issued his Solomon like solution by dividing the salmon resource in half, adding that "off-reservation fishing by other citizens and residents of the state is not a right but merely a privilege."

I spent an hour listening to the commercial fishermen's concerns and said that given their radically changed economic circumstances I would do what I could to help. Several legislators, meantime, grabbed the opportunity to foment the crowd by denouncing Judge Boldt from the Capitol steps. Senator C.W. "Red" Beck bashed Boldt as "a senile judge, almost 80 years old," who had "completely demolished the fish industry of our state." Senator Don Talley declared that the decision "tears this state wide open."

That was precisely what we didn't need.

When I made my appearance, it took me several minutes to calm things down enough to be heard. I vowed to ask President Ford to declare the Puget Sound commercial fishery a depressed industry to expedite relief. "The state does not agree with the Boldt Decision," I said, "but you must remember that the judge is put in office to attempt to interpret laws and treaties. No one but the judge himself knows how he feels about fishing." Unlike many other mass protests, this one didn't get out of hand. But the hotheads were worrisome. Judge Boldt was burned in effigy and received death threats.

I also heard from tribal leaders deeply concerned about the future of salmon runs and the need to protect habitat in Puget Sound streams and rivers. I discovered how intensely all fishermen felt about these amazing fish. They leave the streams where they were hatched, travel to the depths of the North Pacific for five years and return to precisely the place they were born. It's miraculous.

It was nearly impossible to bring sportsmen, commercial fishermen and Indian leaders together to seek solutions for salmon preservation. From wise tribal leaders like Billy Frank Jr. I began to learn about the importance of salmon, not only as a source of food but as a spiritual part of tribal ritual and history. The Fisheries Department gave me a crash course in fisheries management. Two senior fish biologists, Frank Haw and Peter Bergman, were particularly helpful.

With Billy Frank Jr., the Nisqually Tribe's legendary champion of treaty rights. *Washington State Archives*

The Attorney General's office aggressively appealed the Boldt Decision. Slade Gorton argued that the intention of the treaty was that there would be no distinction between Indians and non-Indians. "The Indians—though non-citizens at the time—would have rights 'in common with' the citizens, which of course meant that 50 or 60 years later when the fish began to get scarce and you began to have some kind of conservation laws, the same laws applied to everyone," Gorton said. A formidable lawyer, he was roundly accused of being racist, which was as patently wrongheaded as it was to vilify Judge Boldt. It was a very complicated, emotional issue, settled, legally at least, in 1979 when the U.S. Supreme Court affirmed the Boldt Decision, 6-3.

In Boldt's wake, commercial and sports fishing leaders eventually agreed to join their tribal counterparts in joint management of the Puget Sound and Columbia River fishery. That was the only legitimate response to the specter of open warfare on riverbanks and Puget Sound. A more difficult challenge was to improve water quality and the natural habitat of young salmon. Added conflict developed between fishermen, farmers, loggers, municipalities and industries. The issue was the use of river waters. Hugely expensive attendant issues, including salmon-blocking culverts and dams, are still with us today. It will be a multi-generational struggle to preserve our enviable natural environment while welcoming millions of new citizens to the Puget Sound basin.

I PRESENTED MY BUDGET MESSAGE for the 1975-1977 biennium weeks before the start of the legislative session—a break with tradition. We were plagued by high inflation but the state's economy was still growing steadily. Our Baby Boom bulge was now creating record-breaking enrollments in higher education, while attendance in K-12 schools was beginning to drop. As the economy expanded so did population growth, which put more pressure on state services. Seattle topped livability studies of America's 50 largest cities. The state's largest city—my home town—ranked first in the nation in terms of public safety, health-care, education, cultural and recreational resources. I believed this was the time to act boldly to preserve that progress—and to enhance quality of life statewide.

I proposed funding new and smaller residential facilities for the mentally ill and the developmentally disabled and new community programs for both. I applauded the wisdom of the voters in passage of the Washington Future bond program. It would allow us to issue bonds, which together with matching funds, would provide $500 million for needed new facilities. Further, the budget would fully fund all state pension systems, add resources for higher education enrollment and boost salaries for state employees to at least partially offset inflation. Inflation made it necessary to propose new revenues. I suggested raising the state sales tax by 1 percent but eliminating totally the state sales tax on food. That was mostly a tradeoff, but I proposed using 0.1 percent of the sales tax increase to help fund local governments. The net effect would decrease taxes on low- and middle-income citizens and reduce some of the unfairness in our rigid tax structure. I also proposed an increase in the B & O tax from 0.44 percent to 0.52 percent. It was the first increase in business taxation since 1959. I knew this would be a difficult set of proposals for the Legislature but it was probably my last time to influence our state's direction.

41
DOORS OPEN, DOORS CLOSE

I stared in stunned disbelief as the networks aired the breaking news from Vietnam. It was April 30, 1975. The last Americans leaving Saigon didn't bother to turn out the lights. Our defeated allies were in even greater peril. A column of desperate refugees scaled a ladder to a roof top, clambering for a spot on a U.S. helicopter. The Marines guarding the Embassy nervously fingered their M-16s.

The 18-hour operation carried 1,300 Americans and 5,600 Vietnamese to safety. "Yet in sheer numbers," *Newsweek* reported, "the feat was overshadowed by the incredible impromptu flight of perhaps another 65,000 South Vietnamese. In fishing boats and barges, homemade rafts and sampans, they sailed by the thousands out to sea, hoping to make it to the 40 U.S. warships beckoning on the horizon. Many were taken aboard, while others joined a convoy of 27 South Vietnamese Navy ships that limped slowly—without adequate food or water—toward an uncertain welcome in the Philippine Islands."

Most of these people desperately seeking asylum in the U.S. or with our allies were well educated. They had worked closely with Americans during the war and feared reprisals by the Communists. Yet a Gallup poll found that only 36 percent of Americans favored Vietnamese immigration.

Ralph Munro visits the refugee tent city at Camp Pendleton, Calif. *Washington State Archives*

California Governor Jerry Brown, the unpredictable Democrat who had just succeeded Ronald Reagan, balked at resettling refugees in his state. Dubbed "Governor Moonbeam," by reporters, Brown spun the issue to the dark side, declaring, "There is something a little strange about saying, 'Let's bring in 500,000 more people' when we can't take care of the one million out of work." One of his senior staff even attempted to prevent airplanes loaded with refugees from landing at Travis Air Force Base. Senator Ted Kennedy expressed similar concerns. So much for liberalism! I was appalled and furious. For starters, it wasn't a half-million more people. It was around 130,000. And these were people being driven from their home country. They had no place to go. America, after all, is a nation of immigrants.

Bruce Chapman, Lud Kramer's successor as Secretary of State, had heard the same news out of California. So had Ralph Munro and Chi-Dooh "Skip" Li, my legal counsel, a refugee in childhood from the Chinese Communist revolution.

As my volunteer coordinator, Munro never ceased to amaze me with his resourcefulness. I dispatched him to Camp Pendleton, the West Coast processing center, to see what Washington could do to help. My parting shot as he headed for the airport was "If you see Brown, remind him what it says on the base of the Statue of Liberty."

Munro toured the sprawling refugee tent city before meeting with Camp Pendleton's commander.

"Do you want these people?" he said.

"Yes," said Ralph. "I'm pretty sure we do."

My response was "Absolutely."

"Governor, you won't believe the talent of these refugee families," Munro said. "They are doctors, lawyers, business leaders, governmental officials, all seeking a new life. Great people."

Munro announced that those who wanted to do so could come to Washington state. Many quickly stepped forward. It struck me then that a lot of them probably thought they were going to Washington, D.C.

While the transit of the refugees was being arranged by Tom Pryor and the Department of Emergency Preparedness, my staff was contacting churches, community groups and other possible host families. We found more volunteers than we could handle. We designated Camp Murray, the National Guard headquarters south of Tacoma, as a reception center.

At Camp Murray in 1975, Vietnamese refugee Tony Le, center, a former employee of the U.S. Embassy in Saigon, introduces me to one of the children who accompanied him to Washington. They were part of the first group of refugees arriving in the state. *MOHAI/Seattle Post-Intelligencer Collection*

Soon the first 500 refugees began making their way to Seattle, followed by 3,500 more. On May 8, 1975, I handed President Ford a letter formally advising him that Washington state was agreeing to be involved in the resettlement effort. Ford soon created the Presidential Commission on Refugees and pushed through the $500 million Indochina Migration and Refugee Assistance Act of 1975. Our experience in resettling the refugees helped shape the larger effort. I was honored to be selected as a member of that committee. John Eisenhower, Ike's son, was our chairman. Other members included George Meany, president of the AFL-CIO, Edgar Kaiser, chairman of Kaiser Industries, and Dr. Malcolm Todd, president of the American Medical Association.

Gerald R. Ford doesn't get enough credit for his compassionate heart. At the opening meeting of the commission, he noted that "most, if not all of us, are the beneficiaries of the opportunities that come from a country that has an open door. In one way or another, all of us are immigrants. And the strength of America over the years has been our diversity. The people we are welcoming today... are individuals who can contribute significantly to our society in the future." In less than a year thousands of Vietnamese refugees found new homes and new opportunity in America.

ON A SUNNY MAY MORNING, Nancy and I went to Camp Murray to visit the newcomers. As buses pulled up to the reception center, families began to emerge, some smiling, some wary. Children clutched their parents' hands. Most were bundled in sweaters and coats. We realized that our warm day was chilly for people accustomed to a tropical climate. As they gathered around us, I was introduced and welcomed them to the State of Washington, using a few basic Vietnamese phrases. I described our state's great diversity and said I was confident they would find new opportunity. They were then paired with sponsor families and started new lives, bringing only the clothes they wore, their talent and a fierce determination to succeed.

My namesake, Evans Nguyen, is perched on Ralph Munro's knee at the 10th anniversary of the refugee assistance effort. *Nguyen Family Album*

On the ride back to Olympia, Nancy and I wondered how we would respond if our family with three young boys was suddenly transported 10,000 miles to a new home with no personal resources. We were immensely gratified that we had offered a fresh start to these tragically displaced people.

One of the families we met that day was the Nguyens—Chuong Huu Nguyen and Xuan Hoa Pham: husband, pregnant wife and five children. The young couple soon found jobs, moved into a

Evans is now director of development engineering at NanoString Technologies, a biotech firm in Seattle. *Nguyen Family Album*

modest home, Americanized their names to Colin and Mary Nguyen and devoted their lives to the education of their children. When the sixth was born, they named him Evans Nguyen in my honor. That is one of the most humbling and satisfying moments of my life.

Nancy and I gathered with their family each year for a Christmas time celebration, attended school events and watched with pride as the children graduated from Liberty high school near Renton. Each became a valedictorian. However, when it came time for Evans to graduate we were surprised not to receive an invitation. We discovered his parents were reluctant to invite us because

Nancy and I with three generations of the Nguyen clan in 2019. Evans is holding his youngest daughter. The patriarch is seated next to us. *Nguyen Family Album*

he was not a valedictorian, just in the top 10! We were delighted to attend, of course.

Ultimately all six children graduated from the University of Washington. Two are physicians; one is a director at Blue Origin; one is an architect; one runs an organic food company, and Evans Nguyen is the director of development engineering at NanoString Technologies, a biotech firm in Seattle. There were two shrines in the Nguyen house. One was a religious shrine. The other one was in the living room where the UW diplomas were displayed.

The Nguyens are a stellar example of the success of our Vietnamese immigration program. Washington state has the third-largest Vietnamese population, behind only California and Texas. I'm exceedingly proud of the volunteer sponsors, support organizations and legislators who welcomed these productive new citizens to our state.

The refugee crisis is an event Ralph Munro and I look back on with great satisfaction. When he went on to serve five terms as secretary of state, a child of one of those refugees occasionally would stop him on the street or at a school event, saying, "My grandpa says you saved my life." That's one of the priceless rewards of public service.

HOW I WISH my experience with the 1975 legislative session had been as uplifting.

Exactly 10 years after my first inaugural, I stood before the lawmakers to present my State of the State message. It was not an easy time. President Ford's WIN program was barely denting inflation. At 11.8 percent it was the highest since 1947. And the national unemployment rate was 8.1 percent, highest since World War II. Internal strife raged in the Democratic caucuses in both chambers. A clump of conservatives in the House GOP caucus demanded "smaller" government. The mood was sour. There was little enthusiasm for new ideas.

The 65,000 citizens who responded to the Alternatives for Washington questionnaire saw things through a different prism. They strongly favored moderate economic and population growth. Their top priority was protection of our natural environment and the conservation of our natural resources. Their enthusiasm helped forge my message. I called for comprehensive land resource management. To address concerns about the escalating cost of healthcare, I proposed a bill to provide backup protection for families facing financial disaster. I also said Washingtonians should have a chance to vote on whether to call a constitutional convention, saying we could give ourselves no better Bicentennial present than to re-examine our 86-year-old State Constitution to see if it was still responsive to today's needs. I promised to return to the Legislature within 10 days to deliver a special message on energy and conservation. These were high-octane proposals, but I knew this might be the last time I had a chance to challenge my fellow lawmakers.

I was particularly saddened by their subsequent refusal to even give voters a chance to create a constitutional convention. Our creaky State Constitution is seven times as long as the U.S. Constitution and has been amended more than 100 times. A patched-up Model T attempting to race in the Indianapolis 500, it hampers us in competing in today's international economy.

My healthcare proposal, developed by a task force headed by Richard Roddis, dean of the University of Washington Law School, encountered similar legislative lethargy. I was eager to show the country we could produce a cost-effective healthcare program that ultimately might provide the blueprint for a national equivalent. It was designed to not only cover medical costs of the indigent and working poor, but to provide catastrophic healthcare cost insurance for all citizens. One of the major speed bumps was the opposition of task force member Joe Davis, president of the State Labor Council. "Until we can meet present needs, we're not in a position to start new programs," Davis said.

My special message on Energy, Conservation and Agriculture urged conservation as our top priority in meeting the challenges of energy shortages. The lawmakers stifled a yawn, having often heard all this from me. But I startled them by emphasizing the precious nature of our water resource, "which by law and our Constitution is reserved to the people of this state. It is a public resource which should have its value reflected in public benefits."

Custom and tradition had helped create a system of perpetual and free rights to water. I said there was a more than striking similarity between public water resources and timber on public lands. However, the contrast in income to the public was equally dramatic. "Last year, timber sales brought more than $100 million to the state government for public purposes. Our water brought us essentially no income." I proposed that for large commercial, industrial and agricultural purposes we establish a system of long-term, moderately priced permits instead of perpetual water rights. The income should be utilized in much the same fashion as income from the management of our state lands: 20 percent for continued management of our water resources and 80 percent to help finance the further development of irrigation and water supply for agricultural and industrial purposes.

"My God!" one legislator declared, "the governor has figured out how to tax everything but air and sex." My rejoinder was "Well, now I have two more ideas."

Editorial reaction was mixed. The most strident opposition came from *The Tri-City Herald*. Its editorial said my plan smacked of "fascism" and "communism." When I visited the Tri-Cities shortly afterward, a story in the *Herald* included the agenda for the meeting: "Governor introduced; Governor speaks; Glenn Lee (the paper's publisher) speaks in opposition to Governor's proposal; Resolution introduced in opposition to Governor's proposal." I told my audience it reminded me of Western justice: "Hang him first, then give him a fair trial." They came at me in waves of vitriolic opposition. But just before adjournment an elderly fellow stood up at the back of the room and said, "I want to say something before you quit. I have lived in this area for 78 years and some of you guys who want to draw water out of the river forget how that water got there. It is all in the pools behind these dams, and these dams are paid for by citizens from Maine to Washington and from Florida to California. The taxpayers all over the country helped make it possible for you guys to do this. Governor, I didn't vote for you in 1972, but by God if you run again I will vote for you!" A woman piped up, "I think so too." With that, the chairman slammed his gavel.

I was convinced the proposal was fair and equitable, especially given one contract by the Department of Natural Resources. For the previous 10 years it had leased 600 acres of dry land for cattle grazing at 15 cents an acre per year, producing a whopping $900 in income over the decade. The department then drilled two irrigation wells on the land at a cost of $30,000 and put the property up for another 10-year lease. This time the high bidder offered $170,000, plus a share of the crops, for a total of $525,000 in income over 10 years. The water obviously had great value and just as obviously was a public resource.

Wild opposition in the farm community killed any legislative action. Interestingly, however, a short time later, U & I Sugar Company built a sugar beet processing plant after signing a water permit with the state. It featured a time limit and stipulated payment for the water used.

All these years later, I am more convinced than ever that water will become a more precious resource than oil and we will be forced to use it more efficiently, both for agriculture and industrial purposes.

THE LEGISLATURE was stalled on almost every item of importance. Voters in Puget Sound area school districts had massively defeated special levy requests. What a pickle. We were in a national recession. Interest rates topped 15 percent. Tax reform had been repeatedly rejected, and rural legislators refused any support that would raise taxes. Leading newspapers editorialized piously about the need to support education after many earlier editorials advocating a lid on taxes. Teachers threatened to strike if their demands were not met. Six-thousand rallied in Olympia. Next came a "Children's Crusade" featuring 3,000 students. They descended on the Capitol to plead for adequate support for their schools. It was one of the most or-

Addressing 3,000 students from around the state in the spring of 1975. They staged a rally at the Capitol to demand more money for K-12 public education in the wake of special levy failures. *Washington State Archives*

derly and focused demonstrations I ever saw. I met with 16 student leaders and was thoroughly impressed with their knowledge, ideals and determination.

The kids left town but the grown-ups' problems remained.

I asked for an opportunity to speak to a joint session of the Legislature. In a tumultuous decade, Americans had faced urban turmoil, assassinations, an aerospace recession, energy shortages and Watergate. I noted that Washington had survived each of these crises remarkably well. Despite population growth and increasing demands for government services, our taxes had grown slower than any other state in the nation and property tax burdens were below the national average. Our welfare caseload was a little more than half the national average and our error and fraud rate was among the lowest. Our public schools produced graduates who did well in nationwide tests. I cited two recent national quality-of-life studies: Washington state ranked third, Seattle first. "We are proud of what we have done," I said. "Let us not today destroy it." Turning to the immediate crisis of school funding, I proposed a four-part program:

> State revenue to support 75 percent of the special levy requests for the coming school year.
>
> A temporary 0.6 percent increase in the state sales tax and a 10 percent hike in the Business and Occupation tax. I emphasized that this revenue increase of $127 million would be offset by property tax reductions of $177 million.
>
> A citizen task force to seek alternatives for permanent guaranteed basic school financial support. The group should report back to a legislative session in September to allow preparation of alternatives for a citizen vote in November 1975.
>
> Improved educational management, starting with the office of the state superintendent and right on down to the smallest school district. I mentioned merit pay for teachers, accountability and measurement of educational achievement, tougher accreditation standards, a uniform accounting and information base for all schools and reduction-in-force policies no longer based solely on seniority.

Our forefathers made one thing perfectly clear when they wrote the State Constitution: "The paramount duty of the state" is to make "ample provision for the education of all children residing within its borders." I said it was time to turn that constitutional mandate into reality.

House Speaker Leonard Sawyer represented a suburban Pierce County district, while Senate Majority Leader Augie Mardesich (facing an ethics indictment) was from Snohomish County. Neither felt the urgency of King County legislators over defeated special levies. The longest legislative session in Washington state history—and in my view the worst in 25 years—droned on into summer. Three weeks from the beginning of the new biennium, it passed a budget that failed to relieve school problems and staggered to adjournment, leaving me with an inadequate budget and a fatally flawed transportation package. The Legislature had made a mess of it all. A strange variable gas tax was enacted, automatically raising the gas tax if revenues decreased. But gas tax revenues were decreasing because automobiles were more efficient. The Legislature had enacted a nonsensical direct tax on efficiency. And once again, it refused to allow the governor to appoint the Secretary of Transportation, instead keeping that authority with a highway-oriented commission.

As promised, I vetoed all three transportation bills to howls of rage from highway lobbyists and the construction industry. I knew there would be another opportunity to revisit this issue in six months and I hoped to get a better outcome. I also vetoed the inadequate special levy relief section of the budget and called the Legislature back into session in July to try to ease the crisis facing our urban school systems.

The Senate was not prepared to make any compromise. "Let Seattle take care of itself," said Hubert Donohue, the Eastern Washington lawmaker who headed the Ways and Means committee. After two more brief extraordinary sessions, the House finally accepted the $65 million emergency school relief figure originally proposed in the budget. I was furious. It was obvious, however, that the Senate was unmovable, so I signed the bill and blew my stack at a press conference:

> Unfortunately, this Legislature was in control of the same old gang. "No new taxes," was the cry. Deceit is a better name. Gas taxes, game fees, motor-vehicle excise taxes, cigarette taxes, sales taxes on contracts—$100 million or more of new taxes and new costs were added to the taxpayer while they said no new taxes. Then they rolled over weakly and meekly to special interests. Contractors said "Roads!" and the gas tax was raised. Utilities said "Help!" and they effectively raised the people's utility bills. The small-loans people and banks said "Increase our interest rates!" and they got it. Milk producers wanted more money and the Legislature said, "Raise milk prices!" The only special interest they stood firm against were the schoolchildren of the state—schoolchildren who have no vote or campaign money. I serve notice here that I intend to continue the fight for quality education in the state at every opportunity—this year, next year and in the elections of 1976.

UPI's Gordy Schultz jumped right in: "Does that mean you are a candidate for re-election?"

"No, it does not mean that. It means that I will continue to fight for quality education in whatever way I can during those election years."

"You're mad, aren't you?" said Adele Ferguson.

"You bet I am mad!"

For a decade we had labored to reform our tax system. The bipartisan effort produced a reform that could have amply supported our public school system for many years. But the people turned it down at the polls. Now the bipartisanship was gone and the Legislature divided into rural versus urban, East versus West, and Republican versus Democrat. I knew it was highly unlikely that any significant school reform would occur in the remaining year and a half of my term.

At the end of the marathon legislative session, the *Seattle Post-Intelligencer* released a poll on the 1976 governor's race. I led by a substantial margin over seven other competitors. The surprise contender was Dr. Dixy Lee Ray. The brilliant but eccentric former UW professor and chairman of the U.S. Atomic Energy Commission ran second, ahead of all other Democrats and significantly ahead of King County Executive John Spellman, who was already actively campaigning. That set off a new rash of press speculation on whether I might seek a fourth term—especially with so much unfinished business. I told the press the truth: I had not yet made up my mind. And if I had I wouldn't have said so. Why become a lame duck at the age of 50 with 18 more months at hand? I had not initiated any fundraising or campaign team building but I was confident I could do that promptly if I decided to run.

42
GO FOURTH?

I was truly conflicted about a fourth term. Our economy was on the rebound and I was developing a new Blueprint for Progress, including a call for a constitutional convention, catastrophic healthcare coverage, more educational funding, new environmental protection initiatives and expanded international trade. But our three sons were quickly growing up. I realized we had only a few more years together as a family before they left for college. Our oldest, Dan Jr., was 4 when I became governor. At the end of a fourth term he'd be 20. It seemed like only yesterday that we were building a tree house together.

The decision went on hold until the outcome of what would prove to be an extraordinary legislative session.

While Democrats still handily controlled both the House and Senate, their caucuses were in chaos. Senate Majority Leader August Mardesich had been indicted by a federal grand jury for extorting $10,000 from two garbage company officials and failing to report the income to the IRS—accusations first lodged by his old rival, Bob Greive. Mardesich was subsequently acquitted by a U.S. District Court jury. Nevertheless he was forced to resign as majority leader after the Senate Ethics Board found him guilty of three counts of unethical conduct. He lashed out at his enemies like an old crippled lion, admitting only to benign "errors of judgment." I was sorry to see Augie step down. He was a wily adversary, a capable leader and a force for reform. He had always been a straight shooter with me.

Senator Gordon Walgren, a nimble attorney from Bremerton, became majority leader. The Democratic majority was crippled for the remainder of my term as the bitterness persisted.

House Speaker Leonard Sawyer was "invited" to appear before the Public Disclosure Commission to explain why he had not reported funds he received from a Baltimore engineering firm for work he had done for the newly independent nation of Papua New Guinea. Sawyer claimed his fee was substantially less than $500, but admitted under questioning that the firm had paid more than $2,000 for his airfare.

Sawyer was a bright man, but too full of himself. The younger members of his caucus chafed under his heavy-handed leadership style. As the 1976 session got underway, Sawyer's caucus ousted him as Speaker in favor of Joe Haussler, a well-respected lawmaker from Okanogan County. However, given their schism, the Democrats lacked the Republican votes necessary to elevate Haussler. Wily old John O'Brien, the Speaker Pro Tempore, presided over the session—back in business 13 years after our legendary Coalition coup cost him the gavel.

All that was inside baseball. In the real world, the state's K-12 schools were in crisis, attempting to fund soaring enrollments amid double-digit inflation. I jumped at the chance to address the Downtown Seattle Rotary Club, one of the largest and most influential service clubs in the nation. I was weary of hearing business leaders ask, "Why don't you run state government more like a business?" Well, I said, "Which business should I choose—Boeing and General Motors or Lockheed and Chrysler?" The latter two were in bankruptcy and the former chairman of Boeing admitted that during the "Boeing Bust" his company nearly went under.

I decided to present a program on the fiscal health of our state. My staff and cabinet worked hard to prepare a financial report that highlighted the assets and liabilities of state government and the equity owned by Washingtonians. We included a profit-and-loss statement for fiscal year 1975 and wrapped it all into a little brochure that mimicked a corporate quarterly report. There was one at each place setting.

I told the club their corporation—the State of Washington—was in excellent condition, but its future was murky. In FY-'75 our revenue exceeded expenditures by almost $180 million—earnings of nearly 7 percent. The state accounting system, however, showed a budget barely in balance for 1975. It was dramatic evidence of the difficulty of communicating public budgeting to those accustomed to private industry accounting. As for assets and liabilities, our cash in hand, long-term investments, land, buildings and state highways amounted to $6.5 billion. Liabilities in retirement systems, long-term bonds payable and taxes and wages payable amounted to $4.6 billion, leaving the citizenry with $1.8 billion in equity—a little over $500 per capita. The Rotarians seemed surprised at our financial health, but I was speaking their language.

I turned to the crisis in education, using charts to show the Baby Boom bulge in our school-age population. It now extended from kindergarten to graduate schools. As the property tax burden increased, more levies failed. "We have a choice," I said. "Bold and courageous action to assure our children a basic education or we can succumb to fear and indecision that will haunt us for a generation to come. The financial crisis for our schools is every bit as dramatic as our aerospace decline a few years ago. We rallied then and we must rally today."

I prepared a series of major bills designed to enhance teacher standards, reform school funding formulas and boost per-pupil support. For the first time in almost a decade I proposed raising both the state sales tax and the Business & Occupation tax. The proceeds would help fund education, radically reducing dependence on special levies and stabilizing tuition for higher education. An important part of the package was reform in teacher hiring and accountability. Teacher union representatives bleated that the increased money was insufficient and the accountability measures were onerous. I was always astonished at how often lobbyists for major organizations publicly trashed ideas designed to help them. It is far better to contact the sponsor privately and try to improve the proposal. In this case the teacher lobbyists turned me from a friend to a skeptic in a session virtually paralyzed by conflict.

IT WAS AN ELECTION YEAR. That meant there was little stomach for the tax measures I proposed, even though the revenue would replace increasingly burdensome property taxes for school support. Some who would support new taxes were adamantly opposed to teacher accountability measures; some just as adamantly opposed to taxes backed my reform measures. It was impossible to forge a majority for anything, so basic support for education remained dependent on onerous special property tax levies. Mardesich, meantime, rallied from his troubles and focused his incisive intellect on one of the state's most critical issues: Fully funding our state pension systems. The benefits, particularly in our Law Enforcement Officers and Firefighters system—LEOFF for short—could not be sustained. Years earlier, State Representatives Ned Shera and Homer Humiston separately attempted and failed in earnest efforts to reform the state pension systems. They were defeated at the next election by the combined efforts of state employees, teachers, police officers and firefighters, all determined to protect a status quo whose status was on quicksand. Thanks to Mardesich, pension reform passed in 1976.*

ONE BILL THAT DID GAIN legislators' interest was a proposal for a presidential primary. Oregon had one scheduled for May. Idaho and Montana were interested in some limelight of their own. All three urged us to create a primary on the same day, stressing that a Far West regional primary would generate nationwide interest and entice candidates.

The Washington State House quickly passed a good presidential primary bill. When it arrived in the Senate, Mardesich strolled into my office.

"Boss," he said intently, "do you want a presidential primary bill?"

"Sure. It's a great idea."

Augie smiled. "Well, we have a few little amendments since Senator Jackson is running for president and we want to make sure he gets all the delegates from Washington state."

Aha. I warned him that my support for a presidential primary bill depended on it being fair to all candidates and a good thing for the state in the long term.

"OK, boss." With that, he headed back to the fray.

Sure enough, in the dying days of the session a presidential primary bill was sent to my desk. I learned later that there was a major backroom dust-up in the State Senate when Scoop Jackson's supporters demanded the bill maximize their chances for delegates. That they had prevailed was abundantly clear from the bill in front of me. I really wanted a presidential primary but there was no way I was going to sign this contrivance. My middle name is Jackson and I liked Scoop, but I vetoed it on the spot, saying, "This bill is obviously tailored to enhance the prospects of a single candidate in one year and for one election."

Ironically, by the middle of May Scoop had already retired from the presidential race. On the Republican side Ford and Reagan were embroiled in a fierce fight for the nomination.

AS THE SESSION DRONED ON, new initiatives were clearly futile. Jim Dolliver and I continued to have our regular strategy sessions. One day our conversation turned to our shared love for Olympic National Park, where I took my first hikes as a Boy Scout and Jim had spent summer breaks from Swarthmore working as a forest ranger. He remembered his visits to the fabulous wild and windy beaches bordering the gray Pacific. "It's too bad they're not included in the National Park," he said wistfully, stroking his beard. "They sure should be." We pulled out a map and discovered 7½ miles

---

* August P. Mardesich's storied 28-year career in the Legislature came to an end in 1978. He was defeated in the Democratic primary through the massive efforts of the potential beneficiaries of an out-of-control pension system. Augie fell on his sword but his legacy is a more rational system of public pensions and the savings of hundreds of millions of dollars to Washington taxpayers.

of unprotected oceanfront between the Makah Indian Reservation and the existing Ocean Strip of Olympic National Park. We summoned Elliot Marks, our staff member in charge of environmental affairs, and told him to assemble some detailed ownership charts of that area. Soon the three of us were examining potential boundary lines. We asked Elliot to draw the line along the top of the ridges that could be seen from the ocean, adding some buffer land to the east while including the remaining shoreline of Lake Ozette that was not already in the park.* Virtually all the land was owned by five timber companies. I asked Jim to request a meeting with their executives.

A few days later we gathered in my office. I presented the proposal to the landowners, saying it was only an idea—and one that would require federal legislation, including market compensation for any land acquired and set aside. They were not pleased, to put it mildly. A scheme like that would remove too much of their timberland and cripple lumber production, they insisted.

"Well, I'm really interested in protecting this priceless ocean frontage. What do you suggest?"

Pencils were distributed. Potential boundaries were drawn. I had a flashback to the redistricting battles of the 1960s, with Gorton, Pritchard and I huddled over Shell Oil maps as boundaries were argued street by street. This time it was virtually tree by tree. Gradually we came to an agreement that preserved virtually all of the land visible from the ocean.

I called Senator Jackson and Don Bonker, the young congressman whose 3rd District included the Olympic Peninsula. Both were interested. Scoop was especially enthusiastic. He offered to sponsor a bill in the Senate, an immensely important development since he headed the Energy & Natural Resources Committee. It had jurisdiction over National Parks. The bill moved rapidly, although a few residents with summer places on the shores of Lake Ozette complained vociferously about being included within the park. In a remarkably short time the bill passed and the remaining stretch of wild ocean beach was added to the park. It was one of those marvelous moments when an idea with strong citizen support, coupled with environmental awareness, found a strong advocate in Henry M. Jackson. I was immensely pleased that the casual conversation a few months earlier with Dolliver had produced such extraordinary results.

Scoop Jackson and Don Bonker. *Courtesy Don Bonker*

ASKED ABOUT POTENTIAL vice presidential nominees, President Ford told a press conference I was one of eight potential running mates. The others were Secretary of Commerce Elliot Richardson of "Saturday Night Massacre" fame, U.S. Senators Edward Brooke, Charles Percy, Howard Baker and William Brock, and Governors Robert Ray of Iowa and Christopher Bond of Missouri.

I received a letter from CBS News asking if I would appear on *Face the Nation* on the Sunday "after you are named as the Republican vice presidential nominee." I showed it to Dolliver and we

---

* Marks would go on to become Washington State director of the Nature Conservancy.

laughed, knowing that the same letter had been sent to all of the other potential nominees.

Three weeks later, the annual winter meeting of the National Governors' Conference was held in Washington, D.C. The President sent a White House limousine to the hotel to bring me to a private meeting in the Oval Office. We discussed energy, unemployment and inflation, relationships between the states and Congress and talked at length about the growing intensity of his fight with Reagan for the nomination. I offered to campaign for him wherever and however he thought useful. I got the strong impression he was sizing me up.

The next day I met with our congressional delegation to discuss ramifications of the Boldt Decision, followed by talks with James Lynn, director of the Office of Management and Budget, to urge release of federal funds for the Bacon Siphon, a major irrigation project in the Columbia basin. It was a highly productive four days. I returned to Olympia still wondering about that Oval Office visit.

BY EARLY MARCH I realized it was fourth-term decision time. I was tossing and turning every night, sometimes even dreaming about whether to run. The issue came up at every press conference. Finally, on March 23, I announced I'd reveal my decision two days later.

"What does Mrs. Evans suggest that you do?" said David Ammons, the AP's bright young reporter.

"Well, I suggest that you ask Mrs. Evans, but I doubt that she would tell you. She has learned that much."

We all laughed.

Mrs. Evans, for her part, is such a wise and wonderful wife that she was not about to tell her husband what to do. "Look, this is your decision," she said. "I'm prepared to support you whatever you decide. Do what your heart tells you." Secretly, her heart was telling her it was time for something new.

When I asked the boys at dinner that night I got a mixed reaction. They were apprehensive about moving to a new community and new schools. They really wanted to stay with their friends. But they also expressed some weariness about our fishbowl lives.

I also consulted Dolliver, of course. He was much more than my chief of staff. He was one of my earliest and wisest supporters when I launched my long-shot bid for governor in 1964. We had talked about the long agenda of unfinished business. "There will always be an unfinished agenda," Jim said. "You began with a Blueprint for Progress. You accomplished virtually all of it. Now you have a brand-new agenda in 1976. If you run and win there will be another agenda in 1980 and 1984. When do you step off the train? Don't let the unfinished agenda affect your decision."

On the afternoon of March 24 I sat in my office, pondering what to do. All of a sudden everything seemed clear. I must have startled some of the staff as I hurried out the door.

Across the street at the Governor's Mansion, Nancy was entertaining several hundred people at an open house.

"I've got to talk with you," I whispered, taking her by the arm.

"Just wait a minute," she protested.

"Now," I insisted.

We went upstairs to our bedroom. I took her in my arms and held her tight for several seconds, too choked up to speak.

"What in the world is the matter?" she said, pulling back to stare into my eyes.

"Let's go buy a house," I said.

She wrapped her arms around me and said two words: "I'm relieved."

That evening we told our boys. Bruce, our 10-year-old, laughed uproariously and said, "I won!"

"Won what?"

"I had a bet with our school janitor that you would not run," Bruce said, revealing that he was looking forward to his winnings: a half-pint of chocolate milk.

The next morning my entire cabinet and staff gathered in the ballroom of the Mansion. It was an extraordinary team. Many had been with me since 1965. I saw the many emotions reflected in their faces: Anticipation, wonder, fear, eagerness, even passion. They were ready to fight and win a campaign for four more years. I congratulated our team for its skill, loyalty and friendship. Then tears welled up in my eyes. Fundamentally, it came down to a family decision, I said. "They have contributed all I think they should contribute to this state." There was a collective gasp and scattered sighs. Then, after a few seconds, applause. It grew until it echoed. I reminded everyone that we had still nine months left. We needed to work hard right to the end. There were tears and embraces, funny stories, shared memories. As I walked through the ballroom I saw State Patrol Chief Will Bachofner standing ramrod straight, his eyes filled with tears. I remembered with great admiration the many times we had faced a crisis and how his advice was always wise.

It was time to meet the press. Accompanied by Nancy and the boys and my entire cabinet, I entered the Capitol's ornate formal reception room. Shutters clicked and the TV klieg lights flashed on. As I approached the podium, Adele slipped a small piece of paper in front of the cluster of microphones taped to the speaking stand. I picked it up, laughed heartily, and began by reading my horoscope for the day: "Libra, September 24/October 23. Meet this day with a determination to see its new possibilities and offers—many to be eagerly grasped. Creative pursuits especially favored."

I paused, took a deep breath and said: "I'm deeply proud of the administration of this state. I'm proud of the state itself. Most of all I'm proud of the people of Washington. They are worth working for, and they are worth fighting for. I'm proud most of all of my family and my wife, Nancy, and my boys, my parents and one of the greatest mothers-in-law that you could ever have." I was momentarily overcome with emotion as the reality hit me. Finally, I said, "Because I love my family so much I will end this term as governor and not seek re-election."

Some onlookers raced to the exits to spread the news. Before turning to questions I read one of my favorite Teddy Roosevelt quotes—one that I believe typifies those who serve in public office:

> It is not the critic who counts. Not the man who points out how the strong man stumbles or where the doer of deeds could have done better. The credit belongs to the man who is actually in the arena, whose face is marred by dust and sweat and blood, who strives valiantly, who errs and comes short again and again. Who knows the great enthusiasms, the great devotions, and spends himself in a worthy cause. Who, at the best, knows in the end the triumph of high achievement and who, at the worst, if he fails at least fails while daring greatly. So that his place shall never be with those cold and timid souls who know neither victory nor defeat.

The press rose in a standing ovation, which pleased me greatly. They knew more than most what our administration tried to accomplish. I had presided over more than a thousand press conferences during 11½ years as governor. I was grateful for the press corps' fair and even-handed treatment, and I told them so.

Two days later the Kingdome was dedicated. John Spellman, King County's first executive, had persevered to get it built through a seemingly endless series of setbacks and controversies. Major League baseball was back, together with the Seattle Seahawks of the NFL. Jack Gordon, the master of ceremonies, introduced me. "Governor Evans recently announced that he would step down after 12 years of distinguished service as our governor," he declared.

I was astonished and deeply touched by the response: 55,000 people rose in a prolonged standing ovation. "Be careful," I cracked, "or I might change my mind!"

JUSTICE ROBERT FINLEY of the Washington State Supreme Court, whom I had known for years, died unexpectedly at the age of 70 the day before I announced I would not seek a fourth term. Finley had served on the bench for 25 years. A wise and witty man, he formed a jazz band during the Depression before earning a law degree at Duke University. He had a particular interest in improving the judiciary, in creating better working relationships with the legal profession, the press and the people in state government.

Picking Finley's successor was one of the easiest decisions I've ever made.

In 1970, I had urged the Washington State Bar Association to consider the qualifications of Dolliver to succeed retiring Justice Matthew Hill. "Concerned that he lacked sufficient law practice experience," the association's board of governors, deleted Jim's name from the approved list. Jim asked me to withdraw his name from consideration. I did so reluctantly.

In 1975, I recommended Dolliver for appointment to the U.S. District Court in Seattle. Gallingly, the American Bar Association declared him "not qualified" since he had no prior judicial experience and had not "practiced law for the previous 10 years." I was furious, pointing out that as my chief of staff and trusted adviser, Dolliver had spent 10 years crafting judicious laws, not just interpreting them. His intellect, temperament and wisdom far exceeded that of any other candidate for the position. Scoop Jackson, who knew and admired Dolliver, called to say he wholeheartedly agreed with me. "But I just can't send his name to the Senate without Bar Association approval."

I wasn't going to squander a third chance to elevate an extraordinary legal mind to the bench. A few days after Finley's memorial service I received a call from the Washington State Bar Association. It offered to assist in reviewing names for the Supreme Court vacancy. "Thank you very much," I said crispy, "but I will need no help on this appointment."

I summoned Jim. He was delighted to accept my offer.

I carefully weighed each of my appointments to the judiciary since I realized many would serve long after I left office. During my 12 years as governor I made more than 100 appointments, including Superior Court judges around the state, Supreme Court justices and all 12 members of the new Court of Appeals. In appointing James Morgan Dolliver to the high court, I said he was probably the best qualified person I had ever appointed to any position and predicted he would be "a people's judge."

I was right. In 1993, the Washington State Bar Association honored Dolliver as its "Outstanding

Judge of the Year." Other accolades fill two pages.

OCCASIONALLY I HAD TO CHOOSE between several highly qualified judicial candidates who also happened to be friends. That happened in Walla Walla County several years before. It turned out to have a huge impact on Dolliver's first campaign to keep his seat on the bench.

Art Eggers, the prosecuting attorney in Walla Walla County, was a nominee for the Superior Court. There were three other solid candidates. I chose Jim Mitchell, the top choice of the County Bar Association, instead of Art. Now, fast forward to 1976: I received a letter from Eggers' wife Patsy, chastising me for not appointing her husband and ruining their summer vacation that year. Revenge was on her mind. Somehow she had convinced her husband the best way to punish me was for him to challenge Dolliver for the State Supreme Court. This development was to have uncommonly positive results.

State Senator Fred Dore, a hard-charging populist Democrat from Seattle, had long lusted after a seat on the Supreme Court. He filed to run against Dolliver. Dore was not a particularly distinguished legislator, in my view, and intellectually not remotely a challenger to Dolliver. He did have considerably more name familiarity than Jim. We both knew it would be a difficult race.

Washington has a unique provision in its election laws. It provides that in nonpartisan judicial races, if a candidate receives more than 50 percent of the total vote in a primary election, that person is elected. I was worried that we had less than six months before a primary election to get voters to understand the extraordinary potential Dolliver would bring to the high court.

The campaign proceeded during the summer in the somewhat limited and stilted fashion of judicial races. Dolliver hit the hustings, visiting towns big and small all around the state, just as we had done together in 1964—this time on his own behalf.

On Primary Election night we watched with increasing dismay as Fred Dore ran substantially ahead of Jim and collected almost 50 percent of the total vote. However, when all the absentees were counted, Eggers had received just enough votes in third place to keep Dore from winning the seat. Dolliver went on to win in November by a narrow margin and began an enormously successful 23 years on the Supreme Court. I never heard from either of the Eggers again, although I was mightily tempted to write Patsy a thank-you note.

Jim Dolliver, a man to remember, died in 2004. I miss him practically every day.

43
THE VEEPSTAKES

Despite losing the Iowa caucus and five consecutive presidential primaries, Ronald Reagan pushed ahead in the spring of '76, buoyed by diehard Goldwaterites and the party's rising evangelical wing. Together with North Carolina Governor James Holshouser, I issued a statement urging Reagan to withdraw and get behind President Ford. Several other Republican governors joined us in warning that protracted divisiveness could elect a Democrat in November. Reagan huffed, "You don't take your bat and go home when the game is still in the first inning." He won five of the next seven primaries.

With President Ford, a fellow Eagle Scout. *Evans Family Collection*

I campaigned for Ford in Minnesota, Hawaii, Idaho, Wyoming and California. Reagan for months had been accusing Ford of "negotiating in secret" to give away the Canal Zone, which he proclaimed was "sovereign U.S. territory." I noted that Panama's titular sovereignty over the canal was established in 1904 and reaffirmed by the last three administrations. Further, Reagan's frequent boast that as governor he had returned $4 billion in rebates to California taxpayers was only half the story. He neglected to mention that he was, at the same time, pushing through tax increases totaling $9 billion. Tough stuff, but the whole truth.

On my return to Olympia, I received an urgent call from Joel Pritchard. The Department of Agriculture was urging Ford to veto the Alpine Lakes Wilderness Bill.

The Forest Service objected to preserving thousands of acres of federal timberland. Joel implored me to fly to Washington and lobby the president. The White House reluctantly granted me 15 minutes. The Mountaineers had produced a wonderful book documenting the grandeur of the Alpine Lakes. In the rush, I left my copy at home. A longtime friend and hiking companion, Bill Douglas, lived in Annapolis.* He agreed to lend me

---

* Not to be confused with William O. Douglas, the longtime Supreme Court justice from Yakima, Bill Douglas was the son of my scoutmaster. He joined the troop when I was an assistant scoutmaster.

his copy. I had to promise I'd get the president to autograph it.

Ford greeted me warmly. A couple of White House staffers hovered, intent on reminding him the Forest Service was recommending a veto. I explained the uniqueness of this extraordinary wilderness just a few miles from Puget Sound's urban sprawl. My 15 minutes was ticking away. I opened the book and started showing the president the pristine area encompassed in the bill. Soon he was immersed in the photos, studying each page while talking about his hiking experiences as a Boy Scout.

"Mr. President, your next appointment is here," a secretary announced. Ford waved her away and kept turning the pages. My 15-minute appointment turned into a 45-minute discussion on the historic opportunity at hand. He autographed the book for Bill Douglas. A few days later he signed the Alpine Lakes Wilderness into law. Gerald R. Ford, a man imbued with the common touch and common sense, is an underappreciated president. Luckily, he was also a Boy Scout.

WILL ROGERS ONCE OBSERVED, "I belong to no organized political party. I'm a Democrat." He would have been amazed by the open warfare in the Washington State Republican Party. The "Evans Republicans"—including Evans—were an endangered species. Pitched battles erupted at county conventions. Centrist Republicans were vanquished by passionate Reaganites. Washington sent a solid Reagan delegation to the national convention in Kansas City. That I was summarily left off the delegate list spawned a series of editorials castigating the party for removing the senior Republican governor in the nation from its delegate roster. The race between Ford and Reagan was now extremely close. Every delegate counted. It would have been foolish for the Reagan supporters to give away even one delegate to a Ford backer.

Almost every list of potential Ford running mates now included me. A White House aide sent me a confidential request for a comprehensive background report. I was told other potential vice-presidential candidates were also being vetted. I scheduled a physical exam, assembled tax returns for the previous 10 years, supplied a net-worth statement and provided a detailed biography.

Delegate or not, Ford's campaign asked me to come to Kansas City and be part of the president's team. Besides Pritchard, my contingent included my chief of staff, Bill Jacobs, Press Secretary Jay Fredericksen, and State Patrol Sergeant Bill Lathrop. We were joined by Bud Pardini, one of the few Ford delegates from Washington state. We arrived in Kansas City with the nomination still in doubt. Ford had a small lead. But the delegates the president had won in many primaries would jump ship to Reagan if he failed to secure a first-ballot victory. If Reagan were to win in those circumstances the party would be horrendously divided heading into November.

Wearing my "Committed to President

With press secretary Jay Fredericksen at the 1976 GOP National Convention. *Evans Family Collection*

Ford" button, I began meeting with delegations. Our task was to solidify Ford delegates and sway the uncommitted. At a reception sponsored by Vice President Rockefeller, I saw a tall man with an ill-fitting hairpiece. He was energetically working the crowd, making his way toward me. He shook my hand and boomed, "I'm Harold Stassen and I'm running for president!" Laughing, I said, "I was a delegate in Washington state for you in 1948—28 years ago!" We had a good conversation before Stassen plunged back into the crowd, an old warrior who never stopped dreaming.

I felt strongly that you don't run for vice president. You are selected. Still, our team figured a little publicity wouldn't hurt. We assembled a four-page biography with full-color photos, a much slicker version than the campaign tabloids of previous campaigns. As Pritchard and Jacobs talked to delegates about potential vice-presidential picks, they quietly circulated the biography and suggested I ought to be considered. An added bonus was the news that Republican state chairmen from the 13 Western states—including California—sent a resolution to Ford unanimously endorsing my candidacy.

PRESIDENT FORD CONVENED A MEETING of Republican governors for a strategy session. A dozen of us gathered in his hotel suite. He sought our views on the vice presidency. I suggested that a governor would be a good counter to Jimmy Carter, now officially the Democratic nominee. My colleagues emphatically supported me, noting that I was an experienced governor from the West where Ford had to prevail to win. I was pleased by their enthusiasm and thought the president was impressed as well. *The Seattle Times* featured a story about campaign buttons. A beaded, Indian-style necklace boosting my candidacy was creating a stir among delegates and pin collectors. "Judy Larsen and Nancy Burnett of Spokane were wearing theirs at the Crown Center Hotel yesterday," Dick Larsen wrote, "when a good-looking young man saw the Evans name and stopped to admire the beadwork." It was Jack Ford, the president's son. He extolled my environmental record and said I would add real strength to the ticket. He was supporting me "all the way." Our team was a little giddy at the thought a miracle might happen.

We watched the balloting from our hotel room, confident Ford would win the nomination, though by a small margin. The final count was Ford 1,187, Reagan 1,070. That night, Ford visited Reagan at his hotel to offer him the vice-presidential nomination. It was well scripted in advance that Reagan would refuse. Then, in private, they discussed other potential candidates. The Southerners, led by Jesse Helms, pressed for a conservative acceptable to the South just as they had in 1968 when Agnew was the compromise choice.

We heard the sirens in the distance as Ford's motorcade approached the headquarters hotel. Bud Pardini, sitting next to me, suddenly said, "Governor, you ought to go upstairs and demand to see the president. Tell him directly why you think you would be the strongest candidate for vice president and he might just respond favorably." I seriously thought about it, finally deciding that would be presumptuous. Looking back all these years later, I think it might have been a good idea and probably the only way I could have received the nomination.

Our entire team was staying in the same hotel suite. There was no knock on the door or summons from above. Finally, we went to bed, wondering what Ford would decide. Around 5 a.m. the phone rang. I jumped out of bed, stumbled to the desk, picked up the receiver and croaked a sleepy "Hello." By then the whole pajama-clad team was gathered around me. It was Jim Cannon, one of

Ford's top political aides. "It's Dole," he said. We were all deeply disappointed even though we knew I was a long shot. "I know I'd be a better candidate than Dole," I told Nancy. She agreed, of course, but not just out of spousal loyalty. Nancy, unsurprisingly, given our years together on the campaign trail, is a sophisticated judge of political moxie. Nor was it sour grapes for either of us. We admired Bob Dole for his World War II heroism and leadership in the U.S. Senate—all the more so when I became a senator. But he was a staunch conservative. We were also wary of his sarcastic tongue. The GOP ticket went on to lose to Carter and Mondale in a close election. "That was the one time when I felt the VP choice made a difference," Jacobs says. "Mondale ran a good campaign, Dole a bad one."*

I still wonder what might have happened if I had not vetoed the primary election bill passed by the Legislature in 1976. I am convinced that in a primary election, open to independent voters, Ford would have won handily in Washington state, and that I would have arrived in Kansas City as chairman of a delegation with a substantial majority committed to the president. That additional margin would have given the Ford campaign significantly more flexibility in dealing with both the party platform and the vice-presidential selection. Who knows what might have happened then? It's always fun to dream.

Dixy Lee Ray cuddles her beloved poodle, Jacques. *Washington State Archives*

FOR THE FIRST TIME IN 20 YEARS, I was not a candidate for election. I worked hard for our GOP candidate for governor, John Spellman. His integrity, civility and management expertise had transformed the King County Courthouse. But this was the year of the outsider, personified by a peanut farmer and a 62-year-old marine biologist, Dixy Lee Ray. The former UW professor directed the Pacific Science Center before heading the Atomic Energy Commission under Nixon. She was urged to run for governor by Lou Guzzo, former managing editor of the *Seattle Post-Intelligencer*. Guzzo had grandiose ideas about politics and believed she would not only make a good governor but a great president. She wasn't even sure whether she was a Democrat or a Republican. Guzzo steered her to an expedient conclusion that she was indeed a "D." Her primary election opponent was Seattle Mayor Wes Uhlman, who boldly steered the city during the tumultuous early '70s.

Spellman scored an easy victory in the pri-

---

* Jules Witcover's book on the 1976 campaign, *Marathon*, says Ford and his inner circle began narrowing the field of possible running mates around 3 a.m. With Reagan unwilling to take second spot, "the list quickly boiled down" to a quartet of contenders: Howard Baker, Bill Ruckelshaus, Ambassador Anne Armstrong (soon dismissed as too big a gamble) and Dole, whom Reagan had pronounced an excellent choice. "Polls showed that farm and rural America would be a major trouble spot for Ford, and Dole could help there, as well as shore up the party faithful, keep the conservatives happy and not overly exercise the moderates and liberals. Finally, and perhaps most important after all, Jerry Ford liked him."

mary against perennial candidate Harley Hoppe, the bombastic King County auditor. In a surprising upset, Dr. Ray defeated Uhlman. She exuded a quirky kind of populism. I vividly remembered a meeting with her at the Atomic Energy Commission headquarters in Washington, D.C. I had asked for the meeting because I had worrisome evidence that Hanford Reservation nuclear waste storage tanks were leaking, with potential long-term consequences. Scientists warned that nuclear waste material could reach the water table and ultimately the Columbia River. I was greeted by a stocky, no-frills woman with two poodles. We sat down at a long table, she at one end, me at the other. The dogs started sniffing my ankles. I surreptitiously tried to shoo them away with my foot. I had an almost overwhelming desire to drop kick them out the nearest window. Nevertheless, I explained our findings and concerns and was treated to a terse lecture about the safety of atomic energy and the impossibility of even small leaks reaching the water table. She talked at length about the bright future of atomic energy and bluntly maligned those who raised any questions about its safety. I surmised she would be a contentious governor. I campaigned whenever I could for Spellman and probably ensured that my future relations with her would be bumpy when I declared that the oil companies would "dance in the streets" if she was elected.

PRESIDENT FORD ARRIVED IN SEATTLE a week before the election. Polls indicated Carter's big post-convention lead was rapidly narrowing. On the evening before Ford's visit, the long-running dispute over the Boldt Decision boiled over. Commercial gillnetters defied a salmon-fishing closure on Puget Sound and continued to fish, to the frustration of sports and tribal fishermen. When a young gillnetter attempted to ram a fishery patrol vessel, an enforcement officer fired his shotgun, wounding the fisherman. A fleet of fishing boats gathered to protest Ford's visit. I gave the president a detailed briefing on the incident and the history of the Boldt Decision. He fielded questions about the fishing dispute with aplomb, saying, "We recognize that this is a federal problem with broad ramifications. It seems to me we have to keep our cool until we get corrective action."

Ford carried Washington and every other Western state except Hawaii. A change of 4,000 votes in Hawaii and 6,000 in Ohio would have spelled victory in the Electoral College. I was deeply disappointed since I was well acquainted with Carter from his days as Georgia governor. Ford was a substantially more capable leader. I was even more distressed that John Spellman would not succeed me.

I called Dr. Ray, congratulated her on her victory and invited her to come to Olympia for a visit. Every department of state government prepared an extensive briefing book for the new governor and her staff. We had a good conversation about building staff and preparing for her inaugural.

I was puzzled by her delay in appointing department heads and gubernatorial staff. Quick to fire my department heads, she took office with vacancies in important positions. Not an auspicious start for the state's first female governor.

I was looking forward to a long family vacation when a wonderful new opportunity came knocking.

44
GREENER PASTURES

Herb Hadley, an old friend and former fellow legislator, came to see me when the Ford and Spellman campaigns were kicking into high gear. I figured he wanted to talk politics. It was Herb, after all, who jumpstarted my dark-horse campaign for governor by organizing a "Draft Dan Evans Committee" in 1963.

Hadley was now chairman of the Board of Trustees of The Evergreen State College. He intimated that Charles McCann, Evergreen's founding president, wanted to return to teaching. McCann had labored for a year with a dedicated core of faculty members to invent Evergreen's unique approach to higher education. A strong supporter of Evergreen's unconventionality, I was also well aware that the school faced challenges. Interdisciplinary education, team teaching, narrative grading and free-form, student-designed majors were viewed with deep skepticism by legislators, high school counselors, many parents and much of the Olympia community. Evergreen was "that hippie school."

I was stunned when Herb asked if I would be interested in becoming Evergreen's second president. In the months following my decision to leave office I had received many offers. They included the presidency of a large foundation and a chance to manage a substantial family-owned manufacturing company, plus several opportunities to join large law firms as a non-lawyer counselor. None seemed to be the right opportunity. Herb's idea was fascinating. I told him I would talk it over with Nancy and do some more mulling.

Nancy thought it would be a good fit. Our boys were happy at the prospect of remaining in Olympia.

A few weeks later, Herb reported that a presidential search committee was set to meet on December 22. And if I wanted the job, he was certain it was mine. I was ready to say yes but wanted to meet with the committee to be sure they really wanted me.

As I entered the conference room at Evergreen and introduced myself to the dozen committee members, I thought to myself, "This is the first time I have formally interviewed for a position in 22 years!" There were many probing questions and a lengthy discussion about Evergreen's goals. As a non-academic president, how could I help break barriers? I said the language Evergreen used to describe itself seemed to confuse high school counselors, parents and even potential students. I told the story of a good friend in Olympia whose teenage son was eager to enroll at Evergreen early in its inception. Their family was avid about sailing. After registering at Evergreen, the usually reticent kid came home smiling.

"What are you taking?" his dad asked.

"Sailing."

"OK. What else?"

"Nothing."

My friend blew his stack and called me. "Governor, what the hell is going on out there?" I told him to calm down. I'd find out. There had to be more to the program than that. And there was. "But this story typifies Evergreen's biggest problem," I told the committee. "I think the college concept of interdisciplinary programs, limited faculty tenure, and a broad liberal arts education is spectacularly good, yet widely misunderstood by the outside world. I believe I can tell that story and help ensure Evergreen's future. I don't pretend to have academic management experience so I will need help from a strong provost to handle internal affairs while I spend much of my time with legislators, high school counselors, editorial boards and potential students." Our session lasted for more than two hours.

Herb called to say the committee had voted unanimously to offer me the job. I accepted immediately. At 51, it was a great joy—and relief—to discover a new challenge unlike any I had faced before.

An early sign of the challenges I would face on a college campus came the next day when the *Cooper Point Journal*, Evergreen's student newspaper, protested the appointment. They objected to shortcutting the work of the search committee. The editorialists supported me as the new president but not the method of selection. The two students who collaborated on the article were Matt Groening, later the creator of the hugely successful TV show "The Simpsons," and Joe Dear, later the chief investment officer of CalPERS, the largest public pension system in the nation.

OUR DINNER-TABLE CONVERSATION that evening was spirited, especially when Nancy and I proposed to our boys that we go on an extended trip to Europe since I was not expected to assume the presidency of Evergreen until June of 1977. We told them the story once again of our honeymoon trip 17 years before when I left my job at the Associated General Contractors to embark on a private engineering practice. They were eager to plot their own itinerary. We all agreed the trip would start with several weeks of skiing. The core of our trip was a six-week stay in London where I was to do some consulting work for the Woodrow Wilson Center.

We held a final huge Christmas party at the Governor's Mansion for family, friends and staff. Laughter echoed in those old rooms until late in the evening as stories, both true and fanciful, were exchanged. It was unlikely that we would ever have another opportunity to bring so many of our family together for such a festive dinner at home. Tears were shed as our guests departed.

My last two weeks in office began with a valedictory talk at the Seattle Rotary Club. I said I would always remember the times I stood on the steps of the Capitol, facing hundreds, often thousands of dissatisfied people: the schoolchildren who came with their parents and teachers to seek more funding for education; the hard hats angry over state involvement in minority hiring, and the Black Panthers, who arrived menacingly, some carrying rifles. Behind all that revolutionary bravado they were mostly teenagers. Like the schoolchildren and the construction workers, they were looking for change and their place in the sun. The angry young Black people wanted a more equitable world. Above all, I said, all these people wanted one thing: "They wanted their state government to listen to them."

The Rotarians—foursquare Republican businessmen—were always a skeptical audience when it came to growth in state government and taxation, so I used an analogy I was sure they would understand: We should compare our state to its competition to gauge how well we were doing. I unveiled a chart showing the percentage of change in state taxes per thousand dollars of personal income during the previous 12 years. It was a state-by-state overview. Washington was one of only three states whose state taxes had declined as a percentage of personal income. We were also 50th out of 50 in the growth of state taxes.

I could not pass up the opportunity to comment on a recent *Seattle Times* editorial. It ranted about increased state government spending, concluding, "Each of these and other program proposals have merit, of course, including larger state commitments to such worthies as mental health care, highways, and higher education. But the decision is how much. Critics of Evans' past fiscal policies will contend that his newest budget is a sign that he wants to leave office with his reputation unimpaired, intact as a big spender." I noted that in 1976 the management of the state's largest newspaper had editorialized 71 times on state spending. And 50 of those editorials advocated more spending. "Most of us recognize the need for investment; the need for spending," I said, "but few of us really want to be charged for it."

I summarized the just-completed Alternatives for Washington report, a seven-year project that involved nearly 100,000 citizens. The task force analyzed the costs and trade-offs for each goal—better education, better highways, better social services. "State government is virtually unique in America," I said, italicizing my political philosophy:

> I have reminded members of Congress on numerous occasions that the states invented the Congress; the Congress didn't invent the states. It was the genius of the federal system given to us 200 years ago by the makers of our Constitution. The states represent 50 laboratories of independent government. They are testing. They are trying. They fail sometimes. But in succeeding, the transfer of success is very rapid. The chance for success is even more rapid when there is an opportunity for independence of action among those 50 states, and not a federally imposed mediocrity and sameness. Perhaps our Bicentennial did remind us of our unique governmental heritage, with the states as the keystone of our federal system.

A week later, I presented my final message to the Legislature. The galleries were filled with family, cabinet, staff and friends. As I gazed out at the members of the House and Senate I reflected on the continuity of government in our nation. It was the 45th time since statehood that a new Legislature had gathered in Olympia. Twenty years of memories flooded my mind. In the far corner of the House chamber, I could pick out the seat I occupied as a freshman in 1957. Now it was occupied by a young, fresh-faced legislator, probably as dazzled as I was by the marble majesty of the Capitol and the opening ceremonies. Only 11 of my fellow legislators from the 1957 session were still in office. "It was an easier time," I said. "A true citizen Legislature met only every other year. There were relatively few federal programs and rules. We had not yet seen the trauma brought about by an incomprehensible war, by urban campus unrest, foreign oil boycotts, and a national nightmare called Watergate."

This was too good an opportunity to just say goodbye. I urged the Legislature to address five overriding issues: financing of public pension systems, tax reform, school finance, a constitutional convention, and the need to spend more time reviewing laws and regulations already passed. I also recognized the 30,000 state employees who did so much to bring credit to my administration. "Public service is a profession I view as a high calling," I said. "Neither saints nor sinners, they are every bit as productive, as concerned and as dedicated as their counterparts in private industry. ...The public and the private sectors cannot act as armed camps—one in conflict with the other, but rather as cooperators for the common good."

Nancy and I review 12 years of memories in 1976. The digitized gubernatorial scrapbooks are now available on the Washington State Archives' website. *Washington State Archives*

I saluted my parents, my mother-in-law, my sons, and most of all Nancy Bell Evans. In my view, she had been "a simply smashing First Lady." I had given several thousand speeches as governor. Now, in my last, I had someone else to thank: "the people of Washington, who three times gave me the opportunity to serve as their governor. Through your support I have been given a rare privilege accorded to only 16 men in the history of our state. Through thousands of letters, personal contacts and more than a million handshakes and opportunities to speak to people directly, you have helped to teach, guide and influence my actions as governor."

I wished my successor all the best, and declared: "Twelve years now is all history. Nothing can be changed. Nothing can be added. As years go by, memories will dim, and the impact of these years will diminish. If only one epitaph remains, I hope it will be: 'He left it a better state than when he began.' "

ON WEDNESDAY, JANUARY 12, 1977—exactly 12 years to the day after I walked into the Governor's Office for the first time—I strode in for the last. I calculated that I had served 4,383 days as governor, held 1,262 press conferences, made 1,495 visits to other communities and 160 national and international trips.

Earlier in the morning I brought an ornate wine cooler to the office. It was part of the famous Navy silver service on permanent display in the Governor's Mansion. As a Navy man, the gesture struck me as fitting. A silver service is a tradition in the Navy, particularly on battleships and cruisers named for states and cities. This one was donated by the people of Washington to the battle cruiser *U.S.S. Olympia*, Admiral Dewey's flagship during the Spanish American War. It was returned when the ship was decommissioned. Nancy didn't think the cooler should leave the Mansion, but I plowed ahead. In it I placed a good bottle of champagne on ice, accompanied by a note wishing Governor

Ray congratulations and good luck.*

I walked out the door with my staff, turned and joked, "Now, let's all hear it in unison: 'What's the address of the Employment Security office?' "

Several senators could not pass up the opportunity to challenge my appointment as president of The Evergreen State College. Governor Ray, in her early statements, ranted about Evergreen and suggested that if closed it would make a good state office complex. My challenges were mounting even though I would not assume office until June.

---

* I never received an acknowledgment. Dixy's tin ear for the social graces contributed to the bumpy four years ahead.

45
EVERGREEN

Being away from Olympia for the first six months of Governor Ray's administration was an additional blessing. I did not have to answer questions from the press or Legislature and could not comment on the stormy relations already building between Dixy and almost everybody else. She refused to have regular press conferences, suggesting that veteran Olympia reporters were "too cynical" to recognize the truth. "If you press people continually tell me I have bad relations …I guess I have to give it back as good as I get it," she huffed.

Workmen were still remodeling the college president's home, so Nancy and our boys spent the summer on Bainbridge Island at her brother's summer home. I decided to move into student housing to get a better understanding of student life. On occasion I would find a message taped to my door inviting me to dinner or a student potluck. Summertime was peaceful, with relatively few students or faculty on campus. I roamed the beautiful campus, thankful that trustee Hal Halvorson had found the site and convinced his colleagues to buy 1,200 acres of forest and 3,000 feet of natural waterfront.

The Evanses at The Evergreen State College. *Evans Family Collection*

My first and most important appointment was selection of a provost, the chief academic official of a college. I did not pretend to understand the nuances of academic management, particularly at a school as unique as Evergreen. Happily, Byron Youtz, the most revered faculty member, was serving as provost. The bad news was that he wanted to return to his first love—teaching. He agreed to remain as provost, at least for a time. His wisdom, superb intellect and calm manner were indispensable.

I soon discovered a hidden joy of my new job. There was no faculty dining room, just a series of small tables, reserved for faculty. They were arranged in a wide hallway just outside the student dining hall. When the fall semester started, I went through the student lunch line and took my tray to one of the faculty tables. Soon I was engaged in a conversation on marine biology. The next day it was Shakespearean literature, followed by history and economics.

My biggest initial challenge was enrollment. After the initial enthusiasm over a bold new college, enrollment leveled off and began to slowly decline. There was still enormous interest from across the country. Twenty percent of the student body was from out of state. The Legislature kept reminding us we were established primarily to serve Washington residents and that our out-of-state enrollment was already too high. We were facing a crisis of survival.

I launched a series of speeches to community organizations and met with college counselors at high schools around the state. It was apparent that Evergreen was grossly misunderstood by most of the outside community.

The first faculty meeting in the fall of 1977 was intense. There was no faculty senate since all faculty members wished to be equally involved in academic management. Many of them were obviously sizing me up. I talked about my experiences with high school counselors, legislators and potential college parents. I said that most people were skeptical of Evergreen's liberal approach. They'd heard there were no grades; that students could create their own majors—including some pretty wacky stuff. Supposedly, there were no departments and little academic rigor. Several faculty members hotly replied that it wasn't so. "I know that," I said, "but the perception in the outside community is the reality we have to change."

We developed easily understood responses to the misconceptions. We described the detailed faculty evaluations of student work, an approach that measured student achievement far better than a letter grade. Instead of rigid departments and tightly defined courses, Evergreen had created coordinated study programs especially designed to challenge freshmen. Each program typically combined four faculty members and a maximum of 80 students engaged in a full-time course of study focused on a theme. One early program was "Society and the Computer." The first-quarter students studied the Industrial Revolution and began learning computer programming. In the second quarter, they investigated the onset of the communication revolution and continued their study of computer programming. During the third quarter, students were expected to develop a computer program that would be useful to an Olympia business and write an essay arguing whether the Industrial Revolution or the communication revolution had the greater impact on society. Freshmen were learning in a much more cohesive way than in a series of unrelated courses. Freshmen at my alma mater, the University of Washington, and other major schools were often lumped into lecture-hall classes with hundreds of other students.

I asked faculty member Duke Kuehn to spend an academic quarter as my institutional researcher. It was a challenge. The college was only six years old, with just three graduating classes. Kuehn was enthusiastic about the challenge, and in less than a month returned with his first findings. He unrolled a statistical chart on more than 100 Evergreen graduates who had applied for graduate study in medicine, business and law at some of the most prestigious schools in the nation. Ninety-one percent had been admitted, one of the best records in the nation and far above other schools in the state. I asked Kuehn to interview the admissions officers to see if we could discover why our graduates were so successful. He returned several weeks later. "It's because we don't give grades," he said with a grin. The student portfolios, combined with faculty evaluations, gave admissions officers far more detailed information on student achievement than a mundane grade-point average, he said.

Now I had some factual information to use when communicating with legislators, counselors, parents and prospective students. Later in the year, when *U.S. News & World Report* ranked Evergreen third in the nation among all regional liberal arts colleges, I knew we were now secure from threats of closure. Our reputation climbed rapidly and enrollment began rising as more Washington state high school graduates joined the already enthusiastic applicants from virtually every other state in the nation. Two 1973 Evergreen graduates helped immensely in gaining legislative support. Eleanor Lee was elected to the State Senate as a Republican and Denny Heck—elected lieutenant governor in 2020 after four terms in Congress—joined the House as a Democrat. As they gained seniority, they were invaluable as supporters, counselors and examples of a good Evergreen education.

SCORES OF INVITATIONS flowed in to join commissions and boards. I tried to concentrate on organizations that might be helpful to Evergreen. Clark Kerr, former president of the University of California, headed the Carnegie Council on Policy Studies in Higher Education. He invited me to join the council. It was the working arm of the Carnegie Foundation for the Advancement of Teaching, funded by the 19th century steel magnate Andrew Carnegie. The council members were top leaders in higher education. As we debated ideas on how to improve the student experience, I took copious notes since this was a crash course on effective college management.

I was asked to join a number of corporate boards. I chose three I thought would be interesting and whose time commitments I felt I could handle. I was well acquainted with Washington Mutual Savings Bank and enthusiastically said yes when asked to join their board. As a schoolchild, I brought a dime to school every Tuesday and proudly exchanged it for a stamp to enter into my savings book. That was Washington Mutual's way of encouraging youngsters to save and someday, of course, become clients. Shortly after I joined the board the bank celebrated reaching $1 billion in total assets. Twenty years later, when I retired from the board, Washington Mutual Bank was a national force, with assets of more than $300 billion. The carefully nurtured traditional culture of the bank was still dominant in spite of huge growth. Years later, Washington Mutual chose a riskier path, strayed from its culture, and ultimately failed. That was a sad day.

NINETEEN-SEVENTY-EIGHT began with my investiture as president of the college. I promised to continue Evergreen's philosophy of cooperation among students and collaboration among teachers. My goals included establishing a graduate program; expanding off-campus and affirmative action programs, and encouraging older students to return to college.

Faculty member Ginny Ingersoll asked if I would be interested in joining her in team teaching a program titled Management in the Public Interest. I told her that my education was not in business and that I had never taught in a classroom. She laughed and said, "You have plenty of experience in management and this program, as its title describes, deals with the relationship between business, government, and the consumer." I decided that the best way to really understand Evergreen was to directly engage in the classroom. I was impressed by the enthusiasm and knowledge of the students. They were smart, but also challenging. That experience gave me a new appreciation for how much preparation and skill it requires to be a great teacher.

I WAS SOON EMBROILED in a decidedly different aspect of my presidential responsibilities. Evergreen boasted an innovative theater program. This year, their choice was "Equus," a challenging play featuring a nude scene with sexual overtones between a young man and a young woman. The cast gave a riveting performance that received a standing ovation. But the Olympia Area Ministerial Association told the *Daily Olympian* the play was not suitable as a campus production. Puzzled and annoyed, I contacted the Rev. Paul Beeman, the husband of my personal secretary, Betty Beeman. He was a wise and thoughtful counselor and agreed to call a meeting of the Ministerial Association so I could address its concerns.

A week later, most of the churches in the Olympia area were represented at a luncheon. I asked how many had seen the play. Not a single hand was raised. It was apparent that the resolution was drafted by pastors of several conservative churches. Other ministers signed on without full information. We quickly turned to ways the Ministerial Association could help the college and its students. I realized once again that there was good will in the community yet incomplete understanding of several thousand college students and even the college itself.

I was reminded of an incident earlier in the year when community members complained that Evergreen students were swimming in the nude. The Evergreen swimming beach was in a 3,000-foot forested waterfront owned by the college. The beach could not be seen from any nearby homes. I talked with some of complainers. "Well, we can see them from our boats as we go by," one said. "For heaven sakes," I said, unable to resist laughing, "if that bothers you, just look the other way or put down your binoculars!" I realized that being a college president included part-time parenting, occasional policing and sometimes questioning one's sanity.

MY FIRST GRADUATION CEREMONY at Evergreen was fascinating. The outdoor event was held on the huge central courtyard on a magnificent June afternoon. I was curious about the attendance since the intense student protests of the previous few years had been characterized by rejection of tradition and ritual. Attendance at graduation ceremonies had dipped precipitously nationwide. I wondered what would happen at Evergreen.

I joined the faculty in academic garb. We marched to the podium through a huge crowd of family and friends of the graduates. As I reached the stage I turned and saw the parade of graduates taking their seats. Virtually every graduate was in attendance. Only a handful wore the green cap and gown. The rest varied in dress, from extremely casual to impressively formal. As they walked across the platform to receive their degrees, a number of older graduates strode beside their children. Others carried infants. A few were accompanied by their dogs. I was distressed at first by the casual nature of this traditional ceremony, but soon realized it was an event filled with love and pride. So I relaxed and enjoyed this milestone together with cheering parents and friends. It was Evergreen showing its independent spirit, although I suspect if any legislators were in attendance most were grinding their teeth.

After graduation, the campus quieted down. I thought we could relax for a time from the incessant public and political discussion surrounding Evergreen. Almost immediately, however, newspaper stories charged that the state Fisheries Department was refusing to hire Evergreen graduates as fisheries biologists, the implication being that they were not qualified. Gordon Sandison, the director, had served with distinction in the State Senate and was a good friend. He told me the problem was that the job description stipulated a Bachelor of *Science* degree, while Evergreen issued only

Bachelor of Arts degrees. He also admitted that the bachelor-of-science degree requirement was an unnecessary barrier and several of the Evergreen applicants had all the necessary science education for the position. Sandison observed that it must have been a slow news weekend. Asked for a comment on the story and the bogus crisis, I replied that the whole thing was a non-story, declaring, "I'm madder than spit." It was one more case of incomplete understanding of Evergreen's unique educational methods. Many Evergreen grads went on to hold responsible positions in the Fisheries Department.

We were all anxious about fall enrollment. While applications had increased, our challenge now was to turn applications into admissions and admissions into enrolled students. We were particularly concerned about entering freshmen who came from Southwest Washington. One of Evergreen's original charges was to provide educational opportunity for residents of Southwest Washington, but we were proving to be more interesting to students across the country than across the street. In early September our numbers finally surpassed those of a year earlier and the enrollment decline of several years was finally over.

Unfortunately, the state's economy was beginning to falter and the governor's fiscal management office told all of higher education to prepare for budget cuts. Legislative leaders observed that Evergreen's costs were much higher per student than any of the other colleges or universities. I concentrated on individual meetings with legislative leaders, focusing on the fact that the college campus was constructed for 4,000 students and we had a little over 2,000. As we grew, cost per student would decline and eventually approach those of other schools. Meeting with one skeptical legislator after another I was tempted to just say, "Of course Evergreen costs more per student because an Evergreen education is worth more."

46
EARTH'S HIGH PLACES

A phone call from a park ranger interrupted a leisurely Sunday breakfast. It was March 4, 1979, my saddest day as president of The Evergreen State College. A climbing team from the college had been caught in an avalanche on Mount Rainier. "There may be some fatalities," the ranger said. "We will keep you informed."

There was no one in the world better qualified to teach climbing skills than 52-year-old Willi Unsoeld. The legendary mountaineer had developed Evergreen's nationally recognized outdoor education program. In 1963, Willi and Tom Hornbein, a Seattle anesthesiologist, were the first Americans to traverse Mount Everest, reaching the summit via its West Ridge, a feat never before attempted. Willi and I often talked about our experiences as Boy Scouts. Willi said he once dreamed of becoming an Episcopal priest, but his spiritual horizons broadened immeasurably the first time he tromped into the Cascades when he was 12. Man-made steeples were no match for God's country, Willi said. Nothing could rival the majestic "bare austerities of His earth's high places."

Willi Unsoeld. *The Evergreen State College Archives*

Earth's high places also held high danger, but we both believed the rewards were greater than the risks.

I called Evergreen's provost, Byron Youtz and told him I was headed to the Unsoeld home to break the news to Willi's wife, Jolene, an accomplished climber in her own right.* Byron offered to accompany me. His wife Bernice joined us.

Opening the front door, Jolene greeted us with her signature toothy smile. In a split second, however, she read our faces and knew the news was bad. She crumpled into my arms, but quickly recovered and asked about details, most of which we could not yet answer. I'm sure she realized Willi was likely dead. We all worried about the student climbers. Byron and I attempted to get more

---

* Jolene Unsoeld, whose relentless activism propelled establishment of the Public Disclosure Commission, went on to serve in the Legislature and Congress.

information but communication was fragmentary. A wild winter storm continued to pummel the mountain.

After several hours, we received definitive word that Willi Unsoeld and 21-year-old Janie Diepenbrock had died. The other two members of the rope team Willi was leading were partially buried but dug themselves out. Together with 18 other students, they desperately followed the climbing rope, attacking the now-frozen snow with ice axes, shovels and their hands. By the time they reached Janie and Willi, both were blue and not breathing. Several members of the expedition conducted CPR.

The horror of the event was not over. The surviving climbers needed to reach the safety of the Camp Muir huts, but the swirling snow rapidly erased their footsteps from hours earlier. Visibility was virtually zero, yet the 20 survivors skillfully navigated through the storm to safety.

Now I faced the extraordinarily difficult phone call to the Diepenbrock family in California. Mrs. Diepenbrock answered and I just started to report on the accident when she cried, "I just can't talk now. Please call later." Her husband took the phone and listened while I told him what I knew about the accident and Janie's death. He asked a number of questions and said that the family would travel to Seattle promptly. I hung up and sat shivering in a suddenly cold room, quietly weeping over the tragic loss of a world renowned climber and masterful teacher and a vital young woman just beginning her adult life.

Willi always said that a wilderness experience was not an end in itself. He often posed the question in one breath and answered it in the next: "Why don't you stay in the wilderness? Because that isn't where it is at. …The final test is whether your experience of the sacred in nature enables you to cope more effectively with the problems of people. You go to nature for an experience of the sacred. To re-establish your contact with the core of things—where it's really at—in order to enable you to come back to the world of people and operate more effectively."

A week later, at a memorial service for Willi and Janie, the stories were poignant, sometimes hilarious. They brought two memorable people back to life for a huge crowd of mountaineers and students, family and friends. The gathering ended with all forming a huge circle surrounding the central plaza of the campus singing softly several familiar songs of remembrance. As we left, walking through the large grove of evergreens surrounding the campus, Willi's frequent admonition returned in full force: "Seek ye first the kingdom of nature, that the kingdom of people might be realized."

ON A SUNDAY several weeks later, Nancy and I visited my father who was in the hospital with a serious heart condition. We had a marvelous conversation with my mother and dad about memorable experiences, early-day hikes and building our family's summer home. At the end of our visit, dad asked if I could shave him, saying, "I've got to look good for the nurses." I had shaved myself thousands of times but never anyone else. I said, "OK, Dad, but you may bleed to death from 1,000 cuts!" But my hand was steady. As we left I told Nancy, "Dad looks and sounds terrific. He is going to fool them and walk out of the hospital.

Early the next morning I received a telephone call from my brother Bob. He said Dad was rapidly failing. Nancy and I raced to the hospital. As we neared his room I saw my mother in the hall quietly sobbing. My guide, my mentor, my teacher and, most of all, my friend was gone. Now I was the oldest man in the family and deeply felt the passing of one generation to the next. The entire family gathered at my brother Roger's home that evening. As I sat on the sofa next to Nancy, the enormity of our loss struck. I sobbed uncontrollably in her arms for several minutes. I knew the grandchildren were uncomfortable and I finally wiped my eyes and said, "Who wants to play dominoes?" That was my dad's favorite game. We spent the rest of the evening with raucous and lively bouts of dominoes interspersed with memories of Dad's admonitions and advice on how to play the game well. He played his game of life just as well.

LEGISLATIVE SKEPTICS had a field day trashing Evergreen as budget hearings began in 1979. Several conservative Republicans demanded that the college be closed. They railed against Evergreen's coordinated studies program and declared that a college without grades wasn't "a real college." I contacted the most vociferous critics. After some prodding, they admitted that their own college-age kids resisted admonitions to cut their hair and embrace establishment values. They could reluctantly accept their own children's quirks but were overwhelmed by the specter of 2,000 students from other families with the same counter-culture attitudes. The objections faded, but the news stories documenting the controversy didn't help our enrollment efforts.

An article in *The New York Times* reported that I was one of seven candidates for the presidency of the Ford Foundation. I squelched that immediately, saying that under different circumstances I would be interested. "It would be an enormous challenge, but I cannot walk away from a college I have a great deal of interest in and respect for—especially on the eve of a legislative session." Removing my name from consideration immediately fueled rumors that I would be a candidate for governor again in 1980. I simply could not escape political speculation.

Evergreen was constantly trying to develop closer relationships with the Olympia community. In early spring a group of faculty and staff proposed a year-end celebration that ultimately became known as Super Saturday—a massive open house for the Olympia community and students' families the day before graduation. Tours were arranged for academic programs; the swimming pool and gymnasium were open to the public; games were scheduled for children; food booths were scattered throughout the campus and an outdoor beer garden was created for adults. We were overwhelmed when several thousand people descended on our wooded campus. It was a huge public relations success and helped create a whole new community relationship with the college.

DEFIANT AS EVER, Governor Ray was in constant combat with Democratic legislative leaders, the press and a rising tide of disenchanted voters. Jimmy Carter, the other notable post-Watergate outsider, was also in trouble. Gas pump lines stretched for blocks on Independence Day in 1979. Inflation and interest rates were in double digits; unemployment was climbing. Carter responded with what came to be called his "malaise" speech, characterizing America's problem as a loss of unity and "a crisis of confidence." Jimmy Carter and Dixy Lee Ray had succeeded in creating a crisis of confidence in their own competence.

I received a phone call from Seattle City Attorney Doug Jewett, who railed against current politics and politicians and urged a new approach to politics. He proposed a bipartisan meeting of political leaders and asked if I would attend. I was as distressed as he about the political landscape and agreed to attend. The conversation at the meeting was a delight. Seldom is there an opportunity for political activists of both parties to join in a discussion on how to make government work better.

I should have known that any meeting of that type would become public but I wasn't quite prepared for the publicity that followed.

The *Seattle P-I's* headline the next morning screamed "A crisis in leadership—Evans hints at new state party." A fabulous David Horsey cartoon depicted me stepping off a rowboat onto a beach. Dressed like Napoleon returning from exile, I was being escorted by Jewett. Two frantic bystanders were yelling to one another: "Quick! Get word to Queen Dixy... HE'S BACK!!"

In the middle of all that, Dr. Frank Press, Carter's science adviser, called to say the president wanted me to consider becoming a candidate for chairman of the Nuclear Regulatory Commission. Over lunch in the West Wing, I expressed my reluctance to leave Evergreen. But Press urged me to give it more thought. A few days later, he called to say the president wanted me to know the post was mine if I would accept it. I had already decided the job was not a good fit for me. Also, with all three Evans boys in high school, it would have been a disruptive move, not to mention a relatively short assignment. Nancy absolutely agreed. I have often wondered how our lives would have changed if I had accepted the post and moved to Washington, D.C.

ENROLLMENT IN THE FALL was up substantially and newspaper headlines were increasingly favorable. Evergreen's trustees helped immensely to build the school's reputation. They were part of a powerhouse team that changed the external view of this innovative college.

At the end of 1979, we received the results of our five-year re-accreditation. The report, which had high praise for Evergreen's innovative attitude, essentially quashed any real political effort to close the college. Dr. Aldon Bell of the University of Washington, a member of the accreditation team, wrote a particularly insightful article in *The Seattle Times*: "The dedicated, able men and women of The Evergreen State College faculty, administrators, students, and citizen-friends have created against great odds one of the finest undergraduate educational resources in the United States," he wrote.

Bell detailed the challenges Evergreen faced as an innovator. He lauded our success and dismissed the skeptics: "The truth is very different from common assumptions, which are usually inaccurate and unjust to the college, and occasionally are deliberately destructive and even vicious.... In short, the date for cheap shots at Evergreen should be over. All of us should take the college seriously and recognize what it adds to the Northwest."

WHEN THE 1980 LEGISLATIVE SESSION convened, Governor Ray was feuding with practically everyone except her poodles. For starters, she asked state agencies to cut their budgets by 3 percent in response to a rapidly worsening economy. Inflation and interest rates were in double figures. At Evergreen, we had delayed purchasing and replacing equipment as much as feasible. I kept my head down and tried to avoid political involvement, although the temptation was almost irresistible.

Carter was being challenged by Ted Kennedy and Jerry Brown. Ronald Reagan and George H.W. Bush, the leading GOP presidential hopefuls, also smelled blood. State Senator Jim McDermott, the unapologetically liberal Seattle psychiatrist, was aggressively challenging Dixy for the Democratic nomination. John Spellman, who had done a great job as King County's first executive, was campaigning hard for the GOP nomination.

Though I had been out of office for more than three years, the media were still interested in my observations and perceived ambitions. In an editorial meeting with the *Post-Intelligencer*, I remarked that it was doubtful I would "go beyond one term." I was referring to the fact that Evergreen's presidents are appointed for a specific term of six years, with a proviso for only one additional term. That ignited a flurry of political speculation. The next day, when *The Seattle Times* called, I was exasperated, saying, "I have not talked to the Board of Trustees about my future. Hell, I haven't even talked to my wife about it."

For the first time since I became president, the college was faced with over enrollment. We scrambled to find enough student housing, rearranged some faculty scheduling to handle crowded classes, and recognized that the additional students did not mean any more appropriations from the state. We were left to our own ingenuity and the revenue from low tuitions, which fell far short of educational costs. We were beginning to greet more students from Thurston County and Southwest Washington, which pleased me greatly for it reduced legislative angst about Evergreen's popularity with out-of-state students.

With my newly unveiled gubernatorial portrait in 1981.
Washington State Archives

THAT SEPTEMBER, Jim McDermott summarily put an end to Dixy Lee Ray's career in elective politics. A sitting governor was denied re-nomination. Senator Magnuson pounded the final nail, blistering Dixy at a raucous state Democratic Convention.

Down the stretch, McDermott and Spellman were locked in combat. So too Reagan and Carter.

Reagan's coattails carried Republicans to control of the U.S. Senate. Spellman won a resounding victory over McDermott, and in a stunning upset, Slade Gorton defeated Magnuson to become the first Republican senator from Washington in 28 years. Reagan's charisma—coupled with Carter's haplessness—had generated a political tsunami. Reagan and I had our political differences while we were governors, but now he was head of a revitalized Republican Party and, more importantly, would soon become the leader of a country demoralized by the Iran hostage crisis and battered by recession, astronomical interest rates and inflation.

Spellman, a genuinely optimistic man, would face the challenge of a deepening recession and growing needs for public services. But he was a friend of higher education, and I was now confident any serious opposition to Evergreen's future would be quelled. Evergreen grad Denny Heck was a rising star in the Washington State House of Representatives. He emerged as an articulate foil to the gaggle of right-wing legislators who still demanded our closure. They were generally the same ones who fought Spellman's every attempt to deal with the realities of the recession. The governor famously dubbed them "troglodytes."

47
POWER FOR THE PEOPLE—AND FISH

The economy seemed to be in a free fall, yet conservative legislators were dead set against raising taxes. During the first weeks of the 1981 legislative session, I met with two dozen legislators, and appeared before Senate and House Higher Education and Appropriations Committees. I also met frequently with my colleagues from the state's five other public four-year schools.

Governor Spellman, vowing to maintain essential services, eventually convinced a majority of the Legislature that some new taxes were essential. It was a brave move—one that would cost him heavily in political capital. The concessions eased but did not eliminate the need for us to find ways to cut Evergreen's budget to meet these new realities.

As the legislative session droned on, I was fascinated and delighted as I read the newly-passed Pacific Northwest Electric Power Planning and Conservation Act. Scoop Jackson was the prime sponsor. Congressman Al Swift, a visionary Democrat from Bellingham, helped guide it through the House. For the first time, Northwest states would have a seat at the table when major decisions were made on the development of new resources to meet power needs. The impetus was the growing discontent with the father-knows-best attitude of the Bonneville Power Administration, a federal agency with enormous power. The BPA paid little attention to state governments and made power allocation decisions at odds with local priorities. As governor I opposed a number of BPA policy decisions.

The act created a Power Planning Council composed of two members apiece from Washington, Oregon, Idaho and Montana. Appointments would be made by the governors and confirmed by their Legislatures. It was a rare chance to participate in a game-changing moment in Northwest history. I discussed my interest in the new council with Evergreen's trustees. I believed I could do both jobs without slighting the college. In fact, there would be opportunities for classroom discussions on council issues. Ideas generated by our environmentally-minded students might even steer decisions. The trustees were supportive, worried most about whether I was overburdening myself.

I went to see the governor. It was a moment of considerable nostalgia as Spellman greeted me warmly at the door to the ornate office I had occupied for 12 years. The fumes from his briar pipe wafted through the room as we discussed the economic and fiscal challenges facing the Legislature and the ramifications of the Power Planning Act. I told him I was definitely interested in becoming one of his two appointees to the new council, emphasizing that I had the support of the college trustees.

Spellman appointed me to the council, together with Charles Collins, a successful businessman and former head of Seattle METRO. "Chuck" Collins was a senior adviser to Spellman during his days as King County Executive. I soon discovered that he was a brilliant addition to the council. We examined the details of the act, including the new council's working realities. For starters, an eight-member council frequently might face tie votes and bog down in frustration. Also, although 80 percent of Bonneville's power was produced and used in Oregon and Washington, they would have only four votes out of eight. Final adoption of power allocation and fish and wildlife plans required not only a six-vote supermajority, but at least one vote from each state. It was clear that regional unity was vital if we were to succeed.

When Senator Jackson next returned home, I asked to see him. The enabling act was vague and perplexing in several places, I politely observed. He laughed, saying that if he had been more specific "it would never have passed!" And the ambiguity gave the council more leeway. "This gives you an opportunity to create the specific direction you choose," Scoop said. "Just be prepared to defend it." His sage advice heightened my enthusiasm.

Studying the nuances of the Power Planning and Conservation Act, I discovered it was funded by a small millage charge against the electricity sold by Bonneville. I did the math on the potential income and realized that the council could be amply funded using only a fraction of the potential millage. The basic charge of the legislation was to produce a 20-year electric power plan for the Pacific Northwest. A parallel charge was to protect the environment and restore fish runs on the Columbia River and its tributaries. The stated priority to deal with projected electrical shortages was conservation. Public and private power distribution agencies had been fighting over the sources and price of electric power for a generation. This legislation would require more sharing of the benefits of the federal power system. It gave Bonneville "purchase authority" to acquire conservation or non-federal resources to meet Northwest power needs. New BPA acquisitions would be subject to approval by the Power Council. Now I was really excited. The Power Council would set out with a blank sheet of paper, ample funding, significant authority and visionary goals.

After promising I would keep the Legislature informed of our progress and seek its advice, I was confirmed 41-7. Several senators who had been combative opponents on many issues during my 12 years as governor supported my confirmation.

MY NEW COLLEAGUES were an impressive lot. Oregon Governor Vic Atiyeh appointed his energy adviser, Roy Hemmingway, and Herb Schwab, a former chief justice of the Oregon Supreme Court; Idaho's governor, John V. Evans (great name but no relation), appointed his chief of staff, Bob Saxvik, and a long-time aide, Chris Carlson; Ted Schwinden of Montana appointed his chief of staff, Keith Colbo, and his energy adviser, Gerald Mueller.

We re-read the act and realized its authors had referenced every conceivable open meetings requirement codified in federal law. Several members protested, saying that brainstorming in public could be risky. I felt strongly that we should not conduct closed-door meetings. My suggestion was that at public hearings all eight of us should face the audience. And when we were meeting to create programs, we should sit around the table and let members of the public watch and listen. That turned out to be one of the best decisions we made. At every business meeting we welcomed public comment after we finished discussing the topic at hand. Those sessions produced innovative ideas that became part of our final plans.

We turned next to two important decisions: Who would head the Power Planning Council and

The Power Planning Council in 1982: Sitting, from left, Al Hampson of Oregon; me; Bob Saxvik of Idaho, and Keith Colbo of Montana. Standing, from left, Roy Hemmingway of Oregon; Chuck Collins of Washington; Chris Carlson of Idaho, and Gerald Mueller of Montana. *Power Planning Council Archives*

where would the staff be located? I hoped the council's office would be located in Seattle or Olympia, since our state was by far the largest consumer of electric power. Chuck Collins suggested I be named chairman. The other members agreed. However, as a matter of practical politics, that meant our headquarters would be in another state. Portland was quickly chosen.

We planned a series of public hearings in each of the Northwest states to gain a sense of the challenges and difficulties we would face in attempting to draft a 20-year plan. Our goal was to ensure adequate power while protecting the environment, fish and wildlife. It was urgent that we build a capable staff. We quickly settled on Ed Sheets as our founding executive director. He had served as Senator Magnuson's legislative assistant and special assistant for energy and environmental issues. Sheets was young, brilliant and politically savvy. He set out immediately to build a highly competent staff. Little did we know that Ed would direct the council for 15 years, helping develop innovative plans that have saved Northwest consumers billions of dollars.

THE FIRST ROUND OF HEARINGS in each of the four states demonstrated vividly how tough this task would be. A tricky cast of competing players crossed the stage: the Bonneville Power Administration, private power companies, public utility districts, public power agencies, consumer representatives, environmentalists, state and local governments and a diverse array of citizens determined to have their voices heard. And that was just on the electric power side. We also listened to several hundred representatives of state fish and game agencies, sports fishermen, commercial fishermen, Indian tribes, irrigation districts, local governments and, once again, vocal citizens—all with an intense focus on the parallel fish and wildlife program we were also obliged to produce within two years.

All eight of us grasped the magnitude of our task. I suggested that we divide into two task forces, each manned by a member from each state. The two committees quickly became known as the "Fish Four" and the "Power Four." It was a remarkably unified effort to produce results within 24 months. Members focused on the needs of the region. I do not remember a time when the desires of a single state kept us from unanimity.

The Pacific Northwest Power Act required that we request recommendations on fish and wildlife management from the region's federal and state fish and wildlife agencies, the tribes and other interested parties. If any recommendations were modified or rejected, the Power Planning Council was required to justify the modifications. We were flooded with recommendations, more than 600 in all—2,200 pages. Our public hearings produced 1,728 additional pages of testimony. The hearings were mind-numbing in the complexity and controversy produced by battling factions. Occasionally, however, we received refreshingly clear testimony that buoyed our spirits. During one hearing in Yakima we were attempting to measure salmon run sizes historically, with the handicap that no measurements were taken in the early 20th century. Toward the end of a long day, a 90-year-old Yakama tribal member with a wonderful wizened face, arrived and asked to testify. He said he was sorry to be late but he had been tending his nets on the Columbia River. Asked if he could give us any idea on the size of early fish runs, he nodded and said, "When I was about 18 I was riding my horse and tried to cross the Yakima River. My horse spooked and refused to cross because the river was filled bank to bank with vigorous, splashing returning salmon." I thanked him emphatically, saying it was the most authoritative testimony we'd heard all day.

NOW WE BEGAN the demanding task of sorting through recommendations and deciding whether they made fiscal or scientific sense. It soon became apparent that salmon faced daunting hazards—human and natural—during their life cycle. One of the earliest challenges facing young salmon is getting from their nesting areas to the ocean. When the Columbia River was free-flowing there was natural movement toward the ocean. But now, from Bonneville Dam up river, the Columbia is a series of lakes. We ultimately developed an innovative "water budget" to help increase the survival rate of young salmon headed for the ocean. The "water budget" was a block of water that could be released over the Columbia River dams to speed stream flows during spring salmon migration. We assigned joint management of the "water budget" to state fish and wildlife agencies and Columbia Basin Indian tribes. The concept was controversial but ultimately helped substantially in reviving Columbia River salmon runs.

Since Columbia River salmon spend most of their lifetime in the open ocean and return to their rivers of origin along ocean coastlines, they are subject to catch by Canadian, Alaskan and California fishermen, both sport and commercial. We worked hard to help develop regulations and treaties that would better manage these vital fish runs. The Power Planning Council also dealt with serious controversy over upstream migration, predators, commercial and sports fishing and wildlife protection. We appointed a Scientific and Statistical Advisory Committee, consulted with scores of agencies and utilities and ultimately produced a draft program containing more than 600 recommendations for action. Extensive revisions to our draft program were made as a result of the oral and written comments. On November 15, 1982, the council adopted the Columbia River Basin Fish and Wildlife Program. A proviso in the Northwest Power Act allows expedited judicial review of the program. Not one appeal was filed. We were delighted at the broad support, given the history of disputes and litigation between fish and power interests.

Twenty years later, the salmon runs entering the Columbia River were twice as large on the average as the numbers when the Fish and Wildlife Plan was adopted. Management of water on the

Columbia River now recognizes two vital needs, producing electric power and enhancing salmon runs. That required understanding and cooperation between electric power producers, the BPA, the tribes, environmentalists, commercial fisherman, the Army Corps of Engineers and many activist citizens. That was not easy to achieve. I remember vividly an experience with the U.S. Army Corps of Engineers.

During our early mitigation on fish and wildlife, one of the elements was to provide the tribes access to the Columbia River to mitigate for ancient fishing spots lost over the years with the advent of the dams. Gone was the spectacular fishing site at Celilo Falls where tribal fishermen had harvested giant salmon for thousands of years. Some of the lands best suited for mitigation were managed by the Corps of Engineers. That became part of our Fish and Wildlife Plan, with agreement of the Corps. When nothing happened, I was certain that some Corps officials opposed to the idea simply let it bog down in the bureaucracy.

A year later, as a newly-elected United States senator, I learned a confirmation hearing was on the schedule for a nominee to head the Corps of Engineers. I went to the leadership and declared, "I'm putting a stop on this one!"—a senator's prerogative. Within two days, representatives of the Corps were in my office, beseeching me to tell them what was wrong. "I'll tell you what's wrong," I said, jaw set. "I don't have any problem with the new general you want to install, but here's what happened when I chaired the Power Council." It was amazing how fast the land was distributed to tribal members. Sometimes you just have to know which button to push.

THE "POWER FOUR" initiated an effort to fashion a 20-year electric power plan for the Northwest. It began with the electric energy needs projected by Northwest utilities and the BPA. We all quickly realized that these single-line projections were all likely to be wrong. And since the utilities could not afford to be short of electricity, they consistently overestimated their projections. In the 1950s and 1960s, the cost of overbuilding was low because the electricity from new dams was cheap. As the region turned to more expensive resources we started to see the effects. The wholesale cost of electricity from BPA went up 80 percent in 1980 to pay the first installment on three nuclear plants.

The council started from a totally different perspective. We could not predict with accuracy the need for electricity 20 years in the future, but we probably could calculate the maximum and minimum needs based on historic trends and future economic and population predictions. Observers scoffed at our efforts, claiming our plan showed a difference of more than 10,000 installed megawatts between minimum and maximum predicted needs. "Who can do any planning based on that uncertainty?"

What we knew for certain was that the future was uncertain. We began to plan accordingly, allowing for exigencies. The "Power Four" calculated construction and operating costs and time to completion for each practical source of electric power, including conservation. Chuck Collins observed that we should be able to meet any load growth with an appropriate assembly of electric production methods. He maintained that our task should be to develop a "least cost method" of power planning that would give us the ability to respond to any future load growth at the lowest cost possible. This was a brilliant departure from the previous tendency to overbuild. We quickly began to measure the relative costs of electricity from different production methods, including the cost involved in the time required to construct new facilities.

Nuclear power had high construction costs and relatively low operating costs. Unfortunately, the time required for design, regulatory approval and construction was prohibitively long. Coal plants, hydroelectric facilities, gas turbines, wind and solar energy all had different costs and time of construction, giving planners choices that would allow them to respond in time for actual electrical needs. We also found that electrical conservation and steps to boost efficiency amounted to an enormous resource, one that could be acquired at less than half the cost of any other alternative. As the Power Planning Council built its plan, it focused on energy-efficient building codes and more efficient manufacturing processes. Conservation can be acquired much more rapidly than other alternatives, and is a particularly effective way to respond to unusual and rapid economic growth.

THE FISH AND WILDLIFE and the Electric Power plans were constructed in an extraordinarily public fashion. We requested projections of economic growth from more than 200 businesses and industries to develop our demand forecast. Town hall meetings on regional power issues were held in 22 locations throughout the Northwest, followed by intensive energy workshops. The council inserted 2 million tabloid fliers in the region's daily newspapers to outline the issues in the draft plan and encourage attendance at the hearings. We ultimately received 18,000 pages of comments from more than 1,200 groups and individuals.

We integrated the activities and challenges of the Power Council into several programs at The Evergreen State College. Student questions and proposals eventually influenced the direction of the council, especially on our fish and wildlife challenges.

Our final power plan was adopted unanimously exactly two years after our first meeting. Developed publicly, the plan included contributions from thousands of interested citizens and businesses. It was an extraordinary privilege to head the Pacific Northwest Power Council. Its eight dedicated citizen members focused on the needs of our region rather than just representing their own states' positions. Ultimately the power plan was challenged in the Ninth Circuit Court of Appeals by two groups, the natural gas industry and a home builder's coalition. We prevailed in both lawsuits and were pleased that both plans became law without modifications.

This two-year effort, culminating in two extraordinary plans for the future of our region, was one of the most satisfying in my entire career. Dedicated public employees, carefully listening to citizens and then building dramatic plans for our future, represented the best of public service and contributed mightily to the economic well-being of the entire Pacific Northwest. I was hugely pleased that the Democratic governors of Montana and Idaho joined the Republican governors of Washington and Oregon in appointing members who focused on facts. They did not allow political affiliation to interfere with their effort to find the best solutions to serve the entire region. Their end result was a bipartisan plan for efficient energy use that produced huge savings for our citizens.

In April of 1983, the Pacific Northwest Power Council unanimously adopted what was hailed as a 20-year power plan. Chuck Collins put it best: "It's not a 20-year plan; it's a strategy that may hold up for 20 years. The resource mix will change but all that stuff (in the plan) that says '1990' is going to look laughable by then. And we shouldn't be embarrassed about that." I commented that the strength of the document was that it was designed to be a "flexible, working, continuing concept" updated every two years. I was gratified by the unanimity of the Power Council in adopting both the Fish and Wildlife Plan and the Electric Power Plan. I was confident we had initiated new, and more flexible ways of planning for the future of our region.

The plans have been modified regularly to meet changing needs, but 40 years later they still give guidance to electric power planning and to the restoration of fish and wildlife, particularly in the Columbia River basin. Conservation and efficiency were our guiding principles in the beginning and the results are dramatic. Since the adoption of our first plans, almost two-thirds of the electrical load growth in the Pacific Northwest has been met by conservation and efficiency. The combination of Utility and BPA programs, energy codes and federal efficiency standards have produced over 5500 MWa of energy savings. That is enough electricity to serve the entire state of Oregon. In 2013, it saved consumers of the region nearly $3.5 billion while lowering carbon emissions by 21 million MTE.

IF WE HAD BEEN SMART ENOUGH to create the Power Planning Council 10 years earlier we never would have tried to build the five nuclear power plants that fell victim to soaring interest rates, cost overruns (almost five times the original estimates), and assorted ineptitude. My own culpability sprang from buying into the era's conventional wisdom—namely the wildly inaccurate, survey-based energy demand forecasts of the mid-1960s. "Experts" told us the Northwest would need 20 more nuclear power plants and two more coal-fired plants by the end of the century to meet residential and industrial energy demands. In 1966, our new Office of Nuclear Energy Development unveiled a master plan to make Washington "the nuclear progress state." We needed to get going, I emphasized, if we wanted to avoid a serious power shortage by 1975.

In 1973, the Bonneville Power Administration notified its customers that by 1982 it would not have enough power to guarantee their needs. Two years later, however, a BPA study suggested the region could avoid building 11 nuclear power plants by instituting aggressive conservation. I should have remembered an important lesson from my childhood. The water for the hot water tank at our house was preheated by a coil of pipe routed through the furnace to save power. And when we went on vacation, we turned off the water heater. My folks understood the power of conservation. Chuck Collins, my fellow commissioner on the Power Planning Council, would observe, "If people knew as much about saving energy as they know about growing their lawns, then we would begin conserving and stop wasting."

When WPPSS began scrambling to forestall disaster in 1981, it became clear to the Power Planning Council that the WPPSS board—largely comprised of utility district commissioners—was out of touch with ratepayers and in over its head. But there was plenty of 20-20 hindsight to go around. Critics noted that all five WPPSS plants were approved on my watch as governor, including "the particularly ill-advised" pair at Satsop in Grays Harbor County. Although the state Energy Facility Site Evaluation Council had endorsed the Satsop site, I had misgivings from the outset, especially about the amount of water allowed to be siphoned from the river for the cooling towers. I should have followed my instincts and denied the application. After weeks of contentious hearings in 1979, the Site Evaluation Council allowed WPPSS to increase the levels of copper and other heavy metals that could be discharged into the Chehalis River when the plants became operational. At least it never came to that.

I WAS DELIGHTED to have my mother join us for the holidays in 1981. She enjoyed making cookies and helped unpack our traditional family Christmas decorations. Nancy was preparing a special Saturday breakfast on Dec. 12 when she looked up from the stove and said, "You better go wake your mother." I quietly knocked on her bedroom door. Hearing nothing, I went inside. Mother was still in bed. I gently shook her. There was no response. I felt for her pulse. There was none. She had died during the night. I was devastated at the loss of an enthusiastic and proud parent who thought her son could do anything and always said so. I remembered that after Dad died in 1979 she would often say, "I miss Les so much. I would like to be with him." Now she was, after a life filled with children and grandchildren she adored, political activities that fascinated her and good health until the night she died at the age of 84.

A private family service was followed by a huge family gathering at Christmas time to retell stories of her life. It brought back the smiles and laughter, which is how Irma Alice Ide Evans, an extraordinary woman, wanted to be remembered.

48
MAKING THE LIST

C-SPAN intermittently polls nearly a hundred historians and political scientists to come up with its list of "best and worst" presidents. Lincoln, Washington and the Roosevelts routinely top most. Harry Truman's stock has been ascendant for years and Eisenhower's ratings are now higher than Kennedy's as memories of Camelot dim and Ike's wisdom snaps into focus.

I had a nice new year's surprise in 1982: I was named one of the 10 outstanding U.S. governors of the 20th century in a study conducted by George Weeks, a Kennedy Fellow at the Institute of Politics at Harvard University. The citation said:

> Daniel J. Evans, R-Wash., 1965-1977: For strong administration; for recruiting of highly professional managers; for pattern-setting innovation in environmental, open government, local revenue sharing and other programs; for revitalization of cooperative efforts among governors; for formation of a coalition of state and local governments.

The others on the list, in order of service were: Robert M. La Follette, Wisconsin, 1901-06; Woodrow Wilson, New Jersey, 1911-13; Alfred E. Smith, New York, 1919-21, 1923-28; Huey Long, Louisiana, 1928-32; Earl Warren, California, 1943-53; Thomas E. Dewey, New York, 1943-54; Nelson A. Rockefeller, New York, 1959-73; Terry Sanford, North Carolina, 1961-65 and Reubin Askew, Florida, 1971-79.

The eye-opener for many was the selection of Huey P. "Kingfish" Long. Loved and loathed, the bombastic populist ruled Louisiana like a fiefdom and ascended to the U.S. Senate before he was assassinated in 1935. Often overlooked is the fact that Long presided over a transformative public works program. He also championed better schools and old-age pensions. He certainly adds dash to the list. Can you imagine Huey Long having a conversation with Woodrow Wilson, the prim Presbyterian? One of the great parlor games is to imagine having a party with a guest list that includes famous characters from throughout history—Jesus Christ and Mahatma Gandhi; Elvis and Beethoven; Einstein, Joe DiMaggio and Marilyn Monroe; Donald J. Trump and Thomas Jefferson! I'd like to be at a party with my fellow "Top 10" governors and listen to Nelson Rockefeller swap New York stories with Al Smith, the original "happy warrior."

Making the list was gratifying—all the more so because Rockefeller, Sanford and Askew were colleagues and friends I deeply admired. The *Seattle Post-Intelligencer* featured an editorial headlined "A perfect 10." The editors mulled whether there was "a common trait that marks a politician as an outstanding servant of the people." Their answer was: "Courage, perhaps, and conviction. And the will to lead." I said I was flattered to be included in the top 10. "He needn't be," the *P-I* said. "He earned his place."

I INVITED PROMINENT national figures to speak at Evergreen. Tennessee Senator Howard Baker, a friend, was now Majority Leader of the United States Senate. The library was jammed with students as Baker launched into a cogent analysis of the complexities of American foreign policy. A few students in the second-floor balconies hissed their opposition. It was not disruptive—Baker was unfazed—but it was annoying and rude. When he entertained questions from the audience, I noticed that the hissers were curiously silent.

The next day I tracked down the hecklers and asked them to visit me in my office. It was a vigorous, constructive conversation. I told them that opposition without alternatives is largely empty. And by refusing to take part in dialogue with a leading member of the United States Senate they missed an opportunity to advance their cause. We talked about the Senate's role in government and the need to reach across the aisle in order to make progress, especially in a sharply divided Congress. As the students left, several said they wished they would have challenged Senator Baker to see how he would respond. I just said, "Yes!" It was a memorable teachable moment.

Evergreen entered its second decade gathering national recognition for its interdisciplinary focus, challenging curriculum and the success of its graduates. That did not dissuade a few hardheaded legislators from their campaign to close the college. They were the self-anointed protectors of the higher education system they remembered from their college days and had little stomach for anything different. Fortunately, we were receiving positive editorial support from Washington's newspapers while students voted with their feet to increase enrollment.

The Legislature conducted a hearing at which several Evergreen instructors proposed unionizing the Evergreen faculty. I thought it was a bad idea, especially at a college that depended heavily on cooperation, coordination and interdisciplinary study. I said so at the hearing, which did not endear me to advocates of unionization. I spent considerable time in conversations with them, and the entire faculty, explaining my position. I urged that continuing regular meetings between the administration and the entire faculty would best serve our college and reduce potential tensions. The Legislature refused to act and we continued to seek cooperative rather than confrontational relationships between the administration and faculty.

THE RECESSION WORSENED, ravaging state revenues. I deeply empathized with Spellman, who now faced terrible choices and hostile elements in his own party. All state agencies, including Evergreen, were required to reduce budgets while serving more clients—in our case, students. Faculty, staff and students combined to find ways to be more efficient and still provide a unique Evergreen experience.

I was now deeply involved with the Power Council, while also serving on three corporate boards and two professionally-oriented foundations. Fortunately, family-time requirements eased a bit when Dan Jr. and Mark left for college—Dan at Whitman and Mark at Williams College in Massachusetts.

I lost a valued colleague and friend on January 8, 1983, when former Oregon governor Tom

McCall succumbed to prostate cancer at 69. He was a tall, engaging man whose voice was tinged with the New England accent of his youth. Tom was unpredictable, unconventional and extraordinarily candid. He cared deeply about the environment.

Cecil Andrus, Idaho's admirable governor, had joined Tom and me to create a bipartisan triumvirate to protect the natural resources of the Pacific Northwest. Bill Hall, an award-winning columnist for the *Lewiston Morning Tribune,* wrote this shortly after McCall's death: "On such matters as water and power and fish and, most of all, conservation of the region's boundless treasures, Andrus, McCall and Evans were a clear-eyed oligarchy leading the Northwest out of its wasteful wanton youth and toward the sober management of finite resources and the conservation of fragile splendor."

EVERGREEN FACED one last significant legislative attempt at closure. This time it was State Senator Brad Owen, an outspoken young Democrat from Shelton who had virtually no knowledge of Evergreen and was playing in the Senate sandbox. He did get half his caucus to support him to close the college and use the facilities for state office space. I was irate. "No school can survive a steady drumbeat every year," I told reporters. "They could close Harvard that way. You're damn right I'm mad. Some of these people are using Evergreen to get at me. Others brought this up to trade votes for pet bills because they knew Evergreen was strong in the House. … I don't mind if the attack is against me. I've been in politics and I'm used to it. But when it is against the school, that's another matter."

Congratulating a graduate at Evergreen's 1982 Commencement. *The Evergreen State College Archives*

It only took 24 hours for the Senate to back down. Several senators said they didn't have all the facts when the first vote was taken. Several editorials appeared in support of Evergreen. I loved the one in Spokane's *Spokesman-Review*: "In a single decade, Evergreen has acquired a national reputation for excellence that, in some areas, may equal or surpass what Washington's other universities have achieved in a century. And Evergreen did it on academic merit, not by winning the Rose Bowl."

After my sixth graduation ceremony, Nancy and I talked about our future. Evergreen was consistently appearing on lists of the best small colleges in America. I thought it was time for a new venture, although I had no idea what it might be. Time pressures were building since the Power Council required frequent trips to Portland, and the coming school year would demand my full attention.

49
LOSING A NATIONAL TREASURE

One of the recurring questions of my eventful life is "What next?" In August of 1983, with my six-year term as president of The Evergreen State College nearing its end, I met with Thelma Jackson, the chairperson of Evergreen's Board of Trustees. I told her I believed it was time for an academically oriented president to head the college. My mission had been to shore up the school's political and public support and create a sense of unity and mission among the faculty and students. In my view, I had succeeded. Thelma agreed, expressing regret at my decision. I said I would be happy to stay until June of 1984 to give the trustees ample time to hire a new president. "What do you plan to do?" Thelma asked. "I have no idea," I said with a chuckle. We set a luncheon date for early September to work on a succession plan.

A few days later we waved goodbye to Mark, our middle son, as he departed for Massachusetts and a new school year at Williams College. The next day we took our youngest son, Bruce, to the airport to send him off for his first year at Yale. It was a great adventure for him, but Nancy and I had tears in our eyes as our tall, curly-haired 17-year-old disappeared down the chute to the plane. Dan Jr. had already departed for Whitman College in Walla Walla, Nancy's alma mater.

WE SPENT THE EVENING with my brother Roger at our summer property on Quilcene Bay. The next day, September 1, we returned to a strangely quiet empty house. The shocking news was that Soviet fighter pilots had shot down a Korean Airlines Boeing 747 that had strayed into Soviet air space en route to Seoul. Georgia Congressman Larry McDonald was among the 269 innocent victims. Senator Jackson called a press conference to denounce the tragedy as a "dastardly, barbaric act against humanity." I had rarely seen him more angry—and appropriately so.

We turned off the TV, repaired to our deck and watched Mount Rainier turn an impossible shade of vibrant pink as the sun slowly set. It was gloriously peaceful.

"I guess I better go in and get dinner," Nancy said all of a sudden, which made me smile.

"Why? There's no one home but us!"

"I guess you're right," she conceded, plopping back into her chair.

We settled down for another drink and calculated that it was the first time in almost 23 years that our nest was nominally empty. It was a good time to think about new challenges.

We went to bed early, only to be rudely awakened by the insistent ringing of the night-stand phone. It was my brother Roger. "It's almost midnight," I muttered groggily. He cut me off in mid-sentence: "Have you heard the news? Senator Jackson died this evening!" Nancy and I turned on the radio and TV to learn what details there were. Jackson had just returned from a grueling two-week tour of China with a chest cold and a hacking cough. After the press conference, he saw a doctor and headed to bed at home in Everett. He died that evening, at 71, of a ruptured aorta.

I SLEPT FITFULLY and awoke to a deluge of calls. Reporters wanted quotes for Jackson's obituary. Some also asked my opinion on his successor. Was I interested in the seat? I shut them off quickly, saying such questions were unseemly. Henry M. Jackson had admirably served his state and nation as a congressman and senator for a total of 42 years, I said. He was a patriot for all seasons and a great Washingtonian. I would have nothing more to say until after his funeral.

Twice a viable contender for president, Jackson was number three in seniority in the Senate at the time of his death. He was practically invincible at the polls, drawing votes—and substantial campaign contributions—from both Republicans and Democrats. He stood for a strong national defense, worked hard to protect the environment and led the fight for equal rights. As governor, I often visited Scoop's office for help on state problems. He was always positive and vigorous, frequently enlisting Magnuson to help me. "Scoop and Maggie" for decades were the most powerful tag-team in the U.S. Senate. Washington gained immeasurably from their political strength and loyalty.

Henry Kissinger called Jackson a "national treasure." George Will, perhaps the most thoughtful conservative in America, hailed Jackson as "the finest public servant I have known." Jackson's funeral at the First Presbyterian Church in Everett drew more than a thousand mourners. Vice President Bush, Chief Justice Warren Burger, Kissinger and more than 40 senators were joined by Scoop's friends, neighbors and other admirers. Magnuson best captured the moment, "What he did in Congress ought to make him immortal. But for his headstone they ought to say this: He was a humane, compassionate man."

As the mourners left the pews, the guessing game began in earnest: Who would, or *could*, succeed Scoop?

SLADE GORTON, who had achieved his life's ambition with his election to the U.S. Senate three years earlier, called a few days after Scoop's death and asked Nancy and me to join him and his wife Sally at their summer place on Whidbey Island. Slade and I sat in the sun while he talked with great enthusiasm about the Senate and how wonderful it would be for us to serve together once again. As we drove home that evening I told Nancy I was really unsure that was the right thing for me, assuming that Governor Spellman would even ask me to accept an appointment.

The governor was being heavily lobbied by all sides. Jackson had won re-election in a landslide in 1982, and the Democratic state chairwoman, Karen Marchioro, declared that Spellman should fill the seat with a Democrat. State law imposed no such obligation on the governor. (If it had, Spellman said later, he

With Slade Gorton on the campaign trail. *Washington State Archives*

would have happily appointed Spokane Congressman Tom Foley, whom we both admired.) Washington state last had two Republicans in the U.S. Senate in 1923, and the White House was anxious to build on its Senate GOP majority. *The Seattle Times* suggested Spellman should appoint a caretaker until a special election could be arranged. But the Senate was squabbling over appropriations. Serious international incidents were front-page news. A caretaker appointment did not seem appropriate.

Joel Pritchard and I headed practically every media list of potential successors. Others mentioned were Bill Ruckelshaus, who was overseeing the federal Environmental Protection Agency for the second time, and Congressmen Sid Morrison and Rod Chandler.

Attorney General Ken Eikenberry, a Republican, was besieged by questions: Would the appointee serve for the remaining five years and four months of Senator Jackson's term? Or be required to stand for election in the fall of 1984—or in just two months, in keeping with the recently passed annual elections law?

Eikenberry ruled that an election should be held forthwith. But it was too late for a primary election, he said, so all the candidates should run in November, with the top vote getter to be named senator. Officials from both parties objected strenuously.

I watched the political maneuvering with a certain sense of detachment until I received a wake-up call from Secretary of State Ralph Munro, my friend and former aide.

"Have you talked to the Governor?"

"No. Why should I?"

"Well, you owe it to the governor to let him know whether you would accept an appointment to the Senate if it were offered to you," Munro said. He was clearly annoyed at my lack of action. Even if I was conflicted, he said it was discourteous not to talk with the governor.

I realized how right he was and immediately called the Governor's Office. Spellman invited me to breakfast at the Mansion. As I prepared to leave the house the next morning, I told Nancy, "If he offers me the job, I'm going to tell the governor 'no.' "

"Are you sure?" she counseled. "It might be an exciting and challenging change for you. But it's your decision to make. You do what you want to do. Whatever you choose is fine with me."

Nancy remembers watching me walk down the hall to the garage, shaking my head.

During the 15-minute drive from Cooper Point to the Mansion, I listened to the morning news. The headline story focused on the fallout from the loss of the Korean airliner. Interspersed with the news was commentary on Jackson's long career and his recent trip to Asia. The photo of Jackson and Deng Xiaoping hugging cheek to cheek in the Great Hall of the People was front-page news around the world. I realized these were critical times, and if I could help make a difference by serving in the Senate I wanted to try.

The governor met me at the door. We walked to the sun-filled private dining room added to the Mansion in 1974, thanks to Nancy's renovation efforts.

I realized this was my first private visit to the Mansion since our family's departure in 1977. We talked about the challenges Spellman faced with a sinking economy, looming budget deficits and hardline conservative legislators making his life difficult. Finally, the conversation shifted to the challenges he faced in making an appointment to the U.S. Senate.

"I don't want to put any pressure at all on you," I assured him. "You make the appointment you think is right. But I wanted you to know that if you thought I was the right appointment I would be honored to serve."

The governor was politely noncommittal. We dropped the subject and enjoyed the rest of the breakfast talking about our families and the challenges of living in the Mansion, not to mention being governor in challenging times.

I returned home and told Nancy about my change of mind. "We'd better prepare for some interesting days ahead."

That night, Nancy and I were having dinner at the Washington Athletic Club with friends when I received a call telling me it was urgent that I call the governor immediately. I headed for a phone booth and was quickly connected. "I would like to appoint you to the United States Senate," Spellman said. Without hesitation, I said I was honored and would be pleased to serve. The governor asked me to join him at a press conference set for the next day. Memories flooded my brain. I thought about three young rookie state

With Gov. Spellman at the Governor's Mansion. *Washington State Archives*

legislators who lived together during the 1959 legislative session. Evans, Gorton and Pritchard would now serve together in the United States Congress. But I had an election to win to make that a longer-term reality.

I returned to our group and quietly told Nancy the news. It was the beginning of the most challenging, exhilarating, frustrating, exhausting and ultimately rewarding 60 days of our married life.

REPUBLICAN STATE CHAIRWOMAN Jennifer Dunn was besieged by calls from conservative party leaders, especially in King County, who were opposed to my nomination. Jennifer was the one party leader highly respected by all factions. She helped maintain official party neutrality during the primary. Afterward, she deftly unified factions in support of my candidacy.

The White House, after some quick polls, anointed me as the most electable Republican. Mitch Daniels, director of the national Senate Republican Campaign Committee and later governor of Indiana, met with the state Republican Party leadership. "Senator Evans' occasional differences with party regulars are well-known," he counseled, "but we hope they will be transcended by the great senator he will be."

Spellman, also under fire by conservatives, was annoyed by the squabbling. "I enthusiastically appointed Dan Evans, wholeheartedly endorse and vigorously support him," he affirmed.

The Washington Supreme Court ruled that an election must be held in November of 1983, adding that it could not force a primary election. Spellman, in constant contact with legislative leaders, deftly called a special session. On the following day, in the space of just two hours, the Legislature created a special primary for October 11, with the General Election to be held on November 8.

I was about to become a United States Senator, temporarily at least. I had no staff, no campaign organization and no money. It was an enormous stroke of good luck that Bill Jacobs, who had ably served as my chief of staff during my last term as governor, was living temporarily in Washington, D.C. Having once served as director of our Department of Labor and Industries, he was working as a consultant with the U.S. Department of Labor. I told him I was in the biggest political jam of my career. I needed him to get back in the harness and help create a new team. He was reluctant, saying he had been looking forward to going home to Olympia. After considerable cajoling on my part, Jacobs agreed to take on the task—but only for 60 days. I agreed, telling myself, "Just wait until he gets fully involved in this exciting new challenge."

As we strode out of the plane in Washington, D.C., a few days later, there was Bill, smiling his wonderful smile.

AFTER CALLING the Senate to order, the president pro tem, Strom Thurmond of South Carolina, administered the oath of office.

As fellow senators gathered round to greet me, I discovered I had served as governor with a dozen of my new colleagues. Dale Bumpers of Arkansas and David Boren of Oklahoma were prominent Democratic governors during my time as governor. I was now reunited with my good friends John Chafee of Rhode Island and Mark Hatfield of Oregon, both outstanding governors in their day. And I would soon work closely with another fellow governor, President Reagan. I was thrilled to meet giants of the Senate: Rus-

Strom Thurmond, President Pro Tempore of the U.S. Senate, administers the oath of office. *Washington State Archives*

sell Long of Louisiana, John Glenn of Ohio, Patrick Moynihan of New York and Barry Goldwater of Arizona. The ceremony lasted only a few minutes. It was time to go to work.

50
THE JUNIOR SENATOR

Senator Jackson's talented staff, though still stunned by his passing, personified professionalism. They set aside space for us to operate while they finished packing his files and memorabilia. I asked if any were interested in working in my office. Most of Scoop's senior aides wanted to move on or retire. But some stayed on, including Shirley Harrod, the receptionist. Having worked for both Magnuson and Jackson, Shirley seemed to know everyone. When someone asked her what it was like to be working for a senator who was number 100 in seniority when she used to work for a senator who was number three, she replied, "Honey, in my estimation Senator Evans is number one." That was nice of her to say, but I'm certain she didn't relish the move to a less desirable office when seniority bumped us out of Jackson's spacious suite.

Sam Spina, Lisa Marchese and Irene Winter also joined us from Senator Jackson's staff. Spina, a veteran Senate staffer, became my senior legislative assistant. He guided a growing group of smart, young, hard-working analysts. Marchese was just finishing her law degree. I had the pleasure of watching her being sworn in as a member of the bar by Supreme Court Justice Antonin Scalia. Joe Mentor Jr. was traveling to Washington, D.C., to join Jackson's staff when the senator died. We were glad to add him to our team. I had worked closely with his father, a Kitsap County businessman who served in the Washington State Senate. My new press secretary was Sally Heet, a vice president at Rainier Bank. Bill Jacobs was a godsend as chief of staff.

I was temporarily assigned to Senator Jackson's committees: Armed Services, Energy and Natural Resources and Governmental Affairs. At my first meeting of the Armed Services Committee I also had my first introduction to seniority. The chairman was seated in the center of an intricately carved table, with Democrats arrayed on his left and Republicans on his right. I was a long way from the center.

Seniority rules the United States Senate. It determines your choice of office, committees, parking place and virtually everything else involving choices and perquisites. Each senator is assigned two numbers. One represents his or her numerical seniority dating from the first Senate session in 1789. The second is seniority in the current Congress.

Usually a number of new senators are elected at the same time. In 1958 a tiebreaker system was developed. Since then, former government service decides seniority. Senator Number One after the Constitution was signed in 1789 was Richard Bassett of Delaware. I was assigned number 1,760. Senator Pete Wilson of California was just ahead of me; John Kerry of Massachusetts immediately behind. Arriving by appointment I became number 100 in seniority. Before long, senior senators dropped by to say hello. Mostly they were sizing up Senator Jackson's old office to see if was nicer than theirs. They even eyed the historic roll top desk Scoop used.*

THE HECTIC PROCESS of settling in was now overtaken by the urgency of a special election in less than 60 days. I asked Jay Gilmour, a stalwart in all three of my gubernatorial campaigns, to serve as campaign manager. Jim Waldo, who earned his spurs with Action for Washington in 1968, volunteered to serve as chairman of the campaign. We rapidly built a team composed of veteran foot-soldiers and newcomers. My brother Roger, Dan Jr. and his cousin, Bill Bell, worked tirelessly producing and distributing campaign signs.

Having last run for office in 1972, I felt a little like Rip van Winkle. A lot had changed in 12 years. For starters, winning required a bigger war chest—especially for TV advertising and tracking polls. Political gurus were now muscling aside volunteers. Personal campaigning—including door-belling—was less important than "image" creation. I did not like it much. Our weekly campaign meetings were sometimes so argumentative that I finally banned our out-of-state consultant during the last couple of weeks of the campaign.

When filing opened, more than 30 candidates signed up. It was immediately clear that I had three serious opponents, two Democrats and a Republican: Congressman Mike Lowry, the ebullient liberal from Seattle's 7th District; Seattle Mayor Charles Royer, and former KIRO-TV general manager Lloyd Cooney, who had lost to Slade Gorton in the GOP Senate primary three years earlier. Cooney was a character. He flew ultralights, rode motorcycles and went skydiving. His KIRO editorials generated a lot of controversy. Ed Donohoe of the *Washington Teamster* once quipped that "in a race with a test pattern, Lloyd Cooney would come in second." Maybe, but he was a legitimate contender, actively supported by former governor Ray, who couldn't abide the thought of me serving in the U.S. Senate.

I made seven round trips between the two Washingtons in less than 60 days, campaigning intensely every weekend. Weekdays, I worked long hours to brush up on issues and learn Senate procedures.

The Washington Wilderness bill was a priority, but it would take another year to pass. I was asked to chair a subcommittee hearing of the Energy and Natural Resources committee to receive the Pacific Northwest Power Council's first plans outlining power projections and fish and wildlife protection measures. Keith Colbo of Montana, the new chairman of the Council, presented the report. A month earlier I was chairman of the council, preparing to come to Washington, D.C. Now I received the report I had helped prepare. Moments like that sum up how quickly life can change.

IN A PRIMARY FEATURING 33 candidates, I decided to ignore the others and speak to my own philosophy and views on current issues. The Cooney campaign took a scattershot approach, blaming me for higher taxes, bloated budgets and the WPPSS nuclear plant fiasco since I had signed the permits for the ill-fated plants. Cooney said I was a closet liberal who would not be a reliable supporter of President Reagan. Royer and Lowry, meantime, claimed I was too close to Reagan. It appeared that this hundred-yard-dash election could boil down to a test of Reagan's popularity. "I am a Re-

* Offices were reassigned in January 1984, with the beginning of the second session of the 98th Congress. My old friend, Oregon Senator Mark Hatfield, chose to move into Jackson's suite. I ended up in Hart Office Building, the newest of the three Senate office buildings but farther from the Capitol than the other two.

publican," I emphasized, "but I am an independent thinker. I am also a loyalist."

On October 11, 1983, I defeated Cooney by almost 2 to 1. Lowry, in what was viewed as a mild upset, handily defeated Mayor Royer, a former TV newsman. I was not surprised. Lowry was much more knowledgeable on issues. As a sitting Congressman, he had better access to campaign finances. He also gently reminded contributors that win or lose, he'd still be in Congress.

I received 37 percent of the total vote. The press predicted a hot final race. Sure enough, minutes after the polls closed Lowry challenged me to debate—daily if possible! "Dan Evans is a fine man," Mike declared. "A decent man. A family man. But he's wrong on the issues." My response was that I had known Mike for a long time. "He is a good person, but he is also extremely partisan. His liberalism is more extreme than any other member of the Washington delegation, and more extreme than all but a few members of the House. Either the others are wrong or Mike Lowry is out of step."

Lowry pirouetted like a pro, saying that being called a "liberal extremist" was both "disappointing" and "encouraging." If I was resorting to labels, I must be worried about the election, Mike said, charging that I was avoiding telling voters where I really stood on the issues. Whenever I said I would study an issue, he styled me as indecisive. My rejoinder was that he had neatly italicized "the difference between sloganeering, which he's good at, and thoughtfulness, which I hope I'm good at. You get more than a 'yes' or 'no' vote in Congress. You get to work in committee. You get to craft legislation. You get to amend it, and you get to suggest. Only after all of that is done do you finally cast a 'yes' or 'no' vote."

Lowry attempted to push me to the right and I tried equally hard to push him to the left. Both of us in fact were reaching toward the center and Washington's large bloc of independent voters.

Lowry and I squared off on October 16, my 58th birthday. I was frankly rusty, while Mike was his passionately wonky, arm-waving self. Our differences on issues were clear. The major foreign-policy question of the time was whether the United States should engage in a "nuclear freeze" with the USSR. Or, as the Reagan Administration suggested, initiate a "build down" of nuclear weapons. I believed that approval of the MX missile, a key replacement in our aging arsenal, coupled with an agreement with the USSR to destroy two missiles for every new one constructed, was our most prudent course. Mike pushed hard for an immediate nuclear freeze, claiming that the MX heightened the danger of nuclear war, and that both sides should immediately stop building any nuclear weapons. Neither of us, nor the voters or Soviet experts—let alone Ronald Reagan—had any inkling that the Soviet Union would collapse in less than seven years.

Reviews were mixed, but Lowry gained by the intensity of his views. The most negative assessment of my performance was a column by Shelby Scates, the veteran political columnist for the *Seattle Post-Intelligencer*. In a piece headlined "Why can't Dan Evans be himself?" Scates wrote, "Senator Dan Evans got beat on television last Sunday in his debate with Representative Mike Lowry, and the way things are going in his campaign, it could be a portent of November 8. …Evans supporters, apparently, are of two minds about campaign strategy. Those outside his present inner circle insist Reagan needs Evans more than Evans needs Reagan. Evans' new crop of campaign advisers, all young in age and experience, appear aiming straight for the 128,816 votes Cooney got in last week's primary election. So far they've succeeded in turning gold into lead. It may cost Evans the election."

That was a wake-up call, with only three weeks left before the final election.

GILMOUR WAS OVERSEEING a campaign that featured thousands of volunteers. We mailed more than a million campaign flyers. Money flowed in without my making a single phone call for donations. I discovered that my new Senate Republican colleagues were contacting their closest supporters, saying, "Send money to Evans! He can help us keep Republican control of the Senate." We raised almost $2 million in 60 days.

One new twist was independent expenditures that exploited a loophole in campaign finance laws. The U.S. Supreme Court had ruled several years earlier that independent expenditures could be made without limit during campaigns since they were protected under the First Amendment. The court stipulated that such expenditures could not be coordinated or revealed to a campaign, but must be made independently.

Crude ads began to appear on my behalf. Most were attacks on Lowry's integrity and fitness for public office. I disagreed with Mike Lowry's politics but I respected him. Mad as hell, I told my campaign to find out who was running them and tell them to stop. They reported back that it was illegal to have any contact with groups running the ads. Besides, we wouldn't know who they were until they filed reports with the Federal Elections Commission.

One of our most fascinating joint appearances was hosted by a citizens group that a year earlier had sponsored a week-long "Target Seattle" symposium on the dangers of nuclear war. The symposium featured prominent national speakers. The closing event drew 10,000 to the Kingdome, with Archibald Cox, national chairman of Common Cause, as the keynoter. Congressman Tom Foley and I agreed to co-chair the 1983 "Target Washington" event, which unfolded in the middle of the Senate campaign. The opening symposium was a dramatic event. People jammed the Paramount Theatre to hear speeches by Lowry and me. It would have been hard to imagine a more topical theme than the danger of catastrophic warfare, what with the recent downing of KAL Flight 007, the bombing of the Marine Corps barracks in Lebanon and the invasion of Grenada. The audience was intelligent and passionate. Most supported the nuclear freeze Lowry advocated, but a growing number were deeply concerned by recent aggressive action by the Soviets and new international conflicts. For me, it was the highlight of the campaign. Mike and I made serious and detailed arguments to a thoughtful audience. He advocated a "mutual, verifiable weapons freeze aimed at ending the insane nuclear arms race." I was concerned that a freeze would not reduce nuclear weapons but maintain an aging and increasingly dangerous arsenal. I advocated the "Build-down" policy. The event was in sharp contrast to the emptiness of campaign advertising and time-constrained debates that squashed intelligent exchanges on complicated issues.

A gratifying newspaper ad was headlined "Eight more reasons Democrats are voting for Dan." It featured large portraits of prominent Democrats and quotes saying why they supported my candidacy. "He was an outstanding governor, and he will be an equally outstanding senator," said Cecil Andrus, a former Idaho governor and Secretary of the Interior. "If I lived here, I'd vote for Dan Evans." Stewart Udall, a former Secretary of the Interior, spoke of my environmental leadership. Bill Gissberg, a prominent member of the Washington State Senate, was joined by State Senator Francis Haddon Morgan. I enjoyed the ad all the more when Democratic Party leaders threatened to expel the traitors.

POLLS AND YOUR GUT instincts may give you confidence, but until you hear from the voters you're never sure. It's a scary moment.

The early returns foretold a decisive victory. I won the remainder of Jackson's six-year term with 55.41 percent of the vote and carried 32 of the state's 39 counties, including King by nearly 52,000 votes.

Around 9 p.m. I received a call from President Reagan, who was en route to Japan on *Air Force One*. He expressed delight at my election and said he looked forward to working together. We discussed international problems and I told him about my interest in being on the Foreign Relations Committee. As I hung up, I reflected on our sometimes conten-

A family portrait on the morning after my election to the U.S. Senate in 1983. *MOHAI, Grant M. Haller, Seattle Post-Intelligencer Collection*

tious moments when we were both governors and how much had changed in the past decade.

The next morning, Lowry and I held press conferences. I said I was ready "to find out what it's really like to be a senator—full time!" and noted that environmental, social and civil rights concerns were virtually ignored during the campaign. I said that was most likely because Mike and I were of the same mind on those issues. "I think we will work very well together."

Lowry was gracious: "I think Dan Evans has the ability to be a senator the state can be proud of. I certainly hope so."

We worked well together. And became genuine friends.

Saying goodbye to a host of friends—old and new—was bittersweet.

The Evergreen State College Foundation sponsored a farewell roast for its departing president. Jan Lambertz, the school's athletic director, entered disguised as an 8-foot geoduck, Evergreen's mascot. Nancy was the final roaster. With her droll sense of humor and perfect comic timing, she testified, "Dan is a wonderful man. And if you don't believe it, just ask him."

I said I was exceptionally proud of our college. "Wherever I go, I'll always be a Greener."

AS WE SETTLED IN across the continent, I received word that my brother Bob had succumbed to lung cancer. He'd been fighting its relentless advance for months, but that didn't deter him from pitching in on my Senate campaign. A talented artist and sculptor, Bob had been a stalwart in practically every race I'd ever run. He designed and helped manufacture the yard signs that volunteers distributed by the thousands. I felt an immense loss when my parents died, but they had lived long lives in good health. Now my brother was gone at 56. I felt cheated. Though he was only two years younger, we had not spent enough time together. I wanted him to see all the historic places in Washington, D.C., visit Capitol Hill with me and enjoy the storytelling and memories that were so much a part of our family gatherings. He was a good man and a gentle soul.

51
WILDERNESS WARRIOR

On Capitol Hill at the chilly outset of 1984, I reflected on the tumultuous four months since my appointment to the U.S. Senate. I was beginning to sense the rhythm of the place and had growing confidence in the team we were building. I fought hard to stay on the Energy and Natural Resources Committee, but there were no spots available. Finally, Virginia Senator John Warner offered to relinquish his spot, with the stipulation that he would retain his committee seniority.

I was delighted with my assignment to the Committee on Environment and Public Works headed by John Chafee, who was governor of Rhode Island when we first met as fellow governors. We shared a deep devotion to the environment, and in the years to come pushed the EPA and the Department of the Interior to move faster on environmental protection.

The first major issue of importance to our state during the 1984 session was the Washington Wilderness bill. The federal government had completed a nationwide survey of remote and roadless areas. The survey, dubbed RARE II, identified federal land that had not been touched by mining, grazing or logging. Much of the area was desert. Some 2.5 million acres in Washington state had been pinpointed. Battle lines were drawn. Environmental groups wanted all 2.5 million acres protected, while the U.S. Forest Service, at the behest of the Reagan Administration, advocated a little over 300,000 acres. Senator Gorton and I worked hard with our staff experts, Creigh Agnew and Joe Mentor, to develop a strategy. Our "discussion only" bill would preserve 750,000 acres as wilderness. The challenge we faced snapped into focus immediately as the combatants weighed in. "If this is a trial balloon, I would characterize it as lead," said Charley Raines of the Sierra Club. Gus Koehne, representing the National Independent Forest Manufacturers, warned, "The best way to eliminate the small timber producers in the state is to take away their supply of timber."

Several years earlier, Harvey Manning, an irascible environmentalist and brilliant writer, wrote the narrative for a Seattle Mountaineers' book, *Washington Wilderness: the Unfinished Work*. I wrote the foreword, concluding, "When there is doubt, I hope we will always preserve wilderness. If ultimately we have too much, uses can be changed, but wilderness destroyed cannot be regained." I now proposed to argue our case in the U.S. Senate with that basic principle in mind. A Greener was sticking his neck way out.

With pressures from all sides building, we needed a united congressional delegation to make a Washington wilderness bill a reality. Slade and I asked Congressman Tom Foley, the Democrats' outstanding Majority Whip from Spokane, to host a meeting of our delegation. We were divided right down the middle politically, five Democrats and five Republicans, but we worked together well on issues impacting our state. We had strategy sessions over breakfast once a month. Many of my Senate colleagues were amazed, moaning, "We can't even get our delegation to speak to one another!"

Though we were largely united on expanding the Wilderness Act, the details remained to be sorted out. With 10 members of the delegation and at least 10 staffers in the room, that was quite a crowd. Foley looked around and said, "Let's have just the members meet in my office." We kicked out the staff, which was like "Whoa, what's going on?" But when it was just us—elected officials who understood their constituencies—we hashed it out.

The big conference table in Foley's office was soon covered with topographical maps.

MIKE LOWRY AND JOEL PRITCHARD, two consummate politicians, were also avid supporters of maximum wilderness areas. As urban legislators, they did not face the direct conflict that tortured many other House members. GOP freshman Rod Chandler's district stretched in a huge suburban arc east of Lake Washington. His constituents included environmental enthusiasts and small timber operators. He was understandably wary. Al Swift, a seasoned Democrat who represented large timber communities in Northwest Washington, proposed cautious compromises that went as far as he felt he could go in designating wilderness territory. An Emmy-award winning former broadcaster, Al once joked, "The only way I'll go into the wilderness is on a sedan chair." Don Bonker, a bright young Democrat from Southwest Washington timber country, faced the same sort of pressures. Nevertheless, Bonker proposed significant additions to wilderness from his district. Norm Dicks, the Democrat from Bremerton who earned his spurs as an aide to Senator Magnuson, also represented large timber communities. Yet he boldly advocated additional wilderness on the Olympic Peninsula and new wilderness areas adjacent to Mount Rainier National Park. Sid Morrison, who represented the Yakima Valley, proposed eliminating 500 acres of existing wilderness adjacent to the White Pass ski area in order to

Three old friends promoted to the other Washington: Congressman Pritchard and U.S. Senators Evans and Gorton in 1984. *Washington State Archives*

allow it to expand. I supported him, although this was anathema to environmental leaders who opposed any reduction in existing wilderness. Morrison also proposed surprisingly large additions to wilderness in his district. Environmentalists were troubled. Should they object to the 500-acre removal and risk losing Morrison's support, or should they trade the 500 acres for almost 100,000 acres Morrison supported? Tom Foley added some smaller wilderness areas in his district.

Slade and I helped guide the discussion, identifying areas still in question. The delegation spent one memorable morning studying tracts of wilderness acreage, swapping ideas and suggesting compromises. It was one of the most productive and rewarding legislative negotiations I have ever experienced. As we rolled up our maps and walked out the door we were met by anxious staff members. I briefed Joe Mentor and we sat down to develop our position on the bill I would propose at a follow-up meeting of the delegation. Joe added up the acreage and exclaimed, "Senator, do you know this is over one million acres of new wilderness?" I nodded, saying the plan would surprise and dismay the timber industry. I was equally certain the environmental community would think it was not nearly enough.

The timber industry, awakened to the threat of a large wilderness bill, sent droves of lobbyists to our offices and ran full-page ads in Washington state newspapers. The industry found to its dismay that the environmental lobby had worked harder and longer on the issue.

At the delegation's follow-up meeting, we debated boundaries virtually foot by foot. I was reminded of the redistricting sessions when I was governor. This time the objects were trees and animals, not voters (Too bad trees and critters can't vote!) The debate was intense but devoid of animosity or political posturing. Everyone wanted a solution. After five hours, we backed away from the maps, glanced at one another and shook hands all around. We were united.

Reporters crowded the corridor outside Foley's office. We spoke of the difficulties we faced, and our determination to reach a bipartisan plan. I said our only chance to pass a million-acre wilderness bill was to remain united.

Several timber lobbyists watched the news conference somberly. I was dismayed when I heard one of the environmental lobbyists sniff, "Well, now we'll just go back and get the other 1.5 million acres!" She had no idea how difficult it had been to reach consensus. And she offered not one word of congratulations for the job just accomplished. Too often I experienced obstinate environmental groups unwilling to make progress step-by-step, instead demanding everything and too often ending up with nothing.

Press commentary back home was highly positive, commenting as much on our unity as on the bill itself. "It is surprisingly refreshing," one editorial said. "One million acres comes very close to striking the proper balance among natural resource development, wilderness conservation and political necessity." Another observed, "No other Western state delegation has succeeded so well on the wilderness issue... The team can be counted on to look out for the state's broad interest in the future."

WITH SUCH STRONG SUPPORT from our state delegation, I expected prompt action by the Senate Energy and Natural Resources Committee. To my dismay I discovered that Senator James McClure of Idaho, chairman of the committee, was holding hostage our wilderness bill and Oregon's in a dispute he had with the House Interior and Insular Affairs Committee. Subcommittee Chairman John Seiberling, a Democrat from Ohio, demanded release language in the bill that McClure despised. We were being treated to a showdown fight between two powerful committee chairmen. It was House against Senate, Democrat against Republican. "Release language" is a somewhat obscure but vitally important element of federal land management. "Soft release" allows the Forest Service to decide which areas, not presently selected for wilderness, could be logged and which should continue to be protected for potential future wilderness designation. "Hard release" allows logging on all lands not immediately set aside for wilderness.

The Washington and Oregon delegations had inserted "soft release" language in their wilderness bills. McClure was adamant about changing that language. At one point he talked about the "intransigence" of the House, saying it could take "a keg of dynamite" to break loose the logjam. He counseled patience and compromise. I was furious. "I hope that patience is one of my virtues," I wrote. "If in fact a keg of dynamite is needed, my fuse is lit. ...Intransigence is a two-way street."

Former Oregon governor Mark Hatfield, the chairman of the Senate Appropri-

The Washington congressional delegation in 1984: I'm sitting with Slade Gorton and Joel Pritchard; standing, from left: Rod Chandler, Al Swift, Norm Dicks, Tom Foley, Sid Morrison, Mike Lowry and Don Bonker. *Gorton Center*

ations Committee, joined the battle with a not-so-veiled threat to McClure at a committee hearing on the legislation. "As Chairman of Appropriations, I have tried to accommodate various senators... But, Mr. Chairman, I am a little impatient." When Hatfield slowly italicized *"Chairman of Appropriations,"* the meaning was heard by all. I felt a little like David watching two Goliaths readying for battle. Chairman McClure now proposed a five-week cooling-off period to attempt to find compromise language. Hatfield and I strongly objected, finally agreeing to a two-week delay.

Finally in late April both the Oregon and Washington wilderness bills unanimously passed our Senate committee.

During the congressional August recess, President Reagan signed the bill into law without formal ceremony. Almost immediately, environmental activists began to propose additional wilderness areas. The debate over how much to preserve continues. None of that detracts from a landmark moment in the battle to preserve our most priceless natural resource. Wilderness destroyed cannot be regained. The legislation we passed honored Scoop Jackson's environmental legacy by protecting from development 1.6 million acres of National Forest land in Washington state under the umbrella of the Wilderness Act. The act was also a first step in protecting the National Forest lands along the North Cascades Scenic Highway corridor. Scoop was chairman of the Senate Interior Committee in 1964 when he engineered passage of the original act, which set aside 9.1 million acres across the country as land "where the earth and its community of life are untrammeled by man; where man himself is a visitor who does not remain."

52
FUNDAMENTALLY FRUSTRATED

As our delegation was crafting the Washington Wilderness Bill, the United States Senate turned to floor action on President Reagan's proposed constitutional amendment to "protect" prayer in public schools. It's not enough that students can privately invoke divine guidance whenever in need. Every time some court somewhere in America rules against *organized* prayer, alarmed Christians want to change the U.S. Constitution and the Bill of Rights. In my view, "school prayer" and other proposed constitutional amendments of the same ilk would weaken, not strengthen, our Constitution.

Floor debate droned on for nearly two weeks before I finally joined in:

> I may not be a fundamentalist when it comes to religious practices, as I am a Congregationalist. But I am a fundamentalist when it comes to the Constitution. Our Constitution, any constitution, it seems to me, should have two fundamental elements: the organization of government under which we operate, and the basic rights reserved to all citizens.

I detailed the 16 amendments to the Constitution since ratification of the Bill of Rights in 1791. They are of two types. One is ministerial or organizational; the other deals with fundamental rights or responsibilities of citizens. Only six amendments since the Bill of Rights relate to fundamental rights and responsibilities: Abolition of slavery; citizenship rights not to be abridged by the several states; the income tax, and expansion of the right to vote, first to men of all races, then to women and finally to 18-year-olds. I said:

> The issue before us seems to relate to a concern over the general state of our schools, and probably to the piety of our people. If religion in this country is really weak, does this proposal strengthen religious beliefs? Even though advocates are careful to separate prayer in school from governmental supervision of that prayer, the teacher will end up playing a vital role. If there is one great problem in our school systems today it is that we have overburdened our teachers with many elements beyond their most fundamental role: providing teaching to our children. Harried, overworked teachers are now being called on to be substitute parents, to be guardians, to be policemen. And this will lead to the exceedingly disagreeable responsibility of referee.

If religion is really strong, does this then enhance religious practices in this nation or does it really reduce or dilute the religious practices of many?

I suggest that prayer, whether vocal or silent, if organized and led through the school systems during regular school hours will be unfulfilling for the devoted, puzzling for the questioning and annoying to the nonbeliever. …

I am confident that God will remain in the heart of every child who will let him in, with or without this amendment. But the nation's economic recovery may not last until we pass an effective deficit-reduction program. And none of us may survive at all unless we devise an appropriate way to secure nuclear arms reductions and a more secure peace.

The final vote on the amendment was 56 to 44 on March 21, 1984. Thank God, it failed to reach the necessary two-thirds majority by 11 votes.

I LEARNED EARLY ON that the pressure for more spending on favorite projects overwhelmed the desire to balance the budget. A Democratic House and a Republican Senate fought over priorities. The end result was that few of the appropriations bills were passed by Congress before the beginning of the fiscal year on October 1. As pressures grew for adjournment late in the year—especially in an election year—the appropriations bills were lumped together and passed in one huge document. That effectively denied the president the power of veto since that action would effectively shut down the government. I found out late in the year just how ludicrous our appropriations process really was.

Congress was eager to adjourn and head home to campaign. I was presiding over the Senate early one evening when a messenger arrived from the House. He proceeded down the center aisle, pushing a hand truck loaded with a three-foot stack of documents. He announced that the House had duly passed the Appropriations Bill for fiscal 1985. And here it was!

The majority and minority leaders debated how much time would be allowed to discuss the most important act of the session. *Voila!* It would be one hour, divided equally between the parties. I was stunned, since it was clear that no one outside the Conference Committee that negotiated the Appropriations Bill knew what it contained. And many of the committee members likely were unaware of earmarks inserted at the last minute. Little matter. The urge to adjourn far exceeded any willingness to closely examine the details of the bill. Only one thing was obvious: Total spending would far exceed income and the national deficit would continue to grow.

When spring arrived I still had hopes for some semblance of budget sanity. At the beginning of each day's session senators have an opportunity to deliver 15-minute speeches on any subject. It's called "morning business."

I spoke in favor of a bipartisan deficit reduction proposal—a one-year across-the-board freeze in the federal budget. As co-sponsor of the plan, I asserted that deficit reduction ought to be the top priority of every senator. Annual interest payments on the national debt exceeded 13 percent of our annual budget, exceeding the payments for Medicare and Medicaid combined. In addition we needed to cure a $500 billion unfunded liability in our Federal Civil Service Retirement System. Not once in the previous five years had the Congress passed all 13 of the appropriation bills introduced before the start of the fiscal year. And many were not passed before the end of the year they were intended to fund. Deficit reduction must be immediate and substantial, I said, and it also must initiate a downward trend for future year deficits. "I believe very strongly that a budget process must be established that provides Congress with the procedural tools to responsibly reduce deficits and work toward rationality in our budget activities." We had to work together, across party lines, with everyone sacrificing something to realistically stop the growth and begin to reduce the deficit.

Acknowledging that retired Americans relying on Social Security were worried about a budget freeze, I said immediate action to reduce the deficit would lower interest rates and inflation. That would have a direct, decisive impact on the cost of food, energy and shelter. Further, a lower rate of inflation is a non-taxable benefit. A freeze on defense spending would be offset by an increase in purchasing power, what with lower interest rates and inflation.

I endorsed the Budget Reform Act of 1983 introduced by Senator William Roth, the Delaware Republican perhaps best known as the father of the Roth IRA. His proposal called for a two-year budget cycle, which would allow more time for oversight of current spending and give state and local governments more certainty in coping with federal expenditure patterns.

After extended debate, the Senate rejected the one-year freeze, 65 to 33. Slade Gorton brought forward his own thoughtful plan for significant deficit reduction. That too was defeated, 72 to 23. While virtually every senator spoke of the need for deficit reduction, courage took flight when tough plans were proposed.

AS THE EASTER RECESS approached, I was surprised and pleased to receive a call from Senator Baker. He was leading a congressional delegation to Japan and Korea and asked if Nancy and I would like to accompany him. It was a great opportunity to continue my contacts with Japanese and Korean leaders and to urge opening of these markets to Washington products. Governor Lamar Alexander of Tennessee—who later became Secretary of Education and a U.S. senator—and his wife Honey accompanied us on the trip. We became good friends.

In Tokyo, our delegation met with Ambassador Mike Mansfield for a briefing before we embarked on visits to various governmental agencies. Mansfield, a widely respected Democrat from Montana, was Senate Majority Leader for 16 years before being appointed ambassador. With his courtly manners, our 81-year-old ambassador generated good will in a country where

The Evanses at the U.S. Capitol. *Evans Family Collection*

age is highly respected. Mansfield offered us a comprehensive overview of U.S.-Japan relations, punctuating his remarks with economic and cultural insights. He didn't need any notes. Other embassy officials made special presentations, but invariably Mansfield stepped in. He was clearly in charge and masterfully so.

The next day, accompanied by my legislative aide, Phil Jones, who was fluent in Japanese, I visited the Agricultural Ministry. We pushed hard for eliminating the ban on apple imports. I was reminded of my prior experiences in Japanese-style negotiations. They never said no but listed myriad reasons for not saying yes. We were making progress but it was exceedingly slow and frustrating.

We flew to Korea for another round of meetings with top governmental officials and an audience with the president. But the highlight for me was a visit to the demilitarized zone and Panmunjom. Thirty-one years earlier I was a young naval officer serving as aide to Admiral William Mendenhall, one of the first five members of the Military Armistice Commission. I had been an observer at the first meeting of the commission in the tiny frame building that still sits astride the border between North and South Korea.

My visit to the DMZ was a vivid reminder of the difficult and dangerous world we all inhabit. The long flight home gave me time to think about international relations and our foreign policy and I was determined to seek a place on the Foreign Relations Committee at the beginning of the next Congress.

I WAS PLEASED in late spring to get my first piece of legislation through the Senate: $30.5 million to restore fish runs on the Yakima River. It was one of the highest priority proposals endorsed by the Pacific Northwest Power Planning Council. We felt that the Yakima River projects enjoyed the best cost-benefit ratio of any fisheries enhancement projects in the Columbia basin and were eager to prove we were right. I helped craft the restoration proposal while I was chairman of the council. Now, as a U.S. senator, I was bringing it to reality.

Floor action intensified after the recess. We spent more than a week on defense spending. President Reagan asked for anti-satellite weapons—his "Star Wars" system—and production of at least 40 multi-warhead MX "Peacekeeper" missiles. The nuclear freeze movement was particularly opposed to the MX. I voted to limit the number of missiles to 21, noting we hadn't deployed a new ICBM since 1973. Less reliability might lead to greater danger and instability, I said, noting that the Soviets had superior land-based forces. "I think it's more important to negotiate with the Soviets, than for Congress to spend all our darned time negotiating with the President." More missiles were authorized by Congress in 1985. The wisdom of Reagan's proposals to strengthen our military and space programs while pushing for an expanded domestic economy was proven four years later. The Soviets attempted to match our military and space initiatives but ultimately could not provide adequately for their citizens, nor effectively control their satellite states. In 1989, shortly after Reagan left office, the Soviet Union collapsed.

I WAS CHAFING under the Senate's ironclad seniority system and its maze of 126 committees and subcommittees. Senate leadership, recognizing the growing frustration among younger members, appointed a 12-member bipartisan committee to recommend reforms. Dan Quayle, 37, an up-and-coming first-term Republican from Indiana, chaired the committee. Barry Goldwater, the old conservative lion, observed that the number of committees had grown 20-fold since his arrival on Capitol Hill in 1953.

I jumped at the chance to testify before the committee, saying, "As I struggle with the thicket of seniority, which is probably the bane of every new senator, frustration bubbles over... I have enormous respect for the tradition, the potential and the leadership of the Senate, but great dismay on organization." Much of my frustration centered on the three-day work week of the Senate. No votes were scheduled on Monday and Friday, so most members fled for their home districts Thursday evening and returned to Washington, D.C., late Monday. "The short weeks are a result of our efforts to return to our home states, to the concerns of our constituents. It is even more of a problem for those of us from the West. We do not work efficiently through this short week and we find our limited time at home ineffective as well."

I proposed that the Senate schedule two five-day work weeks, followed by a week's recess. We would get more work done in the Senate and have an opportunity to more effectively meet constituents at home. I also suggested that senators serve on fewer committees and that committee schedules be established to eliminate conflict and overlaps. Also, I said we should set aside occasional late afternoons for live debate on major issues. As things stood, our "debates" amounted to a series of statements delivered to a largely empty chamber. Reading the *Congressional Record* or listening to those hollow voices through an office squawk box is a thin substitute for the traditional debates the Senate was once noted for.

I was pleased to receive a letter from Senator Goldwater. He wholeheartedly endorsed my proposals. "Your biggest frustration in your first years in the Senate is going to be the thing we call seniority," he wrote. "I have never believed in seniority, but I'll swear I don't know how we can get around it. Seniority will put more incompetent people into responsible jobs than any other system that I know of, so if you can ever come up with a dream that can abolish it, we've got it made."

Many significant proposals were recommended by the committee, but little changed. Familiarity and comfort trumped reform. My frustration deepened. There was more of the same back home in Washington.

AS THE 1984 CAMPAIGN season accelerated, I was involved with the Republican State Convention for the first time in years. Militant anti-abortion activists, intent on seizing control of the convention, wanted to impose a litmus test. It would have required all delegates to the GOP National Convention to sign a declaration that they subscribed totally to the state party platform—*before* a platform had even been adopted. That was too much for many otherwise conservative delegates. The leader of the defeated radicals, Dottie Roberts of Snohomish County, declared, "We'll be back in two years and kick butt. The old hacks may be mad at me but that's OK. We don't lose."

The single-issue zealots cared little about budget and education issues, or even war and peace. Banning abortion was their cause, and they eventually succeeded in taking control of the state party. Many successful Republican candidates simply ignored the party hierarchy as a result.

53
DAMNATION DEEP AND WIDE

Senator Howard Metzenbaum, an unreconstructed liberal from Ohio, was lathered up over federal hydroelectric dams. "Where are all those conservatives who talk about government doing business like a business?" he huffed "Where are all of those who make the speeches about the need to balance the budget when it comes to giving away the power developed at Hoover Dam?"

It was August of 1984. The question was whether power from the mammoth Hoover Dam, which harnesses the Colorado River at the border between Nevada and Arizona, should be sold at current market rates or at rates necessary to pay the principal and interest on the cost of its construction during the 1930s. The differential was huge, with market rates as much as 10 times higher. The implications were huge for the Bonneville Power Administration and electrical customers throughout the Pacific Northwest.

The battle lines were fascinating. Staunch liberals and equally staunch conservatives advocated raising rates. Senators were taking sides based on whether their state's power rates would rise or fall.

I noted that the Saint Lawrence Seaway corporation serving Metzenbaum's state was not required to repay one dime for construction costs, interest or maintenance and operation—billions of dollars: "Is the total infrastructure of this nation going to be put up for sale to the highest bidder?" I asked. "Why not put our bridges, our waterways and locks and irrigation projects up for sale?" Barry Goldwater chimed in: "Put another way, the Metzenbaum proposal would tax electric consumers to solve federal budget problems."

The Senate, antsy for its month-long recess, voted 60-28 to limit debate on the issue to 100 hours. It's called "cloture"—rarely imposed since the Senate cherishes the right to unlimited debate.* The bill's opponents finally conceded defeat. The final vote was 64-34 to continue selling power from federal dams at cost. However, the battle was far from over. The Reagan Administration proposed market rates for the sale of Bonneville power in each succeeding budget. Senators from the West rallied repeatedly to defeat the measure.

After Labor Day we faced a huge stack of legislation and appropriations measures far behind schedule. The new fiscal year would begin on October 1, 1984, and none of the 13 bills had cleared Congress. It was apparent that once again the president would be faced with a huge omnibus appropriation bill with the grim choice of accepting all of the pork barrel spending or shutting down all of government.

---

* A vote for cloture brings a filibuster to an end. Cloture once required a two-thirds vote but after Southern senators regularly killed civil rights bills by filibuster, the Senate in frustration, reduced the requirement for cloture to 60 percent. It is still extraordinarily difficult to succeed in a cloture vote.

I strongly supported giving the president line-item veto authority, which I utilized regularly as governor. Senators Mack Mattingly of Georgia and Joe Biden of Delaware joined me as sponsors of a measure that would divide appropriations bills into separate spending items after passage but before they were sent to the president. Under this procedure, the president could sign or veto individual spending items. We eventually added 60 senators as co-sponsors and proposed to add the measure as an amendment to an important highway bill. The Appropriations Committee barons strenuously objected. This time, Hatfield was not an ally. He blasted the idea that a line-item veto could help reduce the federal deficit, saying, "It's simply not true. It's a false, unfounded delusion. It's a phony panacea."

With President Reagan at the White House. *White House Photo*

President Reagan and the head of the Office of Management and Budget endorsed our proposal, which left the Senate stalemated. With members clamoring to return home to campaign, I finally extracted a promise from each of the five senators seeking to replace Howard Baker as majority leader that they would bring the line-item veto issue to the floor early in the next Congress. It was fascinating to watch the thirst for adjournment create opportunities.

As we neared the end of the 98th Congress, I watched with dismay as members lined up to propose amendments to the comprehensive appropriations bill. We all recognized that the appropriations bill had to pass in order for the government to keep operating. Many members saw this as an opportunity to couple a boxcar-load of sidetracked bills to the appropriations locomotive they were certain would chug down Pennsylvania Avenue to the White House. The pressures for adjournment were in sharp conflict with the ambitions of those sponsoring controversial amendments. On several occasions I voted against amendments I favored in order to get an appropriation bill passed. I was rapidly becoming an advocate of the rule that exists in most state Legislatures and the U.S. House of Representatives—the requirement that amendments be relevant to the bill they seek to change.

LATE IN THE SESSION, Ted Kennedy proposed a civil rights amendment to the appropriations bill. It would have reversed a Supreme Court decision that narrowed federal anti-discrimination laws. His amendment deadlocked the Senate for five days as conservatives, led by Senator Orrin Hatch of Utah, used an array of obstructionist tactics to thwart the majority. In the event the Kennedy amendment was adopted, the opponents had prepared 1,300 amendments to keep the Senate in session for weeks. Finally, the Senate voted 53-45 against including the civil rights amendment. Slade Gorton and I voted to set the amendment aside, knowing there was no chance for action in the remaining hours of this Congress. Kennedy thundered, "Shame on this body! If Ronald Reagan should just wink, this bill would fly through the Senate!" Kennedy's co-sponsor, Robert Packwood of Oregon, also voted against the amendment, acknowledging it was a futile effort in a waning session.

Gorton and I were attacked by Nancyhelen Fisher, chairman of the Washington State Women's Political Caucus. "Women and minorities don't count in the present senators' priorities or in their hearts," she charged. It was either a blatantly political statement or Fisher had no understanding of the procedural landmines in the Senate. Slade and I reaffirmed our strong support for the civil rights measure and our intent to push for its passage in the next Congress.

In 1987, when a strong civil rights bill was finally passed. I joined the prime sponsors, Kennedy and Lowell Weicker of Connecticut, in hailing the legislation as an important advance in the battle for equality. Now the support was overwhelming. The bill passed the Senate 75-14, but Reagan vetoed it, proposing a watered-down alternative. I noted that I had received thousands of phone calls and letters expressing concern about the "evils and horrendous effects" of the Civil Rights Restoration Act. I was convinced that most of the critics had been influenced by the gross misinformation campaign waged by the Moral Majority and like-minded groups. The Senate voted 73-24 to override the president's veto—a rare occurrence. The Washington State Women's Political Caucus did not note my vote to override.

I CAMPAIGNED HARD for Governor Spellman and several legislative candidates in the fall of 1984. Every poll showed Reagan way ahead of Walter Mondale. Unfortunately, the president's popularity didn't seem to be boosting GOP candidates in Washington. From his first day in office, Spellman had grappled with tough choices. Faced with a serious recession, he was forced to raise taxes several times in order to balance a precarious budget, much to the disdain of conservative legislators. Spellman's challenger was Booth Gardner, a charismatic millionaire with an admirable record as Pierce County Executive. Gardner was the stepson of Norton Clapp, the powerful Weyerhaeuser executive who had been one of my earliest political supporters. Gardner had publicly identified himself as a Republican as late as 1968. Now he was an enterprising Democrat.

Slade and I barnstormed with Spellman, but a good man with a run of bad luck became a one-term governor. Though there was a lot to like about Booth—we would become friends and allies—I was sorry to see John Spellman leave office. Besides preserving essential state services during difficult economic times and protecting Puget Sound, he had given me two singular opportunities by appointing me to the Pacific Northwest Power Planning Council and the United States Senate.

Reagan won a second term with nearly 59 percent of the popular vote. Republicans maintained narrow control of the Senate. Seven new senators were elected, including John Kerry of Massachusetts and Al Gore of Tennessee. The new Republican senators included Phil Gramm from Texas and Jay Rockefeller from West Virginia. Mitch McConnell of Kentucky defeated the incumbent Democrat, Walter Huddleston, in an extremely close race. Illinois Senator Charles Percy, a formidable three-term Republican, was one of our casualties. After a bruising primary with conservative Congressman Tom Corcoran, Percy lost to bow-tied Democrat Paul Simon in a bitterly contested final. As chairman of the Senate Foreign Relations Committee, Percy had attempted to steer an even course on Mideast policy. But he angered the Israeli lobby when he voted to support the Reagan Administration's sale of AWACS planes to Saudi Arabia. The American Israeli Political Action Committee is a take-no-prisoners lobbying group feared by most members of Congress.

SOON AFTER TAKING MY SEAT in the Senate, I introduced a bill to study wages within the federal Civil Service. As governor years earlier, I attempted to set rational salaries for department heads and senior executives. We were puzzled on how to proceed until we discovered that the private sector faced the same problem. We hired a skilled consulting firm that produced an excellent report that gave us a basis for appropriate salaries for senior state executives. At all levels of state government women were paid substantially less than men doing equivalent jobs. In many cases the discrimination was blatant. I recognized that wages are generally set by the marketplace, but the marketplace was subject to discrimination by race and age, as well as gender. The concept that emerged to level the playing field became known as "Comparable Worth." Our proposal to begin the task of modifying state wages was upheld by Federal Judge Jack Tanner. While I disapproved of the rationale behind Tanner's decision, it did have the effect of initiating corrective measures by Washington state government.

A few days after the 1984 election, the chairman of the U.S. Civil Rights Commission, Clarence Pendleton, launched an attack on my bill, calling Comparable Worth "the looniest idea since Looney Tunes." I was astonished that Pendleton was heading the Civil Rights Commission. I guess I shouldn't have been surprised. A year earlier, the Reagan Administration had fired a number of its appointees, including Jill Ruckelshaus, the talented wife of EPA Director Bill Ruckelshaus. They said she was too liberal on civil rights. Years later, when I asked Jill about her dismissal, she said, "One night I was cooking dinner and the phone rang. Soon I heard the familiar voice of President Reagan thanking me for my service on the Civil Rights Commission. That was the first indication I had been removed."

54
THE GORGE

On a beautiful fall morning two days after the 1984 General Election, I arrived at the Skamania County Recreation Center in Stevenson, Washington. Its front yard was a thicket of signs opposing legislation to protect the Columbia Gorge. The breathtaking ancient glacial canyon stretches for 80 miles as the Columbia River winds its way to the Pacific.

I could barely maneuver my way through a standing-room-only crowd. Some people were clustered outside because the local fire marshal laid down the law on the capacity of the meeting room. I brought the meeting to order and recognized a delegation of Boy Scouts from Stevenson's Troop 321. As they presented the colors, I glanced around the room. I saw a slice of real America—a Norman Rockwell scene. It struck me as a wonderful alternative to a bevy of paid lobbyists in some sterile hearing room in Washington, D.C.

Preservation of the Columbia Gorge, a national treasure, rates as one of the most controversial—and ultimately satisfying—issues of my career in public life. The bill's tortuous path through Congress was a text-book case of dispute, debate, compromise, and finally, success.

For me, the trek began in 1970 when I met with my fellow governor and friend, Oregon's Tom McCall, on the banks of the Columbia to urge that efforts be expanded to preserve the unique beauty of the Gorge. Preservation efforts over many years, especially on the Oregon side, resulted in protection of much of the scenic vista, although interstate highway U.S. 84 slashed along the Oregon shoreline. During intervening years a variety of environmental organizations promoted federal protection of the Gorge. The Friends of the Gorge, viewed by many Gorge residents as Portland do-gooders, was the prime promoter of federal intervention. Residents in the rural counties on the Washington side of the river vehemently opposed any federal role. They detested the "granola crunching" Oregon interlopers.

Competing bills were introduced in 1982 and 1983. Oregon's senators, Packwood and Hatfield, proposed legislation that essentially turned over management of the Gorge to the U.S. Forest Service. That the bill was drafted by Friends of the Columbia Gorge added to the polarization. Jackson and Gorton refused to sign on as co-sponsors. Hatfield introduced another bill, which modified federal control by increasing the powers of a regional commission.

In 1983, Packwood held a Commerce Committee hearing in Hood River. Washingtonians stomped out, incensed that they were granted limited testimony, primarily because Packwood had little jurisdiction over environmental legislation. Before long, Packwood and Hatfield reintroduced their legislation. And two weeks later, Governor Spellman and Oregon Governor Vic Atiyeh teamed up to propose a radically different protection plan featuring a bi-state commission without a significant federal supervisory role. During much of 1984 little progress was made toward compromise. In staff discussions I suggested that a new hearing was necessary to sort out the competing proposals. I asked Senator McClure, chairman of the Energy and Natural Resources Committee, if I could hold a hearing in Stevenson, the center of the Gorge on the Washington side of the river. Warned that it could be a hostile session, I felt strongly that Washingtonians needed to be heard.

WHEN THE HEARING BEGAN, I related the history of Columbia Gorge legislative proposals and set some ground rules. With 200 people signed up to testify, at roughly three-minutes each, we could be there for nine hours. I wondered how I could ever respond to all those who had waited four years for the opportunity to express their opinions.

It didn't take long for pent-up tensions to explode. Governor-elect Gardner's representative, Dave Michener, testified for a strong federal presence, essentially endorsing Senator Packwood's bill. The room erupted in hooting and booing. I banged the gavel repeatedly, warning that I would not tolerate further outbursts.

I emphasized the need for civility to create consensus. Instead, we had the dueling stereotypes of "quiche-eating" urbanites in Volvos and Porsches out to make the Gorge their private playground vs. redneck locals thumbing their noses at conservation. "I've heard enough of that from both sides," I said, "and I just hope we can arrive at some place for everybody to get together." That put a dent in the mutual antagonism. But former governor Dixy Lee Ray earned a standing ovation when she declared, "No more arrogant individual walks this Earth than a Federal administrator coming into your area."

During the dinner break, I toured the Stevenson business district with Gary Olson, the Skamania County Auditor. He was a longtime friend and supporter. Almost every storefront boasted a sign stating "No federal control."

After dinner, the crowd slowly dwindled. No one responded to my call for any additional testimony. I said all those who attended deserved gold stars for patience. "We heard 125 witnesses today, which, if it isn't a new record, it ought to be. It went better than I could have hoped." I thanked the people of Stevenson for being good hosts. Someone in the audience piped up, "You deserve a gold medal yourself!" The applause that followed was gratifying. Giving people a chance to speak out on contentious issues not only reduces tensions but produces some pretty good ideas.

It would take two years and a huge effort to produce an appropriate federal act to protect the Gorge.

I ASKED JOE MENTOR, my staff member responsible for environmental issues, to wade through the maze of testimony and proposals and come up with a plan. It was apparent to me that the federally dominated management proposal urged by Senator Packwood and some environmental groups would not succeed. I was equally dismayed by the intransigence of many of the local residents and county officials who just wanted to be left alone. The Columbia Gorge is a unique natural wonder that belongs to all Americans.

We began by reviewing the Packwood bill strongly supported by environmentalists. Atiyeh and Spellman had proposed a radically different approach based on local control. Environmentalists trashed that proposal, which effectively pigeonholed the Packwood bill as too divisive. We attempted

Hiking with Joe Mentor in 1994, just below Lake of the Angels at the new boundary of the Olympic National Park. *Courtesy Joe Mentor*

to work with Packwood's staff to inventory the land in the Gorge and define critical areas. I thought we might make progress if we analyzed specific land areas to determine what needed special protection. When that effort was completed, we urged Vic Atiyeh and his new fellow governor, Booth Gardner, to sponsor a staff retreat with congressional and gubernatorial representatives to attempt to reach a unified position.

The focus now was on resolving differences. Senator Packwood and some environmental groups insisted that the Gorge be under the management of the National Park Service, but most opted for the U.S. Forest Service since it already had a significant land base in the Gorge. Local officials continued to oppose any bill, but began to realize protective legislation was inevitable. I announced I would only support a measure if the four senators and two governors reached consensus. Senator Hatfield joined Gorton and me to urge Packwood to co-sponsor a reasonable bill.

Mentor was in charge of drafting the bill. I came in early the day it was set for introduction. Joe was sitting at his desk, blank-eyed from exhaustion. He had finished drafting the bill late the night before, but when he hit the "print" button the text of the bill disappeared. We were working with a crotchety pre-Microsoft program called Prime. Joe had worked all night trying to retrieve the bill draft. Finally, in total frustration minutes before I arrived, he typed in "Fuck You!" The machine promptly disgorged the entire bill! The staff concluded it might be a useful new computer command.

IN FEBRUARY OF 1986 the legislative logjam broke. Mike Lowry and a fellow Democrat, Oregon Congressman Jim Weaver, introduced Senator Packwood's old bill. Although there was still some debate on standards and enforcement measures, the four Northwest senators, Hatfield, Packwood, Gorton and me, joined in introducing S.2055. We believed it would be a starting point for further efforts to reach consensus. "There are many who strongly support Federal legislation to protect the Columbia Gorge," I said. "And there are many who vigorously oppose it. Yet we all share a common love for its compelling beauty. We must work together to protect the pastoral environment of this unique area, to preserve its scenic beauty and the lifestyle of its residents for generations to come." Sid Morrison and Ron Wyden, an Oregon Democrat, introduced an identical bill in the House, while Don Bonker of Washington and Oregon's Les AuCoin introduced a parallel version of their own. Now the dance of legislation began.

Establishing the entire Scenic Area as a unit of the U.S. Forest Service was anathema to most local residents, the Reagan Administration, Senator McClure and me. We proposed four large Special Management Areas that would become part of the National Forest system and 12 urban areas exempt from the act. Neither environmentalists nor local residents liked the boundaries of the urban areas. I concluded that our choices were probably pretty reasonable.

In my view, the critical element of the entire bill was establishment of a regional commission, composed of local representatives who would play an important role in planning and administering the act. Adoption of a management plan for the Gorge would require a two-thirds vote of the 12-member commission. The plan would then be submitted to the Secretary of Agriculture for approval or modification. The Regional Commission would retain the authority to override the secretary by a two-thirds vote. That led environmental groups to demand an even larger vote to override since they had little faith in either local governments or citizens of the area. I thought they were overreaching and warned they could end up with nothing.

The legislative process is tedious, but the clear benefit is accurate wording that can be relied upon by administrators and citizens alike. The bill was improved by strengthening standards, protecting several rivers under the Wild and Scenic Rivers Act, and adding modestly to the list of exempt urban areas. In an effort to help local communities, we added an interpretive center on the Oregon side of the river and a conference center on the Washington side. Funding for land acquisition, recreation facilities, and the two centers required a recommended appropriation of $70 million.

AFTER ANOTHER HEARING in Stevenson we four Northwest senators agreed on the amended bill. In August of 1986 it unanimously passed the Senate Energy and Natural Resources Committee.

After the August recess, action shifted to the House, where the urge to adjourn to hit the campaign trail was a strong weapon for opponents of Gorge protection legislation. Conservative Republicans offered scores of amendments as a delaying tactic. Opponents also thwarted attempts to move the bill out of subcommittees. They made a fatal error, however, by not showing up to a key committee meeting. The chairman moved the bill out of committee by unanimous consent even though a quorum was not present. Late-arriving Republican opponents of the legislation sputtered their indignation while the Democratic committee members chuckled.

Nevertheless, Congress was speeding toward adjournment and the Columbia Gorge legislation had not passed either House.

The Senate created another problem. Chairman McClure, Senator Malcolm Wallop of Wyoming and the Reagan Administration declared the bill unacceptable. They were worried primarily about federal authority over private land and the potential cost of the legislation. I told Mentor it was absolutely necessary to retain the authority of the Secretary of Agriculture over the most important lands in the Gorge. We engaged in intense negotiations and ultimately reached a fragile compromise that I felt would preserve the most important elements of the Gorge bill. We found a tiny gap in the Senate schedule and Senator Hatfield succeeded in bringing the revised bill to the floor. Hatfield and I engaged in extended talks with McClure and Wallop to clarify the amendments we proposed. These formal "colloquies" are important to help establish legislative intent on complex or controversial issues.

Finally, the bill passed the Senate by a voice vote.

Adjournment was hours away and the House had still not acted. Now the Justice Department intervened. The Reagan Administration clearly was trying to derail the bill. The House Rules Committee was our last hope. Majority Whip Tom Foley, a masterful tactician, convinced the committee to meet and allow the bill to proceed to the floor, with the proviso that only three amendments would be allowed. That decisive move by our ally from Spokane—a future Speaker of the House—broke the back of the opposition. The bill passed the House with an overwhelming majority. The next day we brought the bill to the Senate floor where it passed unanimously on the last day of the second session of the 99th Congress, October 18, 1986.

Would Reagan sign the bill? The Justice and Interior departments recommended a veto, while we four Northwest senators urged the president to sign the legislation. We received word from the White House congressional liaison that a veto was pending.

I told reporters that a veto would be "an extraordinary slap in the face for the senators, and we may have to go down there and tell them that." Finally, a month after congressional passage and on the last day before the bill would die, Reagan signed it, stating, "While I am strongly opposed to federal regulation of private land use planning, I am signing this bill because of the far-reaching support in both states for a solution to the long-standing problems relating to management of the Columbia River Gorge."

The Columbia Gorge Act was enormously controversial and probably the most complicated measure I worked on during my time in the U.S. Senate. Environmental activists, concerned over protection of this unique place, fought local residents who felt their heritage was being stolen from them. Questions of local control versus federal domination and who should pay for protection had raged for years. Controversy still surrounds the Columbia Gorge Act, although logging has been replaced by tourism as a major source of jobs in the region.

55
EVANS AGONISTES

David Stockman, Reagan's young supply-side guru, oversaw the Office of Management and Budget. They called him "the father of Reaganomics." He was frequently the mother of all duplicity, once admitting, "None of us really understands what's going on with all these numbers."

When Congress convened for a new session in 1985, Stockman proposed that BPA electric power rates in the Northwest be raised to "market rates"—a proposal generated by the Grace Commission, a business group formed to suggest ways to balance the federal budget.

I had thought the irrational idea was dead, if not buried, after the previous year when the Senate voted more than two to one to limit

President Reagan with David Stockman, the "Father of Reaganomics" as director of the Office of Management & Budget. *White House Photo*

increases. When I called Stockman and Secretary of Energy Don Hodel to protest, Stockman retorted, "Show me some numbers."

My staff and I prepared a 24-page report. It documented that the "market rates" plan amounted to a 50 percent electric rate increase that would close nine of the 10 aluminum plants in the Northwest and eliminate 70,000 jobs overall. I was a budget hawk, but this wrong-headed cost-saving measure made no sense or cents. The cost of unemployment would exceed the expected revenue. Stockman, desperate to find ways to reduce the federal deficit, refused to back down. The only good news was that he promised that the administration would not attempt to implement rate increases administratively. When he attempted to reach a compromise on a rate increase, I flatly refused to dicker, saying, "If the thing is wrong, it's wrong."

The fight shifted to Congress, particularly the Senate. I knew we had a winning hand. Gorton and I got Senate leadership to declare that Stockman's proposal would not even be considered as a budget-balancing tool. It helped immensely that Oregon's senators, Hatfield and Packwood, headed Appropriations and Finance, while Senator McClure of Idaho headed Energy and Natural Resources. Leadership immediately grasped the fight was over. We were forced to remove this proposal from each succeeding budget during the Reagan presidency. By August, Stockman was gone.

EARLY IN THE 99TH CONGRESS I joined with Senator Mack Mattingly, a junior Republican from Georgia, to once again sponsor a measure giving the president line-item veto authority. I intended to test the promise made by the candidates hoping to succeed Howard Baker as Majority Leader to bring this measure to the floor early in the new Congress.

Mattingly and I were thrilled when a clear majority of senators joined our effort. However, we were adamantly opposed by senior senators on Hatfield's Appropriations Committee. Mark and I were close friends, having served together as governors, but the gloves were off on this one. Hatfield persisted in calling the line-item veto "constitutional madness" and claimed the proposal was "a mindless affront to the concept of separate but equal branches of government... an open invitation to political mischief... and a nasty swamp that serves as a breeding ground for lawsuits, confusion and escalated confrontation."

I retorted that Congress was in the midst of an institutional crisis. The budget and spending procedures in place were a miserable failure. "We have missed every budget deadline so far this year," I said. "The budget process is in shambles. Is this any way to run a government?" I was surprised, yet pleased when Ted Kennedy joined the fray, saying the deficit was out of control and Congress was part of the problem.

President Reagan called individual senators, urging an end to the filibuster. We voted three times on cloture. Needing 60 votes, we came close repeatedly, the last vote 58 to 40. Exasperated, Bob Dole pulled the bill from the floor, claiming further attempts were unlikely to succeed.

In all, 11 presidents proposed line-item vetoes. Bill Clinton finally succeeded in 1996. The bill was immediately challenged by several senators. The U.S. Supreme Court, in a 6-3 decision, declared the law unconstitutional. Congress and presidents will continue this struggle for power as long as the congressional appropriations system is broken. I was dismayed to be forced to vote, after little debate, on an enormous appropriation bill that no one could fully explain and which contained hundreds of hidden earmarks. At the very least, Congress should be required to vote upon and send to the president separately each of the 13 appropriations bills that are introduced at the beginning of each year.

IN FEBRUARY OF 1985, Reagan presented his budget for fiscal 1986. He was consistent with past budgets, proposing a 6 percent real increase in defense, deep cuts in domestic spending but retaining cost-of-living increases in Social Security. The Congressional Budget Office, a nonpartisan professional organization that provides unbiased fiscal information to Congress, immediately reported that the president's deficit target was far too optimistic. The Democratic leadership in the House vehemently opposed increases in military spending and demanded that cuts in domestic programs be restored. Reagan adamantly opposed any tax increases but just as strongly urged increases for the military. Senate leadership pushed hard for deficit reduction and proposed that all programs share part of the burden. We were heading for a train wreck.

By early May enthusiasm for a one-year budget freeze on all programs, including Social Security cost-of-living adjustments, gained momentum. I was an enthusiastic supporter because all interests would share the pain modestly in an effort to reach a balanced budget. I also recognized that a one-year freeze would set a new base for spending in future years and represented a major step toward a rational federal budget.

One of the dramatic votes in the history of the U.S. Senate occurred on May 10, 1985. It was showdown time on the budget resolution. At 1:32 a.m., the doors to the chamber swept open as Senator Pete Wilson of California arrived in a wheelchair. He was recovering from an emergency appendectomy but insisted on leaving the hospital to take part in this critical vote. We cheered and applauded as he approached the dais. "Senator Wilson votes aye!" he said in a firm voice. That made it 49-49. Vice President Bush broke the tie. Delighted, I thought the vote would put pressure on the House to adopt an effective deficit-reduction proposal.

The AARP claimed we were balancing the budget on the backs of the elderly. Military groups wailed at the freeze on military spending. Not one program was cut, however, and the Senate vote merely required that everyone live within their current budget for one year. We were prepared to assist low-income elderly people during the year, but that voice was unheard in the tsunami of objections by those sucking on the government's teat, predicting national disaster if we even attempted to balance the budget.

House members frantically fled from the COLA freeze on Social Security but pushed for even larger cuts in military spending. Reagan vowed, "I'll repeat it until I'm blue in the face: I will veto any tax increase the Congress sends me."

The president invited congressional leaders to the White House on a hot summer evening. The group gathered on a terrace under a large oak tree. Drinks were served and the group began discussing budget alternatives. Someone, half-jokingly, suggested that a solution should include raising taxes. The president protested loudly. Speaker Tip O'Neill slammed his big fist on the table and yelled, "All right, Goddammit! If that's the way it's going to be, then everything is off the table with me, too!" The exchange caused everyone to attempt conciliation.

O'Neill knew exactly what he was doing. Ultimately he reached an agreement with the president to allow more military spending and protect the COLA increases he treasured. The Senate was double-crossed by the administration with catastrophic consequences. Dole charged that Reagan was surrendering to the deficit. We all felt abandoned. Senator Warren Rudman of New Hampshire said it best: "People feel they flew a Kamikaze mission and ended up in flames and got nothing for it."

In the elections of 1986, Democratic senatorial candidates kept reminding the elderly that Republicans had frozen their COLAs the year before. We lost eight seats and control of the Senate, which we did not regain for eight years. Reagan faced much more difficulty with his legislative program in the last two years of his presidency. Any attempts to control costs of Social Security turned politically toxic and the long-term ramifications were huge. Decades later, the deficit keeps growing. Congress has no stomach to make the tough decisions necessary to stabilize Social Security.

ONE OF THE MOST CONTENTIOUS ISSUES of the 99th Congress was foreign trade. History ought to teach us important things. The competing philosophies of protectionism and free trade divided the Colonies and almost derailed our Constitutional Convention. Ever since, states, industries, regions and politicians have debated this question, usually from their own self-interest. Early attempts to protect American industry from European imports shifted to Asia when burgeoning new economies threatened American producers. Members of Congress from North and South Carolina joined to protect their textile industry from an onslaught of inexpensive clothing imports. The House of Representatives quickly passed a textile protection bill and the Senate faced a wave of demands to follow suit.

New moves toward protectionism were extraordinarily bad news for Washington, the most trade dependent state in the nation. Determined to vigorously oppose the bill, I contacted Clayton Yeutter, our U.S. trade ambassador and volunteered to help. He was enthusiastic about my offer since few in the Senate were willing to oppose the Barons of the South, Strom Thurmond and Fritz Hollings of South Carolina and Jesse Helms of North Carolina. Yeutter scheduled an early strategy session with President Reagan. I was invited to sit in. I liked the strong free-trade concepts championed by Reagan.

When Congress reconvened after Labor Day, 1985, a bill to limit textile and apparel imports was expanded to include footwear in order to expand support of senators from shoe manufacturing states. The battle extended over the next two years in a procedural brawl that was a fascinating test of the Senate's long tradition of extended debate.

Thurmond was a prime supporter and eloquent practitioner of the filibuster. His Democratic seatmate, Fritz Hollings, was equally devoted to extended debate. They joined in introducing a bill to limit textile and apparel imports to the United States. The bill was appropriately assigned to the Finance Committee's trade subcommittee chaired by Senator John Danforth of Missouri. He promptly informed the South Carolinians that their bill did not have the votes to be reported from the Finance Committee. Thurmond waited for an appropriate vehicle, then pounced.

The Senate turned to approval of a major treaty entitled *The Compact of Free Association*, the result of 40 years of negotiations between the United States and the Federated States of Micronesia and the Marshall Islands to ensure independence for the islands while maintaining a special relationship with the U.S. Now, the compact was ready for approval by the United States Senate. Senator Thurmond, fully aware of the compact's importance, deftly appended his textile bill, which was languishing in the Finance Committee. He added 43 other sponsors, including 21 Southerners dedicated to protecting the textile industry, 11 Northeasterners and seven Midwesterners equally dedicated to protecting the shoe industry. It was going to be a latter-day civil war—not between the North and South, but between the East and West. Westerners were generally engaged in newer industries that competed well internationally. I was leading the free trade Western bloc, squaring off with two of the most senior and clever senators in the chamber.

The sponsors of the textile bill were clever to have included shoe manufacturing in their proposal. That secured the support of senators from Maine, Pennsylvania and Missouri. We Western senators, our states deeply involved in trade with Asia, stood firm. Those from agricultural states worried about retaliation if we increased trade barriers. Party lines blurred as the debate turned into regional combat. I said the legislation would ignite an internal trade war pitting one region against another, one state against another, one industry against another and workers against workers.

The failure of a tabling motion by McClure forced Dole to withdraw the Micronesia Bill from consideration to allow other business of the Senate to continue. Since it was already October and late in the session, I thought the issue would die. I underestimated both the determination and craftiness of my South Carolina colleagues. With their original bill now stalled in the Finance Committee, they proposed a new and thoroughly disruptive idea: They would attach it as an amendment to the budget reconciliation bill. Amendments are intended to be germane to the bill, but even that did not slow down Thurmond and Hollings.

This whole episode sums up my frustration with the convoluted duplicity I discovered in the United States Senate, an institution I had long revered.

Hollings soared into one of his famous speeches, hammering at fair trade in his stentorian voice tempered by his honeyed Southern accent. "There is a fierce global competition out there, and our government is just sitting on the sidelines while American industry is getting its hindquarters kicked. The myth is that there is free enterprise on the world marketplace—that world trade is open and fair. This is not just a myth, it is a pipe dream. There is no free enterprise on the world market, only government to government enterprise."

The South Carolina senator detailed examples of countries limiting imports. "They love it because we keep it open to their industries while they shut their own markets to our industries. Good old Uncle Sam has become good old Uncle Sucker." He rambled on for almost an hour.

I jumped in, saying the fundamental question was not textile protectionism. It was whether the Senate would retain its unique position as the only legislative body in the world devoted to unfettered debate. After inserting into the record historic statements by Robert La Follette, John Stennis and Lyndon B. Johnson supporting the right of free debate, I read a similar statement by Thurmond to drive home my point. "Should any simple majority, 51 members, be allowed to silence all other members on any matter before the body … we would, in my opinion, die as a unique body and take our place in a long and dismal line of ordinary Parliaments and Congresses."

In spite of the oratory and the monstrous precedent being set, the Senate voted 57 to 39 to proceed with the textile bill amendment. We finally got to a vote on the major amendment by Thurmond, which carried 54 to 42. This was our high water mark in opposition. It was a battle between East and West all over again, with only five Eastern senators voting for open trade and five Westerners voting for protection.

Leadership finally realized a destructive force had been unleashed. Robert Byrd of West Virginia, the Minority Leader, rose to propose an amendment on behalf of himself and Majority Leader Dole. The essence of the amendment was this: A super-majority would be required to successfully appeal the ruling of the chair. I cheered silently but recognized that this proposal was an amendment to the reconciliation bill, which might not even make it through the Congress.

When the final debate began it was apparent that the vote on each proposed amendment would be virtually identical, with the Eastern senators prevailing over the West. "How can we cohesively move together when we pit East against West, when we trade off a textile worker for an aircraft worker or a farmer for a seamstress?" I asked. "The question at stake here is whether this is in America's best interest? I think not, if the end result is to destroy our trade relationships with two of our strongest allies in the Pacific; if it would cut off our good relationships that currently exist with the People's Republic of China... and especially when, in relationship to Hong Kong, we say we cannot stand the competition of a truly free trader."

The final vote was 60 to 39 in favor of the textile bill. The hundreds of hours of debate, skirmishing, amendments and maneuvering did not change a single vote. Most senators voting in favor were attempting to protect industries in decline, while Western senators, whose states were deeply engaged in foreign trade, rejected this protectionist bill. Reagan promptly vetoed the legislation and I began the task of finding at least 34 senators who would vote to sustain the president. The House of Representatives delayed action on a veto override vote until the next year. The lawmakers used the threat as pressure on the administration while they negotiated a new international agreement covering textile and apparel imports.

In the summer of 1986 I was at a luncheon meeting of the Republican Wednesday Group with about 20 moderate senators when we received word that the House had sustained the president's veto of the textile bill by 14 votes. Other senators congratulated me on leading the opposition. I thought then that we had won the fight. Was I wrong! Textile protection bills kept reappearing in each Congress. Reagan and ultimately George H. W. Bush just as regularly vetoed them.

56
A LESS PERFECT UNION

Senator Phil Gramm's down-home drawl was deceptive. The economics professor with a Ph.D. was one shrewd Texan. Gramm was a former Democratic congressman, jumping ship in 1983 after refusing to toe the party line. He had regularly attempted to install a procedure to automatically reduce spending if the budget wasn't balanced. Now, with all attempts to cut the deficit in shambles, the newly-minted senator dusted off his House proposal and set out to enlist co-sponsors with some seniority. Phil was a take-no-prisoners fiscal conservative, yet he quickly grasped that the Senate looked askance at the raucous combat allowed in the House.

Warren Rudman of New Hampshire, a widely respected, hard-working senator, was disappointed by the gridlock. "This place is 99 percent frustration and 1 percent exhilaration," he once told a reporter. "It's hard to live on that 1 percent." Rudman read Gramm's plan and recognized it was a golden opportunity to require Congress and the president to reach effective budget-reduction goals. When he recruited Fritz Hollings, the wily South Carolina Democrat, as a third sponsor Gramm-Rudman-Hollings was born.

"Gramm-Rudman," GRH for short, mandated automatic across-the-board spending cuts if the president and Congress failed to reach specific targets to balance the budget. It was a draconian approach to what I viewed as a growing crisis. Tom Foley, the House Democratic whip, summed it up with a wonderful Tom Clancy metaphor. He said Gramm-Rudman was "about the kidnapping of the beloved only child of the president's official family" (think Defense) "and holding it in a dark basement and sending the president its ear." But the hostage game worked two ways, Foley said. "Democrats could slice defense's ear only by doing the same to their own 'children.'"

I respected Rudman, and I shared his frustration at the inability of the Senate to make tough decisions, especially on budget matters. The "oak tree" agreement between Reagan and Tip O'Neill convinced me that effective deficit reduction would not come voluntarily. I signed on as a supporter of the Gramm-Rudman-Hollings Balanced Budget and Emergency Deficit Control Act of 1985. Putting the deficit reduction program on autopilot didn't seem like a great idea, but there were no reasonable alternatives. As I watched weeks go by and the rancor grow between the House, the Senate and the president, I became more and more convinced Gramm-Rudman's harsh medicine was the only cure.

After huge floor fights, rancorous conference committees and unbelievable lobbying pressure, Gramm-Rudman passed the House on August 1, the Senate on October 10 and became law on December 12, 1985. Senator Rudman said it best, "It's a bad idea whose time has come."

Analysts predicted debilitating cuts in important programs. Senators and congressmen were frightened by the potential fallout. Lobbyists were terrified. Efforts promptly began to castrate what critics saw as a monstrous animal. To this day, few in Congress enthusiastically support deficit reduction. The politically unpalatable reality is that to effectively reduce deficits we must cut popular programs or raise taxes, or both. Such negative consequences spell doom. It did not take many years for Gramm-Rudman to be dismantled.

A COMPELLING ALTERNATIVE to Gramm-Rudman was the proposal developed by a task force I co-chaired with Virginia Governor Chuck Robb, one of Lyndon Johnson's sons-in-law. The Committee on Federalism and National Purpose worked for a year to produce a final report. When we issued *To Form a More Perfect Union* at the beginning of 1986, Neal Peirce, a distinguished national columnist, wrote: "Two contrasting events occurred as the fortune wheel of our national fate spun wildly in Washington last week. On the one hand, a confused Congress embraced Gramm-Rudman-Hollings, surely the most draconian budget-slashing bill of American history. Yet simultaneously, a task force headed by Evans and Robb announced an intriguing, potentially historic blueprint to straighten out the mess in the American federal system."

Our task force boasted an array of prescient politicians, including governors, mayors and members of Congress, and thoughtful leaders from business, labor, education and law. Thoroughly bipartisan, the task force engaged in lively yet unfailingly civil debate. We learned from each other and from a long list of experts on governmental organization. Gradually the group produced an outline for a major reorganization of responsibility between federal, state and local governments. "A consensus did emerge," Peirce wrote. "There may be a window of opportunity, even in a season of fiscal crisis, to achieve a grand trade-off of functions that would promote a federal system that's both more humane and more efficient."

We proposed dividing governmental functions between those that are national in nature and those that are regional or local. Our fundamental recommendation was that the federal government should assume financial responsibility for the safety net of welfare and medical care. Welfare would be converted into job systems. And benefits would be more uniform across the country. We identified hundreds of current federal programs that were primarily local or regional in nature and proposed that they be returned to states and local communities. We proposed that the transition be revenue neutral, but strongly believed that better levels of service ultimately could be produced at significantly less cost by eliminating duplication of action by federal state and local agencies.

Peirce ended his insightful commentary on the report this way: "Implementing the Evans-Robb proposals would be politically controversial. But there is a certain magic in them: the possibility that while official Washington stumbles over its own errors and excesses, a new national consensus is forming around the two simple ideas: more power to the states and the people, and more equity."

I attempted to translate the report into a legislative package. Unfortunately, few in Congress or the Reagan Administration were willing to assist because our proposal was so far-reaching. The president had other priorities, even though I believe he endorsed the fundamental concepts we proposed. Congressional leaders were so exhausted by the debate over Gramm-Rudman that they were unwilling to propose any new ideas until they measured the results of the fiscal restraint bill they had just adopted. It was apparent that a junior senator could not bring a proposal of this magnitude to fruition, and neither the president nor congressional leaders chose to lead. We lost an unusual opportunity to reconstruct our federal system in a manner that actually would have formed a more perfect union.

The first session of the 99th Congress finally adjourned in exhaustion a few days before Christmas 1985. We failed to finish action on the maze of appropriations bills. More disappointingly, we failed to slow the growth of spending. Notwithstanding Gramm-Rudman, we had done little to dent the deficit. As I surveyed 1986, an election year, I was worried about Slade Gorton and the other first-term senators elected in the Reagan landslide of 1980. The Democrats and their allies, busy raising bundles of campaign money, were itching to regain control of the Senate.

AFTER THE HOLIDAYS, I joined a Senate delegation on an overseas trip to participate in the North Atlantic Assembly in Istanbul, with a three-day stop in Rome and a private audience with Pope John Paul II. He shook hands with each of us and offered a few remarks. He struck me as tired. Given that he was one of the most traveled world leaders in history—and a formidable politician in his own right—that was understandable. The most striking part of his wardrobe was the pair of brown Gucci loafers peeking out from his flowing robe. The high-fashion shoes seemed so incongruous.

Our stay in Istanbul was filled with stultifying meetings of the Assembly, interspersed with rewarding visits to museums and the colorful bazaars that make this ancient city so fascinating. As we boarded our plane for the long trip home I was reminded again of the difficulty of gaining information when you are part of a large congressional delegation. I decided that from then on I would stick to individual trips and pick the nations and officials from whom I could learn valuable lessons on the intricacies of foreign relations.

That opportunity would come quickly. I had scheduled a 16-day trip to the Association of Southeast Asia Nations. I was accompanied by Nancy and Chris Dawson, my foreign affairs staff member. It was a highly rewarding yet exhausting trip, with 68 meetings with high governmental officials in the Philippines, Thailand, Indonesia, Malaysia and Singapore. In each country I met with an American Chamber of Commerce and received impressively candid commentary, both on the difficulties of entering foreign markets and the frustration over the reluctance of American manufacturers to modify products to fit those markets.

Our visit to the Philippines concentrated on land reform and agricultural productivity, as well as the ongoing rebellion of groups in the southern Philippines. The highlight was my visit with the country's new president, Corazon "Cory" Aquino. Earlier in the year, Ferdinand Marcos had called a quick election, believing he could prevail over a divided opposition. He was declared the victor over Aquino, but widespread election fraud caused the Catholic Church in the Philippines and many foreign governments to reject the results. Aquino led a massive peaceful protest that drove Marcos from power. She faced internal opposition from those who could not abide the reality of a woman president.

Aquino greeted us with unexpected warmth and enthusiasm. In her nine months in power she had survived several coup attempts by disgruntled members of the military. We talked of the need for economic revival in the Philippines and the difficulty of responding to the communist insurgency. I was impressed with her plans and determination. I flashed back to a meeting with Marcos a decade earlier. We were ushered into a room illuminated only by a spotlight trained on the president. He was seated at an enormous desk on an elevated platform. We sat in chairs below, gazing up at his ostensibly regal presence. His first two terms had been positive. Then rampant graft and corruption ensued, which led to martial law. He maintained power with an iron fist. Ultimately the people prevailed. They elected Aquino.

In Bangkok, I received word that Nancy's sister, Mary, had died after a long bout with breast cancer. It was terribly difficult to break the news to Nancy, who adored her older sister. In a hotel restaurant specializing in Thai cuisine, we sat together holding hands and quietly watched a young Thai woman carve intricate flowers out of oversized carrots. It was a remarkably soothing and healing experience to see beauty emerge from ordinary vegetables.

The next day we flew to the Thai-Cambodian border to visit the Khao-I-Dang refugee center. The entry lane was dominated by a large sign: "Welcome Senator Daniel J. Evans." I don't know who was responsible, but it was obvious that everyone from Thai officials to refugee camp residents wanted help from the United States. We saw the sobering results of the incessant rebellion in Cambodia: 25,000 refugees lived in tiny bamboo huts, some Cambodian of various factions and some Vietnamese. The primitive medical facilities were hopelessly inadequate to treat the horrifying results of landmine explosions and rapidly spreading infectious diseases. We talked with many of the refugees. Most simply had one dream. As we strode toward the exit, a teenage Cambodian boy ran alongside. "Senator Evans," he cried in impeccable English, "take me to the United States!" I left, knowing it was highly unlikely, given our foreign aid priorities, that the people left behind in the forgotten aftermath of the Vietnamese war would receive any significant assistance from America.

I returned home with a detailed briefing book that would be of great help in my responsibilities on the Foreign Relations Committee. Individual congressional visits are probably an imposition on embassies and officials, but I remain convinced that they are of great value when they clearly fit the responsibilities of the member of Congress—as opposed to sightseeing junkets. Abuses of congressional travel offend me.

THE AGENDAS of the Foreign Relations and Energy and Natural Resources Committees on which I served were packed with important issues. After 2½ years in the Senate, I was learning how to juggle schedules, respond to constant questions from the press, listen to a steady stream of entreaties from citizens and lobbyists, consult with staff on difficult issues, devour information from an endlessly full inbox and still find time for Nancy and family. Anyone who thinks being in Congress is a piece of cake ought to try it for a month. The same naysayers maintain teachers are overpaid because they "get the summer off." Try spending a day in a classroom of first graders.

57
CONTRA-DICTIONS

Secretary of State George Shultz was in no mood for irony in February of 1986 when he appeared before the Senate Foreign Relations Committee to defend the administration's open-ended request to increase aid to the Nicaraguan "Contra" rebels attempting to overthrow the left-wing Sandinista *junta* headed by President Daniel Ortega.*

I noticed that one of the State Department's charts showed rebel strength was actually higher when Congress reduced aid. "Three more years of no aid and the opposition may be larger than the government's army," I observed with a slight smile. Shultz, red-faced, pounded the table. "Is that a flip comment?" he demanded. "It's a very serious subject." I said my remark was made in jest, but continued pressing him on the lack of specificity in his proposal. His testiness betrayed that this was a high-stakes issue for the Reagan administration.

A month later I received a call from the White House. Could I meet with the president regarding "Central American issues"? That was the current code phrase for aid to the Contras. As I awaited the president in the first floor library of the White House, I remembered it was the room where FDR gave his famous "Fireside Chats." There was no fireplace, but leather-bound books filled shelves on all four walls. I was examining the titles with interest when Admiral John Poindexter, the president's stuffy National Security Adviser, entered the room. Just then, Ronald Reagan, rosy cheeked, breezed in: "Hi, Dan, how are things going? How's Nancy?" Every time we met I asked myself, "How can you not like this guy?" I disagreed with Reagan on many issues, but his warmth never seemed contrived.

Reagan emphasized that he was intent on stemming the spread of communism in Central America, particularly in Nicaragua, by providing military and financial aid to the rebels. I questioned him about the wisdom of his plan since it was not enthusiastically endorsed by the neighboring nations. Ever the Cold Warrior, he insisted it made sense. The conversation eventually shifted to free trade issues where I was a strong ally. Afterward, Reagan walked with me to the first floor entrance of the White House. We chatted about our children and our years as governors. Years later, when the Reagan diaries were published, I was fascinated to find an entry on our meeting. "I think I moved him somewhat," Reagan wrote. Actually, no.

When I got back to the office, Bill Jacobs, my chief of staff, and Chris Dawson, our foreign affairs staffer, anxiously wanted details. With some wonderment, I noted that it now dawned on me that in our entire 45-minute conversation, the president never directly asked for my vote on the Contra issue. I drafted the elements of what I thought would be a responsible Central American policy. The

---

* "Contra" is short for counter-revolutionary.

next day I delivered a speech on the Senate floor:

> Oh how quickly we forget! One month ago we all celebrated events in the Philippines. [The "People Power" revolution that ended the Marcos era.] It was hailed as a triumph of American foreign policy, as indeed it was. We should have learned some lessons from the success in the Philippines and from the historical high points of American foreign policy. Three elements seem to continue to be repeated when American foreign policy succeeds:
>
> It is bipartisan. It represents a unity of effort between the legislative and executive branches. And the leadership comes from those countries most directly involved.
>
> All were present in the Philippines. We were united—Republican and Democrat. We were united—Executive and Legislative. And the leadership came spectacularly from the people in the Philippines themselves. We are now headed for votes that I am afraid will violate all three of these principles. We have a bitter, partisan division. We have heard strident voices from the administration—accusations about loyalty, Americanism and patriotism. These have no place in a successful American foreign policy.

I reviewed the history of American intervention in Nicaragua over more than a century, saying we were caught in a Catch-22. We said negotiations wouldn't work and that the left-wingers wouldn't share power voluntarily. So the alternative supposedly was to offer military aid to the Contras. "But I have heard no one yet assert that $100 million in aid would overthrow or assist in overthrowing that government. In fact they say we don't intend that is the purpose. Well, if negotiations won't work and we won't overthrow the government with this aid, where does that leave us? It looks to me like it leaves us with nasty, extended, dirty warfare escalating on both sides. Who will die? Nicaraguans. Who will suffer? Nicaraguans."

Reminding the Senate that we had failed to deliver our promised aid to Central American nations, I proposed a program for a Central American policy: First, foremost and up front, we needed to reassert our commitment to multi-year economic aid to the democratically-elected governments in Central America—Costa Rica, Honduras, Guatemala and El Salvador. The best way to contain a communist-run Nicaragua was to reward our friends in the neighborhood. We also needed to recognize that the problems in Central America were primarily Central American problems. Negotiations to solve them ought to be led by Central Americans. Impossible preconditions were a prescription for failure. To require that the Contras be the negotiators with the Sandinistas "is very much like saying that before Israelis and Jordanians can negotiate, the Palestinian Liberation Organization must be at the same table. Human rights, free elections and national reconciliation are all devout wishes, not preconditions."

Finally, I said we had to reassert our determination to join with others under the Rio Treaty—the 1947 reciprocal assistance pact—in opposing armed aggression by Nicaragua against its neighbors. "This is the core of a comprehensive policy that aids our friends, builds upon their strengths, isolates and confines the Nicaraguan government and gives to Latin Americans the chance to lead in resolving the critical conflict that is rapidly approaching. Unfortunately, none of the current proposals meet this test. I hope that before final congressional action is taken we step back, lower our partisan defenses and seek that elusive but vital strategy that will unite us and that will work."

A number of senators sought me out after the speech to praise the proposal. Unfortunately, the administration was not listening. It continued to insist on more aid to the Contras, without much success and scandalous under-the-table schemes.

LATER IN 1986, the Senate was engaged in an interminable series of votes. I was discussing the Columbia River Gorge Bill with Senator McClure when we were called to participate in the 23rd vote of the day. I voted "aye," believing it was a tabling motion on aid to the Contras. Only after the session ended did I find out I had mistakenly voted in favor of aid to the Contras. I immediately issued a statement confessing I had voted in error. I received plenty of razzing from colleagues, cartoonists and columnists. An editorial in the Vancouver *Columbian* censured me for my error, concluding, "One cannot help wondering how many lives that bit of inattention may cost as Central America continues to flare."

I did not make that mistake again.

Ironically, five years later, democracy came to Nicaragua, not by the force of arms but by the free decision of the Nicaraguan people.

AFTER A 12-YEAR STRUGGLE that began in 1973 when I ordered a study of wage disparity in state job classifications, Washington reached a "Comparable Worth" settlement with its employee unions. I pushed for a similar study at the federal level when I arrived in the U.S. Senate in 1983. While the proposal generated strong support, a filibuster threat kept the bill from even being discussed. I wasn't going to give up.

One of the speed bumps on the road to progress was Jesse Helms. He exuded Southern charm but was relentless in using Senate rules to gain any goal he pursued. One of the Senate's oldest, most contentious traditions is the art of the filibuster—holding the floor to delay action. The filibuster plays a starring role in Frank Capra's 1939 movie, *Mr. Smith Goes to Washington*, when the idealistic outsider portrayed by Jimmy Stewart makes his stand against the Powers that Be. Southern senators repeatedly used the filibuster to stymie civil rights legislation. The speaking record is still held by the late Strom Thurmond of South Carolina, who spoke for 24 hours and 18 minutes against the Civil Rights Act of 1957.*

In recent years the threat of a filibuster is usually sufficient to sidetrack a bill or nomination. A senator merely asks the Majority Leader to put a "hold" on the objectionable item or individual. A real distortion of the original concept of "extended debate," the move extends the tyranny of the minority to a single senator. Senator Helms was a master of this procedure, using it frequently to gain bargaining chips to trade for legislation he wanted. I was soon to experience Jesse's dexterity in the Foreign Relations Committee.

PRESIDENT REAGAN sent to the Senate for confirmation the appointment of Morton Abramowitz

---

* Desperate opponents kept offering Thurmond glasses of water in an effort to force a bathroom break that would have ended the filibuster. Thurmond anticipated as much, installing a urine bag in his trousers!

as Assistant Secretary of State for Intelligence and Research. Abramowitz was a former ambassador to Thailand and an expert on Asia. I met him through Nancy's brother, Bill Bell, who had spent many years in Asia. I found Abramowitz to be a brilliant and perceptive professional who had served the State Department with distinction for decades. But when he came before the Foreign Relations Committee, Helms went to work. He zeroed in on a book Abramowitz had written 16 years earlier, *Remaking China Policy*. Helms aggressively quizzed Abramowitz on proposals he had advanced regarding U.S.-China relations. All had become U.S. policy under four presidents, but Helms charged that Abramowitz was soft on Red China.

Helms, a former journalist, had arrived on Capitol Hill in the early 1950s as administrative assistant to Senator Willis Smith of North Carolina. Helms acquired his ardent streak of anti-Communism from Pat McCarran, an archconservative Democrat from Nevada, and Joe McCarthy, the bumptious Wisconsin Republican who rose to fame—and infamy—by painting the State Department as a coven of commies. He trashed Truman for "losing" China and insinuated that Eisenhower wasn't much of an improvement. Censured by the Senate for his wanton disregard for the truth, McCarthy succumbed to alcoholism. Helms, 64, soldiered on soberly.

Jesse Helms of North Carolina, chairman of the Senate Agriculture Committee, holds court. Bob Dole, left, and other members look bemused. *Courtesy The Wingate University Archives*

Helms insisted on recalling Abramowitz for further testimony before the Foreign Relations Committee, and was mightily peeved when the committee eventually voted 16 to 1 in favor of the Abramowitz nomination. When the nomination came before the Senate, I praised Abramowitz's distinguished record and urged that we proceed promptly to his confirmation. Whereupon Helms served notice he was prepared to kill the nomination with a filibuster "because considerable amount of comment is essential in connection with this nomination." He proceeded to tar the nominee with a broad brush, saying that some of Abramowitz' former colleagues and co-workers—all unnamed—had told him the former ambassador was "an ardent and eloquent advocate, if not an architect, of the policy to betray Taiwan and to normalize relations with the Communists."

A few days later, I was having coffee in the Senate dining room with Dick Lugar of Indiana, Mac Mathias of Maryland and several other senators, mostly members of the Foreign Relations Committee. I asked Lugar, the committee chairman, and the others how I could successfully advance the Abramowitz nomination. No one could figure out a way around the Helms roadblock. When Jim Baker, the Secretary of the Treasury, walked in we called him over. I explained my predicament. Baker, an old hand on Capitol Hill, had been Reagan's first chief of staff. He cut to the chase: "What does Jesse want? When he puts a barrier in the way it's almost always because he wants to trade lowering the barrier for something else he wants."

In a fascinating coincidence, Helms strolled into the dining room at that very moment. Baker, without hesitation, buttonholed him. "Jesse," he inquired earnestly, "I understand you have a problem with Dan over the Abramowitz nomination. Isn't there some way we can work this out?" Helms thought for a moment. "Well, I have a candidate for Ambassador to Belize, James Malone, and the Foreign Relations Committee voted him down by a narrow margin." I thought to myself, "Good God! He's holding up a major appointment to the State Department for a barely qualified applicant to a tiny Central American country." We all turned to Mac Mathias, who had voted against the Belize appointment. Baker leaned forward: "Mac, can't you give one committee vote so that Jesse takes his foot off the Abramowitz nomination?" Mathias reluctantly agreed but didn't promise anything beyond the committee vote. Helms agreed to remove his objection to Abramowitz. With that, we finished our coffee and returned to the Senate for the next scheduled vote. I learned another valuable lesson in the backroom politics of the Senate.

When the Foreign Relations Committee voted favorably on the Belize ambassadorship, the Democrats on the committee were furious. They boycotted the final vote. I quietly tried to explain to some of them what had happened. They were still unhappy.

The Abramowitz nomination cleared the Senate just before the August recess, but the nomination of Malone to the ambassadorship of Belize was delayed by several Democrats using the same tactics Jesse Helms had employed.

Sometimes I had to just shake my head at the tangled web of democracy in action. Get ready for another case in point.

ADVOCATES OF THE GRAMM-RUDMAN budget balancing act now proposed a balanced budget amendment to the United States Constitution. The proposal was strongly supported by President Reagan and avidly endorsed by conservative senators as well as centrists frustrated over the lack of fiscal discipline. I immediately entered the fray.

Over many years I had developed a strong position on amending our Constitution. Often in speeches to various groups I would declare myself a "fundamentalist." That usually raised eyebrows until I explained I was talking about our Constitution. My strongly held position was that a constitution should set forth the basic rules of organization of government and the protection and expansion of liberties for its citizens. I always noted that the U.S. Constitution had been amended only 26 times. Some were structural changes in governmental organization, such as giving voters the right to vote for U.S. senators, the purview of state Legislatures until the 17th Amendment was ratified in 1913. Most amendments expanded citizens' rights. The first 10 amendments, the Bill of Rights, sing out to us as they enumerate our priceless freedoms. Other amendments eliminated slavery and extended the right to vote to all races, women and 18-year-olds. Only once did we attempt to control social behavior with a constitutional amendment. It was a terrible mistake. Prohibition, an exercise in futility that promoted hypocrisy, was duly repealed after 13 checkered years.

I saw extraordinary dangers in the proposed balanced budget amendment and resolved to lead the fight against the proposal. My fundamental objection was that the amendment could not conceivably predict or describe what constituted a balanced budget. Our national accounting system was a jumble of antiquated, inconsistent, sometimes competing accounts—hundreds of them. There was a growing tendency to declare some accounts "off budget" in order to reduce the size of the federal deficit. I was gravely concerned that if a constitutional amendment passed, the federal courts quickly would become involved in interpreting the amendment. The risk was that limitations on our federal budget would be subject to interpretation by federal judges who hadn't been elected by the people.

I enlisted help on both sides of the aisle. We needed 34 votes and immediately discovered that a number of members were either undecided or noncommittal. This issue would clearly depend on the force of argument. Leadership reached agreement on a time limit for debate, equally divided between the two sides. There was no threat of filibuster since the constitutional amendment required a two-thirds affirmative vote, which was more than the 60-vote threshold for ending a Senate filibuster.

I learned early in my Senate experience that no matter how vociferously you opposed a colleague on one issue you should strive to maintain a friendship. You might be an ally on another issue. Howard Metzenbaum, the longtime Democratic senator from Ohio, was an astute businessman and hard bargainer. A week before debate erupted on the balanced budget amendment, we had hotly debated the issue of sale of the Bonneville Power Administration. Now we teamed up to oppose a debilitating addition to the constitutional amendment. The add-on stipulated that the nation's public debt ceiling could not be increased unless three-fifths of both houses of Congress approved. We presented a well-researched staff report detailing the havoc such a proposal would produce. Loans to farmers, student and housing loan guarantees and regular payments from the Social Security and Medicare trust funds would be subject to sudden termination if Congress failed to meet stringent requirements, Metzenbaum warned. I emphasized that the proposed addition would likely swing even more votes against the balanced budget amendment: "It just adds to the long list of reasons why the amendment is neither responsible economics nor responsible politics."

The amendment to the proposal was adopted in spite of our arguments.

Some senators began to realize the enormous implications of the proposed constitutional amendment and made proposals to ease its strictures. Senator Howard Heflin of Alabama proposed that the three-fifths voting requirement be waived for military spending during war time. Even though I opposed the amendment itself I supported the Heflin amendment because it eased voting requirements. At the end of a week-long debate on the Senate floor, I spoke in opposition to the amendment, saying the protection of a constitutional amendment was illusory.

> Responsible budgets are balanced by leaders, not laws. Do we really want to turn over much of our budget-making to the courts, which are the least likely to be responsible because they are not accountable for either the economic or political consequences of their action?
>
> The solution to our current deficit problem is for the Congress to summon the courage, the common sense and the discipline to put together responsible budgets for this country. Our Constitution has endured well for nearly two centuries because we have respected its fundamental principles. Tinkering with the fundamental precepts of the Constitution to mandate fiscal policy would be worse than Prohibition trying to mandate social policy. It would be a grave and dangerous error.

That speech, which many say is one of my best, goes to the heart of my feelings about our constitutional republic.

At the close of debate, Majority Leader Dole postponed a final vote for 24 hours. Clearly the proponents did not have enough votes. Our count was 34 opposed—exactly enough to defeat the proposal. A day later, as the final vote got underway, several of us gathered in the well of the Senate, prepared to offer last-minute arguments to any of our allies having second thoughts. The yeas and nays climbed until all but a handful had voted. The nays stood at 33, one vote short. The yeas climbed toward 66. Finally one of our stalwarts stepped forward and cast the deciding "nay."

Don't let anyone convince you one vote doesn't matter. I was deeply gratified that we had preserved the integrity of our Constitution.

The postmortems were offered to clusters of reporters. Dole argued that a "majority" had voted for the amendment and predicted it might win approval in the future. Senator Orrin Hatch of Utah, who led the effort for the amendment, warned that would be difficult, especially if Republicans lost seats in the coming election.

At a post-vote press conference, I half-jokingly observed: "Prohibition did not keep us from drinking. A balanced budget amendment will not keep us from spending. A drunk always has a way to get a drink, and a spender will always find a way to your wallet."

58
A TRAGIC LOSS

On Capitol Hill one morning in the spring of 1986, I was listening to a presentation before the Foreign Relations Committee when Lee Keller, my assistant press secretary, said she had to see me outside "right now." Annoyed, I said we should wait until the meeting ended. Lee was insistent. I knew something serious had happened. When we reached the hallway, her voice cracked. "Sally has been murdered," she said, sobbing. I was stunned.

Sally Heet, 35, was my talented, vivacious press secretary. She had left an executive position at Rainier

Press Secretary Sally Heet with Chief of Staff Bill Jacobs, center, and Phil Jones, my legislative aide. Sally's murder remains unsolved. *Bill Jacobs Collection*

Bank to join me when I was appointed to the Senate. She was highly regarded by her Senate colleagues and the press corps. I raced back to the office with Lee and found a staff engulfed in grief. We began to piece together the details.

I was surprised when Sally failed to show up for my breakfast meeting with Helen Dewar of *The Washington Post*. Maybe she just overslept? But that wouldn't have been like her. Later, when she failed to arrive at the office, her assistant, Monica Thompson, and her stepbrother, Jim Hudson, went to her apartment. They discovered her body. She had been stabbed to death.

Losing Sally, our trusted friend and co-worker—a loss compounded by the horror of the crime—affected all of us deeply. It also brought us closer. The next day I rose on the Senate floor to give the most difficult speech of my Senate career. My tribute to Sally was not a farewell. It was "a celebration of a short and rich life. Our Senate office deeply mourns this mindless act of violence," I said. "We all feel someone precious has been stolen from our lives. She was a self-possessed, confident professional who was an integral part of a closely knit family of our senatorial staff. Someone has taken Sally's physical presence from us, but no one can steal our memories of her."

A week later, several hundred colleagues and friends gathered for a memorial service in the Senate Caucus Room. I said our memories of Sally should help us be more professional, "to be inspired by her loveliness, her good cheer, her wisdom. In this way, Sally cannot die, but will live on in the memory of each of us."

The case remains one of the D.C. Metropolitan Police Department's major unsolved murders. A $25,000 reward offer still stands. The anonymous tip hotline is 202-727-9099. I keep hoping that someday Sally's killer will be apprehended.

"Closure" is such an overworked word. Justice would suffice.

THE TRAGEDY BLIGHTED an otherwise upbeat spring that brought an interesting new opportunity.

Dick Clark was a personable, principled Democrat who represented Iowa in the U.S. Senate in the 1970s. As chairman of the African Affairs panel on the Senate Foreign Relations Committee, he was the most outspoken congressional opponent of apartheid. There was evidence that the white South African government helped engineer his defeat in 1978. President Carter then appointed him as America's Coordinator for Refugee Affairs.

Clark became a Senior Fellow at the Aspen Institute, a respected international think tank. He had called the previous year to say he was working on a fascinating proposal. Now he shared a document he had written for the institute. It was called *U.S.-Soviet Relations: Building a Congressional Cadre.* "The most important public policy issue we face as a nation is our relationship with the Soviet Union," Clark wrote. "It is the heart of U.S. foreign policy, and a major determinant of domestic priorities. Given the importance of U.S.-Soviet relations to America and the peace and prosperity of the world, a working knowledge of Soviet affairs and the range of U.S.-Soviet issues on the part of our government's leaders is vital to the successful management of the relationship."

Clark suggested that a group of senators and congressmen meet twice a year with a delegation of European parliamentarians and U.S.-Soviet experts. I signed up on the spot. The first meeting was held in Bermuda in the spring of 1986. America's powerhouse delegation included Senators Joe Biden, Al Gore Jr., John Kerry and Gary Hart, all future presidential candidates, plus House Speaker Tom Foley and three other rising congressmen: future Secretary of Defense Les Aspin of Wisconsin, future Vice President Dick Cheney of Wyoming and future Senate Majority Leader Trent Lott of Mississippi. The European parliamentarians were equally distinguished.

When we gathered at a posh club for a get-acquainted dinner, I wondered whether this was going to be a group coveting a swell vacation or an opportunity for real learning. The next morning's opening session set the standard for future meetings. Presentations by U.S.-Soviet experts were thoughtful and provocative. Differences between the American lawmakers and European parliamentarians were aired. We found that the Europeans' views of relationships with the Soviet Union differed from ours primarily because of proximity. In any conflict they would be the first to feel the force of Soviet arms. During the two-day session, not one participant slipped out to sample Bermuda's inviting pink beaches and spectacular golf courses. We all looked forward to the next session, set for six months later. I was actively involved in every meeting until I left the Senate in 1989. Interestingly, not once in the three years of my participation did I hear any political leader or Soviet expert predict the dissolution of the Soviet Union. Yet a little over a year after my last meeting, the Soviet empire collapsed.

ANOTHER INTRIGUING OPPORTUNITY came from the American Friends of Bilderberg. I was invited to its 1986 meeting in Scotland. I was aware of the organization, just not familiar with its aims. I discovered it was founded in 1954, with Prince Bernhard of the Netherlands as its first patron. Once a year about 100 Americans, Canadians and Europeans gather in off-the-record meetings to discuss common problems. The invitation list for 1986 included several European prime ministers, CEOs of large international companies, labor leaders, ambassadors and leading parliamentarians. The date of the meeting coincided with a Senate recess so I decided to attend.

The agenda included the significance of the recent Reagan-Gorbachev summit, international economic issues, terrorism and apartheid. I found the differing opinions fascinating. Leaders could speak frankly and test out new ideas without fear of being quoted or misquoted. The European perspectives were particularly valuable. I came away with a better understanding of issues before the Foreign Relations Committee.

The privacy of the Bilderberg sessions and the Trilateral Commission meetings I had attended earlier prompted the John Birch Society to declare they'd been right all along: I was the handmaiden of One World Government. Political conspiracy theorists on the left also attacked the attendees as a nefarious political cabal out to rule the world. What I experienced at the meetings was a gathering of earnest public leaders of widely varied political philosophies seeking a better understanding of how to create a more just world. Those newly forged friendships could help ease tensions during international crises.

THE REAGAN ADMINISTRATION once again asked for congressional approval for an arms sale package to Saudi Arabia. A few years earlier, after Congress rejected the sale of fighter planes to the Saudis, they promptly purchased $8 billion worth from Great Britain. That made no difference to Israeli lobbyists.

I knew the American Israel Political Action Committee would oppose the new proposal so I asked the Congressional Research Service, a highly respected professional arm of Congress, to conduct a study. I posed this question: "Is Israel more secure or less secure if the United States sells fighter planes to Saudi Arabia?" The answer was "more secure." The main thesis was that the Saudis were going to purchase fighter planes one way or another. The only question was from whom? If the purchase was from the United States, conditions on basing and equipment could be attached. But if the purchase was from Britain or France, no conditions were likely to be required. When representatives of the American Israel PAC came to my office to lobby against the sale, I showed them the report. They brushed it aside, saying it made no difference. They absolutely opposed the sale of any military equipment to Saudi Arabia. They were determined to flex their muscle with Congress rather than listen to the facts.

Eventually the Saudis eliminated the planes from their request, seeking only missiles. Nevertheless, the issue was hotly debated in the Senate, with the outcome uncertain as the roll call began. I came to the floor and cast my vote in favor of the sale. Senator Rudy Boschwitz of Minnesota, whose family had fled Nazi Germany when he was 3, was unaware I had already voted. He asked if I would come with him to meet someone just off the Senate floor. He introduced me to Michael Goland, a businessman from Los Angeles, who proceeded to argue vehemently against the sale of missiles to

Saudi Arabia. I was astonished—first that someone was allowed to lobby from a private reception room during a Senate vote, and second that Goland would be allowed anywhere close to the United States Senate after his strident actions that contributed to Illinois Senator Chuck Percy's defeat by Paul Simon in 1984. Goland's approach with me wasn't the least bit subtle: "Imagine a political ad showing a fully loaded 747 taxiing for takeoff. Then the ad shifts to an Arab wearing a keffiyeh standing at the end of the runway preparing a shoulder-mounted rocket. The plane takes off, the Arab fires a rocket and a huge explosion occurs." He glowered: "What do you think about such an ad?" The implication was clear: Vote against the arms sale or be prepared for a vicious reaction at my next election. Simultaneously offended and furious, I glared back for several seconds before saying, "I think the people of Washington state are too smart to be taken in by such an outrageous ad." I turned on my heel and left.

The Senate voted 73 to 22 to deny the sale, with virtually every senator up for election voting no, a real testament to the strength of the Israeli lobby. The Senate, by one vote, upheld Reagan's veto of the bill. In a *Washington Post* commentary afterwards, Mark Shields told the story of Michael Goland's crude attempt to influence the outcome. "While an individual citizen's contribution to a federal candidate's campaign is statutorily limited to $1,000, expenditures that are independent of any candidate's campaign cannot be legally limited. That joint private appearance by Goland and Boschwitz, while suggesting a scene from *The Godfather*, raises serious questions about the supposed independence of such unlimited spending."

ONE OF THE MORE CONSTRUCTIVE outcomes of the 99th Congress was a major overhaul of our federal tax system. Unfortunately, the plan included a proposal that penalized Washingtonians. Slade Gorton and I were double-crossed by a fellow Republican—a Northwesterner to boot.

Bob Packwood of Oregon, chairman of the Senate Finance Committee, was the major force behind the revised tax plan. The meritorious idea was to drastically simplify the system by lowering marginal rates for both business and individuals. In the process, however, Packwood eliminated deductibility for state sales taxes while maintaining deductibility for state income taxes. Oregon has a state income tax but no sales tax, while Washington has a sales tax but no income tax. Phil Gramm was equally peeved, as Texas also has no income tax. He joined us in prodding Packwood to cease and desist. Packwood eventually promised to support us in return for our votes to defeat an amendment on Individual Retirement Accounts. We soon discovered that if you really want to maintain an element of a complex proposal you better be on a conference committee.

Many complicated proposals pass the House and the Senate with distinctly different elements. To settle conflicting plans, a conference committee composed of senior members of the appropriate committees hashes things out until there's a palatable compromise. That agreement is then sent to each House for an up or down vote. If successful, the bill is sent to the president.

Packwood sold us out in the conference committee for another element he really wanted to preserve. No one on the committee was willing to challenge the Finance chairman. Packwood did put together a compromise that restored 60 percent of the deductibility. But in the end, members of Congress from big states, for whom state income tax deductibility was life or death, prevailed. The final bill did represent a huge improvement in our tax system. I ultimately supported its passage.

The political fallout hit Gorton particularly hard. Brock Adams, the former House Budget Committee chairman challenging Slade's bid for re-election, had a field day asserting that Washington's Republican senators had been outfoxed by an Oregonian. "Slade and Dan" were a pale imitation of "Scoop and Maggie," Adams hooted.

59
CROCODILES

A lethargic floor debate droned on Capitol Hill. It was a sweltering summer day in 1986. I was relaxing in one of the ancient overstuffed chairs in the Republican Cloakroom with Slade Gorton, Bob Dole and several other colleagues when Dan Quayle, the junior senator from Indiana, stormed in. He was promoting the appointment of former Indiana state senator Daniel Manion to the United States Court of Appeals for the 7th Circuit. Quayle asked half a dozen of us to help him advance his embattled nominee. Manion's father, Clarence, was a former dean of the law school at Notre Dame and a national spokesman for right-wing causes, once serving on the executive board of the John Birch Society.

Senate Democrats were stonewalling many of Reagan's nominations since he had already appointed more than half of the federal judiciary in his six years as president. Dan Manion was in their cross-hairs. Not as conservative as his father, he was rated "qualified" or "barely qualified" for the bench by the American Bar Association. Forty law school deans asserted that he was a mediocre lawyer. Manion's controversial father was the lightning rod for the opposition.

Gorton stopped Quayle in his tracks: "Why should I support Manion," he scoffed, "when I can't get Bill Dwyer's nomination for the U.S. District Court in Seattle out of the damn Justice Department?" Dwyer was a brilliant trial lawyer whom Slade and I had known for years. It was Dwyer who secured a new Major League baseball club for Seat-

William Dwyer, a nominee worth fighting for. *Washington State Archives*

tle by humiliating the American League owners in 1976. Gorton put it best when he described Dwyer as "a renaissance man" who loved Shakespeare, mountain climbing and "causes that seemed lost."

Dole summoned a staffer and barked that he wanted Attorney General Ed Meese on the phone right now. Meese was unavailable, so the majority leader told a senior Justice Department official to get the Dwyer appointment to the Senate immediately. I heard the entire exchange and did not believe it was a horse trade, just an impassioned plea by Slade to move his candidate forward. But it was widely reported by the press as a cynical quid pro quo.

INSTEAD OF FILIBUSTERING the Manion nomination, Democrats agreed to a vote they thought they would win. To their dismay, it ended up 47-47. And to the equal dismay of the attorney general and White House, four Republicans voted against confirming Manion. I was one of them. Before Vice President Bush could cast the deciding vote, Robert Byrd, the Democratic leader, alertly changed his vote to "aye" in order to move to reconsider the vote. This time I caught hell for voting against reconsideration, especially when the vote was 49-49, with the vice president casting the decisive vote against reconsideration. (A motion to reconsider a vote must be made by a member voting on the prevailing side.) Dan Manion was declared confirmed, 48-46, although his nomination still faced a potential move for reconsideration.

Slade faced a firestorm of criticism, both in the Senate and back home, giving the Adams campaign new ammunition. Governor Booth Gardner, Brock's campaign chairman, asserted, "An almost subliminal question that the Manion situation clarified is that Senator Gorton does what is in the political and not the public interest. 'Slippery' is back."

That Dwyer's track record was decidedly liberal was ignored by the Democrats. He was a former member of the ACLU and had represented a Black Panther, pro bono. They were intent on derailing Manion. And if that caused trouble for Gorton, so much the better.

Slade responded with a letter to his constituents, noting that Manion was strongly supported by both senators from Indiana, and that he had "great respect" for their judgment. However, when it "became crystal clear to me that we simply could not get Mr. Dwyer nominated without extraordinary efforts, it was not only proper to leverage appropriate treatment for my state and constituents in return for a vote for Mr. Manion, it was, in my view, necessary to do so."

Without Gorton's intervention, I doubt very much that Dwyer's nomination would have ever reached the Senate.

Slade would pay a terrible price for his bold move.

The affair was exacerbated a month later as the 1986 Senate campaign was heading down the stretch. The Senate voted on reconsideration. This time I caught hell for voting against reconsideration, especially when the vote was 49-49, with the vice president casting the decisive vote against reconsideration. Manion's nomination was reconfirmed and Dwyer's was now sent to the Senate. "I hope my original vote on Mr. Manion was wrong," I said, "and that he will be adequate to the job."*

Democrats, infuriated by Gorton's vote on Manion, stalled consideration of Dwyer until Congress adjourned. "It was just a mean little act that was unnecessary," I told reporters. "I think they're somewhat embarrassed."

Dwyer's appointment to the federal bench appeared to be dead.

The fallout was disastrous for Washington state and the GOP's majority in the U.S. Senate. That November, the opportunistic Adams squeaked past Gorton by 26,540 votes out of 1.3 million cast. Democrats had relentlessly styled Republicans as enemies of the elderly because we had voted for a one-year freeze on all spending, including Social Security cost-of-living increases. It was an important, gutsy vote, but we were not supported by the president. Now we paid the political price. Five

---

* At this writing, some 35 years after the controversy, Judge Manion is a senior member of the Seventh Circuit appellate court, admired by his colleagues and members of the Chicago Bar.

other Republican senators elected six years earlier in the Reagan revolution also went down to defeat. In all, we lost eight GOP seats and with them control of the United States Senate. One of the few bright spots for the GOP was Arizona, where Congressman John McCain, who endured 5½ hellish years in a Hanoi POW camp, was elected to succeed Barry Goldwater.

I URGED THE JUSTICE DEPARTMENT to resubmit Dwyer's nomination early in the 1987 session. Weeks passed. Other judicial nominations arrived in the Senate. Dwyer's was not among them.

In March I shifted my lobbying efforts to Howard Baker, who was now White House Chief of Staff. Baker told the attorney general to call me. I heard nothing. By the first of June I'd had enough of the stonewalling. I placed a hold on all judicial nominees to the 9th Circuit Court of Appeals. Based in San Francisco, the 9th Circuit is the largest and busiest federal appellate court in the nation. It had a reputation for liberalism that annoyed Reagan conservatives.

I thoroughly disliked, and repeatedly tried to reform the senatorial "hold" privilege. However, I was so frustrated that I used the blunt instrument as a wake-up call to the Reagan Administration. I told Dole that if the administration dug in its heels I would extend the hold to all judicial nominations. Reminded of my opposition to the maneuver, I shrugged: "The longer you run with crocodiles, the longer your teeth become. You operate within the rules you're given."

That finally got the attention of the administration. I met with Attorney General Meese on July 22. The meeting was cordial enough, but Meese was still tap-dancing. This was a new Congress and Gorton was gone, the AG observed, but if I would send them a new nomination they would work to expedite a hearing. "Slade may not be here," I said emphatically, "but I am, and my candidate is Bill Dwyer, just as it was in the last Congress. The president called and offered him the position last year. I am confident he has not changed his mind." If he had, my "hold" on the 9th Circuit nominees would stand. Six days later the Dwyer nomination was sent to the Senate.

I thought the task was almost complete. I was monumentally wrong. On September 11, 1987, Senator Patrick Leahy of Vermont banged the gavel on what normally would be routine confirmation hearings by the Senate Judiciary Committee. The usual drill was that senators from the nominee's state introduce a candidate, and after five minutes of easy questions the nomination was sent to the full committee and the floor of the Senate.

On this eventful morning four nominees were presented and three were approved with virtually no questioning. None were as highly ranked by the American Bar Association as Dwyer, who was rated "exceptionally well-qualified." I told the committee he would be an extraordinary judge:

> Bill Dwyer merits the unanimous support of the members of this committee—and the Senate—for reasons that transcend the fact that he is bright and honest and fair. He would bring such moral courage and enlightened wisdom to the bench that all those who sit in judgment before him, no matter how unpopular, would receive just treatment. The committee apparently will receive testimony from witnesses who oppose the nominee because, as I infer from their letters and public statements, he is somehow tolerant of child pornography. They, or the groups they represent, have undertaken a mean-spirited and vicious campaign against Mr. Dwyer which I find reprehensible and unconscionable. ... I urge, in the most emphatic way that the com-

mittee act promptly to bring the saga of this nomination to a close and support Mr. Dwyer's nomination. Justice delayed is justice denied, and the people of the State of Washington need this man on the bench at the earliest possible date, not just to clear up the backlog we face, but to provide, in the very highest and best sense, true justice for the people who will appear before him.

Senator Leahy said the Judiciary Committee had invited witnesses against Dwyer's confirmation to testify, but none had accepted. "I suspect that says volumes in itself," he said.

A group called Washington Together against Pornography had written several members of the committee to charge that Dwyer was not fit for judicial office because of advice he gave the Seattle Library Board concerning *Show Me*, a controversial sex education book by a Swiss child psychologist and an American photographer. It was first issued in West Germany in 1974 by a children's publishing company sponsored by the Lutheran Church. While the book featured illustrations of young people engaged in a variety of sexual activity, the text was a straightforward attempt at sex education.

"I am embarrassed to have to say this," Dwyer told the senators, "because I think it should go without saying for all citizens: I am strongly in favor of the vigorous enforcement of child pornography laws." Dwyer explained that *Show Me* had been in the Seattle Public Library's collection for about 10 years on a reference-only basis. It could not be checked out. In 1985, the board was threatened with possible criminal prosecution if it failed to remove the book, while some civil libertarians were arguing that such action would abridge the public's First Amendment rights. "The board sought advice from outside counsel on its legal rights and responsibilities. I was retained to help," Dwyer said. "The board put to me a single question: 'If this book is retained in the library's collection, will the library thereby be violating any law?'... We determined that the answer was probably no. ... If there were a court test, the court [probably] would not find the library guilty of a crime." Dwyer reminded the committee that many libraries in the United States, including the Library of Congress, had *Show Me* in their collections. "The presence of this book in libraries does not mean that the libraries endorse or recommend the book. The legal advice I gave was given to the best of our ability on an objective basis, and did not imply any endorsement of the book, either."

Doug Jewett, the Seattle city attorney, and King County Prosecutor Norm Maleng both agreed with the library board's decision to keep the book in its collection.

I was dismayed when Senator Charles Grassley of Iowa introduced a letter from Senator Strom Thurmond requesting an additional day of hearings on Dwyer's fitness for the federal bench. It was apparent that Thurmond's staff was rounding up opposing witnesses, even though they had more than a month to prepare for this first hearing.

David Crosby representing a group called Parents-in-Arms, gave poignant testimony regarding his young son, who had turned into a "street kid" at age 14, lured by a place called the Monastery. Frustrated and angry, he called Dwyer for help. "At that time, I knew Bill only by reputation. I had never met him. His reputation was that he was the best trial lawyer in Seattle. I wanted the best. The following day, he told me he had discussed the case with his partners, and at his own suggestion—not at my request—he wished to do the case on a pro bono basis." In vivid detail, he told of Dwyer's relentless efforts to close down the Monastery in spite of anonymous death threats. That testimony alone should have sent Dwyer's nomination to the Senate floor for confirmation.

Senator Alan Simpson of Wyoming, a wise and witty man, lifted our spirits. Some opponents were suggesting that Dwyer's previous membership in the ACLU was ample reason to disqualify him. "That is interesting," Simpson observed, adding that he too had joined the ACLU in the late 1950s "and thought they were doing great work in the area of privacy, protection of personal privacy and rights. But they also did some things that just said to me, 'I think I've had enough' and I stepped out." Concluding that Dwyer was an altogether "splendid gentleman," Simpson said, "I hope that we will see a swift processing of his nomination."

As the afternoon hearing drew to a close, Chairman Leahy noted that he had served on the Judiciary Committee for more than 10 years. (Still in office at this writing, Leahy is the only Democrat Vermont has ever elected to the U.S. Senate.) "I have probably been to literally hundreds of confirmation hearings, and it is a common courtesy for the senators from a particular state to come and introduce somebody," Leahy said. "Then, because of their schedule, they leave. Dan Evans has to be one of the busiest senators in this body. This is the only time where a senator stayed through the whole hearing, and if you will allow somebody from the other side of the aisle to say it, I consider Governor Evans—Senator Evans—to be one of the true gentlemen of this body."

The feeling was mutual.

I was determined to stick with Dwyer through the mean-spirited testimony that was now sure to come. His first day of hearings consumed five hours, compared to less than half an hour on the other three judicial candidates.

A MONTH WENT BY. I fidgeted because the first session of the 100th Congress was drawing to a close. Finally on October 22, 1987, Senator Leahy opened the second hearing on the Dwyer nomination. What followed was the most unbelievable, misleading testimony I think I have ever heard in all my years in public life. Andrea Vangor, executive director of Washington Together against Pornography, charged Dwyer with a propensity to distort and misinterpret laws prohibiting child pornography. Bruce Fein, a scholar with the Heritage Foundation, a conservative think tank, pointed to Dwyer's role in a celebrated 1964 libel case. Dwyer had represented John Goldmark, a former Washington state legislator, in a defamation case against right-wingers who had branded him "the tool of a monstrous communist conspiracy to remake America into a totalitarian state." Fein asserted Dwyer was "guilty of the identical smear tactics he so eloquently denounces." To hear Fein tell it, Dwyer believed Strom Thurmond, John Wayne and Ronald Reagan were all members of the "radical right."

Senator Leahy bored in like a prosecutor, starting with Andrea Vangor:

"Do you know William Dwyer?"

"No."

"Have you ever met him?"

"No."

"Have you ever tried to discuss with him his views on child pornography or the book, *Show Me*?"

"No."

"Are you familiar with his legal career?"

"Somewhat. Not broadly."

The chairman asked each of the other witnesses the same questions. None of them had any idea of Bill Dwyer's background or reputation. They had wasted the committee's time for an hour with their crude attempts to smear Bill Dwyer's reputation.

The next panel offered a strikingly different perspective on his fitness for the federal bench. It featured my friend William H. Gates, former president of the Washington State Bar Association; Seattle Police Chief Patrick Fitzsimons; Robert Lasnik, chief of staff for the King County Prosecutor, and Judith Krug of the American Library Association. Gates said, "I just sum it up this way: If federal judges were chosen in our area by polling the lawyers, Mr. Dwyer would be virtually a unanimous choice. And if federal judges were elected in their district he'd be elected by a landslide." Fitzsimons told of the numerous times Dwyer had assisted the police department. Lasnik said prosecutors viewed Dwyer as "exactly the kind of judge we would love to appear before—one who puts us through our paces, but who is eminently fair and tough-minded."

Strom Thurmond, a fossil from the Jim Crow South, took it all in with a jaundiced eye. He quizzed witnesses about their opinions on the sex-education book, totally ignoring Dwyer's ruling on the legality of its possession by the library.

The afternoon droned into evening, with Thurmond exploring Dwyer's membership in the allegedly un-American ACLU and attitudes on obscenity cases. Finally Senator Leahy asked how much more time was necessary, suggesting that the Judiciary committee might have to recess, which would seriously delay other pending nominations. Leahy and Thurmond sparred for several minutes over how much longer he planned to grill Dwyer.

Thurmond, peeved, asked just two more questions. The chairman rapped his gavel for adjournment at 6:45 p.m. Dwyer and I went to the podium to thank Leahy for his patience and persistence. He laughed. "I knew that Strom desperately wanted to go to a Goldwater scholarship dinner tonight since he was one of the hosts. He also has some judicial appointments pending and is afraid that continuing the hearing would jeopardize other appointments. I just had to keep going until he realized that he had a choice: Stop asking questions or miss the dinner."

That brought to a close 10 hours of testimony and 464 pages of committee records. It was one of the longest and most contentious confirmation hearings for a federal district court judge in Senate history. A week later the Judiciary Committee reported the nomination favorably to the floor of the Senate where it was approved by unanimous consent.

Sworn in on December 1, 1987, Bill Dwyer served as a federal judge with enormous distinction for the next 12 years, ruling with clarity and wisdom on some of the most important issues in Northwest history. In 1991, he ordered a virtual halt to timber sales and logging in 17 national forests stretching from the Olympic Peninsula to Northern California. Gorton, who had emerged as the champion of timber communities decimated by endangered-species rulings, called it "a perfect example of anti-human decision making." Slade and I disagreed on that one. When the smoke cleared, his admiration for Dwyer was intact.

Suffering from Parkinson's disease and then lung cancer, Dwyer became a senior judge with a reduced schedule while writing a compelling book on the jury system, *In the Hands of the People*. He died at the age of 72 in 2002.

At great political risk, Slade Gorton had stepped across the aisle to nominate a giant. One of the accomplishments of which I am most proud is the persistence and energy I spent to make sure Bill Dwyer became a federal judge.

60
RADIOACTIVE POLITICS

As I escorted Brock Adams down the aisle to be sworn in as my seatmate on January 3, 1987, I fully grasped that I was now a member of the minority party. The Democrats, in control of both houses of Congress, were practically measuring the drapes in the Oval Office. It would be wise to have a Democrat as a prime sponsor of any bill you expected to pass.

Senator Adams was 10 days short of 60. His boyish smile and ambitious affability made him seem younger. Tom Foley once described him as "the young prince of Washington politics." He was unquestionably bright—the first student body president in University of Washington history to graduate at the top of his class. A Navy man and Harvard Law School graduate, Adams was a six-term congressman before a brief stint as Secretary of Transportation in the Carter Administration. That there was something too facile about Brock was hard to define.

I would sorely miss Slade Gorton. We had been friends and political partners for 30 years. Nevertheless, I sincerely believed I could work well with Adams. We had known each other since the 1950s when we were Seattle Jaycees.

RIGHT AFTER THE DISASTROUS '86 election, I corralled the seven GOP members of the Foreign Relations Committee and suggested we vote to retain Senator Lugar, the outgoing chairman, as the ranking Republican member. Lugar had presided with great skill during the previous two years. He built a strong and competent Republican staff, and we successfully passed a Foreign Operations authorization bill for the first time in years. The vote was 7 to 0 to keep Lugar. Jesse Helms, a doctrinaire conservative, especially on international affairs, challenged our vote. He asked the entire Republican caucus to make a decision. That was his prerogative. I was still confident Lugar would prevail. I was soon to learn another lesson about the preeminence of seniority.

Helms replaced Lugar as the committee's ranking Republican member on a 24 to 17 vote. I was disappointed and angry. A capable former chairman had been cast aside, and a disruptive right-winger would attempt to be the Republican voice for foreign relations in the United States Senate. Helms proceeded to fire almost all of Lugar's talented staff, replacing them with his band of rigid conservatives.

It was going to be an interesting two years. I would visit the White House and State Department many times to help plot strategy to try and pry important legislation out of Jesse Helms' iron fist.

Fortunately, I was once again appointed to the Committee on Committees. This time the job was more difficult for Republicans since we had lost eight seats with a corresponding reduction in the number of seats on each committee. I managed to keep my seats on Energy and Foreign Relations, as well as on the Select Committee on Indian Affairs. Senator Dan Inouye of Hawaii, a charming old pro, assumed the chairmanship of Indian Affairs for the Democratic majority. Inouye's record of service with an all-volunteer Japanese American infantry regiment during World War II was the stuff of legends. He lost his right arm in combat and received the Medal of Honor. At our organizational meeting I was astonished when he announced he would appoint me as vice chairman. Members of the majority party traditionally fill all leadership positions. But Inouye said he wanted to ensure that the committee's actions were truly bipartisan. Several of the Democrats on the committee grumbled to no avail. The chairman prevailed. Working together amicably, we posted a remarkably productive track record. I found that being the ranking Republican on the committee gave me an opportunity to appoint a committee staff member. It was the first glimmering of the good things that come with seniority. I asked Joe Mentor to tackle that job. He handled it with skill and enthusiasm.

THE FIRST OPPORTUNITY for Brock Adams and I to team up arrived early on when the debate over a nuclear waste site bounced back into the lap of the Senate Energy and Natural Resources Committee. I asked Adams to sit in on the hearing, even though he was not a committee member.

Energy Secretary John Herrington faced strong bipartisan opposition to the inept way his department had handled the hot potato. Faced with massive opposition to any potential site, the department had unilaterally decided to abandon any search east of the Mississippi. The selection of Hanford as one of three potential sites in the West seemed at odds with the department's own research, especially with regard to cost effectiveness. A site in Mississippi was safer and less costly than either Washington or Texas, according to Energy Department documents that emerged early in the debate. The department had deleted passages critical of the Hanford site. It was apparent that the Energy Department was ignoring the

Brock Adams on the campaign trail, 1986. *Brian DalBalcon/ The Daily World*

Nuclear Waste Policy Act and its own science and cost analyses. I was determined to get them back on track.

It was an especially difficult year for me on a trifecta of Hanford issues. A complicated question of Hanford contractor liability pitted me against most environmental lobbyists. They also challenged me on my advocacy for completing the Washington Public Power Supply System's unfinished WNP-1 reactor at Hanford to produce a key ingredient for our nuclear arsenal. I also proposed an interim nuclear waste storage facility until a decision was made on a permanent one. The Energy and Natural Resources Committee was the focal point for all three issues. I was in the thick of it for the remaining months of my Senate career.

THE FEDERAL GOVERNMENT has assumed financial responsibility for nuclear accidents ever since the advent of the nuclear industry. No insurance company was willing to accept responsibility for accidents that were difficult even to describe. The new Congress now wanted to change the rules to make the industry fully liable for so-called "gross negligence." It was a popular political issue, the close call at Three Mile Island in 1979 having galvanized the opposition to nuclear power. The massive WPPSS construction bond default in 1982, which generated the "Irate Ratepayer" uprising, was part of the political fallout. Critics of WPPSS noted that as governor I had signed the site authorizations for the plants.

I made a thorough study of the proposed new liability rules and concluded that if they became law it would be impossible to attract contractors to nuclear sites. When the bill came before the Energy Committee it was voted down 10 to 9. I cast the deciding vote and caught holy hell from environmental groups. "We were reamed," said the political director for the League of Conservation Voters in Seattle, adding, "Evans has done voters in Washington a huge disservice by failing to support full contractor liability." I supported an alternative—stiff civil penalties—which I believed were far more practical than the draconian proposals for unlimited liability.

Concurrently, in confidential briefings from the Energy Department and White House, I learned that our nuclear weapons stockpile was facing a potential crisis. Tritium—a radioactive isotope of hydrogen—was an essential ingredient in nuclear weapons. It decayed rapidly and needed to be replaced regularly. South Carolina's Savannah River nuclear plants, which produced tritium, were nearing the end of safe operation. I proposed that an unfinished WPPSS reactor at Hanford could be completed much faster and cheaper than any other replacement and would ensure the effectiveness of our nuclear deterrent.

I didn't need to be told that nuclear politics is radioactive, yet I was surprised by the stridency of Adams' opposition. We'd be building "a bomb factory" at Hanford, he declared. Other critics maintained it would be immoral to use a reactor designed for peaceful purposes to construct weapons of mass destruction. They were unmoved when the State Department sent me a letter stating that the conversion would not violate nuclear nonproliferation treaties. Ultimately new and much more costly reactors were built at Savannah River. In the interim, civilian reactors were used to produce tritium.

ADAMS SHARED my strongly held belief that Hanford was not the right location for long-term deep geologic storage of nuclear waste. When I first proposed a plan called Monitored Retrievable Storage (MRS) as a short-term solution, Adams enthusiastically endorsed it as a badly needed alternative. A couple of months later, he switched positions, saying it was "terribly expensive, very much resented by everyone and not a permanent solution."

I never said it was a permanent solution. I felt strongly that I was right on science and practicality. It was a disappointment to lose his support. One thing struck me as inarguable: The Energy Department had things backwards. It wanted to designate a long-term storage site and *then* focus on interim storage. I maintained we should first develop several above-ground MRS sites. In 40 or 50 years the waste would lose much of its radioactivity and heat. As a result, much more waste could be stored in a single long-term geologic storage site. I also believed that through research we could reprocess and utilize waste materials as fuel for existing reactors, thus reducing further the need for long-term storage. J. Bennett Johnston, the Louisiana Democrat who now chaired the Energy Committee, was interested in the idea. He proposed a trip to Sweden and France during the spring recess to examine their progress in handling nuclear waste.

A small group of us traveled to Forsmark, Sweden, where intermediate level waste was stored. We traveled by bus through a tunnel, 30 feet in diameter, until we were beneath the bed of the Baltic Sea. The enterprising Swedes had carved huge caverns and filled them with concrete cells containing casks of intermediate waste. Ultimately the entire cavern would be sealed. Their monitored retrievable storage at another site, Oskarshamn, was also fascinating. Since all of Sweden's nuclear plants are on salt water, the waste was brought to the storage site by ship. The fuel assemblies, in shielded casks, are transferred to an underwater tank where they are automatically transferred to their final pools far below ground level. The plant ultimately was expanded to hold all of the spent fuel from Sweden's nuclear plants. The Swedes strongly believe this interim storage plan gives them plenty of time to develop smarter long-term storage or even to find alternative ways to utilize the spent fuel.

Next stop was France, where most electricity was generated by nuclear plants. The United States prohibits reprocessing of nuclear waste because it creates more plutonium, a nuclear weapons ingredient. The French reprocess and re-utilize the plutonium as new fuel. The result is that their high-level waste is only 3 percent of ours. That waste is vitrified in a highly automated facility and stored above ground while it cools.

We traveled to the Normandy Peninsula to visit an even larger and more modern reprocessing and storage facility. Virtually everything was controlled by computers and robots.

With fresh evidence that we were seriously behind our European counterparts in both policy and science—still true all these years later—we returned to Capitol Hill with a lot of questions to ask our own Department of Energy. Although several of us, including Senator Johnston, worked hard to bring reason to the nuclear waste debate, we could not surmount the irrational fear of nuclear energy exhibited by some environmental organizations and the parallel opposition of "anti-war" groups that opposed any attempts to reprocess waste.

The United States has paid a huge price for our failure to act rationally. New methods of reusing waste have been discovered. Retrievable storage makes more sense than ever, and nuclear energy is even reviving as a power source in place of coal because of global warming. We stumble along following obsolete policies. We have no permanent storage, no modern interim storage and no provision for handling waste generated by a revived nuclear industry. Hysteria is trumping science.

AFTER WE FAILED to develop a monitored retrievable storage concept, I sat down with Chairman Johnston to decide what to do next. A number of Northwest congressmen teamed up with members from a dozen other states to impose an 18-month moratorium on the nuclear waste program so it could be studied again by a blue-ribbon committee. In the meantime, attempts by House members to shift insurance liability to nuclear contractors were defeated handily. Adamantly opposed to delay, Johnston saw the House vote as a help in the legislative poker game. Oregon's Mark Hatfield joined me in negotiations with Johnston. We were able to insert cost and water quality as major elements in choosing a long-term nuclear waste site. Jim McClure of Idaho was another ally on the Energy Committee. We now had a strong majority for the chairman's amendment, which was also winning support from the Department of Energy. Although it was not stated in the amendment, we all knew, that the proposal virtually dictated a site in Nevada.

I would have preferred to let the selection process continue because I was virtually certain Hanford would not qualify. What did concern me was a delay of 18 months and another commission. It was difficult to know what new mischief would arise, either in Congress or the Reagan Administration. The best alternative was to work with Bennett Johnston, a nimble committee chairman, on a proposal that would speed the process and eliminate Hanford.

Reporters covering the issue didn't have access to this inside baseball. One headline summarized their skepticism: "Northwest delegates 'nuked' in two congressional fights." One columnist wrote, "Hatfield and Evans sat down with one of the masters of legislative poker, a game that's historically best played by Southerners. Now that they've left the table, it's not clear who's got most of the chips."

In spite of the hand wringing and yowling by many environmental lobbyists, the press, and others opposed to the Hanford site, I knew we had won the game. Johnston's bill passed. Yucca Mountain, Nevada, was promptly selected as the site for long-term storage, and the threat to Hanford was over. We used the Energy Department's own analysis to prove the Eastern Washington location made no sense, either scientifically or financially.

I'm reminded of the adage that "Laws are like sausages. It is better not to see them being made." The end result in this case was satisfactory, but power politics prevailed over scientific study and thoughtful debate as the Senate rolled over the two relatively junior senators from Nevada. Lawsuits were filed, administrations came and went. In 2007 an agile new senator from Nevada, Harry Reid, became majority leader of the U.S. Senate. Harry's gone now—all things must pass—but not much has changed on the nuclear waste front. Billions of dollars have been spent at Yucca Mountain and there still is no certified long-term or interim-term storage for nuclear waste.

61
GENUINELY NEAT IDEAS

The Hanford debates were time-consuming and draining. I was still determined to resuscitate two issues I championed in 1986: One was the "Blueprint for Federalism" that evolved from the study I worked on with Virginia Governor Chuck Robb. The other was the appliance efficiency standards President Reagan pocket vetoed even though they were passed overwhelmingly by the 99th Congress.*

The plan to create a new federalism was based on principles as old as our Constitution. What better way to celebrate its 200th anniversary than by strengthening state and local governments while streamlining and limiting federal domestic programs? The Blueprint advocated assigning prime fiscal responsibility for welfare and Medicaid to the federal government. Our goal was to eliminate the hodge-podge of state-run programs. Some were paying five times as much per capita as others. The flip side of the plan was that most local or regional programs—economic development, transportation, education and community services—would revert to state and local governments. We were careful to ensure that these trade-offs were revenue neutral during a transition period. "These proposals constitute the most thoughtful, coherent reform of the federal system since the emergence of the modern system of federal grants," the Brookings Institution wrote.

The monumental proposal now acquired significant bipartisan co-sponsors, which made me optimistic. I didn't grasp just how difficult it would be to convince the status quo to alter its status—even when the end result could be much more efficient and responsive government. The U.S. Conference of Mayors maintained the cities stood to lose scores of important federal programs while state governments reaped the benefits. Seattle Mayor Charles Royer, an otherwise progressive voice, joined the naysayers, claiming that state Legislatures were "rural-dominated across the country." The conservative *Washington Times* parroted concerns expressed by the National League of Cities. "A Reagan veto may be necessary to save the taxpayer from another grand shellacking," it warned.

We received polite hearings in both the House and Senate. But the plan took a grand shellacking from stand-pat local officials comfortable with the money that regularly rolled in from Uncle Sam. I believe the plan would have streamlined government at all levels and saved American taxpayers billions of dollars. When I departed, no one in Congress was willing to continue the fight.

I was much more successful with the National Appliance Energy Conservation Act. I suspected that mid-level conservative staffers at the White House, opposed to any efficiency standards mandat-

---

* The U.S. Constitution requires that a president either sign or veto a bill within 10 days of presentation. If the president does neither, the bill becomes law unless the Congress has adjourned in the meantime. In that case a refusal to sign is equivalent to a veto—commonly known as a "pocket veto."

ed by government, had convinced the president to pocket veto the bill.

With a new Democratic majority in the Senate I was careful to ask Bennett Johnston, my newly acquired friend across the aisle, to be a co-sponsor of the revived energy conservation bill. As chairman of the Energy and Natural Resources Committee, the Louisianan would be influential in speeding the bill toward floor action. I also worked with senior White House staff members and accepted a few minor amendments. The bill passed unanimously. This time Reagan signed it into law. The efficiency of major appliances has risen steadily ever since, providing substantial and continuing energy savings.

THE IRAN-CONTRA AFFAIR erupted again with the release of a Senate Intelligence Committee report. It detailed the ludicrous back-channel effort to divert profits from Iranian arms sales to the Nicaraguan rebels battling the country's ruling party, the left-wing Sandinista National Liberation Front. After reading that report and another by a presidential commission led by former senator John Tower, I was convinced that Reagan's top advisers had created a chaotic environment. In particular, the president was not receiving complete information from the National Security Council. Meanwhile, his chief of staff, the imperious Don Regan, saw himself as a prime minister rather than the president's arguably most important aide. "In the sensitive position in which he sits now, Don Regan has no sympathy for making the relationship with the Congress work," I told reporters. "He is the wrong person in the wrong job and certainly now at the wrong time."

I was joined by an increasing number of senators and congressmen, many calling for Regan's resignation. His undoing was his cavalier attitude toward the First Lady. When Nancy Reagan joined the chorus, Regan was out. His successor, Howard Baker, was exactly the kind of man Ronald Reagan needed at his right hand. A consummate deal-maker, the former Senate majority leader was a moderate conservative with a sunny disposition, liked and respected by Democrat and Republican alike. Relationships between the administration and Congress improved immediately, though the administration's ongoing proposals for aid to the Contras remained a hard sell. The scandal would deepen.

A bill to release $40 million in aid to the "freedom fighters" passed the Senate 52 to 48 after intense debate. Many of those in favor of aid to the Contras warned of the danger of Marxism spreading north from Nicaragua to Mexico—the same old "domino theory" that led us waist deep into the big muddy of Vietnam. "Do we have so little faith in our democratic ideals that we believe dominoes can topple in only one direction?" I asked. "I believe the best chance to restore democratic institutions inside Nicaragua lies in building strong Democratic nations around Nicaragua. ...Growing personal

Two Nancys at a Congressional Wives luncheon in 1986. My Nancy said she felt silly wearing her Red Cross volunteer apron, while the First Lady was dressed to the nines. *White House Photo*

income and economic prosperity in those four nations sends a message to the Nicaraguan people."

Several senators who voted for aid stated it was the last time they would do so.

When full-scale hearings on the scandal commenced in the summer of 1987, a heretofore obscure Marine Corps lieutenant colonel named Oliver North stood revealed as a key player in the goofy scheme. North professed that he thought taking money from Iran and giving it to the Contras was "a neat idea."

The star witness was Admiral John Poindexter, the president's former National Security adviser. The fact-finding committee was furious that important intelligence information had been kept from the president. Congressman Dick Cheney of Wyoming, the newly-elected chairman of the House Republican Conference, told Poindexter, "The reason for not misleading the Congress is a very practical one: It's stupid. It's self-defeating, because while it may in fact allow you to prevail in the problem of the moment, eventually you destroy the President's credibility." Cheney's attitude toward misleading Congress was considerably different years later when he was Vice President of the United States.

Ronald Reagan was already a lame duck. After this tangled web of lies, paper-shredding and obfuscation, his job-approval ratings nosedived—temporarily. "The Teflon President" and I departed office two years later. His approval rating had rebounded to 63 percent. Nobody reported mine.

DURING THE FEBRUARY RECESS, Nancy and I headed home for some fresh air in the other Washington. When we landed in Spokane, Nancy's home town, I received word that her 95-year-old mother had died. I broke the news as we set off on a walk down the familiar streets. We walked quietly for a long time, absorbing the loss of our last parent. Nancy's father and my parents all lived long and productive lives, but Lilith Bell—"Gam" to the grandchildren who adored her, and she them—was an integral part of our family for 20 years. She was a recent widow when she moved in with us in Seattle—supposedly just for a while—to help out as we began the campaign for governor. She moved with us to the Governor's Mansion, helped raise our three sons, helped hostess social events and became an active member of the Olympia community.

In her later years, when I was at The Evergreen State College, we were reluctant to leave her alone when we attended evening events. Our sons took care of the grandmother who had cared for them years earlier. Mother-in-law jokes are legion. Mine was a strong, insightful woman and, for me, a grand friend.

THE ISSUE OF a constitutional amendment to require a balanced budget made a comeback after its narrow defeat in the Senate a year earlier. Proponents had spent several years in the trenches, urging state Legislatures to pass bills calling for a national constitutional convention. Article V of the United States Constitution authorizes such a convention if approved by two- thirds of the states. By 1987, 32 states had passed such legislation. Only two more were needed. Montana represented the penultimate step to a constitutional convention.

When the Montana State Legislature scheduled a hearing, I was asked to testify. It turned out to be an unexpected adventure. More than 500 people packed the galleries and hallways of Montana's House chamber. It was the best attended hearing in the Legislature's 100-year history. When the chairman asked how many in the audience supported a national constitutional convention, several dozen hands went up. When he asked how many were opposed, hundreds shot up. I knew I was in friendly territory—and part of an absolutely fascinating coalition of strange bedfellows. It included Phyllis Schlafly, the firebrand leader of the ultra-conservative Eagle Forum. I had debated Mrs. Schlafly on several occasions and knew her to be a formidable opponent. A constitutional lawyer, she had led the successful campaign against ratification of the Equal Rights Amendment. Our other allies in opposition to a constitutional convention were Common Cause, the Conference of Seventh-day Adventists, a senior citizens association and the Montana AFL-CIO. Supporters of a constitutional convention included the Farm Bureau Federation, Chamber of Commerce and the Montana Taxpayer Association, all of whom wanted a balanced budget amendment.

One of the first witnesses attempted to convince the audience that the scope of a constitutional convention could be limited. And anyone who disagreed was "ignorant and paranoid." Next up, I introduced myself as "Dan Evans, a United States Senator, a former Governor of Washington state—and I am paranoid." The crowd erupted in laughter and applause. I urged the Legislature to oppose toying with the idea of tearing apart the Constitution in its bicentennial year. I pointed out that the original Constitutional Convention was called specifically to amend the Articles of Confederation. After the convention was called, the delegates ignored their original charge and began work on a totally new constitution.

I was pleased when the Montana Senate State Administration Committee defeated the proposal by a vote of 9 to 1. That seemed to be the peak of the effort to call a national Constitutional Convention and no serious efforts have occurred since.

IN MID-JULY, when Congress celebrated the bicentennial of the signing of the Constitution, 55 members of Congress were chosen to represent the original 55 members of the Constitutional Convention. One member was selected from each state, with five congressional leaders completing the delegation. Tom Foley of Spokane, the House Majority Leader, was one of the leaders selected. I was delighted when he asked me if I would represent Washington.

In Philadelphia, we assembled in the room in Independence Hall where the Constitution was debated and ultimately signed. I imagined myself sitting on a bench in the hot, humid summer of 1787. Dressed in woolen knee britches and long coats, the delegates must have perspired profusely. The windows were closed and shades drawn to protect the secrecy of their deliberations. How I wished that the historic room could have talked to us—that the room could echo once again with arguments and oratory of those historic deliberations.

Our ceremonies were air-conditioned. And the blinds were open. Twenty-six senators representing the 13 original states moved to Congress Hall next door where we replicated the first meeting of the United States Senate on December 6, 1790.* The Senate met in the upper chamber. The House of Representatives, a larger body, met on the first floor. We sat in crimson leather chairs at small desks almost identical to those in the current Senate Chamber, except that quill pens were the only communications device back in the day. We listened intently as Vice President Bush narrated proceedings that replicated the first meeting. We could hear the raucous singing of the members of the House of Representatives meeting below us. I was amused by the similarity between this event and

---

* The first Congress met briefly in New York City, but not all of the 13 states had ratified the Constitution.

the observations of a visitor to the Senate in 1796:

> Among the 30 senators of that day there was observed constantly during the debate the most delightful silence, the most beautiful order, gravity, and the personal dignity of manner. They all appeared every morning full-powdered and dressed, as age or fancy might suggest, in the richest material. The very atmosphere of the place seemed to inspire wisdom, mildness, and condescension... presenting in their courtesy a most striking contrast to the independent loquacity of the Representatives below stairs.

It would be wonderful if the current Senate would, in some small measure, capture the "beautiful order" our forefathers exhibited. Unfortunately modern electronics allow members to watch debate from their offices while arguments echo in a virtually empty chamber. I suppose that in some future year we may see on the Senate floor flickering holographs of Senators arguing vociferously but speaking from many miles away. A "virtual" Senate is not what our founders had in mind.

After the ceremonies, we gathered at a helicopter landing pad to catch flights back to Washington, D.C. When Nancy and I got separated, something amazing happened. She tells it best:

"I'm standing in this sort of big area, waiting for the helicopter, together with some spouses and some Senators. Strom Thurmond, at that time the longest-serving senator in U.S. history, came over to where I was standing. He had been governor before his election to the Senate. 'Well, Mrs. Evans, how does Dan like being a senator? Does he prefer being a governor or does he prefer being a senator?' I said, 'Well, he really preferred being a governor because of the ability to set the agenda and organize things a bit more the way you would like to have them.' He patted me on my behind and said, 'Yeah, but the Senate is where the *power* is!' "

IN AUGUST 1987, I attended an Energy Committee hearing on oil exploration in Alaska's Arctic National Wildlife Refuge. A panel of young environmental activists was pontificating about the dangers of oil drilling. Finally I'd had enough. Addressing the president of the National Wildlife Federation, I said I found his arrogance repulsive, especially when he declared, "We represent the public interest." In truth, he represented the interests of some people. And if uncompromising environmentalists continued to oppose development of any new energy sources, we could have "the energy equivalent of an AIDS epidemic unless we are careful," I warned. "There is no one at this table, I would be willing to bet, who did not arrive here from home without using petroleum products. I think I was working on environmental issues when you were all in knee pants."

It was out of character for me. A lifelong outdoorsman, I was a member of the board of the Nature Conservancy and a former Washington Environmental Council "Public Official of the Year." On my watch as governor, we created the state Department of Ecology. Frankly, I was still annoyed over the intense opposition of some environmental groups to any rational solution to our nuclear-waste problems. "He's being a Republican now," one critic told reporters, "not our vaunted moderate-to-liberal representative of the State of Washington."

My monitored retrievable storage proposal for nuclear waste caused much of the fracas. In an opinion piece in *The Seattle Times*, Joan Edwards of the Sierra Club called it "dangerous and expensive and only puts off the problem to the next generation." I was really upset and promised a rebuttal "as soon as I can get the smoke off the typewriter... there is so much bad information around."

The new breed of young urban environmentalists struck me as strident, immature and less analytical. "They have no institutional memory of what has gone on in the past," I said. "They haven't bothered to look, read, understand the nature of what we've gone through." My frustration was a reflection of the difference between being a governor and a legislator. My perceptive wife had said it best: *I missed the ability to set the agenda.* As governor I could shape my own initiatives and present policies to voters and interest groups on my own terms. As a senator I was constantly reacting to other people's proposals. Often I didn't even have the opportunity to add my thoughts to pending legislation. I hated black-white, either-or choices on complex issues. Rarely does a person have 100 percent feelings about something. Sometimes, it's 51-49. Yet I still had to cast a "yes" or "no" vote.

David Ortman of Friends of the Earth observed, "When he's on your side, it's wonderful. When he's not, it's like fighting a grizzly." I liked that. I consider myself a rational environmentalist. When someone tells you he or she represents the public interest, be wary.

62
BORKED

When big news breaks, the buzz reverberates down every marbled corridor on Capitol Hill. On June 26, 1987, everyone knew a potentially epic battle was at hand. Justice Lewis F. Powell Jr., 79, a key swing vote on the U.S. Supreme Court, had resigned due to failing health. President Reagan now had "his long-sought opportunity to put conservatives in control of the high court," *The Washington Post* declared, noting that Powell "had almost single-handedly stymied the Reagan judicial revolution, consistently voting against the administration in close cases involving abortion, affirmative action and separation of church and state."

Democrats, having gained control of the U.S. Senate, had been hoping to deny the president another Supreme Court appointment before the 1988 elections. Reagan said he would quickly nominate a replacement so the court could begin its next term, on the first Monday in October, "at full strength."

"Oh my God!" exclaimed Marsha Levick, executive director of the National Organization for Women's Legal Defense Fund, when she heard the "devastating news." The American Civil Liberties Union noted that during its current term the court had decided 20 major civil liberties cases on 5-to-4 votes. Justice Powell's vote was pivotal each time.

On July 1, Reagan announced his nominee: 60-year-old Robert H. Bork, a former Yale Law School professor whom he had appointed to the U.S. Court of Appeals for the District of Columbia five years earlier. An undeniably brilliant conservative legal scholar, Bork espoused "originalism," the theory that the U.S. Constitution should be interpreted as written by the Founding Founders. As Solicitor General in the Nixon Administration, Bork acquired a cart full of political baggage. On October 20, 1973—the day of the storied "Saturday Night Massacre"—Bork complied with Nixon's order to fire Watergate Special Prosecutor Archibald Cox after Attorney General Elliot Richardson and his deputy, William Ruckelshaus, refused and resigned on the spot. Bork said later that he too considered resigning, but worried it would create another constitutional crisis.*

Within 45 minutes of Bork's nomination, Ted Kennedy—practically apoplectic—took the floor of the Senate to demonize him:

---

* In *Saving Justice*, a memoir published in 2013 a few months following his death, Bork wrote that after he complied with Nixon's order to fire Cox, the president promised him the next Supreme Court vacancy. Whether Nixon actually believed he still had the political clout to get someone confirmed to the court is hard to discern. Perhaps, one historian speculated, he "was just trying to secure Bork's continued loyalty as his administration crumbled." In 2018, Ruckelshaus told historian John C. Hughes that he and Richardson encouraged Bork to carry out the president's order to fire Cox "if his conscience would let him. We were frankly worried about the stability of the government."

Robert Bork's America is a land in which women would be forced into back-alley abortions, Blacks would sit at segregated lunch counters, rogue police could break down citizens' doors in midnight raids, school children could not be taught about evolution, writers and artists would be censored at the whim of government, and the doors of the federal courts would be shut on the fingers of millions of citizens for whom the judiciary is often the only protector of the individual rights that are the heart of our democracy.

That ranks as one of the most outrageously demagogic speeches I've ever heard in my 65 years in politics. Ted Kennedy, admirable qualities notwithstanding, had a tendency to go off the rails. He may even have believed his own bombast. This diatribe against a nominee who had been confirmed unanimously for the appellate court five years earlier was the opening shot in a vicious war of words. Unfortunately, the White House did not respond forcefully for a couple of months. Public opinion was polluted by the intensity of the opposition to Bork. Some even suggested that

President Reagan with Supreme Court nominee Robert Bork in 1987. *Reagan Library*

his bushy-bearded chin and owlish eyes gave him the countenance of a Soviet bureaucrat.

Many of the groups that rallied around causes I championed during my 12 years as governor—civil rights, disability rights, equal rights for women, conservation and the environment—were adamantly opposed to Judge Bork. The easy course would have been to join the parade. One by one, senators began taking sides without doing their homework, just reacting to political pressures. Many never bothered to talk with Bork, attend his confirmation hearings or read the transcripts. I read all 730 pages and met with Bork several times, quizzing him closely on his beliefs about the role of the Supreme Court and the duties of its justices. He struck me as thoughtful and well qualified. When I said I was keeping an open mind, the badgering media wondered whether I was waffling or just indecisive. I was even more discouraged by the invective being hurled from all sides. My office received 15,000 letters equally divided over Bork's fitness for the high bench. Only a few had thoughtfully analyzed his legal beliefs and character. Finally, after 93 other senators had indicated whether they would or would not support Bork, I rose on the Senate floor for one of my most heartfelt speeches:

> From the very beginning, I was inclined to oppose the Bork nomination. As governor, I was extraordinarily proud of the work we were able to accomplish on behalf of the expansion of civil rights for minorities and women. We engaged in one of the very first Education for All bills in the nation, providing extra resources for the developmentally disabled. We began to reach a partnership with our Indian nations.

And we took one of the earliest steps as a state to move strongly in the environmental field. Virtually all of the groups representing those people have opposed Judge Bork's nomination. …

I could have just added my voice to the chorus that began to call for the rejection of Judge Bork, even before the ink on the nomination papers had dried. But I could not do that. Edmund Burke said that "your representative owes you not his industry only, but his judgment; and he betrays you instead of serving you if he sacrifices it to your opinion."

The least responsible opponents have sought to portray Judge Bork as a Neanderthal—someone so hostile to civil liberties that no civilized society could survive the venom of his judicial pen. If the record supported that contention in any way, I would do everything in my power to make certain he was not confirmed. …

Without doubt, the record supports the conclusion that Robert Bork is a profoundly conservative man. It also supports the conclusion that he is a highly intelligent man with superior legal skills. But it does not support the conclusion that he would use those skills to incorporate an unprincipled, results-oriented legal philosophy into the decisions of the Supreme Court. …

He is hostile, however, to the concept of a runaway judiciary. And on this point, Judge Bork and I agree. Nothing will so quickly undermine the public trust in our independent judiciary than judges who seek to impose their own vision of social justice. Imperial Presidents can be voted out after four years, Imperial Senators after six, but an Imperial Judge reigns for life. …

I decry particularly those opponents who hypocritically cloak themselves in the mantle of tolerance while at the same time mounting a vicious campaign of intolerance and demagoguery.

Judge Bork is not a radical. He is not an extremist. He is a man who has a more conservative, more restrictive view of the world than I do. He would not have been my nominee for the Supreme Court. Yet the evidence simply does not support the claim that he has views so extreme that he should be disqualified from service on the court.

In October, Judge Bork's nomination was rejected by the U.S. Senate, 58 to 42, the biggest margin by which the Senate had ever rejected a Supreme Court nomination. The bitter battle changed—perhaps forever—the way in which the Senate confirms Justices of the United States Supreme Court. We have now seen—witness the battles over the Obama and Trump nominees—that with rare exceptions it will be a raucous scrap to put the most devout liberal or conservative on the court. When political philosophy trumps judicial philosophy, the court suffers. So do the American people.*

That I was frustrated was no secret to some of my Senate colleagues. Alan Simpson told *The New York Times*, "Dan has an engineering mind. It's precision and it's putting link on link on girder on

---

* Bork's dubious achievement was to have a word named for him in the *Oxford English Dictionary*. The verb "bork" is used as slang, to "defame or vilify (a person) systematically," with the aim of preventing his or her appointment to public office.

girder, and in this place the sand comes along every four days and washes out the foundation."

FOR MUCH OF THE YEAR, I had been working with my friend Congressman Sid Morrison, an energetic Republican from Yakima County, to produce a comprehensive bill to equitably distribute water in the Yakima River Basin. We teamed up with the Yakama Indian Nation, irrigation districts, local governments, the Bureau of Reclamation and Governor Gardner to resolve some messy disputes. The Yakamas wanted more water in the river to preserve fish runs, while the irrigators complained of an increasing shortage of water for agriculture. Western water law was clearly the elephant in the room. It assigned priority in the use of water to those who used it first. Over time, the irrigation districts, individual farmers and local governments reached agreements on water diversion. There was a tenuous truce until the tribe asserted its water rights—dating from "time immemorial"—especially to retain traditional fish runs. That generated a flurry of lawsuits. We hoped to resolve the issues by increasing water supply, having introduced a bill authorizing $142 million in construction projects to carry out our goal.

On the morning of October 19, 1987—remembered on Wall Street as "Black Monday"— we opened a hearing in Yakima. The irrigators were at the microphones when Joe Mentor, my resourceful aide, slipped me a note. The stock market was down more than a hundred points—a huge decline back then, yet a relative blip today given the market's dramatic rise. Joe kept passing us notes on the latest numbers. But as the hearing proceeded we were heartened by the willingness of all parties to compromise. When we got to the last panel, things took a turn. An old country lawyer identified himself as representing two tiny irrigation districts in the Valley. He testified that they weren't involved in any negotiations or agreement and were not prepared to give up any of the water rights they claimed. Initially I thought this would be a relatively small, easily resolved issue. But the large water districts began to back away, which prompted the tribe to reassert its original position of water rights sovereignty. The carefully constructed compromise crumbled. We now had no chance of getting our bill through Congress. Sid and I left the room, distraught that our hard work would yield no dividends. Nor would the stock market, at least for the time being. We realized we had overlooked a major premise on grand compromises: Make sure you have everyone in the room when you're negotiating. Somehow we had overlooked two small but mighty stakeholders. Best not to make that mistake again.

THE ELEPHANT IN MY OWN ROOM was whether to seek re-election to the Senate in 1988. Weeks earlier I had a scheduled a news conference in Seattle for the day after the Yakima hearing. That gave me a target date to make my decision. When I set out on my three-day swing around the state, reporters kept asking if the campaign was officially underway. I just smiled and said, "I'm still waiting for that bolt of lightning from above." I didn't admit that I was so conflicted I was finding it hard to sleep. Nancy's advice at crossroads moments never varied: "Do what you would like to do. I'll be happy either way." Our three sons felt the same way. I created a mental balance sheet with parallel rows of pros and cons. (I do have an engineering mind!) I started with the firm belief that if I ran I would win. Several Democratic congressmen were weighing the race, regardless of my decision. I believed that only Mike Lowry would have the passion and courage to sign up for a rematch. And he was still a polarizing figure.

After five years in the Senate, I was beginning to understand the pace of the place. Starting to gain seniority, too, which meant practically everything. The challenges facing the Energy and Indian Affairs committees were fascinating. I was beginning to have some influence on major issues. Service on the Foreign Affairs Committee was a delight, even with Jesse Helms as chairman. I would have the opportunity to travel to strategically important regions of the world and meet foreign leaders.

The other side of the ledger was equally long. I was frustrated by the lack of intelligent debate on the Senate floor. Organizationally the Senate was a basket case. Every senator, no matter how junior, was an individual power center with unrestricted access to the ready television cameras waiting in the Senate pressroom. The appropriations process was ghastly. Virtually none of the 13 appropriations bills were being presented to the president before the start of the fiscal year. We lumped them together into a single Continuing Resolution or omnibus appropriations bill, loaded with pork, and presented it to the president, knowing he had no chance to exercise a veto and close down the government.

While I was unhappy about those problems I looked forward to the challenge of making things better. None of the "cons" was sufficient reason to retire from the Senate.

It came down to age. I would be 63 at the end of my term. If I stepped aside from the Senate I could look forward to a variety of interesting new careers. If I ran and won I would be 69 at the end of my next term. The external choices narrow considerably at that age. At that point, another term in the Senate, with more power and seniority, would look pretty attractive. So this was the time to decide: Would I seek a new and as yet undefined career, or stay in the Senate for the rest of my working life—or at least until I was defeated, which often happens when you hang around too long, Slade's victory over Warren Magnuson being Exhibit A. Too many of my colleagues who had stayed too long ended their careers physically and mentally impaired. When I asked myself that final question the answer was easy. It was more like connecting the dots than a bolt of lightning:

There's no place like home.

AROUND MIDNIGHT on October 20 I realized that if I stayed in the Senate I would be a permanent resident of Washington, D.C., and a *visitor* to Washington state. I was a creature of the Northwest, a native son from pioneer stock. I loved our mountains, our lakes, streams, beaches and prairies; our vineyards, rolling wheat fields and vast stands of great-girthed evergreens. On a dazzling Puget Sound morning, you can wake up to the Olympics at your front door and the Cascades in the back yard. I wanted to hike my favorite trails and dive into icy lakes—in the buff if the moment suited me. Above all, I loved our state's diverse population—the people who had trusted me with statewide elective office four times.

I shared my epiphany with Nancy and we called our sons. Early that morning I called my staff in Washington, D.C., to share my decision before alerting the press. Bill Jacobs had led an extraordinary group of young, smart, hard-working yet fun-loving people who collectively made me look better and smarter than I ever could have possibly accomplished alone. I told a press conference in Seattle that it was a fundamentally personal decision, admitting that the tediousness of getting things done was frustrating. "And I think that's probably something that I share with all members of the Senate who once served as governors." Four other senators—two Republicans and two Democrats— had also announced it was time to go.

A few months later, as my would-be successors jockeyed for position, I conveyed my feelings more forcefully in an essay for *The New York Times Magazine:*

> I came to Washington with a slightly romantic notion of the Senate—perhaps natural for a former governor and civil engineer whose hobby is the study of history—and I looked forward to the duel of debate, the exchange of ideas. What I found was a legislative body that had lost its focus and was in danger of losing its soul. In the United States Senate, debate has come to consist of set speeches read before a largely empty chamber; and in committees, quorums are rarely achieved. I have lived through five years of bickering and protracted paralysis. Five years is enough. I just can't face another six years of frustrating gridlock.
>
> Consider the filibuster—speaking at length to delay and defeat a bill. This legislative tactic has an honorable past, but recently its use has grown like a malignant tumor. Now merely a "hold," or threat of filibuster, placed by a senator is sufficient to kill a bill. Senator Jesse Helms's bitter feud with the State Department provides a classic example. The Republican from North Carolina has shown himself particularly adept at using the rules to further his own foreign policy agenda. Only rarely is the Senate willing to go through the pain and time necessary to stop this bullying. The dramatic decline in discipline helped to stretch out legislative sessions interminably, and thus eliminated the extended periods of time that legislators used to spend among their constituents. Most of us have been forced to become only Tuesday-through-Thursday senators, squeezing in brief weekend visits to avoid feeling like exiles from our own home states.

Chances are you're now thinking what I'm thinking: *Not much has changed.*

In 2017—30 years after I announced I would not seek re-election—John McCain delivered a stunning excoriation of "a Senate riven by partisan infighting and almost no effort to work across the aisle." Newly diagnosed with terminal brain cancer, the 80-year-old Arizona senator had flown 2,300 miles across the nation to cast a critical vote against Trump's attempt to dismantle Obamacare. This is what John said:

> I have been a member of the United States Senate for 30 years. ...
>
> I've known and admired men and women in the Senate who played much more than a small role in our history—true statesmen, giants of American politics. They came from both parties, and from various backgrounds. Their ambitions were frequently in conflict. They held different views on the issues of the day. But they knew that however sharp and heartfelt their disputes, however keen their ambitions, they had an obligation to work collaboratively to ensure the Senate discharged its constitutional responsibilities effectively. The most revered members of this institution accepted the necessity of compromise in order to make incremental progress on solving America's problems and to defend her from her adversaries.
>
> That principled mindset, and the service of our predecessors who possessed it,

come to mind when I hear the Senate referred to as the world's greatest deliberative body. I'm not sure we can claim that distinction with a straight face today. Our deliberations today are more partisan, more tribal more of the time than any other time I remember. Both sides have let this happen. Let's leave the history of who shot first to the historians. I suspect they'll find we all conspired in our decline—either by deliberate actions or neglect. We've all played some role in it. Certainly I have.

Let's trust each other. Let's return to regular order. We've been spinning our wheels on too many important issues because we keep trying to find a way to win without help from across the aisle.

We're getting nothing done, my friends! What have we to lose by trying to work together to find those solutions?

The success of the Senate is important to the continued success of America. This country—this big, boisterous, brawling, intemperate, restless, striving, daring, beautiful, bountiful, brave, good and magnificent country—needs us to help it thrive. That responsibility is more important than any of our personal interests or political affiliations.

History will long remember what John McCain said. Now more than ever, the question is, "What will it take, my friends, to thwart the politics of polarization?"

AS WE MOVED from the difficult committee schedules of early spring to floor action in the fall of 1987, the Senate schedule became more frenetic.

One night, several of us were in the Senate dining room having coffee before the next vote. David Pryor, a hard-working Democrat from Arkansas, was also a former governor. We bemoaned our fate. Practically in the same breath, we asked ourselves, "What in the world are we doing here?" Even though I was now a short-timer, I suggested that each of us find two other backbenchers and form a committee to improve quality of life in the Senate. It produced some excellent ideas. We proposed that the Senate be in session Monday through Friday for three weeks, then recess for a week so all senators could return home to consult with their constituents. Four of us from the committee met with Senator Byrd, the Majority Leader, to advocate our proposals. He listened carefully, commented that they were interesting and promised to consider them. Meantime, interminable night sessions occurred regularly.

Then, to our amazement, when the second session of Congress convened in January 1988, Senator Byrd announced we were going to try a new schedule: three five-day work weeks followed by a week of recess. Our committee's proposal was never mentioned. But pride of authorship didn't matter in the bigger picture because we now had an opportunity to create a more effective Senate.

Unfortunately old habits are difficult to change. Senators who lived not far from the Capitol constantly badgered the majority leader to schedule no votes on Mondays or Fridays. Byrd tried hard to make this new schedule work, but the thirst for time to raise money and to visit constituents gradually reduced the work week. Like clockwork, chaos erupted each fall, especially on the budget. Quality of life in the Senate improved, but only marginally.

63
THE SCRAMBLE

David Horsey's brilliant take on "Life After Dan." *Courtesy David Horsey*

My decision to retire changed the political landscape. It would be the state's first wide open U.S. Senate race since 1944 when a young congressman named Warren Magnuson defeated Tacoma Mayor Harry Cain. It was fun to sit back and watch the scramble.

David Horsey, the *Seattle Post-Intelligencer's* marvelous editorial cartoonist, offered his view of "Life after Dan." A middle-aged guy in a wild sport coat is talking to a waitress at the local diner. He says, "Evans isn't running, see?! So... our Congressman runs for the Senate, our legislator runs for Congress, the mayor runs for the Legislature, the councilman runs for mayor, the water commissioner runs for the council, thus paving the way for ME, Myron Torvald, to nab the water commissioner's job! The waitress smiles admiringly. "Myron," she declares, "you are a regular Machiavelli."

As things turned out, all of the congressmen except Mike Lowry and Don Bonker decided to stay where they were, and all the Myron Torvalds never got to be water commissioners. Slade Gorton, who had done a lot of soul-searching since his devastating loss to Brock Adams in 1986, was poised for a comeback.

Bonker, a capable seven-term congressman from Vancouver, styled himself as Kennedyesque. A devout Christian but no Bible-thumper, Bonker was less liberal than Lowry, but he had name familiarity problems outside his district. Lowry's King County base was formidable. He'd run state-wide against me in 1983.

The kinder, gentler 1988 versions of Gorton and Lowry captivated the pundits. Lowry shaved his scraggly Yasser Arafat beard and resolved to stop waving his arms whenever he got worked up. Gorton ditched his horn-rims in favor of stylish new glasses and moderated his perceived intellectual arrogance with "a heavy dose of contrition." During "the unhappy days of 1986, I must confess I lost contact with too many people in the State of Washington," he said. "I was not listening. That will never happen again." Above all, he regretted voting to freeze the cost-of-living increases for Social Security recipients. "I *really* wasn't listening then."

THE PRESIDENTIAL RACE was equally fascinating. Dole and Bush were jetting off to Iowa and New Hampshire at every opportunity. It's fascinating to me that two small states that are not very representative of the nation, nevertheless can play key roles in the making of a president.

I liked Bob Dole. Gravely wounded in World War II, he was a centrist who took his leadership role seriously. He now began to demonstrate the dry wittiness missing from his acerbic performance as Ford's running mate in 1976. I admired George H.W. Bush's thoughtfulness and wide-ranging experience, but I did not know him as well as Dole. Still, I believed Bush would be a stronger candidate and would do a good job as president. It was still difficult to go against my Senate colleague.

I had called the vice president in the fall of 1987, telling him I was inclined to

With George and Barbara Bush. *Evans Family Collection*

support him but we needed to talk. The very next words out of his mouth were: "If you and Nancy are free this evening why don't you come over to the residence for drinks with Bar and me around 6 o'clock?"

The vice president's palatial official residence—once occupied by the Chief of Naval Operations—is on the lovely grounds of the Naval Observatory in northwest Washington. George and Barbara met us at the front door and led us to a sunny sitting room. I said I was interested in what he wanted to accomplish as president, particularly with regard to our out-of-control national budget and peace in the Middle East. He kept returning to campaign tactics. South Carolina's primary would be critical, he said. I found myself listening to him with one ear and to the lively conversation between Nancy and Barbara Bush with the other. They started out talking about abortion, and then began discussing priorities for education. George was so fixated on campaigning that he could not focus on what he wanted to do if he got the job.

The Bushes were delightful hosts, but as we drove home I said to Nancy, "You and Barbara talked more about issues than we ever did, and frankly I wanted to join your conversation. I think George wants to be president but really doesn't know why. I'm going to wait a while to see what he proposes before I make any commitment."

IN IOWA, THE CAMPAIGN got nasty. I wrote a note addressed to both, saying their strident rhetoric left neither of them looking presidential. "For heaven's sakes, ask or demand that your campaign aides keep focused on the right targets." Otherwise, they'd be playing into the hands of the right-wing candidate, TV evangelist Pat Robertson—not to mention the Democrats.

I did not hear back from Dole. Bush responded immediately with a handwritten note: "Dear Dan: you are right. Many thanks for the wise counsel. I'm grateful." That convinced me he had the stature and grace to be president. I told reporters I believed either man would make a first class president. But I had decided to support Bush because he had the best combination of experience, stability, and steadiness America needed. I traveled to several Eastern states during the primary season to campaign for Bush. I also came to realize that an earlier commitment could have brought me closer to the center of the campaign and given me a real opportunity to influence policy proposals.

I returned to my home precinct in Olympia to join our old neighbors for a precinct caucus and was duly elected a delegate to the Thurston County GOP convention. The other precinct-selected delegates were committed to the Rev. Robertson, whose followers were out in force. Unlike presidential primaries, the caucus system tends to attract the most dedicated party workers and partisans.

Our convoluted system of selecting presidential candidates is left over from the 19th century when communication was slow and voter eligibility was limited. Today, we're saddled with a messy mixture of caucuses and primaries, with Iowa and New Hampshire protecting their roles as potential king makers. I think it is time for us to embark on a primary system for all states. Proposals for four regional primaries to be held a month apart strike me as a reasonable solution. Dates for each region would be rotated so that each area of the country would have its turn as first in line. I doubt it will happen anytime soon. Political party bosses are too enamored of power to open the system to broad public participation.

BY SPRING it was apparent that Bush would win the GOP nomination. I thought it would be interesting to see what my 30-person senatorial staff—from mailroom interns to Bill Jacobs, my top aide—would say to the vice president about the campaign, his policies and the future of the Republican Party. I listened with awe and pride as our uncommonly bright, mostly young staffers offered their advice. I distilled their thoughts in a letter to Bush:

> President Reagan's slogan was "It's morning in America." Perhaps the slogan for the next administration needs to be "It's time for America to get out of bed." You should package programs for the future—from the human genome to the supercollider and magnetic transportation—under the major scientific challenges facing us.
> Revisit the notion of what it is to be a Republican. Return to the concepts of

Teddy Roosevelt and put the term "conserve" into conservative. We have a duty to protect the environment for our future as well as utilizing it for the greatest good.

The Republican Party captured many people by its pocketbook issues, tax reductions, and emphasis on free enterprise. Now there is a need to show compassion and help people recognize that effective management of government leads to success in human programs.

Don't squander your credibility on issues like school prayer and a balanced budget amendment. Focus on programs that can bring new hope to people and new opportunity for our free enterprise system.

In foreign policy, attempt in every way to make it bipartisan.

Don't allow too narrow a litmus test on appointments to high positions.

Don't make government the enemy.

It's important to speak out on women's issues specifically. Special mention of child care and preschool education is important for a growing number of women, especially young women, in this country.

The most experienced, expensive campaign consultants in the land could not have put it any better than my staff. The next day I received a reply on the vice president's personal stationery. It reflected one of Bush's great strengths—immediate and personal written communication:

Dear Dan: That letter was superb. Please thank all that highly motivated "focus group" of a staff. I agree with most of the suggestions. I can do better at letting people see the "human side that's there." I do feel strongly about opportunity for women, about finding a non-budget-busting answer to daycare and about better cooperation with Congress. Please thank each and every participant in this unique and extraordinarily helpful exercise. It really means a lot to me. Tell them also to excuse my self-typed letter; but I wanted to fire this off right now. – All best, George

When I read his response at the next staff meeting, the reaction was "Wow! We got through to the vice president!"

NUCLEAR DISARMAMENT and aid to the Contras remained hot topics during the presidential campaign. When the second session of the 100th Congress convened, we were faced almost immediately with contentious Foreign Relations Committee hearings on the Intermediate-range Nuclear Forces Treaty signed in December by Reagan and Gorbachev. Some of the lead treaty negotiators were scheduled to appear before the committee.

Jesse Helms, the committee chairman, quickly derailed our progress. The INF Treaty required the U.S. and Soviet Union to destroy hundreds of intermediate-range missiles. Helms argued that while missiles would be destroyed, the nuclear material from the warheads would be retained. In his own inimitable way, the archconservative North Carolinian argued that "a missile is a carrying case and the warhead is the thing that goes boom and kills you. A missile doesn't kill you unless it falls on your head and cracks it open." The negotiators, taken aback, responded that verification of nuclear material destruction was virtually impossible. One noted, "It's very hard to pick up this nuclear warhead and throw it at someone. That's why you have to have the missile."

Exasperated, I interrupted: "I fear that we will spend most of our hearings over the next several weeks trying to respond to red herrings that are strewn across the path of these treaty negotiations. In fact it is more than a red herring. I'd call it a crimson whale."

Helms' homespun "Go boom" side show was typical of his obstructionist mentality. He sought to amend the treaty, which would require renegotiations. He also was out to thwart a much more significant treaty aimed at cutting long-range nuclear missiles. It struck me as ironic that he was attempting to frustrate the goals of President Reagan, the leader he adored.

The Foreign Relations Committee, by an overwhelming vote, rolled over Helms to ratify the INF treaty.

REAGAN'S REQUEST FOR $36 million to help the right-wing Nicaraguan rebels was rejected by the House of Representatives. That normally would have been the end of the Contra aid saga. But the identical proposal came to the floor of the Senate in an extraordinarily unusual way. In the last days of the previous session a proviso regarding aid to the Contras was attached to the Continuing Resolution. It expedited procedures and waived points of order. The Foreign Relations Committee, in a purely political move, now voted to reject the president's aid package. The action was totally unnecessary since the bill was already scheduled for floor action. Republicans on the committee, in protest, boycotted the meeting.

The calls and letters pouring into my office were running heavily in opposition to helping the Contras. Some opposed aid because they thought it was inappropriate to involve ourselves in the internal affairs of another country. Others opposed aid because they were active supporters of Daniel Ortega and his left-wing Sandinistas. They believed a revolutionary government represented the best future for Nicaragua.

I had been a consistent opponent of military aid to the Contras. This time, however, I supported the Senate proposal, explaining my vote by saying that if both houses of Congress voted against the president it would leave a void, creating huge amounts of apprehension in Central America, leaving no vehicle for crafting a united Central American policy.

A few months earlier, together with Chris Dodd of Connecticut and Nancy Kassebaum of Kansas, I made a quick trip to Central America. President Oscar Arias of Costa Rica was offering a peace plan for the region. He shared some intriguing ideas about how to gain support from the heads of neighboring nations. When we met with Ortega, we pressed him on the Arias proposal for free elections. Eyes flashing, Nicaragua's 42-year-old president declared, "We will never give up the revolution!"

We also spent a fascinating hour with Violeta Chamorro, the widow of an assassinated Nicaraguan hero. She was a vibrant woman who impressed us with her devotion to her country. Two of her four children had joined the Sandinistas. The other two supported her opposition movement. She was obviously a potent political leader, and much more believable than the Contra leadership. On the long airplane ride home we agreed that we would support and advocate the peace plan presented by President Arias. We felt it was imperative to keep pressure on Ortega and his Sandinistas, but not by providing military aid to the Contras, believing they were incapable of winning militarily.

Now, my change of heart generated an intense reaction from many voters. In the final debate on the Senate floor, I proposed an alternative approach:

> Since the time I arrived in the Senate, I have been an opponent of Contra aid because I felt that it simply would not do the job that its adherents suggested it would.
>
> Much has happened in the last two years. I believe the circumstances have changed. Economic aid has helped these fragile democracies, but continued insurgency has made it terribly difficult to make very much progress in otherwise destitute lands. More important, the leaders of all five Central American countries have spoken. They did not say, "Isolate Nicaragua while the other four democracies go their own way." All of them, including the President of Nicaragua, said, "Democracy in all five lands; democracy now, not democracy tomorrow. Democracy under specific plans and very specific timetables."
>
> I do not like the package the president sent to us. It is inadequate. It is aimed in the wrong direction. But it may be better than no package at all. This cannot be the final answer. We cannot simply walk away from Central America. I intend to vote in favor of this package tonight. Tomorrow morning I intend to start working with any and all of my colleagues and with the president and those in the State Department to craft a better policy, one that is bipartisan; one that brings unity.
>
> Do not give up until we find a better, bipartisan answer—one that will truly bring a lasting peace to Central America.

The Senate supported the administration's request for aid to the Contras, 51 to 48. Several of us set out to see if we could find a better answer. Unfortunately, the Reagan Administration was not willing to modify its position. We struggled incoherently and unsuccessfully for the rest of the Congress and the president's term to resolve our differences. It was, after all, an election year. Water commissioner began to sound appealing.

THE COMMITTEE ON ENERGY and Natural Resources was the focus of renewed debate on our energy future. The Reagan Administration regularly sent Congress proposals for energy research, focusing primarily on nuclear and coal while ignoring most renewable resources. We would just as regularly modify those requests by prioritizing research on solar, wind, and fuel-cell technology. As the administration and Congress dithered, the nation imported more oil, leaving the U.S. dangerously more susceptible to pressures from oil-producing nations.

The success of Alaska's North Slope oil exploration and the construction of a trans-Alaska pipeline led to increasing demands to open Alaska's Arctic National Wildlife Refuge for oil exploration. I recalled my work on the Pacific Northwest Energy and Conservation Council where almost a decade earlier we developed a comprehensive energy plan for the Pacific Northwest. Chuck Collins, my colleague from Washington on the council, summed up our approach: "We cannot predict exactly the energy needs, but we can develop a 'least-cost energy' strategy that ranks potential energy sources based on their long-term costs." The results showed conclusively that conservation and energy efficiency were the least expensive and the most productive energy sources.

I joined with two industrious Democrats, Tim Wirth of Colorado and Dale Bumpers of Arkansas, in a bipartisan effort to accomplish the same goals at the national level. We said the Energy Secretary should be required to rank all of the alternatives, giving priority to the alternative or alternatives that were the least costly. We should increase efficient use of our petroleum resources, reducing their impact on the environment, and enhance the diversification of the domestic energy supply base. "No one questions the unique and sensitive nature of the Arctic ecosystems," I emphasized. "And no one questions that the area we are focused on today is undisturbed by man. It is because of the environmental sensitivity of the coastal plain that I feel it is imperative that we stop making energy decisions in a vacuum."

After a vigorous 2½-hour debate, our plan was defeated, 10 to 9. The committee adopted a so-called compromise that authorized a study, but allowed concurrent development of the Wildlife Refuge. All these years later, Congress is still debating oil recovery from the Alaska Native Wildlife Refuge. In 1988, we lost a unique opportunity to develop a sensible energy plan that could have showed the way to energy independence by the beginning of the 21st century.

64
TAKE ALL YOU CAN GET

In the dwindling months of my term in the Senate, I thought a lot about my checklist of issues—ones we had a fighting chance to resolve. High among them was to follow the success of the Washington Wilderness Bill with a proposal to extend wilderness protection within the boundaries of the state's three national parks.

Although Mount Rainier, Olympic and North Cascades were operated as wilderness parks by policy directive, there was no legal protection against excessive development within their boundaries. I decided to delineate wilderness boundaries within the parks, carefully excluding existing road systems and developed campgrounds. There would be no attempt to further restrict access to the interior of the parks since they were already reasonably remote.

Brock Adams joined me in sponsoring the bill. A companion measure was introduced in the House sponsored by Rod Chandler, John Miller and Al Swift. Three members of my talented staff, Joe Mentor, Sara Kendall and Heidi Biggs, worked long hours to produce the detailed wilderness boundaries within the three parks. Our entire Washington delegation supported the bill. Testifying before the House Interior Subcommittee on National Parks and Recreation, I outlined the proposed wilderness boundaries, stressing that their immediate impact was not as crucial as long-range protection. "What this bill would *not* do is keep visitors shut out of the park. I believe that the parks are there to provide for recreation as well as the preservation of a natural ecosystem." Even in the wilderness areas, the National Park Service would be able to construct trails and back-country campsites. Additionally, all the existing transportation and development corridors would be excluded from wilderness designation. Those corridors included areas that the Park Service had deemed necessary for additional campgrounds and other facilities to accommodate visitors.

The bill moved swiftly. Before the end of the session we added 1.7 million acres to Washington's wilderness. Years later I found that every avid environmentalist's legislative motto, "Take all you can get now and come back and get the rest later," was certainly true. My original intent to both protect wilderness and current access was to be seriously distorted. Although we had designated 200-foot wilderness exempt corridors along each existing road, an unusually severe storm occasionally would create raging river torrents that eroded several hundred feet of roadbed. Building better roads to avoid future inundation now required minor modification of wilderness boundaries. That of course would require a bill to be passed by Congress. Some environmental groups immediately opposed any action, claiming that closing a road would create even "deeper" wilderness. While they were technically correct, it also would make access much more difficult for all except the fittest and those with the most time to explore. The battle continues but I believe very strongly that in order to protect our national parks we need a large contingent of supporters. And the best supporters are those who experience the wonders of wilderness. If we continue to make access more difficult we reduce their numbers. Someday we may wake up to discover that our army of defenders has been reduced to a besieged platoon of vocal elders.

ENVIRONMENTAL PROTECTION can occur in strange ways. Shortly after I introduced my National Parks Wilderness Bill, a certificate arrived in the mail. It said, "In appreciation of his services to the people of the State of Washington, the Redwood *Sequoia sempervirens* located at Union and Franklin streets on the State Capitol Campus in Olympia is hereby designated "The Daniel J. Evans Tree."

It was signed by the Washington State Capitol Committee: Governor Booth Gardner, Lt. Governor John Cherberg and Commissioner of Public Lands Brian Boyle. A fancy gold state seal was affixed by order of Secretary of State Ralph Munro. Pleased, puzzled and surprised, I called Ralph to find out what happened. He chuckled and explained that he and Herb Legg, a former chairman of the State Democratic Party, were having coffee one morning when they read in the paper that a downtown lot was to be bulldozed for parking for the Capitol campus. Herb was a marvelously eccentric, independent guy. We had become good friends during my 12 years as governor. Herb told Ralph the lot featured a Sequoia planted in 1889, the year Washington was admitted to the Union.

The two debated what to do. Then Herb had a Eureka moment: If they named the tree in my honor the state wouldn't dare cut it down. They recruited state Supreme Court Justice Jimmy Andersen, an old legislative colleague, to help lobby the Capitol Committee. Boy Scouts cleared away brush, built a fine bench and an appropriate sign commemorating the designation. It was their Eagle Scout project. I was pleased, especially since the Scouts got involved. The tree was saved and the three conspirators hugely enjoyed their triumph.

MY ROLE AS VICE CHAIRMAN of the Special Committee on Indian Affairs gave me insight into the shocking number of unfair, sometimes irresponsible decisions made by the paternalistic Bureau of Indian Affairs during its 150 years of managing tribal lands. Joe DeLaCruz, the charismatic chairman of the Quinault Tribe on the coast of the Olympic Peninsula, contacted me about a long-running dispute over the boundaries of the reservation. A surveying error in 1892 shorted the reservation by 15,000 acres. Decades later, the U. S. Court of Claims ruled in favor of the Quinaults, but stated that if the Bureau could show it had given the tribe more than was strictly required by their treaty it could subtract the difference from the value of the land. Amazingly, the BIA found that it had "gratuitously" given the tribe in "food, rations and provisions" a whopping $6.94 more than the government owed for the disputed land.

I set out to right that wrong, enlisting the support of Congressman Al Swift, whose sprawling district included the Quinault Reservation. We produced a bipartisan proposal that would correct the surveying error without adversely affecting local residents. The U.S. Forest Service was reluctant, worrying that some local counties would miss their share of timber profits from the Forest Service land that would now be in the reservation. It also claimed that sensitive species such as the Olympic Mud Minnow and the Northern Spotted Owl wouldn't do well under Indian management—never mind that it was the white man who had ravaged vast tracts of reservation land—and that it was the

Indians who respected the creatures of the wild.

Happily, local counties testified in favor of the legislation, as did environmental leaders. We were ultimately successful.

JOE MENTOR WAS NOW head of the minority staff of the Special Committee on Indian Affairs. In partnership with Chairman Inouye and his staff, we wrote two bills that would transform the relationship between Native American tribes and the federal government. The first allowed tribes to assume responsibility for spending federal funds appropriated through the Bureau of Indian Affairs. Traditionally, spending priorities were determined by the BIA with little input from tribes. Our bill allowed tribes to set their own priorities. It was a huge step toward self-determination and building tribal leadership expertise.

The second bill arose because lawsuits opening gambling on Indian reservations were proceeding through appellate courts. Our committee began a long and contentious effort to regulate gambling on reservations without interfering with the well-established "sovereign-to-sovereign" relationship between the United States and Native American tribes.

A major dispute developed over casino-style gambling. We produced a proposal for a compact between tribes that wanted to build casinos and the states in which the reservations were located. If the state generally barred casino gambling, that would close the door on tribal casinos. The proposal was opposed vigorously by tribal leaders because it was too regulatory—and by a number of attorneys general who thought it was too permissive. Senator Inouye and I spent hours trying to fashion a solution. We finally brought our proposal to the floor of the Senate and engaged in an extended colloquy to describe precisely what we had in mind. These colloquies—pro and con exchanges—are an important part of Senate debate since they describe legislative intent when future disputes arise over the language of the law. Although several senators indicated they could not support the legislation, the bill passed by voice vote.

I later heard from a number of concerned constituents, as well as Washington legislators flatly opposed to Las Vegas-style gaming. The refrain was, "We don't allow that type of gambling, so why can tribes do it?" I pointed out that the state allowed nonprofit organizations to engage in casino-style gambling once a year for charitable purposes. If the Legislature wished to repeal that law then the tribes could not engage in full-scale gambling. I heard immediately from dozens of community-minded organizations that claimed that their very existence depended on that one night of gambling. It was quickly apparent that the Legislature had no stomach for repealing that act. Several tribes began to negotiate compacts with the state to engage in casino gambling, with major economic benefits to their people.

MY SECOND ATTEMPT to settle the water allocation dispute in the Yakima River Valley failed. Sid Morrison and I had come close in the fall of 1987. When the Yakama Indian Nation initiated a lawsuit to obtain water for irrigation on tribal lands and maintain salmon runs, panic broke out among farm irrigators as well as local communities that depended on the river for municipal water. We now proposed a $500 million package of projects in the Yakima Basin to increase water supply for everyone, but the fear of failure overcame the hope of success. I was deeply disappointed since I strongly believed we had an opportunity to end conflict over water and embark on a new era of economic prosperity for the entire Yakima watershed. When I finally decided further effort was futile, I said the stalemate was going to impact every stakeholder. All the Yakima water users were dependent on each other for a healthy, viable economy. If this controversy was left to the courts to resolve, the economy of the entire region would suffer.

Morrison and I were much more successful in our efforts to preserve the last free-flowing stretch of the Columbia River above Bonneville Dam. The 51-mile Hanford Reach flows through the Hanford Nuclear Reservation and ends at the pool of McNary dam. We immediately ran into a storm of opposition from the U.S. Army Corps of Engineers, which wanted to dredge a barge passage upriver to Wenatchee at the request of the Port of Chelan. Our supporters included environmental, fishing and tribal groups. An array of agencies lined up against us, including WPPSS, the BPA and the Department of Energy. They had no plans for the area at present but piously declared that there might be need for development someday.

We proposed a three-year study of the Hanford Reach to determine what protection was most appropriate, adding a five-year moratorium on development beyond that to allow Congress to respond. The completed study recommended strong protection for the area. Congress attempted several times to establish permanent protection.

It took 12 years—long after Sid and I left office. But the bill we passed in 1988 was the first and essential step. In 2000, President Clinton established a Hanford Reach National Monument by executive order.

IN THE DOG DAYS of an election year, there was still a laundry list of legislation on the calendar, including a messy budget. That did not deter members from proposing bills and amendments to burnish their political records.

Senator Al D'Amato of New York again proposed legislation to allow the death penalty for drug dealers who kill or order murders. Senators lined up to echo his declaration that it was "society's way of saying we are going to fight back." I could not remain silent. The goal was to score points with the voters rather than address America's complex drug problem in a responsible way. We were also aiming at the wrong target. Focusing on the supply side of the equation would not work half as well as reducing demand for illicit drugs. Alcohol and tobacco, both legal drugs, killed far more people than illegal drugs. Reduction in their use came only when we focused on the demand side through widespread publicity and education. After hearing D'Amato's supporters sanctimoniously declare they were addressing "the demands of society," I observed, "I suppose you could say that the demands of society in the Middle Ages required the Inquisition. And that demands of society in revolutionary France demanded the guillotine."

Unfortunately, the Senate was more interested in grandstanding than logic. D'Amato's death penalty bill passed, 65 to 29. I received a number of letters, most wondering how I could be so soft on drug dealers. The most enjoyable came from a self-identified "Missouri mule Democrat transplanted to Texas." He wrote, "I just watched your speech in the Senate…and I want to thank you for having the balls to oppose the strident Alphonse D'Amato. Forgive the coarseness of my praise, but I think you will agree that the moral barbarity of this bill makes blushing at such language the equivalent of straining at a gnat while swallowing a camel."

NEXT CAME A MEASURE to erect a statue of an Army nurse as part of the Vietnam War Memorial. Waiting in the wings were proposals to add statues of paramedics, American Indians and scout dogs. The stark beauty of the memorial designed by Maya Lin offended many veterans of earlier wars. Secretary of the Interior James Watt, one of Reagan's most embarrassing appointees, would not allow construction to begin until a statue of three servicemen was added to the monument. I listened to my colleagues expound on the heroic role played by Army nurses in Vietnam, agreeing with everything they said. The measure passed the Senate 96 to 1. I was the sole objector, declaring:

> On this wall, without discrimination or rank, are the names of all those who gave their lives in Vietnam: young and old, officer and enlisted, men and women, black, white, red, or Asian. There is personal recognition for each who died in their names inscribed on the wall. Collectively there is dramatic proof of the cost of that war in American lives.
>
> While I fully understand the desire of those who seek statuary recognition, I believe it was wrong to add the three statues that are now there; that it is wrong to add a statue of a woman veteran and that it would be wrong to add future statues representing other categories of veterans. This vote is simply a protest against what I view as the diminution of the original concept of the Vietnam Memorial and the stark reminder it gave to all of us. In no way does this diminish my respect for those women veterans who gave their lives for their country. …

After the vote, at least a dozen senators told me I was right, but they just didn't want to go against their constituents. When I arrived back at my office after the vote, I waved a white handkerchief. Women comprised more than half of my staff. They understood my reasoning and were enthusiastically supportive. I was not surprised at the response from many citizens who questioned my patriotism and accused me of lacking respect for women. The editorial voices from around the country were fascinating. "It was hardly an act of bravery in the heat of battle," *The Washington Post* wrote, "but 96 senators fell in line Tuesday behind a project wrapped in the flag and pressed in the name of women who served this country in Vietnam. Only one senator, Dan Evans of Washington, had the real courage to vote against this proposal, for an important and patriotic reason: the measure calls for a statue that would be added to—and clearly would detract from—the already powerful Vietnam Veterans Memorial that so movingly expresses this country's respect for the men and women who lost their lives in that war." Jim Fain, a Cox Media Group national correspondent, reported on the extraordinary clutter of monuments around Washington, D.C., suggesting the city needed a statue shredder—"then add one simple marker to the lasting glory of Daniel Evans, the only senator with the courage and taste to vote against this new desecration of a sacred place."

THE DEPARTMENT OF ENERGY announced a decision was imminent on a site for tritium production reactors. I had obtained a temporary security clearance for one of my aides so we could review the study's assertions regarding the urgency of producing more tritium, an essential element of nuclear weapons. It gave us a rare insight into the debate and led me to believe that Hanford was the best site. Tritium is a radioactive isotope of hydrogen and has a half-life of about 12 years, so needs to be regularly replaced. The information we received predicted a critical shortage of tritium within the next decade unless new production was initiated. A new reactor at the nuclear reservation at Savannah River, South Carolina, would take 10 to 12 years to complete while construction at Hanford could be completed in less than half that time and at much less cost.

Energy Secretary John Herrington announced that new reactors would be constructed at Savannah River and an experimental new reactor in Idaho. An Energy Department advisory board said conversion of the unfinished WPPSS plant at Hanford would cost less and be on line quicker, but cautioned that legal and technical uncertainties could make conversion a riskier option. I was convinced that the major influence on the decision was political. A united South Carolina congressional delegation pushed hard for a new reactor at Savannah River. Senator James McClure of Idaho intervened directly with the White House, urging an experimental new reactor in Idaho. But our delegation was deeply divided. Sid Morrison and I worked hard on behalf of a Hanford decision while Brock Adams, Mike Lowry and Don Bonker actively opposed the Hanford site.

Lowry argued that conversion of a civilian reactor violated global nuclear non-proliferation treaties. The fact was that WNP-1 was half finished and never operated as a civilian reactor. Bonker claimed, rather pompously, that "for once, DOE has looked at the scientific merits of a problem, not just the political considerations... Evans just wants to help Slade Gorton in his bid to return to the U.S. Senate." It was a seat Bonker and Lowry coveted. And the primary election was only a month away.

I was furious over the loss of 6,000 jobs, the delay in production and the higher costs to the taxpayers. I boiled over at a press conference: "I don't remember in my political history any member of the Washington delegation who has ever dealt so crassly with what could have been a very important economic opportunity for the state."

The issue would play a big role in the senatorial race.

65
LAST HURRAHS

As we prepared to leave Washington, D.C., our sense of nostalgia was growing, especially after an evening at the White House for an informal dinner and movie with the Reagans. The small group included George Will and Willard Scott.

During the reception I noticed that Reagan was standing alone, which was unusual since he normally had clusters of people surrounding him. We reminisced about our time together as governors and talked about the difference between being governor and president. He said it was a lot easier to get away from official duties when he was governor. It was a delightful interlude and the most extended informal conversation I ever had with Ronald Reagan.

A few days later I was invited to breakfast by Secretary of State George Schultz. As I waited on the top floor of the State Department building I once again marveled at the grace and beauty of these reception rooms furnished with exquisite furniture from the earliest days of our nation. I wondered a little where the other guests were. When an assistant invited me into the secretary's small dining room I saw that the table was set for two. Schultz and I sat down to an intimate farewell meal. He said that while we did not agree on all issues—Nicaragua for instance—I had always provided thoughtful and reasoned analysis in the Foreign Relations Committee and was a stalwart supporter of the administration on free trade, nuclear arms reduction and foreign aid. I thought George Shultz was one of Reagan's best appointments, certainly a vast improvement over his predecessor, the erratic Alexander Haig.

THE LAST DAYS of the 100th Congress were a blur of legislative activity. Every appropriations bill was festooned with irrelevant amendments as members attempted to get their favorite bills loaded aboard the only vehicles likely to reach the president's desk. I spent those last few days working hard to secure final passage of bills I had developed over several years. One of my last-minute successes was a bill to provide alternative fishing sites for Columbia River tribes whose traditional fishing sites had been inundated by federal dams.

My proposal for a Washington National Parks Wilderness was adopted, together with the land settlement for the Quinaults. A study was authorized on protection of the Hanford Reach. The president also signed the Indian Gaming Regulatory Act and the Indian Self-Determination Act. I thanked Dan Inouye and Sid Morrison for their important support.

My final year had been exceedingly productive. I realized with a degree of wistfulness that had I decided to stay in the Senate the combination of legislative experience and seniority would have yielded even more major dividends. On the whole, I had no regrets about leaving, confident there would be new challenges back home.

I LEFT MY OFFICE in the elegant Hart Senate Office Building one last time, strode through the huge central atrium dominated by the enormous Alexander Calder mobile and descended to the basement station of the Senate subway. Friendly guards greeted me as I hopped aboard for the five-minute ride to the Capitol. As I walked up the stairs to the Senate floor I tried to fix in my memory the historic surroundings. The marble steps were worn from countless footsteps of senators and visitors. Murals covered the walls and vaulted ceilings. I passed niches featuring marble busts of vice presidents who had presided as presidents of the Senate. When I entered the chamber, Senator D'Amato, sure enough, was still thundering that drug dealers deserved the death penalty. When D'Amato finished his latest 10-minute rant, I was recognized and gave my last speech to the Senate. It was virtually an empty chamber but the galleries were filled with visitors:

> I may not have another opportunity before the Senate closes this session to say some things about an experience of the past 5½ years, which for me has been one of the most rewarding experiences of my life.
>
> I do not know what will come next in my own career, but I do know that this might well be the close of 32 years of public service that started the day I took office in January 1957 as a young state legislator. I enjoyed very much the privileges I've had in the succeeding years, as a legislator, as a governor, as a college president and as a senator.
>
> As I leave the Senate, I find that there is an unfinished agenda for me personally and, obviously, an unfinished agenda for the Senate. And, most particularly, an unfinished agenda for the United States of America—because that is the important story of America. There is always an unfinished agenda. We are always attempting to do something better. We are always crafting a freer society. Hopefully a kinder society, one which will give better opportunities to our children than those we enjoy.
>
> I thank my extraordinary staff for their skill, hard work and dedication. They have made me look good. There are no greater accolades to staff than that. And, of course, I must thank my family, particularly my wife Nancy, who never knows from one day to the next when or if I am coming home for dinner. She has been a true partner in everything I have done for most of those 32 years. Nancy married into politics, not knowing just how far and how long this road would carry us.

My seatmate, Brock Adams, was one of several senators who offered kind and thoughtful goodbyes. His gracious remarks reflected the 35 years of friendship we had enjoyed.

With my last words in the Senate, I responded with a bequest to Brock, the promise that in January of 1989 he would become the senior senator from the State of Washington.

Three days later, on October 22, 1988, the 100th Congress adjourned and I headed home to campaign for Slade Gorton and George Bush.

MIKE LOWRY'S 77,000-VOTE CUSHION in King County propelled him to victory over Don Bonker in the Democratic senatorial primary. Pollster Stuart Elway had good news for Gorton: 43 percent of Bonker's backers were now inclined to vote for him rather than Lowry. Slade shrewdly staked out his theme: "I will be a senator for all of the people of the state, not just for a handful of liberals in downtown Seattle."

With only two weeks left in the campaign, negative ads for both candidates were slithering their way into every available second of TV and radio airtime. Most were from so-called "independent groups," ostensibly not connected with the candidates, thus free to spew half-truths and misinformation. Unfortunately, sleaze seems to work. During a Senate debate on campaign finance reform, I added an amendment requiring candidates to take responsibility for their overblown claims. It's easier to OK an ad with anonymous charges than to look into a TV camera and repeat them personally. Though the amendment was adopted, the campaign finance reform bill failed.

The Gorton campaign aired a series of 30-second spots hammering Lowry for voting against a sweeping anti-drug bill. The Lowry campaign fired back, charging, "There's a reason Slade Gorton isn't in the Senate any more. While he was there he voted to deny low-income senior citizens a Social Security cost-of-living increase... and voted 13 times to cut Medicare and health services for seniors." Lowry also noted—correctly—that I opposed Gorton's call for the death penalty to deter "murderous drug lords." The Gorton campaign then aired an over-the-top ad accusing Lowry of favoring legalization of marijuana, which Mike hotly denied. (How times have changed!) I wasn't happy about the marijuana ad or the whole tone of the two campaigns. It amounted to nuclear warfare. In fact, that was next on deck.

I was furious when the Lowry campaign unleashed a last-minute TV ad charging Slade with wanting to create a "bomb factory" at Hanford. A big semi marked "Caution Nuclear Waste" rolls toward the camera as an unseen announcer intones: "The congressional record shows while Slade Gorton was in the Senate he voted with the nuclear industry to make it easier to dump the nation's nuclear waste in Washington state. And after he was defeated, Gorton went to work as a Seattle attorney on a new project—to turn WPPSS into a factory producing highly radioactive fuel for nuclear bombs. . . . Slade Gorton's been working for the nuclear industry for years. Do you really expect him to stop now?" As the truck rumbles past, the camera pans to a group of innocent kids standing by the road.

The bill to modify a WPPSS plant was one I sponsored. It was not to create a bomb factory, but to supply tritium to keep our current nuclear armament functioning. I told reporters the Lowry ad was "ugly and sleazy and absolutely false, and I'm going to say so in a few minutes when I go up to cut another TV ad for Slade!"

Mike McGavick, Gorton's campaign manager, and Gary Smith, the campaign's communications wizard, came up with what became one of the most memorable political ads in Washington state history.

Arriving at the studio, I met with Mike Murphy, a producer who had done first-rate work for the GOP Senatorial Committee. I gave the script a read-through while Murphy sized up the lighting and camera angle. It was good stuff: "Come on, Mike Lowry, clean up your act! Your negative TV ads distorting Slade Gorton's good record embarrass this state. You'd have us think that Slade opposes all environmental legislation and that he would sink Social Security. Actually, he's passed more environmental legislation than you have. And when Social Security faced bankruptcy, Slade helped to save it."

"You nailed it!" Murphy said, suggesting an even punchier ending. It might be corny, he said, but it was worth a try. He brought out a pair of hip boots they had borrowed from Mc-Gavick's grandfather.

I balked.

"Lowry's ad is false and misleading," Murphy prodded, "and this would dramatize your response." I was so mad about Lowry's ad that I finally shrugged "OK."

They rolled film. "Mike, you've been spreading so darn much stuff I've had to change my shoes," I declared. I was wearing a suit and tie, but when the camera pulled back I lifted a leg to reveal the hip boots.

If I'd had 24 hours to think about it, I probably wouldn't have agreed to do it. But I was ticked and wanted to make a statement. Some columnists and letter writers suggested the ad tarnished my "straight arrow" reputation. It was tough stuff, all right, but still well within the bounds of political debate. Gary Smith would maintain that the commercial was the pivotal moment of the campaign. I was dubious because many people had already voted.

A clip from the famous "Hip Boots" commercial. *Washington State Archives*

FOR WHATEVER REASON, a significant batch of undecideds swung Slade's way on November 8, 1988. He edged Lowry by 40,000 votes out of 1.85 million cast. The state's notoriously unpredictable ticket-splitting electorate favored Mike Dukakis over George H.W. Bush by about the same margin, yet Bush was handily elected nationally. And 41-year-old J. Danforth Quayle, who had caused us such grief over the Daniel Manion judicial nomination, was now vice-president-elect of the United States. Unfortunately, Republicans made no gains in Congress.

I sent a congratulatory letter to Bush right away and indicated I would be pleased to serve in his administration. I followed up with a phone call. Bush expressed enthusiasm about my offer. Doubtless he was being inundated with entreaties, but from our previous meetings I could sense his sincerity. He suggested I talk with Jim Baker, his transition chief. I was well acquainted with Baker from his stint as Reagan's White House chief of staff. Detailing my long track record of environmental leadership and my work with the tribes, I told Baker I was particularly interested in the Department of Interior. I emphasized that I was a team player— someone who would never embarrass the president over policy differences. I would simply resign if the differences became too great. My closer was my assertion that my appointment would help erase the stigma attached to Republicans from James G. Watt's wretched two years as Secretary of the Interior. Baker was friendly but noncommittal. I concluded my chances were slim.

Slade got busy and gained endorsements for me from virtually every Republican senator—with a couple of interesting exceptions. Jim McClure of Idaho was not only chairman of the Energy and

Natural Resources Committee on which I had served, but also a close friend and campaign adviser to George Bush. They had served together in the House. McClure was now advising the president-elect on Cabinet appointments. McClure was noncommittal when Slade contacted him. Meanwhile, Bill Armstrong, a conservative from Colorado, was a good friend of mine, but a better friend of ranchers, miners and timbermen. He was afraid I would tilt too much toward the environmental side. "I will work hard to keep you from becoming Secretary of the Inte-

Election night 1988: I'm with Andy McLauchlin, left, one of my Senate aides who was running for state treasurer; Joel Pritchard and Slade and Sally Gorton as the early election returns appear on TV. Joel was elected lieutenant governor. Slade narrowly defeated Mike Lowry to win the Senate seat I was vacating, and McLauchlin lost to Dan Grimm. *Washington State Archives*

rior," Armstrong told me, "but I will work equally hard to help you get any other cabinet position you would like." It was gratifying to have an overwhelming vote of confidence from my colleagues. Yet those two roadblocks were formidable. I received equally gratifying but probably not as helpful endorsements from Democrats Cecil Andrus and Stewart Udall, both former Secretaries of the Interior.

Support from environmental groups ranged from enthusiastic to tepid. The vice president of the Audubon Society offered a glowing endorsement, while the League of Conservation Voters just couldn't put aside its Democratic bias. The league's political director damned me with faint praise: "Well, you have to put it in context... Evans is sort of a moderate on the environment. We've never really supported him, but he's not James Watt either." I chortled over that one, figuring it probably did me more good than a resounding endorsement.

Bush opted for a more conservative choice, New Mexico Congressman Manuel Lujan, who had served with Bush in the House. The League of Conservation Voters certainly did not approve. I'm sure the president-elect's conservative brain trust was apoplectic at the thought of me as Secretary of the Interior. I believe I could have brought rationality to environmental protection and innovative leadership to the Bureau of Indian Affairs. I certainly would have clashed with those who sought a free hand to exploit federal lands. The exploiters had the last say.

I received a follow-up call from a member of the transition team. Bush "really wanted" me in his administration: How about as Ambassador to the Organization of American States? The OAS, which would turn 100 in 1989, is composed of all 35 nations of North, Central and South America. I had no particular background for the position, nor could I speak Spanish, an important attribute for the job. I politely declined the offer, saying I would be happy to support the president in any way I could from my home state. We were there to watch him become the 41st President of the United

States. The ceremonial exchange of power so vital to a democracy seemed a fitting way to end our fascinating years at the nation's capital.

THREE UNEXPECTED OFFERS dramatically affected our future plans: Seattle's KIRO-TV proposed that I become a political commentator and adviser to its Board of Directors; Harvard offered me a fellowship at its Institute of Politics in the Kennedy School of Government for the second semester of the 1989 school year, and I was asked to join the board of the Henry J. Kaiser Family Foundation, a non-profit focusing on national health issues and America's role in global health policy.

All of a sudden we had a tantalizingly full plate. I said yes to all three. Nancy and I headed to Cambridge for an orientation session. We learned we would be living in student housing at the business school. I would be a visiting professor, teaching a class of my choosing, and free to engage in whatever research project struck me as intriguing. The facilities of Harvard University were open to us, including the intriguing dark and dusty stacks of Widener library.

It turned out to be a wonderful interlude at one of the world's great universities. We were like full-ride grad-school students without the pressure of grades. Every morning, I'd head out to my classes. And Nancy would don her winter boots, wool coat, hat and gloves to cross the wintry campus to audit whichever courses sounded interesting. Or as she put it with a happy little sigh, "A college student all over again!" Being musical, she loved a course on Beethoven's symphonies. Together we took a course on Machiavelli and Renaissance politics from a great lecturer.

MY POST-SENATE SEMESTER at Harvard dovetailed with another fascinating assignment.

The identification of the Antarctic ozone "hole" in 1985, followed by North America's hot, dry summer of 1988, prompted intense scientific and media interest in greenhouse gases and the specter of global warming. Congress appropriated funds for a comprehensive study by the National Academies of Sciences and Engineering, and the Institute of Medicine. I was chosen chairman of a panel to oversee a report on the "Policy Implications of Greenhouse Warming." As assignments go, things don't get much more fascinating—or daunting—for a lifelong outdoorsman. The panel included some of America's most distinguished scientists, environmentalists, engineers, economists and academics. Many became guest speakers at my Harvard classes.

Among reputable scientists there was genuine skepticism on global warming. Some noted that we'd gone through millions of years of global climate change. Over eons, our planet has been shaped by ice ages, dramatic thaws, volcanic eruptions, meteor strikes and other cataclysmic events. Washington's diverse topography bears witness—from the Dry Falls in the Grand Coulee to the magnificent Columbia Gorge, created by the massive Missoula Floods some 15,000 years ago. All true, other panelists said, but our modern, industrialized society was accelerating climate change at a rate that threatened catastrophe.

As we gathered data for the report, I was disappointed that the Bush administration joined the Soviet Union and Japan in vetoing efforts by a 70-nation conference on global warming to set goals for reducing carbon dioxide emissions. U.S. representatives claimed piously that more study was required before adopting an action plan. It was the same story we heard from the Reagan administration on acid rain. The end result was no new clean air bill while our air got dirtier and our forests continued to die.

The 918-page scientific report on Greenhouse Warming was published in 1992. We focused on a 40-page policy summary for Congress. Any synthesis is tempered by compromise, including our conclusion that "the full social cost pricing" of energy must be studied. But we achieved consensus, noting that global warming also could be the result of "natural climatic variability." Our report warned, however, that if temperature increases accelerated it could mean "climate warming greater than any in human history." If the higher projections proved accurate, "massive responses would be needed," and the stresses on Earth and its inhabitants could be devastating.

In the decades since, more scientific evidence has documented that reducing greenhouse gases and fossil fuels requires unprecedented global leadership. It's undeniable that Earth's ecosystems are endangered by all manner of human pollution. My memories of Lake Washington awash in effluent in the 1950s are still vivid. I am, however, no fan of former vice president Al Gore. He downplays the scientific truth that humans are not responsible for all "global warming."

WHEN WE FINALLY RETURNED home to Seattle to start our new lives, I joined Foster Pepper & Shefelman, one of the city's oldest law firms, as an adviser. When they made the offer, I protested that I did not have a law degree. They said that many of their clients needed advice on governmental relations and personnel management, and my engineering background would be of real value as well. They authorized one additional staff member and I thought immediately of Cleo Davidson, a valued member of my Seattle Senate office. For the next 10 years we were a team through some fascinating experiences.

66
TEMPORARY TRIUMPHS

Cleo Davidson peered into my office with puzzling news: "President Carter wants to talk with you." Though we had served together as governors, I hadn't heard from Carter since he left the White House. Before long, he was on the line, explaining in his soft Georgia drawl that he now headed the Council of Freely Elected Heads of Government. The council was sending a delegation to observe the Nicaraguan elections, and he wanted me to co-chair the United States delegation. I had little experience in foreign elections but immediately grasped the importance of the election to a beleaguered nation of 4 million people. Nicaragua was ruled by the leftist Sandinista government President Reagan had hoped to overthrow before a ham-handed covert plan to assist the "Contra" rebels was exposed.

I accepted the invitation on the spot. It was December of 1989. The Nicaraguan election was 2½ months away.

In Atlanta, I received an extended briefing on the election process and had a good conversation with Carter on his expectations for the trip. Our first venture was to co-chair a Nicaraguan election symposium at the Carter Center at Atlanta's Emory University.

The protracted war with the Contras and a failing economy had set the stage for the referendum

President Carter and I meet with Nicaraguan election officials. *The Carter Center*

on the leadership of Nicaraguan President Daniel Ortega. Under pressure from his neighbors—El Salvador, Costa Rica, Honduras and Guatemala—Ortega had agreed to free elections "in exchange for promises from the other nations to close down anti-Sandinista rebel bases within their borders."

At the symposium, the President of the Supreme Electoral Council outlined the ground rules for the election set for February 26, 1990. It was clear that the wily Ortega would enjoy enormous advantages in the campaign. He had appointed the members of the Electoral Council. Representatives of the three major contending political parties argued their positions. Elliott Richardson, representing the United Nations, and Mario Gonzalez from the Organization of American States joined President Carter in summarizing our task. This was likely to be the most officially observed election in modern history.

I joined President Carter and Senator Claiborne Pell, chairman of the Senate Foreign Relations Committee, on a trip to Nicaragua to review preparations for the balloting. We worried that Ortega's FSLN revolutionary political party would subvert the process. Most of the media was government owned or controlled, which minimized the opportunity for the opposition to effectively campaign.

Ortega, a vibrant young leader with a rebel's rakish mustache, greeted us with enthusiasm. We met in the living room of his modest home. He served us splendid Nicaraguan coffee and vowed the electoral process would be fully independent. There were no less than 32 candidates running for president. He was supremely confident he would win.

Fanning out to take the pulse of the electorate, we soon learned that 14 opposition parties had formed a coalition called the UNO—the *Union Nacional Opositora*. It was a curious conglomeration of conservatives, centrists and communists. They agreed on only one thing: Ortega had to go. Their candidate was Violeta Chamorro. When they overthrew the Somoza regime, Ortega's revolutionaries had her strong support. But as the new government moved leftward, Chamorro's newspaper, *La Prensa*, became a vocal opponent of the FSLN. Chamorro, who proved to be a delightfully witty person, was nevertheless deeply concerned about the fairness of the election process.

We also met with members of the Electoral Commission to explore how registered voters were identified. It was a surprisingly sophisticated system. It appeared most citizens would be able to cast a ballot. The registration rolls seemed complete. The process for ballot distribution and counting was also well designed, especially considering the primitive road network and the difficulty of safely transmitting ballots to central counting stations. As we left for home I was much more confident that it would be a fair election, though the odds were still tilted strongly toward President Ortega.

WE RETURNED the night before the election and met the delegates from Latin American countries who would join us as observers for the Carter Center. We also met observers from the United Nations, several liberal organizations and leftist celebrities eager to celebrate a rousing Ortega victory.

On election morning we divided into teams of two in order to observe the election from a variety of stations. I was joined by a former Chilean government minister. In a suburb of Managua we were astonished to find voters patiently waiting in a line that stretched for six blocks. They shuffled forward under a blazing midday sun. One couple told us they had walked for four hours from their home to a bus stop and then spent several hours on the bus before arriving at the end of this long line. Frustrated by the weak economy, they were no fans of President Ortega. I began to sense that Ortega was overconfident.

The ballots were spectacular. Almost three feet long, they listed the 32 candidates for president, with colorful symbols as an aid to voters with limited literacy.

As we traveled from precinct to precinct, we noticed that people on street corners were greeting each other with a thumbs-up "I-have-voted" gesture. Their thumbs were blackened by ostensibly indelible ink—evidence they had voted as well as a safeguard against any attempt to vote more than once. A black thumb quickly became a symbol of pride. There was consternation at noontime, however, when our group reassembled at election headquarters. Someone had discovered the ink could be removed with common bleach. Some opposition leaders were threatening to boycott the election. We had a crisis on our hands. I met with President Carter and several Latin American observers. We decided that keeping this news quiet was the best course. We convinced the opposition that few voters would learn of this trick, and even fewer would attempt to use it.

My Chilean partner and I visited a school to observe the ballot count. A single lightbulb dangled from the ceiling. Precinct workers were gathered around a small table. Poll watchers from several major parties looked on. They wore large rosettes sporting the colors of their parties. Each ballot was inspected to ensure there were no irregularities before it was added to a candidate's stack. I was mentally counting as the stacks grew. Chamorro was leading Ortega by a growing margin, which was totally unexpected. She had won this precinct by more than 50 votes. When the session was declared over, the Chamorro observer walked around the table and embraced her Ortega counterpart. They exchanged congratulations, shook hands, and left together. I cannot imagine the same thing happening in an American election.

THE CARTER DELEGATION gathered for dinner. Our unanimous conclusion was that the election had been conducted impartially, with good security. We were all amazed by the turnout. More than 80 percent of Nicaragua's eligible voters had gone to the polls, a far higher response than in U.S. presidential elections.

Counting ballots in an essentially rural country with poor roads and limited communications is always difficult. I thought the Nicaraguan Electoral Council managed the election with great skill. Precinct ballot boxes were brought by truck, occasionally by mule, to one of many regional election centers where the precinct votes were certified and added together to produce a regional total. Each of these centers was connected by teletype to a central counting station in Managua.

I strolled over to the teletype center. Long tables held scores of clattering teletype machines. Grabbing a pad and pencil, I walked up and down the aisles. It was quickly apparent that a huge upset was brewing. I tracked down Jimmy Carter and told him what I had discovered. Just then, all the television and radio stations went off the air. It was obvious that the Ortega government did not want adverse returns publicized. Carter assembled the leaders of our group. We debated what to do. Carter exclaimed that he wanted to visit Ortega and urge him to accept the results of the election. I offered to accompany him, but he said he thought a personal, president-to-president visit would be more effective: "I want to try to convince him that he is a young man with a great opportunity to serve his country and perhaps to run again for president."

We waited impatiently for more than an hour. Finally Jimmy Carter arrived with the news that Ortega had agreed to accept the results, but he demanded that the opposition not gloat over its victory. Next, Carter visited Chamorro, who had polled more than 55 percent of the presidential vote. The opposition had also captured the National Assembly. He urged her to celebrate victory with a call for national reconciliation.

Though it was 2 a.m. back in Washington, D.C., I called Secretary of State Jim Baker, who answered his bedside phone with a groggy hello. "I hate to wake you," I said, "but I thought you'd like to hear the results of the Nicaraguan election: Violeta Chamorro has won a resounding victory." The sleepiness instantly disappeared from Baker's voice. He said I could call him at 2 a.m. any time I had news that good.

Violeta Chamorro receives the presidential sash from Daniel Ortega in 1990. *Fundación Violeta Chamorro, CC0 1.0*

THE REST OF THE STORY is another kind of wakeup call: Democracy is fragile in Third World nations. After leaving office in 1997, Chamorro devoted her energies to international peace initiatives until poor health forced her to retire from public life. Daniel Ortega regained power in 2007. And at this writing is still president, having dismantled nearly all institutional checks on his power, according to Human Rights Watch. "A brutal crackdown…left over 300 dead and 2,000 injured in 2018, and resulted in hundreds of arbitrary arrests and prosecutions. The Ortega government has continued to bring criminal cases against protesters and critics. Impunity for human rights abuses by the police continues," and the government's response to the Covid-19 pandemic was a litany of "denial, inaction and opacity." In a sham election in 2021, Ortega won a fourth consecutive five-year term after jailing his leading rivals and criminalizing dissent.

67

NOT-SO-ODD COUPLES

Settling in back home in Seattle in the fall of 1989, I was busy weighing offers to serve on corporate boards and delivering my first political commentaries on KIRO-TV. Mike Lowry was teaching at Seattle University, having lost to Slade Gorton a year earlier in a second try for the U.S. Senate.

When Mike and I squared off for the U.S. Senate in 1983, David Broder of *The Washington Post* called it "a fight between a junkyard dog and a golden retriever." The race was heaven sent for cartoonists: Mike was the rumpled, arm-waving warrior in a polyester sport coat challenging a straight-backed Eagle Scout engineer. Conservative Republicans had long declared I was too liberal; Lowry conjured up their worst fears. Overlooked in the heat of that battle was the fact that Lowry and I had at least one very important thing in common: Our concern for the environment. Further, it was hard to not like Mike, whose intelligence matched his exuberance. "He's a love," Nancy said after we came to know Mike and his wife Mary. "He really is."

Elliot Marks, the director of The Nature Conservancy's Washington offices, had a great idea: I should call Mike and ask him to be co-chairman of a statewide drive to promote a bond issue to preserve more land for outdoor recreation and wildlife habitat. "We think you two will be the political odd couple that attracts the broad base of support we need. But we don't know how to get you two together." I laughed and said, "I'll give him a call!"

Mike signed up without hesitation.

Full credit to Marks for the inspired idea and tireless legwork that followed. Elliot had served on my staff during my last term as governor, arriving in Olympia from U.C. Berkeley with degrees in divinity and law. Jim Dolliver and I immediately recognized he was a young man with vision and moxie. After we promoted him to serve as my natural resources aide, Marks helped negotiate a major expansion of the Olympic National Park that preserved a large swath of coastal forests. When I left office, Marks joined the Portland office of The Nature Conservancy. And in 1979, he became the first director of the global conservation group's Washington state office.

By 1987, the Nature Conservancy was focusing on wetlands protection, noting that "all life forms are interdependent." The state had lost half of the estimated 800,000 acres of wetlands that existed a century earlier. Governor Booth Gardner and I headed a fund-raising campaign to acquire endangered wetlands around the state, with the hope that the legislature would appropriate $2 million in matching funds.

Re-elected handily in 1988, Booth became an enthusiastic supporter of our plan to form a nonprofit Washington Wildlife & Recreation Coalition, WWRC for short. In the decade prior, the state had allocated, on average, a paltry $2 million per year for new parks and protection of wildlife habitat and farmlands. Lowry and I immediately concluded that a one-time bond issue was not the answer. The urgent mission of saving old-growth greenbelts, protecting habitat and building more parks for a growing population required a commitment by the governor and the legislature to allocate significant funds to the cause in the state's biennial Capital Construction Budget. A major grant from the Bullitt Foundation jump-started our effort to create the WWRC.

I joined Gardner and future governor Chris Gregoire, then the director of the Washington Department of Ecology, at a

Elliot Marks of The Nature Conservancy with the not-so-odd couple: Dan and Mike. *Washington Wildlife & Recreation Commission*

1989 conference in Seattle that drew 500 leaders from business, industry, academia and environmental groups. Booth warned that "Californication" would be our fate unless we were proactive instead of reactive. "No one can do the job alone," I said. "Not the government, not the Legislature, and certainly not the courts." Eastern Washington conservatives branded our plan the "Evans-Lowry land grab." But we had momentum. The coalition soon enlisted influential partners.

The Legislature established the Washington Wildlife and Recreation Program, with an initial appropriation of $53 million in the 1990 supplemental capital budget. The impetus was the breadth and depth of the WWRC. Business giants like Boeing and Weyerhaeuser, plus Group Health, the Washington Forest Protection Association, the Nature Conservancy, the Realtors and the Grange all supported our cause. We established a diverse board of directors. Its notables have included House Speaker Frank Chopp, King County Executive Dow Constantine, Billy Frank Jr. of the Northwest Indian Fisheries Commission, Mark Doumit of the Washington Forest Protection Association, and Joe Mentor, the Seattle attorney who was my natural resources counsel for four of my years in the U.S. Senate. Today, as in the beginning, the Washington Wildlife & Recreation Coalition is the lobbying arm, while a separate Washington State Recreation and Conservation Office reviews and ranks requests for matching funds from state and local agencies and forwards its recommendations to the governor and lawmakers.

The bifurcated yet bipartisan process works so well that during the deep recession that began in 2008 we were able to fend off attempts by conservative legislators to exercise more influence over which projects were funded. From the outset, the Washington Wildlife and Recreation Program has been strictly nonpartisan. Mike and I said the whole program would collapse if it became a political football. He talked to some of the Democratic leaders and I talked to some of the Republican leaders. We got them to back down. We survived that burp. The coalition emerged stronger than ever.

Population growth has driven up construction and land costs and threatened farmlands, green spaces and wildlife habitat. "Some of the Northwest's most iconic plant and animal species are in rapid decline due to habitat loss and fragmentation, declining water quality and ecosystem destruction," we told Governor Jay Inslee in 2018.

We need to remember that our state's enviable yet vulnerable quality of life is also an economic engine. The Washington Wildlife and Recreation Program helps support more than 200,000 jobs. Recreational lands generate more than $26.2 billion in consumer spending annually, plus $2.3 billion in state and local tax revenues. In its 32 years, the partnership between the coalition, the program administrators, the governor and the legislature has generated an investment of more than $1.5 billion for habitat conservation and outdoor recreation. The 2021 Legislature approved a Capital Construction Budget that included $100 million in funding for the Washington Wildlife and Recreation Program, matching the previous all-time record. The outdoors has been my passion since 1941, when a 15-year-old Eagle Scout became a member of R.E.I. Nothing has given me more satisfaction and hope for the future of a truly evergreen state than the WWRC.

ONE OF THE ENDURING LESSONS I've learned in my long and eventful life is that coalition building is sometimes messy but often the best prescription for success. When we ousted Speaker O'Brien in 1963, forming an alliance with dissident Democrats was our only choice.

I admired Booth Gardner for his vision and envied his charisma. He could communicate with kings and kindergartners, popes and politicians on equal terms. Richard Larsen of *The Seattle Times* once quipped that in terms of public affection Booth ranked "somewhere between Donald Duck and fresh-baked bread." I was peeved in 1984 when he defeated my friend John Spellman, a very good governor vexed with a lousy economy and a no-new-taxes legislature. Booth came to Washington, D.C., soon after he took office. I was a little wary, but when he walked in with that quirky little smile, we connected immediately. Our interest in education and the environment created a bond. The first time the Legislature overrode one of his vetoes, I sent him a letter he had framed. "You're not a governor," I said, "until you have been overridden."

In 1991, Mike Lowry, Jim Ellis and I lent our support to Gardner's proposal to lift the state's statutory debt ceiling by one percent to allow a billion-dollar general obligation bond issue. The money was to be earmarked for new schools and university buildings as well as low-income housing. Another sum was to be allocated to preserving recreational land and wildlife habitat. Ellis and I reminded a House committee that the state had borrowed millions of dollars to

Booth Gardner, Mike Lowry and I, together with Judith Billings, the State Superintendent of Public Instruction, testify in 1991 on a proposed billion-dollar general obligation bond issue to boost public schools. *Washington State Archives*

expand public facilities as the population boomed in the wake of World War II, and it issued more bonds in 1971 to keep pace with changing needs. "I think it's time again for Washingtonians to take stock of their future," I said. Governor Gardner emphasized it was vital to protect more land from development "before it's gone forever," while Lowry noted that rising property values and decreasing federal aid were leaving increasing numbers of poor folks out in the cold. This time, we struck out. Dan McDonald, the GOP floor leader in the State Senate, and Gary Locke, the chairman of the House Budget Committee, were worried about what would happen when the bills came due.

IN 2003, BOOTH AND I teamed up to secure more funding for higher education. Neither of us was in political office. We had no campaign money or staff. We didn't know many of the current legislators. But we knew there was a crisis. Earlier, we were at a luncheon that spotlighted the growing technology gap at Washington's universities. Boeing had moved its corporate headquarters to Chicago. Someone asked Microsoft's Bill Gates to cite the most important single thing a concerned citizen could do to promote a better economic future for the state. "Support your local university," he said.

Afterward, Booth called. "Did you hear what I heard?" he asked. "And are you as concerned as I am?" I had and I was. Booth is the one who lit the fire under me. The message at that luncheon was that we were in trouble. The key to our future is how good we are, and how good we are depends on how well educated we are. Brains are now our most important natural resource. Higher education—particularly our research universities—is all about our future. It's truer today than it was in 2003. Booth and I both had experience in academia, he at the University of Puget Sound, me at The Evergreen State College.

Parkinson's disease had reduced Booth to sleeplessness. When the phone rang a 2 a.m., Nancy would just hand me the receiver, saying, "Booth wants to talk."

We visited the state treasurer and received his blessings for a proposal to tweak the state's capital debt limit to fund capital construction projects at the universities. Then we hit the road to sell the plan. We contacted legislators, visited editorial boards and made the rounds of Rotary Clubs and Chambers of Commerce.

Booth's brave battle with Parkinson's was taking a toll, despite innovative deep-brain surgeries. I knew all the implications because my brother Roger had it too. Booth had trouble buttoning his shirt. His voice was frequently reduced to a whisper. The kinetic man who had been a superb athlete in his youth was now walking with difficulty. He called it the "Muhammad Ali Shuffle," in honor of a fellow sufferer. I'll never forget the day when we were walking across the capital campus. I had two bad knees. Booth was alongside me, having a little trouble moving himself. Finally he turned to me with that mischievous smile and said, "What the hell are a couple of old poops like us doing down here?"

What we were doing was helping create a legacy to leave for our grandchildren and the grandchildren of every other Washingtonian. The legislature in 2003 adopted the Building Washington's Future Act, better known as the Gardner-Evans Plan. It authorized $750 million in general obligation bonds to fund new buildings and improve facilities on college campuses statewide over the next six years. We couldn't have done it without another old Olympia hand, Bob Edie. Bob worked for the State Senate for 10 years and was staff director for the Senate Ways & Means Committee in the mid-1980s. Edie later became director of government relations for the University of Washington and a vice president at Western Washington University.

ONE OF THE DOWNSIDES of living a long life is losing good friends. Booth Gardner succumbed to complications from Parkinson's at 76 in 2013. He could have been a millionaire playboy. Instead, he dedicated his life to public service, especially to youth. Mike Lowry died unexpectedly after a stroke in 2017. He was only 78.

Cecil Andrus, Idaho's four-term governor, died the same year, a day shy of his 86th birthday after a long battle with cancer. As Secretary of the Interior in the Carter cabinet, he spearheaded the conservation of millions of acres in Alaska. Andrus, Oregon's Tom McCall and I were dubbed the "Three Musketeers" when we were governors because we agreed on so much. In 1986, when Cecil decided to run again for governor of Idaho after being out of elective office for a decade, I returned a favor. Cecil asked if I would support him against his Republican opponent. He had endorsed me when he was a private citizen. Now I was a Republican officeholder. I sweated over the issue for several days but finally decided to endorse a good friend and first-class public servant, party be damned. I caught hell from the Idaho Republican Party and from some of the more conservative Washington State Republicans. Andrus won the election by 4,000 votes and remained governor for the next eight years. I hope my support helped put him over the top.

In 2018, we lost John Spellman at 91, and a few days later, his wonderful First Lady, Lois. A man of integrity and courage, he deserves to be remembered not just as "Washington's last Republican governor." If not for Spellman, an oil pipeline with a capacity of a million barrels a day could be snaking along the bottom of Puget Sound. In the face of a full court press by the Reagan Administration in 1982, he rejected Northern Tier's pipeline application. Puget Sound is "a national treasure," he declared.

Jim Ellis and Bill Ruckelshaus, two visionary activists, died in 2019. And in 2020, we lost two more extraordinary Washingtonians, Bill Gates Sr. and Slade Gorton. They had been my friends for 60 years.

When time and tide dilute the mourning, what remains are permanent voids. What I miss most is not being able to just pick up the phone and call any of those marvelous citizens.

68
BOARDED UP

"Don't get too boarded up," said Jerry Grinstein, the president and CEO of Burlington Northern Railroad. He was a little late. In addition to the Kaiser Family Foundation, I had become a director of Washington Mutual Savings Bank and McCaw Cellular Communications. KIRO-TV had hired me to do five commentaries a week. And I was now an adviser to the lawyers at Foster Pepper & Shefelman. By 1990 I was also the first Public Leadership Fellow at the University of Washington's Graduate School of Public Affairs, tasked with leading a year-long symposium on "Global Environmental Policy in the Making."

Grinstein's advice was solid. Some of the boards I joined had a country-club atmosphere. I learned quickly that there was a reluctance to challenge the CEO and other top managers. Things had to go seriously south before the directors felt empowered to make drastic moves. That wasn't my style. Nor Grinstein's. A decisive manager, he was a young Harvard Law School graduate back in the 1960s when he joined Senator Warren G. Magnuson's Commerce Committee staff. It was Grinstein who recruited the team of enterprising, idealistic young staffers dubbed "Bumblebees." Many were University of Washington Law School graduates, including Stan Barer, Ed Sheets, Norm Maleng, and Norm Dicks. Another nimble operative, Mike Pertschuk, was wooed away from the staff of Oregon Senator Maurine Neuberger. During my years as governor, everyone knew Magnuson had the best staff on Capitol Hill.

I like everything about Jerry Grinstein, especially his wit and booming laugh. After those formative years with Maggie and a stint as CEO at Western Airlines, he arrived at Burling-

Jerry Grinstein always offers good advice.
Courtesy Puget Sound Business Journal

ton Northern unencumbered by old thinking. "We're not taking steps to modernize," he warned his executives, "and that's a huge mistake." Other railroad executives told him, "You can't fight the government." "The hell you can't!" Jerry said. "Some of these regulations are so antiquated they impede progress, so let's get our act together." He barked at them so persuasively and so often that the industry got the government to modernize regulations regarding train crew staffing.

When Grinstein said he wanted me on the railroad's board of directors, I was flattered and excited. During my years on the railroad's board, I must have absorbed the equivalent of an MBA watching Grinstein in action. I watched him out-maneuver the rival Union Pacific Corp. to engineer the $4 billion acquisition of Santa Fe Pacific Corp. "He never claimed to be an expert on engineering or the intricacies of running what was then the nation's largest rail carrier," the *Fort Worth Star-Telegram* observed in 2003 when Grinstein became CEO at Delta Air Lines. "Instead, he concentrated on long-term planning and investor relations. ... Grinstein traveled widely over the 27,000-mile BN system and gambled with new technology in locomotive power, a risk that ultimately paid off and was widely copied in the railroad industry."

I received many lucrative offers to join corporate boards. I learned to be picky, focusing on integrity, innovation and actual involvement. I wanted to be more than just another name atop the letterhead of a corporation more interested in the gravitas of a former governor and U.S. senator than oversight. Earlier, it was rare for a corporate board to meet in private, away from the CEO. The Enron scandal underscores the importance of a robust, diverse, independent board. In good companies, directors serve on important committees, especially auditing and compensation. Still, a good director knows not to cross the line and try to micromanage.

On the Costco Board during the tenure of the company's visionary co-founder, Jim Sinegal, I watched quality control and disruptive innovation transform Costco from a 1976 startup to a worldwide warehouse retailer. We directly challenged and soon outpaced Sam's Club, Walmart's entry in the bulk retail marketing wars. "In the final analysis, you get what you pay for," Sinegal always said. Costco is now a household word. Its customers value the return on their membership fee investment—high quality at low prices

A metaphor for what I learned on the Costco Board is the power of the $1.50 hot dog, with a 20-ounce soda as part of the bargain. The now legendary food-court deal was introduced in 1985. The price should be around $3.65 today, according to inflation calculators, yet Costco remains committed to Sinegal's loss-leader. In fact, I'm pretty sure the company is at least breaking even, having built its own plant to produce a Kirkland Signature wiener. In 2020, Costco sold 151 million hot dogs and sodas, according to the *Puget Sound Business Journal*. When Sinegal's successor, W. Craig Jelinek, complained to his retired friend that the hot dog deal was proving too costly, Sinegal shot back, "If you raise [the price of] the effing hot dog, I will kill you. Figure it out." And they did. A helluva good buck-and-a-half hot dog personifies Jim Sinegal's marketing genius.

Joining the Costco Board was one of the best decisions I ever made. Bill Gates Sr., a friend for 40 years, was rotating off the board when my term also was up.* That would have left them without a majority of independent directors, so they asked me to stay on for an extra year. It turned into three. Charlie Munger, who together with Warren Buffet ran Berkshire Hathaway, was also on the board, which made for some fascinating meetings. Costco was not the least bit worried about having 80-year-olds on its board. Costco did everything differently. The average employee wage was about $24 an hour, and its entry-level wage was at $15 long before the campaign for that new minimum wage. Arkansas-based Walmart, meantime, was intent on keeping its wages low. Everyone said, "How can you compete when your wages are so much higher? Walmart is a juggernaut." Sinegal's response was that Walmart's rate of turnover was way higher than Costco's. "They can't keep people

---

* His famous son is actually Bill Gates III, or "Trey" to his family and old friends. The future Microsoft founder stayed with us at the Governor's Mansion when he was a teenage legislative page. His parents were the founders of a bridge club we had joined in the 1960s.

with meaningful experience. Our model is so much more efficient. We can pay higher wages and beat the hell out of them. *You get what you pay for.*" Costco's upper management purposely kept their own executive compensation lower than CEOs in comparable industries. It all added up to phenomenal success.

I NEVER REGRETTED my early decision to join the trustees of the Kaiser Family Foundation, a nonprofit focusing on global health policy. Dick Cooley, chairman and CEO of Seafirst Corporation, had joined the Kaiser board in 1987. A Yale graduate, he was a fighter pilot during World War II, losing his right arm in a P-38 crash. You'd never know he had a handicap, even on the golf course. Cooley was an inspirational businessman with a strong moral compass. Right as usual, he said I'd find Kaiser's work inspiring.

Founded in 1948 by industrialist Henry J. Kaiser, the foundation's outreach was revamped in 1991 under the leadership of its new CEO, Drew Altman. I became chairman of the board and served for six years. Our outreach included a survey of health care in South Africa where the state of health care among people of African and Indian descent—especially women, children and the elderly—was miserable.

On three trips to South Africa, I was horrified by the unspeakable poverty of squatter villages, where thousands of Black families lived in shanties built from packing boxes, scrap lumber and corrugated iron. Malnutrition, tuberculosis and dysentery were rampant. I was also deeply moved by the determination of community health workers and the inherent dignity of people who dared to hope better days were ahead. On the day in 1990 when Nelson Mandela was released from prison, we visited a group of South African women lugging building blocks for a health clinic. They were helping to build their own facility. They had heard the news about Mandela. Though I could not understand what else they were saying, every other word needed no translation. It was "Mandela, Mandela, Mandela!" A few years later, President Mandela was a guest at a Kaiser Foundation dinner. What struck me most was his marvelous quiet charisma and aura of forgiveness for the people who had incarcerated him for 27 years. I also met F.W. de Klerk, South Africa's former president, who deserves a huge amount of credit for having the courage to right a wrong even though he knew he would be on the losing side as he set about dismantling the evil of Apartheid.

The Kaiser Foundation's domestic outreach included Project Achieve, a wonderful program to encourage minority students to consider health-care professions. I visited a predominantly black high school in Memphis where 200 of the 800 students were paired with doctors and nurses. "It didn't used to be cool to be a good student," one teenager told me.

IN ADDITION TO my commentaries for KIRO-TV, Ken Hatch, the station's president and CEO, wanted me to serve as adviser to their Board of Directors. I was delighted to discover that Mary Gates and Jim Ellis—two of the brightest people I've ever known—were members of the board.

Doing the commentaries was more challenging than I had imagined. They wanted me on five days a week for 90 seconds. I said it would be hard to get anything of any consequence said in 90 seconds. John Lippman, the news director, laughed and said, "We're more interested in heat than light." That wasn't what I had in mind. "Maybe this isn't a good fit for me," I shot back. Lippman immediately backed off, but I left the interview wondering just how serious he was.

Next, they sent in the clown, which improved my outlook on becoming a pundit at KIRO—or at least my TV visage. My 5 o'clock shadow rivaled Nixon's.

Chris Wedes was a patient instructor on how to apply TV makeup, but more importantly a hero in our household. Chris was also "J.P. Patches," whose Emmy Award-winning children's show delighted youngsters throughout the Northwest. He was a masterful makeup artist, and a charming guy. "When I'm out in public with my family, with the greasepaint off, no one knows who I am, but everyone recognizes you," he said one day. "How did you and Nancy handle things when your kids acted up?" I remembered 4-year-old Bruce Evans's core meltdown when Nancy insisted he meet Vice President Agnew. But that was an aberration—and like I've always said, Bruce somehow smelled a rat. I told Chris, our three sons realized from early childhood that our family was always under public scrutiny.

The pressure of writing something meaningful for a 90-second spot was tough—especially five days a week. Yet I did not lack for material. My career as a commentator coincided with the Gulf War, the rise of Bill Clinton, Rush Limbaugh's daily harangues against "feminazis," and Newt Gingrich's take-no-prisoners Republican politics. During my 3½ years on KIRO, I was a non-partisan griper, going after Republicans as often as Democrats. My first commentary aired on August 28, 1989. I said it was great to be back home in Seattle after an absence of 25 years. Noting that *Money* magazine had recently rated Seattle as America's most livable city, I observed:

> The economy is booming and job openings fill the help-wanted ads in the papers. But look more closely. Homeless roam the streets in increasing numbers. Gangs terrorize neighborhoods. Angry citizens square off on school desegregation and growth limits on downtown. Confrontation is a hammer chipping away at the Emerald City.
>
> I also see hope. The Puget Sound area retains a civility unusual in a major city.... Drivers here, while far from perfect, are models of patience compared to their Eastern counterparts. ... But time is short. Hordes of newcomers seek to share our good fortune. Growth will overwhelm us unless we prepare with skill and understanding (and maybe just a little luck).

I take back the part about drivers here being models of patience.

IN THE FALL OF 1990, I took on President George H.W. Bush and Congress for failing to stand up to the National Rifle Association after two horrific mass shootings. A disgruntled ex-employee at a printing plant in Kentucky had mowed down six of his former co-workers. And in California a drifter with a long rap sheet murdered five school children and wounded 32 others before taking his own life. His victims were predominantly Southeast Asian refugees. "You can bet that if a lunatic sprayed the halls of Congress with an AK47, a ban on their manufacture would occur the next day," I said. "But schoolchildren and printing plant workers are apparently not important enough."

Reading these scripts 30 years later feels like déjà vu all over again.

Advocating a ban on assault rifles was one of my most controversial commentaries. I was branded a "scum bag" and a communist. One writer declared that anyone who backed gun control should be tarred, feathered "and tied to an ox cart to be kicked and stomped and spit on as they are dragged down to the docks to be deported to Russia or Red China." So much for freedom of speech.

To its credit, KIRO aired my blistering 1991 commentary on a series of stories it ran concerning low graduation rates in the University of Washington's football program. KIRO said no less than seven players were facing arrest warrants. I did some math and concluded that Husky football players were more law abiding than the average King County adult. Some said that as a UW alum and football fan I was just sticking up for my alma mater. That was not the case. The stories were riddled with cheap shots and timed to run during "Sweeps" month when viewer statistics were compiled to influence advertising rates.

In 1992, when U.S. Senator Brock Adams, whom I had known for 35 years, left office after a *Seattle Times* investigation revealed multiple accusations of sexual assault, I worried about the precedent being set—that a distinguished political career could be ruined by anonymous accusers. "Perhaps he is guilty," I told KIRO viewers, "but what if he is innocent?" A thoughtful letter from a longtime friend a few days later prompted me to share a new perspective. After the Anita Hill-Clarence Thomas hearings, she had reached the conclusion that men were oblivious to the routine misuse of power by men against women. "I don't know any women who have worked in subordinate positions to men who haven't suffered sexual harassment at least once and quite often several times in their work life," she wrote. Adams' defense was that he had never hurt anyone. "I have decided that he probably believes it," she added. "I think most men just don't get it. Sexual behavior in the workplace hurts!"

Her words were simple, straightforward and honest. "Every man should listen," I told KIRO viewers. "Mutual respect must guide every working relationship."

The race for governor in 1992 was one I thought Republicans could win. Booth Gardner, surprisingly, did not seek a third term. (He would learn later that his peculiar, disquieting mental lapses were early signs of Parkinson's.) The top two Democrats were House Speaker Joe King of Vancouver and Mike Lowry. We fielded three solid candidates: State Senator Dan McDonald of Bellevue, Attorney General Ken Eikenberry and Congressman Sid Morrison, my choice as our best hope. Morrison, a native of the Yakima Valley, was a standout member of the Agriculture and Energy Committees and a consensus-builder.

Down the stretch to the primary, I was disappointed when Eikenberry's campaign sent out a mailer ripping into Morrison in a particularly unfair way, accusing him of being a big spender based on routine votes in Congress. "Remember, as you go to the polls," I said, "if you don't like negative campaigning, vote against those who produce this junk." Eikenberry edged Morrison; Lowry trounced King and went on to defeat Eikenberry by nearly 100,000 votes. I'm convinced Morrison would have won. I congratulated Mike, but told him he had lucked out. He made a very smart decision when he named Morrison to head the Washington State Department of Transportation.

A lot of Republicans who expected me to be a partisan flag-waver were glad to see me go when my days as a daily commentator ended in 1993.

One of my last commentaries—in opposition to capital punishment—especially outraged conservatives. I acknowledged, too, that most citizens seemed to support the death penalty, particularly for the likes of Westley Allan Dodd, who stalked, sexually assaulted and murdered three boys, one a 4-year-old. Molested himself as a child, Dodd asked to be hanged. He even wrote a "coloring book" for parents and children on how to avoid child molesters. Dodd's execution, set for January of 1993, was to be the first execution in Washington in 30 years. "But will we be a better state and will our citizens be better off if we resume legalized murder?" I asked KIRO's viewers. "I think not. It clearly has not worked as a deterrent. We are the only Western industrialized country that uses capital punishment. We have executed 188 criminals in the past 15 years. Yet our murder rate is the highest among these nations and is growing. When I was governor, I visited the state penitentiary and saw 13 men then on death row. I realized I had the last say on life or death for these 13. I believe that is an immoral power and refused to send criminals to the gallows. If we now restart executions, we will all lose a little of the civility which keeps our society strong."

When Dodd died on the gallows, many KIRO viewers called or wrote to say good riddance.

I all but cheered in 2018 when the Washington Supreme Court unanimously struck down the death penalty as unconstitutional, ruling that capital punishment is invalid because "it is imposed in an arbitrary and racially biased manner" and "fails to serve any legitimate penological goal." I thought of my old friend, former Chief Justice Robert F. Utter, who had died four years earlier. Utter wrote a prophetic profile in courage in 1995. After 23 years on the high court, he sent a letter of resignation to Governor Lowry, saying, "I have reached the point where I can no longer participate in a legal system that intentionally takes human life. ...We are absolutely unable to make rational distinctions on who should live and who should die."

69
GRANDPA STAYED ALL NIGHT

One Sunday night in the fall of 1998, the doorbell rang. We were just about ready for bed. Nancy and I exchanged surprised glances. Who could that be? When I opened the door, Dan Jr. brushed past me. "How do you spell 'rhabdomyosarcoma'?" he said, his voice fraught with worry. When we looked it up on the Internet, our hearts sank. His daughter Eloise, not quite 4, was now in the fight of her life.

Our first grandchild was a cheerful, artistic girl with a lovely smile. A few days earlier Eloise had presented me with a birthday-present portrait that resembled a Jackson Pollock. It was clear, however, that she wasn't feeling well. She climbed onto my lap before dinner—which was great with me—but stayed there, listless. Her mom, Celia, had taken her to their pediatrician, who diagnosed an ear infection. Medication didn't help. Then they suspected tonsillitis. Celia wasn't buying it. She took Eloise to Seattle Children's Hospital. "Something is wrong with this child," she said emphatically, "and we need to find out what it is." A CT scan revealed a mass the size of a tennis ball beneath Eloise's brain and behind her nose.

Primary intracranial rhabdomyosarcoma is a rare, rapidly growing, soft-tissue tumor most often seen in children. Eloise's tumor was inoperable because it was so inaccessible. Our only hope was chemotherapy and radiation. A child with a life-threatening disease can bring a family together like there's no tomorrow. Some marriages fracture under the strain. Dan and Celia's grew stronger, with the loving support of par-

Grandpa spends the night with Eloise Evans at Seattle Children's hospital. *Dan Evans Jr.*

ents, brothers and sisters, as well as a network of amazing friends who prepared dinners and box lunches day after day.

During Eloise's hospital stays over the next year, her two siblings periodically lived with us so Dan or Celia could always be with her. Luckily, Children's Hospital is just a few blocks from our house in Laurelhurst. Jackson Evans, seven months old when our ordeal began, was a happy baby. Isabelle Evans, at 2½, was old enough to know something bad was going on, yet still too young to process the disruption in her life. She adored her big sister. "Where is Eloise?" she'd ask. We explained that Eloise was sick. Doctors were helping her get better. Isabelle's plaintive response was perfectly logical: "I don't want to be here. I want to be home."

Eloise endured 13 rounds of chemo, six weeks of targeted radiation, and several surgical procedures. She'd just get to feeling better, then, wham, the side effects would kick in. Back she'd go to the hospital—more than a hundred days in all. The doctors and nurses were amazing. And Eloise was our 40-pound hero. She fought her battle stoically and courageously. On the bad days, her dad or mom held her hand as she threw up. "I'm OK," she'd say between gasps. "Don't worry about me."

We were lucky that Children's Hospital has Doug Hawkins, one of the top rhabdomyosarcoma specialists in the nation. Now also a professor of pediatrics at the UW School of Medicine, Dr. Hawkins prescribed the chemo regimen that saved Eloise's life. Sometimes, however, even the most brilliant, cutting-edge medicine can't save a child from cancer, a crafty, cowardly disease. We came to know families whose suffering was far worse than ours.

ONE NIGHT WHEN I VISITED ELOISE, she looked up at me with those amazing eyes and said, "Grandpa, would you stay with me tonight?" I thought I'd won the lottery! All of the election victories, honorary degrees, awards and accolades I have received pale in comparison to those words from a little girl who needed me—*wanted* me.

The next morning, she asked if I would unplug her from the array of medical devices she wore so she could go to the bathroom. I was overwhelmed by the complexity of the task until she laughed and said, "Just unplug the cord from the wall, Grandpa!" She rode her medication tower down the hall, singing a song as she rolled along. I sobbed at the bravery of this little girl, cheerfully facing a daunting disease.

That was 23 years ago. Today, Eloise Evans is alive and well, making her mark in the world with the same spark of optimism that saw her through those touch-and-go days in the hospital, cheering us up. She graduated from Gonzaga University in 2017 with a bachelor's degree in Business Marketing. Next, she received a certificate in sports industry career opportunities from Columbia University. She was named "Sales Coordinator of the Year"

Eloise with her proud grandparents. *Lynette Johnson Photo*

A recent gathering with our sons, daughters-in-law and grandkids.
Dan Evans Jr.

for 2019 at BDA, the promotional merchandise company headquartered at Woodinville. For several years, she attended Camp Goodtimes, a week-long camp for cancer patients, survivors and their siblings. Her brother and sister went too. Today, Eloise is one of the counselors.

When our three sons were college age, Nancy once admonished them, "Don't even think about getting married until you're 30!" Before long, however, she had second thoughts. "Well, I don't care when you get married," she declared. "Just give me some grandchildren!" I seconded that motion.

Nancy and I are now blessed with nine grandchildren: Eloise, Isabelle and Jackson; Emily, Ben and Grace; McKay, Andrew and John Evans—three apiece for Dan Jr., Mark and Bruce. They're exceptional young adults—imbued with a sense of family, and a commitment to community and country. They also share my lifelong love of the outdoors.

LOOKING BACK AT THE DARKEST DAYS of Eloise's battle with the disease we ruefully learned how to spell, I compartmentalized my anxiety by staying busy.

In the fall of 1993, Governor Lowry appointed me to the Board of Regents at the University of Washington, succeeding my dear friend Mary Gates, who had served the university with distinction for 18 years. She was fighting her own battle with cancer, one she sadly lost within a year.

The 12 years I spent as a regent are among the most satisfying, and challenging, of my public life. For starters, critics charged that my appointment smelled like a payback because I had led the campaign against two anti-tax initiatives also denounced by the governor. Lowry was indignant. I shrugged it off as par for the course from conservatives who viewed me as a Republican in name only and saw conspiracy behind every shrub.

I joined the nine-member board in the middle of a scandal. The UW football program was reeling from penalties imposed over the revelation that Billy Joe Hobert, the star quarterback for the undefeated 1991 co-national champions, had received loans totaling $50,000 from an Idaho businessman. Passionate alums with too much money are a blight on college athletics. But Billy Joe's benefactor—banking on his potential NFL earnings—was not a booster who bled purple. Alleged infractions over summer jobs for other players were largely sensationalism. Nevertheless, the penalties imposed by the Pac-10 were the harshest in conference history. The Huskies lost 20 football scholarships and $1.4 million in TV revenue. They were also barred from bowl games for two years. Don James, one of the top coaches in college football, resigned in protest two weeks before the start of the 1993 season. I was part of a delegation that met with the NCAA's Committee on Infractions to argue that any additional penalties were unwarranted. I was tempted to say that SEC coaches break more rules before breakfast than we do in a year.

I was a proud Husky, but no knee-jerk apologist. Other incidents over the next dozen years revealed troubling lapses. A physician for the UW women's softball team was revealed to have improperly prescribed thousands of doses of banned substances, including steroids and stimulants, to athletes and staff members. In 2003, the university fired its head football coach, Rick Neuheisel, for betting on college basketball. I thought Neuheisel was a bad hire to begin with, overrated and riding on his golden-boy charisma. Documents that came to light a few years later buttressed a 2008 *Seattle Times* series about shocking criminal conduct and hooliganism by UW football players on his watch. The Neuheisel affair was compounded by the fact that the university's compliance officer had issued an erroneous interpretation of NCAA rules against gambling. Though the athletic department's oversight was lacking, there was also a collective failure to instill a culture of integrity and accountability. How you play the game—and represent your school off the field—matters more than winning. I represented the regents during a "culture review" of the athletic department by a panel headed by a former NCAA president. A key conclusion was that there was too much pressure on the football program to bolster athletic department revenues by fielding a consistent winner. Despite recent improvements, the university's athletic facilities were below average compared to other major conferences. We had a lot of work to do.

SOME PEOPLE—administrators in particular—were startled by my inclination to poke for more details. Whenever someone squirmed, I knew I was asking the right questions. Despite my practically lifelong association with the university, I discovered it was more complex than I imagined. My administrative experience at The Evergreen State College, a tiny, idiosyncratic school, was nothing like the complex layers of academic bureaucracy I discovered at a university with 16,000 employees. My inquisitiveness was welcomed by other regents. Mari Clack, from Spokane, one of Booth Gardner's childhood friends, was an especially perceptive advocate for higher education.

The regents were soon caught up in the search for a new president for the first time in 16 years. Bill Gerberding, the university's longest-serving president, gave us six-months' notice that he would be retiring at 65 in the summer of 1995. Some boosters blamed Gerberding for the severity of the sanctions against the football program, claiming he had not fought the penalties with requisite vigor. That was unfair. On Gerberding's watch, the University of Washington had become a dramatically better school in every aspect, from academic excellence to facilities, faculty pay, recruitment, retention and research. He also led a campaign that boosted donations to the university by an unprecedented $280 million. Gerberding, like Henry Suzzallo in the 1920s and Charles Odegaard in the 1960s, was a transformational president.

Talks with three potential finalists fell through after a year-long search. As a member of the negotiating team, I soon learned that top private schools paid more than public universities. They also subjected their presidents to less political scrutiny. Even with the prestige of the UW—34,000 students and four Nobel Prizes—the job was a hard sell. Everyone's finalist was someone else's finalist. After 14 frustrating months, we hired Richard McCormick, a 47-year-old historian serving as the provost at the University of North Carolina.

I WAS PRESIDENT of the Board of Regents in 1997 when we extended eligibility for health-insurance and family housing to same-sex domestic partners of UW students. Eight Republican state legislators promptly accused us of promoting "a pro-gay agenda" on campus by "elevating homosexual relationships to that of married relationships." They excoriated McCormick, too, but it was the regents' call, and the vote was unanimous. I noted that no taxpayer dollars were involved. Health-insurance premiums and university housing were paid entirely by students. Boeing, Microsoft, the City of Seattle and King County had taken the same steps. When Governor Gary Locke, a Democrat, reappointed me to the board in 2000, the right-wing saw it as fresh evidence I had abandoned "Christian values."

There was also a student uprising in 1997, including sit-ins at regents meetings. They objected to the person the Dean of Arts and Sciences had picked to head the American Ethnic Studies program. Her name was Ana Mari Cauce. Born in Cuba, she was an accomplished psychologist with a compelling life story. Nevertheless, student leaders and the campus newspaper believed she was being elevated to kill off the program—that the university was abandoning African American, Asian and Chicano studies. When I tried to address their concerns, they cut me off in mid-sentence and issued demand after demand. They shouted profanities at McCormick and threatened to occupy his office. A year later, her former detractors gave Cauce a "rookie of the year" plaque. I knew she was a star. I hoped we could keep her.

In 1999, Marc Lindenberg, Dean of the UW's Graduate School of Public Affairs, told me the university wanted the school to carry my name. My first reaction was "Good grief! Why can't you wait until I'm dead?" He laughed and said, "We don't want just your name. We want you."

I had thoroughly enjoyed my year as the school's first Public Leadership Fellow, leading the symposium on environmental policy. The faculty was outstanding, the students uncommonly bright and committed to public service. To this day, they recharge my batteries every time I enter a classroom. I accepted the honor with a promise I've kept—that I would be an active participant in boosting an "Evans Endowment for Excellence in Public Service." The endowment supports a Daniel J. Evans Professorship, scholarships, and investments in community problem-solving.

RICHARD McCORMICK'S tenure at the UW was marked by perseverance through severe budget problems. Unfortunately, there were also communication breakdowns, spotty reviews from legislators, and worrisome questions about his personal conduct. In 2002, we nudged him out the door. That diverse, decisive Board of Regents was headed by Jerry Grinstein. It also included Bill Gates Sr., Jeff Brotman of Costco, REI's Sally Jewell (a future Secretary of the Interior), and Shelly Yapp, director of redevelopment for the Seattle Center. When we learned of substantive allegations that McCormick had been involved in an extramarital affair with another UW employee, Grinstein buttonholed me before an executive meeting of the board.* "We gotta get rid of this guy," he said. "Absolute-

---

* McCormick denied the allegations at the time, admitting his infidelity a year later.

ly," I said. The regents urged McCormick to pursue an opportunity at Rutgers, the New Jersey school where he had deep ties. He landed there, boosting his salary from $295,000 to $525,000. Genuine talents notwithstanding, he was not a good fit for the University of Washington.

Dr. Lee Huntsman, our capable provost, was interim president while we searched for McCormick's successor. In 2004, we hired 51-year-old Mark Emmert, the chancellor at Louisiana State University. He was a Washington native and UW political science alum with a Ph.D. in public administration from Syracuse University.

In 2007, soon after I left the Board of Regents, Emmert asked me to head a 12-member committee to develop a long-range plan for improvements to Husky

"Send me in, coach." I suited up as a Husky for my 80th birthday. *UW Special Collections/Mary Levin*

Stadium. The original lower seating bowl had opened in 1920. Rusting rebar poked through cracks in the old concrete. When I was a kid we couldn't afford the price of a football ticket. Probably cost 50 cents back then! At the end of the open horseshoe there was a fence and a row of trees. On game days, we'd climb the trees, get on top of the fence and drop down into the stadium, keeping a close eye on the one guard. As soon as he passed by, we'd disperse and head for the seats. Once you were in, they'd leave you alone. I'll never forget those crisp fall days—how it felt to be a 10-year-old in a roaring crowd. It's still a thrill 85 years later.

Our committee soon discovered that the chosen developer did not grasp what we wanted or how to accomplish the task. After some preliminary work, we decided to change developers. Jon Runstad, a champion oarsman on the Husky crew during his days at the university, now was a member of our committee, and also an outstanding developer. When Jon told me he was resigning from the stadium committee, I protested that he was an essential member. He laughed and said, "No, Dan, I am resigning from the committee so I can seek the contract to rebuild the stadium." That was splendid news. The committee promptly chose Runstad as the new developer. He led a spectacularly successful effort and finished the project on time and more than $50 million under the original budget. The renovated stadium is now not just one of the most picturesque in college football, it boasts 70,000 seats, luxury suites, modern locker rooms, training facilities and offices. We worked closely with Sound Transit to ensure construction of its new light-rail station dovetailed with the renovation.

EMMERT'S TENURE AT THE UW was only six years. Wooed by several prestigious universities, including Cornell and Vanderbilt, he departed in 2010 to become president of the NCAA, a remunerative (at $2.7 million annually) but not exactly low-key job.

In 2007, The UW alumni magazine spotlighted my years as a regent. *Mary Levin/UW Columns*

Provost Phyllis Wise became interim president as the university was struggling with the financial fallout from the staggering recession that began in 2008. She proposed merging the Evans School into a larger division of the College of Arts and Sciences. When faculty leaders met to weigh options, some 200 Evans School students were on hand. They presented a compelling argument that the Evans School should maintain its independence, reminding the administration that the school produces more graduates devoted to public service than the Law School or Medical School. The students carried the day. I was immensely proud of them.

After a brief presidency by Michael K. Young, the regents unanimously elevated Ana Mari Cauce from acting president in 2015. It was an inspired choice. The child of immigrants, she is an extraordinary leader—an intellectual with the common touch, her determination tempered by the heartbreak of prejudice. I believe she will be remembered as one of the great presidents in University of Washington history.

IN 2015, THE EVANS SCHOOL was renamed the Daniel J. Evans School of Public Policy and Governance. I take additional pride that Henry M. Jackson and I are the only graduates to have UW schools named in our honor. I was even more thrilled, however, when the university recognized my wife's impressive career in public service by establishing the Nancy Bell Evans Center on Nonprofits and Philanthropy. Besides serving on the Board of Trustees of her alma mater, Whitman College, Nancy was on the board at KCTS, Cancer Lifeline, and the Northwest Parkinson's Foundation. A music major, one of her signature achievements as a member of the Seattle Symphony Board was generating support for the construction of Benaroya Hall, one of the nation's greatest concert venues.

Besides an extraordinary wife, I have been blessed with amazing friends. Bill Gates Sr., the patriarch of a great UW family, was a visionary civic leader and philanthropist. In 2003, together with Bill Ruckelshaus, Bill Clapp of Global Partnerships, and General John Shalikashvili, the retired chairman of the Joint Chiefs of Staff, we founded the Seattle Initiative for Global Development. It's an alliance of business and civic leaders dedicated to the elimination of global poverty, the root of many of the world's gravest challenges. We now have 300 members in 11 cities and support from the Bill & Melinda Gates Foundation.

I was also a member of an exclusive club. In 1997, the former governors began meeting every couple of years. The first "gathering of governors" featured Al Rosellini, Mike Lowry, John Spellman and me. It was great to see Al, a robust 87. Our differences had long since been eroded by time and

Eight governors—past, present and future—celebrate Al Rosellini's 100th birthday and Gary Locke's 60th in January of 2010. Sitting: Rosellini and Booth Gardner; standing from left, John Spellman, Locke, Congressman Dave Reichert, Chris Gregoire, Mike Lowry, Jay Inslee and me. *Ted S. Warren/AP*

tide, and the realization we had a lot in common. One Saturday we sat together at a Husky football game. In fact, all four of us agreed on practically every pressing issue. We opposed the voter-approved Initiative 601, which indexed growth in spending to inflation plus population growth. We warned that conservative legislators intent on keeping government on "autopilot" were failing to invest in highways and bridges, education and the environment. Rosellini, who had championed development of the UW Medical School, said affordable, quality health care would be a defining issue of the 21st century.

In 2010, Gary Locke, Chris Gregoire and Booth Gardner joined us to salute Al on his 100th birthday. He was still an active attorney, mentally sharp. We lost him the following year. My goal is to outlive Al—hopefully by a ways—and follow his example of not slowing down.

70
"Dan Evans Republicans"

Friends and foes, together with pundits and historians, have been trying to label me for 65 years. I am annoyed that liberal Democrats have hijacked "progressive." Granted, former vice president Henry Wallace was out in left field under that banner in 1948. But Teddy Roosevelt was the genuine article. The former president founded the centrist "Bull Moose" Progressive Party in 1912 when conservative Republicans denied him the GOP nomination. Teddy was my first political hero, a reformer who

On a hike in the Alpine Wilderness Area 2019. *Jim Camden/The Spokesman-Review*

challenged the "malefactors of great wealth" and protected 230 million acres of public lands. I wish he had not felt compelled to leave the Republican Party.

A half century ago, when I banished the John Birch Society, avoided Barry Goldwater, and admitted to being "passionately moderate," some of my supporters began declaring they were "Dan Evans Republicans." There are even a few who still whisper, "I am a Dan Evans Democrat." That is simultaneously flattering and divisive. I am tired of hyphenated Republicanism. "Moderate," "centrist," "conservative," even "mainstream," are adjectives that divide us.

Lately, more than ever, I am asked, "How can you still be a Republican?" It's easy: I don't believe in quitting. I continue to fight for Republican principles because I believe they are right for America. But not all good ideas come from one side of the political aisle. In my 1965 inaugural address, I said I was not afraid of the word "liberal" or ashamed of the word "conservative." At my third inaugural, I uttered my most-quoted phrase: "I would rather cross the political aisle than cross the people." I have never seen a Democratic salmon or a Republican highway; a liberal park or a conservative bridge. But I have seen lots of historic bipartisan legislation.

Today, Republicans who value the rule of law and revere the truth are locked in a struggle with

"Donald Trump Republicans." That's a misnomer if there ever was one. Donald J. Trump is not a Republican. He is a populist—arguably the most extraordinary populist in American history. Huey Long was a piker compared to Trump, who against all odds got himself elected president of the United States. Then he proceeded to create a cult of personality based on our darkest fears and deepest resentments, fueled by bizarre conspiracy theories and bald-faced lies—notably the notion that the 2020 election was stolen from him. During Watergate, *60 Minutes* commentator Nicholas von Hoffman compared the Nixon presidency to "a dead mouse on the American family kitchen floor." My hope is that by 2024, Trump will be like last week's dead fish in the garbage pail.

POLITICAL PARTIES NEED PLATFORMS, but true Americans instinctively share a love of our country and a yearning for civility and common sense. That's the future I envision for my grandchildren, their children and their children's children.

Now, as I approach a full century of life, an old question has popped up: "What next?"

The Wall Street Journal led its features section on February 25, 2021, with a story about senior citizens "building their contemporary dream homes when many their age are hunkering down." Dan and Nancy Evans—95 and 87—were the lead-off couple. Our family vacation cabin at Fisherman's Point on Quilcene Bay in Jefferson County—a project germinating for more than 40 years—was finally under construction.

The reporter's unspoken question was "Why now?" The other optimistic senior citizens interviewed had pretty much the same answer as the Evanses: "Why not?"

Every morning, I crank up the shower to as hot as it gets to sooth my old back. It has climbed a lot of mountains. But my head is still young. And I have no doubts about what it takes to keep America great.

WHEN I ADDRESSED the Mainstream Republicans' annual Cascade Conference in 2015, the Tea Party movement was capturing the headlines, swamping the political establishment and nominating newcomers who articulated their anger. I shared the renegades' concern over political gridlock, unsustainable spending, and a patronizing federal government. But not their virulent tactics. They had even misappropriated the name of our colonial ancestors. When the colonists tossed English tea into Boston Harbor, they were not pro-

By an act of Congress, the Olympic Wilderness Area, comprising 95 percent of the National Park, is renamed in my honor in 2017. My first forays into the magnificent wilderness were as a boy scout. *Steve Robinson Photo*

testing taxation. They were protesting taxation without representation. There is a huge difference between protesting and governing. A lasting political philosophy should focus on how to govern.

I said there are four reasons why I am a Republican, the first is particularly close to my heart, for no honor has pleased me more than Congress's decision in 2016 to rename 95 percent of the Olympic National Park—1,370 square miles, including 48 miles of coastline—the Daniel J. Evans Wilderness. Here are those four reasons:

Conservation: Conservative and conservation come from the same word root. It's a good place for Republicans to start expressing their conservatism. We must conserve our natural resources, protecting unique and rare lands. We occupy space on this planet for a limited time and should leave to the next generation a legacy of freedom, opportunity, and resources that are better than we received. We ought to follow the hikers' creed: Leave your campsite better than you found it.

The Constitution: I am a constitutional fundamentalist. A powerful Constitution accomplishes two goals: establishing the structure of government and protecting and expanding our freedoms. Our Constitution has succeeded because it has been amended so rarely—only seven times for structural reasons. We have expanded our freedoms 18 times. The 10 amendments of the Bill of Rights italicize our fundamental freedoms. Later, we abolished slavery and expanded the right to vote to former slaves, women, and 18-year-olds. Only once have we attempted to regulate social behavior. Fourteen years after Prohibition, we realized our mistake. In recent years we have faced attempts to amend the Constitution to allow prayer in schools, require a balanced federal budget, establish political office term limits, ban burning the American flag, and prohibit abortion. Our Constitution is strong because it is amended rarely—and then to expand freedoms, not restrict them. The flag burning amendment is a solution in search of a problem. It's far better to spend our efforts building a strong and compassionate nation where there is little need or desire to burn the American flag. The question of abortion rights may deeply divide our nation, but I have never heard anyone say that they admired abortion. It is the ultimate and painful choice of those who face irreconcilable conflict. It is far better for us to work together to strengthen families, teach our children about sex and love, and open opportunities for adoption. Those actions will do far more to end abortion than the hate and violence of political conflict.

A strong federal system: More than two centuries ago, 13 fiercely independent states united for their common good. But the Civil War finally defined the United States. We truly became a nation. Our federal system emerged, with defined roles for local, state, and national governments. For the past century, however, the federal government has spread its influence into virtually every facet of public authority. Overlap, conflict, and waste harass taxpayers. I co-chaired a national commission on our federal system. Our report, "To Form a More Perfect Union," recommended returning hundreds of federal programs to state and local control. In turn, our national government would assume the cost of public assistance and health care. It was essentially a financial even trade, but eliminating duplication created huge opportunities for savings. Responsibility for national defense, international relations, a comprehensive domestic safety net for our citizens, and constitutional protection of our freedoms are clearly national responsibilities. I believe strongly in reducing the sweep of federal control by creating active, smart, and able state and local governments that are prepared to meet citizen needs. States frequently are the laboratories of democracy. Most major new federal domestic programs evolved out of initiatives first developed at state and local levels.

Fiscal integrity: Fiscal integrity is not encompassed by "Read my lips, no new taxes!" It arises from defining the real needs of our citizens and finding the most efficient and effective ways to meet them. The constant challenge is to find the right balance between spending and taxes, just as a business tries to discover the right balance between prices and profit. Profligate spending and irrational prices lead to disaster. Every effort to reform and streamline government should happen before we talk of taxes. Fiscal responsibility means paying for benefits we receive. Anything less is borrowing from our grandchildren for the benefits we want but are not courageous enough to pay for.

OUR PRESENT POLARIZATION also reminds me of the address I gave in January of 1995 as keynoter at the annual Economic Forecast conference of the Puget Sound Economic Development Council. I had been out of political office for six years. The 1994 elections—the midpoint of Bill Clinton's first term—gave Republicans control of both houses of Congress for the first time in 40 years. The GOP also elected a slew of new governors and achieved a slender majority in the Washington State House of Representatives. The new majorities espoused smaller government and reduced taxes. But civility and common sense had taken a beating. The Balanced Budget Amendment was a loony idea. Absent a national standard set of books, how is it possible to measure "balance"? I was also outraged by the sanctimonious term-limiters striving to steal my freedom to vote for whom I choose. The voters can turn the rascals out at every election.

It was the nastiest election I'd ever seen. Virtually all of the campaign advertising was enormously distorted and negative. By constantly trashing our political leaders, we were also breeding disrespect for our system of representative government. The new political landscape was dotted with constitutional amendments and initiatives designed to protect citizens from "evil" politicians.

The divisiveness I observed then applies all the more to 2020, which spawned a shocking insurrection predicated on big lies, followed by wholesale efforts to suppress voter turnout.

In 1995, the Economic Development Council audience of 900—the largest crowd in the event's history—personified "movers and shakers." It included the business, commercial, and political leadership of the area. Since we were emerging from one of our regular recessions, bold action was not high on their agenda. The opportunity to speak out was irresistible. It was time for a wakeup call.

I said it was "Day Two of a new era"—or maybe "the Newt era," a reference to Newt Gingrich's take-no-prisoners "Republican Revolution." I proposed several major elements of civic enterprise that could propel Seattle and King County into world-class economic status. Today, all but one of the projects I endorsed have been adopted, including replacing the Alaskan Way Viaduct with a tunnel.

The casualty was the Seattle Commons, a plan to raise property taxes to fund a $111 million down payment on a 61-acre park south of Lake Union. The proposal was narrowly defeated that September in one of the most short-sighted votes in my long memory. We lost a major open space that could have been bordered by the research and commercial enterprises of South Lake Union and nearby housing within walking distance of those jobs.

The audience that day accorded me a sustained standing ovation. The *Seattle Post-Intelligencer* reprinted the speech, stating, "Our editorial board believes the scope and content of Evans' views are of such importance that the speech is reprinted in its entirety." It occurred to me then that last hurrahs are sometimes the most satisfying. I think the best way to conclude this memoir is with the concluding paragraphs of that speech:

"Civic," "city" and "civil" all come from the same Latin root—*civis*, meaning "member of the community, citizen." If we are to succeed as a great city, then we must all be members of the community. If we are to be true citizens, then we must do more than vote. We must be continuing active participants in the civic arena. Once again let us engage in civil debate. Once again let us join together in the generosity of volunteerism. Once again, let us seek progress jointly rather than obstruction separately.

The leaders of tomorrow will not be talk-show hosts who cater to the base emotions of people, screeching about waste in government, nor the politicians who blithely promise what they know they cannot deliver.

It will not be those rigid environmentalists who will see you in court if they don't get all they seek. Nor will it be the business leader who always skirts the edge of appropriate behavior.

Leadership must come from those who have the vision to see tomorrow, the intelligence to plan wisely, and the civility to listen to others.

Economic development is not just about jobs and profit. It is also about building a better community, creating maximum opportunity for all, and leaving a promising legacy for our children.

For all of our children and grandchildren, may you dream grandly and plan wisely in building a world-class 21st century community.

Index

ACKNOWLEDGEMENTS

Thank you to the generous supporters and donors who made this publication possible through gifts to the Evans School of Public Policy & Governance, and the ALL Foundation of Washington.

Dave Ammons
Dean Sandra Archibald
Apex Foundation
Aven Foundation
The Bill and Melinda Gates Foundation
Alex Bolton
John Brewer
John Chapple & Vivian Dixon
Ann Chenhall
Cleo Davidson
Pat & Susan Dunn
Wayne Ehlers
David Elliott
James Elliott
Evans Family Foundation
Jay Fredericksen
William & Mimi Gates
Gery Gerst
Gail Basso Girtz
David Kimball Hansen
Patricia Harper
Heather Hirotaka
Sam Hunt
William Jacobs

Sally & Warren Jewell
Keith & Lynn Kessler
Kristie Kirkpatrick
Mike & Moonbeam Kupka
Karin & R. Paul Larson
Laurie Maricle
Curtis & Patricia Marshall
Bruce McCaw
Craig McCaw
Susan McCaw
Alex McGregor
C. Louise Miller
Laura Mott
Mark Neary
Trova O'Heffernan
Amber Raney
Jill Ruckelshaus
John Stanton & Theresa Gillespie
Quintard Taylor
Charlie & Nancy Wiggins
Kim Wyman
Hans Zeiger

Kim Wyman with Dan and Nancy Evans.
Washington State Archives

Isabelle Evans, a talented artist, gave this painting to her grandparents.